Everyday Life
in
South
Asia

Everyday Life

in

South

Asia

EDITED BY

*Diane P. Mines and
Sarah Lamb*

INDIANA
University Press

Bloomington & Indianapolis

This book is a publication of

Indiana University Press
601 North Morton Street
Bloomington, IN 47404-3797 USA

http://iupress.indiana.edu

Telephone orders   800-842-6796
Fax orders   812-855-7931
Orders by e-mail   iuporder@indiana.edu

The paper used in this publication meets the minimum requirements of
American National Standard for Information Sciences—Permanence of Paper for
Printed Library Materials, ANSI Z39.48-1984.

Manufactured in the United States of America

Library of Congress Cataloging-in-Publication Data

Everyday life in South Asia / edited by Diane P. Mines and Sarah Lamb.
p.   cm.
Includes bibliographical references and index.
ISBN 0-253-34080-2 (cloth : alk. paper) — ISBN 0-253-21521-8 (pbk. : alk. paper)
1. South Asia—Social life and customs. I. Mines, Diane P., date
II. Lamb, Sarah, date
DS339 .E94 2002
306'.0954—dc21

2001007968

2 3 4 5 07 06 05

CONTENTS

Part II   Genders

Part III   Social Distinctions of Caste and Class

ACKNOWLEDGMENTS

We would like to thank each of our contributors, not only for their rich essays, but also for their invaluable suggestions and advice as the volume unfolded. We are both especially indebted to McKim Marriott, whose continuous guidance as a professor and mentor has never failed to challenge and inspire us in our efforts to learn about South Asia. We are very grateful to Rebecca Tolen of Indiana University Press, both for her initial inspiration about the project and for her ongoing patience and confidence. We would also like to thank Susanna Sturgis and Jane Lyle of IUP for their support and editorial wisdom.

Generous funding from the Graduate School at Appalachian State University and from a Mazer Award at Brandeis University helped defray the costs of preparing the manuscript for publication.

Members of each of our families have provided priceless support. Rick Rapfogel, Diane's husband, not only assisted in preparing the manuscript and lending his valuable technical advice, but also gave generously (as always) his intellectual and emotional support. Ed, Rachel, and Lauren were wonderfully generous in their lasting willingness to grant Sarah precious time to write and work while still always welcoming her home.

Boone, North Carolina   D. P. M.
Waltham, Massachusetts   S. L.

NOTE ON TRANSLITERATION

South Asians speak over twenty major languages and even more dialects. In transliterating terms from this rich diversity of languages, we have for the most part employed accepted conventions. We have allowed for some variation, however, to reflect distinctive local pronunciations and to accommodate contributors' preferences. In most cases, terms appear in italics and diacritics only on the first usage in a chapter. Proper nouns—names of places, people, deities, and texts—have been left without diacritics, and they sometimes appear as they are conventionally written, rather than as direct transliterations. Indian words are pluralized in the text in the English manner by adding an 's'. The names of some major Indian cities have recently been changed to spellings that more accurately reflect indigenous names and/or pronunciations that preceded British Anglicization (and colonization) of those names. In keeping with the preferences of India's citizens, we are using the current names. Thus, Mumbai is what used to be called Bombay; Chennai is what used to be called Madras; Varanasi is what used to be called Benares; and Kolkotta is what used to be called Calcutta.

Everyday Life
in
South
Asia

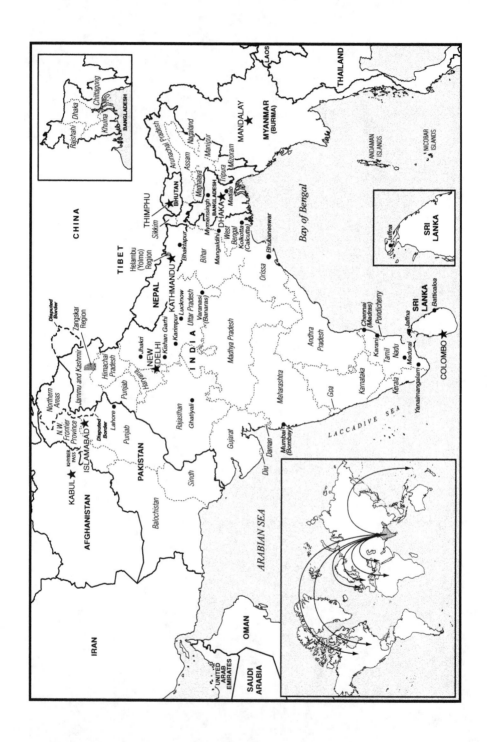

INTRODUCTION

Everyday Life in South Asia centers on the daily lives and experiences of people living in South Asia. Inspired by the focus on practice and everyday life in the work of recent social theorists,[1] we maintain that one can learn much about social-cultural worlds by examining the daily acts performed by ordinary people as they go through their lives. The book explores the ways people live, make, and experience their worlds through practices such as growing up and aging, arranging marriages, exploring sexuality, going to school, negotiating caste hierarchies, practicing religion, participating in popular culture, enduring violence as nations are built, and moving abroad to make new lives. By focusing on the everyday life practices and experiences of particular people, the book conveys important dimensions of social-cultural life in South Asia that could not be imparted solely via abstract theoretical accounts or generalities.

To design the book, we approached leading scholars of South Asian studies (from the United States, Great Britain, and South Asia, and from the fields of anthropology, religious studies, literature, and history) to ask them what they would like, and find important, to contribute to a book on everyday life in South Asia. What we received was a range of significant and engrossing pieces that we then arranged into a series of topical parts—"The Family and the Life Course"; "Genders"; "Social Distinctions of Caste and Class"; "Practicing Religion"; "Nation-Making"; and "Globalization, Public Culture, and the South Asian Diaspora." Although each individual piece can be read on its own, we the editors have written part introductions in which we introduce some background concepts and facts, draw out and reflect upon the common and uncommon theoretical and analytical themes that emerge, and briefly situate the papers in wider contexts.

The book as a whole is intended both to serve as an accessible reader for students of South Asia at all levels and to make a valuable contribution to the academic field of South Asian studies. The papers clearly convey important facets of the history, diversity, and richness of the region's social-cultural life, as well as speak to theoretical questions and concerns viewed vital by a range of contemporary scholars.

SOUTH ASIA

"South Asia," as we use the term in this book, refers to a geographical area—sometimes referred to as the South Asian "subcontinent"—that includes the contemporary nations of Pakistan, India, Bangladesh, Nepal, Bhutan, and Sri Lanka (see map). Sometimes Afghanistan—also part of British "India"—is included as South Asia, as well. The borders of any so-called "cultural area" such as South Asia (or Europe, East Asia, Southeast Asia, sub-Saharan Africa, etc.) are somewhat arbitrary, for the sharing of cultural ideas, practices, and materials is by and large continuous across a territory, not sharply demarcated by national (and, previously, colonial) boundaries. Indeed, the sharing of ideas, technologies, and material is now global in scope (see part VI). In this book we do, however, retain the convention of defining South Asia as a cultural region. Because of a significant number of historical and cultural continuities, South Asians do share many practices and concepts even within the amazing diversity that also characterizes the peoples of that region.

The population of South Asia is quite large considering its relatively small territorial dimensions. India alone supports over one billion people, despite being in area only one-third the size of the United States. With the populations of Pakistan, Bangladesh, Nepal, Sri Lanka, and Bhutan included, the population of the region reaches close to 1.4 billion, nearly one-fourth of the world's population.

In the history of Euro-American scholarship, as well as in the popular imagination, South Asia has often been considered by European and American writers to be a part of the "Orient," an area and a concept that, as Said (1978) has cogently argued, has been constructed as if it were timelessly traditional (instead of historical), basically religious (instead of rationally political), and characterized by Europeans as essentially weak and irrational (and therefore in need of governance by superior outsiders such as themselves). However, such stereotypes are untrue. There is no "timeless tradition." South Asia has its own history: cultural practices, religion, political structures, family structures, values—and all the similarities and diversities of South Asia—are nothing if not historically changing realities that respond to argument, action, and discourse among South Asians themselves.

The layers of history that have contributed to making and remaking the cultures and practices of South Asians are many. Often, textbooks on South Asia begin with the migration of "Aryans" from central Europe into the Indus River valley (in what is now Pakistan) and then beyond. These migrations began around 1500 B.C.E. But of course, there were already people in South Asia before this. The Indus Valley civilization, for example, reached the peak of its urban development around 2300–1700 B.C.E. Others, perhaps the ancestors of the "Dravidians" whose languages still persist in southern India and other pockets through South Asia, were spread further throughout the area. Archaeological evidence shows the area to have been inhabited by humans since the Paleolithic age, as many as 400,000 years ago (Wolpert 1982: 4–28). Aryan culture—from whence came Sanskrit and some of the early rituals of Hinduism—spread over the subcontinent, and it was its culture which became hegemonic, even as it was itself influenced by the practices and ideas of peoples already there.

Since as early as 300 B.C.E., residents of the Indian subcontinent were trading and exchanging ideas and material goods with merchants from Greece, other parts of Asia, Arabia, the Middle East, and, later, Europe. Later, Mughal and Persian cultures, and with them the cultural and religious values of Islam, began to have a profound effect on South Asia. Muslim kings, first from areas now called Turkey and Afghanistan and then, later, from Persia (now Iran and Iraq) ruled much of the subcontinent from the twelfth to the seventeenth century, when it was the British who began to gain control of the area as they established colonial rule. During the centuries of Islamic rule, many South Asians converted to Islam, Islamic forms of art and architecture blended with prior styles, and many new Persian administrative concepts came to restructure South Asian society. When the British began to take control of what they defined as "India" (which then included much of the subcontinent), they, too, introduced new administrative concepts and practices, such as the census (Cohn 1987b), which had broad impact on the structure of Indian society. With the British (and, in smaller numbers, the Portuguese, Dutch, and French), Christianity in various forms also came to influence South Asia, as did the British structure of education, land administration, ideas of private property, and, of course, the English language. In the nineteenth century, when Indian nationalists began to challenge British control in hopes of taking back control of their own political destinies, they, too, altered some of the structures and values of the society (see Chatterjee 1993; see also essays by Kumar and Ghosh in part V).

Contemporary global economic and cultural values continue to shape South Asia: Microsoft has offices in Hyderabad; global customer service lines are staffed by Indians who have been trained to speak in American accents so no one will know they are Indian; Cindy Crawford advertises watches in Mumbai (see Mazzarella, part VI). And South Asia, in turn, shapes other peoples' practices in other parts of the world: Mahatma Gandhi's resistance techniques were used by Martin Luther King, Jr., in the Civil Rights Movement in the United States; yoga is an everyday part of the lives of many people worldwide; Hindu temples are built in suburban U.S. neighborhoods; Sikh temples abound in English towns; clothing styles, music, and food from South Asia can be found in shops from Paris to London to Chicago. Furthermore, many South Asians have relatives living in Europe and America who also influence the shape and structure and values of South Asians, Europeans, and Americans alike as they move back and forth across continents, "transnationally."

What we hope to convey with this all-too-brief outline of some phases of South Asian history is that South Asia has always been a changing, growing, diverse culture area. There is no "authentic" Asia. There are people living their lives and making changes in the structures of their societies as they live. The papers in this volume, as well as the part introductions, clue us in to these lives as well as to some of the changes and histories that the living continue to make in South Asia today.

EVERYDAY LIFE

Why focus on "everyday life"? As Bowen and Early point out in their book *Everyday Life in the Muslim Middle East* (2002: 1–2), to focus on the "everyday" is to focus on the ways people actually live their ordinary, day-to-day lives, rather than on generalities or averages or abstract theories about those lives. Some theorists (e.g., de Certeau 1984) have argued that everyday life is where we can see the actual production and transformation of structures and cultures (Raheja, part III), whereas generalizing analyses and abstract theories tend to "freeze" or "freeze-frame" culture, as well as places and concepts, as Jeganathan (part V) points out. But culture is not a frozen set of rules that people merely enact. Nor do all peoples in a culture abide by the same cultural principles or concepts: the activity of people is heterogeneous, contentious, emotionally charged, and often surprising (see Bakhtin 1981). Our activity is always potentially culturally transformative and historically relevant. In other words, culture *is* as culture *does*. And culture only *does* through active, living human beings. The discourses that are culture may come out not only in words, but also in the way a person walks, where they choose to walk, how they wear their hair, how they dress, how they worship, etc. All of these everyday activities are part of the heterogeneous and always-changing discourse that we call culture.

In keeping with some of these ideas, all of the authors in this volume were invited to write on some aspect of the everyday life of the South Asians among whom they worked. Therefore, while being at the same time analytic and theoretical, each paper gives primary concern to some aspect of the lives of real living and acting people.

HOW TO READ THIS BOOK

There are at least two ways to read the book. One is to focus on the essays in each part as a group. The other is to read across the parts to follow one of the many themes that wind through the whole volume. First, within each of the major parts the individual chapters cover different aspects of the topic named in the respective headings, and as such convey something of the diversity of life in South Asia but within a common theme. In themselves these individual parts make extremely valuable contributions to specific topics in South Asian studies. For instance, "Genders" brings together new research and diverse perspectives on women's and men's lives. This part offers not only revealing explorations of the ways women have been made relatively subordinate within families (via arranged and patrilocal marriages, lack of access to schooling, attributions of bodily impurity, and the like), perspectives which have played a dominant role in existing literature on women in South Asia. "Genders" also offers pieces on male gender and sexuality (a topic that has been largely overlooked in gender studies), same-sex love, the experiences of transgendered *hijras*, and the ways gender relations are changing widely in India's urban centers, as women face increasing opportunities to pursue education and professional work.

The part on "Practicing Religion" likewise brings together a diversity of materials, from Hindu, Buddhist, and Muslim traditions, exploring phenomena such as why women in remote Kashmir fight to join Buddhist monasteries, how lower-caste Hindus use temple rituals to protest existing social orderings, how Nepali shamans heal, why Bangladeshi Muslims are viewed as problematically narcissistic when they sing about themselves rather than God, and what it's like to be a young anthropologist unintentionally intoxicated and caught up with the fervor, ardent devotion, and seeming social chaos of a village festival of the gods.

Because so many of the papers touch on multiple intersecting themes, our section headings cannot do justice to the range of topics and issues addressed. Therefore, the reader may also follow one or more important themes that wind through the sections. These themes include the idea of modernity and its effects on South Asian lives; education and youth; "ideals" versus "realities" of life; competing notions of persons as sociocentrically bound to their families or as individuals pursuing their own, independently defined goals; violence in the constitution of modern nations; globalization; and the impact of colonialism and colonial representations on South Asia today.

So, for example, someone interested in the ways "modernity" is thought about and experienced in South Asia might focus on the readings by Liechty and Wadley (part I), Gold and Seymour (II), Dickey (III), Kumar (V), and Mazzarella (VI), to name a few. These pieces offer various views about how family structures, gender, and visions of a "good" life and society are impacted by the kinds of forces people see as constituting modernity, such as consumerism, a global popular culture, education, and urbanization. Someone interested in youth might fruitfully string together Liechty, Gold, Seymour, Kumar, Trawick, Hall, and Narayan—who examine young people's lives across a wide swath of the South Asian world, from middle-class "punks" in Kathmandu, to working-class Sikh migrants in Leeds, England, to uneducated girls in rural Rajasthan, to second-generation university students in America, to children growing up in the war zone of northern Sri Lanka. Of these pieces, Gold's, Seymour's, and Kumar's also provide a revealing look at some of the dilemmas surrounding education in South Asia today.

Another crosscutting reading might focus on colonialism and its impact on South Asian lives. Mattison Mines's paper explores the autobiographical nature of a merchant's legal will and testament under colonial rule. Joseph Alter shows us what happened to Indian wrestlers after kings no longer patronized them. Gloria Raheja analyzes colonial renderings of caste through proverb collections. Jim Wilce explores the impact that colonial perceptions of India had on the formulation of Islam in Bangladesh. The Introduction and several of the papers in part V discuss the sometimes violent aftermath of colonialism in the construction of independent nation-states. And Richman, Hall, and Daniel in part VI show us something of the lives of South Asians displaced to Europe and North America due in part to their colonial history.

There is no single way to understand people's lives in South Asia. Together these pieces—detailed descriptions of lived realities—hope to convey something of the richly varied, historically shifting, and intensely experienced nature of life as lived in South Asia.

NOTES

1. Scholars such as Pierre Bourdieu (1977a), Michel de Certeau (1984), Lila Abu-Lughod (1993), and Michael Jackson (1996).

PART ONE

The Family and the Life Course

The family is a central site of everyday life in South Asia. It is an arena through which persons move through the life course passages of birth, youth, marriage, parenthood, aging, and dying; it can be a place of love and conflict, material sustenance and want, companionship and painful separations. One term for family in several Indian languages is *samsāra*, which means literally "that which flows together," and also more broadly connotes worldly life in general. In its sense as family, samsara refers to the assembly of kin and household things that "flow with" persons as they move through their lives.

One common assumption held by many both within and outside South Asia is that South Asians live ideally in "joint families," consisting of a married couple, their sons, sons' wives and children, any unmarried daughters, and perhaps even grandsons' wives and children. We see in the following selections that this assumption is both true and not true, and that family relationships and structures are richly complex and varied. In general, urbanites tend to live in smaller, more nuclear households than those in rural areas, and poorer people (with less land and smaller homes to their names) tend to live in smaller households than the wealthier. National and international migration also affects household structures, as many across South Asia are moving to cities or abroad for work, only sometimes bringing the rest of their families with them.

Children are highly valued and loved. The births of boys are often even more elaborately celebrated than the births of girls, but this is not because girls are not equally loved. Parents often worry about the burden of providing a dowry for a daughter's marriage, and they know that a daughter will move away from them when she marries—unlike a son, who could remain with his parents for their lifetime. Most children in South Asia spend at least some time in school (although this school education can be very minimal; see for instance Gold and Kumar); many also play vital roles helping their parents with work; and they also play with friends and receive affection and indulgence from seniors. Liechty explores how many urban youth (in this case in Kathmandu, Nepal) are participating in what is becoming a globalized, cosmopolitan youth culture, with shared forms of popular music, media, slang, dress, and sometimes drugs.

Although not all people get married (see, for instance, Seizer's account of actresses' lives and Vanita's exploration of same-sex relationships in part II), marriage is considered by most in South Asia a crucial part of a person's and family's life. Young people spend much time thinking about their marriages and chatting among themselves about whether traditional, arranged marriages or romantic "love marriages" are better. Even when a marriage is arranged by parents and other senior kin, as is still most common, the young person will usually face the event with, along with some trepidation, a degree of eager anticipation and romantic expectation, having perhaps met the future spouse on one or two occasions, or at least seen and admired a photo. Marriage does not involve only a relationship between two individuals, however; if the wife goes to live with her husband's kin especially, she is not only marrying him, but also becoming a vital part of his family. She is becoming a daughter-in-law, sister-in-law, and later hopefully mother and then mother-in-law.

Aging and dying tend to be accepted as natural parts of life and family flows. The expectation or ideal (one that is not always realized) is that intergenerational ties will be close and reciprocal throughout life and even after death, as parents care for their children when young, and children (especially sons and daughters-in-law) in turn support their parents in old age and as ancestors (Lamb). For the most part, older South Asians practice fewer attempts to fight the bodily changes of age—through the hairdyeing, face-lifting, anti-aging exercise routines, life-prolonging medical technologies, and the like that are so dominant now in Europe and America. (Such techniques are, however, becoming popular among the cosmopolitan South Asian elite.) Hindus, as well as Buddhists, Jains, and Sikhs, view death as not an end but a passage on to new forms of life; the body is discarded and cremated, while the soul moves on to new births, deaths, and rebirths. Muslims bury their dead and imagine an afterlife with the possibility of suffering or bliss depending partly on how much merit or sin one has accumulated. Some Muslims believe that death should not be loudly mourned, for the timing and circumstances of death are in Allah's hands, and one would not want to insult Allah.

One significant theme running throughout several of this part's essays is the idea that belonging to a family whole is more important than pursuing individual aspirations. Susan Wadley quotes a Brahman man using the imagery of the broom to explain the value of a large, interdependent family: "Say there is a broom. If you have one straw separate, it can't sweep. But when all are together, it can sweep." Patricia and Roger Jeffery's examination of a Muslim woman's life in rural north India illustrates how the ideal of a harmonious joint family does not always work out neatly: Sabra's marital family suffers bitter disagreements, separations, poverty, and death. Yet in significant respects Sabra's interdependent extended family ties endure, and it is only through remaining part of her husband's family that Sabra is able to survive as a widow with young children. Sabra's story also demonstrates the importance of a woman's natal ties. Although she moves to her husband's home, her ties to her natal parents and brothers remain valuable lines of material support and affection.

Another theme that appears in these essays surrounds the transformations of modernity. Many in South Asia interpret problems in contemporary families, such as a youth drug culture (Liechty), neglected elderly (Lamb), and a general falling apart of the family, as "modern" afflictions, stemming from forces such as consumerism, urbanization, colonialism, tourism, a globalizing media, and the back and forth of international migration. Some of these modern forces are viewed as coming principally from the "West." In such discourses, the family can stand as a sign of "tradition" and a morally superior national culture (see Chatterjee 1993). But modern changes are also frequently interpreted as stemming simply from a natural propensity for things to change and degenerate over time. According to the well-known Hindu theory of the four *yugas* or ages, things get progressively worse rather than better as time passes, and we are now in the fourth and most degenerate of all ages, the Kali Yuga. Some of the changes of modernity, of course, are welcomed by many in South Asia. For instance, Liechty's urban Nepali youth (below) yearn to be even *more* modern and cosmopolitan than they presently are. Wadley also examines how joint families remain as sound and valued as before, although recent social changes have affected some relationships within families.

* * *

The essays in this section together aim to portray everyday experiences of the family and the life course. Susan Wadley begins by examining the ideology and practice of the joint family in the largely Hindu community of Karimpur in rural north India. People of Karimpur express the idea that power comes through numbers, and that those who wish to sustain a family's honor and vitality should remain together as one whole under a unifying male head. Wadley further examines how, contrary to expectations, the joint family is more prevalent now in Karimpur than ever before, although the nature of some relationships within the family is changing.

Patricia and Roger Jeffery's vivid account of the life of Sabra, a rural north Indian Muslim woman, portrays the phases of a woman's life as she moves from girlhood, to marriage, to motherhood and widowhood; the quest for sons; and the afflictions and sustenance that derive from extended family ties.

Mark Liechty focuses on youth culture in urban Nepal. Middle-class youth, while waiting often in vain for white-collar employment, have the leisure time to join gangs, consort with foreign tourists, sell and take drugs, and consume foreign media—participating in the intermingling of global and local worlds, creating images and fantasies of foreignness and modernity.

Benedicte Grima's piece focuses on the life stories told by Paxtun women. Paxtuns are a Muslim ethnic group living largely in northwest Pakistan and Afghanistan. The Taliban, a regime attempting to set up a pure Islamic state in Afghanistan, and the target of much attention in the world media since 1994, comprises largely ethnic Paxtuns. Grima's essay does not consider the Taliban, however, but rather focuses on the stories rural Paxtun women of northwest Pakistan tell about their lives and families. We see how these women perceive and organize their lives as a chain of crises centering around the family—the death of a mother, abandonment by a husband, the tragic accident of a son. Grima's examination also reveals the importance of narrative or storytelling in everyday life. It is often through telling stories that people express emotion, represent themselves to others, and interpret and fashion their worlds.

Sarah Lamb moves on to explore the ways Bengalis in a rural village and in a Kolkotta old-age home think of aging as a time to loosen ties to family, things, and their own bodies, to prepare for the myriad leave-takings and journeys of dying. She looks also at how discourses of aging are intertwined with discourses of modernity, as an *overly* loosened and neglected old age is represented as part of a degenerating modern society.

Mattison Mines's examination of the autobiographical will of a prominent merchant of Madras City in the early twentieth century speaks to several of the themes of this section. Narayana Guruviah Chetty's will reveals how he sees himself as part of a network of kin that he has had to create through the use of law, affection, and giving rather than through descent, as he was unable to father any children. The will also offers a window into a man's systematic preparation for his own death. Unlike many of the Bengali villagers presented in Lamb's piece, who concentrate on loosening their ties to the world to enable easier dying, Chetty calculates methodically how to leave in the world tangible and enduring signs of himself—through creating charities, schools, and buildings in his name. Mines examines how Chetty's very act of writing a will, and his logic of giving, mixes both Hindu and British colonial sentiments. The British colonial government encouraged charitable giving, and Chetty's bequests to Hindu centers were also perhaps motivated by a desire to provide for his soul after death, especially because he had no children to care for him as an ancestor.

One Straw from a Broom Cannot Sweep: The Ideology and Practice of the Joint Family in Rural North India

Susan S. Wadley

The Indian joint family is built upon the idea and reality that power comes through numbers, and that those who seek to be most powerful, especially in India's village communities, should remain in joint families in order to successfully sustain a family's honor and position. A second, but equally important, component of the success of joint families in practice is the training that children receive that marks their interdependence, their sense of belonging to a group that is more important than individual goals and aspirations. The ideal joint family is made up of a married couple, their married sons, their sons' wives and children (and possibly grandsons' wives and great-grandchildren), and unmarried daughters. In the community of Karimpur[1] in rural Uttar Pradesh, some 150 miles southeast of New Delhi, some joint families extend to four generations and include more than thirty members. For Karimpur's landowning families, which are more likely to be joint than are poor families, separating a joint family is traumatic, rupturing family ties, economic relationships, and workloads, as well as necessitating the division of all of the joint family's material goods (land, ploughs, cattle, cooking utensils, stocks of grain and seed, courtyards, verandahs, rooms, cooking areas, etc.). Separation (*nyare*) is, in fact, most comparable to an American divorce. It also brings dishonor to one's family.

The paradigm most frequently used to regulate social life in Karimpur is that of the ordered family, implying the authority of a male head, a number of adults working together under that authority, and respect for all of those higher in the family (or village) hierarchy. As in many north Indian communities, Karimpur residents use fictive kin terms toward all

Parts of this essay are reprinted from *Struggling with Destiny in Karimpur, 1925–1984,* by Susan S. Wadley. Copyright © 1994 The Regents of the University of California. Used by permission of the University of California Press.

nonrelated village residents of whatever caste group; and traditionally, they have seen the village community as one family.[2] As one elderly Brahman man put it in 1984:

> Where there is cooperation (*sangṭhan*), there are various kinds of wealth and property. And where there is no cooperation, there is a shortage of each and every thing or there is an atmosphere of want.
>
> Where there is cooperation there is no need [of the ambition] to pile up wealth. "The minor streams or rivers go into the ocean but they do not have the ambition [to be big]." So, in the same way, property and comfort accrue without being sought after when there is cooperation: property comes to the properly regulated (*kāydā*) man.

Hence the family is dependent upon a man who has himself, and his family, under his control. This control is attained through a variety of daily practices, as well as a clearly articulated ideology of male superiority. The same elderly Brahman male spoke of women in this way:

> Q: ... how does the man *control* her?[3]
> BM: *Control*? They [women] don't have much knowledge (*gyān*). How is the lion locked in the cage? It lacks reason (*vivek*). Man protects her from everything.
> Q: If a woman progresses, then she would be knowledgeable. Then how can you shut her in a cage?
> BM: I say that if the sun begins to rise in the west, then what? It is a law of nature.

At another time, he added that "a woman cannot think as much as a man" (even though, he went on to state, she might be more powerful). A Brahman widow concurred with this assessment, saying, "The woman is inferior (*choṭī*, literally 'small'). A woman can only work according to the regulations (*kāydā*). She can never leave the regulations." Hence a woman who follows the laws and customs of her family will be controlled and bring honor to her family.

A male gains honor by having land and wealth, by being kind to others, by keeping his word, and by having virtuous women who maintain *purdah* (seclusion). Families can lose honor through their women by having daughters or daughters-in-law who elope, become pregnant prior to marriage, or are seen outside too often. Men may bring dishonor to a household by stealing, gambling, drinking, and eating taboo foods, as well as by being unkind and miserly. A family also loses honor by not remaining joint, in part because control is easier in a joint family.

Karimpur's residents believe that joint families are able to maintain better control of their members, especially young adults. Shankar, a Brahman male and village headman of Karimpur in the early 1980s, suggests that self-control, particularly sexual control, is more easily maintained in a joint family. Several aspects of joint family living relate to his remarks. First, as he notes, no one has his/her own room or even space in the traditional household. In fact, through the 1960s in most joint families, the mother would assign sleeping places on a nightly basis; this gave her immense control over the sexuality of her sons and daughters-in-law. If she felt it appropriate, she would arrange for them to have a place where they could meet at night. A young man, newly married, once complained that he and his wife were being forbidden to sleep together because he had had a bad cold for some time and his grandmother (female head of his joint family) thought that they should remain apart for the good of his health. This raises a second point: many South Asian Hindu men believe that male health is threatened by too much sex, for a man loses vital energy through his semen. Hence controlled male sexuality is especially important. On these issues, the headman remarked:

> But if society lives together (*samāj ikhaṭṭhe*), your self-control (*sanyam āpkā*) is maintained. If you live separately, you lose your self-control. You get a separate room. You get a separate cot. You have separate food. Everything becomes separate. This affects your health (*tandurustī*). But when you live together—you have your mother at one place, sister at another, *bhābhī* (older brother's wife) somewhere else, or a servant at some place—then self-control is not difficult. You don't have any place to indulge yourself [implied is food or sexual indulgence]. This is the greatest factor in good health. That is why it is essential for the family to live together. Now it is important to understand that all this is a gift of nature (*kudarat*). If it is not in men, then how can we blame others? This tendency to live separate is very dangerous. They say that if a young daughter is alone in a room, then even her father should not go into that room. She is the girl whom you have produced out of your own seed, out of your own body, and she is young. So you should not go into that room. So when our family lives together, then we get less time, and we get more opportunities to work. We would not even be able to think about it [sex]. That is why our health used to be good.

Aside from the physical surveillance that is implied in joint family life, other forms of control are vital to the success of a joint family. These include such means as the silencing of women and children (or even adult males younger than the head of the household) through rules that deny them the opportunity to speak, through the seclusion of women (purdah), through rituals which mark the superiority of male kin and the importance of the family unit, and through daily practices such as eating routines that mark the male as superior. For example, a woman should speak only in a whisper, if at all, to her husband's father or older male relatives. A man should not talk with his wife in front of his parents, nor should he do anything disrespectful before his father (such as smoking a cigarette). A woman should keep her face covered before all men senior to her husband, and she should not leave the family home unless accompanied by another woman or male relative and her head and body are covered by a shawl. The yearly ritual calendar is filled with celebrations in which women pray for healthy sons, for long-living husbands, and for their brothers. There are no annual rituals where they pray for their mothers or daughters. Finally, a Hindu wife should never eat a meal before her husband and other male relatives have eaten as this would be enormously disrespectful: the result is that women often eat late at night, after the last men have returned from the town or fields.

These factors are dependent upon and support the powerful male head of the family. The unified, cooperating joint family demands both a trustworthy leader and the respect of the sons. The most powerful Brahman family in 1984 achieved the ideal more successfully than any other Karimpur family: the family was composed of four brothers, the widows of their two dead brothers, their wives, children, children's wives, and grandchildren, who had lived together for over twenty years since the death of the parents. One of the brothers attributed this success to the male head, his older brother, saying, "We understood that he is wise, older, more sensible, would do every kind of good work, but would not do bad work." The family is now separated, but the brother heading the largest portion was described as thinking ahead, having understanding, and seeking peace.

If the family stays together, its power increases. One young Brahman man used the imagery of a broom to explain the need for a large, cooperating family: "Say there is a broom. If you have one straw separate, it can't sweep. But when all are together, it can sweep." One elderly Brahman man used the example of a family with four sons. All have different habits. But the family's power would increase if all four were under the control of one person.

> I am telling what I understand. A family must have one thing. That is, a family is strong when all remain in the control of one [person]. Whatever is said, they must accept that. In other words, having accepted the words of Brahma [the Hindu deity], they have become firm and constant in that, whether it is right or wrong. But the family must be controlled by one, whether or not he has money. Unless there is selfishness [on the part of the leader], the power [of the family] will endure.

On another day, this same man added, "If the family goes every which way, then the whole house is ruined."

Equal treatment of all the members within the family and unchallenged decisions by the head are necessary to the smooth functioning of the united family. I learned this lesson soon after beginning fieldwork in

Karimpur in 1967. I was living in a family that included four married sons, along with their wives and children. Whenever I brought sweets or fruits for treats, I was required to give them to the grandmother who would distribute them among her sons, daughters-in-law, and grandchildren. Her decision as to who got what amount carried weight: mine did not (although I find that thirty years later, I am allowed to make the distribution myself). Further, if I bought saris for the women, they had to be identical, apart from color, for the women at each tier: the brothers' wives all should get one kind, their sisters should get one kind; the daughters all should get one kind, and so on. Likewise, frocks for the young girls or sweaters for the boys should differ in color only, unless I wanted to instigate fights and high levels of tension among the women. So I learned the appropriate buying patterns, those used by heads of households. Thus it is easy at holidays or at more public events like the district fair to identify family groupings, because of the clusters of girls in identical dresses or boys in matching shirts.

My elderly Brahman friend once told his (somewhat idealized) version of the rule within his family:

> In the United States, when people get married, a man becomes master for himself and feels that his duty is to his wife and children. But here in India, whenever there is a guardian and we make the bread in one place [meaning that they cook together], we cannot say, "My wife does not have bread. Bring some for her." Or that "she has no blouse." Whether she has no clothes or she changes into a new sari every day, I do not have the right [to give clothes to her or to complain]. . . . We are either oppressed by the older people or we have respect for them. There is another thing: we cannot say that she does not have a sari so why don't you bring one for her. And I cannot bring another either. The time never came when I had to think about whether she had clothes or not. No one [namely his wife] ever said to me, "I have no clothes or other things." No one ever told me this problem. If she had, what could I have done? That rule has been in my mind till now. But for the past five or six years we have become separate. Now I do all of this that the family wants—saris and clothes for the children. Before, my brother was master of the family and I was always behind. I never was concerned whether my children were in trouble or were happy. I never worried about this.

The unity of the joint family depends, too, on the wife's first duty being to her parents-in-law, not to her husband. As one young man, a Water-carrier by caste, explained:

> First of all she should think about the family. Then me. . . . First of all she should take care to feed them. My mother is old, so my wife should massage my mother. It is her duty to eat the food after my mother, my older brother's

wife, and sister. If my parents want her to clean the pots, she must clean them. Even if she feels that she is a new (*bahū*) (wife/daughter-in-law) and she need not clean the pots now, her duty is to clean the pots.

Another man remarked that the women must also see to equality, not giving bread rubbed with ghee (clarified butter, a prestige item) to one person and plain bread to another. Above all, the good daughter-in-law is one who serves and obeys her father-in-law/mother-in-law (*sās-sāsur*). As a poor Cultivator said, "She should accept what the father-in-law and mother-in-law say, whether they are right or wrong." The authority of the parents-in-law is key, because if a woman seeks favoritism through her husband, the unity of the family is threatened. I vividly remember a young man in his twenties telling us that his mother and aunt (his father's sister) used to like his wife very much, but that he hadn't liked her. (It was an arranged marriage, as are all marriages in Karimpur.) Now he loved her, so they no longer liked her. Without his affection for her, the unity of the family was secured and the power structures unchallenged. Once his affection developed, the power structures that allow for the ideal unity and cooperation were threatened.

Behavior within the family marks the hierarchies. Respect for those senior is demanded: sons respect fathers and older brothers and obey their mothers, with whom a more affectionate relationship exists. Sons cannot smoke, play with their children, or talk with their wives in the presence of their fathers. The Flower Grower's wife says that sensible (literally "understanding," *samajdhār*) boys show respect to their fathers, but some, like one of her sons, refuse to listen to the advice of their parents. Women must also show respect within the household. A bahū asks her mother-in-law what to cook, how much spice to add, whether she can go to the fields, and so on, even when she is forty and the mother-in-law sixty or more. Bahūs also show respect through veiling, by touching the feet of senior women on ritual occasions, and through eating patterns, always eating after both the men and the women senior to them.

The rule of those senior is not always benign, however, and decisions are regularly enforced with physical punishment. The household head (or more senior person) has "understanding" that the others lack. If they do not accept that understanding, that wisdom regarding right and wrong, the message can be reinforced through physical punishment. Husbands can beat wives; fathers can beat sons (and, more rarely, daughters). The Flower Grower's son, a young man then in his early twenties with an eighth grade education who did construction work in Delhi, explained the roles of husbands and wives thus: if a wife erred but did so in public (sitting with her friends, for example), she should not be corrected, for that would be an insult. But in private, a husband could say something or beat her. "In other words, you should scold her, if she makes an error. You must make her understand that she must not do so." A Sweeper woman said, resignedly, "If we don't work well, we're bound to get a beating." A young Watercarrier man told of the time he hit his wife:

> At that time I was studying in high school. It was 1978. One day the food wasn't cooked. On that day, I said nothing. On the following day, I was also made late because the food wasn't ready. Again I didn't speak to her. On the third day again I was made late. In this way, I was late each day. On the fourth day, I went again [to eat, late]. It was summer. I sat on the roof in the air. Then after eating, I hit her four or five times.

So a husband's duty is to make his wife understand things through physical coercion if necessary. A wife can also correct her husband: if he drinks or gambles, she should try to forbid him. But given the limits on female mobility, due to rules of seclusion, she has no real way of intervening in these matters. Moreover, she cannot beat him, although everyone knew of wives who did in fact hit their husbands when angry.

Children should be physically corrected as well. The Flower Grower said, "If he [a son] does some wrong work, beating is a duty." The goal is to teach through fear. My elderly Brahman friend captured the essence of control as understood in Karimpur: physical punishment and verbal abuse are used to instill fear.

> A child who fears that when the parents come, they will shout at me, [that child] won't play in the dirt, won't use foul language, won't fight with anybody. But if he has no fear, he will play in the dirt the whole day. Because he has no fear, he will use bad language toward others. So there should be control—for every man and every woman.

Without fear, according to Karimpur residents, there can be no control, and elders in one's family have the right and duty to "cause understanding." Similarly, those who are senior in the village can beat "understanding" into those of lower status.

In many ways, the village is perceived as one large family. The fictive kin ties that link everyone are one mark of this "family writ large" conception, although there are other ways in which the fictive kinship of one large family is marked. When someone dies, the whole village shares in the grieving by canceling music events or other celebrations. In 1968 a Leatherworker named Horilal died on Holi, the popular spring festival characterized by the throwing of colored powder, raucous play, and role reversals. Within minutes of the news of his death, all Holi celebrations throughout the village came to a sudden halt.

The perceived unity of the village was further articulated when a fire swept through the Brahman section of Karimpur in April 1984. People claimed that the fire was caused by the accumulated sins of the village as a whole, but especially by its Brahman leaders. Just as the sins of a family are ultimately the responsibility of the head, so too the sins of the village are the responsibility of the dominant caste, in this case the Brahman landlords. Here again individuality is muted. Whereas an individual can sin and hence affect his own life course by altering his destiny (*karma*), he also alters that of his family, lineage, caste, and village, for an individual is not a unique entity but shares substance and moral codes with all of those with whom he or she is related, in ever larger circles. All those belonging to the nation of India also share in the same way.

If a family should be united, so too should the dominant group. A retired Accountant by caste attributed the power of Karimpur's Brahman landlords to their unity:

> Those people [Thakurs, commonly landlords throughout northern India] used to understand that they were landlords. Also those [Brahmans] because they were wealthy. Above all, there was unity [*sangthan*] among them whereas elsewhere there was no unity. Everything depends on unity.

By the 1980s that spirit of cooperation was felt to be missing and hence Brahman domination had lessened. In the election for headman in June of 2000, sixteen men ran, including four Brahmans. With no unity amongst the Brahmans, none of their candidates was successful; one garnered all of eight votes of some three thousand cast.

THE CHANGING FAMILY

Numerous factors have begun to put stress on both the united family and the united village. These include increased education, migration, and consumerism. Contrary to expectations, however, the joint family is more prevalent than ever before, although internal arrangements differ from those of the 1960s and before. As table 1 shows, the percentage of all Karimpur families that are joint is greater than at any time in the twentieth century. There is also a marked caste difference in joint families, so that in 1998, the richer Brahmans had 22 joint families and 24 nuclear families, while the poorer Cultivators had 25 joint families and 46 nuclear families. With the average size of the Brahman joint family at 12.2 persons while nuclear families averaged 4.7 persons, twice as many Brahman individuals lived in joint families (269) as in nuclear (112). For the Cultivators, joint families averaged 9 persons while nuclear families averaged 5 persons, and the numbers of persons in joint and nuclear households was almost equal.

The increase in joint families is related to demographic changes as well as to economic changes. In the 1920s, the average life span in India was

Table 1.   Family types in Karimpur

Type	Number of Families (percent)			
	1925	1968	1984	1998
Single Person	13 (8.1)	9 (3.7)	7 (2.1)	13 (3.3)
Subnuclear	33 (20.4)	11 (4.5)	26 (8.0)	23 (6.0)
Nuclear	36 (22.4)	107 (43.5)	143 (43.7)	159 (41.3)
Supp. Nuclear	42 (26.1)	33 (13.4)	58 (17.7)	60 (15.6)
Joint	25 (15.5)	81 (32.9)	91 (27.8)	130 (33.7)
Other	12 (7.5)	5 (2.0)	2 (0.6)	0

about twenty-five years, while now it is over sixty.[4] With many not living past their twenties, joint families were often impossible, because many families didn't include two intact married couples. As table 1 shows, in 1925 families tended to be either supplemented nuclear families (a married couple with one related adult and their children) or subnuclear families (having no married couple). So whereas over 20 percent of Karimpur families in the 1920s were subnuclear, in the 1990s, with greater life spans, only 6 percent are subnuclear. Likewise, joint families have gone from 15 percent of all families to almost 34 percent of all families.

This increase in joint families runs contrary to the expectations of western social scientists who anticipated that family structures in the developing third world would follow the pattern of those of the West, with nuclear families predominating. Many elements work to keep joint families intact, including the role of maintaining honor. But economic factors are also important. The temporary migration of men out of the village to seek jobs in nearby towns or Delhi or Mumbai has increased dramatically in the last fifteen years. Frequently the migrant leaves his family with his parents or brothers in the village, though he may eventually bring his wife and children to join him. Even then, the family may be economically and emotionally joint, as the migrant brother contributes cash to buy fertilizer for the family fields or to pay doctor bills, while also providing housing so his brother's children can attend the better schools found in urban areas. Likewise, the brother managing the family lands contributes food to the migrants and may house young unmarried adults or nieces needed to help with women's household chores. Moreover, it is to the advantage of the migrant to have a trusted relative rather than a land-poor sharecropper working his portion of the family lands. So while much of the time there may be two separate households, one urban and one rural, in fact there is a constant flow of people between the parts of a joint family, as workloads are redistributed around childbirth, holidays, labor needs, etc. Joint families, whether village-based or split between village and city, also benefit from having one adult male freer to manage other family needs such as getting the sick proper medical care, dealing with officials, arranging marriages, or being involved in village politics.

Families with no or little land are most likely to be nuclear or supplemented nuclear households. Here poverty overwhelms the desire for honor, and without land to work and its proceeds to share, with little motivation to enter politics, with no money for complicated medical care, families split more readily. As one woman from the poor caste of Midwives said:

> My mother-in-law separated [from us] because of my children, saying, "You have lots of children. You live hungry. We will live with the other son. That son is in service [has a job]." So because of my poverty, we separated. . . . Now that son is in service. He sends money home. At my place there is nothing. Now that she has left, I have to raise the children alone. Before she used to look after them [while I went with the grazing animals to make cowdung cakes].

In this instance, a mother chose to live with her more prosperous son, creating a supplemented nuclear family. What had once been a joint family, with parents, two married sons, and their children, is now one nuclear family and (with the father dead) one supplemented nuclear family. Most families move through a cycle of at least brief joint status, while sons and their wives are young. As sons achieve differential success in the workplace, and have more or fewer children, the momentum to separate grows. Yet as the same Midwife said, "Living alone is not right." But only those with land, political ambitions, and more favorable economic circumstances can ward off separation.

But even in the joint families, other forms of "separation" are now occurring. Karimpur families are becoming increasingly couple-oriented and challenging the authority of their elders. One manifestation of this change is the use of space. In 1968, only one couple, a young Brahman and his wife, had their "own room"—and only over the strenuous objections of the man's mother. But by the 1980s, many couples in joint families were allocated their own space to set up and use as they liked. This space, often a room of their own, was clearly off-limits to the mother-in-law, who thus lost her control of her son's sexuality. Indeed, I was frequently told that the result of both separate families and "rooms of their own" was a shortening of the time between children, from over three years in the 1960s and earlier to barely over two years in the 1980s.

With these changes came challenges to the authority of those senior. Songs in the 1980s continually spoke of new kinship patterns. For example, in one song a bridegroom is described as very clever because he took his bride to see a movie without asking any of his kin. The following excerpt is from a woman's song that directly challenges the authority of the mother-in-law by reversing roles:

Mother-in-law, gone, gone is your rule,
The age of the daughter-in-law has come.
The mother-in-law grinds with the grinding stone,
The daughter-in-law watches.
"Your flour is very coarse, my mother-in-law,"
The age of the daughter-in-law has come.

While the mother-in-law may still retain authority, songs such as these point to contentious issues in modern joint families where the daughter-in-law is likely to be much better educated than her mother-in-law and more willing to demand some independence and mobility, as well as consumer goods unavailable in earlier decades. With her closer ties to her husband, as symbolized by their personal space, these tensions, though always present in joint families, are greater than ever.

One response to the changing family is the enormous popularity of the goddess Santoshi Ma, the goddess of peace and benevolence but also a goddess whose story speaks directly to women whose husbands are working outside of the village or to women having in-law troubles. In the story told as a rationale for her worship, a young wife has a worthless husband who finally leaves home to seek his fortune. She is left alone with his family. As his absence grows longer, she is treated more and more cruelly, forced to gather firewood from the forest and given rags to wear. On one of her excursions into the forest, she comes upon a group of women worshipping Santoshi Ma. Hearing the story of the goddess, she too begins to worship her every Friday. The husband thus begins to prosper and eventually returns home. When the husband discovers how his wife has been treated, he builds a lavish home for her with the help of the goddess. So those who worship the goddess will prosper, as did the young wife.

The village community is also threatened by similar changes—by democracy, by migration, by education, by right-wing Hindu movements which have pitted Muslim against Hindu in ways unknown in the past, and by new ideas and wants conveyed through films and television. As one of the Carpenters said, "Now there is a headman in every house." In village opinion, what is most damaging is a loss of the village morality that was based on a complex web of mutual obligations between kin and between caste groups. Speaking of the village, people repeatedly spoke of the lack of caring that exists now. While speaking of the family, people lamented the lack of love and of care for one's elders. The cultural code that supported a hierarchy whereby the high had knowledge and might and the right to control the low is now continuously challenged. Thus far, Karimpur's joint families have adapted and met the challenge, so that their unity remains. Meanwhile, the unity of the village is fragile and rapidly disappearing.

NOTES

1. The research on which this paper is based took place between 1967 and 1998 in the village of Karimpur in western Uttar Pradesh. Our knowledge of Karimpur social life is extensive: William and Charlotte Wiser, missionaries with the Presbyterian Mission, conducted research on Karimpur farming practices and social life beginning in the 1920s (see C. V. Wiser 1978; W. Wiser and C. V. Wiser 2001; W. Wiser 1958). I began doing fifteen months of research in Karimpur in late 1967 and have been there twice more for extended research trips and numerous times for short visits: I was most recently there in 1998 (see Wadley 1975, 1994, 2001). Funding came from the National Science Foundation, the American Institute of Indian Studies, the Smithsonian Foreign Currency Program, the National Endowment for the Humanities, and Syracuse University. Portions of this paper are taken from Wadley 1994 and Wadley 2000. A web site devoted to Karimpur with photos and a text by Charlotte Wiser is located at www.maxwell.syr.edu/southasiacenter/karimpur/.

2. India's village communities are facing enormous social change due to economic shifts and other factors related to globalization. The extent to which the village is still a "little community" varies considerably, but in most places is surely less than even two decades ago. Tradition is also a term that implies a lack of change over long periods of time: I do not use it in that sense here, for change is a fact of life in India as elsewhere. But there is a sense of a confluence of factors that before the past two decades was more stable than what exists now.

3. Two asterisks surrounding a term indicate that the speaker used the English word in his/her Hindi sentence.

4. See Wadley and Derr 1993 for a fuller explication of this argument.

Allah Gives Both Boys and Girls

Patricia Jeffery and Roger Jeffery

Since 1982, we have been doing research in rural Bijnor district (western Uttar Pradesh), particularly in two villages, Jhakri (a Muslim village) and Dharmnagri (Hindu and Scheduled Caste[1] village). Throughout our research, we have focused on various aspects of gender politics, especially at the household level.[2] After a year-long field trip in 1990–91, we began thinking about how to portray aspects of domestic life through brief narratives and life stories. In view of the increasing salience of communal politics in India, we were especially concerned with highlighting the notable parallels between the everyday lives of Hindu and Muslim women in the area. This endeavor resulted in *Don't Marry Me to a Plowman!* from which the following story about Sabra is extracted.[3]

Sabra and her husband, Suleiman, were Muslims living in Jhakri, and they became key informants during our research on childbearing in 1982–83 and again in 1985. When we first met her in early 1982, Sabra was about thirty years old and her oldest child was a girl of about eight. Suleiman's father, Bashir, was one of three brothers who had been among the most wealthy farmers in Jhakri. After Bashir's second marriage, however, Suleiman and his older brother, Razaq, had watched helplessly while their father sold land to pay his debts, and their youthful stepmother continued to bear sons who would be entitled to share what might remain of Bashir's land.

Being the son of a wealthy farmer was no guarantee of economic security, and Suleiman and Razaq were compelled to seek other sources of income. For Suleiman and Sabra, though, the issue of security in old age also loomed large because they had no sons to support them when they were old and infirm. Not only that, but the line of daughters born in the quest for a son created worries about arranging their marriages and providing them with dowries. By the time we returned in 1990, however, the significance of these issues had altered in ways that we had not at all expected, for Sabra had been widowed a couple of years earlier.[4]

An earlier version of this essay apeared in *Don't Marry Me to a Plowman!: Women's Everyday Lives in North India*, by Patricia Jeffery and Roger Jeffery. Copyright © 1996 by Westview Press. Reprinted by permission of Westview Press, a member of Perseus Books, L.L.C.

* * *

When we first went to Bijnor in early 1982, people could vividly remember the political Emergency of 1975–77, especially its high-profile coercive population control program. In Jhakri, many people initially suspected that we were somehow associated with the government, and that we had come to pressure them into being sterilized. From the start, though, Sabra had given us a friendly welcome. She would often come through the fields from Jhakri to the Dharmnagri dispensary, where we were living. There was frequently some reason for seeing the doctor. And when she had finished, she would generally take a few minutes to chat with us. Sometimes, too, we would talk to her while she worked at home.

On the first sunny day we had had for a while during the 1982 monsoon, Sabra wanted all the clothes to be dried before nightfall, so she carried on pounding her laundry as she chatted.

"You haven't been in Jhakri for a while," she complained, though with a smile.

"We've been going to other villages and getting women to fill out forms for us. And do you know, the people there haven't been as frightened as the people in Jhakri!"

"I've filled out one of your forms without worrying about it. But I can't say why other people in Jhakri are afraid," she replied.

Indeed, not only did she willingly respond to our requests for information but she was more tenaciously curious about life in Britain than many of the other people we met. One time, Sabra wanted to hear about marriage ceremonies in Britain. Before Patricia could get a word in, our research assistant, Swaleha Begum, said that weddings in Britain were very simple and that the bride and groom simply exchanged rings. Sabra's response was instant:

> That sounds like a good custom. For us a girl seems burdensome. Her parents have to give her a dowry with jewelry, utensils, and so on. They have to give several pounds of silver and gold. And when the girl goes to her in-laws' house, her parents have to fill a whole trunk with clothes. It's a dreadful thing how much has to be given to get a girl married. Nowadays, people want to arrange their son's marriage only into a house from which they'll get a splendid dowry. Meanwhile, who knows how a girl's people will be able to marry her? They just have to get the dowry and jewelry ready. There ought to be a law that dowry should neither be given nor taken.[5]

Another day when Sabra was visiting us at the dispensary, the ANM (auxiliary nurse-midwife) came to confirm that we would take Bhagirthi to the hospital in Bijnor in our jeep.[6] Bhagirthi had been married into a rich-peasant Rajput Hindu household in Dharmnagri. In 1979, she had had a stillbirth because she was given three labor-accelerating injections by the dispensary pharmacist. She was now about to give birth again, and the

ANM had told her that the baby's head was large. The ANM did not want to be held responsible for any further calamity, and Bhagirthi was anxious enough to want a checkup in Bijnor. Sabra asked who we were talking about. The ANM retorted:

> Whoever it is, I don't want to be blamed for any problems. Nor do I want people to think I get women dragged off to hospital to be sterilized by compulsion. Have I ever told you to be sterilized, you with your four girls? And haven't I had you treated for TB [pulmonary tuberculosis] without any pressure for sterilization? And aren't you all right now? And didn't I get treatment for Asghari for TB so that she'd become pregnant? And didn't I help Dilshad's sister Gulistan when she nearly died in childbirth?

Sabra nodded rather sheepishly. Then the ANM asked Patricia to make sure that Bhagirthi had clean cloths prepared for her baby. She turned to Sabra again: "Do you know, when I went [to Jhakri] to help with Zubeida's delivery, there wasn't even a piece of cloth the size of a pocket handkerchief clean enough to wipe the baby off."

Sabra again assented, and the ANM departed, leaving Patricia and Sabra exchanging rather bemused grins as she went. Yet Sabra was a good deal more prepared to seek the ANM's services than many others in Jhakri. She had indeed obtained considerable relief from TB, though it was not completely cleared up.

Some time later, Sabra again came to the dispensary, this time to obtain some medication for her daughter, whose head was covered in boils. As we chatted, we were once more joined by the ANM, who began asking about various pregnant women in Jhakri. She then launched into complaints: "Jhakri women are so unwilling to have prenatal tetanus injections. I give the injections free before the birth. That's much better than having to pay for them afterward. I give freely what comes here free from the government. But I don't give anything from my own pocket. People would become suspicious. But people don't listen to me."

"That's because people are afraid of you," said Sabra, alluding to local people's belief that the ANM would pressure them to be sterilized.

The ANM pursed her lips. She had no answer to that. As she started to leave, Sabra began asking about tetanus injections. Sabra said that she was in the fourth month of pregnancy. Some months later, it was Fatima from Jhakri who told us about Sabra's delivery in early 1983: "She's had another girl, poor thing. That's the fifth."

* * *

When we talked to Sabra about her childbearing career, it became very clear why she was so vocal about the problems parents faced in providing dowries for their daughters. Sabra was married to Suleiman in about 1969 when she was seventeen or eighteen, she reckoned. Her first pregnancy had ended in a miscarriage. Sabra thought she must have been three or four months pregnant, though she was not sure. She had missed three periods.

> But I was young and I didn't know what that meant. I didn't know why periods stopped coming. Nor did I ask anyone. I'd been spreading wheat out on the roof to dry in the sun with my sister-in-law [Razaq's wife]. But in the afternoon, clouds began to appear and we collected the wheat into sacks in case it rained. Then we put the sacks in the grain store in the house. That night I was tired and slept heavily. In the morning, I had stomach pains and bleeding began. I told my sister-in-law that I hadn't had a period for three months and now suddenly one had begun. But she said that I must be pregnant and she called the *daī* [traditional birth attendant] who was living in Jhakri then. The *daī* said that the bleeding had started because I'd been lifting heavy weights. She gave me some pills and told me to eat pulses without chili pepper or spices. But even so, I still had pains and the blood continued to flow. In the evening the baby itself came out. It was just a ball the size of my fist. We called the *daī* again. She said it was hard to stop that happening, as I'd been lifting heavy things, so she gave me some medicine to clean me out properly. The *daī* told my husband the names of the things he had to bring from the bazaar and she ground them and gave them to me to drink.[7]

We asked what had happened in the next pregnancy, but true to form, Sabra reprimanded us for not going on to ask her what food she had eaten after the miscarriage or what she had paid the *daī*. We obediently noted down the details and then asked what had happened in her other pregnancies. "Well, after that baby fell, I had a girl without any trouble," she told us. "But the next time, because I had so little sense, I caused an abortion at five months."

We were astonished at her willingness to mention such a sensitive subject and hardly dared to press her for more details. But after a few moments, we asked—somewhat diffidently—if she would tell us about it. Sabra told us what had happened with hardly any further prompting:

> You see, it was partly that I was lacking in sense, partly that my mother-in-law and my husband's sisters didn't explain things to me. Five months had been completed and sometimes I had spotting like at the end of a period, when just a small amount of blood comes out. At that time I was fighting with my sister-in-law [Razaq's wife]—we weren't speaking to one another. So I talked to a neighbor about the spotting, and she said the baby certainly wouldn't stay in place, it would miscarry. So having listened to that woman, I went to a doctor and told him that I wanted an abortion.

What doctor had agreed to do such a late abortion, when surely she could have died? Did the doctor not even ask why she wanted an abortion? Did he not suggest that Sabra bring her husband with her?

No, he didn't ask me anything. He simply gave me the medicines—just tablets, nothing else. And I took them to my mother's house. My husband didn't know anything about it. You see, a man wouldn't like the idea of an abortion. And also, I was very young at the time, and I just panicked. Now I have five children, and I could cope with another baby, but I didn't think I could then. So I was afraid of my husband, and I took the pills to my mother's house. It was there that I ate them. I didn't tell anyone there first. I just ate them, and the baby was cleaned out. No one was with me at the time. I got pains in my belly, and so I went outside to crap. It was then that the baby fell, and I became unconscious. Sometime later my mother found me, and she carried me inside.

The baby was a boy. Sabra's mother wrapped him up in cloth and buried him. Sabra herself became very weak. Her mother was furious with the doctor and said he should not have done such a dangerous thing. For as long as Sabra's husband was still alive, she told him, he was not to do another abortion for Sabra or he would have to face the consequences.

And out of fear of my husband, I stayed with my parents for a week afterward. But someone had told him about it before I got back to Jhakri. He was very angry. When I got back from my mother's house, he asked me why I was lying down. He said, "Go outside and do your work!" I managed to walk slowly out into the courtyard. But I couldn't work or even sit. So I went back inside. He said some more angry things, and he swore at me. But then he became silent. Having an abortion at five months is dangerous. It's also a sin. It's wrong to kill something with life in it. But I was young, and didn't know any better. Now I'm able to think. Now I'm afraid. I worry about what will happen after I die.[8]

After that, Sabra gave birth only to girls. And yet, when we asked her after the fifth girl was born if she had ever taken medicines to procure a son, she was adamant: "I've never taken any medicine like that. If Allah wants to give me a boy, He'll do so without any medicine. Allah gives both boys and girls, so what's the point of taking any medicine?"[9]

She had not been altogether happy that she had become pregnant again, however, though she had felt she should do nothing about it: "I caused an abortion once and was very troubled after that. And now my health is not what it was then. Anyway, I'm afraid of Allah. Previously, I didn't understand so much." On balance, even though she had no son, she did not want any more children. It would be hard enough to bring up the five girls she now had. "My health is bad. We don't have enough to eat because we don't have enough land from which to obtain grain. These children are too many. It's hard to feed the children and ourselves. Five children are a lot." Not surprisingly, she and Suleiman did not organize any celebrations in 1983 to mark this latest arrival.

* * *

Sabra's situation in Jhakri was in marked contrast to that into which she had been born. Her parents and three brothers lived in nearby Bad-shahpur, where her brothers shared the operation of a farm of over eighteen acres. There was, as Sabra put it, no need for them to seek jobs elsewhere, as the farming kept them fully occupied.

> My father arranged my marriage. My mother also agreed to it, but it was my father who'd seen the boy. I must have been eighteen or so at the time. There were other offers of marriage for me—I can't remember how many— but my father liked only this one. The go-between was a Julaha [weaver] from Chandpuri.[10] He used to go to Jhakri and Badshahpur selling cloth, and he told my father that if he wanted to get me married, he'd show him a boy in Jhakri. The Julaha told my father-in-law about me, and then an offer of marriage was sent to my father. Parents don't ask the girl anything about her marriage. And out of embarrassment the girl doesn't say anything. The parents alone make the decision.

At the time, Suleiman's father, Bashir, operated about thirty acres jointly with his two brothers. He had two adult sons, of whom Suleiman was the younger. Sabra's parents gave her a dowry consistent (as Sabra put it) "with their own standing and the expectations of the time": some fifty-five pounds of brass and copper utensils, eleven pieces of jewelry (silver and gold), thirteen suit lengths of cloth for herself and eighteen for the people of her in-laws' connection. There was also a cycle and watch for Suleiman and the customary bed and stool. Sabra's in-laws had presented her with twelve pieces of jewelry and fourteen suits. Further items of clothing and foodstuffs came from her parents when Sabra went to Jhakri for the second time after the marriage. A year later, her parents sent a buffalo. The clothing and foodstuffs were rapidly used up, as was to be expected. But Sabra was soon forced to succumb to her father-in-law's financial demands.

> There were utensils in my dowry, but I can't remember how many separate items. You see, my father-in-law sold the lot. He also sold two pieces of the jewelry that my parents had presented to me. That was before I'd been married for even a year. My father told him that it had not been his right to sell the things. My father asked him to say where he'd sold the things so that he could get them back. But my father-in-law just asked my father to say how much everything had cost and he'd repay the sum. He still hasn't done so. I even told my mother-in-law that I'd give some other jewelry to them if they'd return the utensils from my parents' house. But they didn't. Then a little later, my father-in-law forcibly took the jewelry that he himself had presented me—apart from two pieces that I hid. At that time, we were still living jointly, and one of the bullocks died. So he [her father-in-law] sold my things and bought another bullock and made all the arrangements to

cultivate the crops. And even those two pieces of jewelry that I managed to hide didn't remain with me. My husband's brother needed money one time and he asked for them, and I've never had them back. And the jewelry from my parents' house got broken, so I sent it to the goldsmith for repair; but he disappeared with it all. So nothing has remained with me.

Sabra's father-in-law's propensity to cheat his relatives and cause them financial worries was widely commented upon in Jhakri, and several people told us about the bad blood it had caused in her husband Suleiman's wider family. It also seems that Suleiman and his brother, Razaq, were hardly paragons themselves. They had reputedly been involved in several thefts in the village. One man alleged that this had prompted Bashir to oust them from his house and refuse them access to most of his land and its produce. Suleiman and Razaq received just one acre between them. A different— though not wholly incompatible—account was given by Sabra. Just before Sabra was married, Bashir had made a second marriage to a woman much younger than himself. Sabra believed that Suleiman's exclusion from his rightful due had been instigated by his stepmother, who wanted to preserve the land for her own children:

> We were all joint with my parents-in-law until after my first daughter was born. But then my mother-in-law made us separate. That was about three and a half years after my marriage. You see, my mother-in-law is a step-mother-in-law. She'd been fighting with me from the day I was married. She didn't want to have her daughters-in-law with her. She began saying that even more often around the time my husband's two sisters were being married. And then my father-in-law joined in all the squabbling, and he made us separate.

This had had several consequences. For one thing, Sabra was deprived of help that she might otherwise have expected, particularly after childbirth:

> My mother-in-law gave me no help with my first baby, and that was when we were still living jointly! She hasn't helped me with any of my other children either. And I can't call my husband's married sisters, since my mother-in-law gets angry that they're helping me. It's a father's job to call his daughters, but my father-in-law rarely calls the older one and he never calls the younger one. His wife doesn't want them to come. And I have nothing to give them, so how could I call them myself?

Sabra had found this particularly trying before and after the birth of her fifth daughter. For most of the pregnancy, Sabra was severely incapacitated with a fever and chest pains (almost certainly TB), yet she was compelled to work right up to the end: "Women should stop lifting heavy loads or making dung cakes, but I had no respite at all. The girl was born at night and I'd worked right into the evening. If I'd had someone to help me, I'd have stopped working, for I wanted to lie down and rest."

Such little help as Sabra had after delivery came from Razaq's daughter and from her own oldest daughter, then eight years old. Suleiman's sister happened to be in Jhakri but could help for only a day in the face of her stepmother's ire.

Perhaps more serious than this, however, were the implications of being cut off with hardly any land. For some time after her fifth daughter's birth, Sabra ran a fever and had pains throughout her body, especially in the pelvic region. After a couple of weeks of treatment from a private doctor in Bijnor—costing Rs. 120—Sabra felt somewhat better. But she still had the sensation of "ants walking all over the body." Over the next two months, the medical expenses mounted to Rs. 1,500, and Suleiman had to borrow money to pay the bills. "My medical treatment is consuming money that should be spent on food. Sometimes we've had to stop the treatment because we were short of money. But then we get medicines when the pain gets too bad again."

Suleiman's brother, Razaq, had not been so short of resources. His mother-in-law in nearby Chandpuri told us she had not wanted her daughter married to Razaq, but her husband had given his word and would not break his promise. After the marriage, her husband frequently gave Razaq financial help for the sake of their daughter. This had enabled Razaq to save some money, and he had bought about two-thirds of an acre of land on his own account before his father cut him off. Razaq's wife died in 1980—according to her mother, during premature labor after Razaq had beaten her severely. Even after this, Razaq's father-in-law continued to provide for his grandchildren's schooling and other expenses.

Suleiman, however, had not had such comprehensive support from his in-laws. Sabra's parents continued to send her the customary gifts of clothing and foodstuffs on festivals and after she gave birth, but they did not send substantial cash gifts. According to Sabra, "Our girls see children in other compounds with toys, but we can't afford to buy things like that. We can afford to eat, but not much more. My father-in-law hasn't given us our share of land, so my husband has to do laboring work."

Was Suleiman not able to rent land or take some land on a sharecropping basis? "He [Suleiman] doesn't have enough money to buy land at Rs. 20,000 per acre," Sabra told us. "For one year, he rented nearly two acres from someone in Dharmnagri. That cost Rs. 900 for the year. But then we didn't have enough money for the rent, so we'd sharecrop and get half the crop instead."

What was going to happen that year? Did people in their own compound not give out land to people who wanted to sharecrop?

We haven't been able to get any land that way this year. The people of our compound won't help anyone. They prefer to get work done by laborers if necessary. That way they can keep all the crop themselves. We used to have a buffalo that gave ten pints of milk a day. But the children got none of it to drink because we used to sell all the milk. With that income and anything my husband could earn from laboring sometimes, we could manage to buy our food. I had to breast-feed the girl older than this baby for longer than I wanted, as there was no other milk in the house to give her. But that buffalo died last year. So now we're very worried about money, as we used to rely greatly on the income from the milk. My three brothers and my father have nearly twenty acres. It's a matter of fate that there's nothing for me in Jhakri.

Suleiman's rights to his father's land and Sabra's control over her dowry had been seriously infringed, with the result that Sabra had grave worries about the future: "Whatever a girl's parents give and whatever clothes and jewelry come to a daughter-in-law from her in-laws belong to her alone. But my in-laws left me with no jewelry and they even sold the utensils that my parents had given. Now I have five daughters, and I'm very worried. If I even had utensils and jewelry, they'd be of use to me. But my parents-in-law left us with nothing. We're just like rats in an unused water pot."

* * *

Suleiman and Razaq, however, were not content with such a position, and they decided to go into business together. They began buying tree plantations—mostly eucalyptus, a cash crop introduced a few years earlier. Then they would fell the trees, sell the wood, pay the debts incurred in buying the plantation, and use the profit to meet their families' needs. Slowly, the business began to flourish: "Whatever profit they earned from the business, the two brothers put to some other use," Sabra explained in 1985. "They saved some money and bought some land. They bought nearly two acres from their own income. We get grain from it; but we also have to buy grain, since we can't be fully fed from the grain that comes from our own land."

By the mid-1980s, things seemed to be promising. Sabra was not so constantly short of money, though they were still living in a single room in the corner of her father-in-law's courtyard. But the children were still a worry. The girl born in 1983 had died, but another one had come to take her place. And there was still no son. As Suleiman put it:

I don't want any more girls—we already have more than enough. I'd like a little bit of a boy. But it's not good to have too many. Two boys are enough; otherwise they'd fight over their shares of land. I can't say that large numbers of children are necessary. In any case, there's a big difference between boys and girls. A man with twenty acres might like a lot of children, but a small person like me needs only two boys and a girl. Then I could give my girl in marriage, and my two boys would each bring in a bride. The boys would be able to help one another, but the land wouldn't be split up too much. God has chosen to give me five girls, and there was one other who died. Parents love boys and girls the same—but a girl goes to her own house after she's married. Boys stay with their father. They do cultivation and animal husbandry, so their father can get some rest when he's old. Girls are fine, but the name of boys is greater. This is the reason: Boys make money for their father.

* * *

Every time we returned to Jhakri, new houses had sprung up. People were shifting from cramped quarters in the center of the village to new sites on the outskirts, where they were constructing kiln-brick houses with higher walls than the older-style houses and with flat roofs instead of thatch. On our return in 1990, one such house was nearing completion. It consisted of a line of three sizable rooms set back from the pathway that had earlier marked the edge of the village. It had yet to be plastered, and several of the windows did not have their wooden frames and shutters. The boundary wall had not been built, and one room was currently being used to house some livestock. The building turned out to be Sabra's.

Our immediate supposition that Sabra's life had changed for the better was dispelled as soon as we met her again. Suleiman had died in a road accident about two years earlier. "He was on his way to Bijnor on his Vikki [motorcycle]. He was hit by a minibus at the crossing with the road from Bijnor to the Ganges. The bus didn't stop. Later a police vehicle came past and they saw him. They took him to hospital but he died later. And now I have six girls and a boy. The boy was in my belly when my husband died. He was born three months after his father died."

Even without being widowed, Sabra would have had great problems in settling six daughters in marriage. Now, there was not enough land to feed the family, and Sabra herself could not cultivate it. Nor could she contemplate engaging in Suleiman's tree business. Without the goodwill and generosity of others, she and her children faced a bleak future.

Razaq had remarried shortly before Suleiman's death. Immediately after, he and his wife established a joint household with Sabra.

My father-in-law never gave his two sons by his first marriage their proper share of the land. But they'd managed to buy land. They'd bought nearly three acres altogether. They used to work it separately. But since my husband's death, the land has been operated jointly, and the cooking hearth is also joint. We also had the Vikki mended, and we sold it. My brother-in-law has bought a new one. My brother-in-law has also taken over my husband's work in Bijnor, checking the men who fell trees.

Since then, Razaq had taken full responsibility for Sabra and her children. In order to lighten the task, his first wife's father had arranged and paid for the marriage of Razaq's daughter by his first marriage. Razaq's daughter explained what had happened one time when she was visiting Jhakri:

> I've been married now for just over a year. My grandfather [mother's father] paid for my marriage. He married me from Jhakri and gave me a very good wedding. There were twenty suits for me and twenty for my in-laws. He gave all the things in the dowry. And the bed was a double one. When the wedding party was departing with me, my grandfather gave my husband Rs. 10,000 and told him to find himself a job. My husband is studying in tenth class [roughly equivalent to tenth grade] at the moment, but he's also searching for employment. After my uncle died, my father began caring for my uncle's children. There are six girls and a boy, so my father couldn't have paid for such a wedding as I had.

Meanwhile, Sabra's oldest daughter was now about seventeen. She had studied only the Holy Qur'ān, for when she had suddenly reached puberty, Sabra had stopped sending her to the *madrasā*, the mosque school in nearby Begawala, where she might have learned some Urdu and Hindi. The girl herself commented that she had been unwilling to attend the madrasā since she was the only "big" girl going. She had remained at home for several years, helping with the family's work. But now she had reached the age to be married.

Razaq had taken the matter in hand. He viewed a boy in a nearby village and decided on the match. There was land in the boy's family, but the boy did not work on the land. He had studied to about fifth class, but he was also *Hāfyz Qur'ān* (able to recite the Holy Qur'ān by memory) and he was teaching the children in his village. Given Sabra's daughter's education, it was a good match. The marriage was to take place in late spring 1991. Sabra, however, had no jewelry to present to her daughter. "A few years ago my younger sister died, but my father had already set aside jewelry for her marriage," Sabra told us. "My father gave all that to me because I had nothing left. I presented that jewelry to my husband's brother's new wife—but that too got stolen. When my husband's funeral procession was waiting at the cattle byre and everyone was there, there was a theft at our house and all the jewelry was stolen."

Fortunately, Razaq also took responsibility for all the details of the marriage arrangements, including the dowry. Sabra's brothers also played their part, for this was the first of Sabra's children to be married and it was incumbent on them to provide the *bhāt*. Sabra received Rs. 3,000, fourteen suits (two for the bride, one for the groom, and the rest for Sabra and her other children), and three pieces of jewelry for the bride—gold nose stud and nose ring and a silver necklace.[11]

This was all a great relief to Sabra, who proudly displayed all the items to us on the wedding day while the wedding party from the boy's village was being received by the Jhakri men at Sabra's new house on the village outskirts. The bride and her female relatives were inside the village, waiting in one corner of the compound of Bashir, Sabra's father-in-law and the bride's grandfather. But when we asked if Bashir was making any contribution to the marriage expenses, Sabra denied it vehemently. "My mother-in-law," she told us, "made a curse that these children of mine would end up in a desolate place with no one to care for them. But did Allah forget them?"

"A person who has killed off someone else's money and land cannot live happily," commented Razaq's wife.

"Yes," said Sabra nodding, "just look how much land our father-in-law has sold. And still one or another person who has lent him money is standing up and demanding his money back. Stealing someone's entitlement isn't right. He'll never be able to live properly. He didn't even give two acres to us out of the ten or twelve acres he used to have."

* * *

Bashir's behavior caused no surprise in Jhakri. The role taken on by Razaq, however, was a source of wonder in the village. One young man reminded us of the thefts that Suleiman and Razaq had perpetrated years back and commented that Razaq was transformed. Maybe the deaths of his first wife and his brother had chastened him; maybe he was afraid of what punishment Allah might bring him next. One woman reported that Razaq had not let his niece sit on the ground during the seclusion before her marriage but had insisted that she sit on a bed. Another woman told us that Razaq had responded to his niece's tearfulness by saying that he would make good directly any shortages she felt there were in the dowry. But she also added a note of caution: "Sabra has six girls, and her brother-in-law has arranged the marriage for one of them. There are still five others. I don't know if he'll do all the other weddings. Uncles like that are rare. But his second wife is from the city, and she's very good."

The future, then, was uncertain for Sabra and her children: "The younger girls are still studying. I want them to study reading books as well as the Holy Qur'ān. But then that'll be enough. What, are they to be made to go out for employment? If there were a school or madrasā in Jhakri, I might let them study more. But no one in Jhakri teaches children. I'd like them to be married into farming families so that they can eat from their own land. But beyond that, it's a question of their destiny what sort of husband they get."

As for the boy, Sabra would also like to see him educated: "There's so little land. What can come from it? If he's willing to study, I'll send him to the madrasā in Begawala to become Hāfyz Qur'ān. Then I'll send him to the government school in Dharmnagri. If he wants to continue further, I'll send him to Bijnor. If he studies, he could get an educated wife, somewhat schooled, too. I want him to study and then get service. But beyond education, Allah is the master."

ACKNOWLEDGMENTS

The research on which this account is based was funded by the Economic and Social Research Council (U.K.), the Hayter Fund at the University of Edinburgh, and by the Overseas Development Administration (U.K.). We are grateful to our research assistants: the late Radha Rani Sharma, Swaleha Begum, Swatantra Tyagi, Chhaya Sharma, and Zarin Ahmed. This research would not have been possible without the warm welcome and willing involvement of the villagers of Dharmnagri and Jhakri, and we are well aware of the debt we owe them.

NOTES

1. Scheduled Castes are castes listed in a schedule of the Indian Constitution as previously having been "untouchable" and therefore in need of protection and positive discrimination.

2. See P. Jeffery, R. Jeffery, and A. Lyon (1989); R. Jeffery and P. Jeffery (1997).

3. See P. Jeffery and R. Jeffery (1996a), in which Sabra's story is chapter 16. All personal names here are the pseudonyms used in our other publications on rural Bijnor.

4. For more discussion of widowhood in India, see Chen (1998); Chen (2000); Chen and Drèze (1992); Chen and Drèze (1995a) and (1995b); Chowdhry (1994: 74–120, 356–377); P. Jeffery and R. Jeffery (1996a), especially chapters 14 and 15; Kolenda (1987a) and (1987b: 288–354). Vatuk (1990) and (1995) discusses widows' fears of dependency on their sons, while Wadley (1995b) presents an account of a woman who overcame some of the difficulties of widowhood; see also Wadley (1994: 25–9, 154–162) and (1995a).

5. There are, in fact, several pieces of legislation relating to the curtailment of dowry, but they have been ineffective in combating the rise in dowry in north India.

6. ANMs had an eighteen-month training, and were employed by the government and posted at dispensaries and clinics. They were primarily responsible for maternal and child health, including prenatal and postnatal care, immunizations for children and pregnant women, and family planning.

7. See P. Jeffery, R. Jeffery, and A. Lyon (1987) and R. Jeffery and P. Jeffery (1993) for further discussion of the dāī.

8. In local understandings of conception and pregnancy, the life or spirit enters the baby only at the end of three months, at which point its sex is also fixed. Only then do women talk unequivocally about "pregnancy" rather than having "periods in arrears." The terms "abortion" or "medical termination of pregnancy" cover actions that are distinguished by women in rural Bijnor: an abortion at five months is considered problematic (and sinful) in a way that one at two

months is not. See P. Jeffery, R. Jeffery, and A. Lyon (1989: 74–77) and P. Jeffery and R. Jeffery (1996b).

9. Women may take so-called *seh palat* medicines at the end of the second or third month of pregnancy to ensure that the baby's sex becomes fixed as male. Many of our informants were skeptical about the efficacy or appropriateness of *seh palat* medicines, but their existence (and the lack of comparable medicines to obtain daughters) reflects the importance of having sons. See P. Jeffery, R. Jeffery, and A. Lyon (1989: 191–193) and R. Jeffery, P. Jeffery, and A. Lyon (1984: 1210).

10. Many castes were associated with occupations. Julahas were generally associated with weaving, although they did not necessarily earn all their income that way. Chandpuri was a mixed Hindu-Muslim village near Dharmnagri and Jhakri, and many of the Julaha homes had working looms.

11. The bhāt should be given by a woman's brothers at the first marriage of one of her children. It is one of many continuing obligations that men have to their out-married daughters and sisters.

"Out Here in Kathmandu": Youth and the Contradictions of Modernity in Urban Nepal

Mark Liechty

Kathmandu's Thamel tourist district is a place where imaginations meet. Every year hundreds of thousands of people from around the world pass through Thamel on visits to Kathmandu and Nepal's "adventure tourism" hinterlands, each carrying with them images of Nepal—mediated memories of an "exotic" and "mysterious" place they have never known outside of magazines, books, films, and travelers' tales. At the same time Nepalis—often young people on the margins of society—come to Thamel with their own mediated images of foreignness. For them the bustling, cosmopolitan streets of Thamel provide the window through which to slip, even if only momentarily, into the imagined pleasures of modernity that they know through magazines, books, films, and travelers' tales. In Thamel Nepalis and foreigners interact, playing roles (wittingly or otherwise) in each other's imaginings of "other" places.

Although Thamel is often so crowded with young tourists that Nepalis sometimes refer to it as *"kuire* country"—using a derogatory term for fair-skinned foreigners—those *Nepalis* one sees in Thamel are mostly young men, the majority of them workers from rural districts around Kathmandu who put in long hours for low wages as cooks, waiters, and dishwashers in the dozens of Thamel tourist cafes and restaurants. But those young men one sees "hanging out" on the streets and in certain cafes and bars are often representatives of two categories: tourist hustlers (who are often drug users) and "*punks*"[1]—middle-class young men who cultivate a tough but suave and fashionable persona. Few tourists are aware of Thamel's unsavory local reputation for drugs, danger, and assorted illicit activities. For many Kathmandu young people, to frequent Thamel is to claim a vaguely sinister tough-guy reputation associated with drug use and/or violence. Most of the city's middle- and upper-middle-class young people congregate in other parts of town; to be in Thamel one should be tough and ready to prove it.

DOWN AND "OUT HERE" IN KATHMANDU: DRUGS AND DREAMS FROM THE BOTTOM

Although a generation ago drugs were an important part of Kathmandu's tourist allure, by the 1990s drug use among tourists was not that common. One Thamel dealer in his thirties remembered "better times" but noted that now maybe only two or three out of a hundred tourists showed any interest in his whispered offers of "hash, real cheap." Ironically Kathmandu's drug market is now mostly propelled by local demand, and the substances of choice are often "harder" drugs like heroin and various commercially produced (and unregulated) pharmaceuticals.

Thamel's reputation for drugs is only indirectly related to tourism; tourists help finance local users. White heroin from Thailand and Burma is too expensive for Kathmandu users; the brown or unrefined heroin from India and Afghanistan makes up most of the local market. In the early 1990s a gram of "*brown sugar*" cost 400 Nepali rupees (compared to Rs. 1,200/gram for white).[2] At this rate, an "average" habit of one-half grams per day required a monthly cash outlay of at least 6,000 rupees, close to double the monthly salary of most civil servants. With the prospects for getting *any* job, let alone a high-paying one, abysmally low for even privileged young people, it is not surprising that most addicts eventually ended up pursuing tourists on the streets of Thamel. Taking profits on hashish or pot, changing hard currency on the black market, or acting as a tour guide, in Thamel a skilled hustler can make enough for a daily fix in a matter of hours.

Ramesh was one such person. Although I had encountered Ramesh several times in previous years, when I met him on a Thamel street one chilly spring morning in 1991 his gaunt and tired appearance seemed to confirm reports that he had relapsed into a heroin habit. As we walked together through Thamel in the months that followed, Ramesh threw light on a dimension of reality around us which was completely new to me. In Ramesh's company places I knew well would suddenly evaporate as glimpses of other (and others') places came briefly into view. Sitting together in a Thamel garden cafe that I had frequented for years, Ramesh opened my eyes to a parallel reality: drug transactions, police surveillance, schoolboys drinking codeine cough syrup, a junkie tottering out of the bathroom, his face flushed from retching, unable to keep down any food. Here was a kind of violence—usually quiet and self-destructive—that, once seen, shattered the tranquil image that I and other foreigners imposed on that place: our imaginations rendered this violence invisible and inaudible.

Ramesh introduced me to friends and fellow street hustlers. For these young men supporting addictions meant maintaining the precarious balance between presenting a "clean" and nonthreatening image to potential tourist clients, and successfully procuring a daily fix. Losing one's composure meant losing customers, which meant missing a fix and further damaging one's ability to make money. One victim of this truly vicious cycle was Tamding, a Tibetan refugee and former monk with a severe heroin addiction. When I met him Tamding was in his late twenties and sleeping on the streets: thin, filthy, and with a full-gram-a-day heroin habit, he was close to death. Reduced to begging and unable to support his habit, he used what money he had on incredible "pharma-cocktails"—seemingly deadly combinations of powerful sedatives, synthetic opiates, and psychiatric drugs that would temporarily induce sleep and mask the effects of heroin withdrawal. In tears Tamding described how a few months earlier his younger brother had died after eating refuse out of a Thamel tourist restaurant dumpster. It was clear that Tamding himself would not survive the next intestinal parasite he encountered.

Ramesh was in better shape, though his personal background would not have suggested his current condition. Ramesh's parents had moved to Kathmandu from an eastern hill district when he was in his early teens. He had attended a respected English-medium high school in the valley and learned to read and speak English. He had first tried heroin as a high school student, but over the course of a few years in which his mother died and his father married a woman with several sons, Ramesh developed a habit that grew out of control. Through a combination of mistrust between him and family members, a slow-burning resentment over his father's remarriage, and an increasingly disruptive heroin addiction, Ramesh began to spend more and more time living with friends and, eventually, on the streets. The previous year, after he went through a detoxification program, his good English had landed him a coveted (though typically low-paying) sales job in a retail shop catering to tourists. He swore to me that he had stayed clean and would still be working had not someone told the manager that he was a former junkie. (Others claimed that he had been caught trying to sell drugs to tourists.) By the early 1990s Ramesh had been in and out of drug rehabilitation seven times and had little more than the clothes on his back and the few rupees in his pocket. He lived by his wits day to day, hustling tourists, selling drugs, taking profits on petty commodity transactions, and running a variety of scams like sewing foreign labels into locally produced garments.

From a middle-class family, the product of an English-medium school, and a heavy consumer of imported Hindi and English mass media, from videos to detective novels, Ramesh had much in common with his peers. As with many others, consuming foreign media had made Ramesh painfully aware of the limitations of his life as a Nepali, a life that he constantly compared to lives lived in distant power centers. Ramesh constantly evaluated his Nepaliness through his media awareness of life in the West and Far East even though he himself had never traveled farther than North India. In my presence, he repeatedly brought up images of "America" compared to which he found his own life one of extreme deprivation.

> R: Out here young people like me, we want a *fast* life, not this slow life.
> M: What do you mean a *"fast"* life?
> R: I mean like in the States where you can stay out all night until you drop. Here there's nothing, no [late-night] bars, and we can't even go anywhere to play video games.

When I asked how he knew about bars and video games, he explained that he had learned all about these things from movies and novels.

Indeed Ramesh was a special connoisseur of films, books, magazine articles—anything he could find—especially those having to do with New York City. He knew all the city's boroughs and landmarks but he was especially intrigued by "the Bronx," a place he brought up again and again in our conversations. From dozens of tough-guy movies and gangster novels, Ramesh had constructed a detailed image of a New York street culture full of drugs and gangs. He frequently compared Kathmandu's street life with that of New York, like when he explained how Kathmandu "gangs" take "tabs" (specific prescription drug tablets) before going to a fight, "just like in the Bronx." Ramesh could quote lines from Mafioso novels, and he frequently spoke of how one's face should never show feeling, a lesson he learned from *The Godfather*. Ramesh's ultimate goal was to move to "the States" and live in New York City. He often spoke in vague terms of a cousin living in Seattle who might help him get there.

Ironically, it seemed sometimes as though Ramesh already lived in New York. "The Bronx" in particular seemed to be a kind of shadow universe where his mind roamed while his body navigated the streets of Thamel. "The Bronx"—with its street-smarts and anti-heroic codes of valor—was often the standard of reality against which he measured his own existence. At times it seemed that Ramesh was only imagining his life in Kathmandu against the reality of "the Bronx," not vice versa. For Ramesh "the Bronx" seemed to offer a way of understanding his own life, a life that he hated, yet which he could link with a way of existence at the modern metropole. Ramesh's vision of "the Bronx" allowed him to identify his own existence as at least some version of "modernity," even if it lacked the all-night bars, video games, and a host of other modern accoutrements that he had never seen in more than two dimensions.

Like many other young adults I met in Kathmandu, when speaking in English Ramesh constantly referred to the place he had spent most of his life as "out here." "Out here in Kathmandu" prefaced so many of his comments that in the course of time the words barely registered in my mind. This persistent self-peripheralization is almost unimaginable outside the context of global media and a host of other marginalizing transnational cultural forces, including tourism and commodity imports. Mass media (as well as tourists and foreign goods) act like a lens which situates the local in an implicitly devalued and diminished "out here" place, while at the same time seeming to provide a window onto modern places that are distant in both time and space. But if the video screen is like a window, it is one with bars that keep viewers like Ramesh outside, "out here" looking in.

THAMEL TOUGH GUYS: FIGHTING BOREDOM

While Ramesh struggled with images of a seemingly foreign modernity on the streets of Thamel, other young Kathmandu men came to Thamel to live out fantasies that were much more localized. If part of Thamel's reputation for "toughness" and danger is tied to its drug culture, the area is also infamous for its gang activity and violence. Ramesh often starred in his own internal dramas, but other young men are tied into a variety of loosely organized, hierarchical factions or "*gangs*" which occasionally enact group dramas of toughness that may become violent. Though by no means the only spot in town that sees gang activity, Thamel is known for having more, and more serious, violence.

For Europeans and North Americans "gangs" and "idle youths" hanging out on street corners ("corner boys") are usually associated with lower- or working-class backgrounds, but in Nepal the poor do not have the luxury of becoming what are known in Nepali as "*punks*." Ironically, in Kathmandu the "tough-guy," "street-fighter" persona is the privilege of a kind of "leisure class." They are members of a middle class that, while not wealthy by first-world standards, would rather have its educated young people unemployed than engaged in anything but white-collar labor. In an enormously glutted middle-class labor market, young people are more or less idle for years between high-school graduation and the beginning of any meaningful employment (Liechty 1995).

Leading lives of essentially forced inactivity and boredom, young people, especially young men, often experiment with fantasies of "action" with scripts loosely based on the media images that fill much of their day-to-day lives. Of the many "action" fantasies available, some are more active and potentially violent than others. Thamel is a popular hangout for a certain kind of middle-class action seeker willing to "*fight* khelnu"—literally "to play at fighting."[3] A Kathmandu journalist in his early thirties described a fight he had recently witnessed in Thamel:

I saw those people and they weren't the types who have nothing, you know. They were like me, just a little younger, that's all. I didn't see anyone who didn't look like [their family owned] a house in Kathmandu. It's all these people who at least have a house and their parents are working—basically middle-class types.

Said another young man, only half sarcastically, "The poor kids have gangs in America then they make movies about them and it's the rich kids who watch them here!" In Kathmandu the areas that have the worst reputations for juvenile violence—where taxi drivers hesitate to go at night—are usually the middle-class neighborhoods in the suburbs, not the poverty-stricken areas in the old city.

In many respects the young men who hang out in Thamel are similar to the Japanese *bosozoku* described by Ikuya Sato (1991). Bosozoku are young middle-class men who live for the thrill of dressing up in tough-looking clothes, and driving their modified cars and motorcycles at suicidal speeds (known as "*boso* driving") down the city streets of Japan. Like the young "*punks*" in Kathmandu, in certain times and places becoming an anti-social and dangerous bosozoku offers young people an expressive experience in what would otherwise be "extraordinarily boring and purposeless" lives (Sato 1991: 4). Yet whereas bosozoku culture revolves around modified vehicles and the potential dangers of hot-rodding, Kathmandu "*punks*" are much more likely to fixate on what one might call "modified bodies"—disciplined through regimens of martial arts and bodybuilding —and the potential dangers of fighting. Bosozoku idolize characters from films like *Mad Max* and fantasize about the "fierce-looking Kawasaki 1000 vehicles they use in the movie" (Sato 1991: 77), while Kathmandu tough guys are more likely to be avid "kung fu" film consumers, and focus on the moves and bodies (of both "heroes" and "villains") depicted in those movies.

More than just a recent media-generated fantasy, the "toughness" projected by these young men in Thamel has an important history in Nepal. From "Gurkha" soldiers to "Sherpa" mountaineers, many Nepalis literally make a living off of the now global image of the fearless, robust, and tireless Himalayan hill man.[4] Indeed "Gurkha" and even "Sherpa" are now essentially professional titles, as often as they designate ethnic or regional identities. Although the image and rhetoric of the brave "Gurkha" soldier is more than simply a colonial fantasy, the fact that British colonizers identified several populations in west-central and eastern Nepal as among the subcontinent's innately warlike "martial tribes" is an important factor in both the historical construction, and continued salience, of an essentialized image of the *bahādur* (brave and courageous) Nepali male. For centuries the British and Indian armies have recruited Nepali "Gurkha" fighters, and many parts of rural Nepal are dependent on this form of mercenary labor (Des Chene 1991).

It is perhaps no coincidence that among those young men in Thamel with the "toughest" reputations, many are from the very "martial tribes" that have traded in toughness for centuries (Gurung, Rai, etc.). Precisely where and how "toughness" as a colonial artifact articulates with new media-generated images such as the kung fu hero is difficult to say. But perhaps most important is how a "deterritorialized" global media genre like the kung fu film becomes embedded in a highly idiosyncratic local history that is itself already inflected by centuries of transnational cultural processes.

In informal interviews conducted in a Thamel restaurant two young men talked about (among other things) their tastes in films. The first—a twenty-year-old Gurung with long hair, fashionable clothes, and a muscular build—explained which kind of "*English*" films he liked most:

> G: I like certain kinds, like *Rambo,* *commando* films, and the *kung fu,* *karate* films, you know, Bruce Lee, Jackie Chan, and all that stuff.
> M: Why these kinds?
> G: Now, while I'm a youth, I like to be brave and active. This is what I like to do.
> M: How did you get into watching English films?
> G: My friends all watch only English films and at first I didn't really like them but after a while, I got into the habit and I could understand what was going on. At first I didn't like them. But now I like them a lot.

His friend, a few years younger but also well-dressed and extremely fit, also claimed English films as his favorites.

> M: For example, what kind?
> F: Let's see . . . Well, there's *kung fu.* I like Bruce Lee *so* much. If I feel *bored,* like if there is some really *boring* time,[5] I like to go watch a Bruce Lee film.
> If I do, *automatically* I begin to feel very energetic, very strong and eager. All these feelings start to rise up! I've probably seen six different Bruce Lee movies already. There was *Enter the Dragon,* *Way of the Dragon,* and others too.

For both of these young men film preference had to do with imagining themselves as particular kinds of youth, ones who are tough, active, brave, and eager.

Part of the "tough guy" persona involves adopting a studied presentation. In addition to fashioned bodies and fashionable clothing, young "*punks*" in Thamel cultivated a kind of expressionless countenance (like Ramesh), slow, fluid body movements, and a variety of striking postures and actions. A tricky way of lighting a cigarette, smoking in a sensual and suave manner, a sophisticated demeanor, effortlessly performing intricate dance movements: in Thamel young Nepalis often surpassed "first world" visitors in cosmopolitan sophistication.

In addition to the often-mediated fantasies of toughness, bravery, and violence, perhaps the ultimate fantasies pursued in Thamel are sexual, and in particular, fantasies of sexual relations between Nepali men and foreign women.[6] An essential part of any claim to distinction in the "play world" of the Thamel tough guys is the ability to attract foreign women (or at least a reputation for doing so). With its bars, music cafes, and hotels, Thamel is the prime location in Kathmandu for engaging in these transnational sexual fantasies. Even if many tales of sexual prowess are exaggerated, there is no doubt that out of the over one hundred thousand Euro-American women who visit Nepal each year, a few bring with them romantic fantasies of a kind that complement those of some young men in Thamel.[7] Compared with male fellow-travelers, young female tourists from Europe and North America seemed more interested in having a "local experience" that included friendships with Nepalis. Because the Nepali people they encounter are likely to be in Thamel, there are fairly frequent opportunities for young "*punks*" to meet foreign women. What for these women may seem like a pleasant local friendship may, for the young men involved, be very sexually-charged. Even if there is no sexual contact, these relationships may be the stuff of erotic fantasies and boasting among friends.

One young man I met came close to epitomizing the Thamel sophisticate. When I met Pradip, the friend of a friend, he was only in his late twenties and already owned a restaurant/bar and a small lodge in a prime Thamel location. Having owned land in Thamel, Pradip's family was able to cash in on the tourist boom of the 1970s and '80s (Liechty 1996). Pradip had received a first-rate English education, had grown up around foreigners, could converse in several European languages, and was a refined and engaging conversationalist by any standards. His reputation for sexual conquest was probably based more on speculation than evidence but on several occasions he spoke of his relationships with foreign women. Pradip identified one woman in particular as his "girlfriend"—an American from California, whom he had met several years earlier. She came to Nepal at least once a year and they were in regular phone contact. Clearly they had a sincere relationship, but, Pradip confessed, deep down, he knew it could not work. He described how one evening on her most recent visit she had been out smoking hash with friends and did not return to the lodge until the early morning. When Pradip angrily demanded an explanation, she exclaimed, "You don't own me! I can do what I like." Furthermore, his girlfriend assumed that he would eventually move to the United States. "Why should I go to America?" Pradip asked.

There I couldn't get a very good job but would just have to work all day for little money. Here I have plenty of money and I don't have to work! Here I have my bar and my lodge. They are both in profit. Why would I want anything different?

In the meantime Pradip introduced me to a young woman from the consular affairs office of the French Embassy whom he had been "dating for the past six months." It was clear that ultimately Pradip was not interested in marrying a Western woman, even though he greatly enjoyed such company. Pushing thirty, Pradip was thinking of "settling down" and had realized that while Western women—witty and unreserved—were good to have in a Thamel restaurant (and possibly in a hotel room), a Nepali woman—obedient and demure—was good to have at home. For Pradip different kinds of imagined women belonged in different imagined places.

"STARS OF ACTION": THE POLITICS OF DESIRE

During the early 1990s Star Beer (produced in Nepal) staked its claim in the increasingly competitive Nepali national alcohol market with an interesting jingle that ran frequently on Radio Nepal. Even though almost all of Radio Nepal's programming is in Nepali, the Star Beer jingle was in English:

> It takes a star of action, to satisfy a man like you,
> Smooth reaction, to satisfy a man like you,
> Men like you who want to see, men like you who want to be,
> Stars of action with Star Beer.

It struck me as no coincidence that advertisers would wish to capitalize on the desire to "see" and "be" "stars of action." The ad seemed to capture, in caricature, the "smooth reaction" of the suave, Thamel tough-guy persona, and then play on the related longing for "action." "Men like you" not only "want to see" the media stars of imaginary action, but also "want to be" those "stars of action."

For the young Nepalis who navigated its streets, Thamel seemed to encapsulate the anxious yearning for "action" and "satisfaction" that the Star Beer advertisement sought to capitalize on. For young men like Ramesh and Pradip, Thamel was a place with a distinctive ethos, a quasi-foreign place in which to *experiment with* and, for those "lucky" enough, to *indulge in* images and fantasies of foreignness and modernity. For Ramesh—the heroin addict who came to Thamel to hustle tourists and dream of life on the streets of New York—dreams of foreign places made Nepal a place to flee. For Pradip and other Thamel sophisticates who successfully enacted the ethos of the Thamel transnational "play world," Thamel was a place to escape from local dramas into the mediated fantasies of a foreign modernity. Thamel was a fantasy space where a global traffic in images of "traditional" Nepal and foreign "modernity" flowed through and past one another, perpetuating the ideological economy in which "Nepali modernity" remained not just a paradox, but an oxymoron.

In places like Thamel, "first" and "third worlds" ("modernity" and "tradition") implode into one another; both tourists and locals come to Thamel to find the "others" they imagine. Although brought together in Thamel by a now global economy of desire for "other" meaning—whether the tourists' nostalgia for the "exotic" periphery or the Nepali youths' desire for the "modern"—the distance between their imagined places (and the fact that only one group may actually indulge their fantasies *in* the "others' space") not only reflects but reinforces the global contours of power and privilege that keep Nepali youth "out here in Kathmandu."

ACKNOWLEDGMENTS

I am grateful to the International Institute for Asian Studies (IIAS) of Leiden, the Netherlands, for a postdoctoral fellowship during which I wrote much of this essay. Parts of this essay were originally published in Liechty 1996.

NOTES

1. Words appearing between asterisks in quoted material designate use of English in colloquial Nepali.

2. In the early 1990s 400 Nepali rupees was equal to roughly 10 U.S. dollars. In 1991 Nepal's average annual per capita income was only 180 U.S. dollars (Central Bureau of Statistics 1994: 260).

3. Unlike *kusti khelnu* (to wrestle), *murki hānnu* (to punch), or *jhagaṛā garnu* (to quarrel, or tussle), "*fight* *khelnu*" is a term/concept that entered local language and practice via films. "*Fight* *khelnu*" refers both to the surrealistic choreographed fight sequences in South Asian potboilers and East Asian "kung-fu" films, and also to the dramatic role acting between individuals and "*gangs*" which occasionally escalates into serious physical violence, especially when weapons are involved.

4. Adams (1996) and Ortner (1999) are two important recent studies of the historical and cultural construction of Sherpa identity.

5. When used in spoken Nepali various forms of the English word "bore" can have meanings slightly different from common usage in the West. In addition to tedium or monotony, in Nepali feeling "*bored*" can imply sadness, depression, and frustration. In fact, the two sets of feelings are not antithetical and seem to be common features of life for many middle-class youth in Kathmandu.

6. As I discuss in detail elsewhere, these sexual fantasies of "other women" are at least in part tied into the heavy consumption of Euro-American and East Asian pornography in Kathmandu (Liechty 1994 [chapter 14]; Liechty 2001).

7. Because Nepali women have far fewer opportunities to interact with foreign men, there seems to be very little sexual contact across this divide. Unlike Bangkok, Kathmandu is not a destination for Euro-American or East Asian male sex tourism, even though it has an active prostitution scene. According to my sources (social workers, medical personnel, journalists, hotel managers), the only foreigners that employ Kathmandu prostitutes are Indians (truckers, businessmen, tourists).

The Role of Suffering in Women's Performance of *Paxto*

Benedicte Grima

Paxtuns were studied and described first by British colonialists stationed in what they called Northern India (present day Afghanistan and Northwest Pakistan) in the mid-nineteenth century. Later, they became of interest to anthropologists as a tribal society and were studied by Jon Anderson (1982), Fredrik Barth (1959, 1981), Akbar S. Ahmed (1980), Charles Lindholm (1982), the Tappers, and others. What most of these studies have in common is that they are conducted by men and focus on male culture and society. Paxtun areas, as viewed from the outside public realm, seem at first very hostile and harsh, and most unaccompanied women do not feel comfortable there. Indeed, the outsider among them is treated with utmost suspicion and aggression, particularly if she happens to be female. The language is difficult and little instruction exists. The result is that few women have chosen to do fieldwork in that area, and so the Paxtun world is presented largely as a men's world. Those women who have written about Paxtun women's culture have so far presented the institution of marriage (Lindholm and Lindholm 1979; Tapper 1987), the position of women in Paxtun tribal society (Ahmed and Ahmed 1981), and women's rebellion in folk poetry (Boesen 1980, 1983).

Anthropologists, travelers, and generalists writing about Paxtuns have never failed to mention the code of honor and modesty/shame, a code with rigid behavioral requirements sometimes referred to as *paxtun-wali*. The word *paxto* itself designates not only the language but also the behavior defined by the code. Almost every Paxtun is familiar with the proverb: "You don't speak Paxto; you do *paxto*." Indeed, people daily refer to "having" or "doing" *paxto* in describing others or in socializing children. *Paxto*, in this sense, is equivalent to honor. *Paxto*, the code of honor, and not just Paxto, the language, defines the person.[1]

So what does it mean to have, do, or perform this *paxto*?

The doing of *paxto* for men generally means showing oneself as strong, combatant, generous, and hospitable. It is the side of the code which has been elaborated by male ethnographers relying on data from male informants. I now turn to what *paxto* means for women.

Just as the gun and turban are typically used as images to exemplify Paxtun manhood, I suggest that tears and the endurance of hardship exemplify Paxtun womanhood. This is true both in the image of women as created by men in popular culture (films, romances, songs, poetry) and in women's images of themselves. I would like to illustrate this notion of honor in suffering by discussing narrative[s] in which women present themselves to each other.

I focus on narratives of the self among Paxtun women. I shall begin by introducing the life story as it is perceived and performed. I am using this data to suggest that the display, or performance, of emotion, in this case of loss and suffering, is related to identity: Paxtun, Muslim, and feminine. It is these stories and events that inform us about people.

When I first did formal fieldwork in 1982, I began by looking for women's performances of the popular romances with which I had previously worked. Actually, I was looking for any kind of household narratives. The following is a passage taken from field notes at that time.

> Shama Babi is both criticized and widely acclaimed in her village for being a great narrator of *qessa* [stories]. Almost daily, she comes to visit the household where I am staying as a guest, and takes and holds the floor for hours with stories defaming other women, or with tragic personal narratives, most of which have been heard numerous times before by this community of women, but which they urge her to tell for me. The first time I expressed interest in Shama Babi's narrative and asked to tape it, she delightedly responded: "Oh, that's the kind of *qessa* you wanted. You should have said so. I thought you wanted *qessa* like *Adam Khan* or *Yusuf Khan* [popular folk romances], and I don't know any of those. This kind, I can tell you many of, and make you cry like no one else can."
>
> I sat with Shama Babi and recorded her for three days. She narrated, and groups of women would come and go in her courtyard as time allowed. Her tales were mostly sad and personal ones, recounting the painful events of her husband's death, her son's car accident when he was a child, and her daughter's wedding. It became clear as I listened and watched the audience that the more personal suffering she could express, aided by tears and outcries and occasional wailed verses, the better her tale was esteemed by the small audience of women.

It was Shama Babi and others like her who slowly led me to acknowledge this neglected genre as what was most told and valued by women. I began to see the personal-event narratives and life stories emerge as the major performance genre both in ritual contexts, which I later describe, and in informal contexts of intimacy. It was a private genre told by women to women, and the more I made my loyalties to the women's domain known by eliminating my interaction with men, the more I became privy to these personal tales. Not only did I become privy, I also gained a reputation as "the one who is interested in our sad tales," which is how I was often introduced to new women by those wanting to have me record all the best stories.

These narratives are a performed and framed genre with defined social contexts and rules. Each time they are told, it is with the implicit message of asserting and reasserting membership and reputation as a good Paxtun in the community. Each is saying: "Look what I've been through. I've suffered one hardship after another, and endured it. I'm still here." The quest for honor is a quest for reputation. In fact, the motivation behind most behavior among Paxtuns is a concern for one's reputation, a fear of being accused of not performing *paxto*. We can extend this interpretation to the way women present themselves in their personal narratives.

In her work on the Bedouin discourse of self and sentiment, Abu-Lughod (1985, 1986) proposed that there exist two ideologies, each with its own models of and for different types of experience.[2] She juxtaposes the poetic discourse of self and sentiment, on the one hand, and the ordinary, everyday discourse of honor and modesty, on the other. Her clear-cut distinction, however, leaves one curious about the array of possible narrative genres among the Bedouin that she does not mention. The life stories told by Paxtun women are also vehicles for sentiment and emotion that are inappropriate to tell out of specific contexts of intimacy and privacy, but at the same time, they are a discourse of honor that gains them reputation. This can perhaps best be illustrated in discussions evaluating the type of narrative being collected, such as the following dialogue I had with a major informant in Ahmadi Banda[3] who was deciding, along with her friends, whom to send me to for a good story. It is the metafolklore that supplies crucial data for research:

> *Selma:* You must go see X. She's really got the best story to tell.
> *BG:* What makes her story so good?
> *S:* She's undergone so much *gham* [sorrow, pain, hardship, suffering]. She's really endured a lot.
> *BG:* Can you or someone else tell her story?
> *S:* No, only the person herself, or someone who knew her very well. The best story is always told by the person herself.

As Selma demonstrates, a longing for truth and for knowledge of each other and of events outside their compound has created a requirement for accurate reporting among women. There is a thirst among Paxtun women for autobiography. There is also a correct way to "seek the person out" with questions. One day, when my daughter's nanny had observed me eliciting a life story from someone, she later tried to correct me on the grounds that I did not know how to interrogate properly. "You foreigners don't know how to search [*latawal*] each other," she reproached me. "When we Pakistanis[4] ask a person's story, we don't let a single detail go by. We dig in all the corners, high and low. We seek the person out. That's how we do things. We are storytellers and story seekers. We know how to draw out a person's heart." Finally, there is a great appreciation for the skilled teller of her own life story. This skill lies mostly in her ability to move her listeners to tears.

I often asked about and sought out the women communally known to have the best stories and to be the best tellers. As it turned out, most of the women with this reputation had experienced difficult and sad lives. Their experience itself, its beauty judged by the appropriateness according to *paxto*, along with the fact that they had not run from the hardship, made for the best story in community evaluation.

Here is an example of how a life story often begins, and the way it advances:

—The story goes like this, *kana*, that my name is Naseema.
—My mother died when I was a child. Those orphan children remained in my care. My father remained in my care.
—My mother, she died. She died in childbirth. My brother remained, only a year old. I took care of him. Then he grew up, *kana?*

—Then I got married. Then my father gave me away. I got married. Those orphans stayed in the house with their father. I have no mother.
—My brother stayed with my father and I would climb over the roof so he could see me. Like, he was sad, *kana?* His mother was dead. He didn't know his mother. He was still crawling on all fours.
—A husband took me. A man married me. My father gave me to him. They all stayed behind.
—Now, they would wait, and I'd bring them bread by way of the rooftops. Bread, which I'd throw down to them. He'd come crawling on all fours, and then would eat it.

—Now, I came by the road. My father beat me. He said, "Why are you running a stranger's house and coming here looking after this boy? You've become a non-kin woman to us. Don't come to my house. You run your stranger's house."

—Now, I had another sister. I had another sister. Then my father gave her away, too. They [father and children] stayed alone.
—Then my father died. I brought them all over with me.

—Then my house fell apart. I had three children. I became a widow with three children. I was a young widow. Then I stayed.

—Then I got to it and took another husband, that fish man.
—My brothers got upset with me. They left. They said that, "You've left us, just like that."
—Now, they cut off relations with me for four years.

—Now, my father went and fell down in the road. His heart failed. He died.
—A whole lot of people came. My father died.
—I cried. My other brother came. I cried. I cried a lot. I cried that: "My father died upset with me. My father died vexed."
—Like, lots and lots of people cried.

—Then, in the meantime, time passed and passed. I left home and went to Kalam. My seven-year-old son died. Then he died in the meantime.
—Lots of people kept coming for us. They all came. The people cried. The boy was dead. Three days. People kept coming for many days. He was dead.

—Then, some time later, my husband performed the *hajj* and took my co-wife.
—My daughter cried. I cried. All my neighbors were upset for me, that he had taken her and not me.
—Then he came back. He had hidden the dates, and those garlands.
—Then again I cried and was filled with grief.

—Then my daughter got married very young. I cried after her. She used to help me with the children. She does that for me, like, the housework. My brother went with her.
—I came in that grief and again cried after my daughter because I'd given her away in tribal area. I'd sold my own daughter. I'd done her an injustice. I cried again.

—Then their father jumped up and he broke my arm. I cried again for a month.
—Then I got upset and I cried a whole lot.[5]

In contrast to the autobiographical life story, I have also collected a few biographical accounts of other local famous women, told by women. These were told with more distance, not so much as a series of woeful events. They were also told after expressing tremendous reluctance to do so. Responsibility for another's life is a burden not many want to be accountable for. Selma's comment above was often repeated to me, that the best story is by the protagonist herself, because only she, as narrator, can tell and elicit from her listener(s) the amount of sympathy needed to make a good story.

Discussions with contemporary Paxtun writers, critics, and audiences have yielded similar conclusions in regard to the story line in novels, romances, television or radio dramas, folk tales, and poetry. *Gham* (pain, suffering) is what determines the best story in any of these.

In an interview with a thirty-year-old unmarried rural school teacher, when I asked her about her own life story, I received the following answer: "I have no story to tell. I've been through no hardships." And when I asked her what gave a woman renown, she replied, "Her hardships. How else can she prove herself? If she takes any independent action to better or escape her situation, she'll be stigmatized and even ostracized, and certainly not held in praise. With age and hardship, a woman gains respect, her story becomes known, and she is respected by all in the community for having undergone so much suffering. Her suffering is perceived as action according to the code of honor and morality. If she goes through troubles, it's for the sake of honor. Otherwise, she could be free and take care of herself."

Both *paxto* and Islam, which supply the grid through which action and experience are determined and evaluated, dictate that women should bear with their hardship and not seek to escape or ameliorate it. This endurance is what earns a woman honor and reputation among other women, and makes her worthy of being called Paxtun by them.

Gham, then, along with shame and modesty, is a key cultural term in women's everyday performance of *paxto.* In a woman's life, *gham* and *taklif* (misfortune, hardship) begin with her marriage, when she is cast from the security of her mother's house into an environment of hostile relationships with a mother-in-law, sister(s)-in-law, and even a co-wife, living day after day in the same house with no release from them. It may also begin with her mother's death, but most often with marriage. Before that, she is not expected to know anything about life, or to share in *gham.* She neither considers herself, nor is she considered by the community, to have begun living or to have any kind of story to tell. She is frequently referred to, in this regard, as *kam-aʿqla,* or ignorant.

Just as marriage marks the introduction of *gham* into a woman's life, so does it mark the opening in the story of her life. In fact, the phrase used most often by women to speak of their lives is *taklifuna che mā bānde ter shəwi di* (the misfortunes which have befallen me), as opposed to the more literary Urdu-Persian word for autobiography, *ḥāl-e zendegī.* Many informants, when I asked them for their story, began before I had even set up my taping equipment with a line such as: "My life has been nothing but misery," or "My life has been that of a dog," or "There's been no joy in my life."

The following are some responses I received when I asked women, toward the end of their tragic tales, if they could recall any joy in their lives at all:

—"None. Since I learned good from bad, there's been no joy at all."
—"No. Only unhappiness has come into my life. All unhappiness."
—"I've never seen any joy. My birth itself is a sorrow, a sorrow. There is no joy at all."

Most of the answers to the question were of this nature. A woman's life is perceived almost entirely within a framework of hardship and suffering, beginning with her being severed from her mother. Many women agreed, upon my asking, that the time before marriage had been one of happiness. But hardly any women admitted remembering anything of this period.

The perception and organization of life as a chain of crises and stresses is particularly true of rural and older women. In urban centers, among the younger generations of upper and upper-middle class, educated and working women, there is resentment about perceiving their lives within this framework. I often tried to elicit life stories from these young women, but they claimed they had no story to tell, as the schoolteacher's reply above, "I have no story to tell. I've been through no hardships."

These women expressed the pressure they felt from relatives in the villages and from their elders in the family, to perform a discourse they no longer identify with. One elite Paxtun woman, divorced and working in a women's hospital in Peshawar, complained that she often felt pressured by her patients who wanted to hear her story in terms of the hardships she had encountered as a result of her divorce. She resented these pressures because she did not perceive the experience as being anything other than positive. "These women like to hear life stories," she told me, "but I have none for them." Another young upper-class urban mother originally from Peshawar and now living in Islamabad complained to me that she felt pressured by her mother-in-law to tell the story of her children's birth to relatives in terms of the pain and difficulties she had experienced. It angered her because she had, on the contrary, perceived the births as elating. She also added that she felt more consciously pressured to display a distressed persona among her relatives in Peshawar than among the younger, less traditional ones in Islamabad.

Although my work was conducted mainly among rural, poor women, the dozen or so urban women I spoke with had responses similar to the ones discussed above and told me they had no story. I could elicit no life narratives. However, they were quick and eager to refer me to an old servant woman or to other women from their family villages who were known to tell the "saddest and most beautiful stories." They appreciated the aesthetic of the *gham* but did not personally identify with the genre, as if the life story, defined in *paxto* as a story of *gham*, could only be told by those who still molded their existence into the traditional pattern. There is no new model for the Paxtun life story. Thus not having a life story to tell becomes a statement in itself. It may be saying, "I defy the traditional cultural model, but must remain silent until a new one is formulated."

NOTES

1. *Paxtun* is the adjective and proper noun. *Paxto* is the word used for the language and the code of honor/modesty. For the language, I have used upper case *P*, and for the code of honor lower case *p*. I have used the symbol *x* to represent the Paxto letter, which is spoken as "*sh*" or "*kh*" depending on the speech group. I represent the letter *shīn* by "*sh*," and *khe* by "*kh*," both of which are invariable sounds in Paxto.

2. See Geertz (1973:93–94) for a discussion of models of and for. He differentiates symbolic models or parallels of social or psychological systems (i.e., theories) that represent patterned processes and provide sources of information, from models *for* cultural patterns (i.e., rites, doctrines, melodies) that are required in the communication of pattern.

3. A Khattak village in the Karak district of NWFP, Pakistan, where I conducted most of my fieldwork in 1982–83 and 1986–87.

4. This woman was not originally Paxtun, but Bengali, and had married into a Paxtun family. Although the Paxtun milieu was that which she knew best and which fed her information on Pakistan, she alternated between presenting herself as Paxtun and as Pakistani. On this particular occasion, in private, she was accentuating the difference between me, a foreigner, and her, a Pakistani. When other women were present, she tended more to speak of herself as Paxtun.

5. The full version of this narrative appears in Grima, *The Performance of Emotion among Paxtun Women: "The Misfortunes Which Have Befallen Me"* (Austin: University of Texas Press, 1992).

Love and Aging in Bengali Families
Sarah Lamb

Early on in my days in the West Bengali village of Mangaldihi, I met a woman called Mejo Ma, or "Middle Mother," sitting in the dusty lane in front of her home. She could not stop complaining about clinging. She worried that her ties to her children, to her grandchildren, to her own body, to the pleasures of this life were so strong that they would keep her soul shackled to her world beyond the appropriate time for moving on and dying. "How will I cut my ties to all these kids and things and go?" she lamented. The oldest woman of Mangaldihi, Khudi Thakrun, did not herself worry about clinging, but rather seemed to embrace her many involvements. She lived in the crowded households of her three sons, which were replete with three generations of descendants, the comings and goings of numerous visitors, and the smoke from several cooking fires. She wandered the village daily to spread news, to lend out money at high interest rates to increase her wealth, and to seek the best plums, mangoes, and papayas. Others, however, worried about her eagerly attached ways, saying that her soul could certainly end up as a lingering ghost after death.

These and other older people's stories and predicaments illuminate what many Bengalis see as an inherent dilemma of the life course: its fundamental intensity on the one hand and its irrevocable ephemerality on the other. Life, with all of its pleasure and ties, seems so real and lasting and vital and important as we live it, and yet ultimately it cannot last—a truth that Bengalis say becomes ever more salient in late life. This chapter takes a look at the ways Bengalis in Mangaldihi, and in a Kolkotta old-age home, think about aging, and how their experiences of aging tie into views of love, family, and the life course.[1] Mangaldihi is a large, predominantly Hindu village of about 1,700, in the gently undulating terrain about a hundred kilometers northwest of Kolkotta.

HOUSEFLOWS: AGING AND INTERGENERATIONAL TIES

Aging for Bengalis is not so much defined in terms of chronological years but rather via one's place in a family cycle. Most rural Bengalis do not keep careful track of or celebrate their birthdays; and few count the particular number of years passed in their lives as markers of identity or of life stage. It is the marriage of children, especially the bringing of a daughter-in-law into the home, that initiates the beginnings of the "senior" or "grown" life phase (*buṛo bayas*). Bodily changes—such as graying hair, weakening, and "cooling"[2]—can also be regarded as signs of aging.

It is at this point, when one's children are married and one's body has perhaps grown weaker and cooler, that the seniors shift to a new phase of life and place in the family. The family heads initiate their transition to becoming "senior"—often over a period of several years of competition and ambivalence—by gradually handing over the responsibilities of managing household funds, decision making, cooking, and reproducing children to sons (or a son) and their wives. In this way, the seniors move increasingly to the peripheries of household life. At the same time, the expectation is that their juniors will care for and serve them. Bengalis say that children have a profound social-moral obligation, in fact, to care for their parents in old age, in part because they owe their parents a tremendous "debt" (*ṛṇ*) for being produced and nurtured in infancy and childhood. Khudi Thakrun's oldest son, Gurusaday, strove to care for his mother assiduously, and explained his practices:

> Looking after parents is the children's duty. Sons pay back the debt to their parents of childbirth and being raised by them. The mother and father suffer so much to raise their children. They can't sleep; they wake up in the middle of the night. They clean up their [children's] bowel movements. They worry terribly when the children are sick. And the mother especially suffers. She carries the child in her womb for ten [lunar] months, and she raises him from the blood and milk from her breasts. So if you don't care for your parents, then great sin and injustice happens.

Another man, whose frail mother was incontinent and bedridden, reflected similarly:

> Caring for parents is the children's duty; it is *dharma* [moral-religious order; right way of living]. As parents raised their children, children will also care for their parents during their sick years, when they get old. For example, if I am old and I have a bowel movement, my son will clean it and he won't ask, "Why did you do it there?" This is what we did for him when he was

young. When I am old and dying, who will take me to go pee and defecate? My children will have to do it.

Women often provide much more care for their parents-in-law, inheriting obligations toward their husbands' parents, than they do for their own parents. Parents with only daughters and no sons, however, sometimes choose to keep a married daughter with them, bringing a "house son-in-law" (*ghar jāmāi*) to inherit their property and to care (with their daughter) for them in old age.

Providing care for parents entails both material support (food, shelter, clothing) and *sevā* (respectful, loving service)—such as massaging tired limbs, combing hair, serving food, reading aloud, offering loving companionship, and (if necessary) cleaning up urine and excrement. Caring for seniors also extends beyond old age, as children (particularly sons) reconstruct ancestral bodies for and ritually nourish their parents as ancestors.[3] Such a system of long-term intergenerational reciprocity contrasts with practices in the United States, where among the white middle-class in particular, the dominant expectation is that parent-child gifts will flow "down" from parent to child in a lifelong unidirectional manner. It would make the child and the parent equally uncomfortable if the child were called upon to provide material support or intimate bodily care for his or her parent.

Intimate, smooth, and mutually supportive intergenerational relationships do not always come to fruition, however. Not only can children neglect their parents, but elders can refuse care in various ways. Some people have no children, and other children may be too poor to provide support. Rabilal, an elderly beggar of the leather-working caste, replied pessimistically when I asked him what happens when one grows old, "When you get old, your sons don't feed you rice." He lived in a small hut right next to his two married sons, but they were poor agricultural day laborers and could not spare enough to support their father. A young girl, Beli Bagdi, replied when I asked her what would happen to her in her old age, "Either my sons will feed me rice or they won't; there's no certainty."

Khudi Thakrun's several sons, daughters-in-law, and grandchildren all professed their desire to care for the elder woman. She lived alternately in the three separate homes of her sons, all within about a stone's throw of each other in the same village neighborhood. At each meal, she was served before all others and had the propensity to eat so many of the treats—milk, cottage cheese, sweets, fruit—that sometimes her juniors confessed (privately, but never to her face) to feeling that not enough was left for them. I would come to one of her homes and see her daughter-in-law massaging her dry skin with mustard oil, or a grandson reading to her from the Bhagavad Gita. But she herself did not seem to wish to become the peripheralized (though served) older person whom others expected her and other elders to be—one who received care mostly only from family members and relinquished control of her own property to them. Khudi Thakrun, at about age ninety-seven, continued to maintain a considerable amount of property and money in her own name[4] and, as mentioned above, she would roam the village to lend out her money to needy villagers, earning interest to increase her wealth. She would also commission people who worked in or visited cities to bring back treats for her, and since it was regarded as a great sin and moral injustice to repudiate the request of one as senior as Khudi Thakrun, most complied. I myself became a favorite recipient of her requests and she would ask me to bring back small things, often sweets, from my trips to town. However, once when I brought her a requested bedsheet from Kolkotta, her juniors found out and chastised her, "Why are you asking some girl who has come here from a foreign country to give things to you? You have three sons. They can give things to you." A neighboring woman exclaimed to me, "Such an old woman with three capable sons is still going around pestering others for food! Chi! Chi! An old woman with three sons like that is not supposed to ask others for things—her sons are supposed to give them to her."

Khudi Thakrun's juniors *wanted* to care for her—out of their sense of dharma and for the honor of their family. And in fact they *did* care for her: She lived with and was largely supported by them; she received their sevā, or service and loving care. But Khudi Thakrun rejected some of their sevā, and continued in part to support herself—a matter that concerned somewhat her kin and neighbors, though apparently not her.

Mejo Ma, on the contrary, lived as people expected, very well embedded in her family web, with her two married sons, daughters-in-law, one married grandson, and other grandchildren—happily receiving their sevā and love as the family's most senior member. Perhaps this was one reason why she felt so close to them and worried about how she would leave them all to depart in death.

Transactions of intergenerational reciprocity are practiced and enjoyed to varying extents. But Bengalis say that it is through such transactions— the gifts and services of food, love, and daily care parents and children provide each other at different phases of life—that family ties are created and sustained across generations.

FLEETING LIVES AND THE PROBLEM OF MĀYĀ

The ties binding seniors and juniors across generations are part of what Bengalis call *māyā*. Māyā is a polyvalent term found in all Indian languages, often translated by scholars as "illusion." In its sense as illusion, māyā refers to the everyday, lived world of experience (known as *saṃsāra* in Sanskrit and *saṃsār* in Bengali)—a lived world that is not ultimate or

1. Khudi Thakrun (right) and her daughter.

everlasting (and is thus illusory) but which people feel very tied to and perceive in their daily lives as being "really real." In its more common, everyday sense for Bengalis, māyā means love, attachment, compassion, or affection. A mother has māyā for her child and a child has māyā for her mother. Husbands and wives have māyā for each other. People have māyā for their homes, the plants they have tended carefully in their courtyards, the possessions they have gathered. People feel māyā when they see a tiny calf bleating for its mother, or when a beloved sari is torn. If a grandmother calls her little granddaughter to her to feed her a sweet (even as she may lie dying), that is māyā. When parents weep seeing their newly married daughter depart to her husband's home, they are crying from māyā.

Maya consists not only of what we might classify as emotional ties, but physical or bodily connections as well. Bengalis refer to māyā as taking the form of "bindings" (*bandhan*) or a "net" (*jāl*) in which people, and all living beings, are enmeshed. It is created through experiences such as drinking a mother's breast milk, sharing food, spending time together, engaging in sexual relations, touching, and owning something for a long time. Persons see themselves as physically and emotionally *part* of and *tied* to the people and things that make up their selves and lived-in worlds. These ties, for Bengalis, are all part of māyā.

On the one hand, māyā is something that is valued and sought after by people at any stage of life. Strong family ties, for instance, are highly prized by most Bengalis, and people will say that a person has had a "good" old age if he or she is closely surrounded by loving kin with whom he or she has created ties of māyā over a long life of living together and giving and receiving things.

On the other hand, having a lot of māyā is problematic, because the more māyā one has for people, places, and things, the more difficult are the separations that inevitably ensue. Once when I was talking with two younger villagers, Hena and Babu, about the meanings of māyā, Hena added, "Māyā is a very bad thing." I was surprised and countered, "*We* don't think of māyā [comparable in my mind here to the American "love"] as bad at all." "Then you must not have much māyā," they both replied straightaway. I came to appreciate how māyā is regarded by Bengalis as problematic, one of even the six human "vices" (along with anger, greed, jealousy, pride, and passion), because it can cause immense pain and suffering. Nothing that one loves, or has māyā for, can last forever. Daughters grow up and marry, beautiful clothing becomes faded and worn, a wonderfully sweet mango is consumed and gone, a strain of lovely music fades into silence, a beloved parent dies, and even one's own place in this lived-in world will soon be gone. Old age in particular poses problems with regard to māyā. Bengalis believe that the ties of māyā tend to grow stronger and more numerous as life progresses, and yet at the same time old age is when one's ties are the most ephemeral, for one will soon be moving on in death.

Bengalis offer several reasons for why māyā tends to increase with the length of life. First, because the number of one's kin increases as life goes on, māyā necessarily increases as well—for all of these kin. As Hena put it: "When you are young, you have māyā and pull only for your mother, father, and older sister. But then when you marry, māyā increases—for all of the people of your father-in-law's house. And then you have kids, and then they have kids. You see, from all of this, māyā is increasing." "Look at Khudi Thakrun," she added. "Almost everyone in the village is her relative! She will never be able to abandon māyā—never."

Further, as life goes on one has the opportunity to accumulate more and more pleasurable experiences. Khudi Thakrun's middle-aged son, Gurusaday, reflected on how māyā increases with age: "For old people, māyā and desire increase and increase! . . . At the time of death, however many possessions [a person] has, that much māyā and attachment will he have—for all of those things." He went on to explain, "If you throw ghee in a fire, then the fire increases. In this way, desire and māyā increase and increase as one gets old. People should think, 'I've received and done [things] all of my life. I won't do any more.' But instead they think, 'Let more happen, let more happen!' You see, it's like adding ghee to a fire. The more he gets, the more he wants!" He then went on to repeat this phrase enthusiastically several times in English, seemingly proud to have come up with such a wise statement in my native language. "The more he gets, the more he wants! The more he gets, the more he wants!" And his mother, Khudi Thakrun, was certainly one who evinced such an eagerly attached demeanor in old age.

As death approaches, one's awareness of impending separations can also cause feelings of connection or māyā to intensify. On another occasion when I asked Gurusaday whether māyā increases or decreases with age, he answered definitively: "Māyā increases." "Why?" I asked. "Because [in old age a person] realizes that he will have to leave everything in this earth and go away," and as he responded, tears rose in his eyes. He added, "When I die, then I will have to leave everyone and everything—my children and everything. Then all of the love and all of the affection that I will have—that is all māyā. It will make tears come."

One of the dangers of having such a lot of māyā in late life is that it can make the process of dying very painful. One older woman, Mita's Ma, who was blind in one eye and lame in one leg, described the process of dying for a person with much māyā as like pulling a deeply embedded thorn from the body. The emotional-physical ties of māyā keep the soul or *ātmā* literally "bound" to the body, making it difficult—emotionally and physically—for the soul to leave. Having a lot of māyā in old age can also cause one to linger on in a decrepit body past the natural time for dying. People say in general that it is much better to die while still "moving" (*calte calte*), i.e., while the body is still in good working condition, and that it is just māyā that keeps some people vainly striving to preserve their naturally aging bodies through tools like false teeth, hair-dyeing, and anti-wrinkle creams that are so popular now among the cosmopolitan elite. "What need do I have of such things?" one toothless woman said to me when I asked her about dentures. "They are just unnecessary forms of dressing up. It is now time for my body to go." Too much māyā at the end of life can also cause the soul to linger on in frustration as a ghost around its former habitat, seeking vainly to be reunited with the scenes of its previous life.

For these reasons, some strive to loosen their ties of māyā in various ways *before* dying, engaging in practices that many associate with old age— practices meant to counteract the natural tendency for māyā to increase. For instance, older Bengalis tend to wear white, a "cool" color associated with detachment, old age, asexuality, spirituality. Once their children are married, they generally refrain from engaging in sexual relations, which serve as an intimate means of creating bodily-emotional ties. Older people often sleep alone for the first time in their lives, and they may take their meals separately and before others. For those who can afford it, old age is also viewed as an appropriate time for going on pilgrimages, a process that helps loosen daily ties to home as one wanders beyond to mingle with holy places and divinities. Some elders, people say, become quarrelsome or petulant, which also (purposefully or not) can help slacken ties of affection with kin. Some strive to loosen ties to their own bodies with denigrating epithets, saying that their bodies have become like old clothing ready to be discarded, or like a rice plant at the end of its cycle, withered and gray. Others prepare their souls for the transition to a more heavenly abode[5] by chanting God's name every night as they fall asleep.

In Mangaldihi, efforts to loosen ties of māyā tended to be of greater concern among the higher castes than among lower-caste and poorer people, for the poor often had to worry simply about getting enough to eat and thus did not have the luxury to become preoccupied with achieving a smooth and peaceful old age and death. Lower-caste people in Mangaldihi also told me that they didn't have as much reason for māyā as Brahmans do anyway, because they owned fewer material things, had smaller families, and possessed frailer bodies from lifetimes of hard work.[6]

Other people, like Khudi Thakrun, a well-off and well-connected Brahman matriarch, simply did not wish to focus their final years on cutting ties to their worlds, so much were they enjoying the pleasures of life. Still others did strive to cut māyā, but felt ambivalent about the process. One man went on a pilgrimage expressly in order to diminish his worldly ties, but confessed to me on the way home, tears coming to his eyes as he sat next to his wife, "I left everything to come, but I couldn't leave her." Most admit that no matter how much one strives to reduce the bodily-emotional ties of māyā in old age, māyā cannot easily be cut. Thus Mejo Ma moaned in the lane in front of her home, "How will I cut my ties to all these kids and things and go?"

People feel contrary pulls. One's life in this world is full of pleasures and experiences that bind the self to cherished people, places, and things. It is also inherently fleeting, only a temporary stopping place on the way to something else.

OLD-AGE-HOME DWELLERS AND THE LOOSENINGS OF MODERN SOCIETY

I have concentrated so far on village life, but I wish to look briefly at the perspectives of residents of one of Kolkotta's new old-age homes. A few old-age homes have recently begun to spring up around Kolkotta, West Bengal's major city, as well as in other urban centers scattered around India. Those who stay in old-age homes are (1) mostly women (men are more likely to have their own property and sons to rely on for support in old age, for property is largely controlled by men, and if a man's first wife dies or is issueless, he will likely be encouraged to remarry);[7] (2) those with no children (such as women widowed at young ages or never-married schoolteachers); (3) those with only daughters but no sons (for Bengalis say it is improper or awkward to live with a daughter, especially if she has parents-in-law in her home); and (4) those *with* children, even sons, but whose children live in small urban apartments in "modern" nuclear households or who have moved abroad to places like America, where the elder parent may not feel entirely welcome or comfortable. Residents of old-age homes are also largely from the fairly well-off middle class, as they must be able to supply a modest monthly fee.

I spent some time in Navanir, "New Nest," north India's very first non-Christian home for the aged, founded in Kolkotta in 1978. (A few Christian homes, largely for Anglo-Indians, originated in India during colonial times.) Navanir is a spacious, comfortable home for about a hundred residents, with three or four women sharing a room, shuttered windows open to the airy outdoors, an attractive front courtyard of scented flowering trees, a central meeting room where people gather to watch TV or chat, a dining hall where simple food is served. Those who are mobile can freely wander in and out, taking walks in the neighborhood, perhaps visiting a local tea stall or simply strolling for exercise.

I was curious as to how the residents felt about living in such a home, being part of a society in which it is so highly valued that seniors will be cared for by their children. Most expressed a relief that they *had* a place to stay and they were very grateful to the woman who had founded the institution. "It's better to be here than on the street," several commented. "I didn't like living in someone else's household," another said of her earlier years with her daughter and son-in-law. "I wanted to get away from the signs of my husband in my home," another explained, "after he died. Here [in Navanir], everything is open and empty—it gives some peace of mind." However, probably the most common way both residents and directors of the institution interpreted the need for such homes concerned the conditions of modernity. In modern (*ādhunik*) times, people said, "family love" —which used to be our "dharma" (religious-moral order, right way of living)—is waning; joint families are falling apart; people who used to be considered close kin or one's "own" people—like a childless aunt—are now considered "other"; the young no longer want to care for the old; sons and daughters-in-law wish to live separately in their own homes; and we now live in very "māyā-reduced" and "independent" times. Such discourses on aging and modernity do not take place only in Navanir, but are being heard across India, as politicians, journalists, social scientists, and ordinary citizens are interpreting what they see as the contemporary "problem" of how to care for the aged as a problem of modernity (Cohen 1998; Lamb 2000: 88–98).[8] Thus, many in Navanir also see old-age homes as quintessentially "Western" institutions. The idea of an institutional "home" to care for the elderly outside of the family came from Britain and the United States, they say, and is part of a general "westernization" and "globalization" of Indian society. In such discourses, old-age homes and neglected elders are presented as signs of a widely degenerating modern society, whereas care for elders within close, multigenerational families are part of a more "traditional" and morally-spiritually superior "Indian" past.

Yet the elderly women of Navanir interpreted their old-age home as a new kind of *Indian* institution as well, drawing here on Hindu textual traditions to make their case. The classical Hindu ethical-legal texts, or *dharmaśāstras,* present a series of four life stages through which a person (specifically, an upper-caste male[9]) ideally moves over a lifetime. A person begins his life as a student, moves on to become a married householder, and then, as he sees the sons of his sons and his own gray hair, he becomes first a "forest-dweller" and ultimately a "renouncer" (Manu 1991). During the forest-dweller phase, the person passes most of his property down to his descendants and moves away to dwell in the forest or countryside in a hermitlike state of relative freedom from ties. As a renouncer, he strives further to become free from *all* attachments to people, places, things, and even his own body, through taking final leave of family, abnegating caste identity, giving up all possessions, performing his own funeral rites, begging, and constantly moving from place to place so that no new connections will develop. Several in Navanir interpreted their stays in the home as being comparable to the traditional Hindu forest-dweller life phase, and thus as having its own advantages, helping to facilitate a peaceful old age of relative freedom from the binding ties of māyā. Like those in Mangaldihi, however, Navanir residents said that reducing ties of māyā in late life cannot be easily done, even as they move away from dear kin and things to the relative serenity and emptiness of an old-age home. The widowed mother of an only daughter reflected as we spoke of her life at Navanir, "For me, māyā hasn't completely left yet." She laughed a sheepish, almost apologetic laugh. "I've only been here for a short time—three years—and I was with [my daughter and son-in-law] for so long. So that's why I still have it. But I'm trying to turn my mind toward God. Because what need have I for māyā now? It's time for me to go. So what need is there for māyā? I try to keep my mind strong. But māyā does not go away easily."

CULTURAL MODES OF "SUCCESSFUL" (NON-)AGING

While some biological processes of growing, aging, and dying are common to us all, the meanings we give to these processes are social constructions tied to the beliefs and values of specific cultural-historical settings. People in West Bengal and in North America have interpreted and dealt with, in varying ways, one of the paradoxical dimensions of the human condition—its compelling intensity, seeming really-real-ness on the one hand, and its irrevocable transience on the other. As we have seen, many Bengalis deal with this paradox by striving to embrace transience and process in late life (though such striving is laden with ambiguities). A dominant European American strategy is to fight against the changes of age, endeavoring to construct in their place a façade of permanence. In closing, I wish to make just a few reflections about these contrasts.

In the United States, scholarly and popular cultural representations of aging have recently sought to define "successful aging" as a process that entails, ideally, no *new* changes or characteristics at all. This "successful" (what I would call) *non*-aging or "permanent persons"[10] perspective on aging is nowhere so apparent as in the American proliferation of technologies for disciplining and reconstructing aging bodies. We are witnessing a surge of new techniques to remake bodies so that they are no longer visibly marked as old—through age-calibrated exercise routines, special diets, hair dyes, anti-aging skin creams, and cosmetic surgery. Our contemporary system of biomedicine (which some are resisting, through living wills and "right to die" initiatives) sustains as well a "permanent persons" mode, with its fundamental aim of prolonging life as long as possible, through ever more successful and elaborate technology. Byron Good reflects on the key soteriological role that biomedicine plays in American culture, where death, finitude, and sickness are found in the human body, and "salvation, or at least some partial representation of it, is present in the technical efficacy of medicine" (1994: 86). "[I]n this country, we spend an astounding proportion of our health care dollars on the last several weeks of life," he observes, "so great is our commitment and our technological capacity for extending life" (p. 87). The *New York Times* and *Esquire* report that American biologists are working furiously to defeat the genetic process of aging (Hall 2000; Dooling 1999). We see here a hoped-for model of the body as a machine that can be repaired and maintained on a youthful plateau until, ultimately, even death is defeated.

My purpose in bringing up such contrasts between Bengali and American perspectives is not to deride the "permanent persons" cultural constructions of aging and the life course. Much of the scholarly and popular contemporary discourse of "successful" (non-)aging has been intended to combat what had been viewed as the purely *negative* alternatives, late life as a period of decline, decay, meaninglessness, and ageism. If later life processes of change are not viewed as meaningful transformations on the way to something else positive, then no wonder people (we) would fight against the changes of age. Bengalis strive in certain ways to take apart the self and its ties in late life, as part of a purposeful process of moving on, and of acknowledging our fundamental impermanence. Both the Bengali and American modes work as cultural ways of striving to make meaningful the end of a life span.

ACKNOWLEDGMENTS

Research for this paper was generously funded by Fulbright-Hays, the American Institute of Indian Studies, and the Wenner-Gren Foundation for Anthropological Research. I am especially indubted to McKim Marriott and Diane Mines for their contributions to my thinking. And of course my deepest gratitude is reserved for the people of West Bengal, especially the residents of Mangaldihi, who enabled me to live among and learn from them.

NOTES

1. For a more in-depth look at Bengali aging and the themes covered in this chapter, see Lamb (2000). Cohen (1998), van Willigen and Chadha (1999), and Vatuk (1980, 1990, 1995) also examine aging in India.

2. Bengalis associate being "cool," *ṭhāṇḍā*, with social-bodily conditions such as old age, death, widowhood, and asexuality. Marriage, sexuality, passion, and anger are all "hot" states.

3. Bengali Hindus say that after death a person's soul (ātmā) ordinarily moves on *both* to be reincarnated *and* to become an ancestor. The two passages can happen at the same time and do not strike most people as incompatible.

4. Although Bengali women tend not to own much property in their own right, Khudi Thakrun was unusual in that her well-off father had not had any sons and had therefore left his land to his daughter. She had married within her own village, so now in old age still lived and owned land in her natal place. Most of her husband's property had gone to their sons, as is most common, upon his death.

5. Hindus tend to think of "heaven" (*svarga*) as a temporary abode where souls can remain for some time before being reborn or achieving ultimate "release" (*moksha*) from the cycle of births and deaths.

6. See part III for further discussions of caste and class. Higher-caste people are not necessarily economically better off than lower-caste people, although they often are, and in Mangaldihi the highest-caste Brahmans were also the economically most prosperous group.

7. Among Brahmans and other high-caste groups, widows are not permitted to remarry, even if their husbands die while they are still young and childless.

8. It should be noted, however, that there is little longitudinal evidence to show that the past really was filled with perfectly harmonious joint families and venerated elders. Although old-age institutions themselves are new, India has long had elderly beggars, spiritual ashrams for destitute childless widows, and the like.

9. In the dharmaśāstra texts, the life stage (*āśrama dharma*) schema applies specifically only to an upper-caste man's life. Little attention is devoted to defining the appropriate stages of a woman's life, which are determined by her relationships to the men on whom she depends for support and guidance—her fa-

ther, her husband, and finally her sons (Manu 1991: 115). Both Bengali men and women, however, not infrequently refer to this classical life stage schema to make sense of their own lives.

10. I use the term "permanent persons" to refer to what I see to be a prevalent desire among many Americans to *be* permanent as persons; that is, to stave off decline or life's end even as one ages.

Memorializing the Self: The Autobiographical Will and Testament of Narayana Guruviah Chetty, Madras City, 1915

Mattison Mines

On the 12th day of October 1915 . . . I Narayana Guruviah Chetty
the son of Narayana Ramiah Chetty of Vysia caste and Vishnu sect
living by trade and residing in the house No. 133, in the North line
of Audiappa Naick Street, Peddunaickpetta, Madras, do with a pure
mind and while in the enjoyment of sound memory and within
good intention, contemplete [*sic*] on the lotus like feet of Sri Ramulu
[i.e., the god Ram] and cause the Will and Testament to be written
as follows: —

> As I have been for about two months past some what suf-
> fering from cough owing to excessive heat in the body and
> as I am not restored to complete health by medicines I
> think it necessary to make a suitable arrangement in re-
> gard to matters to be conducted after my life time and so
> cause this Will to be written.
> —Sreeman Narayana Guruviah Chetty

Narayana Guruviah Chetty died shortly after writing this, his will and
testament. At his death he was a prominent textile merchant in Madras
City, engaged in multiple ventures. As one would expect, Guruviah's will
and testament directs his survivors concerning his wishes for the distribution of his properties, real and movable. But Guruviah's will is more than
a directive, it is also an autobiography. True, a will may seem an unusual
form of autobiography, but consider what an autobiography is. An autobiography is an author's telling of his or her own life story. It is written for
an audience, perhaps even a specific audience of readers, and is, therefore,
a form of public presentation of the author's sense of his or her life course
and of notable events set among the significant relationships that constitute the author's "society." Such a story portrays the teller's life as having

a direction that derives from his or her goals and actions: goals striven for and decisions made to achieve those goals, some accomplished, some not. The story may tell of the author's dreams, of obstacles encountered in life, of successes and failures, of tragedies borne and of future aims. And an autobiography preserves the author's identity and life for the future, a testament against being forgotten. We read such a story with fascination because it invites us to see the world as another has seen it, to see life through the author's eyes. Accepting the author's invitation, we learn how another human being has faced the challenges of life. On occasion, as readers, we may identify with and draw inspiration from the author's emotions or difficulties. Or perhaps we read simply to learn how the teller lived in another time and location, when people lived different lives and encountered different adventures, different adversaries. Then again, some autobiographies are accounts of national or civic leaders who through their lives and examples imagine a new society and help to create a shared sense among their readers of themselves as a people and as a nation.

Guruviah's will does some of these things but not others. His is not the testament of a national leader setting a new course for a nation, or even that of a civic leader struggling for a new urban order. His is that of an influential member of one of Madras City's wealthiest merchant castes, and, having once been very poor himself, he wants to assist others, and especially he wants to preserve his place in this Madras Town society where he has worked hard to achieve a position. In short, he seeks to create for himself a legacy, and, in doing so, he reveals to us his sense of self and of the society in which he seeks to sustain an awareness of who he is. The method he chooses for establishing his memory is to use his self-acquired, personal wealth to create a charitable trust. Guruviah draws his admirers to him and creates his legacy through his giving. Generosity is highly valued in south Indian society, but giving is everywhere a complicated act. To be seen as generous, the giver's motivation must be judged altruistic, and altruism is certainly one of Guruviah's intents. Descendants of kin who were his beneficiaries remember him to me especially for his generosity. But the reader of the will senses that the act of giving also may be used to gain religious merit for the giver, and this, too, seems to be Guruviah's interest when he funds temple needs and sponsors the feeding of Brahmans. But, although he stipulates these religious gifts, his will expresses little passion for this specific giving, certainly nothing to compare to the ardor one senses for the very substantial gifts he bequeaths to particular individuals, even while he also explicitly denies the interests of others. His giving is not wholesale; it is a carefully thought-out plan. Nor did his beneficiaries' descendants draw my attention to this meritorious form of religious giving. But, then, his descendants also made no mention that giving is also a way of dispersing the sins of the giver, as Gloria Raheja's (1988) research in a north Indian village has shown. Nonetheless, reading

Guruviah's will, as discussed below, it is possible to surmise that this is his motive as well. The will leaves unclear precisely what sins there might have been—Guruviah himself may not have known—but there are signs of inauspiciousness in Guruviah's life story. He is childless and his adopted son has died without children. Things have gone awry in Guruviah's life, and one senses a feeling of self-ascribed tragedy, which he seeks to overcome through his charity.

Is Guruviah's will unique? During the early twentieth century, a number of Madras City's wealthy merchants created similar charities, in part because of the value south Indian culture placed on generosity toward others and especially toward the poor, and in part because the British colonial government encouraged acts that benefited the common good and in special cases awarded titles for extraordinary public benefactions. Like Guruviah, most of these donors were childless and shared Guruviah's motivations. One of the most famous of his fellow caste members explained his charitable actions in his will and testament this way:

> I make this Last Will and Testament because I am anxious that the bulk of my properties should be utilised for charities and that my name should be perpetuated not by descendants but by schemes of public benefaction which I am anxious to organise and provide for (Rao Bahadur Calavala Cunnan Chetty, 22 December 1919).[1]

Of course, the first purpose of Guruviah's will is to specify how he wishes his estate to be distributed and used. Consequently, he writes his will for those who knew him intimately, members of his household, the kin of his two wives, his adopted daughter, his adopted son's widow, and the members of his community, present and future. These are his audience whom he addresses. Guruviah tells us he is "Vysia" by caste, a community colloquially known as the Komati Chettys or, more formally, as the Arya Vysyas, the name they prefer today.[2] The Komatis or Arya Vysyas are a Telugu-speaking community in a Tamil-speaking state, historically one of the two major trading castes that originally came to Madras City—they and the Tamil-speaking Beeri Chettys dominated trade with the British East India Company.

But there is much more to Guruviah's will than a mere listing of beneficiaries. A will is a legal instrument the form of which is specified within the institution of law, in this instance British-Indian law. Guruviah's desires for his estate, therefore, are constrained by the rules governing wills and individual ownership of assets, and he necessarily tells his narrative according to those rules. Law is both a limiting and an enabling institution. Thus, law frames his understanding, enabling him to see himself as an individual who has control over the disposition of his own, self-acquired property. In 1915, Guruviah is fully aware that this right, vested in the individual, is established law that counters the claims of agnates, who would be his natural inheritors under patrilineal practice and the law governing the inheritance of ancestral property. Thus, the individual's right to dispose of property he controls is not universal. To claim his right under the law, Guruviah must tell his life story in a manner that demonstrates that his property is self-acquired, and that his patrilineal kin have made no contribution and so have no claim under law. The reader is also aware that Guruviah has no similar need to separate his fortunes from those of his maternal kin who raised him and initiated his career because no claim from these nonlineal kin is recognized before the law. Thus, the story Guruviah tells is shaped by the conditions of the law, requiring him to explain some things and allowing him to be silent on others. Yet, when the preamble of his life story, as told in the will, is juxtaposed with his benefactions, the story he tells is complexly autobiographical. He begins his story simply enough, describing his life in order to establish his rights of ownership (the reader may wish to refer to the genealogy in fig. 2, below).

2. My father Narayana Ramiah Chetty was living in the village called Sholavaram attached to Ponnery Taluk, Chingleput District [the district surrounding Madras City]. Having had no sort of properties he was keeping a sundry bazaar and passing time being hard up for living and died 18 years ago in Sholavaram village itself.

3. In my childhood, that is when I was of the age of 5 years my maternal uncle Chekka Rungiah chetty [sic] and his mother and my maternal grandmother Chekka Mangamma brought me away to this Madras from Sholavaram where I was with my father, retained me in their house, maintained me and educated me and made me enter the service of one Nagasurin Papiah Chetty on a salary of Rs. 4 per mensem [month].

4. Sometime after that, I joined as a partner in the petty business, that is, the business of buying and selling dealwood boxes which my maternal uncle was carrying on. Sometime thereafter I joined as a working partner in Chalavadi Raghavalu Chetty & Company. After having carried on cloth business for some time thereafter as a partner in the firm of C. Raghavalu Chetty, N. Guruviah Chetty & Company, I have been since then the Chief partner now in the firm of N. Guruviah Chetty & Company carried on in godown [warehouse] No. 34 of the Godown Street otherwise called Varadamuthiappan Street, Peddunaickpetta, Madras. [Peddunaickpetta is a section of George Town, the oldest business center of Madras City.]

5. Leaving my father during my childhood itself I came away to Madras and lived *separately*, and without any ancestral property or paternal assistance I exerted myself *independantly* [sic] and have acquired as my *self-acquisitions*, immoveable and moveable properties, in all which properties belonging to me *no others than myself have any sort of right title or interest to any extent.*

6. As I have had no children either by my deceased elder wife or by my second wife now living I herebefore took in adoption as son the boy

named Pabbichetti Radhakrishna Chetty who was the son of my elder wife's younger sister, and also got him married. After that, that boy died by want of Divine Grace. To his wife the girl named Alamelumangathayaramma, I had made ornaments of Rupees fifteen thousand (15,000) [a large sum in those days, perhaps three times the price of a substantial house in George Town] besides the ornaments made with the money which her father had given me. As I have after the death of my adopted son handed over finally in full settlement of Alamelumangathayaramma's maintenance and all such other claims all the above mentioned ornaments to her father Kandagaddala Seshachellam Chetty and as the said Seshachellam Chetty has since then independently married his widowed daughter a second time against the shastras [Hindu customary law] and contrary to the rules of the customs of the country and the custom of the caste and as that girl has since then gone out of the caste [i.e., she was expelled from her caste and ostracized by her former caste fellows] and has been living separately, therefore the said Alamelumangathayaramma has hereafter not the least right or claim of any sort in respect of the properties of my estate.

7. I think it important that after my life time the whole of my remaining estate after excluding the properties which are hereinafter mentioned as those that should go to my wife Narayana Ethirajamma should be utilised for charities and appoint these eight persons, namely, 1. My wife Narayana Ethirajamma, 2. Prathy Kanniah Chetty, 3. Pabbichetty[3] Bashyakarloo Chetty, 4. Pabbichetti Venkatramiah Chetty, 5. Vemulapati Rangiah, 6. Vutukuri Narayana, 7. Pabbichetti Basaviah Chetty, and 8. Pabbichetti Ramanujam Chetty as Trustees to my estate after my lifetime. These alone shall also act as executors to get probate of this Will and to conduct after my funeral ceremonies and such other acts and carry out the presents rewards, gifts and all such other charitable services which are mentioned here below." (Trust Deed of Narayana Guruviah Chetty's Charities, reprinted November 1968, pp. 1–3. Emphasis added)

This, then, is Guruviah's brief account of his life. Of course, it is not the only story he might have told. Here, the story's form is framed by issues of property and by the potential claims of others. Normally, Guruviah's patrilineal kin might have a claim on wealth derived from his ancestral line, but Guruviah makes it clear he received nothing from and owes nothing to such kin. And there is more to Guruviah's story. Guruviah has still to name several others who form his intimate society and to specify their worth. And he has to lay out his plan for his continued place in Madras society. But this first autobiographical outline does tell his reader a great deal about his life, including how he came as a small child to Madras City to live and be raised in the home of his maternal uncle. Apparently, like Guruviah later, this uncle had no children of his own. Madras is a patrilineal society and maternal kin are relations characterized by ties of affection rather than by ties of property and competition. Guruviah has no claim on his maternal uncle, nor does his uncle have one on him. Consequently, Guruviah portrays himself as a self-made man, living "separately" and acquiring his wealth "independently." Whatever his maternal uncle may have given him, it is not ancestral property. Consequently, by the reckoning of custom and law he has no kin with a claim to his self-acquired property. Indeed, except for his deceased father, in his will Guruviah mentions only three other patrilineal kin: the daughter of his father's elder brother to whom he bequeaths Rs. 200, and the impoverished paternal grandsons of his father's elder brother. Writes Guruviah, "I think I should as a matter of favour render some help to them as they are altogether poor" (p. 7). Although Guruviah cannot remember the name of one of the boys, nonetheless, he leaves to each of them five rupees per month, enough to provide for food for themselves and their two mothers. In addition,

> when their [the grandsons'] marriages come off, each shall be paid rupees one thousand for marriage expenses and jewels together[.]
>
> 30. Moreover, when their wives come to live in the house after the marriages, payments shall be made at the rate of Rs. 15 per mensem for food expenses. . . .
>
> 31. Further, when these persons may get issues whether male or female, the trustees shall at the marriages of those children be paying at the rate of Rs. 500 for each child. (p. 7)

Guruviah concludes that should either of these boys follow any profession, then "no assistance mentioned above need be given to them from that time" (p. 7).

It is, then, as if Guruviah has no significant paternal kin. His relatives of import are kin by the artifice of his choice only, although, as described below, in his choice one recognizes the south Indian value for alliances with affines. Here, and elsewhere in his will, he mentions his two wives and their families; his adopted son and this boy's younger brother; an adopted daughter, now married, who is the sister of his adopted son; his adopted-son's widow; and the board of trustees he appoints to act as executors and to manage the charities he wishes to establish. Who, then, are these people?

Guruviah's deceased elder wife belonged to the Pabbichetty family, and in his will Guruviah expresses continued affection for her and her family. His deceased adopted son was this wife's younger sister's son. Relatives told me in 1999 that when his adopted son died, Guruviah wanted to adopt another brother, Pabbichetty Manavala Chetty, but the family declined, fearing that, given Guruviah's misfortune, this son too might die. To be sonless and childless was and is considered a great tragedy in Madras society, and to have an adopted son die prematurely as well indicates causes beyond human control. Perhaps Guruviah's childlessness was a consequence of an ancestral sin or had some other inauspicious source. None-

Narayana Guruviah Chetty Genealogy

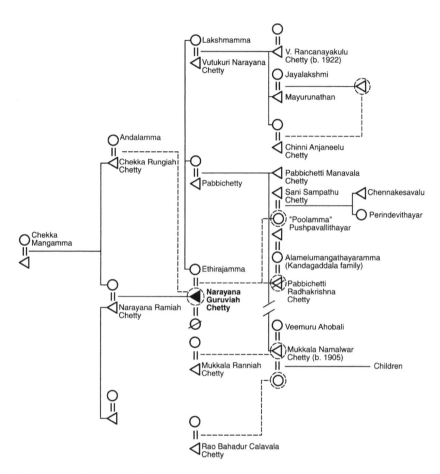

2. Narayana Guruviah Chetty genealogy.

theless, despite being unable to adopt the boy, Guruviah treated Manavala Chetty like a son. In his will, Guruviah specified that the boy live in his house with Ethirajamma, his second wife, that the boy's teacher be paid by the estate, and that Manavala be paid Rs. 40,000 in 10,000-rupee-increments over a four-year period, giving him the advantage of wealth. Guruviah also stipulated that when Manavala reached adulthood, he was then to be appointed a trustee of his estate so as to "carry on the charities arranged for by me" (p. 6). Guruviah also provided for his wife, Ethirajamma, specifying that Prathy Kanniah Chetty (her brother, I believe) and the immediate male kin of his elder wife and each of their respective wives and offspring "should live in my house amicably with and by way of assistance to my wife Ethirajamma, and all of them should so long as my wife lives be messing [eating] together in my house itself. The aforesaid house No. 133. [*sic*] in Audiappa Naick Street shall remain in the possession of my wife" (p. 5). In other words, Guruviah incorporates the affines of his eldest wife and provides for his second wife during her lifetime. It is hard to imagine a stronger expression of what the French anthropologist Louis Dumont has labeled "affinity as a value" in south Indian society.

Later, Guruviah tells us that he has also adopted a daughter, the sister of his deceased adopted son:

> I brought up as a daughter Sani Pushpavallithayar alias Poolamma the daughter of my elder wife's younger sister from her childhood, gave her ornaments for Rs. 2,000 at the time of her marriage and have since then conducted suitable honours to her and to her children up to now. Besides this I intending to buy and give a house for her, caused Rs. 3,155 to be credited in her name in N. Guruviah Chetty and company on 30th May 1914. . . . [Now, Guruviah states, he wishes to add to this amount so that] a house [may be] purchased in (Rs. 6,000) . . . and the trustees shall execute and give a deed of gift to the effect that Poolamma and her children should from generation to generation enjoy the said house. . . . (p. 8)

These, then, are his kin, whom he creates through the use of law, affection, and giving rather than through descent. In each instance, Guruviah's links to males and his adopted children are extended ties established through his marriages. Except for his wives, he owes no obligation to these relations either by law or by any public sense of what might ethically be expected of him, nor are these kin of choice obligated to him. But he draws them to himself by his giving. In this manner, he has made himself the central figure within a circle of kin. He is their household head. Diane Mines (1990) has observed that when kinship ties are created by giving, relationships are asymmetrical: receivers are more related to the givers than vice versa. Expressing this, in Guruviah's case as well, it is the descendants of those who received from him that remember his name and claim connection to him.

But Guruviah's beneficiaries include more than these kin. There is another Pabbichetty brother, as yet unmentioned: Nammalwar Chetty. He, too, is the offspring of Guruviah's deceased first wife's younger sister. And like his brother and sister, he too is adopted by one of Madras City's most prominent merchants, Mukkala Kanniah Chetty. Subsequently, Nammalwar married the adopted daughter of yet another prominent businessman, Calavala Cunnan Chetty. Guruviah also embraces Nammalwar Chetty with his generosity, bequeathing him Rs. 1,500 in "ready money or jewels" (p. 10). Nammalwar's wife's birth family and adoptive family both were wealthy merchant households in Madras City. And like Guruviah the heads of each of these families were to establish important charities in their names: Calavala Cunnan Chetty founded and underwrote numerous schools for the poor, including, in his own name, the Rao Bahadur Calavala Cunnan Chetty School and, in his wife's name, Sita Kingston House. The brothers made their fortunes as proprietors of King and Co., importers of Burmese timber and fine British Scotch. Calavala Cunnan's brother, Calavala Ramanujam Chetty, was appointed sheriff of Madras in 1917, a high honor, and was posthumously awarded the title of diwan bahadur on the king's birthday in 1919 for his many charitable activities. Mukkala (Pabbichetti) Nammalwar Chetty wife's great-uncle was Sri Rao Bahadur Vemuru Ranganadham,[4] the owner of Ananda Press, a famous Madras City press. He founded the Vemuru Ranganadhan Chetty Charities, which included the Sri Venkateswara Students' Hostel, which was founded in 1918 to house university students attending Presidency College. He was awarded the title of rao bahadur by the British in 1922 for his public works. Guruviah's chosen kin, then, were members of the aristocracy of Madras merchant households. And Guruviah, a man without significant blood kin, establishes himself among these families by his generosity, making enduring ties based on affinity where none existed by descent. These families constitute Guruviah's immediate society and mark his place within Madras City society.

What, then, is the sense of self that Guruviah expresses in his will? As G. H. Mead (1934) has observed, a sense of self is always sustained in social relations and incorporates the "rules of the game" governing those relationships. Consequently, self-awareness is founded on the individual's ability to see him- or herself from the perspective of others and to know how to interact with them and to anticipate how they, individually and collectively, will interact with him or her. Since society and its rules are always in process, self-awareness necessarily is a process as well, changing as circumstances change and as the person makes, modifies, and unmakes his or her relationships with others. Guruviah's self-consciousness, therefore, may be seen as occurring at a particular historical moment. Certainly, his is a modern awareness, formed in part by his seeing himself in a set of relationships whose "rules of the game" are framed by the law. Thus, as noted above, he necessarily sees and portrays himself as an individual who has acquired his own wealth independently and separately.

Set within the law, therefore, this individual sense of self—private and dependent on Guruviah's personal efforts and choice—constitutes a first aspect of Guruviah's self-awareness as it is portrayed in his will. But Guruviah also sees himself as a more public figure, and, expressing this, he depicts two additional features or levels of his self-consciousness: One, an intermediate level, is an awareness, which places him among his kin of choice, as has been noted above. The other, encompassing a larger, hierarchical society, is expressed by his intent to construct a lasting place for himself within his larger society of significant others, most particularly among members of his own Arya Vysya caste community; among priestly Brahmans, whom he feeds to acquire religious merit and to counter sins; and, lastly, among others of lesser rank. To position himself within this society Guruviah establishes charities and his kin-based board of trustees to carry out and manage his aims.

This third level of awareness is Guruviah the prominent merchant and generous benefactor, the founder of charities. The nature of the society that Guruviah envisions is apparent from the several forms of charity he establishes. First, he endows religious charities: most prominently he endows the feeding of Brahmans at several temple locations and the monthly celebration of the goddess Thayarlu (the goddess name that women belonging to his elder wife's family incorporated in their personal names). Second, he funds the establishment of three "choultries," or rest houses, each located at a different religious site "for the comfort of Brahmins and Vysias who come on pilgrimage" (p. 12). Third, he specifies the founding of three schools:

> 83. For the education of poor vysia boys in Madras a school shall be established in a place, one or two suitable teachers appointed, and [T]elugu and a little English taught.
> 84. Further, 2 schools shall in that same manner be established in two villages in other places.
> 85. In the above schools, chiefly vysia boys, and if these do not join to the full extent and there are vacancies also brahmin boys and, if there are vacancies still, also sudra [lower-caste] boys shall be admitted. (p. 12)

Fourth, Guruviah specifies that wells be "sunk any where [*sic*] in such places as they will be useful to people" (p. 12). And finally, he specifies small monthly amounts to be donated to two charitable organizations, one of which is the Society for the Prevention of Cruelty to Animals.

In 1915, there is nothing unusual about Guruviah's charitable bequests; they are largely altruistic by design and they portray Guruviah as an ethical man, a religious man of good reputation and intentions. Giving as he does perpetuates his identity among members of his social circle, the Madras merchant community, and especially among his beneficiaries. However, his logic for giving is complex and mixes both Hindu and British colonial sentiments. Thus, his giving preserves a space for him in British-Indian society and earns him public recognition for his "public-mindedness" in the eyes of the British-Indian elite of his day. But his giving also earns him merit because the Hindu logic of *karma* holds that for every action there is a consequence and the consequence of generosity is that things should go well for him. He expressly desires his memory to live on, and one senses a religious desire to provide for his soul after death through his religious giving. He is a good man, a religious man. Perhaps also his charities are designed to counter whatever causes may have left him childless, reflecting a perception of himself as situated within a Hindu-ordered cosmos. But his request for the founding of schools also suggests his awareness of his own childhood poverty and the advantages that education can present to a hardworking boy. Trustees of the Narayana Guruviah Chetty Charities explained that because of financial constraints, only two of the schools have been founded as yet.

On Guruviah's second wife's death, his house also became a part of his estate and was converted for use as a ramanujakutam or "choultry." For a time the house was also used for conducting marriages. Today, perhaps the biggest and most profitable institution run by the Narayana Guruviah Chetty Charities is a large, modern marriage hall located on property owned by Guruviah and now managed by the trust. It is the Ethirajamma Marriage Pavilion (Ethirajamma Kalyanam Mandabam), named after his second wife, located on T.T.K. Road. Everyone in Chennai (Madras City) knows it. And because of its size and popularity, it is booked a full year in advance.

Finally, it is worth considering the relationship between Guruviah's self-awareness and the law. Although law constrains Guruviah's autobiographical depiction of self, he uses his will also as a tool, a legal instrument that gives him the power to affect the future of relationships among those he has drawn around him as kin long after his own death. In this sense, his use of his will is a good example of what Anthony Giddens (1987) labels "structuration," the meeting point of individual actions and intentions and the institutions of society. Structuration is the process that results from this meeting of intent and institutional forms such as the law. Institutions both constrain and enable the actor. In Guruviah's case, he uses his will and the law to create a public presence for himself within his society and among his social circle after death. He wants more than not to be forgotten; he wants to play a continuing role in the lives of members of his community. He wants these future members of his society to know him and to honor him. And he designs his will in a manner to ensure the fulfillment of his intent, that he be a part of these future relations. Indeed, in Chennai nearly a century after Guruviah's death, the descendants of his beneficiaries *do* know him. The vitality of this memory is in part because of his gifts to their forebears, which today's trustees describe as an expression of his generosity. But, more importantly, it is in part because today some of these descendants are also the managing trustees of the charities Guruviah founded. When, in time, each of the first trustees died, the surviving trustees appointed a replacement from among their own close kin, selecting men[5] of good reputation and management skill. Guruviah's charities, then, are living institutions that are actively managed by their trustees, and the board of trustees itself constitutes a kind of evolving genealogy that links Guruviah to the prominent families and men of his caste. In other words, Guruviah created a society in perpetuity with himself at its center. Indeed, Guruviah continues to have a living place in the intimate web created by the marriages and descent that link many of the major Komati families of the city today. And he remains a leading member of the community.

ACKNOWLEDGMENTS

I wish to thank the John Simon Guggenheim Memorial Foundation and the J. William Fulbright Fellowship Program for their support of the research on which this paper is based. I also wish to thank Jonathan Parry, who read and gave me sound advice on an earlier version of this paper. Responsibility for any deficiency is, of course, my own.

NOTES

1. Calavala Cunnan Chetty adopted one of Guruviah's adopted son's brothers. These children were the sons of Guruviah's elder wife's younger sister. This is explained later in the text.

2. "Chetty" and the more formal "Chettiar" are common designations identifying castes whose members historically have been traders. Until the 1960s individuals often used their caste name as a suffix to their personal name, and in this manner the will's author styles himself Narayana Guruviah Chetty. "Vysya" is the third ranked of the "twice-born" varna, the varna of merchants and traders in the parlance of twentieth-century Madras. Members of Chettiar castes today commonly claim Vysya identity. Consequently, there are numerous Chettiar castes and numerous castes that more formally claim Vysya status. The Komati Chettys style themselves Arya [Sanskrit] Vysya to distinguish themselves from other Vysyas and to call attention to their devout lifeways. Feeding Brahmans, particularly members of the Vaishnavite priestly caste, and funding temple supplies and worship are typical examples of Arya Vysya devotion.

3. The reader will note that the author's spelling of this name varies. It is unclear whether or not the individuals spelled their names differently in keeping with the author's spellings. Such inconsistencies are common in practice even today because there are multiple ways of rendering the same sound in roman script.

4. The titles diwan bahadur and rao bahadur are official titles of the Order of British India, which were awarded by the Crown to Indian civilians in recognition of exceptional public service.

5. Reflecting the value of affinity, it is likely that Guruviah appointed his second wife a trustee of his charity because she was his only living kinship link to those whom he wished to manage his legacy and memory. After her death, trustees have been drawn from families linked by descent and marriage to the first trustees, but only men have since been appointed.

PART TWO

Genders

Gender is, for all of us, a part of our identity and how we are socialized. It is implicated in the ways we approach action in the world and make judgments about those actions. It is part of how we organize ourselves into social groups. Experiences and attitudes about gender and what it is to be male or female are an aspect of almost anything we do—a central dimension of everyday life.

South Asian women's interests and positions change in significant respects throughout the life course. Men's positions change, too, although usually in less dramatic ways. Important diversity of course exists in experiences of gender across South Asia. For instance, many women never move in with their in-laws, or marry someone of their own choosing, or even move to the United States for professional work. In general, however, a woman can expect to progress over her life from being a daughter in her natal home, to a wife and daughter-in-law in her husband's and in-law's home, to a mother of young children, to a mother-in-law, and finally to an older woman and, frequently, widow.

Women often nostalgically describe their lives as young girls in their natal homes as the time when they experienced the most freedoms and pleasures, receiving love and affection from their elders and playing with their neighborhood friends. As a young wife and daughter-in-law, a woman is often most constrained. She becomes the newest and perhaps most junior person in an unfamiliar household and must learn to exhibit deference to her husband and his senior kin. As a woman bears children, she begins to feel more and more invested and significant in her marital home and can derive rich fulfillment from being a mother. As a mother-in-law, a woman is at her height of authority in the domestic sphere. She will often be the female head of household (with her husband as the male head), in control of much of the decision making about domestic matters.

As a woman becomes even older, juniors will gradually take over the position of household head. This will mean that the older woman will lose much of her domestic power and authority but will gain in freedoms—to wander beyond the household, to visit faraway temples or married daughters, to play cards with friends, to watch the public performances that come to town, or to expose without care parts of the body such as calves or breasts that were once carefully protected from public view (Lamb 2000). A woman who becomes a widow when she is already at an advanced age with married sons often faces few social and economic consequences, although she may of course profoundly mourn the loss of her husband. In communities where widow remarriage is not practiced (that is, among many upper-caste Hindu groups, and even among many lower castes if the widow already has children), becoming a widow at a young age can have drastic consequences—ranging from poverty, to feelings of being unwanted in either natal or marital home, to being regarded as inauspicious, to facing a precarious old age with no children to support her (see Chen 2001).

Many women work outside of the home, in addition to carrying out their domestic roles as mothers, wives, cooks, etc. The degree and nature of women's work depends profoundly on caste and class. In rural areas especially, upper-status women are often pressed to confine their movements largely to the home and are thus discouraged from taking on outside work. All over South Asia, though, other women can be seen working in the fields, or on road construction sites, or in others' homes as domestic servants. Well-educated urban women pursue a full range of professional careers, as professors, physicians, politicians, travel agents, and the like.

Men do not experience as many marked transformations over their lives. A man may move for the purposes of work, but otherwise he will generally remain firmly rooted in his natal community. Men are expected to marry, to have children, to be economically productive, and as the senior male in a household to assume the role as central authority figure (see Wadley, part I). Like women, when men grow older, they are expected to relinquish much of their authority to juniors (Lamb, part I). Men at any age are generally free to move as they wish in public spheres—working, congregating with friends, hanging out at tea stalls, making journeys to markets, and the like.

Any examination of gender in South Asia must consider the presence of patriarchy. Dominant expectations are that a wife will be subservient to her husband. Hindu ideologies, for instance, proclaim that a husband is in some ways to his wife like a god, and his wife should serve and respect him. Islam also accords men a higher status. In South Asia, sons are generally preferred to daughters for a variety of reasons (see Dube 1988; Jeffery and Jeffery, part I), and because of instances of preferential treatment of sons and the selective abortion of female fetuses following amniocentesis, India is one of the few nations in the world in which there are significantly more males than females in juvenile age groups (Miller 1981, 1987). In many communities, women are regarded as more "impure" than men (e.g., Lamb 2000: 183–87; Rozario 1992: 96–102). Many Muslim and upper-caste north Indian families also expect their women to practice purdah (literally, a "curtain") or veiling, keeping their faces covered when in public and around senior male kin, and striving to confine their activities as far as possible to the inner domains of the home (Jacobson 1982; Mehta 1981; Rozario 1992).

Over the past few decades, reports of "dowry deaths" in India have made it into the world media—cases of newly married women murdered (usually burned to death) by their husbands and/or in-laws over the issue of inadequate dowry (Stone and James 1995). The practice of *sati*, or the burning of a widow alive on her husband's funeral pyre, has also long attracted Western attention; in colonial times, the British were both dismayed by and in awe of women as *satis* (Mani 1998). Highlighting dowry death and *sati* has the potential danger of contributing to sensationalist misconceptions about India. In discussing these issues—which are of vital concern to South Asians as well—it is important to realize that these are not the "norms" of South Asian practices, and are certainly no more "typical" of all South Asians than school shootings or rape are of all Americans.

Earlier studies of gender in South Asia tended to focus on the submission of women to such patriarchal "traditions." This collection of essays, however, fits with recent trends in gender studies in South Asia and elsewhere (e.g., Raheja and Gold 1994; P. Jeffery and R. Jeffery 1996a; Abu-Lughod 1993) in that it looks not only at dominant ideologies but also at the diverse ways such ideologies are experienced, negotiated, made sense of, and reinterpreted in women's and men's daily lives. Ann Gold's essay, for instance, explores uneducated girls' own perspectives on why they remain outside school walls, and Susan Seizer's examines how actresses in Tamil Nadu both violate and conform to the idea of a "good woman."

Most previous studies of gender in South Asia have also concentrated on *women*, and on marriage and married women in particular. Marriage is indeed a crucial dimension of most South Asian women's lives. The dominant expectation is that all women will marry. Girls are taught at a young age to prepare for marriage (Dube 1988, Gold), and even "modern," educated, urban women strive to fit their professional lives into traditional marriages (Seymour). But a unique and important contribution of this collection of pieces on gender is that—along with depicting more traditional expectations regarding gender and marriage—the essays also examine those who do not marry (e.g., Seizer); those who love others of the same sex (Vanita); constructions of masculinity (Alter), for of course men are gendered, too; and *hijras,* an important group of neither-male-nor-female transsexuals (Nanda).

A final note should be made regarding constructions of gender in South Asia, and that is that although South Asian societies are patriarchal in considerable respects, South Asians have long recognized significant female forms of political and spiritual power. In fact, every major nation of contemporary South Asia save Nepal has elected a female prime minister (while the United States cannot yet boast a female head of state)—Indira Gandhi in India, Benazir Bhutto in Pakistan, Khaleda Zia in Bangladesh, and Sirimavo Bandaranaike in Sri Lanka. Hindu religious traditions also include important, powerful, and beloved female deities, such as Kali, Durga, Lakshmi, Parvati, Sita, and Sarasvati (see Kinsley 1986).

* * *

Ann Gold opens this section by exploring why so many female children in rural Rajasthan do not go to school, focusing primarily on uneducated daughters' own perspectives. Some girls, in fact, do eagerly attend school, but others stay home for a variety of complex and compelling reasons—sometimes because their fathers won't let them go, and also because their visions of schooling do not fit with many of their own local values. The messages promulgated by women's development organizations and literacy campaigns seem unfortunately to be pitted hopelessly against local cultural views of family, home, tradition.

Susan Seymour examines the ways gender and family systems have changed over the past thirty-five years in the city of Bhubaneswar in Orissa, India.[1] One of the most dramatic changes concerns how many more girls are pursuing education through college and even graduate school. Very highly educated women, however, are considered potentially too old, too educated, and too independent for marriage by traditional standards. Seymour is struck by how changes in expectations for marriage are not keeping pace with other transformations regarding gender.

Susan Seizer richly portrays the ways unmarried female actresses in Tamil Nadu struggle to conform to the dominant terms of gendered respectability and virtuous domesticity, even while venturing out into the public sphere. They find creative means to configure themselves as "good women," and in so doing subtly reorganize the category itself and throw it into question.

Joseph Alter looks at male wrestlers in Varanasi, India, who are extremely concerned with the nature of their masculinity.[2] He ferrets out underlying reasons behind the almost excessive, bombastic masculinity associated with the sport—as wrestlers often "literally throw out their chests, spread their arms, dramatically cock their heads and, in general, affect a pose which makes their bodies stand for the essence of strength and masculine power." He suggests that the wrestlers' experiences of masculinity not only grow out of Indian "traditions" (surrounding, for instance, patri-archal power and the physical-spiritual value of male celibacy); they are also defined and produced in terms of the anxieties of modern nationalism.

Ruth Vanita's essay centers on representations of love between men in two Hindi films. India now has the largest film industry in the world, and Vanita notes that mainstream Hindi cinema is arguably India's single larg-est common cultural denominator today. As she examines the nature of the same-sex relationships in the two films, Vanita also reflects more broadly upon Indian societal views of homosexuality,[3] and explores the ways love in general is represented in Indian cinematic traditions.

Serena Nanda, finally, focuses on the life story of a *hijra,* an alternative neither-male-nor-female gender role in India.[4] She depicts vividly the way Salima, born in a Muslim neighborhood in Mumbai, is as a child first con-sidered male, but later becomes a hijra. As a hijra, she alternately experi-ences the warmth of being part of a community of other hijras, a marriage-like relationship with a man, and ultimately poverty and degradation on the streets. Salima's story powerfully conveys the potential ambiguity, flu-idity, and not-strictly-binary nature of gender.

NOTES

1. Seymour develops this work further in her *Women, Family, and Child Care in India: A World in Transition* (1999).
2. For a further exploration of the lives of Indian wrestlers, see Alter 1992b.
3. For further examinations of same-sex love in Indian literature, film, his-tory, and society, see Vanita and Kidwai, eds., *Same-Sex Love in India: Readings from Literature and History* (2000); and Vanita, ed., *Queering India: Same-Sex Love and Eroticism in Indian Culture and Society* (2001).
4. Serena Nanda also writes about hijras in *Neither Man nor Woman: The Hijras of India* (1999).

New Light in the House: Schooling Girls in Rural North India

Ann Grodzins Gold

Early in 1997, I spent two months living in the village of Ghatiyali, District Ajmer, Rajasthan. I stayed in the home of Bhoju Ram Gujar, my friend and frequent co-author. Bhoju was at that time a government middle school teacher (he is now a headmaster); his wife, Bali, is not literate. At that time they had three daughters, ranging in age from about ten down to four, and one two-year-old son. During this stay in Ghatiyali, Bhoju and I were engaged in two separate research projects: one on oral histories of environmental change; and the other on environmental education, both formal and informal. For the latter project I sat many whole days in classrooms and school yards, but spent others trekking long distances outdoors as I followed and talked with children between the ages of about ten and sixteen who worked herding goats and sheep, for their families or sometimes for wages. Originally I had no specific focus on the gender gap in literacy, but the more I spoke with children who herded and children who attended school, the more interested I became in the reasons so many female children remained outside the school walls.

In rural Rajasthan, low school attendance and low literacy rates persist in spite of government commitment at national, state, and local levels to universal education. According to statistics drawn from the 1991 Census of India, the statewide literacy rate in Rajasthan was 38.55 percent; broken down by gender, for males it was 54.99 percent and for females it was 20.44 percent. Of the total rural population only 30.37 percent was literate; and the literacy rate for rural females in 1991 was a startlingly low 11.59 percent (Sharma and Retherford 1993; Sharma 1994).

I have spent much of my anthropological career recording, translating, and interpreting oral traditions, and gathering many kinds of knowledge from unlettered persons of both sexes. In the course of that work, my profound respect for the richness and complexity of oral knowledges has been ever increasing.[1] Through nearly two decades of interacting with Rajasthani women, I had failed to contemplate or to conceptualize the disadvantages of being nonliterate—as were most all of my female village acquaintances. Village women to me had always seemed remarkably competent, and confident of their mastery of all skills necessary for their lives. It was they who instructed me, and gently mocked my multiple ignorances.[2] It was only in 1997 when I traveled to Jaipur city with Bhoju's wife Bali that I was hit by the difficulties and embarrassments of being nonliterate in a literate world. While in village and countryside, it was always I who was lost and she who led, now she had to ask me where we were. I could read the signs in Hindi and English.

A few weeks before this excursion, I had a painful encounter that provides a kind of anecdotal context for this chapter, as it highlights the intractable nature of some cultural obstacles that continue to slow the process of schooling girls in Rajasthan, and elsewhere in India. Bhoju and I had gone to interview the father of Arami, Bhoju's cousin Shivji's wife. Arami, like Bali and most young women of the Gujar community in the mid-nineties, was totally uneducated. Gujars' traditional occupational identity is raising dairy animals.[3] In her girlhood Arami had herded family livestock while her brothers studied. After her marriage to Shivji and before the births of her two daughters, she had worked as a laborer to supplement her husband's household income. Now she stayed at home with the baby and the toddler. Arami's father had been in the army, and had a partially transformed perspective on the world that seems to come to farmers with military experience.

Our recorded interview with Arami's father began well. He talked with us at length, very articulately, mostly about changes in agricultural technology. Eventually, we switched to the topic of education, as was our frequent pattern. Bhoju asked him about the choices he had made in educating his children. He told us of financial sacrifices undertaken to prepare his sons for cash-earning jobs by sending them to costly boarding school—an unusual step for a rural Gujar. I then casually inquired whether he had ever sent his daughters (of which he had several) to school. This affable man bluntly replied, "If I send them to school, they might run off, and then I would have to set them on fire, or take my rifle and shoot them!" Our conversation pretty much screeched to a halt, and Bhoju and I soon departed.

Later Bhoju summarized this rough moment, saying to me, "First his brain went bad, and then your brain went bad." Bhoju himself, as a teacher who has seen something of the world, knows the value of educating daughters. As a Gujar, he also well understands how other Gujars feel. Among Bhoju's and Bali's relatives and neighbors, a familiar pattern of boys to school and girls to herding prevails.[4] Bhoju was able eloquently to explain Arami's father's position. A family's entire social status is demolished by one wayward daughter. There are disastrous cases at which it is possible to point. What about the other children? No decent marriages can be arranged for the siblings of a girl who elopes with a school classmate.

Listening to Bhoju, I could not judge Arami's father to be a patriarchal monster or a dull-witted, ignorant man. Like most human beings he wants the best for his children, whom he loves—daughters as well as sons. He makes choices as wisely as he is able, in a society that is rapidly changing but nonetheless socially conservative. For Gujars and other agriculturist communities in Rajasthan, to educate girls is not only to gamble with the family honor, but to do so without visible potential winnings. If Arami's father stressed the dire risks entailed in girls' education as significant disincentives, many others, as we will see, stressed the lack of positive outcomes to be anticipated. This combination leaves little in the balance on the side of schooling daughters.

In this brief chapter my primary focus is uneducated herd girls' own perspectives on school, expressed in recorded interviews and songs. Then I shall turn to the ways some adult Rajasthani women who have awakened to the value of education articulate their views in slogans and moving lyrics. Nita Kumar has suggested in her study of educational history in Banaras (Varanasi) that to cooperate seriously in a process of modernization means necessarily to question existing practices and beliefs (2000: 194). Modernizing projects undertaken by women in Rajasthan not only question but challenge and often denounce existing practices. Such projects metaphorize their aims as to dispel darkness or to climb aboard an accelerating train.

I have one main aim, and one secondary expectation. Most importantly I present female viewpoints: What do daughters, wives, and mothers think of the skewed literacy and school attendance ratios for girls and women? How does lack of education affect their lives and hopes? What do they wish for their own futures or for their children's? Along the way, I hope to reveal something of the existing conditions in which schooling for girls and local values may seem to clash so discordantly that Arami's father—a decent and reasonable man—would be led to take so extreme a position. Attitudes such as his are rooted in complex social and economic conditions, against which girls' education is realistically portrayed in women's consciousness-raising efforts as bringing "new light" into the house.

SCHOOLING FROM THE HERD GIRLS' POINT OF VIEW

One day a very old woman described the sufferings of her youth to me and Bhoju, and contrasted these with modern times (*nayā zamānā*)—"like in the song." She was a member of the Mina community, farmers sometimes described as "settled tribals" and understood to be indigenous to the region. Like Gujars, Minas had been slow to pursue educational opportunities. Her granddaughter, who had been listening, knew the song to which she alluded, and gave us a few lines. I was arrested not so much by the words— which are rather banal compared to many women's expressive lyrics—but by the song's opening image of a flood: two well-known rivers overflow their banks and wash away a major city. This suggests a tide of radical and irrevocable change, although the innovations described in the following lines will strike urban readers as far from revolutionary.

> The Chambal broke, the Banas broke, and Udaipur flowed away,
> Indira got down at the station, what did she have to say?
> I've installed electricity, faucets, street lamps too,
> And installed your sister-in-law's brother [husband] in a salaried job![5]

Electricity means women do not have to grind grain; water taps mean they no longer have to go to the well; streetlights may imply greater freedom of movement. Rural Rajasthani women have experienced these technologically implemented conveniences as a flood sweeping away previous structures of daily existence. But note that the song grants wage-earning careers only to husbands—presumably literate ones.

According to the young singer, this song was still popular among Mina girls, over ten years after the assassination of its heroine, former prime minister Indira Gandhi. Like many Mina girls, this woman had spent her childhood and early adolescence herding. Totally uneducated, she told us that she attended night school in her marital home, where living conditions were more comfortable than those in her natal village. She was proud of her better life in modern times, with nothing like the hardships her grandmother had endured.

Not all nonliterate or marginally literate wives are content with their situations. Other songs, recorded from women and girls, speak of domestic and emotional problems resulting from the skewed education system. These reveal that young women perceive the gender gap in schooling as leading directly to marital trouble. Illiterate brides are badly treated, even abandoned, by literate husbands seeking companionship.[6] Two songs I recorded in 1993 and published in other contexts revolve around this problem. One of these I heard from a group of unschooled preadolescent herd girls of the Mali (Gardener) caste.

> In the school the parrot speaks; in the garden the peacock speaks.
> Over there, husband's sister, your brother went to study,
> From one side comes the motorbus, from the other comes the car,
> Your brother is dancing with the girls. (Gold and Gujar 1994: 80)

Uneducated females married to educated boys fear their husbands will go astray in the world of modern transportation and foreign "dancing." While the Hindi word for "dance," *nāchnā*, evokes veiled women bending and twirling gracefully among themselves with no males present, the English "dance" that appears in this song represents the Westernized disco scene, of which villagers are aware from media images. Forlornly, the un-educated herd girl complains to her sister-in-law of their brother/husband's desertion to that alien world.

The second song is of a genre called *khyāl* ("feelings"), said to be, among other things, a medium through which women may complain about their husbands. I recorded it from adult women of the Nath community (farm-ers, temple priests, and gurus):

> Sold my nose ring and brought books,
> Went and sat in the school,
> Studied fine Hindi, and studied English,
> Became a respected railway clerk.
> Oh stifle my hiccups and stifle my soul!
> "Just now I'll meet with my pretty one."
> Mother is happy, my father is happy,
> but in the bedchamber, pretty one's sad. (Gold 1996: 18–19)

The young wife is emotionally abandoned by her husband, who has achieved success at her expense. He sold her valued ornament, and no longer seems to care for her. Women joke and tease one another about hiccups: "it means your husband's thinking of you." According to exegesis given me in Gha-tiyali, the wife here admonishes herself to cease hiccuping and to keep her soul patient—in other words, to repress her desires. Her husband casually promises his immediate presence, but evidently his words do not console her much. He is just the kind of educated, salaried husband her parents wanted, but for her there is no conjugal satisfaction.[7]

Such songs voice the fears and anticipate the sorrows of unschooled women paired with literate men. Another song, performed by preadoles-cent Mali girls on the night of the harvest festival of Holi in 1993, is the only performance I happened to record in the village that speaks of secon-dary schooling for girls. The young singers had just done a song about Holi, the female demon, about to be consigned to a joyful bonfire.[8] They then spontaneously broke into a rousing tune, its lyrics proposing new, perilous, but thrilling possibilities for women:

> O innocent Shivji, my younger sister is going to school while riding on a motorbike.
> O Shivji, she studied to the sixteenth class and joined the army.
> She beat the policemen with four sticks and hurt them, and the police grabbed her and took her away.

Girls in Ghatiyali have yet to mount bicycles, let alone motorbikes, except as veiled, sidesaddle passengers. Careers in the military and the police are highly respected, desirable, and competitive professional options for edu-cated young village men. This fanciful song seems uncertain where women's educational and professional achievements might lead. It sounds an adventurous note, but also warns of chaos and punishment. It seems to give voice simultaneously to girls' hopes and parents' fears.

Bhoju's niece Kali was an incredibly high-spirited, independent-minded, bright-eyed girl. People shook their heads and said she should have been born a boy. I interviewed her in 1993 when she was probably no more than nine years old. Her pragmatic attitude was already crystallized.

> *Ann:* So, do you go to school?
> *Kali:* School, never! I never went to school, never.
> [She talks about her work helping to graze the family's sheep.]
> *Ann:* Is grazing good or is studying good?
> *Kali:* Grazing sheep is very good.
> *Ann:* Why?
> *Kali:* Sheep give us income, what does reading give? Sheep give us income. Suppose I do go to study, so, I'll hardly get a job!
> *Ann:* So what is good about sheep?
> *Kali:* Our own house's sheep? They give lambs, so we sell them; they give dung, and we sell it.

By 1997 Kali, maybe thirteen, was married but was still living in her natal home, where her work is valued. Her parents will demand that her in-laws give her some hefty silver ornaments before they relinquish their claims on her energetic labor and cheery company. Kali continued to emphasize the economic aspect of her non-education. It struck me, though, that she was well aware now of what she was losing. If not bitter, she was just slightly acid when she spoke of it.

> *Ann:* Your brother goes to school—why not you?
> *Kali:* If I went to school then who would do the housework?
> *Ann:* Do you go to the night school?
> *Kali:* My mother doesn't send me.
> *Ann:* Why doesn't she send you?
> *Kali:* She says, "what's the use of sending you? What kind of master will you become?" [*tum kaun sā mārsā ban javelī*].

Kali's older brother, Shankar, is in school, in eighth grade. He dresses well, but is not very good at his studies. Kali never directly expressed envy of Shankar, but when the girls of Bhoju's extended family prevailed on me to take pictures of them posing in their finery on the roof, Kali disappeared, then returned triumphantly transformed, wearing Shankar's clothes.

Kali's mother's taunt, "What kind of master will you become?" is a painful one, but it reflects perfectly the way families such as hers gauge the potential worth of school education. Even at the younger age, she produced the line "I'll hardly get a job" to justify not attending school. Abraham and Lal, in their excellent account of female education in Jaipur district, confirm this to be a widespread attitude on the part of Rajasthani parents: "Envisaging the future of their children, all the parents saw education as a path to success." And success is defined as "gainful employment in the service or business sectors" (1995: 132–3). In numerous interviews with parents, teachers, and students, Bhoju and I systematically pursued this issue to find education consistently and firmly linked in all minds with the world of jobs (*naukarī*). Yet jobs are scarce, and women's opportunities are especially limited.[9]

THE STICK OF MODERNITY, BROKEN HEARTS, AND WISHES FOR DAUGHTERS

I want to turn now to messages of modernity—specifically of "*mahilā vikās*" or "women's development" as transmitted in activist pamphlets—in the local language. I draw largely on one particular booklet which I first encountered in the hands of men. Anticipating a visit from a district-level officer, Bhoju's fellow teachers in the village of Palasya had decided it was necessary to paint slogans about literacy on every available wall. A pamphlet— not their minds—was their source for slogans, many of which were rhymed couplets in the original. I give a few examples, of which the first seemed to be the most popular in Palasya and environs.

1. One daughter will be educated, seven generations will be liberated!
   ek beṭī paṛhegī sāt pīṛī taregī
2. Every daughter has a right to health, learning, respect, and love.
   har beṭī kā hai adhikār sehat, śikṣā, mān aur pyār
3. If we educate our daughter, we increase knowledge and honor.
   beṭī ko ham paṛhāye jyān aur mān baṛāye
4. Just one vow is to be made: give your daughter an education.
   ek pratijyā lenī hai beṭī ko śikṣā denī hai
5. Let brothers do the housework too, so girls can go to school!
   bhāī bhī ghar kā kām karāye tabhī to bahnā paṛhne jāye
6. Girls and boys one and the same, be it health, education, or virtues!
   laṛkī-laṛkā ek samān, hom svasth, śikṣit guṇavān
7. When a daughter goes to study, our own knowledge will increase.
   beṭī paṛhbā jāvelī apṇom gyān baṛhāvelī
8. Daughters' education is the family's protection.
   beṭiyom kī śikṣā, parivār kī surakṣā

At my request, Bhoju later obtained a copy of his colleagues' source book. Its title, *Preṛṇā gīt aur chetan nāre*, translates into something like *Inspirational Songs and Consciousness-Raising Slogans*. The book is authored and produced by members of a women's collective, working under the auspices of the well-known and successful Jaipur-based Women's Development Program (WDP).[10] An eloquent introduction begins, "The work of awakening human society to women's issues is a very heavy challenge." It ends with a wish for women who read the book to "make these songs and slogans your own," so that "Joining our voices and melodies, . . . one day we will be successful" (Upadhyay et al. 1995: i–ii). Although the introduction is written in Sanskritized Hindi, the songs are in the Rajasthani vernacular, the only language in which most unschooled village women of this region feel comfortable.

Girls are taught to perform such songs for school assemblies. On Republic Day at the big government middle school in Ghatiyali, the spacious courtyard had a single row of chairs for parents to watch their children recite, sing, and dance in honor of the national holiday. On these chairs sat a handful of men—fathers, all in western clothes. Clustered outside the walls, peering over them, were larger numbers of parents in Rajasthani dress, men in loincloths and turbans; women in skirts and wraps, often with veils pulled over their faces. This voluntary and spontaneous segregation by gender and class, or profession, is indicative of ways the school remains an alien space. Nonliterate parents of both sexes feel no sense of belonging there.

Bhoju's own wife, Bali, stayed home claiming child-care burdens, although Madhu, her oldest daughter, was in the show. Girls on the stage sang songs such as this one, which Madhu and two classmates beautifully performed:

> Don't get me married when I'm young,
> Let me study, let me study!
> My sister Kajori is un-schooled, she has eight children,
> and doesn't know how to raise them, so the lot of them are sick.
> Let their sickness be less!
> Don't get me married when I'm young,
> Let me study, let me study!
> Many literate sisters go to work at jobs, but
> The illiterate sit, their veils pulled down,
> In their homes, darkness and shadow.
> Let me bring the new light into my house!
> Don't get me married when I'm young.
> Let me study, let me study!

Self-defined consciousness-raising songs and slogans—heartfelt productions of already mobilized women—hurl themselves melodically against the surrounding culture of gender discrimination, to which uneducated herd girls' songs sorrowfully allude.

Notice that this song unites the idea of education with health, good housekeeping, and even jobs for literate young women. Yet among the herding and farming communities, at least, it is quite likely that the mothers and grandmothers of these girls are happily plotting weddings. Like Kali's family, and even Madhu's female relations, they believe good marriages to be more essential for their well-loved daughters' future well-being than any schooling.

I found many songs in the booklet to be unexpectedly moving, genuinely "inspirational," even when I had never seen or heard them performed. Some have individual named authors, while others were apparently composed by the collective. They carry powerful emotions, persuading me that at least some parts of the modernity project have been fully internalized. I shall give two of these texts in full. One speaks sadly of discrimination between daughters and sons; the other is about the imminent danger, and tragedy, of girls "missing the train" to literacy.

The first is titled "This Evil Custom Goes On (of Discriminating between Daughters and Sons)" [*rīt burī ye chālī (betī-bete mem bhed bhāv)*]:

> *Listen, Listen, O my company of girlfriends,*
> *this evil custom goes on, O sisters,*
> *without knowledge, she remains empty!*
> When I was born, a broken potsherd,
> When brother was born, a nice plate,
>   *O sisters, knowledge.*
> They send my brother to study at school,
> but they have me do the herding work,
>   *O sisters, knowledge.*
> My brother wears pants and a sports-shirt,
> but I'm wearing only a thin cloth wrap,
>   *O sisters, knowledge.*
> My husband's brothers' wives read books aloud,
> But they make me scrub the plates,
>   *O sisters, knowledge.*
> When a gardener plants two trees,
> That gardener alone is the one to water them,
>   *O sisters, knowledge.*
> All sisters, go and study!
> I too shall not stay empty,
>   *O sisters, knowledge.*
> (Upadhyay et al. 1995: 116)

This song aims a direct reproach at parents who practice multiple forms of daughter-neglect and son favoritism, leaving their girls hungry for knowledge, among other things. It is one among many with similar themes.[11]

The upbeat closing refrain of the "discrimination" song is absent in another composition titled "Daughters' Education: The Learning Train." This

3. Madhu Gujar and friends at school assembly, Ghatiyali, January 26, 1997.

one, which has a named author, expresses a mother's acute personal sorrow at seeing her daughter kept away from school due to household needs.

> *The learning train is going along,*
> *Oh, the learning train is going along.*
> See the rich boys slip right inside,
> See the children of the poor remain outside.
> *How many girls are climbing in?*
> *But half of them descend again.*
> *The learning train is going along,*
> *Oh, the learning train is going along.*
> Everyone comes to the station when the train halts there.
> But sometimes money, sometimes marriage get in their way.
> *How many girls are climbing in?*
> *But half of them descend again.*
> *The learning train is going along,*
> *Oh, the learning train is going along.*
> My beloved daughter says, "Please register me at school."
> I say, "I'd really like to but how can I register you at school?

4. The "stick of modernity": Chinu Gujar plays school.

When I go to do labor work, and you go to your school,
Then when we're both outside the house,
Who looks after baby brother?"
My daughter's tears flow, my heart just breaks,
Before our eyes the Education Railroad pulls away.
My daughter's tied down at home,
  But the learning train is going along,
  Oh the learning train is going along.
(Upadhyay et al. 1995: 98; song by Kamalesh Yadav)

Another of the pamphlet songs is called "Times Have Changed!" (*jamān badal gayo*). It begins by promoting literacy, and goes on to praise famous Indian women. This lengthy song then addresses just about every aspect of tradition that modernity rejects, admonishing people to renounce black magic, cease child marriage, reduce population, and live in happy small families, as well as to educate their daughters. Such is the package deal, imposed by what Nita Kumar has called the "stick of modernity" (2000: 199).

School itself is aptly associated with an authoritative stick intended to coerce young persons into new and unfamiliar behaviors and modes of thought. Chinu, Bhoju's middle daughter, decided to play schoolmaster to her younger sister and cousin one day while I was living there (fig. 4).

She was about six years old at the time, and her pupils were three or four. She separated herself from them with a table and took up a stick, doubtless wielding it in imitation of teachers at the village primary school she attended. I have heard teachers harangue village students at morning assembly to "forget" everything they had in their minds before arriving at school, to sweep their brains clean, to erase them like slates. Education thus explicitly pits itself against family, home, and tradition.

In women's activist compositions the New Light prevailing in the New Times shines upon near inversions of familiar gender hierarchies, and not without good reason. As we have seen in the case of Arami's father and throughout this chapter, resistance to girls' education is stubbornly embedded in slow-changing social and economic patterns. It is easy to agree that all the factors disadvantaging women are linked. Child marriage, for example, works directly against keeping girls in school—as Madhu's Republic Day song recognized. Preference for sons, based on their potential future contributions to household income, means that girls are given herding chores so boys can study. Were we determined to pursue root causes, surely (as many others have argued) the fundamental sources of gender discrimination lie in property rights, patrilineal descent, and patrilocal marriage.[12] It is also my hunch that a major fount of many invidious gender practices I encounter in Rajasthan is the ineffable but palpable culture of honor or *ijjat*. Fear of lost honor is what caused Arami's father to make his terrifyingly matter-of-fact statement about the mortal peril of schooling girls.[13]

Women's development organizations are probably correct in perceiving that multiple changes will have to precede gender equity in education, or at least to accompany it. Yet this stand, however logical, perpetuates in the arena of gender the split between home and school that has sabotaged efforts for universal literacy in India for well over a century.[14] Hence, I find myself wondering what would happen if the literacy campaigns in Rajasthan were to renounce their attacks on child marriage, child labor, household sex roles, brother favoritism, and all the rest of it. Could we just have initiatives for nothing but reading, writing, and arithmetic, and miraculously produce literate child bride goatherds? Even as I write this I realize it sounds not only heretical but absurd. Yet I remain troubled, as do many thoughtful authors on education in India, by a situation in which the school system is hopelessly pitted against the culture. Women's development groups—with all the best intentions—redouble this opposition.

One auspicious sign for future female literacy may be found in the wishes expressed by mothers for their daughters' education. Not only activists, but women fully enmeshed in the present gender web sometimes express these aspirations, revealing that even those unable to decipher slogans may nonetheless read the writing on the wall. If change comes slowly to the farming communities of rural Rajasthan, similar processes took place among urban upper classes fifty and one hundred years ago in other regions.[15]

In concluding I turn to words I recorded at the end of an interview with women laborers, young wives cheerfully doing the work of breaking and carrying rocks. A program under the auspices of Rajasthan's accelerated "Total Literacy Campaign" for Bhilwara district in 1997 made participation in adult literacy classes a condition of obtaining work as laborers for the state government. Moreover, their wages were to be withheld until they could successfully sign their names. These women disparaged their own success at the modernizing project, asserting that "wet clay won't stick to a baked pot" (*pākā haṇḍā kā gār na lāgai*).[16] But, with the author of the education train song, they had different aspirations for their daughters' lives. The last words I heard from an authoritative voice among them, as they scattered back to their hard work, were these:

> I may not be literate (*paṛī likhī*) but you should teach my daughter! . . . Our lives are half over, but our daughters [have a future], so take care of them.

ACKNOWLEDGMENTS

I am grateful to the Spencer Foundation and the American Institute of Indian Studies for research support in 1997. Bhoju Ram Gujar participated in every stage of this project, and I also owe enormous thanks to many women and girls who gave me their time and words—especially Bali, Madhu, and Kali Gujar. Many thanks also to Madhu Kishwar for encouraging me to publish this in India in *Manushi*, and to Diane, Sarah, and Indiana University Press for agreeing to let this happen.

NOTES

1. See, for example, Gold 1992 and Raheja and Gold 1994.
2. In Ghatiyali I encountered nothing like the self-disparagement of non-literate women reported by R. Jeffery and P. Jeffery (1996) from Bijnor, U. P. Regional differences are evidently of enormous importance.
3. There are castes called Gujar throughout North India. In Ghatiyali, and generally in eastern and central Rajasthan, Gujar identity—both in folklore and in practice—is bound up with livestock and often most specifically with dairy production. For pastoralists in Rajasthan, including Gujars, see Kavoori 1999.
4. Most boys also drop out relatively early. Young men educated to ninth or tenth grade are often unable to find jobs that suit their educated status; or to feel comfortable herding and farming. This chapter focuses on particular problems for girls, but keep in mind that total male literacy also remains a remote goal.
5. "Sister-in-law's brother" is a common circumlocution for "husband" in Rajasthani women's songs.

6. On girls' education explicitly defined as the production of companionable wives, see Forbes 1996: 32–63.

7. Women's songs recorded in other regions of north India include those in praise of wage-earning husbands and criticizing farmer husbands (P. Jeffery and R. Jeffery 1996a), as well as those that identify employed husbands with the sorrows of separation (Narayan 1997).

8. For the context of Holi in which this song was recorded, see Gold 2001.

9. These days competent, literate women are such a rare commodity that many of them do find minor wage-earning opportunities as workers in numerous development programs. These are often part-time positions they can hold without leaving their homes; as such, they garner neither the prestige nor the income of outside full-time employment.

10. For the WDP, see Abraham and Lal 1995; Unnithan and Srivastava 1997.

11. A number of activist songs critique unfair discrimination between boys and girls, and include in their litany not only the reaction of the family at birth, clothes, and education—as does this one—but food distribution and marriage age as well. Abraham and Lal describe teaching a very similar song to women in a village in Jaipur district. They write, "And soon the whole village was humming the song" (Abraham and Lal 1995: 79–80).

12. For a masterful discussion of gender and property issues, see Agarwal 1994.

13. Manoj Srivastava's recent study offers a new angle on honor, from the advantage of his experience as a government administrator in another low literacy state, Bihar. Srivastava suggests that honor's motivating power may be harnessed and redirected to abet the cause of literacy. Speaking of some success stories in literacy campaigns, he writes, " . . . people felt a sense of honor through a vicarious identification with the prestige that got symbolically, but intensely, associated with achieving a total literacy for the community" (1998: 143).

14. For two illuminating discussions of this, from different perspectives, see K. Kumar 1991; Illaih 1996.

15. See for example many of the writings in Tharu and Lalita 1991. Raman 1996 offers a fascinating portrayal of women's education initiatives, mostly among upper castes, in colonial Tamilnad. Among other things we learn from her case study that marriage need not impede education; and that daughters in families with a "reverence for learning" are likely to be educated. In other words, if schooling is valued it may easily trump gender discrimination, as it has done in Bhoju's own household.

16. See Srivastava for a similar saying used with similar import: "can an aged parrot be ever domesticated?" (1998: 137).

Family and Gender Systems in Transition: A Thirty-Five-Year Perspective

Susan Seymour

> Mrs. Tripathy (New Capital middle-status mother): "Won't you please arrange my daughters' marriages to men in America?"
>
> Mrs. Seymour (researcher's mother): "In the U.S. today young people don't want many children, sometimes none, and you might have no grandchildren."
>
> Mrs. Tripathy: "I should never have had so many children, only one or two. It's a burden. I don't want lots of grandchildren. They're too difficult to educate and to marry."
>
> —Excerpt from January 25, 1987, fieldnotes

INTRODUCTION

This poignant conversation between a mother in one of the twenty-four families I have known and studied for the past thirty-five years and my own mother, who in 1987 accompanied me to my long-term research site —Bhubaneswar, Orissa, India—captures some elements of the dramatic change that has been occurring for many families in this part of India. Mrs. Tripathy[1] spoke in Oriya, the state language of Orissa, and my mother in English, but with my help these two middle-aged women from two different worlds managed to communicate. The topic was the crisis in arranging suitable marriages for the first generation of highly educated young women in Bhubaneswar—a crisis not limited to the Tripathy family. While the problem of marriage was particularly severe in the Tripathy family, where there were seven daughters, only one of whom was married in 1987, it extended to many other families. By 1987 the young children whom I first studied in 1965–67 had not only come of age, but many had received schooling that far surpassed that of their parents and had reached an age well beyond what was previously considered suitable for marriage.

Mrs. Tripathy, for example, had only a few years of schooling and was married at the age of fourteen to a widower with one son. She then produced two more sons and seven daughters—a liability in a society that still requires the parents of girls to provide a dowry (cash, property, and/or goods provided to the groom and his family) as part of marriage negotiations. The Tripathys, a high-caste but socioeconomically middle-class family, had limited resources for so many dowries. Furthermore, they had allowed five of their daughters who excelled in school to continue their education through college and graduate school, making them potentially too old, too educated, and too independent for marriage by traditional standards. At this moment in time changes in expectations for marriage were not keeping pace with other changes in Bhubaneswar. For example, parents were still expected to arrange their children's marriages, but the education and employability of a daughter was not considered a substitute for dowry. In addition, parents-in-law feared that an older, highly educated girl might not make a docile and cooperative daughter-in-law.

To better understand this crisis in marriage and how it relates to changing family and gender systems in this part of India, some background on Bhubaneswar, Orissa, and my thirty-five-year study there is requisite.

RESEARCH SETTING AND METHODOLOGY

Bhubaneswar, an ancient temple town in eastern India and now the capital city of the state of Orissa, has been an ideal microcosm for observing the impact of urbanization and modernization upon traditional principles of family and gender systems. In 1946, just before India's independence from Great Britain, Bhubaneswar was selected to become a new seat of government. With independence in 1947, Orissa became a new state and Bhubaneswar its capital city. Thus began Bhubaneswar's transformation from a small agricultural town renowned for its medieval Hindu temples to a modern planned city of administration and commerce (Seymour 1980).

Within a period of fifteen years Bhubaneswar grew from a large village, where the same families, which for generations had resided in caste-based neighborhoods, knew one another, to a sizable city with many of the institutions of modern urban life as well as its social anonymity. In growth of population alone Bhubaneswar experienced dramatic change. When I began research there in 1965, the town's population had grown from an estimated 10,000 residents to 50,000. By 1999 it exceeded half a million.

Change, however, has gone far deeper than mere demographics would indicate. The establishment of schools—from kindergarten to the post-graduate university level—has provided both old and new residents potentially transformative educational opportunities. Along with schooling have come new job opportunities, ranging from all levels of government service to the many kinds of work that go into building an urban infrastructure—from transportation and lodging to providing food and other goods and services. An age-old agrarian way of life has had to come to terms with a modern life based less upon ascribed caste status and temple rituals and more upon achieved status through education and new forms of secular employment.

My initial research was a two-year study (1965–67) of family organization and child-rearing practices which was part of a larger interdisciplinary study, known as the Harvard-Bhubaneswar Project,[2] to examine the impact of building a new capital city (the New Capital) next door to an old temple town (the Old Town). My strategy was to select households[3] from both sides of town that had more than one child under the age of ten. In addition, I wanted households that represented a range of status in each part of town. In the Old Town caste was used as the diagnostic criterion of status. Accordingly, families ranged from the most pure (Brahman priests) at the top of the caste hierarchy to the least pure or most polluting at the bottom (Washermen and Bauris, an outcaste group of laborers). In the middle were a set of relatively pure Shudra castes (Carpenters, Barbers, and Milkherders). In the New Capital the household head's position in the civil service hierarchy and income were used as diagnostic criteria, and a set of households ranging from top government officials to low-level peons and sweepers were selected to represent a range from the highest stratum of society to the lowest. The result was a set of households that can loosely be designated "upper," "middle," and "lower" status (Seymour 1976, 1999).

Twenty-four households, twelve from each side of town, constituted my 1965–67 sample. They represented a range in structural types: Large joint households (i.e., multigenerational families made up of fathers, sons, and grandsons with their wives and children or sets of brothers, and their wives and children) were predominant in the Old Town, whereas in the New Capital smaller "nuclear" ones were predominant. Middle- and upper-status families had been transferred to the New Capital, often leaving extended kin behind, whereas Old Town families continued to reside in the same houses and neighborhoods that their ancestors had inhabited. However, New Capital families maintained close ties with their extended kin, often hosting a niece or nephew for years of schooling, caring for elderly relatives, and receiving supplies of rice and other foods from rural kin. These webs of responsibility and sharing among extended kin mean that New Capital households are more accurately described as "truncated extended" rather than "nuclear" with its Western connotations. Lower-status New Capital families were also extended: All included maternal and/or paternal grandmothers and other kin, all of whom pooled their resources in order to make a living in the new city.

In 1965–67 sample households ranged in size from five to twenty-four members, with most of the larger households occurring in the Old Town. These households had a total of 130 children under the age of ten who became the focus of my parent-child observations. Since 1965–67, I have stayed in regular contact with all but one of these twenty-four households, returning to Bhubaneswar during the 1970s, '80s, and '90s for further research and to monitor each child's educational, occupational, and marital status.[4] The 1987 trip with my mother inspired research in 1989 that focused upon interviews with mothers, daughters, and grandmothers in order to record *their* reflections about changes that women had experienced during these several decades. It is their insights, as well as my own, that I shall try to summarize below.

PATRIFOCAL FAMILY STRUCTURE AND IDEOLOGY

In 1965–67, Old Town middle- and upper-status family life was characterized by principles of patrilineal descent and patrilocal residence that created multigenerational households with sets of related men, their children, and their wives who had married in from other families. The ideal was to keep together as many patrilineal kin as possible under one roof or to reside close by. Thus, children grew up in enclaves of extended kin. Women, however, were potential strangers who married into their husband's family—usually without even having met the bridegroom before the wedding ceremony—and who had to gradually establish themselves within their husband's family.

These patrifocal families were also characterized by hierarchies based upon gender and age (Mukhopadhyay and Seymour 1994). The oldest male —a father or oldest brother—served as household head, and his wife oversaw the domestic work of the family. While authority formally resided with males, women exerted authority over younger women and over their children, including married sons. The authority of a husband over his wife was in part maintained by his parents' selecting a bride who was significantly younger and less educated than he.

Old Town middle- and upper-status households were characterized by gender-differentiated roles and responsibilities and by some degree of sexual segregation within the house. In addition, purdah (the seclusion of women) was observed for women of childbearing age. Such women could not leave the house alone or in the company of their husbands or other women; they could only leave for special occasions when escorted by older male relatives. A married woman's life was, therefore, highly secluded and focused upon the care of others—preparation of food, house cleaning, and child

5. Old Town middle-status girl (seven years) holding her two-year-old brother.

care. The handling of food and touching of others was periodically inter-rupted by menstruation and childbirth, times when women were viewed as impure and had to observe special restrictions.

Children in Old Town households were provided with numerous care-takers—mothers, grandmothers, aunts, and older siblings and cousins. Early child care and socialization focused upon instilling in children a sense of interdependence—an understanding that they were one of many and that the well-being of the family should always come before their in-dividual interests (Seymour 1999). Both girls and boys were taught to sub-ordinate personal needs and desires in favor of the collective whole. How-ever, for girls who were going to marry out and have to adjust to their husband's family, it was especially important that they learn obedience, modesty, and self-sacrifice. Patrifocal ideology stipulates that it is the bride's responsibility to make the major adjustments in marriage.

Once they had reached puberty, Old Town girls were viewed as highly vulnerable. Their sexuality needed to be protected and guided so as not to bring dishonor upon the family. Hence, the early arranged marriages that characterized Old Town mothers and grandmothers, the seclusion of child-bearing women, and the sexual segregation of homes. In patrifocal ideol-ogy the chastity of women symbolizes family honor, and a virgin daughter is considered a sacred gift to bestow upon another family.

6. Old Town low-status mother and infant.

Life in the New Capital, by contrast, was somewhat different due to the absence of extended kin as well as residence in a new city where not everyone knew their neighbors. In the absence of in-laws, husbands and wives were forced into greater cooperation and allowed more intimacy. For example, some New Capital husbands and wives dined together, something unheard of in the Old Town, where men and children were always fed first, followed by the adult women of the family. Similarly, children were not growing up in large enclaves of extended kin and were more dependent upon the care of their parents. While interdependence continued to be an important value, higher-status New Capital children were also acquiring a greater degree of self-reliance and independence than Old Town children. This, together with an emphasis upon schooling and educational achievement, created a distinctly different climate for these children.

Finally, the life of low-status families, regardless of which side of town they lived in, was deeply affected by economic scarcity. Both men and women had to work outside the home in order to sustain their families, making the observance of such high-caste practices as purdah impossible. Women's work outside the home also meant that household tasks had to be done by a variety of family members: Aging grandmothers and older children, for example, tended to infants and young children while mothers were away from home, and husbands assisted their wives with cooking, child care, and other household tasks when they were home. As a consequence of enhanced cooperation both inside and outside the home, lower-status households exhibited less sexual segregation, less gender-role specialization, and more gender equity (Seymour 1975). And low-status children were expected to become responsible members of the family at an early age (Seymour 1976, 1988, 1999).

SCHOOLING AND THE CRISIS IN MARRIAGE

The remarks by Mrs. Tripathy quoted at the beginning of this chapter reflect not only her anxiety about getting her daughters married but a significantly changed attitude toward childbearing. She asserts that too many children are a burden. As residents of Bhubaneswar have been making the transition from an agrarian way of life to an urban one, the desire for large families has declined. Instead, the emphasis has increasingly focused upon educating one's children and thereby giving them access to new forms of employment and suitable marriages.[5] And as Mrs. Tripathy points out, it is costly to educate lots of children and then difficult to find suitable spouses for them.

Why should this be? Although schooling is state-supported, there are costs associated with acquiring school uniforms and other materials such as pencils and paper. In addition, many Old Town and New Capital families hire tutors to work with their children outside of school so that they will have a better chance of passing the national exams that are part of each level of schooling. Furthermore, more ambitious New Capital parents try to send their children to private English-medium schools that are prestigious and costly.

Another "cost" is what happens to children's aspirations once they are enmeshed in the educational system and the new opportunities it affords. In a society that has emphasized familial interdependence, young people have been expected to follow their elders' directives with respect to educational, marital, and occupational decisions. However, formal schooling often motivates young people to pursue their own interests, and in an urban setting it exposes them to new ideas, people, and career options.

Old Town middle- and upper-status parents carefully tried to invest in the education of some sons while directing others to continue with the family caste-based occupation. While New Capital parents were committed to educating all their sons, in 1965–67 they had little vision of what daughters should achieve educationally. And the idea of girls developing career aspirations was not yet part of their thinking. For example, in 1967 Mrs. Tripathy told me one day that her sons would definitely go to college. Then she added, "Perhaps, the girls will also go to college if they pass their matriculation exams. They might go for a while anyway."

7. New Capital middle-status girls setting off to school.

Yet another "cost" of schooling for girls is a complex social one. How much schooling will improve but not damage a daughter's marriageability in a society where marriage is expected and where there is supposed to be a significant age and educational difference between husband and wife? Furthermore, schooling involves a social danger. It exposes girls to unfamiliar parts of the city and to strange men. As a consequence, many Old Town families viewed sending girls to school as potentially dangerous and opted for local all-girls primary and secondary schools. To attend college, however, required entering the New Capital and attending coeducational institutions that could compromise a daughter's social reputation. For example, one middle-status Old Town mother offered the following explanation for why her youngest unmarried daughter was not in college:

> We had to concentrate on our sons' education both because of expenses and because of dangers. It's a jungle out there, and we live in an isolated house. I had to go with a lantern to meet my son every evening when he came home from college. I have always had to think about my children's safety. (Excerpt from 1989 interview with Mrs. Gauda, an Old Town Cowherder mother)

8. New Capital upper-status school girls.

Despite these various costs, educational change in Bhubaneswar over the past thirty-five years has been dramatic for all families except the very poor. In 1965–67, *all* eligible girls and boys from middle- and upper-status families in both the Old Town and the New Capital attended school. In the Old Town the majority remained in school through the secondary level (11th Standard) with some continuing on to college and even acquiring postgraduate degrees. As table 2 indicates, this represents a significant change in one generation. Sample middle- and upper-status children have dramatically outperformed their parents educationally, especially daughters, who on the average have acquired as much education as their brothers and are now far more educated than their mothers.

In the New Capital, with only one exception, all middle- and upper-status children continued on to college or acquired some specialized training beyond secondary school (table 3). Again, girls have acquired, on the average, as much education as their brothers. All but one has completed a bachelor's degree, and eighteen have continued on to graduate school: fourteen have acquired M.A.s in the arts or sciences; one an M.S. in computer science; two have medical degrees; and one has a Ph.D. in the social

Table 2. Mean Number of Years of Schooling: An Old Town Father-Son and Mother-Daughter Comparison (1989)

Status	Fathers	Sons	Mothers	Daughters
	(N = 26)	(N = 47)	(N = 26)	(N = 35)
Upper/Middle	6.8	11.7	1.5	11.4
Lower	4.0	6.8	0.5	1.4

sciences. By comparison, only one New Capital mother in my sample had completed college. In the span of a single generation these young women have become a highly educated elite in a society where only a small fraction —less than 1 percent—of women acquire a higher education. By contrast, their brothers' mean level of education is not quite as high as their fathers', although several of them have Ph.Ds. and two are now professors in the United States.

While Old Town families have responded somewhat more conservatively to higher education, they too have experienced major disparities between generations in levels of schooling, especially girls. On average, Old Town daughters have completed ten more years of school than their mothers, with many of them completing secondary school and some continuing on for intermediate and baccalaureate degrees. Five completed college, and four of the five have master's degrees in the arts and sciences. My 1989 interviews with mothers, daughters, and grandmothers revealed a longstanding desire for education on the part of many older women:

> I was the only daughter of my father. He was not interested in educating me. Now things have changed. I want to educate my children, and girls in this generation have equal schooling to boys although they should not learn more than boys. (Excerpt from 1989 interview with Mrs. Badhei, an Old Town Carpenter mother)

> My ultimate aim in life was to make my children educated. My father prevented me from studying when I wanted to continue. I don't hold this as a grudge against my children. I wanted them to get an education. I got them educated and then married. I brought them up differently than I was.... With an education women can manage themselves. Also, the cost of living is high. If both men and women are employed, they can manage better. (Excerpt from 1989 interview with Mrs. Mahapatra, an Old Town Brahman mother)

When Bhubaneswar became the capital of Orissa, it also became the educational center of the state. Schools at all levels were established and schooling was suddenly accessible to everyone. In addition, nationalist goals emphasized the importance of education for girls as well as boys.

Table 3. Mean Number of Years of Schooling: A New Capital Father-
Son and Mother-Daughter Comparison (1989)

Status	Fathers	Sons	Mothers	Daughters
	(N = 12)	(N = 22)	(N = 12)	(N = 26)
Upper/Middle	17.4	16.3	9.7	16.0
Lower	1.1	6.9	0.0	3.5

Women such as Mrs. Badhei and Mrs. Mahapatra were able to see their daughters realize the education they had been deprived of but had desired.

Among low-status families, by contrast, there has more limited educational improvement during this same time-span (tables 2 and 3). In a few Old Town and New Capital families sons have been sent to school; several have matriculated (graduated from secondary school) and one has completed a B.A. The majority of girls and boys, however, have received little or no schooling. Most low-status families have not yet envisioned the benefits of schooling, or if they have, they have not been able to afford to have children away at school when they are needed at home to care for younger siblings and to help out with other household chores. By adolescence most low-status sons and daughters have become low-paid workers like their parents.

For middle- and upper-status Old Town and New Capital children, prolonged schooling has resulted in delayed marriage. Whereas most mothers had married at the time of puberty (twelve to fifteen years of age), this generation of girls was marrying no earlier than eighteen years and most not until their twenties. One reason that marriage was such a heightened topic of conversation and concern in 1987 was that by then all my original sample of children were eligible for marriage—they were in their twenties —but many were not yet married. This was considered particularly problematic for parents of daughters. In the Old Town, where attitudes toward schooling and the age of marriage were more conservative, in 1987 only 24 percent of girls remained unmarried. In the New Capital, by contrast, the figure was 48 percent and the mean age of unmarried girls was twenty-seven whereas for Old Town unmarried girls it was twenty, still within the acceptable age range (eighteen to twenty-four years) for marriage. Hence, the crisis of marriage in the New Capital.

While some degree of schooling for prospective brides had become desirable during this period in Bhubaneswar, high levels of education were complicating marriage arrangements. Parents of daughters needed to find prospective grooms of the right caste and class status who were even older and more educated than their daughters. In addition, those who had daughters with career goals sought to identify grooms and parents-in-law accepting of these ambitions—i.e., having a wife/daughter-in-law employed outside the house, which also implied acceptance of a prospective wife/ daughter-in-law's greater independence. Thus, the marriage market had been greatly complicated, and eligible men were scarce. As one unmarried New Capital daughter expressed it: "Candidates come to our house but do not choose us. Men just want less educated wives whom they can dominate; we are not supposed to out-achieve our husbands."

SOME IMPLICATIONS FOR THE PATRIFOCAL FAMILY

Change is neither uniform nor ubiquitous, and in Bhubaneswar the baseline for change varied considerably by Old Town–New Capital residence and by class/caste status. Nonetheless, the establishment of a new capital city has instigated changes that have both immediate and long-term implications for patrifocal family organization and ideology and hence for systems of gender.

Well into the 1960s young men and women married without having met one another. Then, if possible, the bride moved in with her new husband and his family, and the young couple only gradually came to know one another while surrounded by the groom's kin. There could be no expression of intimacy in front of others, and various household practices ensured that they had little time alone together. Furthermore, other practices emphasized the subservience of the wife to her husband and in-laws, and the expectation that the conjugal relationship would always remain subordinate to the interests of the collective family was constantly reinforced.

> *Mother:* At that time [when she married] the husband's ability was like a god. Wives would pray to God but take care of their husband first. That's no longer so.
> *Son:* A wife would never reply, never speak back to her husband. Nowadays they do. They have their education. [His wife and married sister, who are present, indicate agreement.] (Excerpt from 1989 interview with an Old Town Brahman family)

> *Mother:* Give-and-take is what makes a good relationship.
> *Daughter:* Mutual understanding. Both husband and wife must want to work together.
> *Mother:* The wife should give way [when there's a disagreement].
> *Daughter:* No. There is no reason why the wife should give in any more than the husband.
> *Mother:* The husband's voice should come first.
> *Daughter:* I disagree. (Excerpt from 1989 interview with a New Capital upper-status mother and daughter)

These two excerpts from my 1989 interviews with mothers, daughters, and grandmothers, as well as some male kin, are indicative of ways in which people have begun to reconceptualize the husband-wife relationship. There has been movement away from the more formal, hierarchical relationship toward one that exhibits greater cooperation and equity. Most of the young people in my sample share this changed ideology, but it has not always led to harmonious relations. In one case of a New Capital daughter, her husband's domination by his mother and lack of support for her as a working wife and mother led to their separation. Gitali was twenty-six, educated and employed when she entered into an arranged marriage and moved into her parents-in-law's home. There she experienced two serious problems: she and her husband were allowed little time alone together, and her mother-in-law dominated the household and her husband's affections. Gitali, who believed that a husband-wife relationship "should be one of commonality, of cooperation," found herself in a hierarchical setting where her mother-in-law dominated her husband and her husband, in turn, tried to dominate her. It was not the more conjugal relationship she had imagined. After bearing two children and enduring eight unhappy years of marriage, Gitali moved out, taking one of her children with her. In 1989, this is how she expressed her sentiments: "Women feel that they should sacrifice, that they would lose respect in society if they leave their husband. I don't feel so. I don't care [what society thinks]." Gitali considered herself a rebel, someone out of step with society, and regretted not having been born at a time when she could have joined Gandhi in the fight for independence.

In two other cases women have left abusive husbands and have moved back in with their natal kin. And in three additional cases of uncompromising in-laws, both in the Old Town and the New Capital, the conjugal pair has moved to separate quarters. Kalika (aged thirty-three in 1989) began her narrative by saying, "There are some problems. I will tell you now. You can know the problems I face after my marriage. Why I am here alone with no help from anywhere." Kalika went on to tell me about the unusual circumstances of her marriage, that it was not an arranged marriage in the traditional manner but that her husband had learned about her and had selected her. They were both college lecturers, and he wanted to marry an educated woman with a career similar to his. However, his mother, also an employed woman, rejected his bride and did not welcome Kalika to their home after the marriage ceremony—a significant slight. Subsequently, she expected Kalika to behave in an obsequious manner and to do all the cooking for the household despite her responsibilities as a college lecturer.

> They [Kalika's mother-in-law and sister-in-law] forced me to work, to prepare work in the kitchen. They wanted to torture me. My husband came to my defense. He explained that his wife is educated—a servicing [working] woman, who cannot prepare food for the whole family and work. How is that possible? (Excerpt from 1989 interview with a New Capital upper-status daughter)

Things went from bad to worse when Kalika's mother-in-law took away the engagement ring that her father-in-law had given her. Ultimately, her husband became very angry with his family, refused to take food in his parents' house—a highly symbolic gesture—and moved his wife to separate quarters.

The six cases of marriage difficulties that I have documented are small in number but reasonably dramatic within the context of my twenty-four-family sample, and they are indicative of significant change with respect to women's, and some men's, expectations for marriage. Nonetheless, what is perhaps most remarkable is the degree of stability Old Town and New Capital families have exhibited over the past thirty-five years. In the Old Town, all families that were joint in 1965–67 continue to be joint, although some sons have had to reside elsewhere because of their employment, and some families have divided because of space constraints. A few households that were not joint in 1965–67 have become so with the marriage of sons. And the two sons who moved out in order to have greater independence for themselves and their wives and children reside close by.

In the New Capital, some portion of each family continues to reside in Bhubaneswar despite some members having had temporary job assignments elsewhere. Several sets of parents are now retired in the New Capital, and all but one couple has married children and grandchildren living nearby. One father even built a retirement home big enough to accommodate his three married sons and their families, so they have become a joint household.

Thus, most Old Town and New Capital families have incorporated significant changes in gender roles and ideology, as well as in intergenerational relationships, to maintain this degree of stability. While arranged marriage within caste has remained almost universal, parents have made it a more collaborative process by allowing their children to meet prospective brides and grooms and to have a veto power over them before arrangements are finalized. In several cases a son has met and liked a suitable woman and has asked his parents to arrange a marriage with her, and they have complied. With these kinds of adjustments, arranged marriage has remained a stable institution that young people in Bhubaneswar accept. As one young New Capital unmarried daughter put it:

> My parents have left me free. They have told me that if I want to have anybody of my choice, then I should tell them. I don't want to take any such project on for myself because I know my parents are very capable in this matter. It will be according to my choice [i.e., her parents will not force her into a marriage she does not want]. (Excerpt from 1989 interview with a middle-status, employed New Capital daughter)

Furthermore, many middle- and upper-status families have adjusted to daughters/wives/daughters-in-law who are employed outside the home and are combining careers with marriage and childbearing—something that none of their mothers had done. While this phenomenon is rarer in the Old Town than in the New Capital, it has required significant change in gender roles and ideology in both places. Obviously, employed women cannot observe purdah and menstrual seclusion, and thus both the beliefs and practices pertaining to female sexuality and family honor have had to change. Furthermore, employed women are not available to attend to the needs of family members all day long. Thus, mothers-in-law have had to adjust their expectations for daughters-in-law or potentially jeopardize their relationships with their sons. When there is intergenerational cooperation, extended families provide a wonderful solution to child care for working parents. For example, in one Old Town family a husband and wife who have jobs and housing in the New Capital bring their baby to the husband's family in the Old Town each day to be cared for while they are at work.

SOME CONCLUDING REMARKS

There is no question that family life in Bhubaneswar is in transition. Many patrifocal ideals that only some families realized but others valued are being challenged. Central to these are the roles and expectations for women. To varying degrees all middle- and upper-status families have had to accommodate to new ideas about gender and age hierarchies, the education and status of women, husband-wife relationships, and the employment of women outside the home. Ironically, these accommodations make middle- and upper-status families resemble low-status ones, where most women have always worked outside the home, making the seclusion of women impossible and enhancing gender equity within the home—practices that formerly stigmatized these families.

For most low-status families, Bhubaneswar's rapid expansion has brought new forms of employment, some increased economic stability, but little upward mobility. When in 1989 I asked Sopna, a low-status New Capital daughter, who is now married with three children, whether things had changed for women between her generation and that of her mother, she replied:

> I am lucky. Unlike my parents, I did not have to stay in the village. I was brought up in Bhubaneswar with some education. In the village my parents suffered terribly. They had no food. They ate nothing but boiled tamarind leaves during the drought. I am much better off than my mother. (Excerpt from 1989 interview with Sopna and her mother)

Sopna's reply was a sobering reminder of what poverty can mean.

* * *

Changes in family and gender systems in Bhubaneswar are not unique. They resemble processes of change that have been documented in several other longitudinal studies for different parts of India (Minturn 1993; Ullrich 1987, 1994; Wadley 1994). All of these studies identify changes that include the loosening of familial bonds of authority based upon age and gender hierarchies in favor of increased husband-wife intimacy and the relaxation of purdah restrictions on women. The fundamental question then becomes, To what extent will the patrifocal joint family be able to adjust to these kinds of democratizing changes while retaining the general commitment of family members to the well-being of the collective whole? And will India achieve any better solutions to the dilemma faced in Western societies of how to balance the needs of the family, whether extended or nuclear, with the desire to enhance gender equity and provide women as well as men with some degree of personal autonomy?

NOTES

1. All names of family members have been changed to protect their identity.

2. Initiated in 1961 by Cora Du Bois, then Zemurray Professor of Anthropology at Harvard University, the project was to examine processes of rapid urbanization and sociocultural change in an Indian town undergoing transformation from an ancient temple town to a modern state capital. Over some twelve years, fourteen Orissan and American graduate students, representing a variety of academic disciplines, undertook research in Bhubaneswar under the guidance of Professor Du Bois. This research has become known as the Harvard-Bhubaneswar Project and has been synthesized in Seymour 1980.

3. An important distinction is that between "household" and "family." Here I use the term "household" to mean those members of a family residing under one roof who usually share food and other goods, who usually cook together, and who cooperate in child care. The term "family" refers to extended kin who may not necessarily reside together but who consider one another family. See Gray and Mearns (1989) for a discussion of households in different parts of South and Southeast Asia.

4. Since my predoctoral research in 1965–67, I have returned to Bhubaneswar in 1978, 1982, 1987, 1989, and 1999. My 1965–67 research was supported by an NIMH predoctoral research training grant. Subsequent trips have been supported by Pitzer College Research and Awards grants and by a Senior Fulbright Research Fellowship.

5. In 1965–67 most Bhubaneswar residents were not aware of family-planning strategies, despite the presence of a family planning clinic in the New Capital. Subsequently, under Indira Gandhi family planning became a major national objective. More importantly, improved health and a decrease in infant mortality rates, together with education and modernization, have convinced this generation to have fewer children.

Offstage with Special Drama Actresses in Tamil Nadu, South India: Roadwork

Susan Seizer

> The event was absolutely unique, and it was repeated every year. For the event (any event) unfolds simultaneously on two levels: as individual action and as collective representation; or better, as the relation between certain life histories and a history that is, over and above these, the existence of societies.
> —Marshall Sahlins, *Islands of History* (1985)

MISE-EN-SCÈNE

Roads and streets are a common mise-en-scène for enactments of the Tamil popular theater genre known as Special Drama. The obligatory opening comedy scene of these live performance events always begins with a young woman dancing in the middle of a road, a fantastic suspension of Tamil norms of conduct for women. The painted canvas backdrop for this scene displays a wide, generic road stretching off vertically into the horizon. The comic enactment that unfolds rapidly develops into an exploration of illicit love. An unknown young bachelor appears on the road, and all manner of shady business unspools between the young man and woman, including lewd banter, flirtatious spats, boasts laden with sexual innuendo, coy one-upmanship, cooing love songs, and, eventually, elopement.

This opening scene is a dramatization, in a comic mode, of the proverbial bad road for women. Its narrative content perpetuates and encourages a dominant association between public roads and the bad reputation of actresses as public women. This essay concerns how such an association of

This is an abridged and amended version of a paper entitled "Roadwork: Offstage with Special Drama Actresses in Tamil Nadu, South India" that originally appeared in *Cultural Anthropology* 15, no. 2 (2000): 217–259. Reprinted with permission.

ideas shapes Special Drama actresses' offstage lives, and in turn, how their practices "on the road" potentially refigure that dominant discourse.

"Special Drama" (*Special Nāṭakam*) is a contemporary Tamil theatrical genre that began around the turn of the twentieth century. Its hybrid English-Tamil name refers to the practice of hiring each artist "specially" for every performance event. Special Drama is performed outdoors in small towns or villages, either in the village commons or, equally often, at the intersection of two roads. In 1993, sixteen cities and towns throughout the state of Tamil Nadu had actors associations, run by the artists to facilitate a statewide network of Special Drama performers (see fig. 9).

The participants in Special Drama—performers as well as audience members—are predominately working class. In my interviews and conversations with artists, the explanation most performers gave for entering this line of work was "due to poverty." Some Special Drama artists begin performing in childhood, others as young adults; about half come from families that are already involved in some way in the drama world. Though the work is only seasonal, the pay is relatively high when available. For example, a woman who works as a cook or a maid might earn Rs. 75 *per month*, whereas working as an actress she might earn Rs. 300 *in one night*. Such relatively high wages are virtually the sole compensation, however, for the loss of social standing that results from entering this profession. And this cost, to be sure, most severely affects women.

Becoming a Special Drama actress generally means forfeiting any chance of a "normal" marriage (by which I mean a legally sanctioned marriage arranged between the bride's and groom's families), as no self-respecting groom's family will agree to have a son marry an actress (and this often includes families of male actors!) because of a standard view of actresses as public women, aka prostitutes. Indeed, several common Tamil words for "actress" simultaneously denote "whore" or "prostitute." *Kūtti, kūttiyāḷ, tāci,* and *tēvaṭiyāḷ* all mean "dancing girl or prostitute" (Fabricius 1972: 505), "(derogatorily) mistress; concubine" (Cre-A 1992: 349), or "dancing girl devoted to temple service, commonly a prostitute; harlot, whore" (Lexicon 1982: 1825). The combined effect of such stigmatizing terms and the discourses that fuel their existence is to keep most "good" Tamil women from daring or desiring to be actresses at all, and ensuring that most actresses will become "second wives," a euphemism for concubines or mistresses—a lived rather than a legal category.

At the core of this essay are five fieldwork narratives.[1] These retell specific experiences I had while on the road with Special Drama actresses. Each experience helped me to better understand actresses' actions offstage; these were the settings in which I learned, in particular, how and why actresses create private, exclusive spaces in the midst of the Tamil public sphere. Each narrative speaks of one leg in the journey to or from a Special Drama. Together, the five narratives thus make up a single composite jour-

9. The State of Tamil Nadu, showing the location of the sixteen towns and cities in which actors associations are located. These are (in order of membership size) Madurai, Pudukottai, Dindigal, Karaikkudi, Karur, Salem, Sivaganga, Erode, Trichy, Coimbatore, Koyilpatti, Manapparai, Kumbakonam, Perungudi, Namakkal, and Manamadurai.

ney that begins in a calendar shop in town (the first narrative), then heads out by van (the second) or by bus (the third), to the site of a Special Drama stage and its backstage spaces (the fourth), and finally returns home, on foot, to town (the fifth and final narrative).

Through these narratives I aim to convey a sense of the actresses' *road-work* as a set of lived, adaptive practices that operate to foil the dominant notion of actresses as "bad women." When actresses manage to make their behavior indistinguishable from that of good women—in other words, when they appear to comply with these dominant norms—might the norms be somewhat altered by being stretched to accommodate these women? With this question in mind, I suggest that actresses creatively *expand* the category of "good woman" to include themselves. I see this *expansion* of given, exclusive categories of social acceptability as a particular strategy for dealing with social stigma. The theoretical import of this study, then, concerns the larger issue of the effective redress of stigma: I detail a strategy that operates under the appearance of collaboration with social norms while simultaneously refiguring the norms themselves.

THEORETICAL GROUNDS

In her preface to *Imaginary Maps*, Gayatri Spivak uses the metaphor of an intractable obstacle, a roadblock blocking women's movements all over the world, to convey what she calls a "difficult truth": that "internalized gendering perceived as ethical choice is the hardest roadblock for women the world over" (1995: xxviii). In Spivak's vision, internalized gender norms and constraints block both the movement of individual women down particular roads, as well as the progress of collective women's movements worldwide.

Partha Chatterjee similarly stresses the historical importance women's internalization of a properly gendered self-image has had in building the new Indian nation. He argues, however, that women's ability to internalize gender constraints eased rather than blocked their travels out into the world. Chatterjee suggests that it is precisely through their internalization of a self-image of virtuous domesticity that middle-class women have been able to maintain respectability while venturing out into the public sphere; these good women were able to carry their "home" identities out into the "world" with them. This amounts to an ingenious nationalist strategy for resolving "the women's question": the middle-class woman had simply to become so identified with the spiritual and moral sphere of the home that it remained intact wherever she went. As Chatterjee writes:

> Once the essential femininity of women was fixed in terms of certain culturally visible spiritual qualities, they could go to schools, travel in public conveyances, watch public entertainment programs, and in time even take up employment outside the home. (1993: 130)

Moving in public, the respectable woman carries with her an inner strength forged indoors.

The case is quite the opposite for those worldly women against whom nationalism's model middle-class women were explicitly defined—those women, that is, whom Chatterjee calls "sex objects" for the nationalist male, precisely *because* they are seen as "other" than his mother/sister/wife/daughter. Likewise, in Tamil Nadu today, while middle-class women are able to displace the boundaries of the home from its physical confines onto a more flexible psychic domain, Special Drama actresses, who hail from among the urban poor in Tamil Nadu, never had such a proper middle-class home in the first place. For these actresses, the task of attaining the qualities of the good woman—still defined by the virtues of domesticity—requires that they constantly, vigilantly strive in their daily practice to erect those very physical confines the new middle-class woman has left behind. Actresses attempt to better their reputation as women by acting on the dominant script quite literally, throughout their public journeys, by seeking to recreate domesticity in its material form.

In this essay I focus on the problematic mobility of women who do *not* properly internalize gender constraints. I write here about stage actresses in Tamil Nadu, women stigmatized precisely for being too public, and for moving out into the world beyond the bounds of proper, modest feminine behavior. As such, this essay is literally about women and roads; more specifically, it is about my own experiences traveling certain roads, and encountering certain roadblocks, with certain women.

In these travels I began to develop my own embodied sense of actresses' roadwork, of its system of signs and dispositions, indeed of the "imaginative universe within which their acts are signs" (Geertz 1973: 13). I now understand my feelings during our travels as a set of diagnostic signs, signifying to me that I had begun to understand viscerally something of what is at stake for actresses when traveling through the public sphere. I was engaging in the famous ethnographic work of "deep hanging-out" (Rosaldo, quoted in Clifford 1997a: 188), through which I began to understand "the character of lived experience" among actresses. That is, I treat examining my own experiences moving with Special Drama actresses on their turf and in their terms as a classically ethnographic way of gaining insight into their experiences of being "other" in the context of the contemporary Tamil public sphere. "Ethnography . . . has always meant the attempt to understand another life world using the self—as much of it as possible—as the instrument of knowing" (Ortner 1995: 173).

THE STIGMA OF INAPPROPRIATE MOBILITY

Throughout India, as elsewhere, theater actresses have long been the very definition of "bad" women. Unlike the chaste loyalty of the good wife who reveals herself to only one man, the actress's profession requires that she willingly expose herself to the gaze of many unfamiliar men. This blatant step into the limelight of such mobile relations is largely what brands actresses as bad.

There are three highly interconnected dimensions to the stigma of mobility accruing to actresses in Tamil Nadu. The first is a problem with acting itself, the fact of mimetic fluidity—that acting involves illusion and not reality, and offers false selves, making mobile things that ought to be fixed. The second involves the overly fluid offstage behavior of actors in employing fictive kin networks, rather than maintaining normal, orderly, sanctioned kin relations. Actors use kin terms across caste, class, religious, and ethnic boundaries, creating socially expedient relations between them where in reality no blood or marriage relations exist. Such identity shifts onstage (mimetic) and off (in kin relations)—both of which concern normative relations between men and women—taint the reputation of the acting community as a whole, and stigmatize it as excessively mobile and uncontainable.

I restrict my focus here to the third dimension of the stigma that accrues to actresses, their publicity and mobility as they move about conducting their business. The form of this mobility—the very public nature of the actress's line of work—threatens to expose the fragility of the culturally naturalized division of gendered spheres into home and world, as actresses move onto public stages to enact what are meant to be the most private of relations. Added to these other two dimensions of stigma that haunt the acting community (that of mimetic fluidity and of fictive kin), the actress finally is seen as most unsettling precisely in her unsettledness.

Her battle for reputation against this unsettledness is constant, since the very organization of Special Drama depends on performers' mobility. Each artist is contracted individually for each performance. There is no troupe or director for Special Drama. Instead, there are repertory roles, such as Hero and Heroine, Buffoon and Dancer, in a set repertory of plays. It is each artist's responsibility to get to and from each venue on time. During the drama season, the hot summer months of March through August, actresses may appear on a different stage in a different town or village every night. These women travel all across the state to perform night-long shows that begin at 10 P.M. and end at dawn. The primary challenge for these women is how to accomplish their public artistic business with as little tainting publicness as possible.

In moving with Special Drama actresses through the streets of Tamil Nadu, I experienced how they created structures of enclosure even in the most public of places. I experienced viscerally how a dominant "inside/outside" dichotomy of "good/bad" morality informs their every journey. And I grew to appreciate their patient, understated, and expansive response to this oppressive climate. As we traveled, actresses erected enclosures that were their own exclusive, interior spaces, spaces that slyly appropriated for themselves a dominant strategy of exclusion everywhere we went. They strung together little islands, havens of familiarity, and hopped from one to the next as a means of remaining protected while moving through the outside.

Narrative One: Regarding the Gender Dimensions of Booking a Drama

The arrangement of bookings and dates for Special Drama is a side of their business from which actresses often distance themselves, especially because such negotiations concern their own public mobility. Instead of taking bookings directly, an actress hangs her calendar in a booking shop. In 1993, there were five such shops in the city of Madurai, the long-established center for Special Drama.[2] All were very male public spaces; several were printing shops in which booking artists' calendars were a side business, while for others such calendars were the main business. While the calendars of both male and female artists hang in these shops, only men are present physically—in the flesh, that is—sitting around talking, checking on the dates of their next performances, or drumming up business for new bookings. Male representatives from a village or town interested in booking a drama come to the city of Madurai to peruse the posted calendars, check on the availability of specific drama artists, and converse with those in the know about the current crop of artists.

Men who, for a living, help these local sponsors make their drama arrangements are known as drama agents. Together, drama agents, drama sponsors, and male drama actors regularly hang out in and around the five booking shops in Madurai, all of which are located within a small two-block radius in the center of town, a little business district in which actors are kings of the road but through which actresses only briskly pass on their way to and from performance venues.

Inside the shops, the walls are lined with individual artist's calendars. These calendars have a separate thin page for each day of the year. The pages make a square packet, which is stapled onto a cardboard backing where the artist's name is pasted as a heading, and beneath which the artist's bust photo provides further identification and allure. Every artist's calendar provides a book of days that opens out under its personalized headboard like a skirt—or so it appeared to me.

Men interested in hiring an actress do not approach her directly, but rather approach her calendar. An actress's calendar is in this way a material stand-in for her. It provides sponsors with a way to contract an actress without direct interaction, and simultaneously allows the actress to absent herself from the negotiations. Similar to the process by which good Indian girls become brides, here men engage in negotiations in which a woman's person is implicated, but not dialogically involved.[3] While he books an actress, she stays at home; an effigy of her (her personalized calendar) circulates in her stead.

Any man approaching an actress's calendar to book a drama may pick her effigy off the wall, handle it, peruse it, flip through its skirt, and read therein the unfolding story of the actress's public life: where she will be when in the coming days, where she has been in the recent past, how busy this season looks, how in demand (or not) she is this season. Penned onto the back side of her calendar is the actress's performance fee, which is a private note from her, hidden from public view. If he selects her, he pens his name, and his place name, directly onto the front of her calendar. Without her ever having to meet with him, he has arranged for her to come to his place, when he chooses, for a fee.

The shop owner, who functions as a booking agent, has a certain financial stake in these negotiations, as he earns a fee (three rupees was the going rate in 1993) every time an artist whose calendar he posts is booked for a drama. Being financially implicated in this way, the shop owner wants the calendars of popular artists in his shop. He needs to know whether or not a particular artist will actually attract sponsors' bookings; he needs to know each artist's value and reputation. When I asked one shop owner, Mr. Jeyaraman, how he ascertains this, he answered: "I'll ask them to sing. 'Show me how you sing,' I'll say, and they'll sing right here in the shop. I ask many people to sing before I put their calendar up." This surprised me because it was the first I had heard of such a practice. Our conversation continued:

> *Susan:* Really? So, imagine that I want to hang my calendar here. Would you ask me to sing?
> *Jeyaraman:* Oh no! No I won't. I won't ask this of women.
> *S:* Why is that?
> *J:* We can't ask a woman to come here and sing. Can we ask a woman to come sing in a public place? If this was a house, we might ask her; here we can't.

I was intrigued. We were talking about professional performers, stage actresses, the very women who *do* sing in public places—public women par excellence—were we not? I sat there in my sari with my black box of a tape recorder, asking him endless questions, feeling like a gender freak and a bit of a boor. Actresses might be public women professionally and by night, but in their local day-to-day lives, close to home, they tried to maintain a reputation as proper women.[4] In the daytime, in their daily local life, actresses would not come out to a public shop—the very shop where I currently sat and quite publicly acted the anthropologist, asking questions about these very gendered norms and practices—and perform publicly. I realized belatedly and somewhat sheepishly that, when he spoke about asking them to sing, Jeyaraman had been referring only to male artists, the kind of people who *should be* in shops like his.

Before I could even ask how it was, then, that he did ascertain the tal-

10. Jeyaraman's calendar shop, Madurai, Feb. 10, 1992, near the beginning of the drama season. (Mr. Jeyaraman standing left.)

ents of an actress without asking her to sing, he volunteered the following: "Regarding women, if we want a critical assessment, that's easy: many people will be going to see her and will be knowing about her. We can learn from so many people: they'll be saying, 'this is how she talks; this is how she acts.' So therefore I can guarantee her to any town."

Even her booking agent, then, learns of an actress's talents only indirectly, through the eyes, ears, and words of other men who have seen and heard her onstage. Other men speak to him directly about her voice, or else they speak in and around his shop to other men hanging out in and around his shop. It is men, speaking among each other, who determine an actress's reputation, while she sits, quietly or not, at home.

Narrative Two: Regarding Traveling to a Drama in a Private Conveyance

Whenever they can, Special Drama artists travel to their performance venues in private rather than public vehicles. Older artists recall with nostalgia the days when they traveled in the pinnacle of secluded, enclosed, and luxurious worlds: they rode in "pleasures." "Pleasure" is the English word artists still use to refer to the private automobile, the rented Ambassador "pleasure car" that used to pick up actresses at their own door and take them directly to the performance site.[5]

Very rarely are "pleasures" used by drama parties today. Instead, quite often artists pool their resources to hire a private van, the current means of avoiding public buses. Such drama vans are crowded. Sometimes sixteen people squeeze into a space designed for ten, where in addition the back seat is entirely taken up with artistic provisions: a large wooden foot-pedal harmonium, several drums, multiple rolls of painted canvas back-drops for scene settings, not to mention each actor's costume-filled suit-case. People have to sit practically on top of each other in these vans, often for many hours.

Nevertheless, the question of why artists adamantly prefer crowded private vans to public buses is obvious: public-private distinctions as markers of prestige and social status in Tamil Nadu long predate both vans and buses. The reigning logic is familiar: more prestigious persons occupy both more (and more private) personal space, while less prestigious persons occupy both less (and less private) space.

To me, traveling with drama artists in a van always felt risqué. Suddenly the strict women's side / men's side rules of public conveyances were lifted. The two requisite actresses in any Special Drama party would often sit side by side in the van in a two-person seat, but equally often they did not. My own presence could easily instigate multiple shifts: a woman certainly had to be seated next to me for reasons of propriety (so that I would not be forced to sit beside an unknown man), but then what about the other actress? She suddenly had increased mobility, without ever seeming to ask for it. Inside a van, other sorts of allegiances and alliances, even intimacies, emerged easily.

Van interiors provide drama artists a means of moving through and across public roads while carrying a collective interiority, a protective group cohesiveness, with them. The world internal to the drama community creates a bubble of familiarity that stretches to the contours of every space they fill together, and in these cases it was the size of the interior of a van. I felt included in that "inside" familiarity when I rode with them. I felt freer there than almost anywhere else in Tamil Nadu, engaged in a daring squeeze of closeness that was largely invisible to the outside world. I felt inside a family, of sorts, and it was a pleasure too.

Narrative Three: Regarding Traveling to a Drama in a Public Conveyance

Bakkiyalakshmi and I had finally settled on a date for me to accompany her to a drama. Bakkiya is a seasoned actress in her fifties, and we were going to a village in an area well known to her from decades of performing throughout the region.

As this village was accessible by main road, we were traveling by public bus (as there is less excuse for the luxury of hiring a van when a venue can be reached by bus). All Tamil town buses, like those we took that night, have a women's side and a men's side. The words indicating which side is which are stenciled directly onto the walls of the bus. When traveling in a pair, two women need have very little interaction with unknown persons on a public bus, least of all with unknown men. We had none.

We left from Madurai in the early evening and traveled into the night. To reach the sponsoring village we had to change buses at two different stations. In the first station our change was quick and easy, as the next bus was already loading when we arrived. We simply got up from our two-person seat on the women's side of the bus from Madurai, and switched to another two-person seat on the women's side of the bus from Sivaganga.

At the second station our bus was not waiting. Bakkiya told me it would not come for another half an hour. We got off the bus and she led me to a little food stall, one among many lining the road on the side of the bus station. There a man was making a common flamboyant dish, a specialty of the region called "egg parota" (parota is a deliciously thin bread layered in a flat spiral). Its preparation involves terrific energy on the part of the chef. He holds two metal tools—they are shaped more like axes than knives—and bangs them down onto a wide, flat metal skillet, over and over, rhythmically mixing and chopping parota and egg. It is the noisiest manner of food preparation I have ever encountered, entrancing as only an intensely loud barrage of sound can be, starting for a spell of deafening decibels at each new order and abruptly stopping again in equally deafening silence.

The chef at the stall we approached flashed a big smile at Bakkiyalakshmi. They knew each other, though I didn't catch exactly how. He was at least twenty years her junior. She introduced me and he immediately put down his tools and led us back through his stall into a small back room. In it was a desk, a chair, and a cot. The walls were painted royal blue. He made sure I was comfortably seated in the chair and returned to his metal axes and metal skillet. Bakkiya asked me whether I would like to eat, encouraging me to do so here rather than wait for whatever food the villagers had prepared. I agreed. She left the room, and I was alone.

I sat in that little room for what felt like a long time but couldn't have been more than fifteen minutes. The wall of sound just beyond unmistakably delimited inside from outside. Where I was sitting was inside: blue walls swimming around me, a tide of deafening sound reaching me in waves. The other noises and voices and commerce beyond the walls of that room were all outside.

I realized that even on this most public of routes, taking a public bus from a public bus stand two towns away from home, Bakkiya had secured a little private space, which that night she lent to me so that I could disappear into a respite of invisibility. I sat there feeling safe and tiny, and simultaneously out of the loop and bored. How, I wondered, does Bakkiya feel when she sits there?

Narrative Four: Regarding Spatial Arrangements at a Drama Site

When artists reach their performance venue, an outdoor stage has already been erected at the site. The stage is a raised rectangular platform, often with a dirt floor, with palm-frond thatching for three walls and the ceiling. Specifications for the stage require a large playing area and an equally roomy backstage to which the actors may retire when they are not onstage. Actors call the playing space onstage "outside" (*veḷiyē*) and the backstage resting space "inside" (*uḷḷē*).

A central feature of all Special Drama venues is thus that there is a definite demarcation between inside and outside, between a public space where actors are visible to all, and a private space into which they may disappear. This demarcation is provided by the painted canvases known as "scene settings" that stretch from ceiling to floor and are rolled and un- rolled for scene changes throughout the night.

Actors change costumes, touch up their faces and hair, sleep in catnaps between scenes, chat, and snack together "inside" throughout the night. They prepare themselves in this collective space of inside before each stint outside. Inside, they generally maintain the decorum of women's side and men's side arrangements, though not rigidly; inside feels, in short, much like being in a privately relaxed Tamil domestic space, a home, where gender determines behavior somewhat more flexibly than in public.[6] This ability to create a familiar domestic place in the midst of the otherwise unknown and unfamiliar, an inside place where they are shielded from the public gaze and can feel and act in familiar ways, is a skill actresses em- ploy everywhere they go.

Even inside the inside itself, for example, actresses maintain these fa- miliar distinctions. Backstage, they carve out a private space by tying a string across one corner and hanging a sari over it, creating a modest one- woman changing corner.

I found out just how useful a shield from the outside such an inside place could be one night when I needed to empty my bladder and my ac- tress friends directed me to their changing corner. Squatting inside that little triangular women's space, I realized the other obvious resonance of the terms "inside" and "outside," at least in the rural context. Where there is no restroom—and the majority of people living in rural India have none—"going outside" (*veḷiyē pōka*) means literally that. To have to go outside to relieve themselves would have put the actresses on par with the lower-class rural women in the audience, rather than allying them in bodily practice with middle-class women's use of an indoor toilet. Creat- ing inside spaces such as changing corners that double as privies enables actresses to avoid all variety of unsavory outside experiences, and exposures to inclement outside environments, by fashioning inside spaces to meet their private needs.

Narrative Five: Regarding Traveling Home in the Morning

In Madurai I lived with an actress named Jansirani. The apartment building where we lived was smack in the middle of that little two-block radius of a Special Drama business district. Most Madurai actresses try to live as near as possible to this center, which minimizes the distance of their daily travels between home and a van, or home and the central bus stand.[7] Living in the center of town reduces their traversal of outsides, and shortens the distance between insides.

The majority of male actors, on the other hand, still live in their natal villages most of the year and only stay in Madurai during the drama season, when they rent rooms in lodges in the center of town. Lodges are notorious "bad" nightlife spots, such that for a woman with an eye to her reputation, being seen in one (let alone actually staying the night in one) is not a viable option.

Jansi and I returned together from a drama one morning by bus, sleeping against each other in our seat. We arrived at the Madurai station just before 7 A.M., tried surreptitiously to unrumple ourselves, smoothed down our saris, and began walking from the central bus stand to home, a distance of about five blocks.

We walked briskly through the streets. Jansi was moving very purposefully toward home. I stepped outside myself for a moment to wonder what we looked like: Does Jansi look like a woman who simply rose early this morning? Do I? (Not that I ever look simply like any woman here.) Tamil women rising early at home do things around their house, sacred ritual things, the most visible to passersby being making *kolams*, geometric patterns in rice powder that are negotiations of light lines and dark ground at the entranceway of the houses, where street touches home. Kolams are one of so many respectable female daily efforts to keep the street from contaminating the home, to order and purify inner space and separate it from the disorderly outside.[8] Were we, at that moment, the embodiment of the chaotic, disorderly, outside element? The very fact that we weren't at home making kolams suddenly seemed yet another proof of this same distinction. Was it obvious that we had been riding a bus, sitting up all night, our faces bearing as many pressed wrinkles as our saris? What did people think when they saw us?

This felt to me like a particularly vulnerable moment, though at the time I couldn't understand why. Rationally, the kind of danger I was familiar with from generic travels as a woman was over: night was over, we were back on familiar territory, and it was a properly respectable hour of the morning to be out and about. But I saw too how tired Jansi was, and how she had that barely containable kind of morning giddiness that comes from staying up all night. I felt scared that everything we'd gone through was apparent on us—or was I perhaps picking up her fear, as she walked, fast, not stopping to say anything to anyone? I realize now that this was a particularly vulnerable moment for her, a moment of separation from the group: we were no longer in that cocoon of sorts created by all the actors together, inside the inside spaces of their night world and their street-side network of known people. Suddenly we were two tired women alone on the street in the broad daylight that glinted off the stray specks of green and pink glitter still stuck to Jansi's eyelids, and I felt exposed and confused, hurrying after Jansi who was heading home so fast.

CONCLUSION

My own feelings when traveling with actresses reveal an unexpected sense of relief bordering on euphoria at finding havens of invisibility and familiar interiority, as well as a concomitant growing trepidation at being caught alone in public day or night. In narrating these tales from the circuit of actresses' travels between booking shops, vans, buses, backstage spaces, and roads home, I have spoken of instances where I felt uncomfortably "other," as well as of times where I felt included like family; occasions when I felt invisible but somehow safe; and still others where I felt exposed and confused. While some of the sense of marginality and dislocation that pervaded my travels with actresses may have stemmed from my own psychology and cultural baggage, I have been interested here in how I began to experience their roadwork as a sensible embodied practice.[9]

My main aim for the narratives, however, has been to use them to illustrate the artistry of actresses' roadwork. Actresses attempt to resignify and resituate their own social position within a dominant system that persistently casts them as stigmatized other. I have attempted to show how Special Drama actresses struggle to conform to the dominant terms of gendered respectability while also suggesting that in so doing, they subtly alter—by refiguring—these organizing terms themselves. Their struggle readily exposes the extent to which the internalization of a model of femininity based on domestic virtues affects women differently in respect to their class and social status. Femininity based unproblematically on a securely domestic identity is a class-based privilege to which actresses by definition do not have access. Their roadwork is a response to that reality, simultaneously complicitous and resistant: in figuring themselves as "good women," actresses begin to throw that category itself into question.

NOTES

1. These narratives represent the "raw data" of my participant-observation. In a longer version of this essay (Seizer 2000) I have analyzed these experiences in

light of the Tamil classificatory schemes that inform them, and it is only through such analysis that I came to the conclusions I offer here. The actresses' roadwork must be understood within the context and in the light of these broader classificatory schemes, especially that key distinction between complementary spheres of life—known as *akam* and *puram* in Tamil classical literature (Ramanujan 1975, 1985)—that shapes the distinctions interior/exterior, domestic/public, inside/outside, known/unknown, and invisible/visible (cf. Dickey 2000). I urge readers interested in understanding how I reached my conclusions here to read the longer essay in which I develop these arguments.

2. Madurai is an inland city in the south of Tamil Nadu. It is an ancient temple city that still figures largely as a Hindu pilgrimage site. Ramanujan coined the term "rurban" to describe the notion, emergent in both classical and modern Tamil literature, of "a center continuous with the countryside" (Ramanujan 1970: 242). Madurai, a city frequently described as "an overgrown village," is the paradigmatic example of such a Tamil rurban center.

3. In marital negotiations, mothers actively participate. In drama negotiations, as this narrative seeks to illustrate, only men participate. Nevertheless, in both cases the woman whose life is at the center of the negotiation is markedly silent.

4. As the remainder of this essay should make clear, even these women who are the apotheosis of public women care intensely that they not be seen as such, especially locally *where they live*, as is the case for this shop in Madurai for actresses who live in Madurai. For example, many actresses will not perform unless the venue is considered far enough away—generally, at least ten kilometers—from their domestic lives, from where they are known, local women.

Why should women who perform publicly, whose reputations for modesty have already largely been shattered, nevertheless attempt to conform to normative codes of gendered virtue? It seems these are the only codes that matter and that a woman must deal with these in some way. For many actresses, the public sphere seems to be divided into a differentiated continuum of publicness, either relatively more or relatively less proximate to her domestic sphere. Thus there is a proximate public sphere, relatively close to home, wherein a woman's reputation is reflected directly in her domestic life as well as affected by it. In that more proximate sphere a woman attempts to be seen as not an actress at all. In the less proximate public sphere where the woman is known primarily as an actress, she will then attempt to stave off the bad reputation through all the "roadwork" techniques and strategies I speak of in this essay. Thus, the same principles of womanly virtue affect her wherever she goes, though distancing herself from her own home allows her to more easily create a fictive self "on the road" whose modesty is then signaled by her "on the road" actions.

5. Ambassador is the brand name of the first model of automobile manufactured in India.

6. Some gender separations are also maintained in most Tamil homes, for example, women eat separately, after men. Likewise, backstage at a Special Drama event, women and men arrange their suitcases of costumes on separate sides of the available space, and sit behind their open suitcases, each with a hand mirror propped in its lid, to apply their makeup.

7. The towns and cities in which Special Drama artists live function as regional centers for the dense population of villages that surround them. Artists invariably live, and establish their actors associations, near central bus stations so that they can easily be contacted by villagers who travel to these regional centers, on public buses, to engage their services. The occupational need to live close to the central bus stations means that Special Drama artists generally live in the "first" postal code area of their respective cities: the oldest urban neighborhoods,

those established around public transportation lines. Ramanujan's term "rur-ban" (see note 2 above) captures well the way artists live in urban settings pre-cisely because they are continuous with their rural surroundings. Likewise, Oscar Lewis's description of the network of human exchange and interconnection that links persons in different villages in India as "a kind of rural cosmopolitanism" (Lewis 1955: 167) captures the centrality of links repeatedly forged and secured through the continued exchange of services between village, town, and city roads.

8. One account of the function of kolams stresses how they mark the thresh-old of the house as a boundary between the pure and the chaotic: "The mistress of the house, or a daughter, or perhaps a trusted servant, has laid out this pattern upon arising in the morning: she may have selected a traditional design of geo-metric shapes intertwined, or, if her intentions are more elaborate, two peacocks, perhaps, emerging from a maze. One cannot enter the house without passing through this man-made [sic] focus of auspicious forces, which sets up a protective screen before the home. Of course, one cannot see the screen itself, but only its focal point at the threshold, the point at which it emerges into form—a complex form at that, carefully planned and executed, a reflection of some inner labyrinth externalized here at the boundary, the line dividing the inner and the outer, the pure from the chaotic" (Shulman 1985: 3).

9. I have written about certain of the complexities of my own subject position and identity in Tamil Nadu in an earlier essay (Seizer 1995).

Nervous Masculinity: Consumption and the Production of Embodied Gender in Indian Wrestling

Joseph S. Alter

> Every wrestler continues to improve until he has broken the sky.
> —Panditji, Akhara Ram Singh, Varanasi

BREAKING THE SKY: RHETORICAL HYPERBOLE AND HYPERMASCULINITY

Wrestling in India (*pahalwānī*) is a sport engaged in exclusively by men who are extremely concerned with the nature of their masculinity. In contemporary practice it is linked to several historical trajectories, the most significant being the modern history of Indian nationalism. Even though it is regarded as a "traditional" rural sport by some, it is clearly linked to royal patronage and elite sponsorship. Since around the beginning of the twentieth century, however, urban *akhārā*s (wrestling gymnasiums), under the direction and management of *gurū*s (master teachers), have come to define the sport and its associated lifestyle. There are gymnasiums in many Indian cities, with particular concentrations in the states of Maharashtra, Haryana, Punjab, and Uttar Pradesh. In the city of Varanasi—which is unique in terms of the number of wrestlers but otherwise typical—there are several hundred gymnasiums. Gymnasiums are exclusively male, and attract boys and men between the ages of eight and eighty, although young men between the ages of eighteen and twenty-five are most actively involved. Although regional, state, and national champions earn prize money, wrestling is not a professional sport. Gymnasiums are public institutions with informal membership; they are often maintained through gifts, charitable contributions, and solicited neighborhood donations. Usually gymnasiums are nonresidential. Although wrestlers tend to come from lower-middle-class families, and so-called middle- to lower-caste communities, the lifestyle associated with wrestling is explicitly antihierarchical and oriented toward national reform through self perfection rather than toward the development of an exclusive community identity in either religious, ethnic, class, or caste terms.

When I began studying wrestling in the context of Varanasi gymnasiums in the late 1980s I was struck, almost immediately, by the hyperbole and bombastic rhetoric associated with the sport. Wrestlers with whom I spoke would often literally throw out their chests, spread their arms, dramatically cock their heads, and in general affect a pose which made their bodies stand for the essence of strength and masculine power. They did this while recounting in great and specific detail the scale, scope, and sheer effort of their exercise routine, and the enormous quantity of milk, almonds, and clarified butter they ate. Wrestlers often spoke of daily doing thousands of each of the two main exercises—*ḍaṇḍ*s (jackknifing push-ups) and *beṭhak*s (deep knee bends)—and of eating "kilos and kilos" of almonds, and drinking "liters and liters" of milk and clarified butter. Yet, as a participant observer, I never saw anyone do more than a few hundred jackknifing push-ups, wrestle for more than half an hour, or drink more than a glass of milk mixed with a hundred grams of clarified butter.

This "rhetoric of excess," as it may be called, is matched by an equally exaggerated concern with celibacy, disciplined self-control, and the absolute retention of semen. The practice of celibacy in India is linked to many other social institutions and cultural ideals, most notably asceticism manifest in the practice of *sannyāsa* (world renunciation). The principle of celibacy is also linked to broad-based cultural notions of masculinity, since the loss of semen is thought to result in weakness. This cultural notion has taken on specific historical form in the context of Indian nationalism, both through Mahatma Gandhi's advocacy for universal celibacy as a form of sociopolitical action and through the development of a science of celibacy to reform youth—corrupted by licentious cinema and other forms of erotic stimulation—and produce stronger, smarter, more moral leaders (Alter 1993, 2000). Although celibacy is regarded by wrestlers as a very personal issue of self-control—with the "self" clearly marked off as separate from the world but thereby strategically reoriented toward society—it is regarded as eminently hard to achieve due to the intoxicating, dangerous, and debilitating power of female sexuality. As Bhagoti Singh, a senior member of Akhara Ram Singh in Varanasi put it, invoking a phallic fear of the *vagina dentata*:

> The bite of a snake is like the glance of a woman, for both are equally poisonous. But a snake will not go where a woman has gone, for she is more poisonous than it!

This statement resonates with the perspective taken by many psychologically oriented scholars, and relates specifically to a common theme clearly articulated by Ashis Nandy:

[I]n India competition, aggression, power, activism, and intrusiveness are not so clearly associated with masculinity. In fact, in mythology and folklore, from which norms often come for traditionally undefined social institutions, many of these qualities are as frequently associated with women. The fantasy of a castrating, phallic woman is also always round the corner in the Indian's inner world. (1980: 42)

My purpose in this essay is to critically examine the rhetoric of excess in order to rethink the nature of masculinity as it is embodied by wrestlers. Broadly the question posed is this: What kind of power is embodied by men who are obsessively concerned about the nature of their biomoral strength? Is it that they are simply exaggerated stereotypes of male virtue; burlesque performers of an idealized—but clearly over-the-top—Indian masculinity? Do wrestlers take the key cultural values of Indian patriarchy, and, with some novel twists and turns, simply magnify the nature of gender identity until the asymmetry would seem to be so painfully obvious to everyone as to be farcical? Or is there something more complicated reflected within the misogynistic rhetoric of snakelike, destructive, castrating, semen-sucking women, as this rhetoric emerges out of the heroic discourse of men who endlessly produce, but never spend, their vital fluid? Is there something about the nature of gender identity revealed in the extreme case—the perfect, absolute, and categorical opposition of masculinity and femininity (and also its "perfect" resolution)—other than the apparently obvious essentialization of gender identity, the reification of power and the kind of well-there-you-have-it theoretical conclusions to which essentialization and reification inevitably lead?

I would like to suggest that there is, and that gender identity, as it is embodied by wrestlers, is the opposite of what it might seem. Far from being a manifestation of perfectly configured high ideals, masculinity, in the context of wrestling, is a degenerative, nerve-wracking, biomoral dis-ease which has grown out of the historical conjuncture of obsessive desire and a compulsive need to grow bigger and stronger on the one hand, and an absolute need for total self-control on the other. And all of this is set within a context where most wrestlers are relatively poor, and therefore are almost never able to independently support themselves in the manner to which they are accustomed by their "culture."

As a number of feminist scholars have noted, the cultural logic of gender asymmetry is much more complicated than was previously thought (Balsamo 1996; Bolin 1992; Haraway 1991; Ian 1993, 1995; Lowe 1998; Moore 1997). This has to do with the realization that power is not so much a thing that one group has and holds over another group as it is a context which defines the interaction of individuals and groups. Power is understood to be pervasive and comprehensive but never absolute. What is useful about a comprehensive understanding of power as a dynamic field of discursive practice is that it points in a direction where one can look at what might appear to be unambiguous control and see a more comprehensive set of nuanced interconnections. The insights gained by understanding these often invisible, sometimes self-contradictory, and dis-articulated interconnections are particularly valuable when they reveal the unintended social consequences of directed, goal-oriented, purposeful action, and the inherent contingency of apparently coherent systems of meaning.

CONTRADICTION: SOLID BODIES, INFLATED RHETORIC, AND MASCULINITY

Wrestlers seem to embody a contradiction which is articulated in the disjuncture between rhetoric and practice. Almost all practicing wrestlers underscore the importance of a rich and voluminous diet and the ideal of an extremely rigorous exercise regimen. For example, one of the senior members of Akhara Ram Singh in Varanasi, a fifty-year-old gold merchant, made the following remarks while reflecting on his youth:

> I would get up in the morning at 3 o'clock and run 10 times around the park and do 1,000 deep knee-bends before getting to the gymnasium. Then I would wrestle for three hours straight. After a 5 minute rest I would do a few thousand jack-knifing push-ups, climb up and down the rope, lift dumb bells and run around the gymnasium on my hands. I would then go home and drink milk and clarified butter and eat almonds before doing whatever work I had to do. Then in the evening I would do 2,000 or 3,000 more jack-knifing push-ups and deep knee-bends.

By the same token, however, many of the wrestlers who made these and even more exaggerated remarks could not afford liters and liters of milk, kilos and kilos of almonds, and canisters of clarified butter, nor did they have the time, motivation, or even perhaps the requisite energy to do "thousands" of jackknifing push-ups and deep knee bends. Thus, while many echoed the merchant's nostalgia for the bountiful years of eternal youth, many also made remarks about their poverty. Kanaiya Ram Yadav, a senior member of Bara Ganesh Akhara, put it this way:

> As I was saying, back in Calcutta when I wrestled we were fairly poor and I only had 200 grams of milk and a handful of *channā* [chickpeas] a day as my diet, along with whatever else there was, of course. We would fix whatever there was to eat after our evening exercises. I would get up at three or four o'clock in the morning and do 1,500 jack-knifing push-ups. Back then my diet was not much, just a cup of milk. And into that I would mix water and some sugar. I would drink this and then go and practice. I would wrestle with 10 or 12 wrestlers for practice. Even though I didn't have an adequate

diet, I was a celibate, and so combining celibacy and high interest I was able to get it together and make do. And so I wrestled.

Some moments later, in the course of the same interview, he tried to clarify and generalize on the basis of his own personal experience.

This wrestling is a very bitter cup, and is not easy to do. It takes a lot of effort. And like you were saying, these Thakurs [land-owning caste] and Yadavs [dairy-farming caste] are strong. But anyone can do it. If a boy starts exercising it will be good for his body and also for his mind. It is good for everyone. If you have a cup of milk and do 2,000 deep knee-bends, that is not good. One should have a good diet along with exercise. It should be balanced. I regularly did 2,000 deep knee-bends. I was a celibate, and would just eat whatever "dry bread" I could get my hands on. I was satisfied with this, because being satisfied with what you have is necessary.

He then proceeded to contextualize and explain the tension between having an adequate diet and not having enough to eat, and the way in which the price of milk, clarified butter, and almonds is inextricably linked to a particular ideal of health, and how celibacy mitigates inflation, desire, and satisfaction.

But now in this day and age of high costs, a boy needs at least Rs. 20/day to have an adequate diet. After all, milk is rupees 5 or 6 a liter. So, who can wrestle when this is the situation!? And clarified butter is rupees 50/kilo. Now everyone has to work for a living, and only a person who is very interested will choose to wrestle. Only a person who has a good diet will become a wrestler, and that person will stay healthy and not suffer any illness.

Lullu Pahalwan, an enormously thickset senior "akhara brother" of Kanaiya Ram's, echoed this in an interview recorded some weeks later. In a sardonic, wistful tone he said:

Clarified butter is rupees 51/kg or rupees 14/cup; almonds are rupees 70/kg or rupees 35/day, at least; milk is Rs 6/liter; and bread and vegetables about the same per day. This would make the cost of a good diet be around rupees 60/day. Now who has that kind of money to spend!

In a similar vein, Banarsi Pande, a one-time local Varanasi champion, winner of numerous state-level and national competitions and current international referee, made the following remarks in an interview:

B.P.: When I first started wrestling I must have wrestled in two or three hundred competitions. I used to travel around all over the place. We were poor. I would eat just a handful of chickpeas and a cup of milk. I would travel around, compete and spend whatever money I earned on milk.
J.A.: What was the greatest difficulty you faced in becoming a wrestler?

B.P.: The biggest problem was that of diet. I was a hard worker. I would run ten miles every day, do my physical training exercises, dig the pit and then wrestle. The only thing was my diet, because I came from a poor family. I would just eat chickpeas and drink milk when I could get it. But mostly I would eat carrots and tomatoes. I would get 8 annas [one anna equals 1/16 of one rupee] to go to school, and I would buy 4 annas' worth of carrots and 4 annas' worth of tomatoes.

J.A.: So that was your diet.

B.P.: That was my diet.

Most often this "rhetoric of insufficiency" takes the form of a lament tinged either with frustration and resignation, or else an against-all-odds sort of pride. However, there are some telling instances which give this rhetoric a broader, more social, and, as we will see in a moment, specifically historical significance. In other words, some wrestlers made comments in which it is clear that "a dry crust of bread" or a "handful of chickpeas" is not so much a case of negative deficiency as a positive case in which "less is more." For example, Nathu Lal Yadav, a thin man in his mid-forties who helps to maintain Surya Akhara, made the following comment:

No, a good diet is not necessary. If a man is pure; if he always keeps his mind on his goal; then he can eat dry and plain food and still be a wrestler. And in the old days there were men who had no income or resources and they were also wrestlers. I knew a man named Shivnath about 25 years ago. He ate only plain food and dry chickpeas but there was no one who could beat him at swinging the *jorī* ["Indian" clubs]. And he would swing the clubs with one hand!

Although Nathu Lal seems to embody a less-is-more ideal at odds with the rhetoric of excess, it is important to place his remarks within the context of his own specific life experience, where obsession and excess do, in fact, manifest themselves quite clearly.

I used to study in a private college. I did not really study though, because I was completely focused on wrestling. I am "intermediate fail" [completed the equivalent of high school but failed the final exam]; but even that is only in name since I didn't study at all. I ate and wrestled and wandered around. I did not study at all. In those days after practicing I would be so tired that I could not lift a *lota* [pitcher] of water! I would wrestle with 12 or 14 different wrestlers every morning starting at four A.M. and ending at eight. Then I would bathe. If it was summer, Dada would grind fennel and make me a cool drink; if it was winter he prepared *uradh dāl* ["hot" lentils] to warm me up. He used to feed me only pure, *desī* [local] things. The lentils were for stamina and fennel was to keep cool.

In all of these representative comments, the tension and contradiction between more than enough milk, clarified butter, and almonds, and not enough, hinges on the problem of cost on the one hand and celibate purity on the other. Celibacy can transform "plain chickpeas" into highly energized semen and produce, in conjunction with exercise, phenomenal masculine strength. Put another way, the tension is between consumption, production, and expenditure of one kind and consumption, production, and investment of another kind: a kind of embodied balance sheet reflecting a not-quite-clear relationship between consumption and production; profit and loss. A succinct comment by one of the senior members of Akhara Ram Singh reflects the intricate, God-only-knows dynamic of sex, strength, and diet.

> A wrestler will receive *shaktī* [supernatural strength] from God in accordance to the amount of exercise he does. It is all a gift of God. If he eats just salt and bread he may become strong, if it is the will of God. And if it is the will of God, he can drink milk and clarified butter and still be weak! If he abides by his duty and remains celibate, he will become a wrestler. A wrestler's vision should not be corrupted. He must never look at a woman! And the other thing is that he must honor and respect everyone and be humble. He should even show respect to children. So the work of a wrestler is the same as that of a *sadhū* [ascetic]. Wrestler means ascetic. A wrestler should have nothing to do with anyone; he must remain detached. He should eat and exercise. This is wrestling.

With regard to the question of value, semen is often compared to money. As the younger brother of the gurū of Akhara Ram Singh pointed out,

> semen is like money. One must save up semen just as one saves up money in a bank so as to have a reserve to spend. A man with an empty bank account is weak and vulnerable in the same way as a man who has too much sex.

Semen is more often compared to gold than to money as such, and it is thereby regarded as not only extremely precious, but also pure. In this sense it is defined in contrast to, and constantly threatened by, the defiling impurity of sex and the poison of sexuality. Many of the folktales told on the occasion of Nag Panchami, when gymnasiums are repainted and wrestlers perform their identity in the context of the festival's ritualized worship of snakes (see Alter 1992b), reflect Bhagoti Singh's comment, quoted above, about the glance of a woman being like the bite of a snake. One of the festival's "charter myths" recounts how a snake gave gold coins to a man in return for a bowl of milk, but when the man's greedy son destroyed the snake's home in search of what he thought was a treasure trove, he was bitten and killed. In other tales the snake is depicted as a seductive woman who lures men into her hole and kills them with the poison of passion.

It is important to point out, however, that the correspondence between milk/semen/gold and poison/greed/sexuality does not always reflect a simple gender dichotomy. In fact, snakes—such as Nag Raja, who kid-napped the goddess Yamuna until she was rescued by Lord Krishna—are as often male as they are female. Thus the configuration of symbols in the ritual of snakes being offered bowls of milk on Nag Panchami, and the wrestlers' implicit self-association with these symbols, reflect the unam-biguous power of fertility, but the ambiguities—and hence danger—of both male and female sexuality manifest in desire and passion, irrespective of whether it is a "female" desire to consume or a "male" passion to pos-sess, control, and even adore in the enslaved bliss of divine rapture.

It is possible to make sense of this tension, along with the contradiction between the rhetoric of excess and the problem of deficiency, in terms of the contrast and comparison many wrestlers draw between themselves and ascetics. Most often the comparison hinges on the question of celibacy and the extent to which wrestlers feel that they must be more self-disciplined than ascetics; that what they do is more difficult and, therefore, reflects a need to go to extremes in order to retain that which is both precious and produced in mass quantity. Consider a conversation I had with Indramani Mishra, a Brahman widower and celibate for thirty years, and his "akhara brother" Baccha Maharaj as we sat on the wall of Sant Ram Akhara above Mankarnika Ghat in Varanasi.

I.M.: Exercise is like something that pulls something out of something else; like exercise draws out true wisdom. Wisdom is not born of its own accord, it is born of purity, and for this reason one's food has to be kept pure. Pure food produces pure "*rasa*" [a primary fluid distillate of di-gested "cooked" food] and from this the body blossoms. Exercise keeps the mind pure and gives it peace. If the mind is at peace then one can gain strength even without eating.

J.A.: You were saying that ascetics and wrestlers are both celibate, but what is the difference?

I.M.: The difference is that ascetics don't eat food. They do not eat food that gives them strength. They only eat once a day and keep their stom-achs empty. They are ascetics. And for wrestlers things that produce strength are absolutely necessary. Things that are cooling are also ab-solutely necessary. Cold things are necessary so that the strength can be of use. But even with a full stomach wrestlers maintain control. Therefore, the true wrestler is greater than the ascetic.

B.M.: These ascetics do not eat very much at all, and in this present age heat is extreme. Ascetics just eat fruit and things, bathe and mediate for four hours at a time.

I.M.: Actually they do not have that much of a concern with the practice of celibacy because they are already one with the cosmos; with the god-head.

B.M.: Wrestlers eat good things and they digest these things.

I.M.: One must be able to control oneself. This is very important. No one will bother with a woman who is passionate and volatile. A woman

with a correct nature is totally devoted to her husband. And if a married man has strength and does not think evil thoughts then he will be
a wrestler; can be a true wrestler.

B.M.: Even if one is a householder, one can be a celibate as long as one only
goes to one's own wife. But if one goes to another woman, then it is
a sin and one's strength will decrease. This is why they say, *ek nārī,
brahmachārī* [one woman, still celibate]. But those who drink and gamble
and go around with other women, in six months or a year they will be
finished! Their bodies will be finished and they will run against the
grain of society.

In an important way the "rhetoric of excess" and the exaggerated claims
to practice attendant on this rhetoric are qualified by a discourse on sexuality which seeks to reduce sex to a minimum—a kind of emphasis that
turns the minimum into something of maximum and absolute importance.
Thus it is in terms of the discourse on celibacy that the sometimes nervous,
usually ambivalent, always contradictory "less is more" emphasis of some
wrestlers begins to make greater sense. They can choose to see themselves
as either greater than ascetics because they eat more and are tempted more
than them, or greater than ascetics because they eat the same things but
transform their semen into skill and strength manifest in the world rather
than into a state of cosmic consciousness directed away from it. As one of
the senior gymnasium members with whom I spoke at Akhara Ram Singh
pointed out:

Ascetics are celibates and they do not keep company with women. Because
wrestlers must keep company with women they are even more celibate than
sadhūs. Ascetics dream and wrestlers must not even dream! Only the man
who controls his semen can become a wrestler. One must keep a "tight
g-string"; as soon as it is loosened, well, it is all over.

HISTORICIZING HYPERMASCULINITY: POVERTY, POMP, AND THE GENESIS OF A "WRONG SYSTEM"

While I was doing field research in Varanasi in the late 1980s the story of
India's only gold medal Asian Games champion, Malwa Pahalwan, was
still in circulation about ten years after the event. What happened was that
Malwa, after winning the medal and being briefly in the media spotlight,
ended his competitive career and retired. In and of itself this is not surprising. However, several years later, a reporter doing a follow-up story
tried to locate Malwa. Only after extensive searching did he find him and
his family living in a state of poverty. Malwa the national champion had
become a man selling vegetables from a pushcart.

Published in several of the national papers, Malwa's story evoked, among wrestlers with whom I spoke and those who responded to the story in writing, a sense of outraged pity: outrage at the Indian state for not looking after one who had upheld the name of the republic in international competition, and pity for Malwa for what he had become—a poor, power-less, all-but-forgotten, marginalized man. Many wrestlers with whom I spoke about Malwa ended the conversation by simply shaking their heads: in disgust and in disbelief, to be sure, but also in not being able to make sense of something which seemed to be logically impossible—a destitute man who embodied the ideals of a way of life that should have made poverty and powerlessness impossible; a man whose iconic masculinity and national stature could not accommodate personal failure.

But one could just as well see it the other way around. And to do so is, I think, to understand the degree of nervous apprehension that Malwa's story—and also the story of Gama, India's world champion from 1908 to 1950—incites about the nature of embodied masculinity. Although there are wrestlers from elite landed families and relatively wealthy Brahman communities, the vast majority of wrestlers are classed among the peasantry and the proletariat. To some degree, Malwa's story defines the degree to which the "rhetoric of excess" is at odds with, and indeed fabricates, a fragile myth of impossible consumption and misplaced, or displaced, production. Malwa's parents were relatively poor peasants. Wrestling enabled him to momentarily redefine the dynamics of consumption and the production of embodied strength. But when he stopped wrestling, got married, had children, and left his village for the city, he was forced to produce in order to consume rather than consume in order to produce. Although he was a skilled wrestler, he had no other skills. While the body of the wrestler can in some instances smoothly reflect the pretensions of class and nationalism, more often than not it betrays the contradiction between masculinity and class-based identity on the one hand and the question of whether it is strong men who build up and support the nation or the nation that produces and supports strong men.

This did not really become clear to me until I was rereading field notes, since, on the surface, the rhetoric of excess is persuasively compelling as cultural practice, and seems to be logically seamless regarding the structure of interpretation it makes possible. Nevertheless, I was aware of the fact that a few very prominent men—wrestlers themselves who have made a study of wrestling—decry the way in which wrestling has become an obsession with excess, spiraling upward until it "breaks the sky." This is clearly reflected in the remarks of Narain Singh, a professor of physical education and philosophy at Banaras Hindu University.

And one more thing. We talk so much about metabolism and these things; how many calories are consumed and how much energy one can expend. If there is a balance, then the body will grow and develop. I believe that if one is leading a sexual life then one will think of getting a richer diet. You will enjoy the sexual life. Then the whole process is reversed! As the body gets more food, it gets more rich calories and more sexual intercourse. This is a national wastage!! You consume more to expend more energy. This is good for nothing! Absolutely good for nothing!!

Although Dr. Singh was directing these remarks to the larger community of Indian men, it was clear that wrestlers were the primary target of his critique of excess consumption and the imperative to expend, rather than conserve and channel, energy.

Our Hanumanji [divine monkey and servant of Lord Ram] was a great wrestler. But there is no mention anywhere of a huge diet! Twenty liters of milk, one kilogram of clarified butter and too much butter! No. Wrestling means, in the morning you go to the gymnasium, you bathe, dig the pit, do some exercise and then lead a natural life. That is all; it doesn't require a special diet. I find no good reason for these excessive diets. Why should any-one eat so much and then wrestle, wrestle, wrestle and do nothing else. But-ter, milk, clarified butter; wrestling in the morning and then again in the evening and doing no work at all. Is it a life!?

A key to why, in the late twentieth and early twenty-first century, wres-tlers have come to "wrestle, wrestle, wrestle" and aspire to if not actually consume "twenty liters of milk,"—and call this, with the authority of cul-tural logic, "a life"—is found in a comment made by Dr. Singh later in the same interview.

What I think happened to create this problem of excess and exaggeration is that it began with the *rājās* [kings], *maharājās* ["great" kings] and *zamīndārs* [landed aristocracy]. All of these people were involved in pomp and show in everything from sexual activities to music and architecture. These people kept wrestlers, and the wrestlers competed, and this gave their patrons honor. And out of this a wrong system developed.

It is critically important to point out that Dr. Singh's notion that the kings of the princely states are to blame for the development of modern wrestling as a "wrong system" is, to say the least, a minority view, if not all together idiosyncratic. Almost every practicing wrestler with whom I spoke talked nostalgically of the era of princely patronage, roughly the modern period of Indian history from 1860 to 1947, as a golden age for wrestling; a time when kings kept stables of hundreds of wrestlers, and provided them with everything they could possibly want—and more—by way of food; a time when wrestlers did not need to do anything but wrestle, wrestle, wrestle. Published accounts documenting the careers of wrestlers from this era attest to the fact that royal patrons lavished support on their prize wrestlers (see Alter 1992b). As I have written elsewhere, the idea was, at least in part, that wrestlers would come to embody a kind of physical power that directly reflected the political status of their patron within the princely states of India (Alter 1993). Although wrestlers exclusively wrestled, they were, in some instances, called on to stand beside their patron during public audiences in order to give tangible form to the rājā's prestige. Thus, along with his reputation as a skilled competitor, a wrestler needed to be very big and very strong, and so there are life histories of numerous royal wrestlers who are reputed to have been enormous, have had copious appetites, and the phenomenal ability to digest—and transform into energized semen—canisters of clarified butter, kilograms of almonds, and liters and liters of milk. If the rājā was, in some sense, a man greater than other men, his wrestlers had to give physical form to this ever-expanding aristocratic ideal.

Dr. Narain Singh's point, corroborated by Dr. Shanti Prakash Atreya and a few others, is that kings, in their quest for prestige and power within the colonial regime—and their desire to reflect this in the pomp and pageantry of courtly life—turned wrestling into an obsessive compulsion for more and more exercise and the consumption of more and more food, such that, given the financial resources of most kings and princes, only the sky—breakable or not—was the limit.

Although Singh does not make the point, it is clear that almost all court wrestlers were from relatively poor peasant communities, and so the contrast, manifest in embodied practice, between poverty and wealth—a dry piece of bread and a handful of chickpeas on the one hand and milk and clarified butter on the other—was striking, to say the least. The body of the wrestler was made to signify something which the wrestler himself was not, and, to some extent, the greater the significance of the wrestler's body to the state, the less was his significance as a person, until his concept of self was consumed by the state and even within his own village, community, and family his identity was linked to an ideology almost completely at odds with local practice and patterns of consumption, production, and reproduction in the practical sphere of daily life.

With the princely states in place within the colonial apparatus, the obsessive compulsion with excess could sustain itself. With the coming of independence in 1947, however, there was a dramatic change. In independent India wrestlers had to fend for themselves, and what this often meant was that excess very quickly gave way to deficiency. The ideal of celibacy, which was rendered problematic by the stimulating diet consumed by court wrestlers, became less problematic in the early postcolonial period as wrestlers had to make a virtue of necessity and consume smaller volumes of milk, clarified butter, and almonds. But as wrestlers were no longer able to consume canisters of clarified butter and liters and liters of milk, they were still able to think about their bodies—and act upon those thoughts—as though exercise and self-control produced huge volumes of semen. Thus, an obsession with celibacy was able to facilitate a shift from compulsive consumption in itself to a rhetoric of excess which included a preoccupation with sex, sexuality, and generalized self-control.

Although there is no definitive proof as such, it is reasonable to assume that the obsessive concern among contemporary wrestlers with absolute celibacy reflects an orientation toward "modernity"—and the problems inherent in modernity—rather than a revival of tradition. It is highly likely that a wrestler's idealization of celibacy as a means by which to control himself and the conditions under which he lives reflects a broader cultural trend in modern India where celibacy has been translated out of the spiritual domain and into the secular dynamics of national politics, science, and education, to name only a few contexts of practice (see Alter 2000). As Ashis Nandy (1980, 1983) and others (see, for instance, Kakar 1990) have noted, this translation has provoked a great deal of anxiety regarding the terms of masculinity: is a celibate man effete by virtue of his denial of "sexuality," or is he chaste, virtuous, and heroic by virtue of his control over sex? Is he a new kind of modern man, or a man emasculated by tradition?

For the wrestler this is a very particular kind of problem, since he is not just celibate, but either celibate and poor—and thereby somewhat conflicted about his ability to "wrestle, wrestle, wrestle"—or so completely defined by his celibacy that sex would destroy the very essence of his identity as that identity is intimately linked to nationalism. Thus the sense of magnificent masculinity expressed in the bombastic rhetoric of excess betrays a sense of deeply felt dis-ease regarding the competing demands of consumption and the production of gendered meaning in modern India. It is one thing for a wrestler to stand for a powerful, wealthy, clearly defined king. It is quite another thing for him to embody nationalist ideals in a context where the state itself is struggling with the problem of its identity. The wrestler's nervous masculinity, as it is reflected in the "rhetoric of excess," emerges historically out of the obsessive compulsion of kings to make peasants embody the princely state, and the way in which contemporary wrestlers must reconcile this compulsion with the modern conditions of poverty within which they, as marginalized "sons of the soil," have grown up.

CONCLUSION: DRINKING A BITTER CUP AND CHEWING IRON CHICKPEAS

Wrestlers are, like everyone else, not so much in control of culture, or the various things that enable culture to be constructed, as locked in a struggle with history and with the changes of meaning which derive from the interplay of past, present, and future. The story of Malwa, gold medalist of the Asian Games, is noteworthy because it shows how, even in one case where it seemed as though the power of the state was perfectly manifest in the person of the wrestler, there were, in fact, other forces at work.

Wrestlers often euphemistically refer to their regimen as a "bitter cup" or like "chewing iron chickpeas." In drawing these comparisons they are simply pointing out that wrestling is very hard work. Taken at face value, this is true. However, there is, as I have tried to suggest here, another level on which wrestling is not just hard work, but also a kind of work which, in the disjuncture of rhetoric and embodied practice, is, ironically, its own undoing. On this level milk becomes poison when the nation—Mother India—stops giving and only takes. This provokes anxiety. But it is, I think, an anxiety that is not at all about the perfect mother's ability to guard "those dark corners of the inner world," as Ashis Nandy puts it. Nor is it about castration anxiety or the threat posed by aggressively "phallic" women. It is more about what men, enmeshed in history, make of themselves, and the tension created when they are confronted by the demons, and the demonic constructions, of sexuality as sexuality makes reference to things that are meaningful well beyond psychology. On this level it is not so much a question of what the "bitter cup" refers to, and produces in fact—since that, by way of fear, loathing, and rabid nostalgia for eternal youth, leads to both the prestige of a gold medal and the ignominy of peddling vegetables—as a question of how we consume images when the rhetoric of self-control and self-discipline are so perfectly expressed, but so imperfectly embodied as experience. Historically produced and defined in terms of modern nationalism, the nervous masculinity of the wrestler betrays the contingency of masculinity as a psychosocial construct.

Dosti and *Tamanna:*
Male-Male Love, Difference, and
Normativity in Hindi Cinema

Ruth Vanita

In this essay I examine love between men in two Hindi films, *Dosti* (Friendship, 1964) and *Tamanna* (Desire/Longing, 1997), in the context of popular Hindi cinema's conventions of depicting love in general. India has the largest film industry in the world, and mainstream Hindi cinema, arguably today India's single largest common cultural denominator, has an unbroken tradition of depicting intense bonds between men but no tradition of depicting explicit homosexual behavior or relationships. The passionate friendship between the protagonist and his buddy is similar to that found in Hollywood movies, but also draws on older Indian traditions of representing both same-sex love and love in general.[1] I am interested in the continuum between romantic friendship and love, the slippery space where affection slides into or is coded as the erotic without being overtly depicted as sexual.[2] The continuum is evident in the name of India's longest-running gay magazine *Bombay Dost* (Friend), founded in 1990.

LOVE, SEX, MARRIAGE, AND FRIENDSHIP:
THE SLIPPERY CONTINUUM

Sexual activity is not and never has been explicitly depicted in Hindi cinema. Censorship laws forbid explicit sex, nudity, and, until very recently, kissing to be shown on screen. In India today, most heterosexual couples do not hold hands, kiss, or embrace in public or even in the presence of family members.

Same-sex friends engage in these activities more openly, precisely because in their case these activities are presumed to be nonsexual. However, some of these same-sex friends are also lovers. They may be perceived as "just friends" by some people, as "special friends" by others, and as lovers by yet others. As long as the possibility of a sexual relationship between them is not explicitly put into words by them or anyone else, they may be able to publicly engage in a great deal of physical affection and intimacy. Parents and even spouses are more likely to encourage a close same-sex friendship than a cross-sex friendship. It is seen as quite normal for single same-sex friends to share an apartment or even a bed. Problems arise only if a person resists marriage or opts out of a marriage and explicitly cites a same-sex relationship as the reason for doing so.

These facts are central to my argument. When sexual activity is explicitly depicted on screen, as in the Hollywood movie, sexual relationships thereby become clearly distinguished from nonsexual friendships. But when, as in Hindi movies, sexual activity is not explicitly depicted, it can be signaled in other ways.

In Indian social life, heterosexual activity is blazoned in marriage and pregnancy while homosexual activity is invisible. In Hindi cinema, marriage and pregnancy may or may not be connected to romantic love. But romantic love is conveyed through other conventions that operate on three levels: lyrical, narrative, and what, for want of a better phrase, I will call the socioethical.[3] I here examine how these conventions work in the case of male-male love, to figure the lovers as emblematic of a manhood, Indianness, and even humanness that are simultaneously alternative and normative.

The lyrical level functions primarily through song and secondarily through poetic speech.[4] The typical Hindi movie is three hours long and has four to five songs that perform a crucial function. Songs articulate the inner life, stand in for the sexual life, and are a device to demonstrate intimacy between characters. The plot of the Hindi movie tends to be action-oriented. When close relationships are introduced (most frequently between lovers but also between parent and child, siblings, or friends), the degree of closeness is usually signaled by a song sung together or sung by one to the other. Once the song performs this signaling, the narrative is free to proceed to a series of suspense-ridden actions without further exploration of the inner life until the next song. Judged by standards of "realism," characters burst into song at highly inopportune moments, when characters in real life are more likely to be silently overwhelmed by emotion. In the terms of Hindi cinema, these are the most opportune moments for song, because song is understood by the audience as a device for articulating emotions that cannot be articulated through action or speech.

Songs express romantic and erotic longing as well as fulfillment. Frequently, a song and dance sequence is presented as the fantasy of one character in the movie, a fantasy that may or may not be consummated in action. The crucial point for my argument is that since romantic tropes used in song or poetic speech are the primary signifiers of eroticism in cross-sex relationships, the use of the same tropes in same-sex relationships inevitably eroticizes them too.

Many of these tropes are drawn from the Perso-Urdu *ghazal* (Persian-Urdu love poem) since the great songwriters of early Hindi cinema were major Urdu and Hindustani poets, all of whom were steeped in the ghazal. In the ghazal, both lover and beloved are conventionally gendered male, through nouns and verbs.[5] This convention operates even when one of the two is female, as in early Hindi film songs. Even when the gendering changes, as it does in the mid-twentieth-century, to male-female, the earlier convention continues to exercise an influence in the way the beloved and the relationship are figured. Film songs, like ghazals, frequently use the first and second person instead of the third person, thus ungendering both lover and beloved. These ambiguities make for a space that is not exclusively heterosexual and that can function in an erotic continuum.

UNSELFISHNESS AS THE HALLMARK OF LOVE

At the narrative level, the primary formula for depicting love relationships in Hindi films is one of devotion tested by separation and by ordeals that involve sacrifice and suffering on the part of one or both partners, followed by divinely and/or socially blessed reunion. This formula is fairly ubiquitous in most cultures, recalling folktales worldwide, Greek myths, Christian saint stories, and Arthurian romances. But in the Hindi film, it is weighted with particular philosophical significance. For instance, the Radha-Krishna myth and its variants, such as Mira-Ghanshyam or the Laila-Majnun myth, both representing the soul separated from god, often hover in the background of the formula.

The primary source for Hindi cinema's narrative formulae is the cornucopia of epic and Puranic legends. Many ancient, medieval, and modern versions of each legend, both written and oral, exist and proliferate in different regions and languages, and versions differ in the degree of centrality they confer on the same-sex companion of the god or the hero. These legends are cross-fertilized with medieval romances, many of West Asian provenance, which are also central tropes in the ghazal.

At the socioethical level, the good love relationship is one in which lovers each sacrifice their individual welfare for the other's welfare, and also demonstrate their individual and joint devotion to community welfare. Mainstream Hindi cinema revels in explicit, often heavy-handed, didacticism. Intimate relationships, including romantic relationships, are legitimized for the viewer not only by the intrapersonal ethic of sacrifice but by the way the relationship is played out for social benefit. At the narrowest level, the lovers show willingness to sacrifice individual desire to their families' well-being. Frequently, lovers are shown working together to educate, feed, or heal the underprivileged. In vigilante films, the hero's girlfriend aids him in fighting villains who are out to destroy the community or the nation by their antisocial activities.

Community welfare may be represented as requiring the lovers to rebel against norms or as requiring submission to those norms; in either case, the lovers perceive their actions as not merely in their own best interest but in the best interest of all concerned—family, community, perhaps even nation. Family or community may not recognize this until the end, but the lovers will go through ordeals to demonstrate it to them. The happy reunion of lovers at the end represents not just the fulfillment of their personal desires but the fulfillment of social good. In Hindi cinema's socioethics, the individual must suffer to demonstrate that he or she deserves love, that the quest for love is not purely self-directed.

In Hindi cinema, the normative individual is thus constructed as a victim of misunderstanding and a martyr of sorts. He/she is an underdog throughout the narrative, whose worth is recognized only by a chosen few and by the audience, with whom he/she communicates through song. The virtuous individual achieves social recognition and reward only at the end of the film. The Judeo-Christian ideal of "The last shall be first" here intersects with similar impulses in Hindu and Muslim devotional traditions where God is often represented as coming to the help of the outcast.

These narrative, lyric, and socioethical conventions are not confined to the depiction of heterosexual love. They are also deployed to depict other relationships, such as the filial and fraternal. I am interested in the particular ways they work for male-male love.

Eve Sedgwick has argued that denial of homosexuality in patriarchal cultures works through valorizing male homosociality, when men bond, either as comrades or as rivals, over a female body, that is, through a shared misogyny.[6] I argue that in Hindi cinema, there has been no rigid homosocial/homosexual divide. Instead, there is a fluid continuum from friendship to eroticism. To measure the importance of male-male relationships in particular films, I use five indicators that can also be used to measure the importance of male-female relationships: primacy, exclusivity, duration (these operate on the narrative level), intensity (this operates on the lyric level), and the demonstration of moral worth (this operates on the socioethical level). A relationship that has one or two of these features is less significant than one that has four or five of them.

UNITED FOREVER: SELF-SACRIFICING LOVE IN *DOSTI*

The male-male love in *Dosti* demonstrates all five features. Although *dosti* means "friendship," the two male protagonists' relationship is primary and exclusive; it is also very different from other friendships in the film. Neither protagonist has even a shadowy heterosexual romance of any kind on the horizon.

Dedicated to the Mother of the Aurobindo Ashram, the film opens with a football game at a boys' school, where Ramu, who appears to be about sixteen, scores the winning goal. From the camaraderie of this all-male environment he goes home to his ailing mother and her gods. His relationship with her is one of mutual nurturance. He nurses her devotedly and aspires to earn enough to support her in the future, while she aspires to be like the mothers of the Maratha king Shivaji and India's first prime minister, Pandit Nehru. The first two scenes thus invoke Hindu epic ideals (Rama, incarnation of the god Vishnu and hero of the epic Ramayana) and modern nationalist ideals (Nehru) to establish Ramu as a normative youth. The ensuing scenes reinforce sympathy by establishing him as the classic victim of injustice. Poverty and exploitation by a heartless world lead to his expulsion from school for failure to pay the fees, to his mother's death and his crippling.

Ramu saves the life of a blind boy whose pleas to help him across the road are ignored by other passers-by. This boy, about the same age as Ramu, is Mohan (Charming One), one of the names of the god Sri Krishna. The boys' physical disabilities mark them as different from other men, who abuse and taunt them on this account. This difference works in many ways—heightening viewer sympathy, exalting the boys through implicit comparison to such figures as the blind medieval mystic poet Surdas, and also perhaps as a marker of their different way of loving.

Their relationship begins with acknowledgment of likeness: both are homeless, alone, and disabled. It rapidly progresses to a vow of sharing when Mohan refuses to eat without Ramu: "Look, once you have taken my hand don't consider me a stranger."[7] The ritual of holding hands is followed by those of eating together, wiping each other's tears, and making music together (Ramu plays the mouth organ and Mohan sings). The trope of the couple singing together, repeated throughout the film, functions to make them the center of a community. So sweet is Mohan's singing that, like Sri Krishna's flute, it draws large crowds. The crowds are composed of both genders and different classes and religions. Mohan's first song celebrates common humanity, but his later songs, which grow out of the urgencies of his relationship with Ramu, also speak to the crowd. In this, they are entirely within Indian traditions of representing love as occurring in the presence of sympathetic witnesses. For example, the paradigmatic romance, that of Radha and Krishna, is represented both in literature and in visual art as occurring in the presence of fellow villagers. Court paintings and poetry follow this tradition in frequently having friends, go-betweens, or servants present at the lovers' trysts. The convention persists in Hindi cinema where heterosexual love songs are often sung among friends or sympathetic strangers who join in refrains and dance with the lovers.

Intensity between Ramu and Mohan is figured through the conventions of poetic speech, song, and narrative. Soon after they meet, Ramu admires Mohan's eyes: "Such beautiful eyes . . . " and a little later repeats, "Truly, how beautiful your eyes are." The intensity is heightened by the conventional trajectory of undergoing ordeals together. They are abused, jeered at, and beaten by bullies, robbed of their earnings, misunderstood by well-meaning teachers, and despised by the rich brother of a little girl they befriend. This girl, Manju, is the first member of the alternative kindred they assemble. She is a rich but lonely invalid orphan who lives with her older brother, Ashok. From her window she hears them sing and calls them over to talk. They give her the pet-name Rajkumari (Princess) and call her their little sister.[8] She happily accepts them as her brothers. When the boys earn enough to rent a room in a slum, they acquire more kin—the motherly neighbor woman who is addressed as Mausi (maternal aunt) by all the neighbors, and her two children.

Their love grows in the context of alternative family. While the fictive kinswomen foster and delight in the boys' relationship, the fictive kinsman, Sharmaji, proves more problematic. He is an elderly unmarried schoolteacher who recognizes Ramu's brilliance as a student and becomes his guardian since school regulations require every student to have one. Sharmaji is shocked by the conditions under which Ramu lives in the slum (studying by lamplight, disturbed by squabbling families and gamblers) and invites him to live with him, but Ramu refuses, saying he can never leave Mohan.

A clearly gendered difference emerges between men's and women's ways of valuing love. Manju's brother Ashok thinks the boys' relationship with the little girl is nothing but a way of sponging on her. She insists that they love her and that he misunderstands them. Similarly, Sharmaji tells Ramu that his feelings for Mohan are good but he should not spoil his own future for Mohan's sake. So Ramu leaves without saying goodbye, and when the weeping Mohan follows and calls out to him, Ramu, although also weeping, shuts the window in the blind boy's face.

This turning point deepens the relationship's intensity. *Dosti* became a hit largely on the strength of its songs. Composed by Urdu poet Majrooh Sultanpuri and sung by Lata and Mohammad Rafi, they have canonical status today.[9] Mohan's second song presents their relationship as consolation for sorrow: "We may be far from our destination / But our love is enough for us, / Even if thorns prick our feet / This support is enough for us." Putting his arm around the weeping Ramu, Mohan continues: "At least your companion on the journey is someone of your own." The noun *humrah* (companion on the journey) is the same as that used by Humrahi, a short-lived gay men's organization and helpline in Delhi in the nineties.

Other intense moments include Mohan clasping Ramu's hand and swearing that even if he finds his long-lost sister Meena he will never leave Ramu. Holding Ramu's hand to his own cheek, Mohan adds: "God has not united us in order for us to separate." When a bully beats up Ramu, Mohan brings medicine and wishes he had eyes so that he could apply it himself.

Stroking his own cheek with Mohan's hand, Ramu replies, "If you just run your hand over it, it will get well." Ramu studies to fulfill his promise to his mother, but Mohan seems to take that mother's place when he nurtures Ramu, earning money for his fees and buying him a lantern. Ramu acknowledges this when he puts his gold medal round Mohan's neck. When Meena, Mohan's sister, now working as Manju's nurse, shrinks from publicly acknowledging the blind beggar as her brother, Mohan refuses to forgive her. He cries, "I have no one," but Ramu reminds him, "I am yours."

Immediately after this declaration, Ramu abandons Mohan. The film now proceeds to focus on Mohan's devotion. Mohan's third song, "I will love you morning and night, but will never call your name again," is a good example of how the ungendered love song functions out of context. Played on radio and television, it sounds like the lament of the Majnun-type heterosexual lover, because the first and second person ("I" and "you") are used throughout and the words for "beloved" and "friend," such as *yar* and *mitva,* although gendered male, have been conventionally used for a beloved of either sex. The word used for the boys' love both in this song and elsewhere in the film is *chah,* which literally means "want" or "desire."

The song continues on the high road of romantic love, identifying the beloved as the lover's be-all and end-all: "You are my pain, you my rest, you are my eyes. . . . " This is the one song Mohan sings with no auditors and he receives no money for it. His lone figure is silhouetted against the vast clouded sky, siting him as a romantic sign of universal longing and loss. The ailing Mohan, nursed by Mausi, strokes the pillow next to his own and says: "Sometimes I feel as if Ramu is still sleeping beside me." Mausi berates Ramu for his faithlessness and advises Mohan to forget him, but Mohan will not say a word against Ramu. In contrast, when the repentant Meena sends him gifts through Mausi, he throws them away and refuses to meet her.

Following time-honored convention, Mohan proves his love by suffering for his beloved's welfare. When Ramu's teacher and guardian Sharmaji dies, leaving Ramu unable to pay the fee for his final examination, Mohan rises from his sickbed and goes out to earn by busking. He walks barefoot through the rain, singing, "Whatever step I take / Is on your path, / Because wherever you are / I am watching over you." The song goes on to state what is perhaps the most important definition of love in Hindi cinema and in many other older traditions, both Indian and Western: "The bond of pain is true / What separation then? / Only they can be separated / Whose love is false."

Mohan collects enough money to pay the fee but falls seriously ill and lands in the hospital, where he is nursed by Meena and Mausi. In delirium, he talks continually to Ramu. Learning from the newspaper that Ramu has stood first in the examination, he caresses Ramu's photograph, crying, "My Ramu has stood first." The film then ends with the grand reunion, Ramu falling into Mohan's arms and asking forgiveness. Ramu says: "No one can separate us now, Mohan," to which Mausi responds, touching both their faces: "May your enemies get separated. May God keep the two of you united forever."

This final blessing by an older mother-figure is charged with many cultural resonances and is impossible to translate literally: *"Bhagvan kare tumhari jodi isi tarah bani rahe." Jodi* means a couple or a pair. The blessing is one that elders traditionally give to married couples and is thus suitable for the end of a Hindi film. The only heterosexual relationship in the film (that of Meena and Ashok) is presented in a muted fashion. Their involvement is never stated, only suggested through Ashok's protective behavior when Meena's brother rejects her, and through their continued appearance together after Manju's death. They have no song together. The only song that is not sung by Mohan is sung by Meena to Manju, the ailing little girl, and establishes a sisterly bond between them.

SELF-SACRIFICING CO-PARENTS:
MALE PARTNERSHIP IN *TAMANNA*

Made thirty-three years later, *Tamanna* shares the following features with *Dosti:* the opening that establishes the protagonist as a good son to his mother and their love as the touchstone for all love; the trope of physical disability marking the protagonist; the protagonist as a victim of social injustice; the protagonist's unsullied goodness and compassion; the adoption of fictive kin; the benign presence of women as mothers/sisters/daughters in relation to the male couple; the self-sacrificing love that triumphs despite conflict, ordeals, and betrayal.

But *Tamanna* was made in the nineties by Mahesh Bhatt, who has made several groundbreaking films on gender and sexuality, and who has bravely taken a controversial stand against state censorship of pornography. The greater self-consciousness of this film is signaled in its figuring of the protagonist, Tikkoo, as a hijra.[10] We are told that he was born a hermaphrodite. He and others view this as a disability, but it also functions to signal his deviant gender/sexual identity.

The film, however, hedges its bets by its clever representation of Tikkoo in relation to other hijras. The film is based on a true story but the real-life protagonist was a hijra who never attempted to "pass" as a man. Tikkoo's attempts to pass as a man create the emotional drama in the film when his adopted daughter discovers his "true" identity as a hijra. The film thus uses in relation to Tikkoo the tropes of "closeting" and "outing," which are relevant to homosexual people in India today, who often lead double lives, but are not as relevant to hijras, who usually publicly display their difference.

In the film, other hijras live, as most hijras do in modern India, in a group, dressed as women, with female names and personae, but Tikkoo has an aversion to them and asks them to stay away from him. He always dresses as a man, all his friends are men, and he has a long-term unmarried male companion with whom he raises two children. His body language and camp mannerisms are much more suggestive of the self-presentation of many urban gay men in India today than of hijras. By labeling him a hijra the film avoids direct discussion of homosexuality (this distinction is complicated, however, by the fact that many homosexually inclined men of lower-income groups in India today join or live on the fringes of the hijra community). But the film's representation of him allows slippage between the hijra persona and that of a gay man.

The second major difference from *Dosti* is that Bhatt chooses to make his protagonists Muslims and to contrast them with an oppressive Hindu family. That the film did not draw the ire of the Hindu Right despite this daring move is, I think, in part because of its powerful deployment of the narrative, lyric, and socioethical conventions outlined above. Its social critique operates within these conventions. Thus the excessively brutal Hindu patriarch Chopra is the stereotyped archvillain of Hindi cinema—the business magnate cum politician who functions like a feudal lord. Chopra mistreats his servants, humiliates and beats his long-suffering wife, keeps a mistress, and dumps his baby daughters out to die. The alternative family, consisting of Tikkoo, his companion Salim, and their adopted children, works from within the shared Muslim-Hindu space of the Sufi *dargah* (tomb of a Muslim mystic that becomes a site for devotional gatherings).

Tamanna focuses on Tikkoo's love for his adopted daughter Tamanna, with the Tikkoo-Salim love working as an understated but ever-present backdrop. Salim, Tikkoo's hot-tempered but devoted friend, appears in the opening scene, consoling the distraught Tikkoo at his mother's funeral, and is present in the last shot, embracing Tikkoo and their children. Throughout the film he functions as the sensible counterpart to the overemotional Tikkoo. The implicit masculine-feminine coding here, the bearded, silent, and gruff Salim supporting the long-haired, dramatic, often hysterical Tikkoo, is clearer than it was in *Dosti*, where the football-playing, school-going Ramu is nurtured by the sacrificing, sensitive, fair, and delicate Mohan.

Tikkoo's emotion, which initially marks him as "not-man," or not-male, also ultimately marks him as the true "man"—the true human being. The film traces this progress. Tikkoo adopts Tamanna against Salim's advice but she grows up parented and pampered by both men. When the growing girl is endangered by the all-male environment of the slum, Salim berates Tikkoo for his selfishness in refusing to send her to boarding school: "To escape your own loneliness you are destroying the child. If you want to be called Abbu (father) learn to be a father. Learn to suffer, under-stand?"

The term "hijra" is contested when Salim accuses Tikkoo of acting like a hijra, that is, with unmanly lack of fortitude in refusing to send Tamanna to school, while the hijras, also trying to persuade Tikkoo to send her away to school, berate him for pretending not to be a hijra. They tell him that if he ever needs help they will come to his rescue and protect Tamanna from harm. This conflict is resolved toward the end, when Salim and the hijras work together to rescue Tamanna from Chopra's murderous plot.

Tikkoo proves his love for Tamanna by suffering for her. He reluctantly puts on female dress and dances with the other hijras to earn money for her. At the film's climactic moment, when the adult Tamanna realizes Tik-koo is a hijra and rejects him, saying he cannot be her father, an enraged Salim slaps her and cries: "He has stayed awake nights clasping you to his chest so that you could sleep, he has walked barefoot to feed you. [To Tikkoo] Tell her for whom you danced? For her jewelry, for her school fees. And if he is a hijra then shame on us men of the world." He then leads Tikkoo off by the hand, murmuring in standard parental fashion: "These children of today . . . "

OUTWARD-LOOKING LOVE AS NORMATIVE

The Tikkoo-Salim couple is exclusive and primary since neither has any heterosexual involvement or any other close male friend. Their relationship is shown to last from young adulthood to old age. While the youths in *Dosti* are bonded to the community as son and brother figures, the men in *Tamanna* are bonded as parent figures. In both films male-male love is demonstrated to be socially useful and out-reaching rather than inward-turning.

It is important to emphasize that this marking of male-male love as outward-looking stamps it as valuable and normative. This is because main-stream Indian literature and cinema usually celebrates any love, including male-female love, by representing it as unselfish and concerned with the good of a larger community, not merely the good of the two individuals involved. In the rare films where the romantic lovers end up dead rather than united in marriage, they are usually represented as obsessively fo-cused on themselves and one another rather than mutually focused on the collective good. The title of one such Romeo-Juliet type tragedy, *Ek Duje Ke Liye* (For the Sake of One Another) suggests that focus.

The outward-looking love extolled by Hindi cinema marks its protago-nists as both "different" and "normative." They are set apart from average individuals because they excel in compassion, the *caritas* that sanctifies their *amor.* Ramu is repeatedly extolled by elders and teachers as one who will do great things for the country. His drive to study is fueled by his desire to do good, indicated in his passing on the scholarship he wins to a more needy student. At the end, when he tops the examination, all his classmates rejoice, even the bully, his one-time enemy. In *Tamanna* this socially beneficial aspect of the men's love is foregrounded since the main activity they undertake together is that of raising the two children they adopt. The film's theme song, sung by Sufis, points out that to cherish a child is to serve both the community and God: "The mosque is very far from home, let us make some crying child laugh."

The parenting device also works as a safety device, deflecting possible anxiety about the homosexual implications of their relationship. Unlike Ramu and Mohan, Salim and Tikkoo are not shown sharing a house or a bed (though they are always together and Tikkoo remarks that he often sleeps at Salim's house), nor do they sing songs about their love for each other. Their cooperation, conflicts, and bonding through the parenting experience constitute the intensity of their relationship and establish their love as normative and them as ideal men.

Tikkoo's normativity is established both through his self-sacrificing behavior as son and as father and when he continues to act with loving forbearance to his wealthy half brother even after this man insultingly refuses him any share in their father's property or even a loan to get Tamanna married. Witnessing Tikkoo's humiliation and admirable refusal to retaliate against his brother, Salim starts crying. This is the only time he cries in the film, whereas Tikkoo, like the typical Hindi film heroine, cries very frequently. Salim bursts out: "Tikkoo, don't put such a great debt of your goodness on me. I cannot bear this burden, spare me. Make your heart a little smaller just for a while; become human for once. I don't want to worship you, I have to worship God."

In this paradoxical move, Tikkoo, the "abnormal" one, is posited not as subnormal but as supernormal, someone who is the model human being and thereby almost divine. In many religious legends (such as that of Noah), God spares the human race despite its wickedness, for the sake of one virtuous man. In Hindu legend, the divine manifests itself in virtuous beings, both human and non-human. In *Dosti* and *Tamanna,* this virtuous and normative "man" or "human being" is one initially marked as "less-than-man."[11]

Tikkoo and Salim suffer for and with each other, both emotionally and physically. Both are insulted, beaten up, and injured by Chopra and his minions. Salim's tears strengthen Tikkoo's resolve to cross-dress and earn by dancing, even though he feels ashamed to do so. He says: "Salim, I feel greatly consoled by these tears in your eyes. Today, for the first time, someone is crying for me."

Unlike *Dosti, Tamanna* includes the portrayal of a heterosexual romance —that between Tamanna and the other adopted child, Sajid. A parallel between the two couples is subtly suggested at various moments. For example, after both Tamanna and Tikkoo have been crying in despair, Sajid and Salim sing a feminist song ("Rise up, my life, you have to walk beside me"), urging Tamanna, as a type of all women, to fight society's tyrannical forces personified in her father, Chopra. Sajid and Tamanna then stand on a lower level in the *dargah*, his arm around her, while Salim and Tikkoo stand above, Salim's arm around Tikkoo. At the film's conclusion, when Tamanna chooses to stay with her adoptive family rather than go to her remorseful, wealthy biological brother and mother, the same formation recurs, with the two couples embracing.

In both *Dosti* and *Tamanna*, then, established cinematic and cultural conventions as well as nationalist rhetoric are used to legitimize, even celebrate, same-sex love. While this love is not explicitly depicted as sexual, its romantic connotations are suggested. The partners are represented as underprivileged, marked by physical disability and poverty, but, in a move typical for Hindi cinema, they are paradoxically also valorized as normative Indians and human beings through their compassion, integrity, and selfless devotion to the welfare of their love objects who, in some sense, typify the human community.

NOTES

1. For exegeses of these older traditions, see Ruth Vanita and Saleem Kidwai, eds., *Same-Sex Love in India: Readings from Literature and History* (New York: St. Martin's Press, 2000).

2. My thinking on same-sex love in Hindi cinema has profited from discussions with Shohini Ghosh. See her essay "Queer Pleasures for Queer People: Film, Television and Queer Sexuality in India," in Ruth Vanita, ed., *Queering India: Same-Sex Love and Eroticism in Indian Culture and Society* (New York: Routledge, 2001).

3. For an illuminating discussion of Hindi cinema, using different categories, see Ashis Nandy, *The Savage Freud and Other Essays on Possible and Retrievable Selves* (New Delhi: Oxford University Press, 1995), pp. 196–236.

4. Films often sink or swim on the strength of their songs, which are usually released before the film. Songs have a much longer afterlife than films. Songs from films made several decades ago air regularly on radio, audiocassette, and television, and millions know the songs without having seen the films.

5. See Saleem Kidwai's discussion of homoeroticism in the Perso-Urdu tradition and the twentieth-century heterosexualization of the ghazal in Vanita and Kidwai, *Same-Sex Love in India* (2000), pp. 107–125, 200–201.

6. Eve Kosofsky Sedgwick, *Between Men: English Literature and Male Homosocial Desire* (New York: Columbia University Press, 1985).

7. All translations from Hindi are by me.

8. Although the film does not invoke the *Rakhi* tradition, the audience is bound to think of it here. *Raksha bandhan* or *Rakhi* is a festival widely celebrated in north India when sisters tie a thread on their brothers' wrists to affirm bonds of protection and nurturance. There is a long history of fictive kin relations being

established between women and men, even across Hindu-Muslim lines, through the tying of the *rakhi*.

9. The songs in *Tamanna* were composed by a team of poets, including the celebrated Kaifi Azmi.

10. See Serena Nanda's essay in this volume for an account of hijras.

11. Following Ashis Nandy's classic account in *The Intimate Enemy* (New Delhi: Oxford University Press, 1983), several scholars have explored colonial and nationalist attempts to rewrite Indian manhood as more "masculine," thereby disempowering androgynous forms of manhood, which resurfaced in resistance.

Life on the Margins: A Hijra's Story

Serena Nanda

Hijras in India are defined as an alternative gender role, neither man nor woman. The cultural sources for the hijras as a powerful and meaningful gender derive from both Hinduism and Islam (see Nanda 1999). Hijras are born males, and become hijras by adopting women's clothing and behavior, formally joining the hijra community, and (except in the case of born hermaphrodites) undergoing emasculation, or surgical removal of the genitals, as part of their identification with the Mother Goddess. This identification gives hijras the power to bless newlyweds and infants with prosperity and fertility, which is the basis of their traditional occupation as performers at marriages and births.

As devotees of the Mother Goddess, and vehicles of her power, hijras claim to be ascetics, a claim ambivalently regarded by the public. Sometimes, when hijras perform or beg for alms, someone will try to lift their skirts to see if they are truly hijras, or fakes, in which case they will be reviled and chased away.

Hijras are an organized social community with local, regional, and national structures. Basic elements of Indian society such as the extended joint family, the caste system, the hierarchical relationship in Hinduism between gurus (spiritual mentors) and *chelas* (disciples), and local caste and neighborhood councils are all part of hijra social structure. Hijras can be Hindu, Muslim, or Christian, and come from all castes and social classes. Within the community there are no castelike rules pertaining to purity and pollution.

The most important element of hijra social organization is the guru-chela relationship. The hijra guru is both mentor and parent; the chela's role is as a dependent and obedient child and student. Each recruit to the hijra community is sponsored by a guru, who pays the new member's initiation fee and takes responsibility for her material subsistence, receiving a portion of the chela's earnings in return. The gurus in each city form a *jamat*, or council of elders, who regulate the working conditions of the city, act as a dispute resolution forum, and serve as the authorizing body of community membership and exclusion.

Hijra stories compellingly illustrate a basic anthropological theme, most prominently enlarged upon by Ruth Benedict (1934), that the margins of a culture are intimately related to its center and that understandings of the abnormal and the normal reciprocally reinforce each other. The hijra role, both as experienced and as conceptualized by others, also challenges us in many ways, demonstrating the construction of gender dichotomies but also the possibilities of gender diversities. And ultimately, the everyday lives of hijras inspire us, as they reveal the myriad ways that human beings, even under the most adverse conditions, become agents in shaping their own lives, creating meaningful identities and resisting, in small and large ways, the oppression of stigma, poverty, and marginality.

* * *

Salima is a Muslim, born in Byculla, a Muslim neighborhood in Mumbai, where she has lived her entire life. She is a "real" hijra, *born* intersexed, and not, as she says, "converts like those others." When I first met Salima, in November 1981, she was in her early thirties. She was living on the street, sleeping on a tattered bedroll with only a plastic lean-to to protect her from the monsoon rains that fall so heavily in Mumbai. Her clothes were dirty, as were her hands and feet, and she had a beard of several days' growth. We talked about her life over many weeks and, on my subsequent visits to Mumbai, over several years.

In her talk about her childhood Salima emphasized the sad fate of her birth:

> I don't remember much of my early days and only remember the days after my mother married her second husband. I consider this man my father. My parents felt sad about my birth, but they realized it was their fate to have me born "neither here nor there." From my birth, my [male] organ was very small. My mother felt it would grow as I grew up, but it didn't. She took me to doctors and all, but the doctors said, "No, it won't grow. Your child is not a man and not a woman. This is God's gift." My mother also took me to various holy places and made many vows but nothing turned out fruitful. It is God's will—some women give birth to lame children, some to blind children, it is God's will, even the gift of God. My father also made many vows but it was all futile. If I were a boy, I would have had a good job and brought a daughter-in-law into the house, but like this I have been of no use to my parents. They did what they could for me; the rest is my *kismet* [fate].
>
> From the beginning I only used to dress and behave as a girl. I would run off to Chowpatty and beg and fool around. I only enjoyed playing with the girls, even though I got my hair pulled and thrashed for it. I never thought of myself as a boy or that I should behave like a boy or dress like a boy. I would sit with the girls [in school], playing with them, playing with

girls' toys, sweeping the house, cooking, doing all these female activities. My parents gave me a boy's name, but if anyone called me by that name, I would say, "Get lost! Don't call me that! Call me by any girl's name and only then I will come; otherwise, I won't listen to you." I would put on girls' clothes and do up my hair nicely and put on *kajal* [eyeliner] and rouge. People thought of me as a girl and would give me girls' clothes. Even today, my neighbors still laugh and joke with me and the childhood bond is still there. They say about me, "We are childhood friends. It is not her fault— God made her that way."

In school I would never talk to the boys, but only to the girls. The neighborhood boys would tease me and I used to abuse them, as a girl would, and complain to their mothers. Their mothers would say, "Don't complain to us; when these boys tease you, thrash them yourself." So I would abuse and beat them, and these boys stopped teasing me. These boys would call me, "Hijra! Hijra!" My mother would tell them, "Why do you tease like this? God made him like this, and if you tease him, he can make your food go bad. So just leave him alone."

I was sent to my mother's womb by God, like any child; I am a gift for her. When I got older and the children would tease me, I would tell them, "See, today you are doing like this; tomorrow God will punish you for this." When the children would throw stones at me, I would tell them, "This is not good, God will punish you." I would want to abuse them more harshly, but my mother would calm me down, saying, "Never utter anything bad from your mouth, just let it go. Judgment will be given by God."

At around the age of ten or eleven, Salima joined the hijras:

The hijras already knew me and they used to take me along with them when they went begging. At that time my family was in financial trouble, and I helped them by giving them the money that I got on my begging trips with the hijras. One day the hijras came to beg for food at my house. They inspected my body and said, "You're neither a man nor a woman, but you are born this way." So they started accepting me; they would come to see me, bring with them various foodstuffs and other things. They wanted me to come with them, to be a chela (disciple) of their guru. My mother said, "All right, since you are born this way, go wherever you want to go, do whatever makes you happy."

In the beginning I was very scared of the hijras, but they used to talk to me so kindly and gently. I used to run away and hide sometimes, and I never used to listen, but then they were so kind to me, and they didn't beat me or ill-treat me, like I had heard they do, so whenever they called me, I would go running to them. The pain in my heart was lessened and my heart opened up to them.

They took me to live with their guru at Factory Compound and treated me very well. In the beginning they never let me go out; I only worked in the house, like sweeping, cleaning, and cooking. Sometimes I would miss my parents, and even when I was working I would sit and start to cry. I would say, "I'm missing my parents. I want to see my mother." They would take me to meet my mother and would give me 100 or 150 rupees to give her, along with a sari. Like this they looked after me. They kept me like a girl, protected.

Until my initiation, they didn't want me to go out of the house. I wasn't allowed to talk to men or other people. When I first went to the hijras my hair was very short. When my hair grew long enough for it to be tied into a small braid, then the *jamat* [council of elders] came and sat for my [initiation] ceremony. My guru distributed cardamom in my name. Everyone was to know that my guru Sona was taking Salima—that was the name my guru gave me—for her disciple. On a Sunday everyone collected—all the hijras and *naiks* [chiefs or elders]. My nose and ears were pierced. I wore a sari, and they applied turmeric and mehndi [auspicious henna designs] to my hair and hands and feet. They dressed me up just like a bride, gave me a name, and pierced my nose and ears.

From three days before the ceremony they made me sit in the house; they wouldn't let me go out or do any work at all. Everything was brought to me; my movements were restricted. I was not allowed anything salty or too spicy to eat; only I could eat milk, curds, yogurt. On the appointed day they made me wear a green sari, green blouse, and glass bangles. The Marwari jeweler himself came for my piercing ceremony. They made a paste out of rice, and in front of the rice they put plantains, betel nut leaves, betel nuts, and some flowers on a silver plate. Then on another silver plate, they kept one needle made out of gold and some gold wire. I sat on a low stool just like a bride. All the hijras who were there gave some money—five or ten rupees. Whatever people feel like giving they put on the rice. After this was over, the rice was taken by the jeweler along with the coins. The next night all the rich, important people came and gave presents, which were all given in my name, but I must give them to my guru. They garlanded me and all the naiks gave something; one gave silver anklets, others gave a sari, bangles, or eight anna coins, whatever they felt like. In this way they celebrated with so much pomp and show. After this I started going out for the singing and dancing and everyone came to know that I was Sona's disciple.

This was a good period in Salima's life. Along with her "sister" hijras, they went out to beg and to perform. Salima played the *dholak* (two-sided drum), a prestigious role in the group. All day, every day, the group went to Byculla Market to beg cash and kind from the stall keepers or roam their exclusive territories in Mumbai, seeking out weddings or births where they could perform. They made good money, all of which went to the guru, but they were given everything they needed by their guru, "so what need was there for money?" Salima was her guru's favorite because she was a "real" hijra and had been with her guru since childhood.

This was Salima's life for about ten years. During those years she found herself a husband, Ibrahim, a man who was Muslim, like herself.

Only after leaving my house and joining the hijras did I meet Ibrahim. It was at the market where I used to go to beg vegetables and things that my eyes and those of Ibrahim got locked with each other. He used to run a fruit stall. As soon as my eye caught his, he started to give me things—oranges one day, sweet lime the next, one or two kilos of apples, or sometimes a grapefruit. In that same bag that he put the fruit, he would also put twenty or twenty-five rupees. He put it in the bag so that no one would know he gave so much. He did not want me to go from shop to shop. He would say, "In going from shop to shop no man should tease you; you are very young." We would sit together in a tea shop. I would tell the hijras to take the things for the guru so she would think I also was at the market. I told Ibrahim, "If you don't let me beg, then when I go home and the shares are divided up, then won't my guru ask me, 'Where is Salima's share? What did you bring?' I will be caught in my dishonesty."

So, initially, Salima saw Ibrahim on the sly. Gurus disapprove of hijras having boyfriends or "husbands," who compete for a hijra's earnings. Salima's guru did soon discover the relationship, but Salima was able to convince her that the relationship with Ibrahim was no threat to her earnings for the hijra group. The guru then arranged a "marriage" ceremony for Salima and Ibrahim and gave her blessings for them to live together in a separate house. Salima continued to work with the hijras and earn for them.

Ibrahim had told me, "Even when you die, I will pay for your shroud. Don't think that I have taken a young person just to fool around; I'll stay with you until the end." But I used to say, "You're saying all this, but your mother and father will never let you abide by your words." So Ibrahim used to say, "Even if my parents force me to leave you, I won't listen to them." So everywhere they tried to fix a marriage for him, he used to go and attempt to break off the marriage arrangements. But then his brother, that bastard, and his parents, they came and took him away. They told him, "You are not giving us money to run the house; all these years you have spent in Bombay, you never sent any money and we had no news of you." His parents had come from his native place to check on him. When they learned that he got married to me they took him away. Our house was sold, along with everything else. I just took my household belongings and tied them up and brought them back to my guru's house. Again I had to do all the singing and dancing, as well as looking after the dholak and looking after my guru's house. I did all that—I settled down in my guru's house.

At this time the guru was living with a husband of her own. At some point the guru fell ill and went to her native village, leaving Salima living in her guru's house with the guru's husband. Not surprisingly, difficulties developed. Salima's story was that the guru's husband made improper sexual advances toward her, while spreading the story that Salima seduced him. His intention, Salima said, was to undermine her credibility among the hijras and to replace her in her guru's affections so that he could eventually inherit the guru's considerable material assets. He was evidently successful, as on the guru's return, Salima was thrown out of the house and cast out of the hijra community.

This was a serious business: any hijra who would work with Salima, talk to her, or even so much as give her a drink of water, would be exiled from the community herself. In order to gain reentry, Salima had to pay a 500-rupee fine to the council of elders (*jamat*). Unable to earn, much less save, this amount, Salima lived on the streets, where I first met her. Occasionally she begged in Victoria Railway Station but was chased away if other hijras saw her. Sometimes Salima joined a group of *jankhas* (non-hijra female impersonators), looking for work performing or begging alms. This meant long hours traveling on buses or walking to the outer suburbs of Mumbai in the extreme heat and rain of the monsoon season, for the most meager income. As a real hijra Salima was useful to these jankhas because she legitimated their performances. But then she came to owe them money that she could not repay, so she began to avoid them also.

Salima now lived on a street corner under a makeshift tent in the Mumbai Muslim neighborhood of Byculla. She occasionally earned a few rupees caring for some neighborhood children and was given some food by her neighbors. In the monsoon season, she slept under a bus or truck. She sometimes borrowed money from her parents but more often had to lend them money. As a hijra, Salima was the target of harassment from local rowdies. She considered prostitution, but as she so pathetically told me, "No customers are coming." Her general dishevelment, three days' growth of beard and dirty hands, feet, and clothes, made this easy to believe. Salima now talked bitterly about Ibrahim's abandonment, and she was also still hoping to raise the 500 rupees she needed to pay her way back into the hijra community.

> These days I am begging and earning these small sums of money; when the hijras pass by and see me, they turn their face away. I ask Allah, "Have I come to this condition that I am like an insect in a dirty gutter?" Nobody wants me. I don't want to live such a cruel life. If I get a little money, then I can lead a proper life. I can't go on leading this cruel life. Just last night I was sleeping out and at three in the morning four urchins came to harass me. I was fast asleep, and this boy woke me up. He said, "We've been watching you for years. We want to know what your price is—what is the price of your virtue?" I said, "So you want to play with my virtue, do you? Well, while I have breath in my body, you people cannot touch my virtue. If you want to play with my virtue then you will have to kill me."
>
> I have not been feeling well and had to go to the government hospital. If my guru were here, or if I had a protector, I would not have had to go to

this hospital; I could have gone to a private one instead. Never mind, that is life; one minute it's like this, the next minute it's different. So I still pray only to Allah, "If this is the way you want me to live, it's all right, but never put me in such a condition where I'll have to go to the hijras for help. Even if I die on the road, the municipality people will pick me up and take me away." It's all right. . . . I've run my life and it's through.

Salima was at a loss as to what to do to make her life more bearable. It was in this condition that I left her when I departed from Mumbai. When I returned to visit her again about four years later, in the winter of 1986, Salima's life had taken yet another turn. I found her in her usual place on the street, along with a small group of people, which included one hijra and two men. She was dressed nicely, much better than when I had seen her on my previous visits, and she looked in much better health. She gave me a big smile, and very shyly turned to the handsome young man behind her and said, "This is Ibrahim." Salima told me that she had written Ibrahim a letter calling him back to Mumbai and he came.

> Now he wants to do some kind of business, maybe selling fruits, as he did before. But for the past couple of months he is not well; his leg is troubling him so he is not able to go out and do any business and he is not able to earn. He doesn't have any money to start some business. I manage by borrowing a little money, two rupees here, two rupees there. If Ibrahim has earned a little money, he gives it to me to buy food. And now, why hide it, I comb my hair and get ready and go out for business [prostitution]. I have to try for something because my husband is ill and I have to look after him. I ask the customers for twelve rupees; some nights I get two or three customers, but sometimes I just stand there without any business. Thieves and prostitutes, you'll never know what you make in a day. Sometimes in the end I have to borrow money from someone. For the place itself, I have to pay two rupees to do business, even my clothes, I borrow from my friend. I make a little money also from begging, but mostly I stay and pass my day here only. People say to me, "This guy doesn't work, he just sits and eats your earnings. Why doesn't he work for a living?" But how can he? How can my husband go and work? His life is in trouble; do you think he likes to just sit and eat? He would earn money for me himself; how could he just sit and eat but for this trouble? He has a problem, so I have to consider that, too. How can I neglect his trouble? If, by the grace of Allah, he gets some money, to start some sort of business and earns enough money to support us, it will be good. For now, I earn enough to fill our stomachs.

In 1992, six years later, I again returned to India, looking forward to seeing Salima. When I met her I found that her luck had again changed for the worse. Ibrahim had again abandoned her to marry a "real woman," and her health had deteriorated. Because of the Hindu-Muslim riots in Byculla at this time, I did not stay long in Mumbai. When I returned to

Mumbai in 1995, I immediately went to look for Salima but could not find her in any of her usual places. I inquired among the neighbors and they informed me that she had died!

When I tried to find out more details I was told to look for her good friend, Rekha, who lived nearby. Rekha was one of Salima's "sister-chelas," that is, they were both chelas (disciples) of the same guru. Rekha was an older hijra who herself was living outside the hijra community. When I tracked her down, Rekha told me that Salima had died "of a broken heart" after Ibrahim left her. She had started to drink heavily and that, combined with her extreme poverty and depression, "led to her end." Rekha spoke warmly of Salima's character, describing how Salima had "saved her" from the streets, taking her under her wing. Her guru, whom I met the next day, also spoke of Salima's kindness to everyone, the help she had provided to Ibrahim, and his callousness in leaving her. The guru, who was very elderly, was now depending for support on Rekha, who, although lame, was full of vitality and hope.

It was a sad visit for me. I liked Salima very much and had great admiration for her strength in trying to fashion a meaningful life out of the barest of resources. But even with all of her survival skills, Salima was ultimately no match for the hurdles of poverty and marginality of life on the streets of Mumbai.

PART THREE

Social Distinctions of Caste and Class

"Caste" is a term of European origin that is used to describe the social groupings that many South Asians recognize as distinguishing different kinds of human beings from others. The term "*jāti*," which is the Sanskrit-derived term that most South Asian languages use to refer to these groupings, in fact means "kind" and is applied not only to kinds of humans but also to kinds of other things as well: animals, minerals, vegetables, genders, seasons, etc. Human jātis, or castes, are endogamous, that is, people tend to marry only within the caste to which they were born. Many people also prefer to eat only with others of their same caste for reasons that will be addressed below. Caste names sometimes, but not always, correspond to occupational groupings, too. That is, people may be born into a Barber or Potter or Blacksmith caste and *may* follow that profession as well. Often, however, people engage in occupations other than that suggested by the name of their caste, and often caste names do not designate a particular occupation at all. Caste is sometimes confused with *varna*, which is a common term used to describe an ancient textual—and for north Indians at least a contemporary practical—four-class division of humans into Brahmans (priests and scholars), Ksatriyas (warriors and kings), Vaisyas (commoners, including merchants and farmers), and Sudras (servants of the other three). While there are four varnas, castes number in the thousands, with different ones in different parts of the subcontinent.

Probably the first word that comes to mind for most readers when they see or hear the word "caste" is "hierarchy." Indeed social rank is an important aspect of caste distinctions. It is not, however, the only aspect of caste recognized by South Asians. Here we will outline some of the main aspects of caste as the phenomenon has been studied over the last several decades.

ANTHROPOLOGICAL MODELS

Some of the first anthropological models recognized that caste was based on a form of non-monetary, non-market agricultural exchange found in many villages throughout India. In 1936, William Wiser coined the term "jajmani system" to describe this pattern as he found it in a north Indian village. He found that the non-Brahman landholders (*jajman*) in this village gave shares of their grain harvest as well as cooked food and other goods to other occupational castes such as Barbers, Potters, Washermen, Carpenters, and Blacksmiths, in return for long-term service. Wiser characterized these exchanges as "mutual" or "symmetrical." That is, Wiser saw the jajmani system as a division of labor where landholding castes exchanged—tit for tat—grain for the services of the other castes, exchanges that apparently worked for the mutual benefit of all involved.

Wiser's characterization of these exchanges as mutual and reciprocal aroused debate among a later generation of researchers. These later researchers, influenced in part by a Marxian model, saw such exchanges to be coerced and asymmetrical, where services were given to the powerful landholders who then redistributed grain in return. That is, while Wiser saw the landholders engaged in reciprocal, tit-for-tat relations with occupational service castes, others realized that the landholders were politically and economically powerful groups, with privileged access to the food supply, who controlled these exchanges using their power as the "dominant" castes (e.g., Harper 1959; Gould 1958; Beidelman 1959). Whether viewed as "mutual" or asymmetrical, however, all of these researchers shared a view of the jajmani system as a more or less bounded, interdependent, and self-sufficient village exchange network among permanent, hereditary occupational groups, or castes. This was their "caste system." It was primarily an economic system of non-market, non-monetary exchange at the village level.

A second, and subsequent, set of studies on caste concentrated on analyzing caste as primarily a religious, as opposed to an economic, mode of social organization. The most influential theorist to propound this model of caste was Louis Dumont (1970). He argued that Indian society is fundamentally hierarchical in form. He chose a single dimension of contrast—pure to impure—as the framework for this hierarchy, and located castes along this scale depending upon their relative involvement in biological or organic substances (the impure). Thus, those who were scholars and never ate meat (e.g., Brahmans) ranked above those who tilled the soil and were involved in the life-and-death practices of cultivation. They, in turn, ranked above people who washed the soiled—including bloodied—clothes of others (Washermen) or shaved their hair or cared for corpses at death (Barbers), who in turn ranked above those who made leather goods from the carcasses of dead animals (Leatherworkers) (see Parish, this part). This hierarchy was seen as "religious" because the valuation of substances and people as "pure" or "impure" was seen to come from priestly, Brahmanical Hindu texts, beliefs, and practices (see Introduction to part IV for a discussion of Brahmanical Hinduism).

ETHNOSOCIOLOGICAL MODELS

Another approach to caste rankings was put forward by McKim Marriott and some of his students. Unlike Dumont's, Marriott's models were based not only on textual ideas, but also on observational data he and his students collected doing field research, primarily in rural areas throughout India. Most of these studies have had as part of their aim to understand India as Indians themselves talk about it. That is, they have worked to construct their models about social life out of the terms and categories that Indians themselves use to discuss their lives. One of Marriott's overarching aims has been to understand how Hindus understand the concept of "person." Caste was part of this inquiry, because caste—or rather *jāti*—is an aspect of person. Indeed, jāti is simply the "kind" of person one is.

According to ethnosociological models derived from Hindu concepts, humans are thought to differ from one another as well as from other kinds of creatures and things in the universe because they all have different proportions of the same set of substances. These substances include the elements (fire, water, earth, wind, and ether), the humors (bile, phlegm, and wind), and the three qualities of *sattvas* (goodness and light), *rajas* (action), and *tamas* (darkness or inertia) (Daniel 1984: 3–4; Marriott 1990: 6–12). Marriott and Ronald Inden (1977) argued further that many Hindus understand themselves not as "individuals" in the post-Enlightenment European sense of bounded, integral wholes. Rather, they argued that Hindus operate as "dividuals," that is, as divisible persons made up of particulate substances that can flow across boundaries, and thus be shared, exchanged, and transferred. Much of the energy of personal action is devoted to maintaining one's own "nature" in part by not mixing with things, places, or persons that might alter you in a disagreeable manner, and, conversely, by seeking out transactions—such as with pure and beneficent gods—that might at least temporarily enhance your qualities, or "polish" them (*samskāra*). Hence some Indians, for example, saw their own bodily nature to be affected by the soil on which they lived and from which they ate food (Daniel 1984: 84–85), as well as by their proximity and intimate exchanges with others (e.g., Trawick 1990: 99; Lamb 2000: 31–35). Marriott further showed that different kinds of jātis use different kinds of strategies to maintain their varied natures: central, landowning castes engage in many different transactions with all sorts of different people, while being careful to avoid polluting substances; Brahmans tend to give much more than they receive, hence sending out their relatively pure and cooling (*sattvas*-containing) substances but not taking in the substances of others. Lower castes tend to receive more than they give, partly because the higher jātis do not wish to receive from them because of their chaotic, hot, and impure natures, and partly because they require more inputs from others in order to survive. And some jātis seem to avoid transacting with others in any direction, setting themselves apart almost as islands in the otherwise flowing seas of inter-jāti transactions (Marriott 1976).

AN ASPECTUAL MODEL

Writing and researching in the wake of all these approaches, Gloria Raheja (1988) developed a comprehensive model to explore some of the dimensions of meaning surrounding caste as it played out in Pahansu, a village in north India. Raheja brought together (and altered) many of the ideas outlined above, and identified three intersecting *aspects* of intercaste relations that helped make sense of villagers' actions. These three aspects she named mutuality, centrality, and hierarchy, or rank. No one aspect alone expresses the realities of caste for the villagers, yet one aspect or another may be contextually foregrounded at one time (or place) or another.

"Mutuality" refers to those reciprocal exchanges identified by Wiser. Indeed, Raheja found, village residents did talk about their interrelations this way: the Farmer who owns the lands gives grain in return for services provided by hereditary occupational castes such as Washermen, Barbers, and Brahman priests. "Rank" or "hierarchy" refers to those vertical relations of relative purity, where persons of castes that are more "pure" rank higher. Concerned with maintaining their own, purer bodily natures, members of relatively high jātis will regulate quite carefully whose substances they will consume in the form of cooked versus uncooked food, or exchanges of bodily fluids through sharing a pipe or a sexual relationship. "Centrality" is perhaps the most complex aspect of all. Centrality has to do with the fact that the powerful landowning castes are at the "center" of a distribution network, but that this distribution is not only political and economic. It is also a ritual distribution, where the landowners send out to other castes on the "periphery" (all the so-called service castes listed above, *including* the high-ranking Brahmans) their negative karma, their faults, evils, and inauspiciousness. Those on the periphery accept these negative substances in part because they are able to and in part because they must: if the central landowners are to succeed in growing the food that the whole village eats, they must be relatively free of these incapacitating karmic substances. D. Mines (1997b) has reported similar concepts at work in south India, where Brahman priests, Washermen, Barbers, and others receive evil-bearing gifts from dominant landowners. Evils are transferred from the landowners to objects and foodstuffs through rituals and mantras, and these items are then passed on to the "peripheral" castes, who are thought capable of absorbing or digesting them (see also Good 1991; Parry 1994).

CRITICAL STUDIES

Last, but by no means least, many critical studies of caste have highlighted the ways that anthropologists have sometimes treated caste ideas as "traditional" and "frozen" forms of meaning. In fact, caste—like any conceptual and social reality—is historically constructed, variable, and changing. Some have cogently argued that many scholarly concepts of caste have been, in part, influenced by British colonial categories, not to mention by anthropologists who themselves "construct" more than "reveal" knowledge of caste. Bernard Cohn (1987b: 195–96), for example, argues persuasively that even Indians' own concepts of caste were altered historically by British colonizers who, in attempting to control the Indian population through the census, actually concretized caste into a frozen set of ranked groups that became, subsequently, real social and political categories within which Indians had to operate (see also Dirks 1992). Chris Fuller (1989) has revealed how the so-called jajmani system was neither universal in South Asian villages, nor was it nearly the closed and self-sufficient system that anthropologists imagined (or wished?) it to be. Others, especially those influenced by subaltern studies, have pointed out that many anthropological models of caste derive from textual, Brahmanical models of caste, thus ignoring possible alternative understandings of the non-elite (see Raheja, this part, as well as Kapadia 1995; Prakash 1991; Trawick 1988; and Wadley 1994). And contemporary Indian fiction also offers its own critique of caste in South Asia (e.g., Anand 1990; Bardhan 1990; Mistry 1997; and Murthy 1989).

The meanings and uses of caste are also changing. Today, in parts of South Asia, caste associations are becoming important political parties, and as they come to define their identities as political ones, they also redefine their membership to include more and more people who might previously have been considered to be different castes. In parts of South Asia, social movements that have formed among both lower-caste and higher-caste groups have led to violent clashes as each strives to define their own community struggles against the discordant struggles of the other. Among these must be included Dalit movements. "Dalit" is a politicized self-referential term used by many persons and groups that have otherwise been labeled "Untouchable." At least since the beginning of the twentieth century (S. Dube's 1998 work demonstrates much earlier beginnings), but more so since the 1970s, many Dalits have organized forthright resistance movements to protest caste-based inequities in Indian society. They have agitated for structural change as well as for changes in cultural values in an effort to move India toward egalitarian structures and values (see Zelliot 1992; Omvedt 1993; Moon 2001). These movements, too, have resulted in violent confrontation between Dalits and the powerful caste and economic interest groups that would oppress them. To begin to get a sense of contemporary debates about caste and its changing meanings—both among scholars and among Indian citizens—see Fuller (1997).

Finally, in many places all over South Asia, class is in some respects and for some people replacing caste as the dominant mode of social ranking in everyday life. While class analysis has long figured in studies of land tenure and peasant labor (e.g., Epstein 1973; Gough 1989; Beteille 1965; Kapadia 1995), in recent years historians as well as anthropologists have accelerated our understanding of class relations in South Asia by analyzing labor relations in colonial history (Basu 1994; Chakrabarty 2000; Daniel 1993; Gupta 1994), factories (Parry, Breman, and Kapadia 1999; Holmstrom 1976), domestic service (Adams and Dickey 2000; Ray 2000; Tolen 1996), as well as other aspects of class and class relations in urban settings (Breman, Das, and Agarwal 2001; Dickey 1993; and see also Dickey, Hall, Leichty, Mazzarella, Richman, and Seymour in this volume).

*   *   *

The essays in this section reflect some aspects of caste and class as these personal cum social distinctions affect people in their daily lives. Steven M. Parish starts us off with a portrayal of the city Bhaktapur in Nepal. In Bhaktapur, caste, city geography, and ritual all work together to make and remake a set of caste values that provide residents a way to think about who they are relative to one another. As Parish describes the city as a template for caste relations, he also illustrates at least three of the aspects of caste defined above. He fleshes out some of the everyday realities of caste rank based on purity and impurity, he shows how the so-called Untouchables who live on the periphery of town serve as the repositories for the city center's impurities, and he shows that Untouchables are not uncritical of their position in society.

Viramma offers us a first-person account of caste relations in her village in rural South India. A Dalit (formerly "untouchable") woman who labors in others' fields, Viramma describes the different castes in her village from her own point of view. She tells stories of real events in her life. Some are humorous and reveal easy interactions between people of different castes and others reveal some of the harder inequities of everyday life in a village where caste matters.

Gloria Raheja's piece offers us insight into the way that British colonial understandings of caste were distorted by their own colonial agendas of command and control. She shows how the British misused and misinterpreted Indian proverbs by taking them out of the everyday contexts of their telling and using them, instead, as evidence in support of the British position that Indians were controlled by ancient custom and in need of governance by the more "rational" British. In other words, the British "entextualized" these proverbs by placing them within the context of their *own* agendas.

Sara Dickey's portrayal of the life decisions of Anjali, a young woman in Madurai, provides us with a needed shift in focus from caste to class. As Dickey's portrayal of Anjali shows, in urban settings today, economic class and the cultural signs thereof are often more salient considerations than caste for many people as they struggle to make their way through life in the city.

This part concludes with a table on "Seven Prevalent Misconceptions about India's Caste System." This table, which appeared originally in *Ghanta* (vol. 3, no. 2 [1992]: 7), summarizes a few of the most common misunderstandings about the meanings and realities of "caste" as it is lived in South Asia.

God-Chariots in a Garden of Castes: Hierarchy and Festival in a Hindu City

Steven M. Parish

My Kingdom is the Garden of the Four Varna and the Thirty-Six Castes.

—King Pṛthvī Nārāyana śhāha of Nepal

THE CITY

The Hindu city of Bhaktapur in Nepal's Kathmandu Valley is a place where caste and religion came to dominate much of everyday life. Located on an ancient trade route to Tibet, Bhaktapur sits on a rise above a river. Viewed from the south, from the fertile rice fields on the other side of this river, the city presents a face composed of four- and five-story redbrick houses thrust up like a kind of urban cliff, breached by narrow streets that climb up and into the interior. The great pagoda temple of a goddess towers above the rooftops, and beyond the city rise the snow peaks of the Himalaya.

Inhabited by an ethnic group called the Newars, the city was once the royal center of a small Hindu kingdom. Later it was conquered and made part of a larger multiethnic Hindu state. Throughout its history, it has been shaped to religious conceptions of the moral and cosmic order. Today, it remains a harvest of much of the meaning, much of the sense of reality, generated in South Asia over the centuries. The city embodies Hinduism in urban space and form, and makes it part of everyday life in myriad ways. Dense, compact, stratified, Bhaktapur is not just a city, built of bricks and timbers alone; it is a sacred city, a Hindu city, a city of castes—built of rituals and religious meaning within an encompassing social hierarchy.

Parts of this essay appeared in *Hierarchy and Its Discontents: Culture and the Consciousness of Politics in Caste Society* by Steven M. Parish. Copyright © 1996 University of Pennsylvania Press. Reprinted by permission.

THE JOURNEY OF THE CHARIOT, I

In Bhaktapur, myth comes to life with the music of drums and the clash of cymbals. A festival marks the turning of the year. To celebrate it, the gods and goddesses of the city leave their temples to journey through its streets, to rest beneath the eaves of their god-houses, to receive offerings from their worshippers.

Each spring, in rites that mark the passing of the year, the people of Bhaktapur pull two Hindu divinities, Lord Bhairav and the goddess Bhadrakāli, in chariots through the streets of the city, and then out to the edge of the city. Before these set out, expectant crowds begin to gather in the square of the five-storied temple where the journey begins, several days before the new year. The celebration fills the town with joyful crowds, with a sacred tumult, as other divinities are also taken in procession.

During these festivals, I have seen the deities associated with various quarters carried in torchlit processions on the shoulders of ecstatic, intoxicated men. Carried away, they sometimes surge through the crowds that have gathered in the narrow streets; the rush of the men carrying the litter holding the divinity adds to the general commotion and excitement. Those who live along the procession's path crowd into their doorways and lean out the windows of their multi-storied houses to watch the gods go by.

The festival's main event, however, is the journey of Bhairav. At rest, waiting for its ceremonial progression to begin, his chariot is an echo on wheels of the two monumental pagoda temples that flank the city square where it sits. Standing motionless, the chariot rises into the air above the heads of the crowd. It is a mobile temple, a god-house on wheels, several times the height of the people who gather around it to watch and worship.

Moving, the chariot of the god surges through the crowd like a ship on the ocean, parting swirling masses of people, who stream away from it on nimble feet to avoid being crushed beneath its great wooden wheels, each taller than a man. The wheels have painted eyes. The chariot has a kind of prow that stretches forward and up, where an image of another god is attached, a mask that stares outward with blind eyes. The men of the city pull the chariot by ropes attached front and back. In one of the central acts of the festival, they pull it first forward, then back, chanting the rhythm of their efforts, in a sacred tug-of-war. The men of one half of the city vie with those from the other half, each group attempting to pull the chariot and the god it houses into their section of the city. Each side wants the blessings of the god, and the honor of being the first to take the god through the streets of their part of Bhaktapur.

Having the chariot pass through the city is a form of *darśana*, an opportunity to witness the god, offering people a way of coming into the presence of divinity.

The priests do not always have an easy ride during the journey of the god through the streets, either during the tug-of-war or afterward. I have seen the chariot pulled with such energy that it collides with houses along the street as it does not quite make a corner, gouging holes in brick walls, damaging the chariot itself. Bhairav is a dangerous god of force and motion, and the force with which his chariot is drawn through the city seems somehow appropriate, as a kind of metaphor for social and psychological forces that pulse just beneath the surface of Bhaktapur. Composed of human emotions and dissatisfactions, these forces sometimes break through the redundant constructions of reality and common sense that help establish a cultural and political order for Bhaktapur.

The chief Brahman priest of the Taleju temple rides the chariot, carrying a sword that represents the royal power of Bhaktapur's long-vanished kings. Another Brahman rides with the king, representing the king's own Brahman priest and royal adviser, his *guru-purohita*. Thus, the apex of the caste hierarchy is represented in the (symbolic) persons of king and Brahman. They ride with divinity: their proximity to the god declares their status, and lends it an aura of legitimacy.

Their importance is dramatized in the way they make an entrance onto the scene, with pomp and ceremony, before the ritual tug-of-war and hauling of the chariot through the streets begins. Shaded by a ceremonial umbrella carried by an attendant, accompanied by music, they march from the Taleju temple in the old royal palace complex to the temple square, where the chariot waits. Arriving in the square, the priest-king commands that Bhairav's image be brought. The image of the god is placed in the chariot and "the king" worships it. The Brahman representing the king takes a seat on the god's right. The Brahman representing the royal priest takes a seat on the left. Members of other castes take positions in the chariot that reflect their positions in society. Four Carpenters stand at the four corners. An Astrologer and a non-Brahman priest seat themselves behind the priests representing the king and his royal adviser. A *jyāpu*, a member of the farming castes who make up a majority of Bhaktapur's inhabitants, also takes a seat behind the king, the royal Brahman priest, and the god. In this way, a kind of self-image of caste society is composed, and then pulled through the streets of the city.

THE CASTE HIERARCHY IN BHAKTAPUR

While the festival offers a tableau of the caste order, the practical organization of the festival depends on the cooperation of many of the castes of the city. The division of labor that makes the festival possible reflects the division of labor, and the division of symbolic roles, that underlie the social and symbolic order of the city.

Caste is integral to the city. Nurtured by Hindu kings over the centuries, caste civilization flourished in the Kathmandu Valley. Cities, towns, and villages became extravagant flowers in royal gardens of caste, representing a cultural efflorescence of the idea of hierarchy, as caste practices were propagated and cultivated as the essence of the body politic. Society came to embody the ideal that humans are unequal. The propagation of ideas and images of inequality as legitimate and sacred values shaped not only the structure of society, but also the intimate consciousness of men and women, giving them both a fixed place in society and ways of thinking and feeling about themselves and others.

After the defeat of the Newar Malla kings and Bhaktapur's incorporation into the larger kingdom of Nepal, the early Shaha dynasty and the succeeding Rana regime continued to give legal support to caste hierarchy. By the middle of the twentieth century, the larger social and political context was quaking with radical structural change, but change tended to come later to Bhaktapur than to other places. In Bhaktapur, caste continued to be one of the key cultural axioms of local social existence even as the legal and political foundations for caste were swept away. By the early 1980s, when I arrived, some castes had vanished or abandoned their symbolic roles, but the caste system as a symbolic and moral system survived in Bhaktapur, and continued to grip people's minds, to define their social identity.

What we term "caste," Newars call *"jāt."* However, although "jāt" denotes those hierarchically organized divisions of society designated by the word "caste" in English, it refers also to occupational and ethnic groups and to gender—or to any other distinct category. It is used broadly to mean "kind." When used in the sense of "caste," Newars say there are as many as thirty castes in Bhaktapur. Some of these may recently have disappeared as families left Bhaktapur, and a few may be present only cognitively and symbolically—they are there in thought, not as actual groups. In terms of ethnic identity, most of these castes are considered Newar, but some belong to other ethnic groups.

No one—not I, and not any of the Newars I know—would deny that the opposition of pure and impure is one basis for the caste hierarchy (Dumont 1980), one of the key models for social relations, although it is only one among several. States of purity and impurity separate Newar castes, and purity is one key idiom of rank: higher castes are relatively more "pure" than lower castes. Among Newars, this is expressed concretely in a number of ways. As in much of South Asia, food is one medium—patterns of sharing and not sharing food and other items have hierarchical implications. High-caste Newars will not accept boiled rice or certain other foods from individuals of any caste lower than their own; they will accept nothing, not even water, from members of some still lower castes.

Some castes are dangerously impure or untouchable. Members of these castes cannot enter the upper stories of houses of high-caste Newars (the bottom story being conceived either as outside the house or as impure in its own right). They were barred from entering certain temples, though some Untouchables have the right to act as attendants at certain other shrines. They perform stigmatizing roles: accept polluting offerings in death rites, handle excrement, kill animals for a living.

In the past, exclusion was practiced in a variety of ways. For the most part, the higher castes lived in the center of the city while lower castes lived on the peripheries. Some of the more stigmatized castes lived in separate neighborhoods; the untouchable Sweepers, the Pore, lived outside the traditional boundaries of the city, in an area near the river, across from one of the city's cremation grounds. This location resonated with their symbolic association with filth, decay, and death. Certain occupations were reserved for certain castes; occupational mobility was limited. Education was limited to members of high castes. Members of the lower castes were required to wear distinctive dress. Among other legal disabilities, the untouchable Sweepers could construct only one-story houses with thatch roofs. Untouchables could not use the same water taps as "pure" castes. Untouchables could not enter the city after sundown. This was enforced by royal will, by state power. In the past, many still recalled, any wealth Untouchables might accumulate would be seized by the old kings. Power and force kept Untouchables in their places in the caste hierarchy.

The state no longer enforces this system of exclusions, which so powerfully symbolizes hierarchy, but the basic pattern persists, suggesting that it is not only the actions of the state that sustain caste. Given the social, economic, and political changes in Nepal, the persistence of the caste system is remarkable. In Bhaktapur, untouchable Sweepers still live outside the city. Untouchables now use water taps once reserved exclusively for use by the traditional "high" and "pure" castes, but they may still be met with verbal abuse, and be made to feel unwelcome and inferior. Members of the traditional "pure" castes of Bhaktapur object to Untouchables entering tea shops in their neighborhood. Traditionally they could be served outside, and would wash their own utensils. They would risk being beaten if they did not accept these exclusions, if they did not conform to expectations held by members of other castes. Many high- and low-caste persons recalled such incidents of violence for me.

Practices that exclude or stigmatize people, that put or keep them in their place in the caste hierarchy, may no longer receive the active support of the state, but groups, households, and individuals remain under pressure to conform to such practices or else leave Bhaktapur altogether. Although legal and political constraints have eroded, the social and cultural constraints of caste life continue to have power, to be central to people's lives.

Much of the ritual life of the city still rests on its complex caste system; the caste system constitutes a division of labor, not only for economic activity, but for citywide ritual activities (Levy 1990). Brahmans and other religious specialists have essential roles in the temples of the cities, and officiate at some of the domestic rites of families. Several castes have symbolic roles that are stigmatizing, but essential to the traditional social and symbolic life of the city. The impurity and inauspiciousness of untouchable Sweepers, for example, is necessary to the purity and the fate of the city; the impurities, misfortunes, and suffering of the city are conceived to flow into the Untouchables, who live in a separate area outside the old boundaries of the city. Their impurity thus defines the purity of the city.

In a sense, they suffer for the city: they absorb in a symbolic way the suffering of the city. Their symbolic presence helps relieve the existential anxieties of higher-caste actors; through some process of symbolic displacement they become living symbols that condense meanings and possibilities that high-caste actors want to cast away, reject, throw off, keep away from self. In the words of one high-caste Newar, Untouchables "soak up" impurities and inauspiciousness, "like a sponge." They are seen as having a "nature" that fits them for their work of collecting dirt, feces, and garbage.

In a set of conventional stigmatizing stereotypes, the people of low and untouchable castes are seen as dirty, disgusting, impure, as highly sexual and promiscuous, as ignorant and lacking the discipline and mastery of language that would make them truly human. In total, they embody an "otherness" that for high-caste individuals is disturbing and yet reflects a natural order that is necessary, ordained by the very structure of the universe. High-caste actors view low-caste actors, individually and collectively, as deserving their fate. The low castes are polluted, that is, naturally defiled, a notion based on a complex physical theory of the flow of person-defining substances. They are also viewed as realizing the fruits of the sins of previous lifetimes—their fate is justified by *karma* (one's destiny based on one's actions in this or previous lives) and ordained by the *dharma* (moral and religious law) which caste society embodies.

In sum, a hierarchy constituted by power (the king and state) fuses in experience and in practice with a ritualized hierarchy constituted in terms of purity and impurity. This fusion in turn interacts with other formations of hierarchy. It blends with a moral hierarchy of action and knowledge, of sin, virtue, and fate, and finds expression in a religious hierarchy of proximity to sacred values and access to spiritual power. In my view, caste hierarchy is all these, locked together in a dynamic propelled by struggles for domination and emancipation.

Lower-caste actors (Farmers and below) often resent the way they are stigmatized and excluded in the caste system. For them, the garden of castes yields a harvest of discontents. In the past, however, there was often not much they could do about their discontents, since the power of the state weighed in on the side of keeping them in their place. Despite the formal removal of legal sanctions, there is still not much they can do to escape being stigmatized, to escape the life chances offered by that caste system. Overcoming the initial set of life chances determined by their caste standing remains exceedingly difficult, and for most perhaps virtually impossible. Since caste standing is linked to subsistence and survival, the historical reality is that very few could readily act on whatever critique of caste society some of them may have developed. Furthermore, since caste life generates a sense of moral community, shapes personal identity, and offers a number of satisfactions and meanings, it is not surprising that people are ambivalent about caste society. As we will see in testimony from several participants in the system, moral discourse in caste society does not reflect ideology alone; it expresses profound ambivalence.

Caste practices are potent forms of life and thought; they help constitute lived worlds for actors. It is as such that they pose quandaries for the moral imagination. Some actors find their social position and identity disturbing, and reject the reality and justice of the system that positions them in society and shapes the way others perceive them. They are disquieted by cultural life, even as they live it. Such perplexities and quandaries haunt the imagination of any complex society, including my own racially polarized and class-divided society of North America.

Perhaps the symbolic action of Bhaktapur's chariot festival helps quiet the moral imagination disturbed by the inequities of the caste hierarchy. Perhaps it helps reassure some social actors that the way things are represents the way they ought to be, affirming their identities and practices, guaranteeing privileges and compensating for subordination—perhaps. In any event, the festival does display, for social actors to see, images of a sacred and moral order. These images affirm hierarchical interdependence as the basis of social reality.

THE JOURNEY OF THE CHARIOT, II

At one point, the ritual progression of Bhairav and Bhadrakāli takes them out of the city; at least, they leave the city's symbolic core as high-caste actors define it. After their progression through the two halves of the city and certain other events, the chariots descend the hill on which the greater part of the city is built, down a steep, crooked street, down to a wide field on the edge of Bhaktapur, near the river that passes by the city.

This passage to the edge of the city is not difficult for the smaller vehicle of the goddess, but can be a dangerous process with the larger chariot of Bhairav. Two special ruts have been built of stones in the surface of the street to guide the wheels of the chariot and keep it on track. Even with this, the chariot sometimes rushes out of control, endangering bystanders.

I used to watch from the window of one of the houses that line this street. I once observed the chariot break away and rush with great speed and force down a stretch of the road. A man ran alongside the chariot as it crashed down the street. He sped downhill in the narrow space between the chariot and the houses lining the road. Running all out, he virtually bounced off the walls of the houses, and careened back into the chariot, pumping his legs fiercely all the time to keep up with the chariot. I had no doubt that he was at risk, that he could fall and be killed.

I am not sure what he thought he was doing, although he may have been one of those responsible for seeing the wheels did not get stuck in the ruts built into the road for them. (They were in no danger of doing that in the moment I saw him.) I am even less sure how he managed to survive. He looked out of control, pacing the chariot as it accelerated out of control. Running along with the chariot seemed to have taken possession of him.

Caught up in the moment, he appeared in the grip of an adrenaline rush, caught up in some state of palpable religious enthusiasm. Others are swept up in the excitement of the festival as well, are pulled out of their everyday lives and mundane selves, if not as intensely and dangerously. In a variety of ways, festivals offer excitement, danger; they generate palpable sacred thrills. Experienced actively or vicariously, these are encompassed in a religious context, making the body's arousal a sensual chord in the mytho-sacred performance, a felt sign of the presence of the sacred.

At the bottom of the hill, where the street issues into the open area on the edge of the city, a crowd will have gathered to watch the chariot arrive. It emerges suddenly, bursts out of the city, plunging down the hill, rolling with great force and speed. The part of the crowd nearest it scatters to avoid being run over.

The chariot rolls to a halt in the broad field at the foot of the hill that spreads out toward the river. One corner of the field adjoins the segregated ward of the untouchable Sweepers, the Pore. When the chariot rolls to a stop, men again pick up the ropes to pull it into position for the next stage of the festival. Bystanders toss coins at it as it passes, offerings for blessings.

Robert Levy, who has also observed Bhaktapur's chariot festival, describes the selection and raising of a god-pole which now becomes the focus of events on the edge of the city. The god-pole is made from a tree, which may be as tall as seventy feet, cut in the forests east of the city. The pole is treated as a god itself; the life or force of divinity is awakened or installed in it. Envisioned as a kind of body, the tree is stripped of branches, except at the very top, where some are left to represent the god's hair. A crossbar made of part of another tree is attached near the top of the pole, representing the arms of the god. Branches and leaves are tied to the arms to represent the god's hands and fingers. Two banners are tied on to the god-pole. The chariots of the god and goddess are pulled near the site where the god-pole will be raised in celebration of the passing of the old year and the coming of the new, "so that the two deities can watch" (Levy 1990: 476).

Thousands of people gather for the taking down of the god-pole, going first to take a ritual bath in the river. After esoteric and secret rituals are performed in the Taleju temple, the surrogate for the king, carrying the royal sword, and his Brahman adviser leave the temple and go out through the golden gate into the royal square. Joined by their charioteers and musicians, accompanied by an attendant carrying the royal umbrella, they return to the field where the chariots have been left and the god-pole stands. After some preliminary rites, they take their seats in the chariot. From there, they watch the god-pole lowered.

Levy's account describes the process this way: "First the god-pole is rocked back and forth in an east-west direction, in motion called 'rocking to sleep.' The god is said to be tired . . . for 'he has been standing all year'" (1990: 485). The ropes represent the city's protective goddesses. Seeing the god-pole now as Bhairav himself and these goddesses as his consorts, Bhaktapurians interpret the rocking of the pole and motion of the ropes as sexual intercourse between the god and the goddesses. Levy goes on: "The pole is slowly rocked back and forth, and finally, after perhaps ten minutes to half an hour of swaying, eased down to the west. . . . When the pole falls, the new year begins."

This is a high point of the festival, one of its key moments as a signifying practice. While the festival has many meanings, it is crucially a ritual construction of order. The order it constructs has universal dimensions: it is social and moral, cosmic and sacred. These aspects of order are linked; the ritually declared connection to the cosmos and divinities helps give legitimacy to the royal and caste order. Human and divine actors witness the beginning of the new year, participate in it. The festival is, among other things, a pageant of hierarchy and a spectacle of order, in which, as Levy says, "the king and his entourage and the god Bhairava are moved by immemorial ritual order, as the sun moves through the year" (1990: 493).

Much of the ritual activity of the festival takes place not far from where Bhaktapur's untouchable Sweepers live. What part do they play in this pageant of hierarchy, this construction of the order that subordinates and stigmatizes them? The traditional terms of their participation have them enact their own subordination; yet on occasion they have attempted to turn the event against itself through symbolic acts that disrupt it. Levy (1990: 486) describes an event that seems to signify much about dominance and subordination, inclusion and exclusion:

> Now some of the [Untouchables] take hold of the ropes at the back of the chariot, and other men, mostly Jyapus [Farmers], take hold of the ropes at the front. Again a tug of war begins . . . The Jyapus are trying to pull the chariot back toward the city, while the [Sweepers] are trying to keep

the deity in Yasi(n) . . . the area where they live, just outside the symbolic boundaries of the city. This struggle does not (at least in the memory and expectation of present informants) lead to fights, and gradually the more numerous Jyapus with the advantage of the two extra ropes at the front of the chariot prevail. (Levy 1990: 486)

In contrast to the tug-of-war between the city halves, where one side or the other might prevail, it seems unlikely that the Untouchables could ever "win" this tug-of-war. They are less numerous and they have fewer ropes to pull: the deck is stacked against them. We should perhaps see this as a ritual of social positioning that acknowledges their existence but asserts their subordination and marginality. They were not allowed to participate in the other tug-of-war, in which only men from higher castes pulled on the ropes. Unlike the two halves of the city, they do not get to draw the chariot through their quarter, which is symbolically "outside" the city. The unequal contest asserts the power of the castes of the city over those outside the city, the Untouchables. The god and goddess are pulled away from the Untouchables, back into the city.

Untouchables do not always permit the construction of hierarchical order to go unchallenged. In one of the years I observed this event, the pole broke as it was lowered. Rumors quickly spread of how a group of Untouchables—who were supposed to pull on only one of the ropes used to lower the pole—had grabbed more than one, and pulled in such a way that the pole snapped. In breaking out of the place assigned them, and in breaking the god-pole, the Untouchables disrupted the construction of the unity of the social, moral, and cosmic order. High-caste actors argued that this had ominous implications. They felt that the disorder that had taken place at the event would be repeated in a variety of misfortunes and disturbances in the coming year. They blamed the Untouchables for this in advance of any actual misfortune, and turned this blame into another layer of stigma to attach to Untouchables, who were called an unruly mob and denounced as sources of social and cosmic disorder. As this suggests, the symbolic construction of the dominant order does not always proceed smoothly; it may be disturbed by protests and disquieted by the social anxiety such protests release. Even such disruptions, however, may be turned by high-caste actors into reaffirmations of hierarchy, stigmatizing Untouchables as a source of disorder and legitimizing the caste hierarchy as necessary to prevent chaos.

SOME PEOPLE

In Bhaktapur, I lived on the upper floors of a house owned by a Brahman. The entrance was on the second floor; to get to the door you had to walk up a flight of stairs. In Newar culture, this is a walk up to a state of purity; the upper stories of a house are considered purer than the ground floor. Low-caste people are barred from entering the upper floors of a high-caste house. I had two friends who would sometimes come to see me, to help me by talking about their thoughts and experiences, by discussing a variety of cultural topics. They had very different ways of making their presence known when they arrived at my house, and I believe this expresses, in a small way, the reality of caste differences. Shiva Bhakta, a high-caste man, would run confidently up the steps, pound vigorously on the door, call out my name in a loud voice. Kancha, an Untouchable, would come into the tiny courtyard of the house, and sit down on a stack of lumber. He would quietly smoke a cigarette, waiting until I came down or poked my head out the window to see if he was there. I asked him to come to the door and knock, so that I would know that he was there, but he refused. He did not refuse directly—he always bobbed his head affirmatively when I explained to him that he should do this—but he would not make the journey to the top of the stairs. I would poke my head out the window the next time we had arranged to meet, and would find him sitting at the bottom of the stairs, smoking.

The contrast was striking. Some of Kancha's behavior was a public presentation, intended for a possible high-caste audience; when he got to know me, he would in private let much of the diffidence drop. In our interview sessions and conversations, he usually voiced his opinions in a direct and self-confident manner. He did not possess the self-assurance and authority that characterized Shiva Bhakta, but he was not at all passive. He felt it necessary to present himself as yielding—as unchallenging—in public. What we see in his behavior is the culture of dissimulation that develops in caste society and perhaps in any stratified society where power may be used in arbitrary ways.

Kancha did not, dared not, assert himself in public. I did not observe such a radical split in high-caste friends and acquaintances, although they too had public faces and private selves. Shiva Bhakta, far more than Kancha, could both assert himself and embed himself in historically determined patterns of group behavior—without radical self-contradiction. Positioned in society in different ways, and having different kinds of meaning in social life, people of different castes experience life and view the world in rather diverse ways that reflect their place in the caste order.

Let me sketch in the life circumstances of several individuals, beginning with Kancha and Shiva Bhakta.

Kancha, an Untouchable. Kancha is a middle-aged man, usually dressed in dirty, ragged clothes and carrying the tools of his trade as he goes about his business. He is a member of the Sweeper caste, the Pore. Sweepers like Kancha are employed by the Bhaktapur Town Committee (Nagar Panchayat) to clean the streets, and by private householders to clean their courtyards or latrines. As an Untouchable who does such work, Kancha exists on the margins of society, lives on the underside of hierarchy, in its stigmatizing depths.

This is expressed by where he lives: not near the center, where the highest castes are concentrated around monumental temples, but on the very edge of the city. The Sweepers live in a separate quarter, which is considered to lie outside the city. Unlike the houses of others, many of the houses in the Untouchable quarter have thatch roofs. In the old days, these Untouchables were not permitted to have tile roofs, or to live in houses as tall as those of other castes.

Kancha undergoes a social metamorphosis as he leaves his home and goes up "into" the city to work, walking up the same street the god-chariot came rolling down and "out" of the city during the festival. In the social gaze of high-caste actors, who bring a hierarchical sensibility to what they see, he undergoes a transformation. They see an Untouchable.

At home, he finds meaning in domestic life, finds a measure of psychological security—"my caste is good for me," he will tell you. There, he sees himself (and wants to be known) as a good father, a husband, a head of household, and a person with aspirations for himself and his children; but he must leave this psychological cocoon to make a living. As he leaves the Untouchable quarter and enters the city, he enters a world where his presence and being have other meanings. He walks the streets as a living symbol of the caste hierarchy. Here, in contrast to the domestic scene, he has no active role in constructing his own meaning: he simply exists for others as a living symbol of hierarchy. High-caste people view him as a member of a functional and symbolic category that performs needed, but degrading, work. In the symbolic social ecology of the city, they see him as a remover of pollution—of physical filth, but also of impurity and inauspiciousness. They see that his hands and clothes are dirty from contact with feces and filth. I have seen people shrink away, assume disgusted faces in the presence of Untouchables. Being harangued, ordered around by words hurled across the social distance that separates them, may be Kancha's dominant experience of interacting with high-caste people.

Arguably, for the high-caste community, the Sweepers have a special, psychosymbolic value—the Untouchable is one of many "others" who define "self" through contrast and complementarity. Kancha is a source of impurity, a polluting presence; but perhaps even more critically, he absorbs, soaks up, the most disgusting, dangerous, contaminating residues and effluents of higher-caste bodies and selves. He is a receiver of impurity, of inauspiciousness, of what others reject and seek to keep away from themselves. Newar Sweepers have a multiple sociocultural identity, since they are conceived of as polluting in themselves, serve as removers of polluting and disgusting filth, and receive or control inauspicious qualities or forces that bring ill fortune to others. Kancha's caste is associated with an inauspicious celestial demon, Rahu, responsible for eclipses and human misfortune. Some say that the goddess of cholera used to dwell in the Untouchable quarter, near one of the cremation grounds.

Kancha does not seem bitter about his status. At times, he even defends the caste system; indeed, at times, he defends it more vigorously than some high-caste Newars. How, he wants to know, would he survive without it? But he wants something else for his children, and there are moments when he denies that the caste hierarchy has any moral reality, any ultimate justification.

Shiva Bhakta, a high-caste merchant. If Kancha is a marginal man living on the margins of the city, Shiva Bhakta inhabits the center, in a physical and social sense. Indeed, Shiva is a man of many centers, within a lived world that contrasts sharply with Kancha's world. Some of Shiva's many centers, his personhood and status, his prospects and possibilities, his class and caste position, are defined in part by where and how Kancha lives, by what Kancha is. Shiva is not Kancha—this is an existential and social fact of no little significance.

Shiva is a dweller in the city, the head of household of one of the large houses in one of the central neighborhoods of the city. In the local status system, only the Brahmans are higher in status, and even they may not be more central to the social and economic life of the city, although they are to its religious and ritual life.

Befitting his status and prosperity, Shiva dresses neatly, with a kind of precision, in traditional fashions. With a formal black hat settled on his graying hair, there is nothing diffident about Shiva. He is a merchant, and relatively prosperous, with a social network radiating out through and beyond the community. He lives in a larger social world than Kancha, who has few contacts outside of the city.

One center of life for Shiva is the modern economy and the opportunity it represents; he tells me life is getting better, that you have to seize the day. He applies this philosophy to business and pleasure. He has a certain zest for life.

If one center of Shiva's life is commerce, the effort to generate wealth and through it prestige, he is also centered in a moral world, in the traditions of family, religion, and city; he identifies with the dharma, the moral order and rightness, integral to each of these. I believe this gives him what Erik Erikson called an ordering core; for Shiva this ordering core is socially and psychologically attuned to the moral order of his city, his family line, integrating past and present, himself and significant others through whom he integrates self and culture. As the key concept of the Hindu moral order that Shiva identifies with, dharma offers Shiva a firm basis for his sense of self, and yields him moral insights for living his life, yet also helps constitute a society that oppresses others, such as Kancha.

Shiva's confidence also, I think, reflects a sense of position and entitlement, based not just on relative wealth and power, but also on caste status and family history. This is combined with the sense of purpose and fulfillment that doing dharma gives. Shiva characterizes himself as *calak*—vocal, articulate, clever—and I think he is right. Language, the power to use it to express social values and achieve goals, is another one of his centers; he is a man of words and means, grounded in dharma and family, who speaks and acts from the center of a community and tradition.

Kedar, a low-caste man who rejects caste. A member of the Jugi caste, Kedar is an angry man, unafraid to voice his fear and loathing for the caste system, his contempt for what he sees as the bad faith and illusions involved in it. He voiced rage and a sense of powerlessness, too, in a less veiled fashion than some others. Unlike many other low-caste informants, he consistently rejected caste, stressing its oppressiveness and his impotence to change it. He often spoke with irony and sarcasm, pointing out what he felt was bad faith and hypocrisy, insisting on a kind of dual perspective. The caste order had no moral reality for him, but it nonetheless formed a social reality that he could neither ignore, nor deny, nor totally break free from. His goal was clearly freedom: he wanted to break from caste interdependency, to become a man of independent means. He expressed great pride in a small entrepreneurial business selling chickens and goats that he felt made had him relatively free of his caste's former dependency on caste roles. It may be this relative capacity to support himself that made him feel free to scorn the caste system, in ways that others somewhat shared, though they would temper and hedge, worried about what others might think and about their own need to perform caste roles in order to survive. Perhaps it is because he has come to think of himself as a man of independent means that he also insists on defining himself through his own independence of thought. He was willing to concede, even underscore, his powerlessness in the face of the realities of caste. Why would he stress this, if he has achieved more independence than many? Perhaps because in his "inner" world he imagines and strives to create himself over and against the caste system. By claiming that he did not make the world of caste, he emphasizes that he did make himself, in defiance of the caste system and the place it allotted him. He values his hard-won relative independence, the freedom of choices he has earned, in contrast to his sense that he lived in a world that he did not make and would never have chosen.

Krishna Bahadur, a low-caste ritual dancer. Krishna Bahadur dances myth in the city, as a member of a ritual troupe that visits each neighborhood to perform rites that protect the city and its inhabitants. He has danced in the streets of Bhaktapur as a divinity. This role is his center, offering him an ordered and ordering core, a sense of identity. He wishes for his son to follow him, to share this identity, to dance for the city, to have a sacred role. Yet this identity is not without its cost, for it cannot be separated from his low-caste status. He is highly critical of the "closed" hierarchy of caste and proposes an "open" hierarchy based on knowledge—such as he himself possesses of sacred dances and Tantric divinities, knowledge of the kind he knows he has the capacity to master. A thin and intelligent man, brooding and yet gentle, he has given some thought to these matters, and speaks with some rhetorical force. Yet I do not think he can be said to have resolved anything; perhaps this is why he broods.

Dharma Raj, a Brahman priest. A priest and a reflective man, Dharma Raj sees the city in terms of the religious symbols and meanings that compose and integrate it. He supplies others with interpretations of cultural tradition, of religious reality. He performs domestic rites for people, using Sanskrit texts, as he was taught by his father. Like Shiva Bhakta, he sees the city as his; his caste provides the chief priest of Bhaktapur's main temple, in the old royal palace complex. In the days when Bhaktapur was the capital of an independent kingdom, members of his priestly caste served as advisers to the kings. In that role they shaped the ritual cycle and religious landscape of the city. Indeed, as we've seen, Brahman priests have in some ways been amalgamated with the old Newar kings, blending the symbolism of king and priest together in ways that help sustain the Hindu core of Bhaktapur.

Dharma places himself in a line of teachers and students, predecessors and successors, from whom he received the knowledge of tradition (including secret religious knowledge), and those who will receive that knowledge from him. His most important teacher was his father, but other Brahmans also shared their knowledge and helped shape his view of the world.

His concern about change runs deep. He foresees that Hinduism will become more and more a private matter—religion will be confined to the household, and no longer centrally involved in the life of the city, as it is today, as it was in his father's time. Caste is the focus of some of his concern: to be what and who he is, he needs other castes. People will still need Brahmans for domestic rites but they will not care about the web of rites that link divinity to the life of the city, with many castes working together to please the gods and goddesses and perform the obligatory rites. Still a powerful social reality, a breakdown of caste relations seems inevitable.

With this withdrawal of commitment, the means of maintaining the public ritual system of the city will vanish. He does not expect the caste system to vanish, only to change; it is the citywide ritual system based on caste specialization that he sees as threatened. Rather, he expects, with some reason, that the caste system will survive as the basis for identity and exclusion, competition and politics, but will no longer unite the city into a religious community. Already, gaps have grown where special castes once performed symbolic roles; so far, the system has enough resilience to absorb these losses. Dharma Raj lives in a state of quiet, anticipatory mourning, grieving for what is passing, and for what is still to pass.

AFTER THE FESTIVAL

The god and the goddess return to their temples, the people return to their homes, the chariot is dismantled and stored by the side of the Bhairav temple. The passing of the old year and the coming of the new has been celebrated. The order of life has been displayed. People have had their chance to come into the presence of divinity, and to view a kind of tableau vivant of the caste order, a living symbolic display of the caste hierarchy in which members of certain castes get to pose as themselves. The tableau presents an eternal, unchanging image of the way things are—hierarchical, fixed, sacred. It proposes that actual life is no different, that each actor is also a symbol in everyday life, an element in the cultural order. If this display cannot actually contain reality, if disturbing elements and ambivalences enter stage left, nonetheless life must go on. Having seen world-images and visions of themselves, people return to their routines, settle back into the habits of everyday life. Krishna broods, Dharma reflects, Kancha goes up into the city to sweep in the morning. The farmers work in their fields, and Brahmans perform rites.

High and Low Castes in Karani

Viramma, with Josiane Racine
and Jean-Luc Racine

Editors' note: Viramma is a member of the "untouchable" Pariah caste, working as a mid-wife and agricultural laborer in the small Tamil village of Karani near Pondicherry. Like the rest of her family, Viramma is bonded to Karani's richest landowner, the "Grand Reddiar." Viramma: Life of an Untouchable *records Viramma's life story as told to Josiane and Jean-Luc Racine over a period of ten years. She describes her brief, happy childhood; the ordeal of marriage as a young girl and her subsequent fulfilling relationship with her husband; her experiences as a mother of twelve children, nine of whom died; and her days of hard work under the burning sun. She tells of the mutual support the un-touchable castes provide each other in their* ceri—*the low caste residential quarters separated from the main village (*ur*) of the higher castes—as they lend each other rice, sing together, and share confidences. She witnesses as well the growing politicization of caste in her community, as various political party members come to encourage the local low castes to fight the caste system and call themselves "Harijan" (people of God) and, subsequently, "Dalit" instead of "untouchable." (Indeed, in India, the title of her narra-tive has been rendered—perhaps more appropriately—as* Viramma: Life of a Dalit.) *In this selection, Viramma tells of the various castes making up her village of Karani. Being "high" or "low" is tied here to owning land versus working on others' land; giving cooked food to others versus being regarded as so low or impure that one may only receive it; and possessing money versus having none. One can see in her narrative that it is possible to be "low" in terms of caste purity, and at the same time be "high" in terms of possessing wealth and power. Viramma's wit, strength, and sense of pleasure in life also come through in her story, even as she describes many of the hard inequities she has faced.*

All my family is employed at the Grand Reddiar's. My husband takes care of the pumps. The Reddiar owns two which irrigate every day. I collect the cow dung and clean the stable. My daughter Miniyamma helped me until she got married. Sundari has done the same and now it's my daughter-in-law Amsa who works at the Reddiar's. Anban started by looking after the cows. Now he does the important cultivation work with my husband. The reason is that we don't own any land. God only left us these eyes and these hands to earn our living. By working hard at the Reddiar's we've been able to lead our lives in the proper way. We've been able to give Miniyamma and Sundari away in marriage with silver ankle chains and some clothes. We've paid our share of funeral expenses when we've had to. I've been able to buy these jewels for my ears. And when we married Anban, the Reddiar gave Amsa her gold *tali* [marriage necklace] and her sari. Thanks to the Reddiar, thanks to his fortune—and it's a great one, especially in land—we have enough to eat without worrying. The Reddiar is an important man. Every day or nearly every day he goes to Pondy. The serfs who work at the Reddiar's have their rice guaranteed!

Of all the castes in the *ur* [village], the Reddiar caste is the highest. They have no equals. The others come after them: the Mudaliar, the Naicker, the Gounder. The Reddiar are the people who don't go to work, they put others to work: fifty, sixty, ninety, two hundred people. Their women don't work and they never go out.

I take twenty Paratchi [women Dalit laborers] to plant out the Grand Reddi's paddy fields, and they are paid by the day: it takes four Paratchi to plant out four hundred square yards. When we work for the Reddiar, there's no question of us singing. We keep our mouths shut out of respect for the Reddiar, because they're always there in the field watching over us, sitting on their cord bed under a coconut grove or even closer, on the dyke under the shade of an umbrella. Their serf—for the Grand Reddi, that's me—directs the work and checks to see that everything is going right, 'Hey, plant out here! Hey, Saroja! That corner over there's not done!' But towards midday, as soon as the Reddiar goes home to eat, I start up with the first song. After our husbands, the Reddiar are the people we respect and fear the most. We are their serfs. It's different with other landowners, we sing as much as we want and anyway, they like it. Sometimes when we work for the Naicker, we joke with him. We can even make fun of him. We shout, 'Yennayya! You never stop giving your wife children! She's pregnant every year like a bitch and you'll lose your strength, you won't have anything left, even if you eat melted butter and curds. Come over here a bit, ayya, come and see if your strength is a match for us beef eaters when it comes to real work like this!' It makes him laugh to hear us going on like that! That's how we joke with him, Sinnamma, and with the other landowners for whom we're not serfs. The Naicker own lots of land. They've got some rented out, and pumps and stables full of animals: cows and goats, and they make plenty of milk.

We make fun of Brahmins as well, Sinnamma. When the *pappan* [Brahman priest] is about to walk past on the dyke, we quickly make up a little song about him like this:

> It's the *pappan, adi-pappan* [top Brahman]
> Who irrigates by digging a hole,
> Who fishes in there for a dish of crabs,
> Who fishes in there for a dish of crabs,
> While drinking the juices of a young girl
> That very night, there was no moon
> And his sleep was troubled,
> That man with the *pottu*[1] in the shape of the moon,
> Wants to welcome Virayi so much!!
> Nanna, nanna, nanana,
> Nanna, nannana, nananana . . .

The bile wells up in his mouth when he hears that. It disgusts him, he spits on the ground, wipes his lips and hurries on. Have you seen Brahmins eat crab? Even just hearing about it makes them want to throw up! Brahmins own nothing or almost nothing apart from the temple land. We never go and work for them, they only employ Kudiyanar. That's why we can make fun of them. The *pappan* are the Reddiar's priests for marriages, the *puja* [worship] of the ancestors, for this or that rite and for the funeral ceremonies on the sixteenth day as well. They are lower than the Reddiar and like the other servants, they get uncooked food from them. They take it raw because they're in contact with God and they must be pure: they have the food cooked at their homes. We prefer to get it cooked: it saves us the time and cost of cooking. One day at the Reddiar's, I heard the Brahmin mumbling his prayers as he raised the sacrificial fire. (*Laughs.*) I was looking through the window when the Grand Reddiar's mother saw me and chased me away: 'Eh, Velpakkatta! Get out of here! Get out of here! Don't look at that!' And it's true that we mustn't see any of it. The Reddiar and the Brahmins speak both languages, Tamil and Telugu. They are vegetarians, they eat lots of melted butter, yoghurt and fruit, and they drink milk. In the country there are no other castes that can match them.

But Karani has definitely got castes! Reddiar, Mudaliar, Gounder, Udaiyar, Tulukkan, Vaniyan, Ambattan, Komutti, Vannan. In the *ceri* [low-caste residential quarter] there are Koravan, Sakkili, Vannan as well, *talaiyari* [assistant to the village accountant]. There are Tomban towards Selvipatti and Pakkanur. No one accepts them into the castes.[2] They're pig rearers. They live with their animals. The Tomban is very low, but I've already told you, Sinnamma, he's become very rich. His pigs breed fast, he feeds them on abandoned ground, it costs him nothing and he earns plenty of money selling them. One year we had a big argument when I had rented a plot of land near the temple of Aiyanar from the Reddiar and I'd sowed it with *ragi* [grain]. One afternoon I was at my door oiling my hair when Sinnappayya ran up to tell me, 'Aunt! Aunt! Tomban's pigs are wrecking your *ragi* field! Come and see, quickly! Quickly!' I put up my hair, tying it up on one side, and followed Sinnappayya who ran ahead. The kids who used to graze the cows over there had discovered the pigs and sent Sinnappayya to tell me. 'You know, aunt, when the Tomban kids saw there was nobody in the field, they brought their pigs right up to it and went swimming in the river. When we were going past with the cows and saw the pigs in the field, we let you know straightaway, aunt!' I was boiling with rage. I told the kids to catch the pigs, but those dirty beasts, they're smart! They made us run all over the place and they kept on getting away. The Tomban kids saw what was going on from a distance and quickly got out of the water to round up their pigs but even so Sinnappayya managed to capture a piglet which we tied to a stake. Then the Grand Tomban arrived and beat his little pig-keepers. I said to him, 'Innappa! Your pigs got into my field. They've ruined part of my crop. What are you going to do?'

'Please don't get angry,' he answered, 'I didn't know what was happening. We didn't let them loose in your field on purpose. I'll be very careful next time!'

'Ah! That's what you think! You think we're going to let it drop. A crop ruined, a crop filled with such beautiful ears! I want compensation. I'm going to appeal to the Reddiar: he'll decide for himself!'

That's how I answered the Tomban and Sinnappayya ran to tell the Reddiar but he was having a rest. Sinnappayya waited for the Reddiar to get up and told him the story and he told him he'd come after he'd drunk his milk. Meanwhile we'd left the piglet tied up and gone into the shade. I had enough time to make myself a chew of betel. When I heard the Reddiar arriving on his motorbike, I got up and spat out my betel. I went towards him and said, 'Innanga! I've had my grain ruined! How do you expect us to pay you rent now? What do you think of that?'

The Reddiar turned to the Tomban and said, 'Innappa! What do you have to say to that? I see only two answers: either you let her have the piglet or you compensate her in money for her losses.'

The Tomban, squeezing together his legs and hugging his chest with both arms, begged the Reddiar, 'It's my fault but what's to be done? I didn't do it on purpose. I can only give ten rupees. Next time I'll make sure the kids don't bring my pigs this way, Sami!'

But I didn't want to hear any of it and I argued, 'How do you expect me to pay you the rent, Sami? How could I give you five sacks of *ragi* after this damage? I want thirty rupees in compensation!'

The Reddiar calmed both of us down by suggesting twenty-five rupees.

Then the Tomban said, 'Have that pig untied and give it to the woman who cultivates your field. I cannot pay that amount!'

And that's how I came home with a piglet. I gave half a rupee to Sinnappaya and ten *paice* to each kid. They went and bought doughnuts at Kannimma's. As for me, I raised the piglet, and he grew big and fat very fast. My husband and Selvam the cobbler killed it, quartered it and sold it at Tirulagam market. We got twenty-five rupees—the same as Tomban's fine—and on top of that we treated ourselves to a pork curry—and Selvam too: of course we gave him a helping. Because we like pork very much, Sinnamma! Sometimes we club together to buy one on the days of festivals, for Dipavali, Pongal or for the festival of Kartikkai, and we share it.[3] There's a little song about it:

> The one who's bred the pig is the Raja Pandya
> The one who's made the most of it is the Chetti-who-burps . . .

It's pork eaters who know how tasty it is and not the people who breed them on their land. Anyway the Tomban have got rich. They're farmers now: they grow rice, sugar cane, aubergines, chillis and they all get me to hire the manual labour. But in the end, even if they're rich, they're still very low. The Kudiyanar agree to work for them but they don't get any cooked food. Although all that's changing in this *kaliyugam* [Kali Yuga, the degenerate age]. Now you see Tomban living in the *ur*. They used to be only just a little bit above us and now they're much higher thanks to their money! Or rather, we've stayed poor and we find ourselves even lower than before, still accepting cooked food from the Tomban.[4]

In this *kaliyugam*, money's the master and when you know how to earn it, you make yourself higher than you were the day before. It's the same in the city—everywhere it's a question of money. Look at the Kudiyanar. In the past they only worked at the Reddiar's. They did housework, they cooked the gruel for the serfs and the agricultural workers, they did the washing up, they helped in the kitchen. Always at the Reddiar's. Nowadays they'll do hard work in the fields like us, at our side, and they'll even do it for the Tomban. Because you have to fill your stomach and so you'll work for anybody as long as he pays! But one of these Kudiyanar families moved to Madras and a girl from our caste has been doing their housework for a while. It's a different world far away from the village where you were born, especially in the city.

Just as there are the rich high castes, so there are the poor low castes. God gave the land to the rich high castes and he gave the poor low castes the duty of cultivating the land. The duty of the rich high castes is to employ us, us the Palli, the Pariahs, the Kudiyanar. But there are some

Kudiyanar who own land, sometimes as much as twelve acres: they don't go and work. Other low castes have their particular trade. They are a little higher than us because they don't eat beef. They eat eggs, vegetables, fish, poultry, they drink milk like you. But meat is unclean, it's waste. Milk is pure. And as we eat waste, we're unclean. That's the difference between low castes and high castes.

There are all sorts of low castes in Karani that are higher than us. There are three families of barbers, brothers, who moved in next to the temple of Perumal. They're barbers for the Reddiar and the Gounder. They cut their hair, shave their armpits, cut their nails, massage them with oil. Generally they work on the steps of the lotus pond and for our Reddiar they move to his house and do their work on the *tinnai* [verandah]. These families work as barbers for the people of the *ur*, but the Sanar and the hunters sometimes go and borrow their scissors or razors secretly. We do that as well when our barber is away. We quietly borrow a razor from a barber in the *ur* and we quietly give it back to him, because if people ever knew that the same razor had shaved a Pariah and a Reddiar—ayoyo! there would be one of those arguments! That's impossible! But all the same, a barber agrees to it for some money or a little bit of grain. Those barbers are the temple musicians as well and they get some grain for that during the year. They play at puberty ceremonies, engagements and marriages; only auspicious celebrations. It all gives them extra income. Each of them plays a different instrument: the eldest plays the *ottu* [oboe], the youngest the *nadesvaram* [large wind instrument], and the youngest child the drum, dum, dum, dum, dum . . .

Two families of potters live opposite the barbers. They're not high or low, because everybody needs them, from the Reddiar to us. In the past the potter used to make enormous jars which contained thirty or forty measures of *kanji* [gruel]. If you knew how long it took to move those! If anyone carried them on their heads out to the fields, that made the shit come out of their hole! Nowadays the *kanji*'s put in a big aluminium pot which is fixed to a pole. Two men on each side carry it and it's much easier. The potter makes much less crockery than in the past; he mainly makes jars, tea sets for celebrations and dolls. I had all the crockery for my children's marriages made by him. The jars for Anban's marriage were very prettily decorated! I paid the potter in cereals: he's higher than us, but he accepts our grain.

The joiners have built their houses behind him. They are lower than the Gounder and they only marry amongst themselves. Next door there are the carpenters as well. Who else is there? If you come out of their houses and go straight ahead, two blacksmiths have moved in near the Reddiar's quarter. They're never short of orders and they work for us as well. Before the harvest they're asked for thirty to forty sickles. They sharpen old blades and repair carts. One also forged the trident under the banyan tree and the one in our house: you saw how well I decorated it! I never forget to perform the *puja* to that trident, to light some camphor for it. When a house is built in the *ur*, the blacksmiths are asked to make bars for the windows, hinges and bolts for the doors, pulleys for the well, all that sort of thing. The blacksmiths aren't low caste, they're free to go into the Gounder's and Reddiar's houses. They even get to eat with the Grand Reddiar, I've seen them there for a wedding. One of their sons is in teaching now. He married a girl from Pondy where he works and he lives there.

Opposite the blacksmiths are the goldsmiths. There were two families in the past, the big and the small goldsmith. The first made *tali* for the Reddiar and the Gounder. The small one made them for other castes, including us. But he wasn't very honest, that one. I could see that for myself when I gave him an earring to mend. He gave it back much shinier but it was very light. Danam took him her *tali* and she got it back much lighter as well! But we didn't dare complain. They say he cheated a lot of people in Karani and stole a little bit of gold dust from each of them. He got rich that way and chose to leave the village to flaunt his wealth somewhere else. Apparently he set up in his wife's village but sister Virayi who comes from there never saw him again. No one knows what country he's in, that thief! The big goldsmith stayed. Since he had more work than before, he went and got a little shop on the main street of Tirulagam: now he employs three people. Goldsmiths are lower than the Reddiar but, like blacksmiths, they can go into their houses and eat there.

Near the pond, at the entrance to the *ur*, there are two families of traders, they're Komutti. That caste has no other trade apart from business, you can see them in any town. The Komutti speak Telugu, like the cobblers and the Reddiar. But they don't mix either with the Reddiar or with us. We never go to their houses and we don't get food from them. When they celebrate a marriage, they only give betel to the cobblers and even then it's behind their house. They get married discreetly, without making a big noise. Unlike all the other castes, they marry in the month of Adi. I like them a lot, because their wives are always very friendly when they talk to us.

I'd forgotten that the launderers are one of the low castes in the *ur*! They live in four or five houses next to each other and they own a donkey. We have launderers in the *ceri* as well. They're lower than us and we take turns giving them the evening meal. They are pretty poor, but they still manage to hold their yearly festival. They worship Mayilaru and their god resides in their laundering oven. On the day of the festival of Mayilaru, the one in the family who carries out the *puja* takes a bath, puts on new clothes, changes the oven and lights camphor in front of the stone for beating linen. The families cook four jars of *pongal* [a special rice dish] with rice flour and coconut. Some slit the throat of a chicken or—less often—bleed a pig.

There's never any shortage of betel, bananas and flowers. Everything is handed out between them. We don't get anything, even though we contribute to their festival, just as the Reddiar contributes to our own festival of Periyandavan. It's the same, anyway: the launderers work for us and we have to give them something for their festival. No one can refuse. When Arayi, the launderer's wife, arrives with her basket to collect what she's owed—a measure of grain or a cup of oil—we give it to her but we don't miss the chance to have a moan, 'Those people, they're always ready to worship Mayilaru but they haven't even brought our clothes back yet! They're nothing like the launderers in the *ur:* now *they* work!' Then Arayi goes into a corner, scratches her head and always comes up with a reason: it's rained and the linen hasn't dried: or it hasn't rained and there's not enough water in the river: or any old thing. We don't get a share of their offerings but sometimes our kids do. They always want to know what's going on and if they're there when the *puja*'s performed, the launderers give them a little *pongal*. As it's sweet and tastes good, the little ones eat it without thinking or realising that the launderers are lower than us. Don't forget that the launderers of the *ur* are higher than us as well as lower than the Gounder. I always speak with respect to the launderers of the *ur*.

The Sanar are also people of low rank. They're only just above us. A Sanar ought to act pretty much the same as us when the Reddiar goes by: he should stand up and speak to him humbly. Sanar and Pariahs talk to each other almost like equals in the fields. We call out to each other and say, 'Hey, big sister Kuppu! Ho, big brother Kannan! Uncle Viran!' You know my friend Vanaroja well, the palm juice seller. We love each other. Every day in the summer she goes through the *ceri* shouting, 'Palm juice! Palm juice!' She gives me a glass of it and in return I leave her a measure of paddy each year. Sometimes if the harvest looks like being scarce and I think our share is going to be small, I pinch one or two measures of paddy which I go and drop off at her house. Vanaroja keeps them well hidden for me and gives them back to me the next day without anybody seeing. To thank her I leave her a little share. We get on well, the two of us, even if our castes are different!

There's also the Sakkili, the cobblers. They're much lower than us. You know Selvam, the horn player: he gets cooked food from us. When there's a marriage, we give him a measure of rice and a rupee. His duty is to play the horn for us every time it's needed. We never go and drink or eat at his house, but we talk together normally, and we're warm to each other when we meet. He also often comes and sits on our *tinnai* to talk and joke (but never in a crude way) or simply to chew. Then he asks us, 'Give me some betel, aunt' or 'uncle' or 'big sister'—that's how he talks to us. That reminds me, Sinnamma, I'm going to stop for a bit. I want to chew some betel as well. Hey! Look: your little Rajini has two spirals on her head. That means she'll have two husbands! (*Laughs.*)

NOTES

1. A *pottu* is the mark many Hindus wear on their foreheads.

2. Viramma's list is not exhaustive and needs a certain amount of explanation. Of the castes in the *ur*, the Udaiyar are farmers and landowners like the Reddiar and Gounder, the Reddiar being the most powerful caste of landowners and the Gounder the largest. There are no Mudaliar in Karani in the main sense of a high caste of landowners, but the Kepmarithe caste of thieves give themselves this title. Tulukkan is a general name for Muslims and Viramma is probably thinking either of the civil servants sometimes appointed to the village or the tradesmen from Tirulagam. Viramma leaves out the main caste in the *ceri*—the Paraiyar, with their two sub-castes, the Vettiyan and the Pannaiyar—and she describes them in the next chapter. The Vannan here are the launderers of the *ceri* and the Sakkiliar the very low caste of cobblers. There are no Koravar—members of the Nari Korava tribe in the *ceri* as such, but some pass through and the Sakkiliar are often treated as being like them. *Talaiyari* is more a profession than a caste—the position of assistant to the village accountant—and the Tomban are misleadingly described as being completely outside the caste system. Their low rank confines them to the outskirts of the *ur*, and Viramma's exaggeration could be due to her argument with a particular Tomban which she goes on to describe.

3. Kartikkai, the eighth month of the Tamil calendar (mid-November to mid-December), is when the festival of Kartikkai dipam is celebrated. Lamps are lit in every house to evoke the ceremony to Siva at Tiruvannamalai on the same night.

4. The rules governing the exchange of food are an essential aspect of the caste system. The orthodox view is that cooked food can only be accepted from someone of an equal or higher caste. So, although the Kudiyanar are economically dependent on the Tomban, they assert their caste superiority by refusing cooked food. Raw food and basic foodstuffs, like grain, are exchanged more freely—as Viramma goes on to say, the potter accepts grain from her.

The Erasure of Everyday Life in Colonial Ethnography

Gloria Goodwin Raheja

For Michel de Certeau, the understanding of "everyday life" is bound up with the question of how groups or individuals *re-appropriate, use,* and *operate with* the categories, cultural routines, spaces, and structures that are organized by various techniques of sociocultural production (de Certeau 1984). For de Certeau, what is essential to an interpretation of everyday life is an understanding of how, through everyday re-appropriations and operations, actors *transform* a space or cultural routine or set of categories. The users of social codes, according to de Certeau, "turn them into metaphors and ellipses of their own quests." The social codes themselves, then, do not regulate or control, but can be seen "as the equivalent of the rules of meter and rhyme for poets of earlier times: a body of constraints stimulating new discoveries, a set of rules with which improvisation plays."

Colonial ethnographic writing, on the other hand, saw the colonized "native" as incarcerated in his cultural codes and "traditions," wholly controlled by what the colonizers took to be ancient "custom" and "tradition," and thus in need of governance by the supposedly rational and scientific and "modern" colonial power. The notion of a rigid and determining "custom" was of course an illusion created by colonial ethnographic and administrative practice, partly through the systematic erasure of all traces of what de Certeau would later call "everyday life" in the colonial ethnographic record. This paper explores the question of how and why such an illusion was created.

This paper originally appeared as a portion of "Caste, Colonialism, and the Speech of the Colonized: Entextualization and Disciplinary Control in India," *American Ethnologist* 23(3): 494–513 (1996). Reprinted with permission.

TALK ABOUT PROVERBS AND TALK ABOUT "TRADITION"

Proverbs, like other forms of verbal folklore, are situated communicative practices that particularly positioned speakers draw upon to define, reinforce, redefine, or critique prevailing social formations.[1] Yet, when a proverb is recorded, translated, and published in various kinds of administrative and scholarly texts, the inscription of these texts fixes them, decontextualizes them, and the immediate situation of the utterance and thus its communicative and social functions in a speech community are often obscured.

The entextualized proverb[2] lies, in fact, at the intersection of the colonial agendas of mastering and codifying Indian languages and of characterizing and classifying castes during the late nineteenth century and the beginning of the twentieth.[3] In specialized linguistic works like William Crooke's *A Rural and Agricultural Glossary for the N.-W. Provinces and Oudh* (1888) and J. Wilson's *Grammar and Dictionary of Western Panjabi* (1898), and in caste compendia such as Denzil C. J. Ibbetson's *Panjab Castes* (1916) and Crooke's *The Tribes and Castes of the North Western Provinces and Oudh* (1896), so-called "caste proverbs" are given in great numbers; apart from a few caste origin myths, these proverbs are the only "native" speech that is ordinarily recorded in these compendia. Proverbs are regularly quoted in such administrative documents as the district settlement reports and the caste handbooks published by the Indian Army, and in 1908 Risley devoted an entire chapter and an appendix in *The People of India* to "Caste in Proverbs and Popular Sayings." Colonial administrators throughout northern India routinely issued instructions to their subordinates, both Indian and European, to record caste proverbs in their ethnographic investigations and in the ordinary round of their official duties (e.g., Ibbetson 1882: 3, 14; Luard n.d.: 64; Risley 1907: 18). Thus, while other varieties of "folklore" (folktales, songs, riddles, and so forth) were of course collected, translated, and published in almost staggering numbers, proverbs were the only genre systematically associated with the classification and description of castes, and the only genre that appears in the more immediately pragmatic settlement reports and army manuals.

Proverbs drew the attention of colonial administrators for a variety of reasons. At the most general level, proverbs were of interest because they were seen as tokens of the mode of thought characteristic of a particular people. R. C. Temple, for example, frequently expressed the prevailing view that knowledge about the "folklore" of India, including proverbs, was seen as benefiting Englishmen and facilitating in some small way at least their governance of the country:

> The practices and beliefs included under the general head of Folk-lore make up the daily life of the natives of our great dependency, control their feelings,

and underlie many of their actions. We foreigners cannot hope to understand them rightly unless we deeply study them, and it must be remembered that close acquaintance and a right understanding begets sympathy, and sympathy begets good government. (Temple 1886, quoted in Dorson 1968)

To know the people of India thus required a knowledge of folklore, because Indians, unlike Englishmen, were "controlled" by ancient and traditional custom.[4]

Colonial writers saw both proverbial speech and the institution of caste as primary examples of the hold that "custom" exerted on the natives of India. C. E. A. W. Oldham set forth the general view that proverbs are incontrovertibly persuasive to any of the "country folk" who heard them:

> From time to time I made some collections of proverbs current in the local vernaculars, because I have always held that you cannot get into real touch with a people in the stage of culture in which these country folk live and toil, you cannot fully appreciate the working of their minds,—and therefore, the reasons for their actions,—unless you know something of their folklore and proverbs. It is not easy to realize to what extent these terse, pithy sayings, conveying maxims of conduct and practice embodying the experience of past generations, regulate their conservative lives. (Oldham 1930: 320–321)

In speaking thus of the authority of "custom" and the proverbial utterance, and the "conservatism" of the peasantry, these authors assume the existence of a homogeneous and uncontested moral terrain in India, and they assume that proverbs provide colonial officers with a map of this otherwise inaccessible and unfamiliar territory.

These considerations, then, form a backdrop to the nineteenth-century interest in the collection of proverbs in India, but they do not tell us of the specific uses to which talk about proverbs was put in the construction of a colonial discourse about caste and Indian society. The quotation of proverbs in fact contributed very specifically to two aspects of this project: to the articulation of a set of assumptions about caste ideology as a whole, and to the development of a perspective on the characteristics of particular castes. In both instances, the insertion of proverbs into the colonial text was connected explicitly with the surveillance and disciplining of the Indian population, viewed as a congeries of castes.

THE TEMPORAL DISLOCATION OF RECALCITRANT TALK AS AN ENTEXTUALIZING STRATEGY: ASSERTING THE "INVIOLABILITY" OF CASTE IDEOLOGY

Writers who give special attention to proverbs place no less stress on the rigidity and unquestionability of caste ideology than other colonial ethnographers. H. H. Risley, who was appointed Census Commissioner in 1899 and Director of Ethnography for India in 1901 and who became president of the Royal Anthropological Institute in 1910, was particularly interested in proverbs "which are concerned with the caste system as a whole and illustrate the extent of its influence" (1908: 150). In *The People of India*, a book based on his report on caste in the 1901 decennial Census of the Empire, he exhibits specimens of proverbial speech that appear to give credence to his views on the "inviolability" of caste:

> The authority of caste is of course uncompromisingly asserted. "When plates are interchanged," that is to say, when members of different castes intermarry, is a proverb of the impossible. "The high-born man mourns the loss of his caste as he would the loss of his nose," and "The caste killeth and the caste maketh alive," seem to refer to the vital issues involved in the decisions of caste tribunals which may make or mar the lives of those who come before them. In view of these grave possibilities, the discreet advice is given, "Having drunk water from his hands, it is foolish to ask about his caste." To take water from low-caste people is to incur ceremonial pollution, entailing expulsion from caste pending submission to a disagreeable purificatory ritual and the payment of a heavy fine; the least said, therefore, the soonest mended. "A low caste man is like a musk-rat, if you smell him you remember it." "As the ore is like the mine, so a child is like its caste." "The speech fits the caste as the peg fits the whole [*sic*]"; the idea being that you can tell a high-caste man by his refined language and accent.

We note that Risley does not comment on how these proverbs might be used in everyday life by, say, high-caste people as they attempt to discipline or censure people of lower castes, or how they might figure in strategies of persuasion and dispute. And Risley does not describe the situation in which such proverbs were elicited, nor does he describe the ends a high-caste native assistant might have had in view as he dictated certain stretches of speech and not others to the proverb collector. For Risley, the proverbs he produces tell us only of invariant custom and "the supremacy of the caste sentiment in India" (1908: 130).

Risley notices, however, that for every proverb that seems to ratify the ideology of caste, there are several that undermine it. The entextualizing strategy used to cope with the difficulty this poses for colonial perspectives on the supposed inviolability of caste is remarkably ingenious. The preceding passage from Risley's *The People of India* is followed immediately by these observations:

> Along with these sayings affirming the supremacy of the modern doctrine of the necessity and inviolability of caste, we find others which seem to recall an earlier order of ideas when castes were not so rigidly separated, when members of different castes could intermarry, and when, within cer-

tain limits, caste itself was regarded as a matter of personal merit rather than of mere heredity. "Love laughs at caste distinctions." "Caste springs from actions not from birth." "Castes may differ; virtue is everywhere the same." (Risley 1908: 150)

Thus, when Risley was confronted with voices that challenged the authority of caste and the authority of his own pronouncements, he dismissed them as mere "survivals" of an earlier less rigid caste ideology. He refused to consider the possibility of dissent, the possibility that anyone, but perhaps particularly a person of low caste, might deploy a proverbial utterance to subvert or at least comment ironically upon notions of the hierarchical ordering and the separation of castes. Though the idea of "survivals" from earlier evolutionary periods was of course prominent in nineteenth- and early-twentieth-century social theory in general, it is an idea that is readily deployed at certain junctures in colonial writing on caste, because of its usefulness in abolishing the contemporary salience of recalcitrant talk.

Though William Crooke, for example, was a "confirmed survivalist" (Dorson 1968: 343), and though his work is obviously informed by evolutionary thinking more generally (Cohn 1968: 16–17), he invoked the notion of survivals to cope specifically with just such multiplicity of perspective. The festival of Holi is a well-known ritual involving, among other things, the temporary ritual reversal of caste hierarchies. In an article analyzing the ritual Crooke points out that in the course of the annual rite, low-caste people may heap abuse on high-caste people, sometimes using poetic or proverbial verses. But even these temporally contained verbal and ritual challenges to caste status must be interpreted as survivals from an earlier age.

> Among the Ramoshis of [Balaghat District in the Central Provinces], on the day after the [Holi] pyre is lighted, they throw filth at each other, pour mud out of a pot on any respectable man they chance to meet, and challenge him to a wrestling match; the next day cowdung is flung on all well-dressed people. (Crooke 1914: 68)

Crooke also quotes from a letter written in 1809 by T. D. Broughton, describing other Holi activities and the proverbial or poetic stanzas that are voiced at the time:

> In Central India the Mahrattas "cast the ashes [of the Holi fire] upon one another, and throw them in the air, repeating their favorite extemporary stanzas, full of the grossest indecency, into which they freely introduce the names of their superiors, coupled with the most abominable allusions." (Crooke 1914: 63–64)

As Crooke describes these and other similar Holi observances, he cannot envision any contemporary relevance of these ritual challenges to the supposedly rigid ideology of caste. Like Risley, he invokes the notion of survivals precisely when a voice of challenge is heard:

> The rites are purely animistic, or pre-animistic; at any rate, they have no connection with orthodox Hinduism. The otiose legends which profess to explain the rites are figments of a later age invented to bring it in line with Brahmanism. (Crooke 1914: 77)

Ram Gharib Chaube, an educated Brahman man who served for many years as Crooke's assistant, used much the same discursive strategy to dislocate recalcitrant speech when he encountered oral traditions that may have challenged caste hierarchy. In 1894, he published a brief notice of a Dusadh song in which a man of this low caste defeats a Brahman man in hand-to-hand combat and marries the Brahman's sister. The song appears to be at odds with the idea of unchallenged Brahman superiority, and so Chaube, like Risley and Crooke, resorts to the notion of "survivals" to cope with this disorderly discourse: he remarks at the outset that "[t]his is a very curious legend, which illustrates the condition of things before caste as we see it came into existence" (Chaube 1894: 62).

If Crooke's assistant had himself been a Dusadh rather than a Brahman, he might have seen things rather differently, and acknowledged the possibility that Dusadh oral traditions, like the traditions of many low castes (e.g., Prakash 1991; Trawick 1986, 1988; Wadley 1994), might contain critiques of the ideology of hierarchy, and he might perhaps have communicated this to Crooke himself.[5]

I suggest that what is at issue for Risley, Crooke, and Chaube in these discussions of "survivals" is not simply the nineteenth-century preoccupation with evolutionary theory. As they write about caste, the notion of "survivals" is deployed at the precise point at which a crack in this set of colonial representations widens before them. Thus, while the evolutionary concept of a "survival" is generally prominent in nineteenth-century social theory, the particular disinclination of Risley, Crooke, and Chaube to imagine a contemporary India in which voices of dissent could be heard is more immediately significant. When they hear a proverb or a song that seems to deny or to challenge caste hierarchies, they can only conjecture that it is an innocent relic of a bygone age; it cannot be, for them, a particularly positioned and knowingly critical commentary on a living social form. Temporally dislocating this disorderly talk is an entextualizing strategy that allows the colonial commentator to preserve his vision of the authority and homogeneity of "tradition" and the peasant's capitulation to it, and his vision of the uniformly consensual character of caste ideology.

ANNOTATION OF PROVERBIAL SPEECH AS AN
ENTEXTUALIZING STRATEGY: THE CRISIS OF REVOLT
AND THE EXTRACTION OF LAND REVENUE

A second aspect of the appropriation of Indian proverbial speech by colonial administrators as they developed a set of perspectives on Indian society concerns not caste as a system or overall ideology but the purported characteristics of particular castes and their status in local hierarchies. Here another set of entextualizing strategies is brought into play, strategies of annotation and decontextualization.

Colonial writers repeatedly insist that the natives of India speak in their true "authentic" voices when they speak in proverbs. On the very first page of the preface to the first edition of *The People of India,* Risley writes that he has included the chapter on "Caste in Proverbs and Popular Sayings" in an effort "to give a much-described people the chance of describing themselves in their own direct and homely fashion" (1908: vii). It is important for these writers to stress the notion that proverbs represent the true sentiments of the Indian people; as they annotate these proverbs that appear to them to be about caste, they appropriate them into the imperial project of defining and characterizing castes, making Indian proverbial speech appear to be congruent with their own judgments and their own disciplinary measures. Thus, though they may imagine that they are letting the colonized finally "describe themselves," the proverbs are in fact selected, decontextualized, and interpreted to create descriptions that are very much the contrivances of colonial administrators (with the help, perhaps, of local elites), contrivances that create the illusion that colonial pronouncements are entirely congruent with Indian speech about caste.

The annotation of proverbial speech is particularly evident in the caste compendia authored by Crooke and Ibbetson,[6] and in the district-by-district settlement reports that were written to describe patterns of landholding in particular districts and to facilitate the collection of land revenues. Two major administrative issues come to the fore in these documents: the problems involved in extracting revenue, and the problem of explaining why some people and not others participated in the rebellion of 1857. Proverbial speech is regularly quoted in these texts, as colonial authors address these separate but related crises of colonial rule.

Annotations of proverbial speech appear with great frequency in discussions of the specific patterns of rebellious activity in 1857 and of the causes of later revolts. Colonial authors were eager to explain differential degrees of rebellion in terms of the inherent characteristics of particular castes. For castes they perceived as having risen up against the British in the rebellion of 1857 or ones that are perceived as generally hostile to British rule, the code word is always "turbulent." In the case of castes such as the Gujar and the Meo, whose members did tend to actively rebel in 1857, nearly every author cites proverbs that appear to evaluate the caste in an unfavorable light, and comments on the veracity of the proverbial utterance. It is in descriptions of the "turbulent" castes that we encounter a veritable torrent of proverbs. In describing the Meos, for example, Crooke writes:

> In the Mutiny, they and the Gujars . . . were notorious for their turbulence, and seriously impeded the operations against Delhi. The popular idea of them is quite in unison with their history: *Pahle lat, pichhe bat; Dekhi tori Mewat; pahli gali, pichhe bat* are common proverbs, which mean that, in dealing with a Mewati, you had better kick or abuse him before doing business with him; their niggardliness is recorded by *Meo beti jab dee, jab okhali bhar rupaya rakhvale:* "the Meo will not give his daughter in marriage till he gets a mortar full of silver"; his blood-thirstiness—*Meo ka put barah baras men badla leta hai:* "the Meo's brat takes his revenge when he is twelve years old"; his toughness—*Meo mara jab janiye, jab tija ho jae:* "Never be sure that a Meo is dead till you see the third-day funeral ceremony performed." (Crooke 1896, III: 493)

For Crooke, proverbial speech justifies the harsh retaliation meted out to those who participated in the rebellion; even Indians themselves say that you've got to beat or kick a Meo.[7] Similarly, in his description of the Gujar caste, Crooke quotes from the emperor Babar's memoirs, in which he wrote that Gujars "were the wretches that really inflicted the chief hardships and were guilty of the chief oppression in the country."[8] Crooke continues, again producing proverbial speech to validate his assertions:

> They maintained their old reputation in the Mutiny when they perpetrated numerous outrages and seriously impeded the operations of the British Army before Delhi. According to the current wisdom of the countryside he is an undesirable neighbor—"The dog and the cat, the Gujar and the Ranghar, if these four were out of the world a man might sleep with his doors open" [and] "When the Dom made friends with the Gujar he was robbed of house and home." (Crooke 1896, III: 448)

Denzil C. J. Ibbetson, the Superintendent of Census Operations in the Panjab in 1881, also appropriated proverbial utterances for similar imperial purposes and integrated them almost seamlessly into his accounts of "turbulence" and insurrection. In the portion of the census report that was published under the title *Panjab Castes*, Ibbetson describes for example the Kharrals, a Muslim Rajput community, as "notorious for turbulence"

(1916: 174) and he quotes at length from Elphinstone's description of the caste in the Montgomery district:

> Their most celebrated leader, Ahmad Khan, who was killed in September 1857 by a detachment under Captain Black, headed the combined tribes . . . in no less than five insurrections, which to a certain extent all proved successful. . . . This success had spread his renown far and wide, and had given him a great influence over the whole of the [area], as was proved by the outbreak of 1857, which appears to have been mainly planned and organized by him. In stature the Kharrals are generally above the average height. (Quoted in Ibbetson 1916: 175)

Note how the description of a Kharral leader's "turbulence" is situated within Ibbetson's caste compendium, on a par as a caste characteristic with purely physical traits, and note also how after reproducing Elphinstone's comments, Ibbetson fully integrated Indian proverbial speech with imperial assessments:

> In Lahore they appear to bear a no better character than in Montgomery; and there is a Persian proverb: "The Dogar, the Bhatti, the Wattu, and the Kharral are all rebellious and ought to be slain." Sir Lepel Griffin writes of them: "Through all historic times the Kharrals have been a turbulent, savage, and thievish tribe, ever impatient of control, and delighting in strife and plunder."

British administrators were not in the habit of admiring Indians who were "impatient of control," and thus Ibbetson's account of the slaying of a Kharral leader by the British troops concludes with a proverb, deployed here to make the reader envision a world in which even Indians themselves believe that a Kharral should be killed, and believe also that revolt itself is merely a manifestation of innate Kharral violence.

These examples of proverbial speech that supposedly characterize wandering groups or groups whose members may once have engaged in peripatetic and/or thieving activities were particularly singled out by the British, as they defined categories of crime and criminality for colonial India, and as they attempted to naturalize revolt and non-compliance by confining it to certain castes supposedly set apart from the main body of the rural populace. As Bayly (1983: 220–222, 318) and Freitag (1991) have shown, peripatetic banditry was, in pre-British India, often seen as an acceptable mode of establishing political authority, for Gujars and other similar groups. During the nineteenth century, however, critical changes in colonial and Indian elite perception of these groups had occurred, partly as a result of the expansion of the land-revenue-based colonial state. Thus, as Freitag points out, "British administrators used as their informants members of the elite stratum of landed society," and thus the legal institutions and cultural valuations that emerged from this encounter "reflected an amalgam of sedentary South Asian values and British priorities" (1991: 229). It is entirely likely then that these proverbs about Gujars, Meos, Kharrals, and the like gained significance as a result of the transformation of rural society in the nineteenth century, and that they reflect the particular position of an agrarian elite struggling to safeguard its own political authority. And it is also possible, in some parts of northern India, that members of the landed elite told such proverbs to administrators as a means of deflecting the responsibility for plundering that they themselves coerced some members of the so-called "criminal castes" to carry out, providing protection and support in exchange for a large share of the booty (Nigam 1990b). Informants' elite identities were no doubt decisive, as British administrators questioned them about rural society and collected proverbs as specimens of the "ideas of the common people." Yet this positionality is thoroughly erased, as the speech of a particularly situated set of informants was entextualized as "the current wisdom" and as invariable "popular ideas."

The relation between proverbs and the disciplinary thrust of the colonial government against the "turbulent" castes is nowhere more explicitly set forth than in C. E. A. W. Oldham's essay "The Proverbs of the People in a District (Shahabad) of Northern India," originally read as an address before the Folklore Society in London. He remarks at the outset that his observations are based on materials gathered during twenty years of administrative service in the district of Shahabad in Bihar. He describes the geography of the district in two sentences, and then refers immediately to the "warlike" races of the region: "It is part of ancient Karusadesa, the 'country of the Karusas,' referred to in the old Sanskrit texts as a very warlike race" (1930: 322). He writes at some length of the "martial races" of the Bhojpuri region, and of the Bhojpuri Ahir caste in particular:

> [T]he Bhojpuri Ahirs (the cowherd caste) are specially noted for their daring and skill as thieves and burglars, the more law-abiding people in other parts regarding them with terror. . . . During widespread disturbances in 1917, which broke out without previous warning in this district, and threatened to involve the neighbouring districts in grave communal strife, I had to call in a large force of military and armed police (about a thousand in all) to quell promptly and effectively the lawlessness abroad.
>
> Several proverbial sayings might be cited as exemplifying these characteristics. For instance, there are some very popular verses in praise of their favorite weapon, commonly called the 'Song of the *lathi* [stick]' telling of its uses in crossing a stream or ditch, in dealing with enemies human or canine, and how necessary it is to carry one, even if you have a sword hanging by your side. There is a well-known proverb that says,—"Don't go into

Bhojpur; if you go, don't stay; if you stay, don't eat; if you eat, don't go to sleep; if you sleep, don't feel for your purse; if you should feel for your purse, don't weep!" (i.e., you will not find it!). . . . Then we have a proverb which means "If hit, hit back, and don't stop to consider whether you are committing a sin or virtue." And there is a delightfully terse and suggestive saying, specially quoted of the Bhojpuri, as representing his attitude toward others. The words mean simply "Is the dish thine or mine?" A Bhojpuri is supposed to ask this question. If the person addressed answers, "Mine," a blow of the lathi at once settles the proprietorship. . . . "The clenched fist for an enemy"; "the powerful man's lathi hits the very middle of the forehead"; and so on. So much for the mere joy of fighting. (Oldham 1930: 323–324)

The naturalization of rebellion here could not be more direct. Oldham characterizes the 1917 events in Shahabad only as "disturbances" that might lead to "communal strife." Violence had in fact erupted in Shahabad in 1917 over the issue of Cow-Protection, but to argue as Oldham implicitly does here, that this was simply a manifestation of age-old Hindu-Muslim conflict exacerbated by the violent nature of the Ahirs, is to erase the specifically political meanings of the events, just as Risley's notion of "survivals" robs subversive proverbs of their political meanings as tokens of resistance. Ahir participation in the riots was, as Gyan Pandey argues (1983), a response to severe dislocation of social and economic relations brought about under colonialism, and a move on the part of this lower ranked caste to assert a Hindu orthodoxy that would secure for them a higher status vis-à-vis the upper-caste zamindari communities, in the wake of Risley's attempt to list castes in an unambiguous "order of precedence" in the 1901 census. And Oldham does not tell the reader that these disturbances in Shahabad had followed Gandhi's mobilization of peasants in the neighboring district of Champaran against European indigo planters, that Shahabad had for some time been the scene of organized peasant struggle against the colonial government, zamindars, and moneylenders (Roy Choudhary 1966: 86; Nath 1980: 228), and that the issue of "Cow-Protection" had become intertwined with rumors about the end of British rule (Sarkar 1983: 157).

In Oldham's text these "disturbances" that are quelled by a thousand armed military police are instead explained by quoting or paraphrasing proverbial speech purportedly referring to the inherent and invariant nature of the Ahirs, a "martial race." Since Oldham sees proverbs used by the people of India as exemplifying the "working of their minds" (1930: 320), as a "guide to their character and their actions" (321), as "regulat[ing] their conservative lives" (320), and as accurate portrayals of the traits, habits, vices, and propensities of particular castes (335), his citing of these proverbs about the lathis of the Ahirs thus establishes to his satisfaction that the Ahirs are by nature prone to violence, and as he recounts these proverbs in connection with the mention of his prompt deployment of the police and the military, the reader is thus expected to discern that the exercise of the armed might of the colonial government was necessitated by the violent nature of the Ahirs as a caste, and not by their response to the burdens imposed by the revenue demands of the landowning zamindars and by the colonial government. The reader is also expected to discern that "the country folk" themselves feel exactly the same way about the Ahirs, because proverbs show us the "working of their minds" (Oldham 1930: 320–321). The essentialization of Ahir character accomplished through this embedding of proverbs in the colonial text serves both to naturalize revolt and to legitimate in Oldham's eyes the deployment of the military police as a disciplinary measure.

Proverbs figured prominently in discussions of land revenue as well. The district-by-district land settlement reports that focus on patterns of landholding and the social characteristics of the district expected to affect revenue collection often contain lengthy quotations of proverbs that allegedly provide an understanding of the character of specific landholding castes and their inclination or disinclination to meet land revenue demands.

The 1880 *Report on the Revised Land Revenue Settlement of the Rohtak District of the Hissar Division in the Punjab* by W. E. Purser and H. C. Fanshawe provides examples of the entextualizing strategies through which a text about caste and compliance with revenue demands was constructed. For castes that were understood to have rebelled in 1857 and were also perceived to chronically fail to meet their revenue demands, proverbs again were used to illustrate the justice of British reprisals. Muslim Rajputs, for example, are universally decried in colonial writing, as bearing "the worst possible reputation for turbulence and cattle-stealing," and for giving the British "much trouble in the mutiny" (Ibbetson 1916). Purser and Fanshawe wrote at length of the Muslim Rajputs, the Ranghars.

> The conduct of this tribe [the Ranghars] in the Mutiny . . . bears the worst possible character among the people of the countryside. . . . Their turbulence and lawlessness is [sic] commemorated in the following well-known lines—"Though Kanhaur and Niganah are but 35 kos from Delhi, the people eat themselves what they sow, and pay not a grain (of revenue) to anyone."
> (Purser and Fanshawe 1880)

In the section of the Rohtak Settlement Report entitled "Social and Administrative," Purser and Fanshawe list the castes of the district and comment on their supposed habits, level of industry in agriculture, conduct in the 1857 rebellion, and cooperation insofar as revenue collection is concerned. The deployment of proverbs in order to construct a discourse on the latter issue is particularly obvious in their text. The castes of the district are divided into two groups: the agriculturalists and the "non-agricultural portions of the population." The former section contains numerous proverbs, utilized especially to comment on the ease or difficulty attendant on the collection of land revenues; but the descriptions in the latter section are far briefer and contain no proverbs at all; the quotation and annotation of proverbial speech here would apparently have served no useful administrative purpose for Purser and Fanshawe.

A similar tendency to quote proverbial speech only in administratively useful characterizations is evident in Ibbetson's *Report on the Settlement of the Panipat Tahsil and Karnal Parganah of the Karnal District, 1872–1880*. In this report, Ibbetson provides no examples of proverbial speech about the Rajputs, whom he praises as "fine, brave men" whose leaders have preserved a commendable degree of "feudal" authority. But for Gujars, who are said to practice cultivation "of the most slovenly description," the reader again encounters a torrential flow of proverbial quotation, ending with *jitte dekhen Gujar, itte deyie mar*, "wherever you see a Gujar, hit him" (1883: 83–84). Similarly, Brahmans are described as "vile cultivators, being lazy to a degree; and they carry the grasping and overbearing habits of their caste into their relations as land owners, so that wherever Brahmans hold land, disputes may be expected. The local proverb goes *Brahman se bura bagar se kal*, 'As famine from a desert, so comes evil from a Brahman'" (1883: 86–87).

The annotations of proverbial speech produced by Crooke, Ibbetson, Oldham, and others were deployed principally, as we have seen, in accounts of various castes and their supposed predispositions to engage in revolt or resistance to revenue demands, in the project of naturalizing these challenges to the notion that India was governed with the consent of the colonized. In imperial ethnographic accounts, people were seen as rebelling against British rule not for political or ideological reasons, but because they were by nature predisposed to "turbulence."

In colonial writing in the second half of the nineteenth century, proverbs were wrenched from the social practices and improvisations in which they were used, and interpreted not as situated commentaries but as abstract and literal renderings of caste proclivities. These renderings were then quoted or paraphrased and deployed in colonial writing, principally in connection with the "naturalization" of revolt and of revenue non-compliance, and also as guides to military discipline. The discursive reifications of caste, intimately tied at their genesis to the politics of colonial rule, became later the foundation of much anthropological and historical writing on Indian society.

The discursive practices through which proverbial speech was embedded in colonial texts of the late nineteenth century rendered invisible two moments of entextualization: officials render invisible their own links to

212 / Social Distinctions of Caste and Class

proverbial speech by not recognizing the fact that proverbs may be told to them selectively by "informants" (especially members of the local elites) who thus position themselves in relation to members of other local groups as they present themselves to the colonial state; and by speaking of proverbs as indices of consensus and of invariant "custom," they render invisible the everyday rhetorical and discursive strategies in which proverbs by their very nature figure as situated communicative practices, as modes of persuasion and contestation rather than agreement.

NOTES

1. On the situated pragmatic meaning of proverbs and the strategic use of this speech genre, see Abrahams and Babcock 1977; Briggs 1985; Burke 1973; de Certeau 1984: 18–21; Gossen 1973; Raheja 1995; and Seitel 1977.

2. The process of entextualization is one through which speech is detached from the situation of its utterance and interpreted without regard to the conditions of its production or the operations embarked upon by the speaker, and thus understood as a fixed or "authentic" cultural text. This process is, as Bauman and Briggs (1990) and Kuipers (1990) point out, an act of control, an instance in which the political economy of cultural discourses comes to the fore; marking a body of utterances as a text or ahistorical "tradition" is frequently part of a larger set of strategies for seizing or consolidating discursive control or authority.

3. Cohn (1985) has brilliantly described the general relationship between the "command of language and the language of command" in late-eighteenth- and nineteenth-century colonial India. For a discussion of colonial representations of African languages, see Fabian 1986 and Irvine 1993. Rafael (1993) analyzes the politics of translation in the Philippines under Spanish rule.

4. For discussions of the broader political ramifications of this colonial discourse that speaks of Indians as in thrall to "tradition," see for example Chatterjee 1989; Inden 1990; and Mani 1984, 1989.

5. I have elsewhere discussed at greater length the role played by native elites in the construction of a colonial discourse on Indian society (Raheja 1999).

6. Neither Crooke nor Ibbetson agreed with Risley's view of the immutability of caste, and Ibbetson repeatedly stressed the fluidity of caste (Pinney 1990: 257). Further, Crooke and Ibbetson differed between themselves as to the assessment of the centrality of the Brahman or the kingly Rajput in caste organization, but they both nonetheless produced torrents of proverb quotations to illustrate what they apparently regarded as essentialized caste characteristics. The developing formation of a colonial discourse on caste and the developing imperial uses of essentializations of caste identity seem to have been so powerful that they eclipsed some of these important theoretical differences among them.

7. Mayaram (1991) describes colonial appropriations of the oral narrative of Darya Khan used to construct a history of Meo "criminality." The paper effectively critiques essentializing characterizations of Meos as predatory and turbulent, but does not discuss the larger dimensions of colonial representations of caste and caste ideology.

8. For some contemporary Gujar views of their actions in 1857, see Raheja 1988: 4–5, 255 n. 3. Stokes (1978, 1986) and Bhadra (1985) document the extent of

Gujar participation in the rebellion, but Stokes also rejects the view that patterns of rebellion can be accounted for in terms of caste. Thus, although Stokes's approach to the rebellion of 1857 is limited because it resolutely avoids attributing any causal force to political ideology on the part of those who rebelled, he does critique, indirectly, the colonial tendency to "naturalize" revolt by accounting for it in terms of the inherent traits of particular castes.

Anjali's Prospects:
Class Mobility in Urban India

Sara Dickey

In 1985, I took my first research trip to Madurai, a large city in southern India. After moving into an apartment in a downtown neighborhood, I started walking through the nearby streets, wondering how I would ever get to know my neighbors. In this densely built part of the city, brick and plaster houses are constructed wall-to-wall, and doors open right onto the street. Through those doors, I could sometimes glimpse passageways that led back to other homes. Late one afternoon, in front of such an entryway, I saw a group of children playing. A small boy and girl called me over, and all the children crowded around asking me to take their picture. The mother of the boy and girl heard the clamor, looked out, and invited me in. I followed her into their one-room house, which was long and narrow and ran along the street. There were several similar homes in the compound, all linked by a single roof, adjoining walls, and a central courtyard.

Anjali and Kumar, the two children, turned out to be seven and five years old. Their father was out working that day, driving a cycle rickshaw, and their three older siblings were still on their way home from school. From that day on, over the next fifteen months, Anjali and Kumar taught me Tamil proverbs and stick games and movie plots, and were delightful companions. We have remained close. Each time I return, we smile over a favorite photograph of the two children sitting on a windowsill in my old apartment, reading a picture book together. Then they pull down another photo from the same time, in which I am typing field notes for my dissertation, and they point out that back then my hair was long and braided, as a woman's should be. All of our lives have changed since then. I have short hair and a college teaching position and a child of my own. Anjali became the first person in her family to go to college, and then she became a computer graphics designer. With the wages that she and her siblings make, her parents have been able to pay off old debts and buy a television. But Anjali's father was injured recently and can no longer drive a rickshaw, and as his children marry and start to use their earnings for their own new households, his family's hard-won financial security becomes threatened. At the same time, his wife is trying to arrange Anjali's marriage. Yet despite all these changes in our lives, most of us are living out predictable life cycles and circumstances. The only one of us whose material circumstances may eventually be substantially different from her parents' is Anjali.

In both the United States and India, myths of upward class mobility are common and important. In both countries, most families actually maintain similar socioeconomic circumstances from generation to generation (e.g., Featherman and Hauser 1978; Driver and Driver 1987: 39–52; Rao 1989: 24; Béteille 1991; Solon 1992; Conley 1999). Movement out of the lower strata is especially difficult. Yet many of us know someone whose class is dramatically different from his or her parents', and in India there is other anecdotal evidence to support the myth. For one thing, economic circumstances often do vary within a single generation. As in Anjali's family, household income can rise and fall significantly according to how many children are employed, while daughters' marriages or family members' illnesses can require huge expenditures that deplete savings and increase debt for years. Changes like these are usually cyclical. Recently, liberalization of the Indian economy has created potentially longer-term social change. Loans for small business enterprises are now more easily acquired, newly available consumer goods serve as investments as well as signs of class achievement, and new technological sectors provide a host of skilled jobs. All of these changes appear to have contributed to noticeable growth in the Indian middle class since the mid-1980s (Kulkarni 1993; Mankekar 1999: 8–9, 75–76). Nonetheless, upward class mobility remains elusive for most people.

Class is one of numerous systems of hierarchy that shape everyday life in India. Social hierarchies such as class, caste, gender, and age help a person determine, among other things, how to interact with other people—how to act toward and speak to them, what responsibilities might be had for them, and what kinds of help might be requested from them. Of course, like any other system of rules, these are frequently broken or manipulated; but they are followed more often than not, and they help people know what their ideal behavior should be—at least according to a particular set of rules.

Of these different forms of hierarchy, class has arguably received the least attention from scholars, and is often ignored in favor of caste. Caste is a form of rank that, like class, has social and economic aspects, but also carries ritual implications. It is embodied—embedded in the substance of people's bodies—and is passed on from parents to children. While caste provides a group membership that people retain throughout their lives, class standing can change both upward and downward. Although statistically there is some correspondence between class and caste rankings—

people of higher castes *in general* are wealthier than people of lower castes
—there are numerous exceptions. There are many people like Anjali (who
belongs to the high-ranked Pillai caste) who are high-caste but not wealthy,
and many lower-caste people who are economically well-off.[1] There is no
straightforward correspondence between class and caste rankings, and any
person can at least theoretically be or become a member of any class.

Class is one of the most salient idioms of identity in contemporary India, especially in urban areas, and wealth and education provide two of
the most direct means to social and political power (Kumar 1988; Dickey
1993; Kapadia 1995; Fernandes 1997). Furthermore, class is recognized as
a potent social force by Madurai residents. All of the people I interviewed
during my research in 1999–2000 and 2001 said that class had a greater impact on their life opportunities than did caste. Such impressions are a sign
of the salience that class holds in the everyday lives and imaginations of
urban residents.

One reason that class is so significant in urban life is that class standing, unlike caste membership, is highly visible. This makes it an important
indicator of social position in the relatively anonymous setting of the city.
Unlike villages and small towns, where families have generally known one
another for generations, and where the number of castes to be identified is
relatively small, in more urban areas it is difficult to judge caste accurately
by looking at or speaking briefly with a person. Many symbols of class, on
the other hand, are immediately evident upon meeting someone, including
clothing, hygiene, speech, manners, and movement, and sometimes education, occupation, and housing. If you speak for a while with people or visit
their homes, you may also learn which books and newspapers they read,
whether they drink tea or coffee, how they decorate their homes and what
kinds of consumer goods they display, what kind of cooking fuel they use
and which vegetables they cook with it. All of these are signs of class.

Such symbols are important to understanding the nature of class because class is both an economic and a symbolic system. By this I mean that
economic and symbolic factors work together to produce an individual's
class. In my view, class derives not only from income, material assets, and
occupation—the economic sources that usually come to mind when we
think of what determines our class—but also from such cultural and social
"capital" as education, consumption habits, fashion, and ways of speaking (see also Bourdieu 1984; Caplan 1987: 14; Liechty forthcoming; Ortner
1991: 170, 1998: 3–4; Tolen 2000). As I have argued elsewhere (Dickey 2000:
467), what makes class a distinct form of hierarchy, and not just a variation
on caste, is its more fundamental basis in economic power, combined with
the status markers that financial resources can produce—such as education, honor, and conspicuous consumption—which themselves become
sources of economic power.

My argument runs counter to most sociological and anthropological theories about class, which generally view economic factors as fundamental to class, and symbolic features either as derivative of economics or as irrelevant to class per se. Most of these theories derive from the work of Karl Marx and Max Weber. Marx argued that the mode of production determines a society's economic base, which in turn determines its legal and political superstructure (with the latter including all the "cultural" elements that I refer to as symbolic) (Marx 1994a, 1994b). Weber, on the other hand, divided economic and symbolic factors between two types of social stratification, class and status. He argued that class standing is determined by the market value of property, skills, and services, while symbolic forms of identity are much more relevant to a person's status group, which is defined by its "style of life" (expressed especially through consumption) and ranked according to level of honor (Weber 1968). While both these writers and their followers recognize the impact of symbolic aspects of culture on class to some extent, the notable difference in my approach remains that I view these symbolic aspects as themselves playing a *fundamental* role in producing a person's class. The value of examining symbolic and material features together is demonstrated by Anjali's case.

What is the locus of class? Put another way, where does a person's class come from? I contend that, in India, the family is the source of an individual's class.[2] This argument counters some of the only other discussions of the locus of class in India, such as those by Karin Kapadia (1995) and Selvy Thiruchendran (1997), both of whom argue that class is an individual phenomenon and must be defined for each person separately from the family. Kapadia, for example, argues that family members in the same household can be of vastly different classes, since in her assessment class derives from occupation and education, which can vary widely within each family (Kapadia 1995: 251–252). This is a provcative argument that, among other things, helps to highlight the widening gap in the opportunities available to women and to men, but it does not isolate the locus of class effectively.

I contend that the family serves as the source of an individual's class in two ways. First, other people judge an individual's class standing by looking at the individual's family, using signs such as family members' occupations, education, housing, and consumer goods. Second, it is primarily the family that provides and decides upon the resources and opportunities available to each individual (Béteille 1991). Family members share a pool of material resources, and the family head makes decisions about how to divide those resources. Family members also play a large part in deciding how much education individual members receive, and which if any jobs or careers they should aim for. Finally, each generation passes on cultural and social as well as economic "capital"—including knowledge, values, and social networks—to the next generation (Peace 1984, Béteille 1991: 16–19).

Unlike most other urban residents, Anjali appears poised to move up in class standing. How might this happen? How does class mobility occur in urban India, and how secure is it? The story that Anjali tells helps to answer these questions. It reveals the importance of education, the role that family plays in passing on class and making decisions that affect its members' class, and the role that both symbolic and economic features play in determining a person's class and the chances of improving class standing.

What is Anjali's class? Most visitors from affluent foreign countries, along with well-to-do Indians, would look at Anjali's family and judge them to be poor. They would probably base their judgments on the parents' occupations and education, on the size of the family's house, and on the work the children do. But Anjali's family, like other people of similar means in Madurai, do not view themselves as poor. They describe themselves as "in the middle" (*naṭuttaramānavarkaḷ*) or, using the English word, "normal."[3] (Although the Tamil term "naṭuttaramānavarkaḷ" is similar to the U.S. English phrase "middle class," in Madurai this category denotes a position of significantly less financial security than it usually does in the United States.) They use indicators such as the children's education, types of food eaten in the household, the family's financial security and debts, family members' clothing and neatness, and the sturdiness and location of the housing. According to their categories, people who are poor, for example, have only enough money to buy food and other necessities for a single day at best, live in cheaper housing (made of mud, metal sheets, or cardboard), eat fewer meals and less nutritious and high-status food, have less education, and have almost no "modern" consumer goods such as cassette players, televisions, or refrigerators. Some of the difference in our respective judgments lies in varying perceptions of the status of occupations, and some of it lies in uneven knowledge of which signs to use and how to discriminate between what seem to outsiders to be fine gradations but are in fact significant cultural distinctions.

When I first met Anjali and her family, Anjali was in the third grade and very interested in reading and in language. Her parents, like most parents without much money, decided how long to keep their children in school by balancing each child's interest and success in school against the expenses of sending them there. They were also typical in seeing education as the single most important factor in improving their children's chances for the future. Educating children is expensive, however. Private schools are popularly viewed as providing the best education and the strongest chances of succeeding on standardized examinations (which will eventually determine entrance to and scholarships for postsecondary educational institutions), and the fees for these schools can be extremely high. Even government schools, which do not charge high fees, still require additional expenditures on uniforms, books, paper, pens, and other school supplies. In addition, children who attend school cannot work for the small wages that in some families are crucial for meeting housing, food, and medical expenses.

Anjali's family's income was small, but it was enough to get by on without sending the young children out to work. Anjali in particular was very interested in studying. She eventually completed secondary school, a relatively high level of education. Her parents had studied only through the fifth grade, but had educated all of their children through the ninth to twelfth grades. It is rare for a daughter to receive more education than her brothers (her sister, for example, finished the tenth grade and then married a doctor's assistant and moved to another city), but from the tenth grade onward, Anjali began hoping to go to college. She told me, "I was interested in studying computers. I wanted at the minimum to finish a degree. I thought that at least I should study, since no one else in the family has gone to college. And my older brothers told me that they would help since I was their only younger sister." When she finally told her parents, however, they resisted.

> *A.:* They said, "We don't have the money—how can you possibly go to college?" So after completing +2 [the final year of secondary school], I went to take a typing course. My parents had said, "All right, go ahead and learn typing. We will support that." The director at the typing center asked me—he said, "You have a tough situation. There is a job open here. Would you like to work while you are studying?" So I took the job typing and was able to study for my B.Com. [bachelor of commerce] degree.
>
> *S.:* Your parents didn't continue to say you couldn't study?
>
> *A.:* No. Because I was so interested, they said, "Okay, you can study. We will adjust [financially] and help you."

Anjali was able to cover most of the costs of her studies with her typing income, and her parents accommodated the loss of her income toward other household expenses. She worked full-time, and completed her entire degree through a three-year correspondence course from the university. She would work at her job all day, study at home in the evenings while the rest of the family was socializing in the same room, and then get up early in the morning to attend two hours of "tuition" (tutoring) with dozens of other students in the nearby home of a university professor, before going to her job again. Anjali said that the time in a day was "just exactly long enough" to fit everything in. She did find studying difficult. It wasn't just that she had no quiet place to read, but also, as she said, "There was no one at home who could teach me; they are all uneducated." No one could help her study, or empathize with the problems and pressures she faced in finishing a college degree.

Anjali was interested in working with computers, and her parents agreed that the computer field was promising for her future career and marriage prospects. After finishing her B.Com. Anjali took a six-month computer certificate course that taught her the rudiments of computer hardware and software. This training makes her part of the growing but still tiny minority of computer-literate people in Madurai. With it she obtained a position two years ago in a small graphics design office near her home, where she was taught to create the calendars, business cards, and invitations produced by the company. When I saw her a year into this work, Anjali confided that her dream was to obtain a degree in computer programming, work for a technological firm, and eventually run her own business, but her family's limited economic resources, as well as their lack of the social contacts that are so crucial to gaining placement in competitive professions (cf. Béteille 1991: 19 and passim), appeared to prevent her from taking any of these steps.

Anjali's position gave her family an additional Rs. 1,000 per month. It also placed her in a social environment that would have been inaccessible if she, like most other women of marriageable age, had stayed at home after finishing her education. The office on the floor above hers holds a small videography business specializing in wedding and party videos, and down the corridor is a computer and Internet center. She has made close friends with people her age working in these offices. Puri, who works next door, has taught her how to find affordable stylish clothing and to groom her hair in new ways. Both women are close friends with Murugan, one of the videographers. Until recently, such a friendship with a young man was unheard of for proper young women. Anjali's work has given her a new sophistication, which derives not just from her contact with computers, but also from her knowledge of fashion, casual friendships with men her age, a confident way of speaking, and an awareness of the world outside her family and neighbors. She is experimenting with modernity, an important element of a higher-class image (Hancock 1999: 25–27; Mankekar 1999: 48–49, 74–89).

Anjali's arrival at this point has not simply been an individual accomplishment; it has required the joint efforts and support of her family members. Her parents kept all their children in school through high school, despite their difficult financial circumstances. Anjali's parents and elder brothers had the authority to say whether and what she could study. They allowed Anjali to go on to college and get computer training because they felt these courses would be good for her intellectually and economically, and because she was able to finance her studies by working full-time. They too contributed financially. Anjali herself was an agent in this project, persuading her parents to let her study, working full-time as she carried a full courseload, and shouldering the pressure of a college education largely alone. Her family was willing to support her because of her academic interest and success, but also because her education and computer-related career give the family prestige and enhance Anjali's prospects of making a "good" marriage. Through everyone's efforts, Anjali has gained the education, work skills, sophistication, modern sensibility, and even social connections that could make her eligible to join a higher class.

In the meantime, with Anjali and her three brothers working, her family had become more comfortable financially. For a brief period, her mother—who manages the household finances—felt secure enough to stop worrying about how to make ends meet. She paid off debts, put money aside for her eldest son's wedding, and began to consider what kind of groom to find for Anjali.

But then Anjali's father was seriously injured. One day about six months after Anjali began her new job, her father had picked up a heavy parcel from an office for a delivery and was carrying it down several flights of stairs. He slipped on a step and the box struck him on his upper spine. That night he began to have seizures. His frightened family rushed him to the Government Hospital, which offers free care to all patients. When they arrived, however, they found there was a strike at the hospital, and felt forced to take their father to a private clinic. X-rays there showed nerve damage that required surgery in order to avoid paralysis. Because like most Indians Anjali's family has no medical insurance, they knew they would be liable for all medical costs. The surgery alone amounted to well over a year's income for any member of their household, and X-rays and medications were also prohibitively expensive. But as Anjali said, "We thought, 'We have to get him treatment even though it means going into great debt. Our father has to be there for us.'" Without telling their father, they used the money that had been put aside for the eldest son's wedding, sold the mother's jewelry, and borrowed the rest from neighborhood moneylenders at the high rate of 10 percent interest per month.[4] According to Anjali, the physician they consulted was shaken by the extremity of their circumstances and would not charge them for his or his clinic's services. He cautioned, however, that they would have to pay the surgeon, "otherwise he will not come." This same surgeon, Anjali said, would have treated her father "for free at the [Government] Hospital, but because he treated him outside, he wanted Rs. 15,000" before he would begin the surgery. Currently one person's wages—a third of the household income—go to pay off the interest and principal on the loans each month. Their father has recovered somewhat, but he is unlikely to work in the future.

Anjali is twenty-three, older than most unmarried women of her caste and class. Marriage, which is almost always seen in India as an alliance between families rather than a romantic partnering of individuals, is a key point at which family statuses are negotiated, effected, and displayed to the social public. Anjali's parents had decided to delay her marriage until after her oldest brother's so that they could augment her dowry with the money the new daughter-in-law would bring.[5] Now her brother has been married, but the money his wife brought offset only a small portion of their father's medical expenses. Anjali's parents are now looking for a husband for her at a time when they have not only lost the father's income, but have also incurred significant debt.

Searching for a groom is always a complicated business of finding the best combination of a "good" family (one that is sufficiently respectable, financially secure, and good-tempered) with a "good" son (someone who has the proper personality, job prospects, and horoscope), and then attempting to provide the dowry that such a family demands. Dowries vary according to caste and the earning potential of the groom, but in general they represent a very large outlay, usually at least five years' worth of income among the middle classes and mid- to high-level castes. Anjali's parents hope to find her a "government servant" (a member of the civil service or other branches of the government), or at least a business owner. These positions are a large step up from Anjali's father's occupation as a rickshaw driver, and the class standing of such men's families is ranked much higher on the local scale. Anjali is educated, sophisticated, and personable enough, however, to attract a family with such a son.

I asked Anjali about the differences between these types of grooms.

S.: When I was talking with your mother about your marriage, she said that your life would be better with a husband who has a government job. What would the differences be between marrying someone with a government job and someone with his own business? Do you know what I mean?

A.: Yes. For a person employed by the government, things [i.e. his salary and position] can only improve, they can't get worse. And after retirement, he will get a pension and all that. If he dies suddenly, his children or wife will be given a position. They will get a pension. Throughout their lives, there will be something [i.e., some income to rely on]. For someone in business, sometimes things will be good, sometimes there will be losses. When they lose money, they can't look after the family. It will be hard. So people prefer government jobs.

I asked Anjali whether her parents would look for a groom of their own class, or perhaps of a lower or higher class. Whereas most people I interviewed said that parents prefer to find grooms from families of similar means so that their daughters will be comfortable in the social setting of their new home, Anjali replied, "My parents will look for a little higher level. They'll think, 'So far she has lived in hardship. At least her life could be different after her marriage.' They will do that with the hope that at least after marriage, I can be comfortable compared with the hard life I have led so far." I asked, "Won't it be hard for you to live in such a place?" She answered philosophically, "I will have to change to fit with the way they are. That's all. It will be a bit difficult in the beginning. But I can observe what they are like, and I can change." This is the stock response of young women as they prepare for marriage in an unknown household, but in Anjali's case it also evokes the difficulty of adjusting to the material surroundings, consumption practices, manners, and social assumptions of people raised in a different class. As Tamils say, she would have to learn to "move" in such company, speaking and dressing and behaving appropriately.

As Anjali points out, government servants in India have secure employment for life; they are also guaranteed a pension and a position for a child or spouse upon the employee's death or retirement. Yet government servants ask for such high dowries—in the Pillai caste that Anjali's family belongs to, 20 "sovereigns" of gold jewelry (160g, 5.5 oz.) and Rs. 15,000–20,000 in cash, according to Anjali's mother—that such a groom may be out of reach for her family. Families of young men who have their own businesses ask for about half of these amounts, still a huge expense for a family whose primary wage-earner made Rs. 1,000 per month when he was working, and which has no savings remaining. Yet if Anjali could marry someone with financial security, she would not have to worry about poverty herself, and she might eventually be able to help her parents and her siblings. Given Anjali's skills and the immense security such a marriage could bring her, the step is worth taking if at all possible. Before her father's injuries, with five household members working and her brother about to be married, this goal seemed realizable. Now, it feels farther off, but remains something they still work toward.

Recently the family made another decision that keeps Anjali's prospects open. When Anjali's employers decided to move their business across town, Anjali suggested to her parents that they get a bank loan to open her own design business in the old office. Anjali had plenty of experience both with design and with managing the company's daily affairs, and those skills, along with the advantage of retaining the same office—and therefore the same customer base—made her confident that she could run a successful business on her own. She could also employ her brother Kumar, whose screen-printing skills would add to her output. When I last saw Anjali and her family, they had refurnished the small office, completed most of the arduous process of securing a bank loan for computer equipment, and obtained a new computer from one of Anjali's old classmates who sells computer hardware. The classmate's father happens to be the manager of the bank where Anjali's family has applied for the loan, and as he knew that his father had already promised to provide the loan, he was thereby assured that the purchasing price would be forthcoming. In the meantime, Anjali's mother had stopped talking about finding a groom. When I asked why, she said they were waiting to get the business well established because they hoped its income would substitute for a portion of the dowry. In the meantime, Anjali and her two unmarried brothers will continue working, and every rupee left over from household maintenance and loan repayment will be put toward the rest of her dowry—at least until another emergency strikes.

In the United States, middle- and upper-class people tend to think of class mobility as an individual endeavor. If you work hard enough at getting an education or earning a living, you can get ahead. In India, the vision tends to be one of group effort: if you educate your children and pick the right careers and then the right marriage alliances for them, their lives will improve and so might yours. Through a combination of joint financial effort, careful strategizing about Anjali's education and career, effective use of social networks, and Anjali's own talents and drive, Anjali's family seems poised to attain this ideal.

At the same time, the family's own history shows how difficult reaching this point is. Simply *maintaining* current resources can become impossible when illness strikes, or when a wage-earner dies or is incapacitated, since there are no "safety nets" of health and disability insurance, retirement plans, or even low-interest loans. Such events can immediately wipe out a family's savings in cash and assets, and plunge them into debt. Even children's marriages can increase financial hardship, since they may remove wage-earners from the household, and daughters' weddings often require an extremely high outlay of cash and goods. Expensive marriages also bring honor to the family, by demonstrating the family's resources and indicating the type of people willing to create an alliance with them; but like the losses incurred by illness or unemployment, they reduce the savings and other financial capital available to the family for making other long-term investments or for providing a safety net when other tragedies strike.

Anjali's potential gains have also been limited by her family's lack of cultural and social, as well as economic, resources. Their lack of experience with higher education, for example, made Anjali's college experience more challenging than many of her peers', and their lack of contacts in prestigious professions and institutions limits Anjali's ability to obtain a high-status and lucrative career.

Even education, that most vaunted social, cultural, and economic resource for upward mobility, is itself insufficient as a means of entering a higher class. A degree must be accompanied by other symbolic attributes that make one a proper member of a higher class. To be seen as an appropriate addition to a civil servant's or business owner's family, Anjali must adapt her dress, grooming, speech, and manners. She has already been able to learn much of this as a result of her education—by reading, by learning about computers, and by adapting to the social environments she has observed among fellow students at "tuition" and her peers at work. People in Madurai frequently ridicule those who use their money or educational attainments to act "high-class" but retain the values and behaviors of the lesser class in which they originated. If Anjali does marry into a higher-class family, she will have to continue to mold herself into the proper image.

Moreover, she will be viewed by friends and acquaintances as a member of a higher class not merely because of how she presents herself—although this will suffice for casual encounters—but primarily because of the circumstances and image of the family she has married into. Before her marriage her natal family has determined her class, and as a married woman her marital family will provide the context by which others will judge her. Thus Anjali's class standing, like other people's, comes from her family in two ways: her class is judged on the basis of her family's circumstances, and the opportunities she has to change or maintain those circumstances are determined and decided upon primarily by her family members rather than by Anjali herself.

Even with the economic opportunities provided by the contemporary Indian economy, upward class mobility remains difficult to achieve because of the barriers to financial security faced by lower- and middle-class people. When class mobility is realized, education, family contributions and status, and the acquisition of both symbolic and economic criteria are critical to its achievement and maintenance. Anjali's family provided financial and emotional support that have allowed her to gain an education and other symbolic attributes of a higher class status. Anjali and her parents may be able to consolidate these gains through marriage with a more socially prestigious and economically secure family. Whether they are finally able to overcome the odds against her long-term upward mobility, however, remains to be seen.

ACKNOWLEDGMENTS

I am grateful to Susan Bell, Stephanie Dickey, and the editors of this volume for their close readings and thoughtful comments on this chapter. Mary Hancock also provided suggestions that helped refine my concepts and arguments. A version of this essay was presented at the Women, Culture, and Development Colloquium of the University of California, Santa Barbara.

NOTES

1. These exceptions also appear at the aggregate level. The Nadars, for example, have a low ranking in the caste system but are one of the wealthiest groups in Madurai, while Brahmans, the highest-ranked caste, are not among the very wealthiest castes. On the other hand, the lowest castes do tend to be the poorest ones.

2. By family I refer specifically to a person's family members who live in the household and to other members who may live away but still make regular finan-

cial contributions to the household. I do not include the larger extended family of kin who live separately and do not contribute financially to the person's household.

3. People of Anjali's family's socioeconomic standing and higher generally use a three-part model of class, including poor people, middle people, and wealthy people. Poorer people usually employ a two-part model, composed of poor people and rich people. Because all of these class categories include people with a wide range of socioeconomic circumstances, when Anjali wants to be precise she qualifies her family's "middle-class" ranking by saying they are "between the low rank and the middle rank."

4. Lower-interest loans from a bank are generally available only to government employees and others who have the necessary social connections. In addition, because they require a long application process and are targeted for specific needs, such as business equipment or housing finance, they are not useful for emergencies.

5. There are two components to what is popularly referred to as "dowry" in India (*varataṭciṇai* in Tamil). The first includes gold jewelry, cooking vessels, and other gifts of household items bestowed upon a daughter. The other consists of cash, jewelry and other gold items, and large consumer goods given to the groom and/or his family. Giving the second type of dowry is illegal in India, but the practice is almost universal (see Caplan 1984).

Seven Prevalent Misconceptions about India's Caste System

1. *The caste into which one is born determines one's occupation.* False: People in the same caste engage in (and historically have engaged in) a wide variety of different occupations. Confusion arises from the fact that according to the mythical "varna" system of the idealized law books, everyone is supposed to carry out occupations that match their "varnas." The mythical "varna" system and the actual caste system are two very different things.

2. *Caste designations are changeless.* False. There are many historical instances of castes changing (or trying to change) their caste names and behavior in order to receive advantageous treatment. Some of these efforts have succeeded; others have failed. There also are instances of caste groups moving to a different area and being given a new caste name in that area, for example, "chettiar" (merchant), "brahman" (priest), "pahari" (mountain people), etc.

3. *Castes relate to each other in mutually accepted hierarchical patterns.* Frequently false: In any given locality some castes are likely to differ from other castes in their perceptions of what the "correct" local hierarchical patterns are. Disputes regarding the "correct" local hierarchy occur (and have occurred) frequently.

4. *Everyone called by the same caste name is related to everyone else called by that same caste name.* False: Castes are assigned names by other castes living around them. Labeling coincidences frequently occur. Thus there are numerous castes, some of whose members perform priestly functions, that are called "brahmans" by those around them. However, they are not related to all other castes that are called "brahmans." Similarly there are castes that are called "patels," "deshmukhs," or "rajputs" (honorific civil titles) by those around them that are not related to all other castes called "patels," "deshmukhs," or "rajputs." Similarly, there are numerous castes, some of whose members make (or did make) pots, that are called "potters" by those around them that are not related to all other castes called "potters." Every "Gandhi" is not related to every other "Gandhi," etc.

5. *Castes are uniquely Hindu.* False: In India castes exist among Christians, Jains, Sikhs, Buddhists, and Muslims. Frequently the rules about marrying within one's caste and avoiding interactions with other castes are as strict among Christians, Jains, etc., as they are among Hindus.

6. *Hinduism legitimizes preferential treatment according to caste.* Occasionally false: Throughout history, movements have appeared within Hinduism denouncing preferential treatment according to caste (see some of the Hindu devotional bhakti movements, groups like the Lingayats, and certain Hindu philosophers and intellectuals, e.g., Mahatma Gandhi). Throughout history, movements have also appeared on the Indian subcontinent denouncing Hinduism's preferential treatment according to caste (see Buddhism, Jainism, Sikhism, etc.).

7. *Castes have been abolished.* False: India's constitution declares that "untouchability" is abolished and anyone discriminating against "untouchables" can be prosecuted. However, India's constitution says nothing about abolishing castes. Similarly in the United States discrimination on the grounds of race or gender has been declared illegal. However, the U.S. has no laws abolishing race or gender.

Ghanta 3, no. 2 (Spring 1992): 7.

PART FOUR

Practicing Religion

The "world religions" of Hinduism, Buddhism, Islam, Jainism, and Sikhism as well as Christianity and Judaism have long found a home in South Asia.[1] Perhaps it is this flowering of so many religious traditions that have led many westerners to imagine that South Asia is a very "spiritual" place. For many middle-class Americans and Europeans, as well as Asians, the practice of yoga, meditation, and other "eastern" traditions has been promoted as a healthy, spiritual alternative to our harried, anxiety-filled and materially overwhelming lives. That is, South Asian religions have, since the nineteenth century, been structured by westerners in opposition to capitalist values and economic culture. However, looking at the practical religious experiences of residents of the region, it turns out that material well-being, politics, power relations, and the violence these sometimes entail are also aspects of South Asian religious life. The intertwining of religion with politics and economics can be discerned in even the briefest outline of the histories of these religions in South Asia.

What today we refer to as "Hinduism"[2] is practiced by the majority of Indians and Nepalis as well as by a large minority of Sri Lankans. Hindus trace the roots of their religion back at least 3,500 years to a set of Sanskrit texts called the Vedas. The Vedas, which include mythology, ritual instruction, magical formulas, philosophy, and criticism, formed the basis of what is often referred to as Brahmanical Hinduism. Brahmanical Hinduism took the form of "orthodox" or "orthoprax" sacrificial rituals performed and controlled by Brahman priests, who, for the most part, were the ones who wrote, read, and studied the Vedas. These Brahmans were considered to be the highest class in a four-class (*varna*) system that some see as the beginnings of what is now commonly called "caste." Davis (1995: 12–16) describes how, beginning perhaps around 500 B.C.E., some scholars became impatient with and critical of Brahmanical hegemony over the rituals of sacrifice. These scholars began to reflect critically upon the actual meanings of the sacrifice and the Vedas. In a set of texts called the Upanisads, they developed philosophical concepts such as *moksha* (release), *sannyāsa* (renunciation), *karma* (actions), *samsāra* (transmigration or rebirth), *yōga* (disciplined practice), and *dharma* (codes of conduct appropriate to different classes of creatures), among others. These still form the basis of much Hindu thought and action.

In fact, it wasn't until about the seventh century C.E. that Hinduism started to shift significantly toward a theistic imagination, where gods like Siva, Visnu, Sakti, among many others, were represented in images and worshiped in temples. This marked the beginning of a new religious focus on *bhakti*, or devotion, a mode of worship that emphasized a direct (that is, unmediated by Brahman priests) emotional connection between worshipers and the gods they loved. Bhakti remains today the dominant, some would say "popular," mode of Hindu practice, and as Eck (1981) has shown in an engaging introduction to popular Hindu worship, it is eyesight (*darshan*), the exchange of vision between devotee and god, that lies at the heart of bhakti worship (see also Fuller 1992, and Mines, this part). Historically, Hindu kings, who allied themselves variously to competing sects associated with certain gods, e.g., Siva as opposed to Visnu, used temple construction and patronage as one important means of asserting hegemony over a territory (see Mines, this part). In cities, towns, and villages today, the establishment and patronage of temples remains closely tied to social, political, and economic power (see, for example, Appadurai 1981, Fuller 1992, Dirks 1987). In this way, Hinduism has been part and parcel of power struggles and historical changes since its inception. To cite another example, responses of Indian nationalists to nineteenth-century British colonial concepts of the religion and nation are part of what informs today's Hinduism (and, as Wilce shows, Islam as well). Today, for some, Hinduism has become linked to the politics of the nation-state in the form of Hindu nationalism, a religious politics that has led in recent years to sometimes violent clashes between interest groups defined by religious identity.

Buddhism and Jainism both developed out of the same period of reflection and the same critical reassessment of exclusionary Brahmanical control of sacrifice as did the Upanisads. Both religions stress that the path to liberation or enlightenment is one of austerity and renunciation. Both encourage monastic orders for both men (monks) and women (nuns). And both teach that enlightenment can be achieved by anyone, regardless of social class or standing. Jainism was founded by Mahavira, or "Great Hero" (599–527 B.C.E.). Born a prince in a warrior family, Mahavira renounced attachments to the material world and defined the path that today Jains strive to follow. The basic principle of Jainism is "that all living things have an immortal soul (*jīva*) that should strive to be liberated from matter (*ajīva*)" (Levinson 1996: 101). Matter, in the form of karma (action), clings to the soul, thus tying the soul to the material world in an endless cycle of rebirth (*samsāra*). In order to be liberated from this cycle, one should follow an ascetic path that includes renunciation of sex, vices, anger, greed, ego, and even attachments formed by love, pain, and pleasure. Prominent in Jainism, too is the practice of *ahimsa*, nonviolence to all living things. Mahatma Gandhi's influential method of resistance through "nonviolence" is based in part upon this Jain concept. Such a path is too difficult for most humans, who must do the best they can and work for a higher rebirth that will provide them the opportunity and strength to renounce the world, to become a nun or monk and then, finally, achieve liberation. Most of the world's Jains, numbering about three million, live in India.

Buddha was born as Siddartha Gautama (566–486 B.C.E.). Like Mahavira, he was born a prince in a kingly family whose company and values he renounced. After years of ascetic wandering, Buddha achieved nirvana while meditating under a fig tree. Out of compassion, Buddha devoted his life to teaching others how to follow his example and break the cycle of death and rebirth—a cycle that causes only suffering—and attain nirvana or enlightenment. The path to nirvana resembles in many ways the Jain path: practice self-discipline, meditation, and wisdom (Carrithers 1983:71). Buddhism was a proselytizing religion and as a consequence it spread very quickly all over Asia, where it is still widely practiced in many places (Sri Lanka, Nepal, Southeast Asia, Japan, China, Tibet, and Korea). Though it is no longer widespread in India, Buddha's message that enlightenment is available to all and not just to the higher classes of society is one reason that beginning in the 1950s, the social reformer Ambedkar encouraged India's so-called Untouchables to convert to Buddhism. Islam and Christianity, too, are often attractive to the lowest castes for their emphasis on human equality (parity, more accurately) in relation to God.

Islam is the religion of the majority populations of Pakistan and Bangladesh, with minority populations throughout South Asia. Islam was founded in 610 C.E. in Arabia when Muhammad began receiving the revelations now collected in the Qur'an. The Qur'an is considered by Muslims to be the word of Allah as revealed to Muhammad. Along with the Hadith (books recording Muhammad's own words and actions in life), the Qur'an is the authoritative text of Islam. The religion spread very quickly, moving west throughout the Middle East, across North Africa, and into Spain and moving east into what are now Iraq, Iran, Afghanistan, and parts of Pakistan. Islam did not establish itself firmly in the rest of South Asia, particularly India and beyond, until 1206, when Qutb al-Din declared himself the sultan of Delhi after defeating the Hindu ruler. In 1526, this sultanate was supplanted by the Mughal Empire when the Emperor Babar entered India from Central Asia and established wide hegemony over much of what is now north India and Pakistan (Davis 1995: 32). Just as Hindu kings established their territories in part by building and patronizing temples, so, too, did many Muslim rulers establish territories in part by constructing and patronizing mosques. It is important to note here that the vast majority of South Asian Muslims today did not migrate to India from elsewhere, but rather are the descendants of indigenous South Asians who converted to Islam as many as seven hundred years ago. Such conversions continue today, though not in large numbers.

Islam in South Asia can be described along two dimensions: orthodox Islam and Sufism. Both Orthodox Muslims and Sufis follow Islamic texts and codes of action such as the "five pillars of Islam."[3] But while orthodox Muslims adhere strictly to textually prescribed behaviors and laws and "submit" to the authority and power of Allah as revealed in the texts, many Sufi movements emphasize less the textual and more the personal and mystical relation between humans and Allah (Davis: 35). Some Sufi sects believe that certain persons—saints—are specially endowed with God's power and can channel and dispense that power to other people, places, and things. Because these sects emphasize the presence of God's power in persons and places, they have often resulted in syncretic movements attracting Hindus who, too, see divine energy enlivening objects and humans and places on earth. Many orthodox Muslims—usually urban and educated—challenge the validity of Sufi sects because they regard Sufi saint veneration as somewhere between ignorant folk practice and heresy. "Islamization" refers to the religio-political process whereby orthodox Muslims work to get all Muslims to adhere to a more orthodox understanding of Islam. The conflict between different forms of Islamic practice is clearly illustrated by Jim Wilce's essay in this part.

Sikhism was founded by Guru Nanak (1469–1539), the first of Sikhism's ten gurus. Guru Nanak was born to Hindu parents, and as an adult renounced his settled life and wandered South Asia in search of truth. The religion he founded is often described as a syncretic blend of Hindu and Muslim traditions, though today Sikhs see their religion as independent and true, not derivative. Sikhs believe that a person can unite with God (Sat Nam, literally "True Name") through discipline and purification, which help one overcome the five vices of greed, anger, self-centered pride, lust, and attachment to material things. By acting, instead, with contentment, honesty, compassion, and patience, a person can attain a higher rebirth, and eventually, through many rebirths, can attain union with God (Levinson 217–219). Meditation is a primary form of worship for Sikhs, and the primary Sikh text is called the Granth, a compilation of verses by many authors that is used as an authoritative guide to beliefs and attitudes. Sikhs worship in a temple called a *gudwara*, the most famous of which is the Golden Temple in Amritsar, India, in the state of Punjab, a site with its own history of political violence. Observant Sikhs are recognizable by their adherence to the "five k's": *kesh* (uncut hair, including beards—men usually tie their head hair in a turban) *kangha* (a small comb worn in the hair), *kara* (a steel bracelet), *kachhahera* (knee-length "britches" usually worn under other clothes), and *kirpan* (a ceremonial sword).

Unlike Buddhism, Jainism, and some forms of Hinduism where renunciation is the key to release from samsāra, in Sikhism it is believed that a person can obtain union with god while living everyday life as a married, family person, what South Asians sometimes refer to as a "householder." Furthermore, Sikhs do not find it necessary to follow a path of "nonviolence"—they may eat meat, fight in the military, and kill in good cause. Most of the world's twenty million Sikh's live in northwest India, in the Punjab, but many have migrated to Europe and North America as well (see Hall in part VI).

Christianity, practiced by only about 3 percent of South Asians, also has a surprisingly long history in the region. Myth has it that St. Thomas came to Kerala in 42 C.E. and established a Syrian Christian community there. Whether or not this is true, it is certain that the roots of the large Syrian Christian community in Kerala do date from the first century C.E. Jesuit missionaries brought Roman Catholicism to South Asia beginning in the early sixteenth century, when the Portuguese Jesuit St. Xavier arrived in Goa, on the west coast of India, and as other Jesuits arrived in Sri Lanka. In Sri Lanka, Dutch colonizers brought Calvinist Protestantism in the seventeenth century, when the British, too, brought Protestantism to India. More recently, evangelical Protestant Christianity has spread in South Asia with foreign, and now native, missionaries "spreading the word." Judaism, too, is practiced in India, though by only a few remaining souls (most of the already small Jewish population in the coastal city of Cochin migrated to Israel in the 1950s). There are records of Jews living in what is now the state of Kerala as early as the tenth century C.E., though the earliest (and still active) synagogue there dates from the sixteenth century, in Kochi. Parsis, or Zoroastrians, who follow an ancient religion that originated in Persia, also live in South Asia in very small numbers.

Many studies of South Asian religions focus primarily on their textual traditions (the so-called "great traditions"). The essays collected in this part demonstrate a long-standing anthropological concern with how people practice or "do" religion in their lives. The religious "doctrines" of the great traditions outlined above only sometimes, and only partly, inform the way that people today practice religion. Practice, some of the essays show, may sometimes even contradict doctrine to the point of being considered heterodox by religious elites.

* * *

People often speak of "the Hindu Pantheon" as if it were a closed set of gods related in definite patterns of which all Hindus are aware. It is true

234 / *Practicing Religion*

that most Hindus will have no difficulty talking about major gods such as Siva, Visnu, Krishna, and forms of the Goddess such as Kali, Durga, and Parvathi, as well as some of the relations among them. However, every place—be it a village, urban neighborhood, or town—has its own distinctive set of gods. This set may include the pan-Hindu gods mentioned above, but they also include local gods whose identities are unique and tied to the history of the people and events of that particular place. Mines's essay describes the gods who inhabit one village in south India, and explains some of the ways in which gods and humans are considered alike and different.

McKim Marriott's famous essay revels in a north Indian Hindu festival called Holi, a riotous spring festival that celebrates the god Krishna in all his youthful exuberance. In Holi festivals all over north India, revelers spray each other with colored powders and waters in a wild carnivalesque party. In Marriott's depiction, we see how villagers use Holi to critique the everyday forms of gender and caste relations, making their Holi into a "ritual of rebellion," that is, a ritual that exposes and critiques the power structures of everyday life.

Kim Gutschow's essay takes on squarely the differences that often exist between "doctrine"—the texts and rules, both written and spoken ideals of a religion—and "practice," the religious life that persons enact in their everyday lives. Here we see that while Buddhist doctrine states that gender is no more a hindrance to enlightenment than caste or class, the reality of the situation is very different for Buddhist nuns in Kashmir. Gender does make a difference.

In his essay, Robert Desjarlais introduces us to another aspect of religious experience, ritual healing among the Yolmo, a Tibetan Buddhist ethnic group living in Nepal who practice their own form of shamanic healing. Desjarlais argues that Yolmo healing rituals work not so much because the clients experience a psychological or metaphoric healing, but rather because the rituals actually "wake up" the clients to the sensory world around them. That is, they do not feel better because they "think" they are better; they *are* better because they "feel" the world again. The shaman's work is to re-attune the person whose spirit is lost to the here and now of the sensory world. By attuning us to the sensory aspect of human experience, Desjarlais broadens our concept of religion to include what we "feel" as we exist in our worlds.

As a kind of counterpoint, Jim Wilce shows us what can happen in Bangladesh when persons express too openly how they feel. Wilce shows us how prayerful laments by two Bangladeshis become a source of conflict in their Muslim community. Here, two people enter into spontaneous, emotive prayers that are also laments about the conditions of pain in their lives. In their region and culture, such prayers had been accepted and even valued as powerful, involuntary expressions of faith. Yet, now these forms of prayer as personal lament have come under criticism by more educated elite Muslims in the community who would like to "Islamize" the more syncretic forms of Islam that have pervaded Bangladesh. Wilce points out that this parallels, and is perhaps in part caused by, the rationalization brought to South Asia with colonial Protestant values, where all South Asian religions were judged to be "irrational" *because* they were emotional and subjective. Now those who lament aloud are called "mad" for their prayers. Wilce suggests that they are "mad" because they do not fit into the rationalized "norms" of the more powerful elites in their society.

NOTES

1. Statistics compiled from 1995 to 2000 by the U.S. Department of State (http://www.state.gov/www/background_notes/sabgnhp.html) indicate the following religious populations: INDIA: Hindu 81.3%; Muslim 12%; Christian 2.3%; Sikh 1.9%; other groups including Buddhist, Jain, Parsi 2.5%. PAKISTAN: Muslim 97%; small minorities of Christians, Hindus, and others. BANGLADESH: Muslim 88%; Hindu 11%; Christian, Buddhist, and others 1%. NEPAL: Hinduism (86.2%), Buddhism (7.8%), Islam (3.8%) and others (2.2%). SRI LANKA: Buddhist 70%; Hindu 15%; Christian 8%; Muslim 7% (Sri Lankan statistics compiled for 1999 by Worldatlas.com (http://www.graphicmaps.com/webimage/countrys/asia/lkcia.htm).

2. I put the term "Hinduism" in quotation marks because the term was not in use throughout the history of the religion. "Hindu" derives from "Indu," a term used by Muslim migrants to mean something like "all those people over there who are not Muslim and who live on the other side of the Indus River." It was not until the nineteenth and twentieth centuries that the term became consistently applied to a religious community. Throughout the long history of "Hinduism," there has not ever been a unified community, text, or set of universal beliefs, though today's Hindu Nationalist movements would argue otherwise.

3. These five pillars are (1) *Shahadah,* the declaration that "there is no god but God and Muhammad is his messenger;" (2) *Salat,* or prayer, which is ideally conducted five times a day, facing Mecca—and all over South Asia, one can hear the call to prayer coming from the mosques five times daily; (3) *Zakat,* a tax levied on all Muslims that is used to support members of the Muslim community who are in need; (4) Fasting during Ramadan, the month during which Muhammad is said to have received the Qur'an; and (5) *Hajj,* or pilgrimage to Mecca—all Muslims who are able to do this at least once in their life should do so.

The Hindu Gods in a South Indian Village

Diane P. Mines

In Yanaimangalam, a village in Tamil Nadu, south India, residents compare both castes and gods along several dimensions. They describe castes as relatively high (*ocanta*) versus relatively low (*talnta*), as big (*periya*) versus little (*cinna*), as pure (*cuttam*) versus impure (*acuttam*), the latter correlating roughly with vegetarian on the one hand and meat-eating on the other. They describe gods in similar terms, as high to low, big to little, vegetarian to meat-eating, and also as soft (*metuvāka*) to fierce (*ukkiramāka*). Both humans and gods may be further distinguished residentially. Higher and "bigger" (powerful, landowning) castes live in a central residential cluster, while the lower and "little" (landless, service-providing) castes live on the peripheries of the village and in small hamlets out across the fields. It is the same with gods. The higher, more "pure" gods live in the interiors of the central village: in temples on village streets and in alcoves and framed posters on the walls of residents' houses. Low-ranking, "impure," meat-eating gods live outside: out in the fields or the wastelands beyond, outside the house in back courtyards facing away from the house. Given these parallel associations between humans on the one hand and gods on the other, it is certainly easy to see why many scholars have presented analyses where the pantheon of ranked gods "symbolizes" ranks among humans (e.g., Fuller 1987: 33; Dumont 1986 [1957]: 460; cf. D. Mines 1997).

In this essay, I wish to introduce some of the gods of Yanaimangalam by briefly describing some of the stories and histories of temples and gods in that village. In every Hindu village and neighborhood in South Asia reside many gods, but in no two places does the very same set of gods live. Some gods, such as the universally recognized gods Siva, Vishnu, Krishna (an avatar, or incarnation, of Vishnu), and the goddess Kali, can be found all over South Asia, in villages, towns, and cities both north and south. Others, such as Yanaimangalam's Vellalakantan, are unique to one place. Scholars have sometimes described the distinction between universally recognized gods and strictly local ones as a distinction between a "great tradition" and a "little tradition" of Hinduism. But residents of Yanaiman-galam have their own set of distinctions, too.

Residents of Yanaimangalam distinguish among three kinds of gods, what I will gloss here as Brahmanical ("great tradition") gods, village goddesses (*ūr ammaṉ*), and fierce gods (*māṭaṉ* or *pēy*, lit. "ghost"). As noted above, residents compare these gods along several dimensions of contrast —high to low, pure to impure, vegetarian to meat-eating. But the dimension of contrast they stress the most is that of soft to fierce. For example, when I asked a neighbor, Ramayya Thevar, why the village goddess went on procession through the village streets while the fierce god Cutalaimatan ("Fierce God of the Cremation Ground") did not, he spoke not of relative rank but of relative benevolence. The goddess is mother (*tāy*), he said. She protects people and the village. Fierce gods like Cutalaimatan, he said, are dangerous to people in the village. Similarly, one day when I was hiking across the burning dry summer fields from the fierce Cutalaimatan's temple with two young priests, Subramaniam and Venki, I asked these young Brahmans why the Brahmanical god Murukan, son of Parvathi and Siva and brother of elephant-headed Ganesh, lived in the village's central residential area, nestled among houses and freely gazing down residential streets, while Cutalaimatan lived so far out across the fields in the wastelands around the cremation ground. They replied that Murukan, like the rest of his *type* (using the English word and meaning Brahmanical gods such as Siva, Krishna, and Ganesh), is soft (*metuvāka*) while fierce gods are cruel or fearsome (*payaṅkaramāṉatu*).

From one end of the spectrum to the other, soft gods (of which the Brahmanical are the softest) are those who are generally calm, stable, and beneficent. Fierce gods on the other hand are wild, unstable, and unpredictable. The fierce gods may prove protective and beneficent at one time, then cruel at another. They may unpredictably attack a person if they feel the slightest insult or if they simply feel overheated by, for example, seeing a beautiful young woman walking by. The village goddess belongs in between, as befits her well-known dual or "ambivalent" nature (Doniger 1980; Ramanujan 1986: 55–61; Kinsley 1986), where sometimes she is identified with the Brahmanical and benign, cool goddess Parvathi, devout wife of Siva, while at other times she is identified with the fearsome Durga or Kali, unmarried forms of the goddess who, in a not really very mother-like manner at all, wield weapons, ride lions, crack skulls, and drink blood to match their hot nature.

BRAHMANICAL TEMPLES

On the day of my first visit to Yanaimangalam, well before I had moved in, I was invited to "see" the gods in the Siva temple at the end of the Ag-

raharam street, the traditional Brahman community of the village. Offi-
cious elders sent a boy to fetch the temple's priest. The priest arrived. He
was blue-eyed blind with cataracts, a bit plump, and he wore his white hair
in the manner of Brahman priests, shaved in front and with the long hairs
in back tied behind his head in a knot. I followed him down the street and
a dozen or more children followed behind me like an eager wagging tail.
At the end of the street loomed the temple—the largest structure in the village. Weeds grew from fissures in the weathered stone walls, long ago
painted in red and white vertical stripes. In front of the temple, a square
tank choked with lotuses gave way to the flooded rice fields beyond. The
priest unlocked the thick, castlelike wooden doors with a prodigious skeleton key. They creaked open and we, along with the sun's light, entered
the temple's dank interior. The light startled temple bats, and as we ducked
through the ever lower doorways that led further into the temple toward
the interior "womb-rooms" (*garbhagraha*) that housed the images of gods
(see fig. 11), surely hundreds of bats shot past us out of those same doorways in through which we had ducked. The blind priest walked smoothly
through their parting rapids and I, *knowing* bats to be good at avoiding
even moving objects, tried to follow smoothly in his wake. My failure in
this endeavor to "look cool" worked much to the amusement of the giggly
tail of children who squirmed so close behind me. Once we had all traded
places with the bats and approached the shrines (there were several in the
many-halled temple, to different forms of Siva and to his consort goddess
Parvathi), the priest lit camphor to show us the deities one by one. A bronze
image of Nataraja, the "Dancing Siva" (fig. 12) was clothed in leopardskin
cotton and draped in wilting flowers from the morning's *puja*, or worship.
The flame sparkled off his chiseled features and off the bronze flames that
framed him. As the priest circled the camphor flame, we looked at the god,
obtaining darshan. Then the priest, with batlike radar, passed a tray of purifying ash (*viputi*) out to the few worshipers present. I placed two rupees
on the tray as an offering, took a pinch of ash to smear my forehead then
headed outside, now shielding my eyes from the open sunlight.

After visiting the Siva temple, I was beckoned down a wide earthen path
leading between the rice fields to the river that flowed on the north side of
the village. There, another priest, who specialized in serving Vishnu, conducted me through another large temple. There I received not ash (ash is
Siva's special substance) but some red powder (*kumkumam*) to dot my forehead and some leaves from Vishnu's favorite plant, *tulsi*. This temple, I later
learned, was much older than the 300-year-old Siva temple. The Vishnu
temple was 600 years old. This village, I realized, had a long history.

The stone walls of both the Siva and the Vishnu temples are adorned
with inscriptions that bear witness to regional and village history. The inscriptions are chiseled in several languages, including Telugu, Malayalam,
and old Tamil interspersed with Granta script, all unreadable to average

11. Darshan. Worshipers look into the "womb-room" while a Brahman priest bathes the Murukan, son of Siva, in cooling milk.

modern Tamil readers. The inscriptions are, however, clear signs—indexes —of the kingly past of temple and village patronage. The inscriptions tell of the founding of the temples, name the kings who founded them, and record important transactions, gifts, patrons, and hereditary servants of the temples. Smaller village temples to Krishna (an avatar, or incarnation, of Vishnu) and Ganesh (the elephant-headed son of Siva) also bear such inscriptions.

Yanaimangalam's red-and-white-striped temples to Siva, Vishnu, Krishna, and Ganesh put Yanaimangalam on the map of history. They link the village both to the administrative present and to official histories, to Sanskrit myth, to high art and architecture, and to literary languages. These are temples that—along with Krishna, Pillaiyar (Ganesh), and Murukan temples and shrines—make Yanaimangalam part of the "great" tradition of Indian Civilization (the Classical, Sanskritic, Male, Universal, etc., to borrow from Ramanujan's 1973 description of great traditions). These temples are nothing less than historical data, data recorded in stone and then recorded again in colonial and Indian government documents that detail the bronze sculptured images, the dates of temple construction, the kings that commissioned them. All of this information is based on the inscriptions etched into temple walls, translated into English (the language of the great

12. Waving a camphor flame around Nataraja, the "Dancing Siva."

bureaucratic tradition) in epigraphical records that may be found in libraries at the University of Chicago, at Harvard, and at Berkeley, too. When I
lived in the village, government officials would come to Yanaimangalam
in their jeeps to record again an inscription, or to show the new District
Collector the glory of the region's past inscribed in the *paṭṭikāṭus* (the "rustic," "hick" villages) of the region. Village residents are aware of the historical interest outsiders have in these temples, and are eager to show them off
to visiting officials and, it seems, anthropologists. Today these old Brahmanical temples are administered centrally from Ambasamuttiram, a large
temple town about twenty-five kilometers west of Yanaimangalam.

VILLAGE GODDESSES

Despite the historical and artistic significance of the Brahmanical temples,
very few villagers spend much of their time or many of their economic resources worshiping in those temples. Occasionally a Brahman family from
Mumbai or Delhi, or Chennai or Tirunelveli Town, or, in one case, from
Monterey, California—strangers to Yanaimangalam's current population—

would come to visit one of these gods whom they claimed as their lineage (*kula*) god (usually it was Vishnu by the riverbank they came to visit and claimed as their own). But everyone in the village worships the village goddess. To her is attributed the power of fertility—fertility of soil, of humans, and of animals. There is no one in the village unaffected by her power (*cakti*) to assure good crops of rice and to help the living bear healthy children.

Eleven goddess temples and shrines dot the map of Yanaimangalam. Each of the five residential areas that Yanaimangalam comprises has its own goddess temple. In addition, several lineages sponsor their own temple to the village goddess. Though the goddesses have different names (Yanaiyamman, Uccimakakkali, Muppatatiyamman, Mariyamman, among others) as well as independent temples on different sites, all eleven are said to be the same power (*orē cakti*). As the Tamil saying goes, "The life is one, the forms are two [many]" (*uyir oṉṟu, uruvam iraṇṭu*). There are some other goddesses, such as the "fierce goddess" named Issakkiyamman, who are said to be a "different power" (*vēṟu cakti*).

Puzzling over the many forms of the one life that is the village goddess, I asked a respected older man in the village, Virapandi Muppanar, to relate the "birth story" of the goddess named Muppatatiyamman who lives in a small alcove built into the wall of a house compound. I noticed her one day as I was passing by. He denied any knowledge of her "birth story" and suggested I ask someone else. Obviously I had asked the wrong question, so I rephrased it. This time I asked how it was that the same goddess could be in so many places at once. He then started to tell me the story I had been hoping for. It wasn't the story of her birth, but the story of how she came to be in Yanaimangalam, in this place and that.

He started out by relating a little about how in the old days, long before there were people in the village, the goddess had come down from the north and passed through the area, wandering about, pausing to rest here and there. As she walked, small traces of her powerful substance, her sakti, were left behind in the places she traversed. In the places she paused or stopped to rest, her sakti soaked into the soil and there it remains to this day. Sometimes her presence in the earth is discovered by people. Other times her image might appear on its own, as they say about the main village goddess, Yanaiyamman. Virapandi Muppanar continued by telling me how her presence on the spot by the wall was discovered.

It was a long time ago, about five generations ago, about the time of the white man, and about the time of the Vikkayamarattin Kottai story. There was an unmarried boy, about eighteen years old, one of four children in his family. The goddess was always possessing him. She would possess him and he would dance from village to village. His family picked a fight with him over this strange behavior, so he ran away. But a few days later he came back.

He said to his mother: "I'll show you the truth." He took a clay pot full of burning rags and danced with it all night around the village. A lot of people figured he was just pretending to be possessed, and they spoke disparagingly about him. He went all around the village and early the next morning he came back. He went straight into the shed under the tamarind tree in his family courtyard, and there he put down the burning fire pot, came out, and locked the door behind him. A few days later, he returned. It was a Tuesday. He took up the pot again and went around the village. Even though several days had passed, the pot was still aflame! It was still burning, just like that! Seeing this, the people changed their mind and thought that there must be a goddess in that place [in the shed by the wall].

As far as the human residents of Yanaimangalam are concerned, goddesses have "always already" been in the village. Marking the earth with her wanderings, she is rooted in the soil, and her image might spring up anywhere, like a tree's root might throw up shoots far from its trunk. Her power is a quality that shapes the villages's topography: it create zones of greater and lesser energy (sakti), and discovering those places links human beings to that power.

FIERCE GODS

In Yanaimangalam, there are at least sixteen temples and shrines to fierce gods and goddesses. Most of these gods live on the margins of the village territory, outside of the residential areas, out in the fields or beyond in the wasteland (*kāṭu*) (fig. 13). Even those that live within the residential village are nonetheless talked about as living outside. Outside is, after all, a relative term: outside the house in the courtyard (fig. 14), or outside the courtyard on the street. Unlike the village goddesses and unlike Brahmanical deities, fierce gods are not paraded through the streets in processions, nor are they generally brought inside the house for worship. If a fierce god residing in a house courtyard proves too violent or touchy for peaceful daily life, families have been known to remove them as they brought them —in a handful of earth—taking them out into the wasteland, further away from settled areas.

As unpredictable and unstable as anger itself, these gods may protect or attack. Residents of Yanaimangalam give them wide berth in many daily contexts, choosing their paths of movement to avoid directly passing by or standing in front of the hot gaze of a fierce god. In myth and ritual, these gods are often subordinated to the village goddesses as guardians who live near but outside her temple, much like the humans who live outside the central village residential area are thought by many higher-caste residents to be subordinate and unruly as well.

13. Vellalakantan, a fierce god out in the fields.

While kings and, more recently, wealthy upper-caste residents established and patronized Brahmanical temples, and while the goddess traveled to what is now Yanaimangalam independently of humans, leaving powerful traces in the places she moved and rested (hence "self-appearing"), village residents see fierce gods as having come to Yanaimangalam in two other ways. More rarely, fierce gods are created in the village itself: as gods or goddesses born from men or women who have met violent deaths. All over Tamil Nadu, fierce gods are born in violence and injustice. Their stories of origin are sometimes local stories of humans murdered and then reborn as violent deities (Blackburn 1988; Trawick 1991; D. Mines, in press). Or, their origins may be linked to Brahmanical mythologies (*purāṇas*) where fierce gods are the offspring of anger, intrigue, and violence or injustice among those gods thought more benign (Knipe 1989; Hiltebeitel 1989). Either way, the violence of their origins and vengeful natures is often reflected in their murderous depictions as sword-wielding mustachioed heroes ready to fight (fig. 13) or as fanged, terrifying women who look ready

14. Cooking rice for "Backyard Maṭan." This fierce god is present in the small white-washed earthen image on the lower left.

to bite. The following case illustrates the ferocity of these gods. Here is what I learned in 1990 when I asked Picchaiya, an "untouchable" resident of an area of Yanaimangalam called Middle Hamlet, about a small, faceless clay image in a palmyra tree grove at the edge of the village. (This is my retelling of his explication.)

> One day, about forty years ago, a Thevar youth—unmarried and about eighteen years old—was walking up the road to the main village. He walked past a temple festival that Middle Hamlet S.C. [so-called "untouchables"] were conducting to their god Panaiyatiyan ["He at the foot of the palmyra tree"]. The higher-caste Thevar youth threw out some derogatory remarks as he walked past the festival, angering the fierce god. A few yards further up the road, just before entering the first residential street, the youth suddenly fell to the ground vomiting blood. He died as suddenly as he fell, and everyone attributed his death to the fierce god's anger. In 1990, the youth's lineage members conducted a puja for their ancestor. At this time the identity of this Thevar youth [whom they referred to as "grandfather"], was becoming conflated with Panaiyatiyan himself. The victim was becoming a lesser form of the god who had killed him.

Second, and more often, fierce gods come into Yanaimangalam from elsewhere, often through the agency of village residents who, often unwittingly, transfer these gods—or spread them, rather—to the village. They bring gods bodily and they bring them in substances, such as trees and, commonly, in "handfuls of earth" (*piṭimaṇ*) (see also Inglis 1985), as the following story, summarized from the stories told to me by several village residents, illustrates.

Many years ago, a group of men from Yanaimangalam went up into the forest near Cabarimalai [a nearby mountain that starts in Tamil Nadu and peaks in Kerala] to cut a tree for the flagpole in front of the Siva temple. In the tree-cutting party was a Carpenter to do the cutting, a Thevarmar man, and two Pillaimar men [these are caste names]. They ascended the mountain and searched the forest for a tall tree. They found it. They cut it down. They brought it back to the village and set it up in front of the Siva temple. Then, all at once, the four men were struck violently ill. A specialist determined that ghosts and other fierce beings inhabited the tree they had brought down from the mountain. Being deprived of their home, these evil beings had grabbed hold of [*piṭiccatu*] the culprits, that is, possessed them. One remedy was available. The families of each of the men were instructed to go back to the place where they found the tree, take a handful of earth from that spot, and bring it back to the village. There they should deposit the earth near their houses and on those spots build permanent shrines to these fierce beings, adopting those gods into their lineage as lineage gods (*kulatēvaṅkaḷ*). This way the gods would leave the men alone. And that is how the temples for Kalamatasami, Talavaymatasami, Cappanimatasami, and Cutalaimatan-by-the-Carpenter's-House were established.

A similar story, first told to me by a woman from the Thevar neighborhood and retold here, reveals how the god Sivalaperi Cutalaimatan came to Yanaimangalam.

One day, a Thevar man went all the way to a village called Sivalaperi about thirty miles from Yanaimangalam in order to swear an oath to the god Cutalaimatan who lived in that village. The man had been accused of theft in the village, and the accuser agreed that if the suspect swore his innocence in front of this fearsome god, he would let the matter drop. So, the accused went to Sivalaperi and there he apparently lied to the god, judging from the subsequent events. A black goat followed the man all the way home from the temple. Once home, the man tried to kill the goat (for curry), but the goat grew huge and attacked both him and his kinsmen with disastrous and deadly consequences—a pregnant woman in the family was killed. To quell the god's righteous anger, only one recourse was available: the accused had to not only admit his guilt, but also establish a shrine to the god in his backyard. He did this by returning to Sivalaperi with surviving family members. From there he took a handful of earth from the earthen temple floor, and brought it back to Yanaimangalam where he "planted" it, and thereby the god's power, in the courtyard outside his house.

Just as the goddess's sakti resides in the soil, so too does the power of fierce gods. Even the images of these fierce gods themselves are most often formed from earth (fig. 14). These may be simple temporary mounds of earth formed by devotees for worship, mounds which then erode back into earth with wind and rain, only to be reformed for the next puja, or they may be terra-cotta images sculpted by Potters (Inglis 1985).

* * *

In Yanaimangalam, there are thirty-five temples to the three kinds of gods described above. Most days, the temples are quiet places. Priests go there daily, or maybe only twice a week in some cases, to feed and bathe and care for the gods. Passersby may drop in for darshan, to offer a prayer, or make a request. On their way home from morning baths in the river, many drop by the Vishnu temple or the goddess temple to see the gods and obtain some red powder or white ash to smear on their clean foreheads, a final cleansing ritual to begin the day. For most of these temples, there are also occasional festivals—in some cases there are several festivals a year, others are annual, and some are even less frequent. Some festivals are relatively small, limited to just one lineage in the village. Others are multicaste affairs in which most village residents participate.

I wish to end this descriptive essay with one more story. This is a story that was told to me by Andi, a low-ranking man of the Dhobi, or Washerman, caste. Though low-ranking, he is a powerful man in the Cutalaimatan temple because of his ancestor's link to that god. This story is about how gods can alter human relations, including relations of rank between caste groups in the village. This story hints of how temples serve as venues where caste rankings can be undermined, challenged, and sometimes even reversed.

> One day, about a hundred years ago, a man of the powerful, landowning-dominating Muppanar caste was out working in his field by the riverbank. He saw something floating down the river toward him. He fished it out, and found it was a banana shoot. He planted it on the edge of his field.
>
> It just so happened that his field lay in the line of sight of the fierce god Cutalaimatan, whose stone, power-filled image stood nearby positioned to look across this field. Cutalaimatan is the god of the cremation ground and he has a propensity to attack—sometimes quite violently—passersby who displease him or who make him jealous. So, people tend to avoid him, to tiptoe around him. But this fellow's field lay right in the god's line of sight, and there wasn't much he could do about that. His best recourse was to defer to the god, to soften him up, and to hope for the best.

The Muppanar farmer's strategy was simple. He tried to win over the god by making a vow. He promised Cutalaimatan that he would give him the first stalk of bananas that his new tree produced, in return for the god's protecting the plant and field.

A year passed and the banana plant flourished and produced a big stalk of bananas. The owner came out and cut the stalk and took it home, forgetting his vow to Cutalaimatan. He took one banana from the stalk, peeled it, and took a big bite. Immediately he choked, spat out the banana, and could eat nothing from then on.

He realized that the fault was his for forgetting his vow and so this higher-caste man went to see a local man favored by Cutalaimatan, a lower-ranking Dhobi (Washerman) named Mukkan, to enlist his aid and find a solution. He went to Mukkan because he and his entire lineage were the special devotees of Cutalaimatan. They took care of him and he took care of them. Mukkan was the one whose connection to the god was closest: Cutalaimatan regularly possessed him and communicated his needs through this human god-dancer/host (*cāmiyāṭi*). The solution that the Dhobi and the god offered was that the Muppanar man and his whole lineage should adopt Cutalaimatan's younger brother, Mundacami, as their own special god. They should construct a shrine to Mundacami opposite Cutalaimatan's shrine, and worship there from now on, side by side with the low-ranking Dhobis, *as equals*. So, to this day the Muppanar and the Dhobis are equal (*cammam*) in that temple.

A chance event (a banana shoot floating down the river) led to a vow made, and then a vow broken. A vow broken established a permanent relation between a low-ranking, peripheral god and a relatively high-ranking, central caste. This relation between the god Mundacami and the Muppanar lineage is understood as an enduring, substantial, bodily relation between the god and lineage members and it cannot be attenuated at will. The Muppanar lineage (which corresponds roughly to the local Muppanar caste grouping) in Yanaimangalam is forevermore substantially connected with their new god. The god inhabits their houses, bodies, and lives. The god eats what they eat, the god possesses them, the god fills them with energy and can also cause them illness if displeased. The new relation of "equality" established between Muppanars and Dhobis takes on a social, publicly enacted reality in temple festivals that take place three times a year at the cremation-ground temple that houses both lineage gods. South Indian temple rituals, as is widely reported, are venues where ranks among participants, as well as community inclusions and exclusions, are established through multiple ranked transactions from the god to the devotees in an idiom of "honor" (*mariyātai*) (see, for example, Appadurai and Breckenridge 1976; Appadurai 1981; Dirks 1987; and Dumont [1957] 1986). During the festival at the Cutalaimatan/Mundacami temple, one of many ways that ranks are established are through ordered transactions in which the Dhobis receive first honors and the Muppanars receive second honors (and others in order afterward). That is, the Dhobis receive their shares (*paṅku*) of the temple leftovers first, and have authority over the distribution of remaining shares. Moreover, when devotees make their rounds, visiting the gods at the shrine, they pay homage first to Cutalaimatan and his Dhobi god-dancer and only second to the Muppanar's lineage god and god-dancer. The Dhobi, being connected to the older brother god, is, it turns out, first among equals.

The Feast of Love

McKim Marriott

I shall try here to interpret Krishna and his cult as I met them in a rural village of northern India while I was conducting my first field venture as a social anthropologist. The village was Kishan Garhi,[1] located across the Jumnā from Mathurā and Vrindaban, a day's walk from the youthful Krishna's fabled land of Vraja.

As it happened, I had entered Kishan Garhi for the first time in early March, not long before what most villagers said was going to be their greatest religious celebration of the year, the festival of Holī. Preparations were already under way. I learned that the festival was to begin with a bonfire celebrating the cremation of the demoness Holikā. Holikā, supposedly fireproofed by devotion to her demon father, King Harnākas, had been burned alive in the fiery destruction plotted by her to punish her brother Prahlāda for his stubborn devotion to the true god, Rāma.[2] I observed two priests and a large crowd of women reconstructing Holikā's pyre with ritual and song: the Brahman master of the village site with a domestic chaplain consecrated the ground of the demoness's reserved plot; the women added wafers and trinkets of dried cow-dung fuel,[3] stood tall straws in a circle around the pile, and finally circumambulated the whole, winding about it protective threads of homespun cotton. Gangs of young boys were collecting other combustibles—if possible in the form of donations, otherwise by stealth—quoting what they said were village rules, that everyone must contribute something and that anything once placed on the Holī pyre could not afterward be removed. I barely forestalled the contribution of one of my new cots; other householders in my lane complained of having lost brooms, parts of doors and carts, bundles of straw thatch, and an undetermined number of fuel cakes from their drying places in the sun.

The adobe houses of the village were being repaired or whitewashed for the great day. As I was mapping the streets and houses for a preliminary survey, ladies of the village everywhere pressed invitations upon me to attend the festival. The form of their invitations was usually the oscillation of a fistful of wet cow-dung plaster in my direction, and the words, "Saheb will play Holī with us?" I asked how it was to be played, but could get no coherent answer. "You must be here to see and to play!" the men insisted.

I felt somewhat apprehensive as the day approached. An educated landlord told me that Holī is the festival most favored by the castes of the fourth estate, the Śūdras. Europeans at the district town advised me to stay indoors, and certainly to keep out of all villages on the festival day. But my village friends said, "Don't worry. Probably no one will hurt you. In any case, no one is to get angry, no matter what happens. All quarrels come to an end. It is a *līlā*—a divine sport of Lord Krishna!" I had read the sacred *Bhāgavata Purāna's* story about Prahlāda and had heard many of its legends of Krishna's miraculous and amorous boyhood.[4] These books seemed harmless enough. Then, too, Radcliffe-Brown had written in an authoritative anthropological text that one must observe the action of rituals in order to understand the meaning of any myth.[5] I had been instructed by my reading of B. Malinowski, as well as by all my anthropological preceptors and elders that one best observes another culture by participating in it as directly as possible.[6] My duty clearly was to join in the festival as far as I might be permitted.

The celebration began auspiciously, I thought, in the middle of the night as the full moon rose. The great pile of blessed and pilfered fuel at once took flame, ignited by the village fool, for the master of the village site had failed to rouse with sufficient speed from his slumbers. "Victory to Mother Holikā!" the shout went up, wishing her the achievement of final spiritual liberation rather than any earthly conquest, it seemed. A hundred men of all twenty-four castes in the village, both Muslim and Hindu, now crowded about the fire, roasting ears of the new, still green barley crop in her embers. They marched around the fire in opposite directions and exchanged roasted grains with each other as they passed, embracing or greeting one another with "Rām Rām!"—blind in many cases to distinctions of caste. Household fires throughout the village had been extinguished, and as the assembled men returned to their homes, they carried coals from the collective fire to rekindle their domestic hearths. Many household courtyards stood open with decorated firepits awaiting the new year's blaze. Joyful celebrants ran from door to door handing bits of the new crop to waking residents of all quarters or tossing a few grains over walls when doors were closed. As I entered a shadowy lane, I was struck twice from behind by what I thought might be barley, but found in fact to be ashes and sand. Apart from this perhaps deviant note, the villagers seemed to me to have expressed through their unified celebration of Holikā's demise their total dependence on each other as a moral community. Impressed with the vigor of these communal rites and inwardly warmed, I returned to my house and to bed in the courtyard.

It was a disturbing night, however. As the moon rose high, I became aware of the sound of racing feet: gangs of young people were howling "Holī!" and pursuing each other down the lanes. At intervals I felt the thud of large mud bricks thrown over my courtyard wall. Hoping still to salvage a few hours of sleep, I retreated with cot to the security of my storeroom. I was awakened for the last time just before dawn by the crash of the old year's pots breaking against my outer door. Furious fusillades of sand poured from the sky. Pandemonium now reigned: a shouting mob of boys called on me by name from the street and demanded that I come out. I perceived through a crack, however, that anyone who emerged was being pelted with bucketfuls of mud and cow-dung water. Boys of all ages were heaving dust into the air, hurling old shoes at each other, laughing and cavorting "like Krishna's cowherd companions"—and of course, cowherds they were. They had captured one older victim and were making him ride a donkey, seated backward, head to stern. Household walls were being scaled, loose doors broken open, and the inhabitants routed out to join these ceremonial proceedings. Relatively safe in a new building with strong doors and high walls, I escaped an immediate lynching.

I was not sure just what I could find in anthropological theory to assist my understanding of these events. I felt at least that I was sharing E. Durkheim's sense (when he studied Australian tribal rates) of confronting some of the more elementary forms of the religious life. I reflected briefly on the classic functional dictum of Radcliffe-Brown, who had written that the "rites of savages persist because they are part of the mechanism by which an orderly society maintains itself in existence, serving as they do to establish certain fundamental social values."[7] I pondered the Dionysian values that seemed here to have been expressed, and wondered what equalitarian social order, if any, might maintain itself by such values.

But I had not long to reflect, for no sooner had the mob passed by my house than I was summoned by a messenger from a family at the other end of the village to give first aid to an injured woman. A thrown water pot had broken over her head as she opened her door that morning. Protected by an improvised helmet, I ventured forth. As I stepped into the lane, the wife of the barber in the house opposite, a lady who had hitherto been most quiet and deferential, also stepped forth, grinning under her veil, and doused me with a pail of urine from her buffalo. Hurrying through the streets, I glimpsed dances by parties of men and boys impersonating Krishna and company as musicians, fiddling and blowing in pantomime on wooden sticks, leaping about wearing garlands of dried cow-dung and necklaces of bullock bells. Again, as I returned from attending to the lacerated scalp, there was an intermittent hail of trash and dust on my shoulders, this time evidently thrown from the rooftops by women and children in hiding behind the eaves.

At noontime, a state of truce descended. Now was the time to bathe, the neighbors shouted, and to put on fine, fresh clothes. The dirt was finished. Now there would be solemn oblations to the god Fire. "Every cult," Durkheim had written, "presents a double aspect, one negative, the other positive."[8] Had we then been preparing ourselves all morning by torture and purgation for other rites of purer intent? "What is it all going to be about this afternoon?" I asked my neighbor, the barber. "Holī," he said with a beatific sigh, "is the Festival of Love!"

Trusting that there would soon begin performances more in the spirit of the *Gītagovinda* or of Krishna's *rāsa* dances in the *Bhāgavata Purāna*, I happily bathed and changed, for my eyes were smarting with the morning's dust and the day was growing hot. My constant benefactor, the village landlord, now sent his son to present me with a tall glass of a cool, thick green liquid. This was the festival drink, he said; he wanted me to have it at its best, as it came from his own parlour. I tasted it, and found it sweet and mild. "You must drink it all!" my host declared. I inquired about the ingredients—almonds, sugar, curds of milk, anise, and "only half a cup" of another item whose name I did not recognize. I finished off the whole delicious glass, and, in discussion with my cook, soon inferred that the unknown ingredient—*bhāng*—had been four ounces of juice from the hemp leaf known in the West as hashish or marijuana.

Because of this indiscretion, I am now unable to report with much accuracy exactly what other religious ceremonies were observed in the four villages through which I floated that afternoon, towed by my careening hosts. They told me that we were going on a journey of condolence to each house whose members had been bereaved during the past year. My many photographs corroborate the visual impressions that I had of this journey: the world was a brilliant smear. The stained and crumpled pages of my notebooks are blank, save for a few declining diagonals and undulating scrawls. Certain steaming scenes remain in memory, nevertheless. There was one great throng of villagers watching an uplifted male dancer with padded crotch writhe in solitary states of fevered passion and then onanism; then join in a remote *pas de deux* with a veiled female impersonator in a parody of pederasty, and finally in telepathic copulation—all this to a frenzied accompaniment of many drums. I know that I witnessed several hysterical battles, women rushing out of their houses in squads to attack me and other men with stout canes, while each man defended himself only by pivoting about his own staff, planted on the ground, or, like me, by running for cover. The rest was all hymn singing, every street resounding with choral song in an archaic Śākta style. The state of the clothes in which I ultimately fell asleep told me the next morning that I had been sprayed and soaked repeatedly with libations of liquid dye, red and yellow. My face in the morning was still a brilliant vermilion, and my hair was orange from repeated embraces and scourings with colored powders by the bereaved and probably by many others. I learned on inquiry what I thought I had heard before, that in Kishan Garhi a kitchen had been profaned with dog's dung by masked raiders, that two housewives had been detected in adultery with neighboring men. As an effect of the festivities in one nearby village, there had occurred an armed fight between factional groups. In a third, an adjacent village, where there had previously been protracted litigation between castes, the festival had not been observed at all.

"A festival of *love?*" I asked my neighbors again in the morning.

"Yes! All greet each other with affection and feeling. Lord Krishna taught us the way of love, and so we celebrate Holī in this manner."

"What about my aching shins—and your bruises? Why were the women beating us men?"

"Just as the milkmaids loved Lord Krishna, so our wives show their love for us, and for you, too, Saheb!"

Unable at once to stretch my mind so far as to include both "love" and these performances in one conception, I returned to the methodological maxim of Radcliffe-Brown: the meaning of a ritual element is to be found by observing what it shares with all the contexts of its occurrence.[9] Clearly, I would need to know much more about village religion and about the place of each feature of Holī in its other social contexts throughout the year. Then perhaps I could begin to grasp the meanings of Krishna and his festival, and to determine the nature of the values they might serve to maintain.

There were, I learned by observing throughout the following twelve months in the village, three main kinds of ritual performances—festivals, individual sacraments, and optional devotions. Among sacraments, the family-controlled rites of marriage were a major preoccupation of all villagers. In marriage, young girls were uprooted from their privileged situations in the patrilineally extended families of their birth and childhood. They were wedded always out of the village, often many miles away, to child husbands in families that were complete strangers. A tight-lipped young groom would be brought by his uncles in military procession, and after three days of receiving tribute ceremoniously, he would be carried off with his screaming, wailing little bride to a home where she would occupy the lowest status of all. Hard work for the mother-in-law, strict obedience to the husband, and a veiled, silent face to all males senior to herself in the entire village—these were the lot of the young married woman. Members of the husband's family, having the upper hand over the captive wife, could demand and receive service, gifts, hospitality, and deference from their "low" affines on all future occasions of ceremony. Briefly, sometimes, there would be little outbreaks of "Holī playing" at weddings, especially between the invading groom's men and the women of the bride's village: in these games, the men would be dared to enter the women's courtyards in the bride's village and would then be beaten with rolling pins or soaked with colored water for their boldness. Otherwise, all ceremonies of marriage stressed the strict formal dominance of men over women, of groom's people over bride's. When married women returned to their original homes each rainy season for a relaxed month of reunion with their "village sisters" and "village brothers," the whole village sang sentimental songs of the *gopīs'* never-fulfilled longing for their idyllic childhood companionship with Krishna and with each other. Sexual relations between adults of humankind were conventionally verbalized in metaphors of "war," "theft," and rape, while the marital connection between any particular husband and his wife could be mentioned without insult only by employing generalized circumlocutions such as "house" and "children," and so on. The idiom of Holī thus differed from that of ordinary life both in giving explicit dramatization to specific sexual relationships that otherwise would not be expressed at all and in reversing the differences of power conventionally prevailing between husbands and wives.

Aside from the Holī festival, each of the other thirteen major festivals of the year seemed to me to express and support the proper structures of patriarchy and gerontocracy in the family, of elaborately stratified relations among the castes, and of dominance by landowners in the village generally. At Divālī, ancestral spirits were to be fed and the goddess of wealth worshiped by the head of the family, acting on behalf of all members. The rites of Gobardhan Divālī, another Krishna-related festival, stressed the unity of the family's agnates through their common interest in the family herds of cattle. On the fourth day of the lunar fortnight which ends at Divālī[10]— indeed, on certain fixed dates in every month—the wives fasted for the sake of their husbands. On other dates they fasted for the sake of their children. The brother-sister relation of helpfulness, a vital one for the out-married women, had two further festivals and many fasts giving it ritual support; and the Holī bonfire itself dramatized the divine punishment of the wicked sister Holikā for her unthinkable betrayal of her brother Prahlāda. At each other festival of the year and also at wedding feasts, the separation of the lower from the higher castes and their strict order of ranking were reiterated both through the services of pollution-removal provided by them, and through the lowering gifts and payments of food made to them in return. Since the economy of the village was steeply stratified, with one third of the families controlling nearly all the land, every kind of ritual observance, sacramental or festival, tended through ritual patronage and obeisance to give expression to the same order of economic dominance and subordination. Optional, individual ritual observances could also be understood as expressing the secular organization of power, I thought. Rival leaders would compete for the allegiance of others through ceremonies.

A wealthy farmer, official, or successful litigant was expected to sponsor special ceremonies and give feasts for lesser folk "to remove the sins" he had no doubt committed in gaining his high position; he who ignored this expectation might overhear stories of the jocular harassment of misers at Holī, or of their robbery on other, darker nights. Once each year, a day for simultaneous worship of all the local deities required a minimal sort of communal action by women, and smaller singing parties of women were many, but comradeship among men across the lines of kinship and caste was generally regarded with suspicion. In sum, the routine ritual and social forms of the village seemed almost perfect parallels of each other: both maintained a tightly ranked and compartmentalized order. In this order, there was little room for behavior of the kinds attributed to Krishna's roisterous personality.

"Why do you say that it was Lord Krishna who taught you how to celebrate the festival of Holī?" I inquired of the many villagers who asserted that this was so. Answers, when they could be had at all, stressed that it was he who first played Holī with the cowherd boys and with Rādhā and the other *gopīs*. But my searches in the *Bhāgavata's* tenth book, and even in that book's recent and locally most popular adaptation, the *Ocean of Love*,[11] could discover no mention of Holī or any of the local festival's traditional activities, from the bonfire to the game of colors. "Just see how they play Holī in Mathurā district, in Lord Krishna's own village of Nandgaon, and in Rādhā's village of Barsana!" said the landlord. There, I was assured by the barber, who had also seen them, that the women train all year long, drinking milk and eating ghee like wrestlers, and there they beat the men *en masse*, before a huge audience of visitors, to the music of two hundred drums.

"I do not really believe that Lord Krishna grew up in just that village of Nandgaon," the landlord confided in me, "for Nanda, Krishna's foster father, must have lived on this side of the Jumnā River, near Gokula, as is written in the Purāṇa. But there in Nandgaon and Barsana they keep the old customs best."

The landlord's doubts were well placed, but not extensive enough, for, as I learned from a gazetteer of the district, the connection of Krishna, Rādhā, and the cowgirls with the rising of the women at Holī in those villages of Mathurā could not have originated before the early seventeenth-century efforts of certain immigrant Bengali Gosvāmin priests. The Gosvāmīs themselves—Rūpa, Sanātana, and their associates—were missionaries of the Krishnaite devotional movement led by Caitanya[12] in sixteenth-century Bengal, and that movement in turn had depended on the elaboration of the new notion of Rādhā as Krishna's favorite by the Telugu philosopher Nimbārka, possibly in the thirteenth century, and by other, somewhat earlier sectarians of Bengal and southern India.[13] The village names "Nandgaon" (village of Nanda) and "Barsana" (to make rain—an allusion to the "dark-as-a-cloud" epithet of Krishna) were probably seventeenth-century inventions, like the formal choreography of the battles of the sexes in those villages, that were contrived to attract pilgrims to the summer circuit of Krishna's rediscovered and refurbished holy land of Vraja.[14] Of course, privileged attacks by women upon men must have existed in village custom long before the promotional work of the Gosvāmīs—of this I was convinced by published studies of villages elsewhere, even in the farthest corners of the Hindī-speaking area, where such attacks were part of Holī, but not understood as conveying the message of Lord Krishna.[15] But once the great flow of devotees to Mathurā had begun from Bengal, Gujarat, and the South, the direction of cultural influence must have been reversed: what had been incorporated of peasant practice and local geography into the *Brahmavaivarta Purāṇa* and other new sectarian texts must have begun then to reshape peasant conceptions of peasant practice. At least the Krishnaite theology of the "love battles" in Kishan Garhi, and possibly some refinements of their rustic hydrology and stickwork, seemed to have been remodeled according to the famous and widely imitated public performances that had been visible in villages of the neighboring district for the past three centuries or so. The Mathurā pilgrimage and its literature appeared also to have worked similar effects upon two other festivals of Krishna in Kishan Garhi, in addition to Holī.[16]

To postulate the relative recency of the association of Rādhā and Krishna with the battles of canes and colors in Kishan Garhi was not to assert that the entire Holī festival could have had no connection with legends of Krishna before the seventeenth century. Reports on the mythology of Holī from many other localities described the bonfire, not as the burning of Holikā, but as the cremation of another demoness, Pūtanā.[17] Pūtanā was a demoness sent by King Kamsa of Mathurā to kill the infant Krishna by giving him to suck of her poisonous mother's milk. The Pūtanā story could no doubt claim a respectable antiquity, occurring as it did in the *Viṣṇu Purāṇa* and the *Harivaṃśa*; it was known in Kishan Garhi, although not applied currently to the rationalization of the Holī fire, and represented an acquaintance with a Krishna senior in type to the more erotic Krishna of the *Bhāgavata Purāṇa* and the later works. Even if I peeled away all explicit references to Krishna, both older and more recent, I would still have confronted other layers of Vaiṣṇavism in the Holī references to Rāma, whose cult centered in the middle Gangetic plain and in the South. And then there was the further Vaiṣṇava figure Prahlāda, another of ancient origin. Finally, I had to consider the proximity of Kishan Garhi to Mathurā, which was more than merely generically Vaiṣṇavite in its ancient religious orientations: Mathurā was thought to have been the original source of the legends of the child Krishna and his brother Balarāma, as suggested by Greek evidence from the fourth century B.C.E. as well as by the Purāṇic traditions.[18] Assuming that urban cults may always have been influential in villages and that such cults often carried forward what was already present in rural religious practice,[19] I thought it probable that the ancestors of the people of Kishan Garhi might well have celebrated the pranks of some divine ancestor of the Purāṇic Krishna even before their less complete adherence to the cults of Rāma and other gods later known as avatars of Viṣṇu. If these historical evidences and interpretations were generally sound, if Krishna had indeed waxed and waned before, then what both I and the villagers had taken to be their timeless living within a primordial local myth of Krishna appeared instead to represent rather the latest in a lengthy series of revivals and reinterpretations mingling local, regional, and even some quite remote movements of religious fashion.

Beneath the level of mythological enactment or rationalization, with its many shifts of contents through time, however, I felt that one might find certain more essential, underlying connections between the moral constitution of villages like Kishan Garhi and the general social form of the Holī festival—so the functional assumption of Radcliffe-Brown had led me to hope. Superficially, in various regions and eras, the festival might concern witches or demonesses (Holikā or Holākā, Pūtanā, Ḍhoṇḍhā), Viṣṇu triumphant (as Rāma, Narasiṃha, or Krishna), Śiva as an ascetic in conflict with gods of lust (Kāma, Madana, or the nonscriptural Nathurām), or others.[20] Festival practices might also vary greatly. Were there enduring, widespread features, I wondered? From a distributional and documentary study by N. K. Bose, I learned that spring festivals featuring bonfires, a degree of sexual license, and generally saturnalian carousing had probably existed in villages of many parts of India for at least the better part of the past two thousand years.[21] Spring festivals of this one general character evidently had remained consistently associated with many of India's complex, caste-bound communities. Even if only some of such festivals had had the puckish, ambiguous Krishna as their presiding deity, and these only in recent centuries, many seemed since the beginning of our knowledge to have enshrined divinities who sanctioned, however briefly, some of the same riotous sorts of social behavior.

Now a full year had passed in my investigations, and the Festival of Love was again approaching. Again I was apprehensive for my physical person, but was forewarned with social structural knowledge that might yield better understanding of the events to come. This time, without the draft of marijuana, I began to see the pandemonium of Holī falling into an extraordinarily regular social ordering. But this was an order precisely inverse to the social and ritual principles of routine life. Each riotous act at Holī implied some opposite, positive rule or fact of everyday social organization in the village.

Who were those smiling men whose shins were being most mercilessly beaten by the women? They were the wealthier Brahman and Jāṭ farmers of the village, and the beaters were those ardent local Rādhās, the "wives of the village," figuring by both the real and the fictional intercaste system of kinship. The wife of an "elder brother" was properly a man's joking mate, while the wife of a "younger brother" was properly removed from him by rules of extreme respect, but both were merged here with a man's mother-surrogates, the wives of his "father's younger brothers," in one revolutionary cabal of "wives" that cut across all lesser lines and links. The boldest beaters in this veiled battalion were often in fact the wives of the farmers' low-caste field laborers, artisans, or menials—the concubines and kitchen help of the victims. "Go and bake bread!" teased one farmer, egging his assailant on. "Do you want some seed from me?" shouted another flattered victim, smarting under the blows, but standing his ground. Six Brahman men in their fifties, pillars of village society, limped past in panting flight from the quarterstaff wielded by a massive young Bhaṅgin, sweeper of their latrines. From this carnage suffered by their village brothers, all daughters of the village stood apart, yet held themselves in readiness to attack any potential husband who might wander in from another, marriageable village to pay a holiday call.

Who was that "King of the Holī" riding backward on the donkey? It was an older boy of high caste, a famous bully, put there by his organized victims (but seeming to relish the prominence of his disgrace).

Who was in that chorus singing so lustily in the potters' lane? Not just the resident caste fellows, but six washermen, a tailor, and three Brahmans, joined each year for this day only in an idealistic musical company patterned on the friendships of the gods.

Who were those transfigured "cowherds" heaping mud and dust on all the leading citizens? They were the water carrier, two young Brahman priests, and a barber's son, avid experts in the daily routines of purification.

Whose household temple was festooned with goat's bones by unknown merrymakers? It was the temple of that Brahman widow who had constantly harassed neighbors and kinsmen with actions at law.

In front of whose house was a burlesque dirge being sung by a professional asectic of the village? It was the house of a very much alive moneylender, notorious for his punctual collections and his insufficient charities.

Who was it who had his head fondly anointed, not only with handfuls of the sublime red powders, but also with a gallon of diesel oil? It was the village landlord, and the anointer was his cousin and archrival, the police headman of Kishan Garhi.

Who was it who was made to dance in the streets, fluting like Lord Krishna, with a garland of old shoes around his neck? It was I, the visiting anthropologist, who had asked far too many questions, and had always to receive respectful answers.

Here indeed were the many village kinds of love confounded—respectful regard for parents and patrons; the idealized affection for brothers, sisters, and comrades; the longing of man for union with the divine; and the rugged lust of sexual mates—all broken suddenly out of their usual, narrow channels by a simultaneous increase of intensity. Boundless, unilateral love of every kind flooded over the usual compartmentalization and indifference among separated castes and families. Insubordinate libido inundated all established hierarchies of age, sex, caste, wealth, and power.

The social meaning of Krishna's doctrine in its rural North Indian recension is not unlike one conservative social implication of Jesus' Sermon on the Mount. The Sermon admonishes severely, but at the same time postpones the destruction of the secular social order until a distant future. Krishna does not postpone the reckoning of the mighty until an ultimate Judgment Day, but schedules it regularly as a masque at the full moon of every March. And the Holī of Krishna is no mere doctrine of love: rather it is the script for a drama that must be acted out by each devotee passionately, joyfully.

The dramatic balancing of Holī—the world destruction and world renewal, the world pollution followed by world purification—occurs not only on the abstract level of structural principles, but also in the person of each participant. Under the tutelage of Krishna, each person plays and for the moment may experience the role of his opposite: the servile wife acts the domineering husband, and vice versa; the ravisher acts the ravished; the menial acts the master; the enemy acts the friend; the strictured youths act the rulers of the republic. The observing anthropologist, inquiring and reflecting on the forces that move men in their orbits, finds himself pressed to act the witless bumpkin. Each actor playfully takes the role of others in relation to his own usual self. Each may thereby learn to play his own routine roles afresh, surely with renewed understanding, possibly with greater grace, perhaps with a reciprocating love.

NOTES

1. "Kishan Garhi," a pseudonymous village in Aligarh district, Uttar Pradesh, was studied by me from March 1951 to April 1952, with the assistance of an Area Research Training Fellowship grant from the Social Science Research Council. For his comments on this paper, I am indebted to David E. Orlinsky.

2. In this local version of the Prahlāda story, King Harnākas will readily be recognized as Hiraṇya Kaśipu of the Purāṇas, e.g., *Viṣṇu Purāṇa* 1.17 (p. 108 in the translation by Horace Hayman Wilson [Calcutta: Punthi Pustak, 1961]). Holā or Holākā, in the oldest texts a name for the bonfire or festival and unconnected with the story of Prahlāda or other scriptural gods (see the sources cited by Pandurang Vaman Kane, *History of Dharmaśāstra* [Poona, 1958], Vol. V, pp. 237–239), appears only in recent popular stories as a female, and as a relative of Prahlāda. For Holī stories of the Hindi region generally, see William Crooke, *The Popular Religion and Folk-Lore of Northern India* (London: Archibald Constable & Co., 1896), Vol. II, p. 313; for similar tales from Delhi State, see Oscar Lewis, with the assistance of Victor Barnouw, *Village Life in Northern India* (Urbana: University of Illinois, 1958),

p. 232; and from the Alwar district of Rajasthan, see Hilda Wernher, *The Land and the Well* (New York: John Day Co., 1946), pp. 199–200.

3. Some of the cow-dung objects for the Holī fire are prepared after the Gobardhan Divālī festival in autumn, with the materials of Gobardhan Bābā's (= Krishna's ?) body. See McKim Marriott, "Little Communities in an Indigenous Civilization," in McKim Marriott, ed., *Village India* (Chicago: University of Chicago Press, 1955), pp. 199–200. Other objects are prepared on the second or fifth days of the bright fortnight of the month of Phāgun, whose last day is the day of the Holī fire.

4. Books VII and X, as in *The Śrīmad-Bhagbātam of Krishna-Dwaipāyana-Vyāsa*, J. M. Sanyal, trans. (Calcutta, n.d.), Vols. IV and V.

5. Alfred Reginald Radcliffe-Brown, "Religion and Society," in *Structure and Function in Primitive Society* (London: Cohen & West, 1952), pp. 155, 177.

6. Bronislaw Malinowski, *Argonauts of the Western Pacific* (London, 1932), pp. 6–8.

7. "Taboo," in Radcliffe-Brown, *Structure and Function*, p. 152.

8. Émile Durkheim, *The Elementary Forms of the Religious Life*, Joseph Ward Swain, trans. (Glencoe, Ill.: Free Press, 1947), p. 299.

9. *The Andaman Islanders* (Glencoe, Ill.: Free Press, 1948), p. 235.

10. Details of some of these festivals are given in McKim Marriott, *op. cit.*, pp. 192–206. The social organization of Kishan Garhi is described more fully in McKim Marriott, "Social Structure and Change in a U.P. Village," in M. N. Srinivas, ed., *India's Villages* (London, 1960), pp. 106–121.

11. Lallu Lal, *Premasāgara*, Frederic Pincott, trans. (London, 1897).

12. Frederic Salmon Growse, *Mathurā: A District Memoir* (2nd ed., 1880), pp. 72, 93, 183–184.

13. *Ibid.*, pp. 178–221; John Nicol Farquhar, *An Outline of the Religious Literature of India* (London: Oxford University Press, 1920), pp. 238–240.

14. Growse, *Mathurā: A District Memoir*, pp. 71–94.

15. Women beat men at or near the time of Holī among the Gonds of Mandla district, according to Verrier Elwin, *Leaves from the Jungle* (London: J. Murray, 1936), p. 135; in Nimar, according to Stephen Fuchs, *The Children of Hari* (New York: Praeger, 1950), pp. 300–301; and elsewhere in Madhya Pradesh, according to Robert Vane Russell and Hira Lal, *The Tribes and Castes of the Central Provinces of India* (London, 1916), Vol. II, p. 126, and Vol. III, p. 117. The usage is reported also from Alwar in Rajasthan by Hilda Wernher, *op. cit.*, p. 208, and from Delhi by O. Lewis and V. Barnouw, *op. cit.*, p. 232.

16. At Krishna's birthday anniversary, biographies of his life by poets of Mathurā are read. At the Gobardhan Divālī, the circumambulation of the hill by the pilgrims is duplicated in model; see McKim Marriott, "Little Communities," in *op. cit.*, pp. 199–200.

17. See W. Crooke, *op. cit.*, Vol. II, pp. 313–314; and Ṛgvedi (pseud.), *Āryāncā Saṇāncā Prācīna va Arvācīna Itihāsa* (in Marathi) (Bombay, n.d.), p. 399.

18. F. S. Growse, *Mathurā: a District Memoir*, p. 103.

19. R. Redfield and M. Singer, "The Cultural Role of Cities," *Economic Development and Cultural Change*, III (1954), pp. 53–74.

20. W. Crooke, *op. cit.*, Vol. II, pp. 313–314, 319–320; P. V. Kane, *op. cit.*, Vol. V, pp. 237–240; Ṛgvedi, *op. cit.*, pp. 399–400, 405.

21. Nirmal Kumar Bose, "The Spring Festival of India," in *Cultural Anthropology and Other Essays* (Calcutta, 1953), pp. 73–102.

The Delusion of Gender and Renunciation in Buddhist Kashmir

Kim Gutschow

> In the enlightened mind, there is no male or female.
> In the Buddha's speech, there is no near or far.
>
> *Byang chub sems la pho mo med;*
> *rgyal ba² bka² la nye ring med.*

This Buddhist proverb from Kashmir illustrates the ideal doctrinal view that gender is supposed to be an illusion and not an obstacle on the path to enlightenment. In practice, however, gender appears to be a considerable obstacle on the monastic path. The manner in which the Buddha first founded the nuns' and monks' orders enshrined the dialectic of power between those orders. By making nuns subordinate to monks, the Buddha enabled the latter to amass considerable social, symbolic, and economic capital at the expense of nuns, their female counterparts in the Buddhist order. Despite recent challenges from feminists and international Buddhist reformers, nuns in Buddhist Kashmir have faced a glass ceiling in terms of ritual knowledges and practices. As a result, nuns were assumed to count less than monks and were also "left out of the count" in literature on Buddhism in Kashmir.

My method of emphasizing nuns over monks, as well as practice over doctrine, diverges from earlier scholarly approaches to Tibetan Buddhism. It pursues a heuristic laid out by Michelle Rosaldo (1980) and Sherry Ortner (1996), who have argued that one should not study women in isolation from men, nor should one isolate gender from other axes of social asymmetry.[1] While previous studies of Buddhist nuns (Barnes 1987, 1994; Tsomo 1988, 1996) have attempted to reconstruct the history of nuns, they have overlooked the dynamics of power between monks and nuns by which nuns have come to be second-class citizens in the monastic realm. Lopez (ed. 1995, 1998) has shown how Buddhist studies has long privileged the text and doctrine over the informant and her practices, while offering an essentialized and timeless Shangri-La image of Tibetan Buddhism. I follow Lopez's call to deconstruct the myths about Tibetan Buddhism, by looking at the tropes which have been used to describe Buddhist nuns in literature on Buddhism in Kashmir.[2]

Until recently, much of the scholarship on Buddhism in Kashmir either ignored or misrecognized nuns due to a narrow doctrinal image of what a nun should look like. The absence of nuns in much of the literature on Buddhist monasticism in Kashmir is especially disconcerting given that nuns make up nearly two fifths of the resident monastic population in the Kashmiri subdistrict of Zangskar.[3] This ratio, which may be one of the highest in the entire Himalayan realm, is twice as high as the ratio of nuns to monks in the Indo-Tibetan borderlands before 1959 and eight times as high as the ratio in Tibetan refugee monasteries by the late 1980s.[4] Zangskar, which comprises the southern and safer half of Kargil district—the site of the most recent military clashes between India and Pakistan in the summer of 1999—has been Buddhist since at least the tenth century, although it is also home to a minority of Sunni Muslims. Although it covers an area roughly twice the size of Rhode Island, Zangskar's meager population of 12,000 makes it one of least populated regions in India.[5] The inhabitants, who live in over a hundred hamlets and villages at elevations between 3,000 and 4,200 meters, sustain a resident monastic population that makes up nearly 4 percent of the total population.

Although most of the monastic population of Zangskar lives in its seven monasteries and nine nunneries, nuns have more unorthodox residential arrangements. While most ordained nuns reside at a nunnery in monastic cells, some nuns live temporarily in the village caring for their aged parents. Regardless of where they reside, all nuns must work daily in the village in exchange for their daily bread. Some nunneries also house elderly women who are not ordained but take on five precepts—not to kill, steal, lie, commit sexual misconduct, or take intoxicants. This state of affairs was so confusing for many scholars that they often lumped ordained novices together with such elderly precept holders who had never been ordained and had no religious function in village life. While both these women are called "nuns" (*jo mo*) in the local vernacular, lay precept holders are also known as "village nuns" (*grong pa'i jo mo*) and never as ordained novices (*dge tshul ma*).[6] While the association between ordained nuns and elderly spinsters has contributed to a degraded image of Tibetan Buddhist nuns, past scholars failed to ask several critical questions: Why do ordained nuns work on village farms? Why don't they have the same institutional support that monks do? Why have nunneries become retreat centers for merit-making, while monasteries have served as centers for art, education, politics, business, and philosophy? To answer these questions, let us consider how nuns came to be second-class citizens within the Buddhist monastic order.

THE LAW OF THE BUDDHA

According to canonical texts, the Buddha allegedly accepted women into his monastic order on one condition: that they adopt the so-called Eight Chief Rules (*Garudhamma*). These rules specified that nuns may neither censure nor admonish monks and that nuns must take their ordinations, bimonthly confessions, rainy season retreats, and penances in the presence of monks. The Buddha's aunt objected to only one of the eight rules—the one specifying that even a senior nun who has been ordained one hundred years must bow down to a youthful novice who has been ordained but a day—but her objection was overruled by the Buddha himself. While scholars have suggested that these baneful rules may never have been spoken by the Buddha, their lasting legacy is undeniable (Falk 1980; Gross 1993; Horner 1930; Paul 1985; Sponberg 1992; Willis 1985). The cumulative effect of the Eight Chief Rules was to give monks the pastoral rights to discipline and punish nuns. Monks came to regulate the traffic in nuns, by controlling women's admission to and exclusion from the nuns' order at all stages of the process. In Kashmir today, monks still officiate most rites of passage which nuns must undergo, including first tonsure, novice ordination, entrance into the monastic assembly, absolution, penances, expulsion, and final cremation (Gutschow 1998, 2000).

When the Buddha subordinated nuns to monks, the nunneries were never able to gain the same power and wealth that monasteries could and eventually the nuns' order died out in many parts of South and Southeast Asia. As popular and devotional forms of Hinduism grew in the first millennium, the newly formed Buddhist orders had to compete for a shrinking base of donors. During this period, Buddhist nuns could not command the same educational and ritual prestige that monks could. Due to decreasing patronage, lineages of fully ordained nuns died out one by one across the subcontinent, as region after region lost the ability to form the requisite quorum of ten nuns to ordain the next generation of nuns. The monks' order also suffered and was nearly wiped out in medieval Sri Lanka and Tibet for instance. Yet by importing monks from elsewhere, often at great expense, the royal patrons in these places managed to perpetuate the lineage of fully ordained monks even in times of considerable social and political turmoil.[7] In contrast, little effort was made to revive the nuns' order when and where it collapsed.

By the twelfth century, women could no longer seek full ordination in much of South and Southeast Asia. While Tibetan Buddhist orders allowed women to ordain as novices, they never supported a lineage of fully ordained nuns. In Sri Lanka, Burma, Thailand, Laos, and Cambodia, women have the option of holding between eight and ten precepts as de facto rather than de jure nuns.[8] By 1988, of the 60,000 women worldwide who held some form of Buddhist precepts or monastic vows, only one-fourth were fully ordained nuns, who lived mostly in China, Taiwan, Korea, Vietnam, and the West.[9] The recent efforts to reinstate a full ordination lineage in the Tibetan tradition and in Sri Lanka with the assistance of East Asian nuns from Taiwan or Korea has not had much impact in Kashmir.[10] Although the Dalai Lama has given his support, many monastics and some feminists remain opposed, albeit for different reasons. Senior monks argue that formal teaching structures are not yet in place, while feminists hold that female renunciants are better off outside this disciplinary gaze of monks.

In Buddhist Kashmir, the lack of full ordination left novice nuns at the mercy of fully ordained monks who amassed enormous amounts of symbolic and economic capital. Monks became virtuoso ritualists, philosophers, and bureaucrats, while nunneries devolved into impoverished and politically irrelevant retreat centers.[11] While renowned religious women like Machig Labdron, Yeshe Tsogyal, and Nangsa Obum taught unconventional Tantric teachings outside the monastic framework, nuns rarely had the chance to transmit esoteric teachings to their own disciples. Each generation of nuns had to go to the monks for further teachings and advanced ritual training. The exclusion of women from philosophical dialectics and esoteric ritual practices was maintained in each of the four schools of Tibetan Buddhism (Gelug, Kagyud, Sakya, and Nyingma). Until recently, nuns were ineligible to attend the highest monastic and ritual colleges of the Dalai Lama's own Gelug school of Tibetan Buddhism. Western feminists have asked the Dalai Lama to accept nuns at his exclusive philosophical academy in Dharmsala, the Namgyal Institute of Dialectics. Other initiatives have led the avant-garde nunneries in Kathmandu, Kyirong and Kopan to teach nuns sacred arts like the construction of sand mandalas (*dkyil ʿkhor*), burnt offerings (*sbyin sreg*), and meditative dances (*ʿchams*).[12] Significantly, these are the ritual practices which have earned Tibetan monks fame and cash in their travels abroad.

While the Buddha clearly disavowed the role of the priest in purifying others, Buddhist monks in Zangskar have monopolized many ritual practices, including the expiatory and purificatory rites which are so essential to the maintenance of village and household space. In Zangskar as elsewhere in India, the female body exemplifies an innate impurity which the male does not.[13] Due to menstruation and childbirth, women's bodies are conceptualized as inherently impure and thus offensive to the deities of place and space which guarantee household, village, and monastic prosperity. Even though nuns are never mothers and, if elderly, have ceased to menstruate, they remain excluded from many places and rituals of power where Tantric deities, local guardian deities, or underworld spirits are worshiped. Monks have preserved the sole authority to officiate the expiatory and propitiatory rites (*gtor rgyab, brgya bzhi, mdos, glud*), ritual ablutions (*khrus*), and agrarian circumambulations (*ᶜbum khor*) which cleanse monastic, village, and household spaces from ritual pollution. At routine life-cycle events to which both assemblies of nuns and monks are invited, such as funerals and weddings, the ritual roles for nuns and monks are carefully segregated. Only monks may officiate the cremation rite (*sbying sregs*) and the transfer of the corpse's consciousness (*cho ga*), and only monks conduct the ritual transference (*g.yang ᶜgugs, zor*) of the bride from her natal to her husband's household and clan deity. Despite their textual and ritual literacy, nuns are called to perform basic household rites only as substitutes when monks are unavailable.

THE ECONOMY OF MERIT IN KASHMIR

Because the monks' order is still considered to be a higher "field of merit" than the nuns' order in Kashmir today, villagers channel their donations and alms to the monastery. Historically, giving to monasteries offered donors both political prestige and private merit. The historical record for Zangskar and Tibet offers many examples of kings and nobles who gave land grants to charismatic monks during times of political or social crisis in order to demonstrate their piety.[14] By the time of the Permanent Settlement in 1908, local monasteries held one-tenth of all cultivated land in Zangskar. By 1994, Zangskar's largest monastery still owned 90 times the average private holding of 2.8 acres per household.[15] Even today, one out of four households in Zangskar still sharecrop one or more fields from a monastery and some sharecroppers own no land whatsoever. Monasteries command enormous rents, as well as customary donations of corvee labor, grain, butter, firewood, dung, and other services. In contrast to the monasteries, most nunneries collect neither rents nor other tithes. At present, five of nine nunneries in Zangskar have no fields at all, and the other four own a handful of fields from which they harvest a pittance. The monastery in Karsha annually earns one hundred times as much grain as the nunnery, although there are only four times as many monks as nuns.[16] Because nunneries have so little endowment, they cannot afford to feed their members on a daily basis. Karsha nunnery's rites are sponsored on a rotational basis by nun stewards who solicit donations of butter, flour, and other staples.

Institutional poverty forces Zangskari nuns to toil selflessly on their parents' farms in exchange for their daily bread. Even as their shorn heads and sexless maroon robes signal a lofty intent to renounce the worldly life, nuns are pulled back into productive roles by households unwilling to lose an able-bodied servant. According to a common Tibetan proverb, "If you want to serve, make your son a monk, if you want a servant, make your

daughter a nun." The dutiful daughters and sisters who toil on their father's or brother's estate years after taking monastic vows ensures the
agrarian prosperity of lay households as well as monasteries. Classical Buddhist injunctions against nuns performing chores for monks are overlooked by monks who recruit nuns to wash, sew, and cook for their private
benefit. Moreover, the monastic community has no compunction about re-
cruiting nuns to perform the most menial and labor-intensive tasks on the
monastic estates, like weeding the monastery's fields, tending huge flocks
of monastic cattle and yaks at the high pastures for half the year, washing,
drying, and roasting thousands of kilos of grain which the monastery collects from its sharecroppers, and baking thousands of loaves of bread for
two annual festivals—around winter solstice and before spring plowing.
In theory, compassion is supposed to be applied universally; in practice, it
is exacted along lines dictated by custom and kinship.

While renunciation is a full-time occupation for monks, it is an unpaid
but meritorious vocation for nuns. Sending a daughter to the nunnery is
like placing her in a state school without a scholarship. She may have access to peers, knowledge, and travel which take her far beyond the provin-
cial village life, but she must pay her own way. On the other hand, sending
a son to the monastery is like enrolling him in an Ivy League or Oxbridge
college with a full fellowship. Not only is he guaranteed a handsome sti-
pend for his studies, but his elite education and status will provide him
with ample opportunities for privilege and private profit for the rest of his
life. The senior monks and reincarnate[17] priests graduate into more ob-
scure offices for which the duties are less and less understood but the re-
muneration in cash and kind ever more handsome. In recent decades, increasing opportunities for employment in the civil and military sectors of
the state economy have left monasteries struggling to attract young members. Monasteries are rapidly losing monks to the pull of the secular and
consumer world, while some nunneries are gaining members and others
are being founded in villages where there have not been nuns for centuries.
How can this be?

WHO BECOMES A NUN IN ZANGSKAR?

Given the patriarchal nature of Buddhist monasticism, why would an able-
bodied woman in the flower of her youth still wish to join the nunnery?
Why do young women continue to pursue the Buddha's discipline of detachment in a region where the economy of merit is giving way to an economy of consumption? Let us look at the narratives told by a few nuns at
the largest nunnery in Zangskar, Karsha.

Tsering was raised by her mother, who had never been married to Tsering's father. Although customary law gives the father custody of his child

after she is weaned, Tsering's mother simply refused when her father came to collect her at age four. She pointed out to her former lover that while he had a wife and children, she was single and would need Tsering's help on her fields. Tsering and her mother lived together until she was sixteen, when she got the shock of her life. One day, she came upon her father telling her mother that a neighbor had sent the "asking beer" (ᶜdri chang), the first of many negotiations necessary to arrange Tsering's marriage. Tsering spun on her heels and took to the hills behind the house, climbing up and up the cliff until she was dizzy, only stopping when the village and her house were no more than a speck far below. While her father and mother called her all afternoon, she remained hidden in the safety of the red rocks. She sat and thought about how to avoid the indignities under which her mother had chafed. Her mother's first liaison, with Tsering's father, had been disastrous. As the youngest and most spoiled of five sisters, her mother had inherited a parcel of land and some livestock from Tsering's grandfather. With the security that property brings in a land where most women are disenfranchised by virtue of their sex, her proud mother was unwilling to submit to Tsering's father's illicit affairs. Her mother's next affair was with an abusive drunk. As Tsering sat and recounted these relationships, she decided she would never marry. She waited until night fell, when she heard the jingle of her father saddling his horse and the familiar clop of the hooves fading in the distance. As she came down, her mother teased her about getting married but agreed to let her become a nun, as she asked. She realized how helpful it would be to have a daughter close by for daily chores.

Palmo told me about the misfortunes that brought her to the nunnery. Because Palmo's mother was only a mistress and never a wife, she was forced by custom to relinquish her rights to raise her daughter. Her mother's role as clandestine mistress of several brothers in the same household gave her little respect and no authority over the children she bore. Palmo's paternity was decided by lottery among the three brothers who had shared Palmo's mother's bed. Following customary law, Palmo was taken away from her mother to be raised by her father, who would have the rights to her labor until she was married. Palmo's father came to take his daughter away from her mother when he moved to a distant village, where he married his brother's widow. Palmo was an outsider twice over in her new stepmother's house. Her father was a powerless second husband who would never fill his deceased brother's shoes while Palmo was a sign of his past infidelities. Palmo was only fed the leftover scraps after others had eaten and clothes which her stepsister had neglected. Palmo lost count of how many times she ran away to her mother's village, before her father came to beat her and take her back home. Palmo vowed never to wind up a spurned mistress like her mother, and asked her father's permission to join the nunnery. When her father and stepmother stalled in hopes of keeping Palmo at home to do chores, she threatened to kill herself. After years of private study and a steady resolve to join the nunnery, Palmo convinced her father to take her to the nunnery, although he has barely supported her since that day.

Chosnyid had to struggle to renounce for she was an eldest daughter who flagrantly disobeyed both her parents and society. Shortly before she and her best friend were to be married, they went to hear the Kalachakra teachings given by a famous monk. They were so moved, they offered their hair and jewels to the monk, begging him to shave their heads and allow them to take up five precepts. When her parents heard that their daughter had shaved her head and given away her jewelry, they were livid with rage. Her father came to fetch her at the nunnery, telling her that he'd been negotiating her wedding for five years, with considerable expense. Thrashing her soundly, he tied her onto the horse in front of him like a child and took her home. When his daughter outwitted him and fled back to the nunnery, her father came to fetch her once again. For a year, Chosnyid and her father were engaged in this tedious game of hide-and-seek until she could bear it no longer. When the snows melted, she fled over the passes to Dharmsala, where she became a nun and settled near the Dalai Lama's personal monastery. She has never returned to Zangskar, although twenty-five years have passed.

THE STRUGGLES AND MOTIVATIONS FOR RENUNCIATION

What do these stories tell us about the struggle for renunciation in Zangskar? A propensity for religious study or devotion, the words of a charismatic teacher, and childhood hardship or abuse all influence the choice to renounce lay life. Yet one cannot leap to facile generalizations. While domestic abuse, jealous stepmothers, and illegitimacy crop up in the lives of many Zangskari women, only a few will reach the nunnery gates. There is no single factor that determines who becomes a nun, yet a few patterns emerge. Over half the nuns at Karsha come from homes where there is only one parent due to parental death, divorce, or illegitimacy. Nearly two-thirds of the Karsha nuns were sent to live with relatives as au pair girls during their childhood. During this period away from home, many of them may have learned the self-abnegation and stoicism essential to the celibate life. Oldest daughters from unbroken homes, who would ordinarily be destined for marriage, almost never become nuns.[18] While there is no bar against wealthy or aristocratic daughters joining the nunnery, most nuns come from households at the middle-to-lower end of the income spectrum.

Caste, rather than class, presents one of the more salient obstacles to the religious life in Zangskar. Women who belong to the lowest strata (*rigs ngan*), which is made up of three named clans, Gara, Beda, and Mon, are ineligible to join the nunnery, without exception. Although Zangskar does not have a caste system of hierarchically ranked *jati*, the members of these three clans are treated like outcasts and denied intermarriage and commensality with the rest of the population. They cannot join a monastic assembly because, as one nun put it quite pithily, "If the blacksmith becomes chantmaster and must sit at the head of the seating row, where shall we sit?" In other words, she could not imagine a reversal of the traditional seating hierarchy (*gral*), in which the members of these lower strata must always sit at the end of the row, nearest the door.

While the women in these stories share a determined desire to escape the inevitable hardship of their lot, joining the nunnery does not happen overnight. Even those young women who flee to the nunnery somewhat abruptly must dedicate themselves to a lengthy period of tutelage. While many young women dream of becoming nuns or later regret that they didn't, the educated elite who actually become nuns must persevere through a lengthy apprenticeship and training period. Because in these changing times when Urdu and English literacy are critical to desirable government jobs or military service, young girls are taught Tibetan even more rarely than young boys. Those who make it into the ranks of the nunnery or the monastery are few and far between. Young women who become nuns must show extraordinary aptitude in order to grasp the archaic syntax of classical Tibetan while memorizing abstruse philosophical texts of which little is understood or explicated. Women do not arrive at the nunnery gate "by accident" as much as by sustained efforts. Those women who join a monastic assembly are not unwanted spinsters, widows, and divorcees with no other options in life but to get themselves to a nunnery. None lack the endurance necessary to stick to the straight and narrow path while avoiding the seductive lure of mundane desires and affairs in which they must learn to play no part.

> Everything by your own will is blessed happiness,
> Everything by another's will is suffering . . .
>
> (*Rang dbang thams cad dge ba yin*
> *Gzhan dbang thams cad sdug bsngal yin*)

Several nuns recited this popular Zangskari proverb when asked to explain why they became nuns. What they meant was that the freedom to make merit rather than babies or more housework was one of the most important reasons for joining the nunnery. The two most common reasons given for joining the nunnery were (1) to earn merit to avoid a female rebirth the next time around and (2) to avoid the suffering of marriage and maternity. Merit is seen as the vehicle that takes one out of suffering and transports one into a better rebirth. In fact, many nuns explain that they are at the nunnery not so much out of choice but because of their destiny or karma. In other words, the merit they have accumulated in their previous lifetimes is far more important than any choices they may have made or failed to make. Yet seeing one's position as a karmic boon does not deny agency or prevent nuns from surmounting considerable obstacles, as the stories above suggest. Adversity forges determination as much as endurance for those who are truly dedicated to the renunciant lifestyle.

Many nuns told me quite explicitly that they became nuns to avoid the pain of abusive marriages, miscarriages, and infant deaths that they have seen their sisters and girlfriends experience. These fears are not exaggerated in a region where one in three children die under the age of five. The local prevalence of alcoholism, domestic abuse, and rape results in unhappy marriages and a fairly high rate of divorce, while fears of rape are a constraint on women's freedoms and vocational opportunities.[19] The nunnery still serves as a haven for those women who aspired to freedom from domestic drudgery despite the recent increases in educational and vocational opportunities. While a small percentage of students actually complete ten years of education at shoddy government schools in Zangskar, nearly 99 percent fail the secondary leaving exam and are thus ineligible to obtain most higher government posts. In recent decades, some of the rare women who have passed the exam have become nurses, teachers, and medical orderlies. Yet many still lack the wealth and prestige to secure a job in the lucrative government sector, for which there are always far more applicants than positions. Yet women may still choose the nunnery over a secular career, which does not free a woman from her husband's or brother's authority. Nuns, in contrast, gain a "room of their own" at the nunnery, which leaves them relatively free to pursue meditations, studies, and merit.

Why would parents want to send a daughter to the nunnery? Yalman (1962) has argued that poor families in Sri Lanka benefit by sending their children to the monastery. This rational choice framework does not apply in Zangskar for several reasons. Firstly, Zangskari families who give up their daughters to a nunnery still have a mouth to feed, because of the institutional poverty of nunneries. Secondly, a more important motivation from the parents' perspective is gaining an adult worker who will help on the family estate. Unlike elsewhere in South Asia, Zangskari households face shortages of labor rather than food. The recent migration of young men out of Zangskar for education or jobs in the military and civil sectors have reduced the pool of available adult labor and made it even more desirable to have a daughter become a nun and servant. Poor households who cannot afford the costly ritual sponsorship required of nuns who join the monastic assembly may choose to keep their daughters at home as spinsters rather than letting them become nuns. Lastly, prospective nuns face significant emotional and psychological obstacles, not the least of which may include their families. One cannot treat monasticism as a solution to the problem of rural poverty. If poverty was the main reason that children joined the nunnery or monastery, these institutions would be overflowing with members. The spiritual gains of monasticism are tempered by the obstacles and difficulties of maintaining lifelong vows. Sometimes these include the families themselves. While some parents welcome the prospect of a daughter at the nunnery because they gain both merit and a lifelong servant, others are hesitant to commit their children to such a path. The risk of being forced to leave the monastic life for breaking one of the root vows hinders many prospective applicants from even joining.

MODERNITY AND MONASTICISM IN KASHMIR

In recent years, local and foreign feminists have made attempts to revolutionize the education of nuns in the Kashmiri regions of Zangskar and Ladakh. The Ladakhi Nuns Association has been founded by a charismatic local nun, Ani Palmo, to benefit some two dozen nunneries in eastern Kashmir, while harnessing the more recent flood of foreign sponsorship. Kashmir's Buddhist nunneries came onto the map of global feminism after the Fourth International Conference on Women and Buddhism was held in Leh, Ladakh, to promote Buddhist women's education, ordination, and religious training (Gutschow 1995). The entwined flows of capitalism and feminism have resulted in a flurry of expansion and building at over a dozen Ladakhi nunneries, several of which were founded in the last decade. Many of these nunneries face severe shortages of housing, land, and educational resources. In an effort to educate nuns about the value of the monastic discipline, Ani Palmo organized a series of innovative monastic conferences in the late 1990s. Learned Ladakhi monks holding doctorates of theology explained the meaning and importance of the novice precepts to nuns, using explanatory texts such as *The Essential Ocean of Vinaya*. The instructors explained that every monastic bears a karmic burden, not only for him- or herself, but as an example for laypeople. Ani Palmo concluded the conference with a memorable speech about how a nun's virtue is like a white cloth: once stained, it can never be clean or pure again. It is far too early to tell if these efforts will lift the glass ceiling on the nuns' vocation or simply reinforce yet again the subordination of undereducated nuns to monks.

Whether the Buddha intended it or not, the monastic order was adapted to prevailing social hierarchies from the moment of its inception. Impoverished and undereducated communities of nuns have had little opportunity to learn the ritual practices and knowledges controlled by monks. While Buddhist doctrine has attempted to transcend gender by arguing that it has no bearing on the potential for enlightenment, Buddhist practice maintains disparity at every turn. When parents send their daughters to the nunnery in exchange for merit, they also earn a share of her labor henceforth. Although Buddhism is often portrayed as having a politically correct ideology on many issues, including the environment, its stance on gender has been not as enlightened as it could have been.

ACKNOWLEDGMENTS

Tibetan terms are written following the standard Wylie system of transliteration although Kashmiri spellings may vary from Lhasa Tibetan. I thank the nuns, monks, and individual families who have hosted me in Zangskar for their boundless patience, compassion, and generosity. The Jacob Javits Foundation, the Mellon Foundation, and the Harvard Department of Anthropology funded my research between 1991 and 1997. Thanks to Michael Aris, Hanna Havnevik, Arthur Kleinman, Sarah Lamb, Sarah Levine, Diane Mines, Jan Willis, and Nur Yalman for helpful comments and conversations.

NOTES

1. Ortner (1996) follows Rosaldo (1980) in arguing that the issue of male dominance is less interesting than the study of how that dominance is framed differently according to the relations between the sexes and the interrelationship of other asymmetrical relations in any given society.

2. Lopez's (1998: 211) critical deconstruction of Tibetan Buddhism repeats the common tropes about nuns when it notes, "Unmarried daughters often became nuns (sometimes remaining at home). Other women became nuns to escape a bad marriage, to avoid pregnancy, or after the death of a spouse." Such images do not represent the current reality in Kashmir, where not one of the 115 resident nuns I have interviewed in the last decade was a divorcee and only one was a widow.

3. Scholars who have described Zangskar's seven monasteries while ignoring its nine nunneries include Crook and Osmaston (1994), Dendaletche (1985), Dargyay and Dargyay (1980), Dargyay (1987, 1988), Petech (1977, 1998), Schuh (1976, 1983), and Snellgrove and Skorupski (1980).

4. Shakabpa (1967) reports the ratio of one nun for every nine monks in Tibet before 1959. Havnevik (1992: 85) reports 653 nuns and 6,337 monks in India, Nepal, Sikkim, and Bhutan before 1959; and 340 nuns and 6,278 monks in Tibetan refugee monasteries by the late 1980s. Gutschow (1998: 97) reports that Zangskar's nine nunneries housed 116 nuns while its seven monasteries housed 297 monks in 1997.

5. Aridity and altitude allow for the cultivation of three subsistence crops— barley, wheat, and peas—as well as extensive flocks of sheep, goats, cows, yaks, and crossbreeds (*mdzo*). Most villages have between 50 and 500 inhabitants, who

are bound by a patrilineal kinship system, which permits a medley of patrilocal and matrilocal polyandry, polygamy, monogamy, and monastic celibacy.

6. Scholars who describe the pathetic status of "village nuns" in Kashmir but largely ignore monastic nuns include Crook and Osmaston (1994) and Dollfus (1989). Compare Klein's (1985) description of unordained and unmarried women in eastern Tibet known as *ka ma*, who dressed like Buddhist nuns and could join the circle of monks' tents in order to concentrate on religious practices. Ortner (1989, 1996: 119) also describes unordained women (ʿkhor ba) or "peripheral ones," who are affiliated with Sherpa nunneries in Nepal.

7. Falk (1980) and Barnes (1994) describe the devolution of the nuns' order in India. Gombrich (1971, 1988) notes that each time the monks' order was in danger of collapse in Sri Lanka—in 1065, 1596, 1697, and 1753—a quorum of either Burmese or Thai monks came to revive the monks' ordination lineages.

8. Tsering and Russell (1996) indicate that between the twelfth and the sixteenth century, several Tibetan women may have been ordained as nuns by monks alone, without the benefit of quorum of fully ordained nuns.

9. Tsomo (1988) notes that 60,000 women hold Buddhist precepts throughout the world: 15,000 are fully ordained nuns, 5,000 are novices or probationers, and 40,000 hold a varying number of precepts (five, eight, or ten).

10. The debate about reestablishing the nuns' full ordination tradition is discussed in Bartholomeusz (1992), Gombrich and Obeyesekere (1988), Li (2000), and Tsomo (1988, 1996).

11. Although Buddhist discipline actually forbids monastics from handling money, most Zangskari monastics accept payment for their ritual services and some serve the monastic treasury which loans cash to local villagers in addition to managing other endowments. Gutschow (1997, 1998) describes the historical origins of the economy of merit which enfolds the monastery, nunnery, and village households in Zangskari society.

12. Kerin (2000) describes the Kyirong Thukche Choling nunnery in Nepal, which has begun to teach sacred arts with the support of the Dalai Lama.

13. Gutschow (1998) summarizes the exclusion of women from sacred space in Zangskar, while Ortner (1973) and Daniels (1994) describe the role of women in the purity and pollution dynamic of Tibetan culture.

14. In the sixteenth century, for instance, an abbot paid the ransom fee for the king of Zangskar during a war with the Kashgar chieftain, Mirza Haidar. In return, his monastery was rewarded handsomely with huge estates throughout western Zangskar and in the neighboring kingdom of Ladakh.

15. Gutschow (1998) and Riaboff (1997) have discussed the statistics on land ownership in Zangskar.

16. If the membership were proportional with its sharecropping income, the monastery should have 2,000 monks. Karsha nuns receive 8 kilograms of grain every three years, while Karsha monks receive roughly 60 kilograms of grain per year. Compare the nunnery in Nepal which provided each of its twenty-three members with 84 kilograms of grain per year, as Fürer-Haimendorf (1976) and Aziz (1976) noted.

17. A reincarnate priest or monk is one for whom a rebirth is actively sought out and identified after his death. Although there are thousands of recognized reincarnate monks in Tibetan society, the most famous example is the lineage of Dalai Lamas, who served as spiritual and political leaders of Tibet from the mid seventeenth century until 1959.

18. Out of over one hundred nuns I interviewed in Zangskar, not a single one

was an oldest daughter. Chosnyid, who was an exception to this rule, had to flee Zangskar in order to evade the marriage her parents had arranged and desperately sought to consummate.

19. In one Zangskari village of over four hundred persons, there was one rape per year between 1993 and 1997, which is was more than thirty times the all-India rate between 1985 and 1995 according to one estimate (Chaturvedi 1995). Zangskar's estimated infant mortality rate of 250 per thousand was over three times the all-India rate (75 per 1,000) for 1996.

Presence:
Yolmo Spirit-Callings in Nepal

Robert Desjarlais

"We must go like thieves," Meme Bombo, a Yolmo shaman, said to me one afternoon as we sat by the hearth in his one-room house in the Yolmo region of north central Nepal, "without ghosts, demons, or witches knowing of our presence. Otherwise, they will attack." He was speaking of the magical flight he and other healers undertake to search for and "call back" the lost spirit of a sick person.

For over a year in the late 1980s I lived in a village in the southwest of the Yolmo region. Serving as a shamanic apprentice to Meme Bombo, I participated in some two dozen healing rites and tried to learn something of the craft of this "grandfather shaman." Since the first nights of the apprenticeship, I have been trying to understand if, how, and to what extent his spirit-calling rites work to rejuvenate a spiritless body. My understanding is that the rites do, at times, have a positive effect, tending to work through indirect, tacit means to negate a sensibility bound by loss, fatigue, and listlessness and create a new one of vitality, presence, and attentiveness. Simply put, Meme changes *how* a body feels by altering *what* it feels. His cacophony of music, taste, sight, touch, and kinesthesia activates the senses. The activation has the potential to "wake up" a person, alter the sensory grounds of a spiritless body, and so change how a person feels.

This take on Yolmo spirit-callings, in which the sensory dimensions are crucial, goes against the grain of the dominant anthropological interpretations of ritual healing, which tend to privilege the symbolic, intellectual, and social features of such healings. The distinction is, I think, worth exploring. To better appreciate what Meme's rites can tell us about the performance of healing in Nepal and elsewhere, we need to understand something of spiritlessness among the Yolmo people, how the rites work to recover lost vitality, and how the acts intrinsic to these rites compare to those found in other soul-calling ceremonies in the Himalayas.

SPIRIT LOSS

Yolmo wa, or "Yolmo people," are an ethnically Tibetan, Buddhist people whose ancestors migrated in the eighteenth and nineteenth centuries from the Kyirong region of Tibet to the forested foothills of the Yolmo or Helambu valley. They speak a Tibetan-derived language as well as Nepali. Commerce, land rentals, pastoral grazing, and the farming of maize, potatoes, and other high-altitude crops provide the main sources of food and income, although recently tourism and "factory" employment in Kathmandu, India, and elsewhere have brought additional material wealth.

Yolmo wa are devout practitioners of the Ningmapa or "Old School" of Tibetan Mahayana Buddhism. Male religious specialists known as *"lamas,"* who maintain village *gompa* or "temples" inherited through patrilineal descent, conduct most of the Buddhist rites, while lay families regularly sponsor and participate in these rites. One of the main sets of rites that lamas regularly perform are the cremation and funeral ceremonies conducted on the behalf of recently deceased persons. A central purpose of these rites is to help a deceased person to achieve a good rebirth.

Quite different from the village lamas, and usually lower in social status, are the *bombo* or "shamans." While many of the ritual practices of the bombo draw from the same Buddhist imageries and pantheons of gods that lamas do, Yolmo wa do not think of bombos as religious specialists per se. Rather, they are thought of primarily as healers. As Yolmo wa themselves often put it in speaking of the lama's skill in performing funeral rites and the bombo's ability to cure illnesses, "We need lamas when we die; shamans, when we're alive."

Many of the rites performed by Yolmo shamans work to recover life-forces lost by their clients. Yolmo wa possess several kinds of life-forces, each of which can depart from the body. The *la* or "spirit" is one such force, and its absence from the body leads to a dysphoric state that we might gloss as "spirit loss." For Yolmo wa, the *la* or "spirit" implies the vital essence of a living person, a spiritual force that courses through the entire body and upon which rest other psychological functions (volition, motivation, energy). La (written as *bla* in classical Tibetan) bestows energy to the body and volition to the *sem*, or "heartmind"—the locus of personal knowledge, desire, and imagination. It is a spiritual essence that provides the volitional impetus to engage in life—the spirit to get out of bed, eat, and walk up a hill to talk with family. The la typically leaves the body when a person is startled: a sudden fall, birds rustling in a dark forest, or a nervous, solitary walk near a cremation ground can spook the spirit from the body. Once parted from the body, the la can fall into the hands of a ghost or witch (*shindi* or *boksī*), and so be carried into the land of the dead.

Since a person might not know for several days that his or her la has been lost, spirit loss can be an insidious process. Within a few days or weeks, a person begins to lose the volition to act. The body feels "heavy," lacks energy or "passion," and the afflicted does not care to eat, talk, work, travel, or socialize; he or she has trouble sleeping, witnesses ominous dreams, and is prone to further illnesses. "When the spirit leaves, no passion comes," one villager told me. "When the la is lost," another recalled, "a man feels tired, sleepy, lazy. He cannot get up quickly, he can eat just a little, and he wants only to stay at home." "Dullness" wells up in the sem, dimming the afflicted's thoughts, memory, and sense of alertness. The pulse slows and becomes irregular "like a watch that is not ticking properly," as one woman put it. The ill person also loses the sense of kinesthetic attentiveness or "presence," as I call it, that characterizes local states of health. In contrast to Balinese, who, according to Gregory Bateson and Margaret Mead (1942: 7), occasionally drift off into detached moments of "awayness," Yolmo wa, wary of life's vicissitudes, constantly attend to the flux of life around them, chatting with others, smoking cigarettes, shooing fluttery chickens. Yet when the "spirit" is lost, so is the sense of presence.

Although bouts of spirit loss bear a common sensory range, which in many respects compares to what Westerners call "depression," each incident presents a slightly different form and etiology. A middle-aged woman named Nyima lost her spirit while crossing a stream on her way to participate in a funeral rite; she lost the desire to walk, eat, work, and socialize. Yeshi, a young Yolmo bride, also lost her spirit; she displayed a lethargy of body and spirit, a lack of emotionality, and a general apathy toward her surroundings.

SPIRIT-CALLINGS

Dawa, a priest in his early thirties, also lost his la a few years back. "I was so sick," the lama recounted one afternoon. "My body felt dizzy, heavy, and I kept fainting." Several days after Dawa fell ill, his family summoned a renowned shaman, who ritually called Dawa's spirit from the land of the dead. "When the spirit returned to my body," Dawa recalled, "I felt well. I felt happy, comfortable. I felt a bit lighter by the next morning. Slowly, slowly, within ten, fifteen days, I was fine." Dawa's newfound health was further signaled by dreams: after the healing, he dreamed of walking uphill and of seeing a bright, clear light—both signs, for Yolmo wa, of health and prosperity.

Other villagers speak of similar events. In general, if a villager suffers from spirit loss, his or her family will summon a bombo; this shaman then arrives at the sick person's home around sunset one evening to perform an elaborate, all-night healing ceremony in which he divines how the la was lost, searches for the itinerant spirit, and tries to return it to the person's body.

Meme Bombo prepares for a night's work by constructing a sacred altar that serves to both represent and embody the various deities that he calls upon. Once the altar is constructed, Meme begins the ceremony proper by singing of the mythic origins of each ritual item in his altar and equipment. Maintaining a fast-paced drumbeat, he similarly consecrates the lamp and grains of his altar, as well as his bells, belt, prayer beads, and drum, by citing the five directions from which each article comes: east, south, west, north, and the center "above." He then offers "incense" (*sanrap*) to the gods and goddesses of Yolmo and neighboring lands, including Tibet and India. The "incense-recitation," in which the healer charts a score of place names, serves to purify deities and their locales by offering a cleansing incense. Beginning in the *beyul* or "hidden country" of Tibet, Meme tours "with his sem"—with his mind's eye, as it were—the numerous locales and shrines to the east of Yolmo as they descend south into the Kathmandu valley and India. He returns upon a westerly route back north to the Himalayas, then locates the sacred geography within the Yolmo region itself, situating the divine within a range of "cliffsides, big rocks, and tall trees," as Meme spoke of the telluric haunts of his tutelary spirits. After identifying each set of deities, Meme requests the gods to "purify all that has been affected by pollution." The journey is lengthy and encompasses over four hundred sacred sites: from north to east, south, west, and north again.

After taking a break, during which time the host family serves food and tea to Meme and the various relatives and neighbors who have come to watch the event, Meme calls several deities to "fall" into his body to "show," through the vehicle of his voice, the cause or causes of the sick person's malady. If the malady is the result of a lost la, Meme ritually searches for and attempts to "call" the spirit back into the sick person's body by performing a "spirit-hooking" ceremony (*la kug*) in which he journeys on a magical flight to the land of the dead. He begins by playing his drum while summoning the fierce *khyung*, the eagle-like Garuda deity of Buddhist lore. Once the khyung responds to the call, the shaman stops drumming and his heartmind leaves his body with a joyful, ecstatic shout and glides through space, clinging to the bird's chest as it escorts and protects him in search of the lost spirit.

While the shaman's heartmind travels through the air, scavenging "like a hawk," his body remains motionless. Occasionally, the shaman confronts malevolent spirits—from "witches" to angry deities to the shades of persons deprived of proper funerals. In a struggle to escape the clutches of these forces, the shaman's body shakes, causing the bells strapped around

15. Yolmo healing ritual.

his chest to ring out in the otherwise silent room in which the sick person's family waits. These events Meme described as follows: "We go like a hawk hunting a chicken, looking far away, then coming to snatch it. Sometimes along the way a tiger comes to 'cover' [attack] us. Sometimes an ox comes to hit, some dogs come to bite. We get startled."

While Meme searches everywhere for the spirit, "in someone's house, in the forest, in the land of the dead, the land of the gods, above, below," the sick person sits, with legs crossed, hands held in prayer, and a white shawl draped over the head and body, behind the shaman, on a sacred symbol composed of rice kernels (see fig. 15).[1] Once Meme "hooks" the spirit, which the khyung snaps up in his claws, his heartmind returns to his body and a flurry of ritual activity ensues: the participants of the healing shout out in celebration; two assistants pass a bowl of incense around the sick person's body to purify it; and a third man touches the bowl containing the enhanced "life" and other sacred objects to the person's scalp, shoulders, chest, hands, and feet.

As soon as Meme recovers from the flight, he holds his drum so that the skinned surface lies horizontal and drums fiercely upon the bottom surface while chanting sacred prayers. If the spirit has been hooked success-fully, it falls onto the drum surface in the "image" of three white "flowers" the size of specks of dust (which are typically spotted by flashlight-bearing assistants). After each flower appears, Meme lowers the drum—while still drumming—closer to the foods and drops the flower into one of several foods (milk, meat, egg, curd) set in bowls upon a tray before the sick per-son. By eating from each of the foods, a person reincorporates lost vitality.

Finally, Meme touches a magical dagger to the person's forehead to im-bue it with renewed "power," and then, after one more break, he ends the ceremony by chanting a prayer of "departure" that asks the various deities to leave the altar and return to their respective "domains." By this time, his client is usually asleep in bed.

MAKING SENSE OF HEALING

Not all villagers respond to spirit-calling rites. Often the rites evoke a sense of vitality, but occasionally that feeling does not lead to a full recovery.[2] For those who do feel better either during or after a spirit-calling, however, feelings of newfound health typically assume a common pattern: bodies become "lighter," heartminds become "brighter," and the sense of fatigue and listlessness that troubles a spiritless person is "cut" from the body. "When the spirit returns," Nyima said, "it feels like a jolt of electricity to the body. . . . The body feels good, and we feel good in the heartmind. After it returns, you can sleep well. Sleepiness comes. Afterwards, I don't see the bad dreams of before." "After the spirit returns," Lakpa told me, "we feel like eating again. Energy returns. After two or three days, the body feels light, the heartmind brightens, it becomes clear, lucid. The eyes become brighter."

The core phenomena of Yolmo healings, in which eyes brighten, the body electrifies, and the heartmind renews, lead me to advance a model of Yolmo spirit-callings that contrasts sharply with anthropological ac-counts that focus on the ideational or symbolic aspects of ritual healing. My thinking on the subject has evolved out of dissatisfaction with the te-nets of such approaches—particularly with "intellectualist" and "symbol-ist" explanations of the effectiveness of ritual healing—for they seem un-able to explain either the ritual techniques or the effectiveness of ritual among Yolmo wa.[3]

The intellectualist position of British social anthropology, developed most recently by John Skorupski (1976), holds that the shaman's and the sick person's concern for efficacy is an intellectual one. The shaman acts in order to instill faith and belief in a person's mind that something can be done to ameliorate his or her malady (see Frank 1974). Such acts work because they have worked in the past and are expected to work in the present. As Bronislaw Malinowski (1948) suggests, ritual acts are geared not to mean something, but to enact something. Through this enactment, people are said to gain faith in the curing process and begin to think differently about their conditions.

In contrast to the intellectualist stance, "symbolist" positions, the products of French structuralist and American semiotic approaches to ritual performance, contend that curing rites work chiefly by provoking transformations either of the worldview held by a person or of the symbolic categories that define the lifeworld of that person.[4] Here, the shaman typically evokes symbols or metaphors that provide a tangible "language" through which ill persons can express, understand, or transform the personal or interpersonal conflicts underlying their illnesses. These orientations follow the spirit of Lévi-Strauss' classic essay "The Effectiveness of Symbols" (1950), which argues that a Cuna shaman's articulation of a mythic realm affects transformations in the physiology of his client.

While both the intellectualist and symbolist positions have helped to explain the structural logic of religious rites throughout the world, I find neither to be especially useful in explaining how or why Yolmo shamans heal. The intellectualist position, for instance, does not account for why Yolmo healers work to the extent they do to recover a person's vitality. According to this model, ritual acts simply aim to achieve what they purport to achieve—return a spirit, exorcise a ghost. As far as Meme's practice goes, he would need only to call a spirit back in order to instill the personal conviction that something substantial is being done to improve a person's condition; he does not need to carry out a vivid and lengthy rite. And yet he does. In an attempt to explain why he does so, I want to suggest that *how* a Yolmo shaman searches for a spirit is as important as actually finding it.

At the same time, I do not believe that Meme recovers a spirit primarily through the use of metaphors, symbolic transformations, or rhetorical tropes, as recent formulations of "symbolic" healing hold. While these representational models, which have dominated ethnographies of healing for several decades now, apparently identify the general structure of ritual healings in many societies, they cannot fully account for a Yolmo calling of spirits. Yolmo healings imagine a symbolic ascent from weakness to strength, fragmentation to integration, disharmony to harmony, and defilement to purity. Yet the symbolic shift from illness to health here is not the method, but simply the scaffolding, of the rites. Generally, spirit-calling for the Yolmo people is less like a mythic narrative, progressing from one stage to another, than an imagistic poem, evoking an array of tactile images which, through their cumulative effect, evoke a change of sensibility in the bodies of its participants—a change, that is, in the lasting mood or disposition that contributes to the sensory grounds of a person's existence. Seen in this light, it is more the poem's visceral impact than its metaphoric structure that effects change.

The impact ties into the senses. Meme's craft involves a healing of bodies, of sensibilities, of ways of being in the world. His spirit-calling rites might change how participants think of their conditions and how they might alter the symbolic categories that define those conditions. But if the rite is to be considered successful, it must change how a person feels. This is because Yolmo criteria of efficacy rest largely on the lack or presence of visceral evidence that a person feels better in the days following a rite. These rather sensorial criteria relate to Yolmo takes on illness and healing. In illness, a villager cannot know the cause or course of her plight until its signifying symptoms (bodily pains, bad dreams) become manifest. Similarly, since the spirit is an intangible force, a villager can only determine its return by interpreting how body and heartmind feel in the hours and days after a rite.

The shamans have their own, more divinatory ways of assessing a person's welfare. But while a person can take a healer's word that the spirit has been recovered, such talk, I was told, is occasionally "like the wind," and villagers sometimes consider a shaman's "rhetoric of transformation" (Csordas 1983) to be merely rhetoric. As Lakpa put it, "Shamans and lamas tell us 'The life has come back,' but we don't know this, we can't see this. When we feel better, then we think it has returned."

A person, therefore, cannot be sure that the spirit has returned to the body until the sensibility of spirit loss (heavy body, weak eyes, weary heart) has been "cut" from the body. The visceral sense of renewed health, which usually takes hold in the hours after a rite and must last if the rite is to be considered successful, is the major criterion upon which Yolmo wa judge rites efficacious. In Yolmo, a person does not feel better after being cured; she is cured after feeling better. Whereas all rites, by definition, effect symbolic transformations, Yolmo wa do not consider all rites to be efficacious. These facts suggest that if we are to develop a model of Yolmo healings, the model must not simply sketch out possible mechanisms of healing, but also tie in to the particular ways that a shaman's clients know themselves to be healed.

In an attempt to develop such an understanding, I want to build on the work of several anthropologists who emphasize the performative and dramaturgical aspects of ritual healings.[5] While this research attributes ritual efficacy to a variety of factors, from acts of catharsis and an increase in self-understanding to resolutions of social conflicts and the ritual reframing of cultural realities, a constant concern is for the ways dramatic actions and aesthetic performances engage participants and evoke emotional responses. To date, however, this work has focused more on the social and psychological, rather than the sensory, dimensions of such engagement. There is something at work in Yolmo healings for which this literature does not fully account: the presence of the senses in the rites and the extent to which ritual performances change how people feel.

"HERE, HERE"

Meme's search for a lost spirit parallels shamanic itineraries enacted by other peoples who live in the foothills of the Nepal Himalayas, such as Gurung, Tamang, and Magar peoples. A Gurung shaman ventures on an elaborate search of cosmological domains, first calling out the names of goddesses "of rock, soil, rivers, and trees" to ask if the soul has been hidden in these domains and later enticing the soul from the land of the dead (Mumford 1989: 170–175). Tamang healers journey to divine "hidden" lands to recover lost shadow-souls, and Magars descend into the "underworld" to overtake a soul before it reaches "the Waters of Forgetfulness" (Holmberg 1989; Watters 1975).

Of particular interest is the way healers carefully pronounce concrete details of what they encounter during their flights. The chant of a healer of Kham-Magar ethnicity, for instance, mentions a half dozen hamlets, two river crossings, a cave dwelling, a monastery, a sacred shrine, and a "place of origin and fertility" (Allen 1974: 8). A Tamang shaman calls out places where lost souls can "get stuck":

In a heaven of the homeless,
In a heaven of confusion,
In a heaven of distress,
In a heaven of rumorous gossip,
In a heaven of cannibals,
In a heaven of closed mouths,
In a heaven of licentious sex. (Holmberg 1989: 164–165)

If the healer does not leave his body in an ecstatic search for a person's spirit, he calls out to the spirit, imploring it to return to the body.

In Tibet, lamaic lurings assume a similar form: an elaborate, imagistic litany portrays a tangible expanse upon which the singer plots the soul's travels. In a lamaic rite to "call the *bla*," the summoner enumerates a divine pantheon in the hopes of recovering the soul.

. . . Ye, the fire god, rakshasas, the wind gods,
and the powerful ones in the four intermediate points,
Ye gods of the earth below,
All ye gods of the ten points of the universe,
If ye have snatched [the soul] . . . (Lessing 1951: 272)

The litany climaxes with a bystander shouting at the top of his voice:

> Soul and life of such and such a person,
> of such a family,
> of such and such an age,
> bearing such and such a name,
> whether thou hast come to a royal palace,
> or a mansion of a nobleman,
> or a Buddhist temple,
> or a place of worship . . . (Lessing 1951: 273)

The litany ends with a general summons, the power of which might be best grasped if we mold its conclusion into projective verse.

> . . . or an island or islet,
> a rock or a cave, or
> a thoroughfare, or
>
> a place noisy with human activities, or
> a place inhabited by malignant spirits or
> mischievous demons,
> or whether thou art traveling or
> drifting in the wind or
> floating on the water, or
> scattered about,
> whether thou art snatched away or
> carried off,
> I bid thee come back.

The lama's chant turns on a point by point appeal to the imagination. Each image, standing alone, acts as a lure. A mind leaps from island to islet.

The curative power of the chant apparently ties into its style of presentation, and into how people respond to that presentation. On many occasions, Himalayan healers do not say whether or not they have found the souls they are looking for. In my estimation, they do not need to, for it is the search, rather than any ostensive result, that is of fundamental importance.

In my own encounters with soul-calling rites, I find that many of the chants' images leapfrog into the imagination in such a way that they engage the listener not through any threaded storytelling but through a random and roundabout slide show of perceptions—a rock, a cave, a thoroughfare. The chants set up a chain of alternatives—"*or* a mansion, *or* a temple, *or* a place of worship"—that opens up a range of possibilities. Through the imaginative engagements prompted by such possibilities, a chant hooks a soul: it draws a person out of his or her spiritlessness to invoke a sense of presence, volition, and attentiveness. The heartmind opens up to a world exterior to itself and "noisy with human activities," and the heavy slumber marking spirit loss can be countered.

That such rites work to induce sensory attentiveness is further evinced by other chants, whereby Tibetan Buddhist priests lure vital souls by detailing what exists "here," in the felt immediacies of a person's world:

> Your parents are HERE.
> Your brothers and sisters are HERE.
> Your friends and neighbors are HERE.
> The three white and three sweet foods are HERE.
> If you would drink tasty beer, it's HERE.
> If you would eat fat meat, it's HERE.
> If you would eat boiled-down [thick] food, it's HERE.
> Plentiful, sweet tasty food is HERE.
> If you would wear good clothes, they're HERE.
> If you would ride a good horse, it's HERE.
> Don't go there, there! Come HERE, HERE!
> Don't follow to the land of the deathlords!
> *A-bo-lo-lo*, come HERE![6]

The summons begins by acknowledging, and potentially engaging, the sick person's family and friends, then sets acts of drinking, eating, and riding in a fan of alternatives ("if . . . if . . . if"). "Don't go there, there! Come here, here!"—the hurried deictics suggest that the healer seeks to recover lost vitality by pointing to the taste and feel of the present. Fat meat, sweet beer, and a fine horse lie at one's side, close enough to touch. I have indicated the radical need for presence in Yolmo life, and how a sense of "hereness" is lost when the spirit is lacking. Possibly this sensibility is salient in other Tibetan societies also. If so, then a calling of souls works to draw a person into the here and now by selectively attending to the sensory footholds of his or her environment. All told, the rites provoke a stance toward that environment, urge a rush of activities, open up a range of possibilities, and instill a deliberate attentiveness that is absent when the soul is lost.

A HEALING TOUCH

In Himalayan soul-calling rites, the soul returns to the body by attending to what lies outside the body. A similar preoccupation characterizes Yolmo healings. By calling forth a distinct spiritual geography throughout an evening of chants and drumbeats, Meme works to recover lost vitality through a selective attention to detail, an active engagement, a quickening of the senses, and an invocation of presence. The cure tacitly but directly confronts feelings of spiritlessness, crafting apathy into attentiveness and fatigue into vitality.

Common to the opening chants is a flickery, place-by-place slide show of perceptions that has the potential to divert, excite, and engage. Although villagers often do not grasp the specifics of the chants, they do appear to sense their underlying poetics. The prayers transform. As Meme mumbles his chant, cleansing the hills and forests of Yolmo, one catches snippets of meaning. The directional notation is clear: *shar ... lho ... nub ... chang ... uie* repeatedly mark the five directions: east, south, west, north, center. A person soon finds herself at the heart of the center, the four corners of the earth encircling her form. The articulation of place names leads a person to imagine and attend to specific locales—well-known hamlets and hill-sides realized through a rapid, freeze-frame singsong.

It may be that the presentation of this terrain, which plays such an important role in how Yolmo pastoralists make their livings, kindles attention and recalls healthy ways of moving the body. The geographic leitmotif—focused, complete, controlled—commands attention. As shamanic speech orchestrates the five directions, bodies become centered, alert, enraptured. The nomadic focus on an expanse of foothills, mountains, and forests draws the heartmind out of the body to move imaginatively through a rocky landscape in which a person has walked, climbed, and bathed. Meme brings to life a sacred yet tangible geography that centers around a person's body and induces that person to attend more sensibly to that geography.

The body of a sick person is a key player throughout a Yolmo healing, and this physiology takes center stage at the conclusion of the spirit-calling rite. The acoustics of the spirit-calling rite—Meme's "startled," bell-clanging body, the driving drumbeats, shouts from the audience—maintain a high level of intensity throughout. The flicker of candles, the aroma of incense, and the taste of foods adds to the supple fusion of senses. The Buddhist symbols on which a client sits "awaken" his or her body. The various ritual items, which "touch" a person's head, shoulders, chest, hands, and knees when the spirit returns, work to "empower" the body. I once asked Meme why he needed to touch so many parts of the body during this act. "We need to touch everywhere," he said, "to assure that the spirit returns to the body, and to give power to its different parts." The contact takes several forms: incense encircles the body to cleanse it of lingering harm, a magical dagger imbues a person's forehead with renewed vitality, and the body reincorporates its "spirit" by consuming it with the most desirable (and protein-rich) of Yolmo foods.

Ritual sentience helps to renew a person's felt participation in the world. "When the spirit returns," Nyima tells us, "it feels like a jolt of electricity in the body." Bodies lighten. Eyes and heartminds brighten. A person wants to eat and walk and sleep again. "Bad" dreams are cut from the body. The potent blend of image and sensation intrinsic to Yolmo spirit-callings, and the effect that this blend typically has on people, suggest that shifts in how a person thinks of his or her condition (the spirit has returned), or in the symbolic identity that defines that condition (renewed health, transformed contexts), can only partly explain how vitality is restored. For healing to be effective, Meme must alter the sensory grounds of a spiritless body. How does he do so? Our findings suggest that a less cerebral model than those noted above can account for Yolmo spirit-callings: Meme tries to change how a person feels by altering the sensory stimuli around that person. His cacophony of music, taste, sight, touch, and wild, tactile images activates the senses and the imagination. This activation can "wake up" a person, prompt new sensibilities, and so reform the cognitive and perceptual faculties that, in large part, make up a person. "If the sick person is asleep," Meme once said, "he won't get better." Since much of the ceremony does not require a sick person's participation, Meme's rule speaks more of a craftsman's know-how than any ritual imperative: one cannot feel fully if asleep, and by adding to what a person tastes, sees, touches, hears, and imagines, a Yolmo healer jump-starts a physiology.[7]

ACKNOWLEDGMENTS

The present essay, which extends the analysis of an earlier publication (Desjarlais 1992: 198–222), is a slightly modified reworking of a version published in a volume edited by Carol Laderman and Marina Roseman (1996). Special thanks to the residents of Yolmo, especially Meme Bombo, who kindly taught me something of his craft.

NOTES

1. If the sick person is female, a swastika is drawn with rice kernels; if male, the *dorje*, a sacred Buddhist symbol, is composed. These two Buddhist symbols, which stand for health, wealth, and fertility, are said to "awaken" and give vitality to the person's body.

2. The failure can occur either because other dynamics are involved in the illness which spirit-calling rites themselves cannot ameliorate, or because other pains continue to linger after the ceremony is performed. A person might therefore report a renewed sense of vitality, but will continue to suffer malaise in other domains of life. Or he or she will feel well in the hours and days after a healing, but since Yolmo spirit-callings address only the symptoms—not the causes—of spirit loss, the afflicted suffers from the symptoms anew several days after a rite. Since the cure sometimes does not last, shamans often repeat the same rite on several occasions before a person feels that he or she has fully recovered (see Desjarlais 1992 for a more extensive discussion of why Yolmo healings as a whole succeed or fail).

3. These are by no means the only positions. Csordas and Kleinman (1990)

note, for instance, the existence of at least four models of "therapeutic process," which attribute therapeutic efficacy to either "structural," "clinical," "social," or "persuasive" elements. In my estimation, however, the most influential orientations toward ritual healing are the "intellectualist" and "symbolist" positions.

4. See Kapferer 1983; Dow 1986; and Kleinman 1988, for instance. I use the term "symbolist" more broadly than Skorupski (1976) defines the term.

5. See, for instance, Turner 1967; Schieffelin 1976, 1985; Feld 1982; Kapferer 1983; Laderman 1987, 1991; and Roseman 1991.

6. Collected by the Tibetan encyclopedist Kong-sprul from some "exorcists" in the late nineteenth century; as cited in Martin (n.d.).

7. For what it's worth, when I returned to Nepal in 1997 I visited Meme in his home in the Yolmo region and reviewed with him the contents of the present paper. Listening carefully, he nodded his head in agreement to the main gist of what I had to say, as he heard it.

Tunes Rising from the Soul and Other Narcissistic Prayers: Contested Realms in Bangladesh

Jim Wilce

This essay examines why most Bangladeshi Muslims' tuneful (melodic, sung) prayers are condemned while others are legitimated. The many functions of language include establishing and maintaining a sense of well-being, indexing or pointing to oneself or some shared identity, and asserting authority. Yet language (e.g., in prayer) used to maintain well being can increase conflict if its self-authenticating moves—its claims to legitimacy—fail.

Utterances and whole performances experience a better or worse "fit" with genre categories. Failure to find such a fit may have tragic consequences (Crapanzano 1996; Wilce 1998). Prayer balances individuated and corporate voices, personal and conventionalized idioms, sometimes uneasily. The functions of genre in general and of prayer genres in particular—to make story content generic—are transpersonalizing, typifying, and social. That is, to conform a bit of speech to a genre is to transcend the personal and associate one's speech with past and future speech events. Muslim prayer in Bangladesh, as I understand it, points to the corporate more saliently than it does to the personal. Still, whatever corporate realities it invokes, it also allows for the emergence of individuated voices. It is the high personal and social stakes of the forms and functions of prayer that result in unholy fights over it.

At the intersection of ideologies and actual instances of prayer-language in Bangladesh we find at least two tensions: (1) tuneful prayers and prayerful laments are traditionally available yet are now widely disapproved, and (2) tuneful prayer is accepted in the mouths of the powerful but otherwise considered narcissistic. Bangladeshis, Islamist and otherwise, are quick to state that lament tunes rise from the heart irrepressibly; yet in their next breath, Islamists condemn these heart expressions as willful attention-seeking.

This chapter deals first with the tuneful prayers and laments of two individuals whom we might call virtuosi of subjectivity; they stand out in Bangladesh for the degree to which they explore their own experience. An anecdote helps illustrate the disdain some Bangladeshis feel toward the exploration of one's subjectivity. Dr. Reba Chowdhury, a woman psychiatrist in the capital city, Dhaka, told me of the disgust in the voice of a Bangladeshi woman with whom she had to deal in order to apply for a passport to visit the United States for postdoctoral training. When the woman bureaucrat learned that Dr. Chowdhury was a psychiatrist, she said, "Both psychotherapy and the behavior psychiatrists treat are pure *bilāsitā*," luxurious self-indulgence.[1] Many Bangladeshis share with the bureaucrat a sense that the subjectivist-virtuoso's elaboration of selfhood is a bilāsitā.

RELIGIOUS DISCOURSES IN HISTORY AND CULTURE

When Islam came to South Asia centuries ago, it was taken up into a rather syncretic and pragmatic orientation to religion which gave way only gradually to boundary-forming around "Islam," "Hinduism," etc. (Eaton 1993; Wilce 2000). The Islamization of what is now Bangladesh includes recent historical stages in which elites, tract authors, and pilgrims returning from Mecca with new notions of orthodoxy vigorously challenged rural Bengalis' syncretic and pragmatic use of some Islamic forms. Nineteenth-century "reformists" called on rural Bengalis to rid their religion of excessive passion—in commemorations of the martyrdom of early Muslim saints but also in observances they saw as Hindu holdovers. This reformist Islam reflects some longstanding discourses of Islam itself combined with a concern to make all things rational that reflects modernity and specifically the politics of colonialism. One must keep in mind that colonial administrators and Christian missionaries characterized their own faith as rational and Muslims in South Asia and elsewhere as "backward." Nineteenth-century reformist Muslims were thus reacting to the rationalism of colonial versions of modernity and not just imposing a putatively pure Islam drawn straight from the Middle East or the Qur'an.

Traditional forms of verbal art, particularly those genres most typically put to the service of subjectivity, seem at risk in reformist-Muslim-dominated areas of rural Bangladesh. Conventions governing genres of expression become ideological badges. Linguistic conventions in prayer, for instance, become badges of subjection to the divine will. Hence prayer-language comes under religious scrutiny and is subjected to a particular kind of regimentation (Kroskrity 2000). Much social control or regimentation is asserted via explicit utterances about the way one should talk, i.e., metadiscourses—in this case about the proper stance or attitude that prayer should enact. That is the case in Bangladesh. In a religious society prayer might seem beyond critique, safe from attack; yet this essay describes circumstances under which tuneful prayers, and laments that include prayerful verses, attract criticism. Specifically, Bangladeshi Islamists consider *personal* prayers that are sung and wept a narcissistic indulgence. "Sincere prayer" cannot be tuneful or loud.

A well-analyzed historical analogy from the United States can help us understand the values Bangladeshis might attach to silent personal prayer, to tuneful public prayer by a recognized *imām* (Islamic prayer leader), and to tuneful personal prayer. Late colonial America epitomized a trend noted by Michael Warner: the premium placed on anonymity by authors, which he labels "the principle of negativity" (1990). Laura Graham glosses this principle as the formal "negation of self . . . as a [required] condition of legitimacy" (1993: 720). She contrasts it with the "principle of notability." The principle of negativity corresponds fairly well to what Weber associates with Protestantism. A preference for self-distancing, dispassionate discourse even in religious contexts reflects what Weber labeled *entzauberüng*, the demystification or rationalization of the world—replacing a magical sense of ritual participation with actions understood as rational. Bangladeshi Islamists might seem far removed from rationalizing European Protestants. In fact, Geertz (1960, 1968) demonstrated the connection between a "protestant" sort of reformist religious movement in Asia—what he called "scripturalist Islam"—and the capitalist spirit. Reformist, scripturalist Islam often fits Weber's description of Protestantism, particularly in its attack on emotionalism and mysticism. The voices in Bangladesh that would purge the personal and affective from the language of personal prayer represent a trend homologous with that which Weber associated with Protestant spirituality, and with the principle of negativity.

TUNEFUL PRAYERS IN BANGLADESH

The interactions transcribed in the next pages reflect conflict over what is proper in prayer. The first examples are the tuneful, texted, wept prayer of Latifa and the singsong prayer of Suleyman. Admittedly, the content of Latifa's and Suleyman's prayerful performances drew the ire of their kin and neighbors. Yet it was also the form—and particularly the tunefulness —of their sad prayers that attracted criticism.

Laments as Prayers: Latifa and Suleyman

I recorded and transcribed several performances by Latifa and Suleyman. But what was largely hidden from me were the moments when their performances were violently shut down.

Latifa was, when I met her, in her mid-twenties (Wilce 1998). Her mother was the child of one of my fictive uncles in the extended family compound on which I lived in a village in Matlab (Chandpur District, Bangladesh). She had been an outstanding student in high school. After graduating, her brothers had arranged for her to marry (it seems her father had by that point already become infirm or at least distant from the management of family affairs). Two years before I met her, her brothers had stepped into a fairly typical moment of difficult adjustment to her in-laws' home by beating her husband, forcing a divorce, and attempting (in vain) to recover the fixed sum of money in the prenuptial agreement. When I met her, she was singing laments to motivate her maternal uncles to intervene with her brothers and force a reconciliation with the husband for whom she longed. My fictive cousins dragged Latifa from my field home after one nighttime performance—a scene they warned me not even to watch. When they reached her brothers' home miles away, they put her in chains. Very near the Latifa events in time and space, Suleyman (Wilce 2000)—an in-law of Latifah's cousins—was put in chains. Insights into these events come from dozens of informal interviews I conducted with rural Bangladeshis about tuneful weeping. Since the spontaneous response of Latifa's and Suleyman's audiences evinced strong moral censure, I asked others from their area about the moral values attached to mournful, tuneful prayers. Those rural Bangladeshi Muslims, like those who had responded "on site" to Suleyman and Latifa, judged tuneful weeping or tuneful private prayer to be somehow un-Islamic—or, in other cases, embarrassingly traditional or local in contrast with modernist values they associated with either urbanization or *reformist* Islam.[2]

It is noteworthy that both Latifa and Suleyman were labeled *pāgal*, "mad." Are their prayers dismissed only because they were already "known to be" mad? Actually, people labeled them "mad" in large part *because of* their tuneful, prayerful lamenting. As is so often the case, norms are revealed in their violation; responses to the so-called deviance of these two individuals reveal norms of expression. The assumption that tuneful speech and prayer indicate madness is itself an ideological barrier against forms of expressivity, a barrier with which the two individuals collided.

What madness reveals in Bangladesh—and it is of the utmost relevance to our understanding of Bangladeshi values surrounding prayer—is an ethic of sociocentricity, the sense that fitting in is more important than exploring or asserting one's subjectivity. It is not that "the South Asian self" is always and uniquely sociocentric (vis-à-vis Westerners, for instance). To claim that is a dangerous essentialization.[3] It is true, nonetheless, that sociocentricity is ideologically normative for South Asians, as Dumont argued in *Homo Hierarchicus* (1970). It should thus come as no surprise that Bangladeshis construct madness as a sort of individualism, and individualism as a species of madness. Here my rural interviewees and the passport-granting bureaucrat agree—the virtuoso's elaboration of selfhood is a narcissistic luxury, a *bilāsitā*. Thus, both madness and eccentric tuneful prayer paradoxically highlight the sociocentric moral norms that they violate.

Example 1

My first transcript is an excerpt from a long performance of tuneful, texted weeping by Latifa. Lines 1–3 are relevant here because, though Latifa's whole lament was not exactly a prayer, these lines are addressed to *Mābud* (Arabic for "Lord"). (Note: •hh represents sobbing inhalation.)

1.1	*(mābud)* •*hh*	Lord •hh,
1.2	*āmi to (hay nā) (ār ki dure) bujhi nā* •*hh,*	I cannot understand it at all •hh,
1.3	*mābu::d* •*hh.*	Lord •hh.

Latifa sang laments like this for a week before the men of my field home carried her violently back to her brothers' home and she was forced to abandon the hope that had motivated her to prayerfully, mournfully sing for my field family (her mother's natal family). Despite other Bangla-

16. Latifa's lament.

294 / *Practicing Religion*

deshis' success in using such lament to move families to act on their behalf (Doreen Indra: personal communication, 1992), Latifa's family remained unmoved. Had her theme been the death of a blood relative, or had she argued conversationally rather than tunefully to be reunited with her husband, the outcome might have been different. In much of South Asia, gendered divisions of communicative labor are inverted at times of death; women, normally unheard in public, receive "the task of bearing witness to the grief and the loss that death has inflicted" (Das 1996: 88).

Example 2

My second example, Suleyman's tuneful blessing, shares features of the prayerful laments sung by Latifa. When I described his tuneful prayers to people in rural shops and asked them about whether melody could serve the purposes of prayer, Muslims said it was shameful. Why? The answer has to do with tunefulness as narcissism. If he were sincere, why should he draw such attention to himself by praying that way?

Suleyman was about seventy when I met him in 1992, and he reported having a history of being pāgal, "mad." This he usually blamed on a female familiar spirit that he had inherited from his grandmother; he described it as a form of succubus and reflected the shared belief that nocturnal emissions blamed on such spirit-encounters sap one's vitality and health. Sometimes he called the misinheritance from his mother a matter of the blood. The chief sign of his madness—the feature of his behavior that struck those in my field home as so very odd that they had to take me to meet him—was his musical speech. They told me that he had overstepped the bounds of piety and zeal, commandeering the microphone at a mosque. He announced that he would both give the call to prayer and lead prayers (CAPS indicate word stress in the original:

> 2.1   *āmi āzān diBO,*   I will GIVE the call to PRAYer;
>
> 2.2   *āmi nāMĀZ parāBO!*   I will LEAD worSHIP!

The contrast between stressed and unstressed syllables here graphically reproduces the rhythmic, singsong quality with which Suleyman's teenage relatives spoke in imitating his words. They found him very amusing. Months after his attempt to lead prayer, and after his family members had chained him to the posts of his house to prevent him from transgressing boundaries both physical and behavioral, he still performed his sense of personal injustice. His prayers became laments directed at Allah and anyone else who would listen, tuneful narrations of how his family had deprived him of his rights.

After meeting Suleyman and hearing him relate his troubles, my relationship with him took on a deep filial affection. But I admit that it began out of an interest in local views of how madness was linked to marked speech.[4] Whether or not my fictive cousins' report of his speech was accu-

17. Suleyman's lament.

rate, it is still revealing that the Suleyman character they animated was linguistically egocentric. They quoted Suleyman repeating the "I" in each line of his rather poetic attempt to become imām for a day. Along with the singsong intonation, the pronoun *āmi* (I) adds to the color of the utterance by enhancing its rhythmic complexity while maintaining its balance. Even more clearly—since the Bengali word for egocentricity is *āmitva* ("I-ness," from *āmi*)—Suleyman's grammatically superfluous repetitions of āmi underline, in the view of his audience, his selfishness (Wilce 1998).

As Example 3 shows, much of Suleyman's verbal behavior was so multivocal as to be regarded as blasphemous—rather than invoking God in the "voice" of simple faith, he juxtaposes invocation and prayer with cries of abjection. It threatens normative religious ideologies. The criticism he attracts reveals an ideology centering on a religious seriousness epitomized by that monovocality which Weber called "rationalization." Most of Suleyman's neighbors expect prayers to be uttered in one voice—i.e., seriously, with no irony. The playfulness, irony, or double-voiced aggression seen in Suleyman's speech fractured religiously normative monovocality. On one occasion Suleyman said, "My son is a fool," but followed that with *"Āl-hāmd-ul-illāh!"* ("Praise Allah!") The effect was ironic and disturbing. Protestant or Islamist rationalism demands monologic allegiance to clearly stated propositions of the faith; Suleyman's play resists such demands and thus shakes religious rationalism.

On one occasion several months after the seizure of the mosque mike, my colleague Faisal visited Suleyman and audiotaped the event partially transcribed below:

Example 3

NOTE: Underlining indicates Suleyman's neighbor's interruption.

3.10S	*āmār bhāgye*	In my fate . . .
3.11N	*sunen. ey rakam karen nā.*	Listen—don't do like that!
3.12S	*ey::::: nāy je āllāh.*	. . . There is no God [for me].

There was something about this tuneful lament to God that Suleyman's neighbor Nabal felt he must silence. Nabal interrupted it, objecting to Suleyman's performance and probably to his self-inflating mention (in lines of the prayer not represented in the transcript) of having led public prayers several months before. The prayer seemed to Nabal an invocation of God out of mere self-interest, and a poignant expression of doubt as well.

Analyzing these transcripts in the light of interviews with other Muslims led me to see that Suleyman's tuneful prayers were marked theologically as well as intonationally. I say "theologically" because the advocates of an increasingly dominant modernist Islam regard tuneful prayers as "unorthodox"—inappropriately self-indexing (drawing attention to themselves) or primadonna-ish. Again, this rural opinion resonates with the bilāsitā ("luxurious self-indulgence") critique by the bureaucrat whom Dr. Chowdhury encountered.

Prayer Songs: A Children's Rain Song Rebuked by an Elder

The prayers of Suleyman were personal, as were Latifa's tuneful invocations of Allah. A rain prayer sung by children differs in two respects—in its "key" (much lighter) and its more corporate theme and participant structure—but parallels the prayers examined thus far in its tunefulness and in the angry reaction it provoked. A group of about six children sang the song outside the door of my field home, asking Allah for rain. They were loudly interrupted, as was Suleyman in Example 3.

Example 4

Interspersed with verses, the children's song repeated this chorus:

4.1	*āllāh megh de, pāni de, chāyā de re tu*	Allah, bring clouds and rain, give shade.

This provoked Habib's response (in relation to the unedited interaction, about six lines later):

4.7	*Bandho—gān nāi!*	Stop! No singing!
4.8	*āmrā (x) āllāh-e dite haibo*	We [believe?] God must give [the rain when He pleases]
4.9	*(xx) gābrāi*	We're getting irritated!

Example 4 reflects events in April 1992, just before the monsoon season would bring cooling rains. The heat leading up to the monsoon is hard on everyone. The children who lived with me in the large and relatively well-off extended family rural compound that hosted me had been practicing this traditional Bengali rain song that week in their public school. It became clear that day that the older generation in their compound considered this public education as offensively secular.[5] It was my fictive father, Habib, who shouted at the children to stop, as I stood by open-mouthed and silent. Habib implied that *gān* is forbidden even, or especially, in a religious context. By deploying the genre label "gān" ("song"), Habib constituted the children's performance as secular, thereby backgrounding or effectively denying its prayerful content, since the category gān excludes sacred Muslim performances.

Habib's deployment of "we" in line 4.8 indexes a generation gap within the extended family; he was speaking for the elders of the compound. A few hours later, I asked another elder—Habib's brother, Meherban—about the incident. Meherban is the imām (leader of prayers, preacher) of the mosque next door to our shared residential compound. Hadn't he also sung that song as a child? Yes, and he supposed his ancestors had sung it. So, why would he oppose this seemingly pious and traditional (albeit musical) prayer for rain? Scripturalist Islam (Geertz 1968), in his understanding, clearly laid out the proper ritual prayer for rain (presumably in Arabic) and the precise manner in which it is to be performed by the whole congregation with proper leadership (i.e., by an imām like himself). Bengali prayers sung by "armies of wandering children" (the phrase used by another elder in another context) not only fail to constitute legitimate prayer but violate the aesthetic of orderliness (reminiscent of Weber's Protestants) that Meherban propagated.

INDIVIDUAL PRAYER PERFORMANCES
IN THE BROADER BANGLADESHI CONTEXT

But the situation is not quite that simple. The reader might be surprised at this point to be told that the congregational liturgies led by the imām Meherban sound melodic, but are not called "gān," not regarded as "song." Even on the less Qur'anically prescribed occasions when folk gather to celebrate God and His Prophet, congregational performances that to me sound like song receive labels setting them apart from gān. They are *hāmd* (worshipful praise) if they are sung to Allah, and *nāt* (celebration falling short of worship) if they are sung to the Prophet. Bangladeshi Muslims perceive a difference in lyrics but also in musical qualities—parallel to the Western musicological distinction between song and "plainsong" ("chant").[6] These differences are not straightforwardly "there" to be reflected in different genre labels; the labels help make the difference perceptually real.

Bangladesh is religiously plural, and even the so-called "Muslim community" is internally diverse—richly so. It includes a Sunni majority, a Shi'a minority, and a great many Sufi orders varying from mystical and licentious to legalistically disciplined.[7] Bangladeshi Muslims tend to agree, however, in typifying several forms of "prayer." *Sālāt* or *nāmāz*, ritual worship that includes prayers of self-dedication, is one of the central requirements or "pillars" (Bengali *stambo*) of Islam. Recitation of Qur'anic passages during sālāt or nāmāz is obligatory but corporate only in a loose sense. Individuals choose a passage and recite it with flat intonation. One of the most common surahs or chapters to be memorized and used in sālāt / nāmāz is a prayer for guidance. Such prayers are recited in Arabic, a ritual language whose sonic form is regarded as sacred but whose syntactic and semantic structure is opaque to many Bangladeshis who use it in prayer. Despite the privileged status of prayers in Arabic, it is permissible for Bangladeshi imāms to tack on to them a Bengali translation for the sake of the congregation. In Arabic or Bengali, in Bangladesh or any other Muslim society, imāms are expected to intone the prayers and calls to prayer with an almost musical contour (Nelsen 1985).[8] Thus, prayer in Bangladesh is a field of action onto which are projected a set of crosscutting, ideologically freighted polarities—ritualized versus improvised, Arabic versus vernacular, corporate versus private, and Qur'anically prescribed versus locally traditional. But melody attaches to only certain prayers in that field. Hence, the fact that Meherban leads public prayers with a singsong contour but opposes the children's prayer song is far from idiosyncratic. It represents a rationalizing trend well over a century old.

For evidence of the unreflective acceptance of tuneful prayers led by imāms, I turn to a wedding that I was encouraged to videotape for my friend, the groom. It was an elite affair on the military cantonment in Dhaka. The imām prayed for the congregation and the bride and groom. (The honorific pronoun *āpni*, "you," is labeled V in the transcript to associate it with French *vous*.)

Example 5

5.1	*Rab ul ālāmin*	Oh Lord of all worlds,
5.2	*āpnār (V) sāhi darbāre*	to your (V) royal court we come,
5.3	*āmrā (katoguli lok)*	(just) several people

5.4	*hat (gure) uṭheyāchi.*	lifting our hands . . .
5.5	*meherbāni kare āpni (V)* *āmāder duāguli*	Please, the prayers we lift to you (V),
5.6	*kabul karen*	hear them.

Not only did the imām's prayer have a melody to it—Middle-Eastern, to me—it is also striking in using the formal-distant V form of the second person singular pronoun for the divine. Of the hundreds of Bengali prayers I have heard—by Muslims, Hindus, and Christians—this one was unique in not addressing the divine intimately by using the T or "thou" form (*tumi* or *tui* [as in line 4.1], parallel to the French *tu*). The V form of "you" is consistent with a distanced anti-emotionalist, rationalized religious performance.

Those who attended the wedding accepted the tunefulness of this imām's prayer as so much a part of Islam that I gather it no longer seemed tuneful. Such performances are defined as "not song," despite the way they strike my ear. How can it be that such perfectly legitimate Bangladeshi Muslim prayers are tuneful, yet the tunefulness of private, improvised, locally traditional forms (children's rain song, tuneful prayer by Suleyman, laments) is rejected as narcissistic? It seems that the more legitimacy one possesses (from institutional recognition and successful public reassertions in the past), the less one needs to explicitly reassert it, in keeping with the principle of negativity (seen, for instance, in the denial of personal authorship) discussed earlier. This leaves the moves of subalterns—attempts by subordinate individuals to reach for power or legitimacy—naked, open to view. Kroskrity (1998) argues that, among ideologies, the most legitimated are the most implicit. If this is so, then exposing the fact that another party is using any sort of strategy ipso facto demonstrates that party's illegitimacy. Thus, when my interviewees expose the implicit (e.g., melodic) and explicit self-assertions of authority (āmitva, "I-ness") in speech acts of a man like Suleyman who lacks any sort of publicly legitimated grounds to make such assertions (and who, if he had such grounds, would not assert them), they officially delegitimate his speech acts.

Suleyman made a grab for legitimacy at the mosque, staking a loud and melodic claim on an authority that was not legitimately his. He became the prototypical impostor; his speech was taken as "insane discourse" (Bourdieu 1977b: 650). It was the felicity or contextual appropriateness of his melodic words, not their grammaticality or coherence, that was in question. It is the "principle of negativity" which constitutes legitimacy for the *muezzin* (caller-to-prayer) in rural Bangladesh—their calls are valued for repeating the sacred Arabic words in a standardized chant form, not for idiosyncratic signatures, detectable though those may be. To say that Suleyman's taking of the mosque's mike was illegitimate because it violated the principle of negativity is to call it bilāsitā. Claims to legitimacy are, at least in local mosques, dismissed as foolish selfishness, even signs of insanity. Only those who have already won a standing—those who are "in a *position* to speak" (Bourdieu 1977b: 650)—have the right to speak in this context.

CONCLUSION

Conventional prayer exemplifies the way genres transform the idiosyncratic and particular into the conventional and shared. But prayer becomes resistance when people like Suleyman and Latifa use it to bend genres to very idiosyncratic purposes, pushing the envelope of recognized genre, or seizing control of a genre "off limits" to them. Suleyman did such pushing as a man who is not an imām but who made a verbal grab for that office. Latifa did so as a woman, none of whose kin had recently died and who was thus unauthorized to perform prayer-as-lament. Her tuneful performance asserted her desires as well as her rage at her brothers—problematic enough!—and did so, in part, in a religious idiom, thus introducing what is seen as a clash. Although the conventions of religious language form a kind of a moral center from which the distance of prayers is measured, the ideological center nonetheless forms the context for contestation. If prayer —its postures and its words—is a way of "being more than yourself," it is at the same time an activity in which some have more right than others to enlarge the self and its voice.

Opposition to "song"-like tuneful prayers and tuneful, texted weeping targets not only particular sentiments and words—potentially subversive, as when Latifa's lament thematized the injustice of her brothers' violence (Wilce 1998)—but *speech as performance per se.* Reformist Muslim scruples parallel those of Weber's Protestant reformers who worked, even at gravesides (Weber 1958: 105), to replace performed emotionality with cool, distanced rational reference to religious emotion. Such references become the sign of proper religious seriousness and bourgeois modernity.

Songlike speech in Bangladesh cannot be regarded as coming from Allah, since the orthodox Islamic sources on which the dominant metadiscourses draw condemn gān as defilingly secular. Thus, tunefulness must result from human intentionality (Arabic *niyat,* a term borrowed into Bengali), and its specific intent in personal prayer is assumed to be to draw attention to the person praying. Such improvised prayers will not please God. To flatly intone the words of the Qur'an in one's mosque prayers, and not stand out from others quietly doing the same, is to subjugate one's intent and one's voice to the divine word. Suleyman's and Latifa's potentially manipulative deployment of verbal art in prayer and lament runs up against an ideological embrace of submission, including the submission of one's own verbal-performative creativity to God and His Prophet.

Ideologies of language and self-expression co-occur with particular epochs, social formations, and cultural constructions of self. The eroding of ideologies—including cultural concepts of self, affect, and expressivity—that once encouraged lamentlike genres of poetic prayer has undermined public deployments of poetic language. We are witnessing a transformation of selfhood in South Asia—the sense of what the self is and how it should relate to others—across epochs and the ideologies dominating them. This transformation entails the ideological dethronement of the mystical religious self, constituted in musical and poetic performance, by a demystified modernist self constituted in "rational" speech that may still be religious but with a "Protestant" flavor (Weber 1958). Bangladeshis I know are under pressure to distance themselves from self-performed-in-song, to weep silently at someone's death, to construct self privately and yet not celebrate or explore that subjectivity. This substitution of selves is inseparable from changing genres of self-construction. Genre shifts affect forms of gatekeeping, changing who is allowed to performatively constitute himself as a legitimate pray-er. Bangladeshi Muslim ideologies of speech (and of speakers) place increasing restrictions on who may tunefully construct a charismatic (and prayerful) self in public.

If we fail to record and transcribe speech events like those represented here—on the possible grounds that they are microscopic, exceptional, or deviant—we run the risk of overlooking particular moments of profound change. Tambiah has argued (1990) that South Asian cultures have tended to hierarchically rank, but nonetheless include in the range of the acceptable, all sorts of ways of being; this inclusion has to some degree extended to socially recognized forms of "madness" that have remained in dialogue with "reason" (McDaniel 1989; Foucault 1973). This inclusivism may well be giving way to a new era in which even the madness of private tuneful prayer moves beyond the pale. Yet, despite threats to inclusivism, *Homo hierarchicus* (Dumont 1970)[9] seems destined to live on in a transformed state to the extent that self-assertion continues to be disapproved—but now as "madness" or "self-indulgent luxury." In any case, such historically decisive moments reflect and are constituted in relation to ideologies of—and unequal rights to—performance. Such ideologies include the power-informed selectivity of perceptions vis-à-vis who prays well, who prays tunefully, who gets the cultural capital, and who is left holding the empty narcissistic bag.

ACKNOWLEDGMENTS

This essay had its genesis in a paper presented at the panel "The Pragmatics of Prayer," organized by Lanita Jacobs-Huey at the American Association for Applied Linguistics meetings in Seattle, March 1998. My introduction is in essence a meditation on Elinor Ochs's very stimulating discussant remarks on the whole group of papers. I gratefully acknowledge the support of Dean Susanna Maxwell, and Northern Arizona University's Organized Research Committee, for supporting the 1996 visit to Bangladesh in which I was able to conduct broad interviews reflecting on the practice of tuneful prayer, as well as two summers of writing the book (Wilce 1998), in which I hit on the general outlines of the analysis presented here.

NOTES

1. *Bilāsitā* is "a luxurious pastime, self-indulgence, self-gratification" (Ali, Moniruzzaman, and Tareq 1994: 561).

2. C. M. Naim (1999) points out that Islamic reformist movements have more than a thousand years of history, and that a sustained cultural critique of lamentation, especially by women, has always been a part of such movements. Its critique as "rural and backward" is, I suspect, strictly modernist.

3. Dumont 1970 and Shweder and Bourne 1984 are, in my view, guilty of essentializing. For more recent ethnographic views, see Appadurai 1986; McHugh 1989; Derné 1995; and Wilce 1998.

4. I wondered, for instance, how my direct perceptions of his speech would differ from that which my "brothers" had conveyed to me, how their representation of his speech might conform to stereotypes—issues taken up in Wilce 1998. In my ten encounters with him, Suleyman's speech only rarely took on the singsong quality that they reproduced. That is, it was clear when he was performing tuneful prayers and when he was engaged in conversation; only rarely did I hear the marked tunefulness of lament break into his unmarked talking.

5. Secular government schools contrast with the mosque schools, though the latter also receive government funding.

6. To me, *hāmd* and *nāt* are just as musical as *gān,* though my Bangladeshi reformist Muslim friends might one day help me hear the difference. It seems to me (and my musicological training is strictly Western) that, although equally musical, "Islamist" forms draw on a "musical" tradition that has come to Bangladesh from points west, viz., the Middle East.

7. Sunnis adhere to an "orthodox" tradition of Islam that acknowledges all caliphs as rightful successors of Muhammad, whereas Shi'a Muslims regarded the first three caliphs as usurpers of Ali, Muhammad's nephew. Sufi sects collect those willing to engage in special disciplines and religious practices; they bear some resemblance to Catholic monasticism and Protestant Pietism.

8. There is an extensive oral and written literature—again internally diverse, for instance in the four subtraditions of *fiqh,* Islamic law, recognized within Sunni Islam—guiding the faithful to reproduce the sacred sonic qualities of the call-to-prayer (*āzān*) and the recitation of the Qur'an. For instance, marked nasalization of vowels, which is stylistic rather than phonemic in Qur'anic Arabic (and eastern dialects of Bengali), is prescribed for the call-to-prayer (Nelsen 1985).

9. Dumont argues that South Asian societies have encouraged a form of human existence, which he calls "Homo hierarchicus," which valorizes the practices of ranking and relating selves to collectivities that are regarded as prior to and definitional of self.

PART FIVE

Nation-Making

Colonialism had a profound effect on the structure of all South Asian societies, and like many "post-colonies" in the world today, the move from being a colony to being an independent nation-state has been accompanied by struggles to define anew national identities and boundaries. Violence has often played a role in this process of nation-making.

By about 1800, the British had effectively colonized most of South Asia. British presence in mainland South Asia started in the 1600s with the British East India Company. The British colonized Sri Lanka a little later, in 1796, when they took over territories held there by the Dutch, who had colonized the island from 1658 to 1796. (The Dutch themselves had taken over from the Portuguese, who controlled the island from 1605 to 1658.) In India (which included Pakistan and Bangladesh), to protect company interests in the face of an attempted mutiny by Indian soldiers, the British established direct colonial rule during the mid–nineteenth century, and only let go of political-economic control in the middle of the twentieth century. India and Pakistan (including what is now Bangladesh) achieved independence in 1947. Sri Lanka (previously Ceylon) followed shortly thereafter in 1948. Nepal, while never directly colonized, nonetheless was politically structured in part by British policy, having entered into enduring treaties with the British in the nineteenth century. The struggles of many colonized peoples to redefine territories and national languages, histories, and ideologies began, in most places, well before Independence, as Chatterjee (1993) points out.

If we can think of the "state" as the political and legislative apparatus of a country, then what is the nation? According to Benedict Anderson (1991), the nation is an "imagined community." That is, the nation is in

large measure formed upon an idea of belonging that is based on the construction of a common culture through such things as speaking the same
language, reading the same newspapers, constructing a shared history and
sense of the past, and practicing a common ideology (such as equality or
democracy) or religion or heritage (see Bate, this part). Importantly, none
of these shared cultural features are a priori, that is, none of them pre-exist
the human beings who create them. Because of this, it is also important to
understand that imagining a nation also involves some persons or groups
having the power to influence and define what those common ideas, languages, ideologies, and pasts will be. Whose version of the past will become the defining concept of nation? Whose language will become "official"? Whose life practices will become the "norm"? Who will be excluded,
or granted second-class status in a nation not of their own making?

In India (which then included Pakistan and Bangladesh), the very moment of Independence was already a startling challenge to the struggle to
define independent nations. Outgoing British and incoming Indian leaders
came to an uneasy agreement to bifurcate India into two nations, India and
Pakistan, a trauma known as Partition. Partition was the result of contentious and difficult agreements reached by three parties: the British, led by
Lord Mountbatten; the Indian Congress Party, led by Jawarhalal Nehru
(Mahatma Gandhi was against Partition); and the Muslim League, led by
Muhammed Ali Jinnah. While the historical causes leading to Partition
are complex (see Lapierre and Collins 1975), among those causes was a fear
on the part of Muslims that they would be a loathed minority in a majority
Hindu state, and the fear on the part of all parties that violence and even
civil war might erupt. Partition was no peaceful solution, however: no less
than a million people on both sides of the new border lost their lives in the
mass migrations that followed as Muslims whose homes were now in "India" fled to Pakistan, and Hindus who found themselves in what was now
Pakistan fled to India (see Ghosh, this part). The aftermath of Partition
continues to be felt today in the conflicts over Kashmir as well as in other
parts of India. Kakar (1995), for example, demonstrates how Partition remains a motif in current Hindu-Muslim violence in India, and two essays
in this part (Kumar and Ghosh) address some of the ramifications of Partition for the everyday life of both Muslims and Hindus in India today.

Pakistan itself was further divided in 1971, when Bangladesh (previously East Pakistan) declared independence from West Pakistan (see Sisson
and Rose 1990). Among the causes for this declaration was the fact that East
Pakistan was culturally and linguistically distinct from West Pakistan
(not to mention over a thousand miles distant!), despite their shared religion. East Pakistanis "imagined" themselves to be a distinct people (Bengali Muslims), and they resented West Pakistan's hegemony (see Ghosh).

Even within a nation, certain groups might feel excluded or threatened
and thus wish to break off and form their own nation. In the 1920s, Tamil

nationalists in south India called for a separate Tamil nation. Their argument was that the linguistic and cultural heritage of the Tamils was different from numerically and politically more powerful northern Indians and was therefore endangered by the hegemony of the Hindi language and north Indian cultural values, which the Tamil nationalists constructed as Other. (Such conflict marks other nations, too, including the United States, where the Civil War has become a symbol that continues to contribute to the construction of a "Southern" identity and as debates rage about the meanings and uses of the Confederate flag.)

These conflicts over national belonging are not remnants of the past. Today in India, for example, the leading party is a powerful party of Hindu nationalists (the BJP, or Bharata Janata Party), which came to power on a platform of religious and caste identity politics. In their efforts to build a constituency, they constructed a revisionist history of India as an originally Hindu nation—glorious, peaceful, and beneficent—that was destroyed by Muslim invaders. They assert that their hopes for the "recovery" of this Hindu nation is still threatened, now by affirmative-action-type programs and legislation that favors so-called minorities. Among these "minorities" are Muslims whom Hindu nationalists defined as outsiders, despite the fact that Muslims are Indians, too. In order to proclaim a "nation," in other words, they created a nationalized past that would help create an imagined community who would vote to re-gain their "lost" community (see, for example, Kakar 1995; Ludden 1996).

Today in Sri Lanka the nation is being torn apart by the violence that has resulted from redefining the ethnic and territorial boundaries of the nation in the wake of colonial rule. For historically complex reasons (see, e.g., Tambiah 1991 [1986]; Daniel 1996), Sri Lanka's population has come to see itself as divided between two ethnic groups: Tamils and Sinhalese. The Tamils are a numerical minority, though in previous decades they were seen by some as economically privileged, in part due to the position that many Tamils held in the British colonial government. Some segments of the Tamil population, perceiving themselves to be disadvantaged in the new democratic nation of Sri Lanka, sought to establish an independent Tamil enclave on the northeast portion of this small island nation. The warfare and violence that have resulted from these and other factors has left Sri Lanka a maze of checkpoints and military outposts, and a place where violence has become a part of everyday life (see Jeganathan and Trawick in this part, and Daniel in part VI).

* * *

The essays in this part all address how constructing political communities—nations—of shared language, history, and/or heritage impact the everyday life of citizens. Bate's essay focuses on how the everyday activity of "reading the newspaper" creates political identities and emotional ties to state-level political leaders in Tamil Nadu, south India. Politicians take out newspaper ads featuring poems that praise the Chief Minister of Tamil Nadu, and in so doing create for themselves a political identity. Bate argues that these ads—as well as posters and arches that mark the city of Madurai—are effective in rendering power precisely because in both form and content the ads evoke emotional responses in those who view them (including the politicians themselves). The "state" becomes then not only "imagined" but also "felt" as a wondrous object, objectified in glorifying poetic and print images of its leader.

As noted above, one of the defining moments of national inclusion and exclusion in South Asia came in 1947 with the Partition of India and Pakistan. The essays by Kumar and Ghosh show how Partition continues to influence life experiences of Indians today. Ghosh looks into how Bengali Hindus who were displaced by Partition work to construct a Bengali identity that connects them to the homes they left behind in what is now Bangladesh. What is it like to lose your home? How can you hold on to a home identity, yet also fit in to the new nation that both claims you and in some ways rejects you? Kumar provides an ethnographic depiction of several schools in India, where Muslim and Hindu children are taught Indian history. She argues that learning about the history of one's nation is a creative, imaginary activity that aims to turn students into a homogenized citizenry that will carry out national agendas into the future. She goes on to discuss the cost of a homogenized national history: less powerful, minority communities "lose out" on the chance to maintain and create their *own* history and identity.

While Bate's essay describes the south Indian city of Madurai as a place displaying a profusion of evocative political images in newspapers as well as on streets and walls, Jeganathan's depicts another city—Colombo, Sri Lanka—and another space of everyday life, where it isn't a politician's decorative arch that one walks through. Rather, residents of Colombo walk through a city marked by bombs, and walk, too, through checkpoints manned by police officers checking identities and deciding who can pass through and who cannot. Jeganathan both describes the process of moving through a checkpoint and presents us with a challenging theoretical query. He asks us to consider, and critique, some of the ways in which anthropological depictions of culture—such as some of those that might even appear in this book—sometimes "freeze-frame" culture as if it were a stable, graspable entity. He implies that such an act of freeze-framing a culture, like mapping a place or pinpointing an "identity," is an act of power that in fact does violence to the everydayness of life, where it is not stability and singularity that characterize our lives, but rather movement and heterogeneity. How can one "map" a city, or a culture, or an identity, when every movement—or in Colombo, every bomb that goes off—changes one's lived reality?

Margaret Trawick takes us from Colombo to a rural area in northern Sri Lanka, home to a substantial Tamil population and also home territory for the Tamil Tigers (LTTE), the revolutionary insurrectionists whose bombs —along with the bombs of others—alter the topography of Colombo. Trawick interviews schoolchildren about the impact that the civil war in Sri Lanka has had upon their lives. In an area decimated by war since before they were born, these children have grown up with violence, death, and fear as a part of their daily lives. How, Trawick wonders, can children who live so close to death every day still have the courage to continue to think of their futures and work to build lives of peace?

Political Praise in Tamil Newspapers: The Poetry and Iconography of Democratic Power

J. Bernard Bate

O, Auspicious Leader
Who has ushered in
  a Golden Era of Rule!
O, Revolutionary Leader
Whom we worship daily
  turning evil-doing wastrels
  into question-marks . . .
Every movement of your tongue
Results in beneficial development schemes!
Even wastelands flourish
If your foot steps there!
I bow my head
  at the coming of your golden feet
I put my hands together
  and it cools my intellect
  to welcome you
  bowing down to worship your feet.

> —Advertisement placed by Sathur K. Sundarapandian,
> Kamarajar District Secretary, AIADMK
> (*Malai Murasu* 22.VIII.94: II)

The poem above, entitled "I Worshiped Your Golden Feet," exemplifies the kind of poetry that dominates the pages of Tamil newspapers when a major politician comes to town. This one is different from others only insofar as it is somewhat more original. Most of the poems I take up in this paper are far more formulaic: they frequently slap together stock phrases of adulation to weave a new poem that says nothing different from a hundred others in the newspaper that day. But they all attribute to J. Jayalalitha, the Chief Minister of the state of Tamil Nadu, India (1992–96), a certain divinity worthy of worship, even of the most physical forms of worship such as prostrating at one's leader's feet or self-mutilation; they all attribute to her sole agency of the state ("every movement of your tongue [*nāva-caippellām*][1] results in beneficial development schemes [*nalattiṭṭam*]"); they all assert that her mere presence in a particular place will bring forth abundance and fertility, growth and greenness ("Even wastelands flourish if your foot steps there!"); they all claim she is the very embodiment of such qualities as love, compassion, intelligence, the Tamil language, and history itself; and finally, they all address her in very familiar terms such as "family deity," or "deity of my heart," and most significantly, as "Mother" —as an intimate, powerful being.

This essay outlines two interrelated projects. In the first project I examine some of these poems in order to describe an aspect of the imaginings of power in the political practice of Tamil Nadu. In the case of the Chief Minister, the notion that her bodily presence in a wasteland will produce abundance or that her tongue is the source of all development projects suggests that the image of Jayalalitha in these poems is an aestheticized image (Daniel 1996) of an abstraction, i.e., the state (Abrams 1988). I evoke the concept of the "aesthetic" to suggest the "fixing" or "objectification" (Cohn 1987b) of otherwise fluid sociocultural categories in discursive interaction. I also use the term to suggest that the discursively constructed object is imbued with emotional charge, plus or minus, attraction or repulsion. The realm of the aesthetic might be characterized as occupying one end of a continuum of possible takes on the world, from an embodied, emotional, "gut" reaction to a more "rational"—perhaps (better) rationalized—"ideology" of human action, products of action, and institutions. Both aesthetic and ideology are in constant interaction in people's everyday practical engagement with the world. And both, in turn, are the templates for that engagement. The "state" (or other aestheticizations of power), in no matter what form it may be imagined, probably partakes more of the embodied aesthetic end of the continuum than of the conscious rationalizations of ideology. The "state" is never a neutral imagining but always an image to which we either tie ourselves in devotion or patriotic love, or defy with parricidal hatred.

But these imaginings do not merely follow some logic peculiar to the nation-state, whatever that may be (cf. Chatterjee 1993; Anderson 1991 [1983]). Rather, imaginings of the state are informed by common potentialities peculiar to Tamil society which are produced and reproduced in the practices of everyday life. Praise, what we will call *bhakti*, or "devotional love," appears to be a master aesthetic of the practices discussed in this essay.[2] Praise, I argue here, is an ancient Indian cultural logic (Appadurai 1990; Ali 1996) that informs the discursive practices whereby one aestheticizes power as an intimate being, such as a family deity or mother, who will grant us the benefits of her presence and respond to our appeals.

Appadurai describes the praise of superiors in Hindu India, especially kings, as anchored in the logic of worship. Praise is, above all, a ritual activity, which produces a "hierarchical intimacy" (Babb 1986, quoted in Appadurai 1990)[3] between the worshiper and the worshiped, which is, often enough, a deity. The ritual practice, though intimate, is performed for others to see; it is meant to be observed and evaluated by onlookers. As such, it is an aesthetic practice both as one that can be evaluated positively or negatively and also as one which has emotional content—in the case of the praise poetry the content of devotional love, bhakti. As I will discuss below, contemporary political praise poetry draws on, and is structurally similar to, at least three other genres of praise in Tamil Nadu: the contemporary practice of greeting a leader who has graced a public meeting with his or her presence, the ancient praise of kings in inscriptions of their accomplishments, and medieval bhakti poetry.

The second project looks at the medium of this discourse, the newspaper, as an object of inquiry in ethnographic research: What importance does the newspaper have for the ethnography of a place, a practice, or a people? The newspaper as an object of ethnographic inquiry violates traditional categories of anthropological research (Herzfeld 1992: 120–21, n. 5): an anthropologist of a nonliterate society spends time "in the field" whereas scholars of literate civilizations work in archives or libraries. And as Akhil Gupta remarks, the newspaper also appears incompatible with traditional notions of ethnographic time and practice in the anthropology of the present:

> Treated with benign neglect by students of contemporary life, [newspapers] mysteriously metamorphize into invaluable "field data" once they have yellowed around the edges and fallen apart at the creases. And yet it is not entirely clear by what alchemy time turns the "secondary" data of the anthropologist into the "primary" data of the historian. (1995: 385)

The newspaper, though, is a textual artifact that is an integral part of daily life among vast numbers of people, even among those who may read nothing else. An ethnographer "in the field" of an Indian city would be missing much if s/he ignored the newspaper not only as a cultural text but as the focal object of a wide range of practices. It is also a medium accessible to a wide range of people, a means to advertise one's business, marriageable son or daughter, or political patronage. The newspaper, in other words, has a social life far livelier than most ethnographic research has so far given it credit for. My second concern, then, is to explore how the newspaper, as a widely accessible mode of mass media, can be a space, like other spaces in the society—the street or the political stage—where people announce their allegiance to their political leaders through praise, tie their names to them and, in so doing, make themselves great.

I will begin with a discussion of the Tamil newspaper as a focal object in daily practice and as a medium of political patronage. After briefly outlining some of the major themes of the poetry I will then discuss its layout on the page and its iconography. The newspaper image or text does not exist in a vacuum, though, either in terms of its placement on a page or section of the newspaper or in its wider resonance with the world around it. In the end, I will explore how these textual and visual images fit into the wider world in which the newspaper is produced and read by examining some of the textual, visual, and architectural images of praise found (almost) every day on the streets of Madurai.

I

Newspapers, those daily, sometimes twice-daily, mediations of the social world beyond our immediate face-to-face interactions are time-bound textual objects. While Benedict Anderson called them "one-day bestsellers" (1991: 35) they are quite different from books, bureaucratic documents, or other textual artifacts which are produced to stand the test of time, to "record," to transcend the ephemerality of the spoken word, to endure.

They do resemble at least some books, though, such as the Bible, the Qur'an, or other such texts, insofar as they occupy a central place in many people's daily rituals, often in the mornings, but at other specific times of day as well.[4] In the city of Madurai, Tamil Nadu, men (particularly men) gather at tea stalls early to smoke, drink tea or coffee, and read the newspaper or listen to a reading of it. The tea-stall owners keep a few papers around that are taken apart page by page, each leaf passed around so one paper can be read simultaneously by a number of people. Frequently, someone will read an article out loud, his recitation sharply marked as the written form of the language—indeed, his language is even marked as "journalese," that form of written Tamil massively influenced by the grammar of English newspapers. The ritual of early morning reading is often repeated, somewhat more diffusely, after six when the evening papers are delivered. In this way, newspapers are part of the daily rhythm of life in Madurai, like meals, prayers, going to work or temple, or taking an afternoon siesta, activities which vast numbers of people regard as integral, essential aspects of their days.[5]

But unlike a book, a particular edition of a newspaper is an artifact of and for the moment, a punctual object whose value (under ordinary circumstances) is limited to a few hours. In a city like Madurai, with three main morning papers and two main evening papers, the value of the morning paper is at its greatest at sunrise, far less at midday, and by dusk it is worth only its weight as scrap.[6] A half-day bestseller, at best. At the same time, the fact that someone took out a political ad or published an article or poem in a particular newspaper can point to that particular moment, those particular people in those particular relations. Similarly with articles that concern an individual: these become objects the individual might keep folded up in the back of his or her bureau, mementos of a moment in which his or her name transcended everyday life and became a part of history.

Finally, as Anderson has famously argued, the newspaper allows the imagining of a community far beyond the face-to-face world in which it is read (1991: 32–36; 61–65), i.e., the "imagined community" of the nation-state. But these imaginings are closely tied to the particular discourses or events occurring at that particular moment in time. And the community imagined is internally differentiated, politically contested, hierarchized, and bounded off from others in particular ways. Each newspaper in Tamil Nadu has very definite political party affiliations or sympathies, so the multiple imagining of community will have differing evaluations from paper to paper. The "community" imagined on any given morning by *Thikkathir* ("Ray of Fire"), an organ of the Communist Party of India (Marxist), will be very different from that imagined by *Thina Thandhi* ("The Daily Wire"), Tamil Nadu's most popular daily which was originally modeled on the British tabloid *The Daily Mirror* (Jeffrey 1997: 254). What Anderson calls the "fictive reality" of an imagined collectivity generated through the daily reading of the Tamil newspaper, then, is a highly political reality, and that politics is constantly changing.

II

The advertisements I examine here were taken out by local politicians on days of their leader's arrival in their towns or districts.[7] The hundreds of ads that dominate the pages on those days spill over the regular sections into special sections (*ciruppumalar*) issued by the newspapers in order to hold them all. The sudden appearance of the very excess of Jayalalitha images and the sudden storm of praise—O, Amazon Warrior; O, Protector Deity; O, Doctor Revolutionary Leader—never effaces the fact that these ads are taken out by locally well-known people who direct their messages not only to their leaders but to their constituents, their colleagues and competitors within the party, and their political enemies. The larger and more extravagant the ads, the greater one's presence in that town's political organization, and certainly the greater one's image in the sight—in the literal, early morning gaze—of the visiting leader thumbing through the local newspaper. Invariably, a politician's welcome contains a large image of "The Big Person," the leader's name or appellation in the boldest print, and a poem addressed to her. The local politician's photograph placed prominently at the bottom of the page, his or her name always in the second boldest print, ensures that this "enchanted forest of adulation" (Mbembe 1992)

18. Jayalalitha as Andal. "O, Reincarnation of Mother Andal! / O Excellence whom All the World Praises! / Welcome! / Shower Riches upon Us! Placed by P. B. Selvasubramaniyaraja of the Revolutionary Leader Front, Rajapalaiyam, Kamaraj District." Quarter-page ad, *Malai Murasu*, 28 August 1994: 1.

never entirely bewitches us as some "authorless" text expressing timeless truth.

The overall structure and main motifs of these poems have a number of antecedents which reveal the overall logic of praise. Of many possible, I mention here three: the welcome address of stage speaking; medieval bhakti poetry; and the praise of kings found in *prasasti* and *meykkīrti* poems of kingly praise. The "welcome address" (*varavērpurai*), a performance genre of *mēṭaittamiḻ*, or "oratory," ends with the phrase *varuka! varuka! eṉru varavērkirōm*, "We welcome you with (shouts of) 'Welcome! Welcome!'" The most common vocatives—what we might call *hailing utterances*—printed boldly in the advertisements also resonate with the moment of welcoming a leader to a speaking event. The event organizer at the microphone shouts out "O, Doctor Revolutionary Leader"—and the crowd responds, "Long Live!"; he shouts: "O, Amazon Warrior Who Protects Social Justice"—they respond, "Long Live!"; "O, Family Deity"—"Long Live! Long Live! Long Live!" The event becomes marked by the rhythm of the chant-and-response (which may last for five minutes or more), the passion of the party cadres as they throng the stage, and the frenzy that frequently erupts as the faithful struggle with organizers and bodyguards to garland their leader or give her a gift with no regard to the proper time and place for such things. The welcoming of the big person and the vocative chanting is always a moment of intense energy and enthusiasm, one of the aspects of political meetings that mark them as sites of intense desire and longing.

Looking at these vocatives we get a sense of the range of appellations Jayalalitha's supporters generate for her as well as of the variety of images that are deployed in the aestheticization of the state. She is hailed, firstly, as a leader of specific groups such as "the poor," the "common people," or the "the Tamil lands"; she is a "Golden Leader," a "Leader equal to a Lion," a "Leader whom all the world praises." Secondly, she is characterized as a reincarnation of famous historical figures: kings (e.g., Pari, a Sangam-age king known for his philanthropy), queens (e.g., Jansi Rani, a Rajasthani queen who is said to have strapped her newborn crown prince on her back and fought off the Muslim invaders of her kingdom), and literary figures (e.g., Andal, the famous author of bhakti poetry; see fig. 18). Thirdly, she is hailed as a deity: "O, God of Our Heart," "O, Goddess of Dharma," "O, Protector Deity of Social Justice," "Family Deity," and "God of Our Hearts." The remainder of the vocative appellations can be broken down into such categories as history/literature/language (O, Tamil; O, Golden Book of History); light/lamps (O, Sacred Lamp of the Southlands); the heart (O, Vital Heartbeat of the Poor); land or architecture (O, Land That Sprouted Heroism); intimate beings (O, Mother); and a series of abstractions such as bravery, love, statecraft, sacredness, and motherhood. It is precisely the combination of all of these qualities and identities that are woven together in this aestheticized image of Jayalalitha as the sole agency of the state, indeed, as the state itself. Her appearance at opening ceremonies for multimillion-rupee state development projects—which are the impetus for the praise poetry—become celebrations of her personal largesse; her movement across the landscape of Tamil Nadu is praised as the movement of state power itself. Most of these themes are represented in the following two poems.

Poem 2

O, Jansi Rani of the Tamil lands
    who has come to bestow
    the Anna medal on police officers!
O, Land that sprouts victory!
O, Doctor Revolutionary Leader,
    esteemed Premier of the Tamil Lands,
Welcome! Welcome!

O, Amazon Warrior who protects social justice
    who has won
    69% caste reservation
    which will bring well-being

for tomorrow's society
and will make the dispossessed prosper!
Welcome! Welcome!

By your arrival
Madurai achieves excellence!
I welcome you
in praise and worship

> Your true servant
> T. K. Rathakrishnan, B.E., M.L.A.
> Thirmangalam Assembly District
> Madurai District
> (*Malai Malar* 19.IX.94: V)

Poem 3

O, Mother
Who has given us life
Our God of personal grace
The very embodiment of
    Intelligence, Ability, Refinement, Discrimination, Love, Compassion,
    Achievement, History, Epoch, Honesty,
    Ability, Strong Will, Political Strategy
Welcome! Welcome!

We touch your feet and worship you.

> C. Singam, Asst. Secretary, Madurai District AIADMK, Madurai
> Sellur K. Raji, Secretary, 16th Ward, AIADMK, Madurai
> (*Malai Malar* 19.IX.94: XI)

The second most obvious antecedent for the praise poem, as suggested at the outset of this chapter, is bhakti poetry, or the poetry of devotion to a personal deity. Newspaper poems seem to particularly resemble the poetry of the medieval devotional text of Tamil Saivism, *Tēvāram*. The fact that one reads the same basic structure in the newspaper poems over and over again is similar to a reading of the *Tēvāram* which is organized in thematic cycles of praise to Lord Siva. One example taken from the *Appar Tēvāram*, composed as early as the seventh century, might suffice to indicate the obvious connection between the two poetic traditions:

. . .
bright flame, celestial being
who stands as the pure path,
bull among the immortals,

honey who dwells in Tiruvaiyaru!
I wander as your servant,
worshipping and singing your feet.
(*Appar Tēvāram* IV.39; trans. Peterson [1989: 286])

Compare the above with the poem below placed in the *Malai Muracu* by a minister of the Tamil Nadu Legislative Assembly from Kamarajar District, Mr. J. Balagangatharan:

Poem 4

O, sacred lamp of the Southlands!
O, light of the Dravidian family!
O, burning torch of poor people!
O, Athiparasakti
vital ruler of this earthly world!
O, esteemed Doctor Revolutionary Leader
who transforms these Tamil lands into a Golden Realm!
I welcome you
I touch your golden feet and worship you!

> J. Balagangatharan, B.Sc., B.L., M.L.A.
> District Secretary
> Revolutionary Leader Front
> Kamarajar District
> (*Malai Muracu* 22.VIII.94: III)

Obviously, a number of motifs have been borrowed directly from medieval bhakti poetry, not least of which being the evocation of lamps, lights, and fire: elements of worship and icons of power. The mode of worship is hyperbolic (at least from some points of view), intensely emotional, and aesthetically crafted. Today, these same poems are recited in the evenings at major Saivite temples throughout Tamil Nadu.

Thirdly, the contemporary praise poem appears to partake of the same logic of the pan-Indic Sanskrit *prasasti* inscriptions dating in Tamil Nadu from the same period as the first bhakti movements (Appadurai 1990: 110ff, note 1). Prasasti were inscriptional "praise prefaces" which identified the king as a divine descendant of a deity and bestowed titles (*virutu*), "emblems," or "honors" upon the king from a subordinate. The Tamil counterpart of the prasasti prefaces, which developed during the Chola period (9th–12th centuries, C.E.), are *meykkīrtti*. Meykkīrtti differ from prasasti prefaces by their far more standardized formats and their attention to the achievements of the king and not to his genealogy (Davis 1985: 5). For a variety of reasons, genealogical claims were absent. Rather, the Chola king was praised for his conquests on the hot battlefield and the protection of his home landscape, cool and green under his all-encompassing royal parasol. In other words, the king's actions and accomplishments are more important than any authorial claims of legitimate pedigree. Meykkīrttis praise the king's works by which the land is transformed, made lush and fertile ("even wastelands flourish if your foot steps there").

In each case, the welcome address, the bhakti poem, and the prasasti/ meykkīrtti inscription, the leader is praised publicly, emotionally, and hyperbolically. The following poem, sponsored to celebrate the inauguration of a number of state-run development schemes, appears to touch on all of the above categories:

> O, Sacredness! O Sacred Lamp!
> O, Great Light of Dravida!
> O, Encyclopedia of History
>   who achieved (a policy of) 69% caste reservation!
> O, Fantasy who brought the Kaveri River
>   to fatten this golden fertile country for all of history!
> O, Lamp of the Lighthouse!
> O, Golden Light of the Lion Throne
>   which is the cradle of the Child who came to show
>   the world the Grammar of Motherhood!
>
> O, Our Goddess of Love
>   who has placed her foot
>   in Anna District!
>
> O, Leader equal to the Lion!
> Mother, May you (nī)[8] come! O, Welcome!
>
>   Forever Your Faithful Servant,
>   P. Kumaraswamy, B.Sc., B.L., M.P.
>   Palani Parliamentary District
>   (*Malai Malar* 23.IX.94: V)

The member of parliament's poem contains aspects of all three of the antecedents mentioned above. It is firstly organized as a complex vocative phrase directed toward Jayalalitha. Secondly, its characterization of the leader by the use of motifs such as lamps, lights, and majestic creatures such as lions, as well as its overall mood of praise, resonate clearly with medieval bhakti poetic practice. Thirdly, Kumaraswamy publicly praises the Chief Minister's achievements, such as her political struggle to ensure that 69 percent of state government appointments will be filled by members of Scheduled Castes and Tribes and the Backward and Most Backward Classes. And despite the fact that Tamil Nadu's ongoing dispute with neighboring Karnataka over the free flow of the Kaveri River had not been resolved at that time, the poem attributes to Jayalalitha not only the successful settlement of the problem but the very flow of the river itself and the unending fertility of the Tamil lands! The invocation of such images of lamps and lights—common among all the Dravidian parties—suggests that her presence casts a light in the darkness (of opposition rule), brings cool greenness to the lands that were parched; the imagery appears to parallel the old meykkīrti opposition of arid battlefields and the cool, fertile lands of the landscape under the royal parasol.

III

The layout and iconography, too, like the poetic description of Jayalalitha as a deity, king, or queen, suggests the imagining of both hierarchical and intimate relationships to the leader. Her image is literally framed in borders and boxes that confirm her royal cum divine identity. In addition to rather standard borders of the red, white, and black colors of her party, the AIADMK, Jayalalitha stands framed by temple pillars or in a *maṇṭapam* (a pillared hall frequently in a temple); she is shown shaded by the royal parasol; she is seated in the Lion Throne reviewing her all women police brigades—which she has just instituted—marching by. The lion, so frequently mentioned, has numerous resonances in contemporary Tamil culture. The Lion, as in Europe, is the sign of royalty par excellence; it is also said to be Jayalalitha's zodiac sign. One woman examining a page featuring a number of lions—which had been arrayed around Jayalalitha in an ad placed for a ceremony to decorate police officers—suggested to me that the lions were policemen standing guard around the Chief Minister. Finally, just as each deity has a vehicle, so too does Jayalalitha have the lion— the same vehicle, by the way, of the pan-Indian goddess Durga and the local Tamil deity Mariyamman.

The hierarchical distancing of the leader as god or king is fused with a sense of intimacy. Hierarchy is expressed in top/bottom oppositions, and intimacy in the choice of portraits as well as their orientation vis-à-vis each other. One P. Balasubramanian, head of the Tamil Nadu Produce Sales Board, placed a full-page, full-color ad in the *Malai Murasu*, an evening paper (fig. 19). Other than a small picture of himself with some text at the bottom of the page, the ad features a large central photograph of the Chief Minister, dressed in a white sari, smiling pleasantly and gazing down and off page. The central photograph is surrounded by sixty smaller images of exactly the same image, the larger one and most of the smaller ones appearing to gaze warmly at Bala himself! Orienting the Chief Minister's picture such that it smiles at the ad's sponsor is a frequent technique in these ads.

Hierarchical relationships are equally transparent. Numerous ads feature the hierarchical ordering of Jayalalitha just below figures such as the founder of the Dravidian movement, Thandai Periyar E. V. Ramaswamy,

19. Multiple JJ. Ad placed by P. Balasubramaniyan, Chennai. Full-page ad, *Malai Malar*, 24 September 1994: XXXV (Special Section).

and the DMK and AIADMK founders Ariñar ("The Scholar") Annadurai and "Doctor Revolutionary Leader" M. G. Ramachandran (MGR), respectively (see note 8). In such a position she mediates the relationship between those late, great political figures and the local politician pictured at the bottom of the page. This same logic is repeated by lower-level political workers inserting their district-level leaders in between themselves and Jayalalitha; or to foreground their local patronage to an even greater degree, the local leader's picture is placed by his or her subordinates in the same line as the former leaders.

IV

These ads constitute but one of a series of activities local politicos undertake to welcome their leader and, importantly, to tie their names to hers. The placement of the praise poem is, thus, a practice that shares a contexture— "the texture that surrounds and the texture that constitutes" (Daniel and Peck 1996: 1)—with a wide range of related practices. The most notable of these practices include street-level activities which are structurally similar to the newspaper poems. Ceremonial arches are inscribed with the same

20. Mural at "The Space of JJ." (*JJ tital* near Cimmakkal, North Veli Street junction.) Commissioned by "Coconut Shop" R. Mariyappan (pictured lower right). The two standing figures are Ariñar Annadurai (left) and M. G. Ramachandran. The two leaves are the official voting sign of the AIADMK. The image in the circle at center is Periyar E. V. Ramaswamy. The mural reads, "O, Lioness who appears as a burning lamp to light the Tamil lands which have been cast into darkness! O, Goddess of Revolution! O, Mother! O, Tamil!" The writing at the bottom of the mural notes that this painting was sponsored by "The Madurai City Self-Protection Force."

vocative salutations, especially "Revolutionary Leader," "Mother Tamil," "Family Deity," etc., and during the caste reservation agitations, "Amazon Warrior Who Protects Social Justice." The very same phrases taken out in newspaper ads appear on posters, banners, and wall paintings such as the mural sponsored by one of Madurai's most prominent supporters and (therefore) benefactors of Jayalalitha, "Coconut Shop" R. Mariyappan, at a place he dubbed "*JJ tital*," or "The Space of J. Jayalalitha" (fig. 20):

> O, Lioness
>   who appears as a burning lamp to light the Tamil lands
>   which have been cast in darkness!
> O, Goddess of Revolution!
> O, Mother!
> O, Tamil!

This painting, along with several others in Madurai commissioned by Mariyappan's supporters, has the same structural properties as many of the ads examined above as well as other poetic and iconographic repre-

21. Mural at Workshop Road. The mural was sponsored by Pon. Arumugam, R. T. Paramasivam, and M. G. Pandikumar, subordinates of "Coconut Shop" R. Mariyappan, whose name is prominently featured in the picture itself. Above the image of Jayalalitha and Coconut Shop are portraits of M. G. Ramachandran (left) and Arinar C. N. Annadurai. The heading reads: "34th Ward Revolutionary Leader Front."

sentations of praise. Mariyappan's supporters commissioned a number of painted images on structures throughout Madurai in 1994 and '95. There appears in this and other paintings a crisscrossing of gazes and postures, from Mariyappan in the lower-right-hand corner worshiping Jayalalitha; to Jayalalitha on the left worshiping MGR and Annadurai (who appear to float like ghosts); and back again to Periyar, framed not unlike a revered ancestor's portrait hanging in the hall of someone's home.

This spatial logic is equally evident in the painting on Workshop Road (fig. 21). Also commissioned by political workers of Mariyappan's camp, this brightly painted mural depicts Mariyappan reverently saluting Jayalalitha, who lights a lamp over a sun-drenched Madurai, a landscape dominated by the Meenakshiyamman Temple's towering gateways (*kōpuram*). The portraits of their political forebears above (MGR and Annadurai) appear here, too, to balance off the names of the mural sponsors below. Again, as in bhakti poetry, praising the servants (e.g., Mariyappan) of the servants

22. Mural at the Ganesh Temple, Cimmakkal.

(Jayalalitha) of the lord (Meenakshiyamman) is a long and fruitful strategy in Tamil practices of the production of political power. But not merely this, Mariyappan and the Chief Minister appear framed in a tableau, a domestic scene of husband and auspicious wife of childbearing years (*cumaṅkali*) reverently worshiping God. Taking in this image in one glance, our minds shift back and forth from an image of hierarchical salutation to a fantastic Holy Family wherein our local leader—himself a source of great benefit—dwells married to the our Mother/Goddess. What fruits, what benefits, such a union produces!

A final mural commissioned by Mariyappan's nephew, M. G. Pandi Kumar, and his nephew's colleague, Pon Arumugam, both replicates the logic of the two murals discussed above (and, mutatis mutandis, the visual structure of the newspaper advertisements and posters) and pushes the extremes of the identification of god and politician (fig. 22). The mural was painted in celebration of Jayalalitha's accomplishment of inaugurating the Eighth World Tamil Conference in Thanjavur, January 1995. The phrase printed in the painting is rather standard for these kinds of images and hails the Chief Minister: "O, Historical Achievement of establishing the 8th World Tamil Conference! O, Mother Tamil!" The painting is exceptional, though, for several reasons. Firstly, Jayalalitha is seated in the royal "Lion Throne" (*cīmācaṉam*) guarded by a lion lying to the right of her chair. Opposite her, and slightly below, is painted a framed portrait of Coconut Shop Mariyappan, who is depicted in a reverent posture facing Jayalalitha.

Despite the fact that his portait appears slightly below the image of Jayalalitha, the image of his face is larger than hers (and I can't help but find his gold watch and ring, prominent on his left hand, significant in announcing his status as a professional man). Images of MGR and Annadurai, like the portrait of Periyar in the JJ Tidal mural, are framed as ancestors on the walls of someone's (Mariyappan's?) home.

v

It is exactly this contexture of the newspaper image with different discursive practices taken from a wide range of different domains—from the public meeting and wall murals and posters that saturate Madurai's landscape to the practices within domestic spaces and temples—that demonstrates the power of the image of praise. I've begun to show here how the newspaper page resonates with other spaces, and how the very placement of the praise poem is but one of a series of related practices. We praise our leader, and weave together as many images of power as we have available to us, creating something very new in the deployment of material very old. In this, the praise of Jayalalitha is like so many other practices of nation-building: the elements strike us as very old but their deployment in contemporary practice is quite new.

This personification and aestheticization of the state, and the decorating of her with images that span both history and the domains of royal cum devotional practice is a product of the production of power. And, as an aesthetic practice, the omnipresence of Jayalalitha in textual, visual, and architectural images does invoke a wide range of emotional responses. I have dealt here only with the positive emotions expressed by her loyal servants. As this is a political practice, you can be sure that negative responses to these images are also expressed, and just as vehemently (e.g., Geetha and Rajadurai 1995: 201–203).

ACKNOWLEDGMENTS

This essay is based on research conducted between 1992 and 1995 in Madurai, Tamil Nadu, India, as an aspect of my inquiries into Tamil oratory and democratic practice. Research and writing were funded through a Junior Research Fellowship of the American Institute of Indian Studies, a U.S. Department of Education Fulbright-Hays Dissertation Fellowship, a Charlotte W. Newcombe Fellowship offered by the Woodrow Wilson Foundation, and by two years of generous support by the Committee on Southern Asian Studies at the University of Chicago. A previous version of this paper was delivered in "The Hidden Manifest: Newspapers in Ethnographic Research," a session of the 96th annual meetings of the American Anthropological Association, San Francisco, 22 November 1997. Thanks to Akhil Gupta, John Kelly, McKim Marriott, Sarah Lamb, Diane Mines, Mary Scoggin, and Gregory Starrett, who offered substantive comments on earlier drafts.

NOTES

1. I use standard English spellings for the names of places (e.g., Madurai), persons (e.g., Mariyappan), or institutions (e.g., newspapers such as *Malai Murasu*). All other Tamil terms are transcribed according to the method outlined in the Madras University Tamil Lexicon.

2. Usually translated as devotional love, *bhakti* has characterized many moments of South Asian devotional practice over the centuries and among certain sects (Ali 1996; Cutler 1987; Davis 1991; Peterson 1989; Ramanujan 1992 [1981]; Singer 1972). But the logic of bhakti—not strictly a religious logic per se—informs not only the devotional practices associated with deities, but relationships to powerful entities in general. Richard Davis's tripartite definition of bhakti, "recognition of the god's superiority, devoted attentiveness, and desire to participate in his exalted domain" (Davis 1991: 7, as quoted in Ali 1996: 144), serves equally well to describe the practices of local politicians vis-à-vis their sponsors and political leaders. As the poems and images that saturate city spaces on walls, over streets, and on the pages of newspapers described below demonstrate, these three characteristics—praise of superiority, devotedness, and participation—are integral aspects of Tamil political practice.

3. The concept of a "hierarchical intimacy" was first mentioned to me by A. K. Ramanujan in 1992. McKim Marriott also notes that the concept was discussed widely in seminars and classes during the 1970s at the University of Chicago (personal communication, 15 November 1999; cf. also Marriott 1978). Such a mode of intimacy is common between parents and children, beloved teachers and students, and, of course, between a devotee and his or her deity. In contemporary American Christianity, for instance, the relationship between Jesus and those who call him "my friend" certainly qualifies as "hierarchical intimacy."

4. This is not the case, however, with Tamil devotional literature in which the textual artifact bears the same relation to the "text" as a musical score bears to the music, i.e., the traditional Tamil text has its reality in performance, not necessarily in its artifactual form. For a discussion of the Tamil text as a performative practice, see Kersenboom 1995.

5. Contrast the image of the tea-stall newspaper reading with Anderson's description of it, following Hegel, as a prayerlike activity which takes place individually "in the lair of the skull" (1991: 35).

6. During my research I examined five newspapers daily (along with a variety of weekly and monthly magazines): the three morning papers, *Thina Thandhi, Thina Malar,* and *Thina Karan,* and two evening papers, *Malai Murasu* and *Malai Malar.*

7. Given limitations of space, I cannot even begin to do justice here to the rather baroque political situation in Tamil Nadu today. I therefore have limited my discussion to advertisements taken out by only one of the Tamil nationalist, or Dravidian, parties—the ruling party during my inquiries in 1992–95—the All India Annadurai Dravida Munnerta Kazhagam (AIADMK). The AIADMK was formed as a breakaway party from the Dravida Munnetra Kaghagam (the Dravidian Progress Association or DMK) in 1972 by the great cinema idol, M. G. Ramachandran (MGR). His lover and frequent leading lady, Dr. J. Jayalalitha, succeeded MGR as leader of the AIADMK after his death in 1988. Much to the chagrin of the DMK—which was founded by Ariñar C. N. Annadurai—MGR named his new party in memory of *Aṇṇā,* "Elder Brother," Annadurai. Both the DMK

and the AIADMK look to Thandai Periyar, "The Great One," E. V. Ramaswamy, as the philosophical founder of the Dravidian movement.

8. The use of the second person singular pronoun, *nī* (the equivalent of the French *tu*, German *Du*, etc.), would not be used in face-to-face interaction with such a high-status person as the Chief Minister; one would rather use the second person plural *nīṅkaḷ* (French *vous*, German *Sie*, etc.), or, better yet, the third person plural (rational) *tāṅkaḷ*, literally "they," in addressing Jayalalitha or other supernal beings. *Nī* is used to address children, intimate friends or family members, and—most significantly for our purposes here—*one's deity*.

Outsiders at Home? The South Asian Diaspora in South Asia

Gautam Ghosh

Distance is not a safety zone, but a field of tension.
—Theodor Adorno[1]

Once a refugee, always a refugee.
—Somdev Das Gupta[2]

INTRODUCTION: DISPLACEMENT AND DIGNITY

The modern age is also the age of nations. It is, putatively, an age where people are rooted on their land and ensconced in the warm embrace of their national culture, their free expression guaranteed by a stable government that represents their collective will. Then why is the modern age, and the twentieth century in particular, the age of massive, often involuntary, population displacements?

Perhaps, as some scholars have recently suggested, it is unwise to see any sort of social life as *inherently* in happy equilibrium. From this perspective social life—including national life—is better seen as in flux, characterized by ongoing tensions and negotiations.[3] The presumption of social stability has, without question, kept "dislocated peoples" from receiving adequate attention in academic inquiry. Exile, in its myriad forms, has been assumed to be evanescent and therefore an inapt object of investigation. This neglect is evident in the case of South Asia's largest migration: the population movement precipitated by the 1947 partitioning of British India into the independent nation-states of India and Pakistan. The significance of this monumental event—arguably the largest and fastest population displacement in world history—remains as perplexing to scholars as it is a pervasive concern for South Asians.[4] This essay analyzes how forced migration is interpreted by a particular group displaced by the Partition, and describes how this group actively represents daily life in the past in such a way as to orient life in the present.[5] It is hoped that, in this way, intellectual pursuit and everyday experience will shed light each on the other and, moreover, suggest the continuities between them.[6]

BACKGROUND

The *bhadralōk*, or "the respectable people," typically comprised upper-class upper-caste Bengali Hindu professionals and property owners. They saw themselves as uniquely progressive, educated, and refined.[7] The class came into being in the context of the colonial encounter: they received their formal education within the framework of the British Raj and often worked, directly or indirectly, in its administration.[8] In spite of this close association with the ruling regime—or perhaps precisely because of it—they emerged at the forefront of the anti-colonial nationalist movement in Bengal. In fact, they claimed for themselves the position of the intellectual, cultural, and political stewards of all of India, not just Bengal. In his important nationalist tome, *The Discovery of India,* Jawaharlal Nehru—a leader of the nationalist struggle and the first prime minister of India—argued that a dynamic, enterprising middle class was a prerequisite for progress (1995: 499–515). The bhadralōk apparently felt that they were precisely what was prescribed in this regard. This self-proclaimed and self-aggrandizing trajectory, however, was undermined when portions of British India were segmented and placed in Pakistan.

On 15 August 1947 British India found itself both independent and divided. In a final act before their departure, the British colonizers hastily (and somewhat arbitrarily) drew the borders which created independent India and Pakistan, vivisecting Bengal and Punjab in the process. Consequently, many people found themselves in the "wrong" country. The process, often violent, of "sorting out" the population left one million dead and ten million uprooted. It was at this time that many of the bhadralōk felt compelled to leave their homes. Between 1946 and 1952 about two million refugees migrated from East Bengal (which became East Pakistan and, in 1971, Bangladesh) into West Bengal (which remained in India). A sizable number arrived in Calcutta (now Kolkotta), drastically depleting the city's resources and helping to transform it, in the views of many, from a city of the future to one of terminal squalor. It does not come as a surprise, then, that on 15 August 1997, the fiftieth anniversary of the independence of India, the popular press in Calcutta lamented the tragedy of Partition as much as it celebrated the nation's emancipation.

A PASSING PREDICAMENT?

In the subcontinent as elsewhere, being displaced can itself leave one denigrated in the eyes of others, as if one is uprooted not only physically but morally and psychologically as well (Ghosh 1998; Malkki 1992; Bandyopadhyay 1970). Indeed, many of the displaced found themselves disparaged by their "hosts" once they arrived in India. The tide of immigrants was described as coming, not in a "tide" actually, but *pilpil*. Pilpil can be used to describe an endless stream of insects, such as ants. For their part the displaced bhadralōk rejected the idea that they were "refugees" who needed to be "rehabilitated": they who had been on the forefront of the nationalist movement, shouldn't they be revered rather than reviled?[9] The displaced responded by declaring "this 'independence' is a lie!" and, in turn, denigrating their hosts. It was, in their view, the Calcuttans who were corrupt, craven, and conservative, whereas those who had come from the East embodied what was good and progressive in India. Comparing their displacement to the flight of the Puritans to America, these "refugees" began a struggle to restore their pride of place in the Indian polity.[10]

One way in which the displaced sought to retain and reproduce the relatively high status to which they were accustomed was to deny that the Partition was permanent. Their dislocation, therefore, did not reflect on either their character or their future. To the contrary, they represented the displacement itself as another hardship they were enduring on behalf of the nation. Their insistence that their stay would be temporary resonated, in fact, with India's policy of providing, in Bengal, "relief" rather than "rehabilitation." This, in turn, reflected Prime Minister Nehru's concern that automatically giving citizenship to Hindus who came in from Pakistan would undermine his vision of a secular India and could, moreover, precipitate a total transfer of "minority" populations from both sides.[11]

The displaced bhadralōk had other reasons, or rationales, for believing the Partition would be temporary. First, there was precedent: in 1905, decades before the 1947 Partition, the British had partitioned Bengal. That division had been reversed and Bengal reunited, in 1911, largely due to the activism and agitation of the bhadralōk. Indeed the 1905 Partition and its reversal became an enduring emblem for the nationalism of the bhadralōk, and provided the backdrop for the fleeting discussions, in 1947, about the possibility of forming a separate independent nation-state of Bengal, in addition to India and Pakistan. Second, there was a belief that Bengal was simply a natural and essential whole that could not be divided, let alone so suddenly. These sentiments are evinced in the saying, heard to this day, "The Partition left the kitchen on one side and the living room on the other." Consider, in a similar vein, this recent recollection:

There was a rumor about Partition which we, the housewives, did not believe. Then one day we learned that it had happened! [Our village] was a Hindu majority village. But after Partition my father-in-law made arrangements to leave his ancestral home of more than seven generations. We were stunned, but what else could we do? . . . I was at the point of breaking down. My husband said that this would probably be a temporary affair, and we would return [to the village]. So I buried my cooking utensils under the ground in the yard.[12]

Third, and most important here, they constructed an account in which they had been forced to leave the East not by Bengali Muslims but by non-Bengali Muslims—by, in particular, the Biharis who had migrated to East Pakistan from India so as to reside inside *their* (new) homeland, (East) Pakistan. The displaced now claimed that East Bengal—the "true" East Bengal of pre-Partition days—was empyrean. People were honest and generous there, in comparison to the manipulative materialism of Calcutta life. Liberty, community, and prosperity—the sine qua non of nationalist aspirations—were all to be found not in newly independent India, dark and industrial, but rather in the golden, giving lives the East Bengali bhadralōk had secured (in both senses) prior to the Partition. They embodied the nation, and would have continued to perpetuate it if India had been truly liberated in 1947. Partition was wrong and unnecessary—the work of non-Bengali "outsiders"—and, in this sense, not a viable reality.[13]

DISTRICT ASSOCIATIONS OF THE DISPLACED: CITIZENS OR REFUGEES?

In 1971, after a bloody secessionist war with West Pakistan, East Pakistan separated from West Pakistan and eventually refashioned itself as Bangladesh, the homeland of the Bengali people and Bengali language. Many of the displaced bhadralōk saw this as both a repudiation of the "two nations" theory, which had contributed to the partitioning of India in the first place, as well as a vindication of the idea that "Bengali" identity transcended religious differences.[14] This view was reinforced when Mujibur Rahman became the first prime minister of Bangladesh. Sheikh Mujib, as he is affectionately known, not only had invoked a pan-Bengali identity but had made overtures to India before and after the emergence of Bangladesh as an independent nation.[15] Some of the displaced envisioned themselves returning home.

A series of events in Bangladesh through the 1970s and 1980s, however, made it necessary for the bhadralōk to reformulate the narrative that their displacement was temporary. These events included the assassination of Mujib in 1975 and a perceived increase in the influence of Islam in Bangladesh, both of which were great disappointments to these bhadralōk.[16] Was Bangladesh to be just another incarnation of Pakistan? they asked. The displaced responded to these new circumstances and uncertainties by recalibrating their identity *and* allegiance, shifting them from East Bengal as a whole to the particular districts in East Bengal they were originally from. The district, rather than their identification with East Bengal/Bangladesh in its entirety, came to serve as the point of reference for their claims to dignified treatment in India.

There has been, since the 1980s, considerable growth in the creation of "refugee" district associations. Thus those who originally hailed from Mymensingh District in the East have organized a Mymensingh District Association, those from Chittagong a Chittagong District Association, and so on. The Mymensingh Association drafted its constitution in 1987. Its purpose, the constitution says, is (1) to bring together the various "isolated" (*bicchinna*) and "scattered" (*bikshipta*) members of Mymensingh District so that they can know and love each other, (2) to preserve and transmit the glory of Mymensingh culture, and (3) to carry out social welfare projects.

Among its signature activities are the reunions (*sammilanis*) the association sponsors, often (and significantly) at the time of the holy *pūjās* or the New Year. The largest gathering draws up to four hundred people for a day-long program that includes games for children, a raffle, and catered meals, much of it carried out in the dialectical Bengali of the East. But the focus of the fete is on the stage where attendees step up to the microphone and recite (original) poetry about pre-Partition Mymensingh, or sing a song which evokes the old days, or eulogize the luminaries from their district.[17] Consider, for example, these excerpts from a poem recited at a sammilani:

Mymensingh, Our Country (āmāder deś)

Mymensingh, our country, remains forever
   in the necklace of our memory.
Our country, encircled by hills rivers forests,
   could one forget all this? . . .
From the rivers full of fish, from the golden fields of paddy,
   we hear you beckon,
And our minds sway, there and back,
   looking for peace. . . .
[The rivers] swing on your sides,
   your heart is full of care.
Many of your sons [*chele*] gave their lives
   for freedom . . .
    could one forget this all?
    . . . Let us not forget.

Poetry, it may be noted, is considered in Bengal to be among the most refined of literary forms—both an expression and an emblem of a "civilized" people.

An indispensable feature of the reunion is the production of the annual souvenir. These souvenirs (*smārak pustikā, smaraṇikā*) are pamphlets of about forty to fifty pages. They are distributed at the reunion and the members later take them home, often stowing them carefully with their other important documents. These smārak pustikā have certain consistent themes. They begin by laying out the association's organization: its constitution, president, vice president, treasurer, various subcommittees, etc. They list by name and address (including those from abroad, e.g., the United States or England) those who have donated funds to the sammilan and the amount of their contribution.

Typically, a souvenir includes an exhortation that a history of the district must be written. Why? So that the nation and indeed the world can apprehend the greatness of, in this case, Mymensingh culture. Increasingly, the history itself (i.e., not just the need for it) is presented in the pamphlets.[18] Among other things, these writings offer (1) descriptions of the local "folk" culture (arts, crafts) and (2) accounts of all the efforts the bhadralōk made, ironically, to "develop" the very folk whose culture is lionized on the other pages. It is averred, accordingly, that the bhadralōk tended to the bodies and the minds of the populace: they promoted medical care, athletics (one essay says that the "father of Bengali cricket" hailed from Mymensingh), and, most important, popular education. Indeed education is consistently emphasized, with particular attention given to the schools built, in rural Mymensingh, specifically for Muslims and for women.[19] Moreover, much is made of the fact that anti-colonial nationalism grew up in this district's schools, in the interaction between students and the (predominantly Hindu) educators that they allegedly emulated. The schoolroom, in short, is presented as an incubator for patriotism. Narratives about educational patronage remain popular among the displaced to this day: "even now," a "displaced" person said, "that school my grandfather built, and which is named after him, well it is still standing, and our family remains revered in that village."[20]

At the reunions and in the souvenirs the association recognizes the academic achievements of their own by giving awards and scholarships to those who have performed well. All of this is set in contrast to West Bengali society, putatively one which was physically effete and educationally conservative. Moreover, these histories seek to demonstrate that the bhadralōk —unlike the decadent aristocratic class, the big rajas of Mymensingh— truly identified with "the common people" (*sādhāraṇ mānuṣ*) and sought their betterment. The bhadralōk, that is, were uniquely concerned with the welfare of all, and were imbricated in the people's daily lives, whereas the aristocrats saw themselves as utterly separate. This line of argument suggests that if there had been any oppressive treatment in Mymensingh society—vis-à-vis differences in religion, status, or wealth—the culpability lay with the aloof aristocracy, not with the bhadralōk.

The souvenirs also seem concerned to claim that the bhadralōk are Aryan in regard to both race and religion. The Aryan race, after all, was seen as being vital and progressive. In a 1981 souvenir the eminent historian R. C. Mazumdar, an ardent opponent of Partition, is quoted at length:

> [I]n Bengal most of the Hindus have broad heads. According to some the ancestors of the Bengalis are the race called Homo *alpinus* who were inhabitants of the regions Pamir and Taklamakhan. Although their language was Aryan in character, it was different than the ones of the Vedic Aryans. It may be mentioned that the European Nordic Aryans differ in features and characters from the Aryans who live in the Alps region. Such a difference might have come about due to the difference in climate. But they are all part of the Aryan group [*goṣṭhī*].[21]

In short, the Mymensingh bhadralōk had and still have what it takes: an appreciation for the cultural authenticity of the common people, a dynamic, progressive impulse, and the proper racial and religious pedigree (Aryan). They genuinely sought, the souvenirs suggest, the progress of the people and the *nabo-jāgoran* (new awakening, renaissance) of the nation.

Why this new and increasing investment of energy in re-creating the distant district in this fashion? One could, of course, make a sort of demographic argument: the generation that most remembers pre-Partition Mymensingh is about to pass on. They know it, and they want to transmit their knowledge to the next generation before it is too late. An explanation of this sort, however, would not adequately account for the substance of these representations, e.g., the move from foregrounding East Bengal to foregrounding the district, the concern with authenticity, and the emphasis on education. It would fail, furthermore, to provide a cogent interpretation of the participation of younger generations in these associations, i.e., what their motivation might be to engage in these activities (beyond, for instance, simply pleasing their elders).

Perhaps, then, this new energy can be understood as a consequence of "East Bengal" having, in a sense, disappeared as a meaningful point of reference. In the period from the Partition till the 1970s the displaced bhadralōk grounded their claim to honored citizenship in India, in part, on the idea that East Bengal was the true India. East Bengal may have been in temporary disruption, suppression, and abeyance as a consequence of the Partition, but it was nevertheless the embodiment of the nation. The possibility of return was, in this narrative, not unthinkable—and it offered, furthermore, a perspective from which to critique their present condition in Calcutta. After 1975, however, it became increasingly clear that East Bengal/Bangladesh was not going to reunite with India. This collapse of "East Bengal" as a symbol also meant that the narrative of return was undercut, for they would only return to their homeland if it were part of the (true) Indian national homeland—and a district by itself—e.g., those celebrated by the various district associations—is not going to be reclaimed by India. Therefore, the displaced bhadralōk change the justification for their proper place within the Indian nation. They create anew the district of old, and claim its virtues as their own.

An important question arises, however: if everything was so appealing in the district, why did they leave it behind for the dystopia of Calcutta and, in some cases, for refugee camps? Is it, perhaps, because there is some awareness that their activities and relations were never as utterly benign and noble as they now have it?

Among the questions I asked in my fieldwork were "What were the specific circumstances that provoked you to leave the East?" and "Why did you leave the day you left and not days or weeks before, or after?"

"We left because of the insecurity," I was initially told. "We feared for our religion, or our jobs, or 'our women-folk.'"

But these insecurities were just as prevalent months before, I asked, were they not? Why then at the specific time you chose?

The decision to migrate involved many factors, I concluded, but the fear of losing the privilege, status, and respect these bhadralōk had come to enjoy was particularly pivotal. Accordingly, the catalyst which caused many to leave for India was when someone from the locality transgressed a well-established social boundary. A Muslim, who would have never before dared to walk into the Hindu household, did exactly that. Or a servant made an impudent remark. Or the (lowly) shopkeeper refused to sell something at the usual price, saying, "In the era of Pakistan, you are no longer the bosses." That is when they knew they could not stay—when, that is, their elite status, their privilege, was contravened in some such fashion. One might say that, with the Partition, the Indian nationalism which they had envisioned (with themselves at its helm) suddenly left them behind, abandoned, and they then "followed" it to India, seeking to preserve their central role within it.

How do these historical experiences square with the idealized Mymensingh they now re-create? They do not. Consequently, replacing those painful realities with glowing, progressivist memories requires a great deal of collective reiteration: reunions, publications, scholarships for school, and more. Most significantly, these activities are carried out with a great deal of *authority* and *officiality:* a governing body constituted of a president, vice president, executive committees, and a treasury; histories presented with the patina of academic expertise; formal speeches; even a sovereign territory of one's own—indeed all the pomp and circumstance of the modern nation-state. If successfully executed, it would seem, their love of the daily rhythms of the past, combined with their patronage of progress at that time, ensures in their view their rightful place in the Indian present.[22]

CONCLUSIONS: THE PARTITION AND EVERYDAY LIFE

Those displaced by the Partition had to give meaning to their displacement as part of the process of fighting for a "suitable" place within the Indian polity. The bhadralōk did so first by creating an idealized image of their "homeland." Over time, however, they were compelled to adapt their idealized images to historical events and changing circumstances. Thus large-scale events and grand narratives (such as migration and progress, respectively) come to reverberate in present life. However—between broad events and daily life, between historical upheaval and present aspirations, between outsider status and insider agendas—there are self-styled "cultural brokers" who mediate meaning through idioms of authority and officiality. The relations, that is, between the simple but heroic daily life of the past, the everyday present, and possible futures are largely governed by the sammilan, which has taken on the task of producing images and analyses—and punctuating them periodically. The sammilan's occasional though important gathering, then, produces images of daily life in the past and links them to the present and future through the idiom of the nation.

What does this imply, more generally, for studies of diasporic populations? It was noted earlier that social scientists have increasingly recognized the fluctuating and transitional nature of human social forms. Yet this perspective has often been lacking, ironically, in discussions of diasporic social forms. Although studies have noted the complex and negotiated interrelationships between various diasporas and their homelands, less attention has been given to the internal tensions and processes within displaced populations (including populations for which "home" and "diaspora"— and their relations—are acutely vexed). This sort of inattention has resulted in a homogeneous view of diasporic populations, which are consequently presented, generically, as the "other" of the nation-state. Moreover, those particular segments of displaced populations who take on the role of promulgating authoritative understandings of the group's history and identity—the understandings, arguably, through which a displaced population comes to represent itself as being in some sense "in diaspora"—have been overlooked. This implies that the "daily life" of "diasporic populations" should be conceived not as a particular class of social interaction reproducing itself rhythmically. It is rather produced, intentionally or otherwise, through the *activities* of particular people pursuing their goals within the context of ever-changing circumstances.[23]

NOTES

1. Adorno 1974: 127.
2. *Statesman* (Calcutta), 1986. Note that, here, becoming a refugee is sort of "rite of passage," which cannot be reversed. Das Gupta is a well-known Bengali writer in Calcutta.
3. See Clifford 1997b; Appadurai 1996; and Appadurai and Breckenridge 1989. See also Kelly 1995 and Peabody 2000.
4. More scholarship has been done on the Partition in the West of the sub-continent than on the Partition in the East. It is hoped that research on the latter will, among other things, provoke new questions about the former.
5. What counts as "forced" migration is a problematic issue—and, often, a political one as well. Limitations of space prevent me from dealing with this important issue here.
6. Indeed, social science has often sought to capture the texture of everyday life through its scholarly texts.
7. The bhadralōk, called the "nationalist elite" by Partha Chatterjee (1993: 36), included those in West Bengal who did not migrate with Partition, but the focus here is on those who were displaced, and displaced to India in particular. There is some disagreement about whether Muslims were included in the bhad-ralōk category, but there is little doubt that the vast majority were Hindu.
8. "Raj" refers to the period of British rule in India, in particular that period after the Uprising of 1857 when India became formally part of the British Empire.
9. Rehabilitation" is *punarbasati* (re-home). Terms for the displaced included *bahirāgato* (outsiders), *āśraya prārthī prarti* (shelter seekers), *saranarthi* (shelter seek-ers), *udbāstu* (uprooted), *nirāśraya* (shelterless), *bāstuhārā* (homeless), and *bāstutyāg* (home-abandoned).
10. Not everyone, of course, responded with defiance. Some recall that there was a sudden increase in despondency and even suicide among older displaced men as a result of having to abandon their homes. This theme is reproduced in the 1992 film *Tāhāder Kathā* in which the protagonist, a bhadralōk nationalist and schoolteacher from the East, goes mad upon hearing that Bengal has been parti-tioned (Das Gupta 1992).
11. This must be seen in the context of the Nehru–Liaquat Ali Pact. This pact, signed in April 1950, was a bilateral agreement providing for the safety of mi-nority communities in Pakistan and India, with each national government taking responsibility for minorities in its country. In India, especially among displaced populations, it was widely believed that while India honored its obligations in this regard, Pakistan did not.
12. Interview with Sneha Lata Biswas in Sandip Bandyopadhyay, *Deśbhāg/ Destyāg* (1993: 87–88).
13. Immediately after the Partition some of the East Bengali bhadralōk feared there would be armed conflict or even war between India and Pakistan, and hence considered migrating. Yet this possibility was imagined as a conflict between the *West* Pakistani state and India. In this rendition, that is, conflict had little to do with social relations within the Bengali Hindu and Muslim community of East Bengal / East Pakistan.
14. One of the justifications for Partition was that Hindus and Muslims in

South Asia represented two separate nations, and therefore required two separate states.

15. Mujibur Rahman's daughter, Sheikh Hasina—who currently heads the Awami League in Bangladesh—is accused by some of her opponents of being a lackey for India.

16. East Pakistan's opposition to West Pakistani domination was shaped, largely, through Sheikh Mujib's leadership—for which he was often imprisoned. His Awami League party won a majority in Pakistan's 1970 elections, but (West) Pakistan wouldn't accept the results. This led, ultimately, to the creation of independent Bangladesh. Sheikh Mujib was later slain in a military coup.

17. Sometimes, prominent personalities who are of the district are invited onto the stage for significant portions of the proceedings.

18. Younger scholars—e.g., students from local universities—have at times been commissioned to write these histories. "Sammilan" is typically used to refer to the association itself whereas "sammilani" is used for the particular gathering.

19. This more recent construction should be taken, perhaps, in the context of reports of discriminatory practices against Muslims, prior to Partition, in the field of education. One interviewee recalled, for example, that the schools and colleges were often called "Hindu Academy" or the like, and Muslim students would be required to reside, along with the lower castes, outside of the campus. In addition, while Sanskrit was taught on campus, Persian and Urdu were often taught outside.

20. In novels, plays, and films about East Bengali displaced families, the father is invariably presented as an educator of some sort: a school headmaster or a Sanskrit pundit.

21. Mazumdar, here, is clearly drawing on knowledge produced by the colonizers: "A final movement, which appears to have been integral to the building or rationalization of the European imperial polities in the later half of the [nineteenth] century, consisted of the attempt to order and explain differences by constituting races as the major agents of an evolutionary history" (Inden 1990: 88–89). See van der Veer and Lehmann on the links between religion, race, and nationalism (1999: 6–7) and Dirks (1997, 1990) on (post)colonial knowledge. Bhabha takes up the relation between time and nationalism (1994: 139–170).

22. This is not to gainsay the real threats that the displaced faced. In fact these transgressive acts might well have been perceived as violent acts themselves or, at least, as portents of violence to come. Nor is it suggested that their current idealized reconstructions are simply delusional and separate from the "real world"—but limitations of space prevent an elaboration of this issue here.

23. It is worth underscoring that "daily life" is often produced precisely, and perhaps ironically, through the argot of intellectual insight. On a related point: I have argued elsewhere that behind claims to being a "diasporic" population lurks a claim to being a (de-territorialized) "civilization" of global stature.

Why Do Hindus and Muslims Fight? Children and History in India

Nita Kumar

I

Why do Hindus and Muslims fight? The partition of India in 1947 into "Muslim" and (putatively) "Hindu" nations forces one to pose this grave question—or so one would presume. But for those citizens of India born after 1980 (that is, those who were teenagers when the research for this essay was done), the partition of 1947 is only a distant event with which they have at best tenuous relationships. To investigate these relationships is to raise questions about the way history and histories are created and how the arts of memory are exercised.

At the very least there is an official history to which all historians have a certain relationship. Set beside these official histories are other ways of grouping the events of the past, and we experience or observe their presence as alternative or competing histories. The children of modern India may be (1) aware of their official history, which they integrate into other aspects of their being; or (2) aware of their national history but separate from and uninvolved in it. Alternatively, they may be (3) unaware of their official national history but aware of other histories; or (4) unaware of their official history and of any other history.

This essay is chiefly about children in the first three categories, and indeed these may be the only three that are socially possible. In the first and longer section, I look at children of category (3), children who clearly have other histories. How are the arts of memory exercised in their case?

This is a revised version of "Children and the Partition: History for Citizenship," in Suvir Kaul, editor, *The Partition of Memories: The Afterlife of the Division of India,* by permission of Permanent Black, New Delhi.

This section, prefaced by a set of two interviews, concerns the children of Muslim weavers in Varanasi. I have chosen weavers because this community has been historically regarded as "communal," "bigoted," and "backward," and today its members are regarded as much of the same, but more eloquently as resistant to the secularizing and modernizing efforts of the nation.

In the second section, I look at children of categories (1) and (2). They are from the class that forms the backbone of the nation, that wants liberal education and secure "service" jobs for its sons, marriages into service families for its daughters and maybe, now, careers as well, if in proper establishments. This class reads and comments on national politics and takes issues of inflation, corruption, production, distribution, etc., very much to heart. The children confidently regard the lessons of history and society which they learn in school as gospel truth, and, what is important to my argument, there is no contradiction to these lessons at home.

I want to show how weavers' children fall between the arts of memory of a "premodern" and the history of a "modern" epoch. They certainly know their history. But a secular and disciplined national identity is created only through suppression of minority, or local, or deviant cultures. Given their stubbornness in sticking to their own histories, it is the weavers who are losing out on their legitimate place in the nation. But what is not often recognized is that the middle-class children are losing out on the memories and cultural funds that should be theirs also.

Interview no. 1: The son of a weaver in Varanasi, about thirteen years old

Q: Who are you?
Shahzad: My name is Shahzad Akhtar. I am in class IV, in Jamia Hamidia Rizvia.

What do you like to do?
I like to play marbles in my free time. I play bat and ball in the field occasionally. I don't like to stay at home.

What do you know about 1947?
1947? I can't remember. I don't know.

You must have studied it in your history?
History? We don't do much . . . Nothing much is taught in our school. We will have our exams soon. Yes, I know, the Slave Dynasty . . . the Slave Dynasty . . .

Yes?
I don't remember. The Slave Dynasty . . . blast! Many of our periods go free. Let me tell you what happens. The teachers get together in groups, talk, eat, and drink. They eat in the classroom and don't let the children eat anything. No, we don't have tiffin [snack] time. If we try anything, they beat us.

You do have a history book don't you? Maybe Hamari Duniya Hamara Samaj?
(Our World and Our Society—*the government board textbook in social studies*).
Yes, but we—er—we haven't begun it yet.

Shahzad is then asked many random questions in history but cannot answer a *single* one of them. He keeps explaining that he has forgotten or they haven't done it yet. Then he volunteers certain answers he remembers, in a subject called "Malumat-e-Amma" (General Knowledge).
He repeats the answers in a monotone, accompanied by a swaying of his
body, as habitually done by those reciting what is learnt purely by rote:
"What is *haj*? . . . What is *namaz*? . . . What is *roza*? . . . Who invented the
needle? . . . Who invented soap? . . . " The speed of his answers precludes
getting them down exactly, and he is unable to repeat them slower. His
mother enters at this point and interrupts occasionally.

Q: How will you do your exams?
Shahzad (doubtfully): Yes, they are in May, no, in June. . . .
    Mother: We want him to change schools. He is not learning anything.

Is he fond of learning?
Mother: No, his father is very fond of having him learn.

Are there any activities or functions in the school? Do they celebrate 15 August?
26 January? [I refer to the Indian Republic Day and Independence Day.]
Shahzad: Nothing. Nothing at all.
    Mother: There were when I was small. I studied in the same *madrasa* you
    know [a madrasa is an Islamic school]. On 15 August we were all taken
    to Jai Narain [the oldest "modern" school in Varanasi] to participate in
    a parade. The management of this madrasa eats up all the money. They
    do not bother about studies at all.

Can you not complain about this as a guardian? And about their not getting time
for a snack?
Mother: No, because we are "low" (*niche hai*) (I am not sure of her nuance
    here but cannot ask her because she leaves the room.)

Shahzad has a little sister of six or seven whose doll has recently had a
wedding with a doll in her paternal aunt's house. Shahzad recounts it with
enthusiasm. The two children, with two other siblings, show all the store
of things now owned by the doll: fridge and kitchen items, clothes, jewelry,
furniture. . . . Shahzad is very interested in every part of the proceedings
and exhibits a necklace that he has made, one of many such little pieces he
has made for the doll's apparel.

Do you have any teachers at all that teach?
Mansoor master is a good teacher. He even jokes a little.

Interview no. 2: Teacher ("Mansoor master") at Jamia Hamidia Rizvia

Q: Who are you?
A: Mohammed Mansoor Alam Khan, from Bihar, here for ten years. I teach
    maths in VI and VII, Urdu in IX and X, history in VI and VII, geogra-
    phy in V, VI, VII.

What is special or different about the teaching in this school?
For a long time, this school was till class V–VI only. Those who are in the
sari business do not want their children to get ahead. Then it was till VIII
for a long time. For the last four years we have IX and X. There are obstacles
from guardians.

What kind of obstacles?
Greed for money (*paise ka lobh*). Also, the economic condition is not good.

*Regarding that—if the children need to sit at the loom—why not adjust the school
timings?*
We have. The timings are 7:30 to 12. About 40 percent work at the loom plus
studying.

How are the studies here?
Good. Which subjects are good? Hindi and Urdu are good. Sociology [*sic*]
is okay. Science is not. Why? It is tough for them. They cannot work hard
enough.

What is the advantage of learning these things if they will only weave in the future?
Oh, there has been *some* improvement in the condition of the people.

*Is there any direct teaching on the subject of citizenship, social interaction, behavior,
etc.?*
There is Dinyat (Religion), a subject from class II onwards. There is Civics,
part of the U.P. [Uttar Pradesh] Board syllabus from VI onwards.

Is there any indirect teaching? Do you have any functions or programs?
On Republic and Independence Days, we have flag hoisting, sweets. On 23
December, ten days before Ramadan [the month of ritual fasting for Mus-
lims], we had our annual function. We gave awards and a farewell to class
X. There were seven this year. Their guardians came. No, we have no plays,
music, recitation, satire, etc.

What are the main problems you encounter as a teacher?
There are many. Guardians don't take enough responsibility. There is poor
attendance at parents' meetings, or the guardians simply never come. We
tried monthly meetings, classwise. There is great illiteracy among them. In
my own class, V, out of some 28, 20 do come. They listen, but they cannot
do what they are told.

   They drop out after class V because they've finished the Qur'an Sharif
[the respectful term for the Quran]. This place has no society, no culture.
Since this madrasa is free, only the poor send their children to it. They are
also indifferent to other schools because there is no Urdu there.

What do the children learn at home?
How to weave. The traditional work (*gharelu karobar*). Things related to weaving.

Anything else? What about TV?
That influence is restricted to clothes.

No, what about cricket?
Yes, now cricket is such a thing that you can get carried away during a game. But it only lasts as long as the game. They cheer for the Pakistani team. Then they forget. It is a temporary phenomenon. One of my friends currently supports the South African team.

So it is not an indication of communalism?
No, it is only cricket.

Let us explore the arts of memory as they are exercised by the weavers. Weavers' children, like Shahzad, have the following experience. A son, for a weaver, is an extension of himself. As an infant he is only semihuman; the other half of him is divine, toylike, princelike: "A child is an emperor" (*bachche to badshah hote hain*), people say. Fathers give sufficient indication of this by enthusiastically playing with their infant children in their free time, cuddling them, commenting on their abilities, indulging their whims. From as early as four or five years onward, a weaver's son becomes street-wise. He is sent to the shops for tea and *pan* (betel nut), for small purchases, to send and bring messages. He is not disciplined regarding his use of space or time, and he is expected to be mobile. In this respect he is a minia-ture version of his father and other males in the family, whom he begins to resemble more and more. He shares in the male popular culture of Varanasi.

Of the many leisure activities of the weavers, such as fairs, festivals, pro-cessions, annual celebrations at shrines, gatherings for music and poetry, and wrestling and bodybuilding, the most important for them is *ghumna phirna* (wandering around), including both wandering around the city and going "outside" for *saill-sapata* (pleasure trips). In all these activities, espe-cially the last, "freedom" is a concept idealized by weavers and all artisans. It reflects partly the actual freedom inherent in the piecework that charac-terizes artisan production, and is partly an ideological reflex to the inse-curity and inflexibility of such labor. That the idealization of "freedom" reaches the heights it does is a testimony to the self-conscious ethic of the city, based on its corporate character, its patronage of the arts and letters, its pride in more mundane pleasures associated with open air, mud, and water; and a refinement of "tradition" as expressing the excellent in many areas of cultural life.

While Muslim weavers hold this view of the city, of freedom, and of themselves as inheritors of this tradition in conjunction with other arti-sans, their view of "history" and "geography" is parallel to but separate from that of their Hindu counterparts. Certainly, if we reflect upon it, they could not be expected to share in the familiar, dominant Hindu view of the city as the center of civilization and the bestower of release after death, or in its fecundity with regard to temples and icons and holy bathing places.

For the Muslim weavers history dawns with the coming of Islam to the region, approximately around 1000 C.E., when Salar Masaud Ghazi, a semi-legendary general of Mohammad Ghori, was supposedly martyred nearby and the remnant of his force settled down in the region. They became the kernel of the present population of Muslims. Bearing evidence to this his-tory are scores of graves, shrines, and mosques to the *shahids* (martyrs) who sacrificed their lives for the spread of Islam. This history is kept alive in everyday existence by the weekly worship and annual celebrations that mark the most popular of these shrines, as well as in their quieter role as places of rest and meditation at any given time.

While women, children, and whole families go together to shrines on special days, the places are cultural centers for males typically, as are mosques and *chabutaras* (open cemented platforms) in every neighborhood. A little boy may accompany his male relatives and experience, in ever-increasing degrees, the openness and benignity of the city. Like them, he wanders around anywhere in his free time, may be traced to one or two favorite haunts, like an outdoor space, playing or watching cricket at a friend's home, or simply "in the lane" (*gali men hai*). He does not get em-broiled in domestic activities, unless, like shopping, they involve the out-doors. Teenage boys, when interviewed, provide reports of the outdoors, of free time and open space that are identical with those provided by adults.

Shahzad Akhtar stands at a bridge between childhood and the teen years. He was "caught" by me on the street, engaged in nothing in particu-lar, accompanied by a few friends who hastened to blend into the back-ground. Rather than surround me with curiosity, they preferred to remain "free." To shake me off, Shahzad first reported that he was on his way to weave. But when my insistence made him surrender and we were sitting and chatting in his home, two of his friends looked in to find out where he had disappeared to. At the same time, he showed evidence of enjoying quieter, more "feminine," pastimes at home, including sewing and thread-ing necklaces for his little sister's doll, although he did not mention any such interest when reporting on his pleasures.

He began weaving at least two years ago. The vocation of the weavers lies with the pit loom, and the training of all of them starts with their sit-ting at the loom from about the age of eight onwards. This may be with the father or with a master weaver in exchange for a small apprenticeship. He starts with the simplest processes and is made to "embroider" the narrow borders at each end of the sari under the adult's guidance. He is simply inadequate physically to use the loom fully until he matures.

Shahzad Akhtar lives in Madanpura, the center of the silk-weaving industry. To be from a weaver's family is to "be" an *Ansari*, a nomenclature adopted by weavers in preference to the derogatory *"julaha,"* the term commonly used for weavers in the 1930s. Upward mobility through a change in name and the composition of valedictory history is a process that characterizes every caste and castelike group in twentieth-century India, and began too far back for any weavers to retain oral memory of it. Ansaris consider themselves a lineage and an endogamous group. They cite as their specific personality traits pacificity, kindheartedness, and love for freedom. The last is expressed and reconfirmed in lifestyle and leisure activities. Pacificity and the less easily translatable *narmdil* or *dilraham* ("kindheartedness") are perhaps demonstrated in their relations with middlemen and agents. Weavers are consensually accepted as being easy to deal with in matters of buying and selling. Their love of freedom does pose a danger in that they miss deadlines and shut up work at any small pretext, but in the process of transaction, they display no acerbity or aggressiveness.

It is difficult to state precisely where a weaver's son like Shahzad would pick up these preferred qualities of Ansaris except to say that he does spend hours with male relatives, first while sitting at the loom in the dusky workshop amid the clatter of anywhere between two to eight looms, then in occasional trips with his father to Chauk, the central wholesale and retail market of Varanasi, carrying finished saris. Otherwise he hangs around in his neighborhood and rarely if ever goes outside it.

The founding of Shahzad's school, Jamia Hamidia Rizvia, and other such madrasas or Muslim religious schools in Varanasi are both part and result of the educational history of colonialism. The Dispatch of Sir Charles Wood in 1854 provided grants-in-aid to establish new schools in India, for both vocational and ethical reasons. The new schools were favored by some because they trained boys for an official or professional career, but local Muslims failed to "take advantage" of them. As the government was told by assorted members of the public, "The Ansaris already have a profession." Nor could the weavers resign themselves to sending their children to schools where no character formation would take place. Together with other castes and communities, Ansaris came to found their own institutions, in which, they believed, a synthesis between the spiritual (*dini*) and the worldly (*duniyayi*) could be effected. In the process of doing this, they worked along denominational lines: The Muslim sects Deobandis and Ahl-e-hadis set up separate madrasas, as did the Barelwis (Shahzad Akhtar's sect). Their teachers were hired accordingly and their textbooks chosen or even written according to sectarian loyalties.

Shahzad Akhtar's school, Jamia Hamidia Rizvia, like other madrasas, had to develop its own curriculum once a government board syllabus was substituted for the accepted classical Islamic syllabus. Histories and geographies had to be written, since such subjects did not traditionally form part of the Islamic syllabus. Let us look at only one issue as it is treated by the school's fourth-grade social studies text. The book discusses the name and location of the Jama Masjid or Friday mosque in the heart of Varanasi, the Gyanvapi mosque, one of significant interest to historians because of the threat it poses today as a target for the wrath of fundamentalist Hindus, who consider it symbolic of Islamic iconoclasm. Then: "This Jama Masjid was built approximately 315 years ago in 1070 *hijri* (c.1664 c.e.) by the renowned emperor of Hindustan, Alamgir. Hindus claim that it was built by destroying a temple on this site. This is wrong. The foundations of this mosque were laid by the great grandfather of Emperor Alamgir, Akbar, and Alamgir's father, Shah Jahan, had started a madrasa in the mosque in 1048 hijri that was named "Imam-e-Sharifat" (from Maulana Abdus Salam, "Geography District Varanasi," p. 15).

Of course the status of the iconoclastic activities of Alamgir, better known as Aurangzeb, and the origins of the Gyanvapi mosque are far from resolved. While Indian textbooks have unreflectively presented, and continued to present, Aurangzeb as among the most fanatic of Muslim rulers (and for them there are many to choose from), and the destruction of any temple by him as a most credible, unquestionable fact, contemporary research has also shown that complex political motives lie behind seemingly simple religious ones. The Hamidia Rizvia textbook is therefore "right" in its denial of guilt to Aurangzeb but "wrong" in the reasons it gives for this.

What is of immediate relevance here is that textbooks of this kind create a history and consciousness on questionable premises. In this case a community is being set up which includes Alamgir, an emperor whose sway extended over the whole of Hindustan, and weavers in Varanasi, mostly poor and illiterate. The dividing line is between this community, whose members worship at and therefore build mosques, and those who worship at temples and therefore mourn their destruction. Such divisions and constructions do not have to be anything more than suggestive and associative to make an impression on minds of every age. The most powerful kinds of evidence used in these constructions seem to be those from the most fantastic and dramatic epochs of the past, those in stark contrast to the humdrum existence of poverty-ridden everyday life.

Does all this, however, match what we hear from Shahzad Akhtar about his own experiences? We can discount his mother's testimony that things were much "better" in her student days as the romantic nostalgia of a parent frustrated by a child's failure. But while in conversation, Shahzad and I were surrounded by four other children from the same madrasa who assented to everything he was saying, qualifying it for their own teachers and classes. Shahzad is an attractive, cheerful, intelligent, sociable boy, who is articulate on all subjects, but specifically effective on certain chosen ones (his teachers' injustices, his sister's doll).

Shahzad does not know what happened in 1947. Shahzad cannot remember any episode or personality from Indian history. More than that, he cannot make up, improvise, or just invent anything, as one might imagine a child to be able to do who has some elementary training in answering questions of a "textbook" character, or demonstrate experience plus an active imagination in dealing with questioning adults.

His responses constitute a damning indictment of his school. First, no history has apparently been taught him even within this rote-learning system. Second, no overall pattern has been revealed to him regarding how to field questions or spin tales, that is, to construct narratives. Third—a fault the madrasa shares with most other schools in India—no connections have been suggested between his own life and larger historical developments.

If we turn to the second interview, with the teacher that Shahzad admires, we find part of the key to the puzzle. If Master Mansoor may be taken as spokesman for the madrasa, as he and I both consider him to be, his answer to the poor learning of students like Shahzad is that Ansaris in general are apathetic to learning. They should support the schools and the students. In "other" schools (i.e., where guardians are more active), schools do 25 percent of the teaching, guardians the rest, but here the school has to do 95 percent of the teaching. The Ansari guardians are not only lacking in "society" and "culture" (i.e., they do not share in middle-class ideals of progress); toward schooling they are particularly *udasin* (indifferent, because interested only in the child's learning the Qur'an).

The guardians, on the other hand, imagine that the child's learning will naturally take place in the school (what percentage was not specified to me, but I repeatedly got the impression that it was almost 100 percent). Since madrasas are known to be government-aided institutions, which also receive charitable endowments, it is a common speculation that their funds are being misused by their managers. Why else would the kind of descriptions that Shahzad gives of classroom conditions be given? Why else would the child learn so little?

My approach to the "problem" is to try to see it as a condition within a certain faultline between discourses, that of the modern and that of the premodern. The madrasa would like to expect the guardians to behave like "modern," participating citizens and prepare their children socially and psychologically for an educated future. Such a future would be bounded by practical considerations such as health, nutrition, and family planning; and by ideological ones such as awareness of constitutional rights (distinguishing between the hierarchical values of "freedom") and participation as a full citizen of a democracy (distinguishing between "myth" and "history"). The guardians, on the other hand, are still part of a "premodern" world, one that has been trying for at least the whole of the twentieth century to come to terms with the demands of modernization and that has claimed to leave the task for schools. If indeed it was still an older world where an Ansari worldview was fully legitimate and the outside world condemnable, socialization could be left to the family. If, similarly, it was a newer world where a modern nationalist world-view was hegemonic, socialization could be left to the schools.

As things stand, Shahzad learns little in the school. The school blames the parents for their ignorance of the modern educational agenda. The parents blame the school for not fulfilling the agenda, conscious that they are being treated as inferior in this old-new dichotomy.

Of course, while Shahzad does not know what happened in 1947, what is important is that he does know and is learning many other things. Together with other Ansari boys, he is learning the craft of weaving, both its technique and its ethic, or how a weaver is expected to conduct himself. He is learning the pleasures of the outdoors and the established pastimes in Varanasi's popular culture. He is gradually being socialized into gender role playing (even the sewing and necklace making that impressed me so much has much to do with his learning to weave and embroider). Every part of his work and leisure underlines his maleness first. And since he does go to school and passes exams, he is learning to think of himself as "educated." An educated person is necessarily superior to an uneducated person, but inferior to others educated in more normative ways. Madrasa education is on the brink between non-education and education in the eyes of the system and its supporters, and almost everyone else as well.

There is a structural congruity here. Either Shahzad will not become a well-educated person, or he will not become a good weaver. Good weavers, the majority of weavers, are those who are tied to their occupation as an inevitable one, justified to themselves as the best occupation in the world. They are free and unreformed, skeptical of the values of control, discipline, citizenship, and progress. The practices of Jamia Hamidia Rizvia effortlessly guarantee Shahzad's fit for this role. And all madrasas are like that, erring, according to educators, on the side of religion in the balance they try to maintain between *dini* and *duniyayi* (spiritual and worldly) instruction.

One conclusion that emerges effortlessly is that community-based schools such as the madrasas of Varanasi must be sacrificed for national(ist) schools. The needs of a community, whether religious, occupational, or linguistic, have to be erased in deference to the needs of the nation. This is a violent, arbitrary, colonial solution. Madrasas and such schools may be pedagogically weak, but they are not "symbolically violent" (Bourdieu 1977a); they do not impose the "cultural arbitrary" of the dominant group of society on other groups. At the same time, they are repressive in that they restrict the choices of children. If we acknowledge the value of freedom, not in the weavers' sense of strolling around and spitting everywhere, but in the sense of the equality with other citizens to choose occupation and lifestyle, then it is the madrasa that precludes such freedom totally.

Part of being a good weaver is to be rooted in local culture, protective of a particular history, ignorant of and indifferent to the nation and its history, unaware of 1947, aware of being a Muslim, a Barelwi, a Banarasi, and an Ansari, unreflectively supportive of the Pakistan cricket team, and resistant to the condemnations of ignorance and backwardness because the community is self-sufficient in itself. There is a close tie between history teaching and citizenship. The madrasa children do not reproduce their lower-class identities through resistance to their schools, as do the working-class children in a modern British school (Willis 1977), but directly through it.

II

The second section of this essay is prefaced by a set of two descriptions of participant-observation situations and two interviews.

Participant-Observation no. 1: I teach History in class V in Qudrutullah Gulzar-e-Talim, a Muslim school (not a madrasa, or religious school) for girls in Varanasi

Class V has fifty students, of which some five are absent. It is a spacious, well-lit, airy classroom, with bare walls, serviceable desks and benches, a large blackboard (for which a child produces the chalk from inside her desk). They are all wary of me in the beginning, and warm up slowly.

I ask them about 1947. There is a prompt response from the same child regarding both aspects of the event, independence and partition, as well as to my third question, regarding five important freedom fighters. The hesitation in answering among the other students is so extreme, with the same child attempting the next few questions also, that I wonder aloud if she stands first or second in the class? She does not. Now the two who do shake themselves up slightly.

I ask them to attempt a map of India on the blackboard. They will not. I show them the trick of making it with a triangle. With vast prodding and help from me, some two or three come up and make a hash of it. None of them have a picture in their minds of India, its states, or its neighbors. They cannot place any of them on the map, or any cities, or anything else. When questioned orally, they know the main mountains, rivers, and cities.

They have obviously never used the blackboard, drawn anything, or attempted anything visually or tactically.

Does anyone know a story or song regarding 1947? No. With some help from me, a couple mention a song or two, such as *Sare jahan se achha* ("Our land is the best in the world"—a popular children's nationalist song). Has anyone heard a story? No. I mention stories, songs, scenes familiar to me from television. It seems to me that their general knowledge, even regarding TV and film content, is very poor. Even more, their *level of interest* is very poor in what is shown or could be shown on TV.

I try to probe into their identities. What is their father's occupation? After a long bout of tongue-tiedness, one ventures the euphemism "loom *ka kam*" ("working on the loom"). Almost all are from weavers' families. Do their mothers work? Upon their saying "no," it is to their credit that they all look embarrassed when I wonder aloud if housework is not work. They vow to never consider their mothers non-workers again.

Their identities are securely gender based. They laugh heartily when I suggest that their fathers may provide them with clean uniforms for school. They associate intimately with their mothers. All are eager to claim sharing in her work: washing and ironing clothes, washing dishes, cooking, and cleaning up. They love it when I ask a question regarding their dolls and how many were married. Hands shoot up with alacrity. Smiles flash on most faces.

Their subjects are all the same as in a madrasa, including Urdu, religion, and Arabic in addition to the board-required subjects. Many of them have tutors.

When I discover they have no music, dance, or drama, and that the school merely gave a holiday on Republic Day instead of celebrating it, I heave an involuntary sigh of disappointment. "One *should* have some music, dance, or drama" escapes me. Such is the rapport built up in the class by now that they wistfully agree with me.

Participant-Observation no. 2: I interact with class XI in the same school, Qudrutullah

There are eighteen girls, most between fifteen and seventeen years old, sensible, confident, and pleasant looking. They are sitting temporarily in a classroom not theirs, so when I look around for their *naqab*s (full-length veils), I don't see them; they are hanging up in their own room. A couple of voices murmur, "We don't all wear *naqab*s." (The principal had earlier told me that *naqab*s were compulsory.) Throughout the class the teacher of economics, Indrani Tripathi, sits with me. They have no choice of subjects: all do Hindi, economics, and home science. They are just the second or third batch to be in class XI, and the second one from whom the school can hold some hope of future collegians.

They answer promptly all my questions regarding 1947 and freedom fighters. They remember at least the film *Gandhi* and have heard nationalistic songs on TV. They even have some idea of what to do for the country —work to solve the problems of poverty, illiteracy, and so on—especially one who is a doctor's daughter.

They are unselfconscious about Pakistan. Many have relatives there who visit often. One narrates the tale of an aunt who does not like it there because she does not feel at home (*apnapan*) there and is greeted with empathy by others.

All help at home. One even makes candles and pickles, presumably helping in her mother's work.

They meet each other, go out for shopping, watch TV, read Urdu magazines and *Stardust*. Two respond "yes" to having Hindu friends, one the daughter of her father's friend, the other a neighbor in the mixed Hindu-Muslim neighborhood of Shivala.

The girls seem relaxed about themselves and their future. Some five will seek a bachelor's degree from Basanta College. One can *picture* them as promising undergraduates, in veils or not.

In my view the greater "secularization" and "national identification" of these girls is due partly to their belonging to a different class of Ansaris, those who would prefer non-madrasa to madrasa (religious) schools. Within these schools, it is due further to their having some Hindu teachers, like Indrani. These are modern, secular, nationalist women who are subtly Hindu; friendly observers of the girls, but their critics and reformers as well. My most powerful impression of the teacher was that she was a trifle bemused by Muslim customs and commented negatively on them to the children's faces, neither of which would happen with Hindu children getting a Muslim teacher. The students learn in a myriad of subtle ways how to conform to "majority religion" and "national" culture, and because they and their families have the will to do so, they conform and "progress."

* * *

The second part of this second section moves to a different stage of action, Calcutta. The children studied here are all sons and daughters of refugees who left East Pakistan in 1947–48. The families are Hindu, but secular and liberal. They are upwardly mobile and universalist, and believe in progress. All the children go to schools that are overtly religious: Loreto House (Christian), Future Foundations (Hindu, based on Sri Aurobindo's philosophy), and Ramakrishna Mission Vidyalaya (Hindu, based on Vivekanand's philosophy). I take these schools as typical of those that project a national, secular version of India's history. The families concur in this version, regardless (or some may say because) of the past that individuals from these families have experienced.

Interview no. 3: Daughter of a refugee from East Bengal, ten years old, student of Loreto House, a Christian missionary school

Q: Who are you?
A: I am a girl. I like badminton and cycling and my favorite food is cheese. My hobby is reading. My favorite subject is Science . . . I'm short, I have black hair and brown eyes. [There is no response to stimulus from my side for more community-oriented definitions of the self.]

What do you know about 1947?
It was an important year but I can't remember what happened. Yes, India got independence from British rule.

Do you know about Partition?
There were lots of riots going around. India got divided into two. All the Hindus came to India and all the Muslims went to Pakistan.

What are Hindus?
It's a religion? [I encourage her.] Hindus are a kind of people.

What kind?
Their language is Hindi and most of them live in India.

Who are they different from?
Sikhs.

Anyone else?
Muslims?

What are Muslims?
Muslims are just another kind of people. They go to mosques and do a few other things differently.

Do you know any Muslims?
No.

How would you know a Muslim if you saw one?
They dress differently. The girls wear veils. The boys wear salwar-kameez— no, kurta-pyjama [loose shirts and pants]—and caps.

Do they speak Hindi?
Yes. [She realizes sheepishly that earlier she had said that only Hindus did.]

What about Masroor [a friend of hers who is Muslim]? How is he different to you? What is the difference?
He is not. There is no difference.

What is your father?
He is the director . . . [gives occupation]. His religion? He is a Hindu.

How do you know?
I *know* he is.

Does he do puja [Hindu religious worship]? Go to temples?
He doesn't go to *mosques.* No, he doesn't go to temples. He *visits* temples.

Puja?
(Doubtfully, then humorously) I've seen him light a wick.

Tell me about your father's father.
He was a zamindar[1] and used to own a lot of property and then he sold it all. I don't know when. Was he a Hindu? I don't know. I think he was. No, I haven't seen any pictures of him or his house. [I know that such pictures hang in their family house.]

How do you know all this?
My father told me.

Do you know where he lived? Anything else?
In Bengal, but I don't know where. I don't know anything else.

Would you like to know?
Yes.

Do you know any stories about Muslims?
Id is their festival. They go to mosques and they pray. Once in my old school on Id we had a poetry competition. In one book I saw they were hugging in a special way, on both sides of the neck.

Do you know that Hindus and Muslims fight?
Yeah, I don't know about what. I know that one of our neighboring countries wanted to take Kashmir ... it was China or Pakistan ... Why Kashmir? It makes a lot of things. It's clean and pretty.

Would you like to fight? For Kashmir?
Yeah. (grins) No! I don't like fighting. I would not do it because I would like to do something else.

For yourself? Or for India?
I don't know. Yes, for both.

Interview no. 4: Son of a refugee from East Bengal, thirteen years old, student of class VIII in Ramakrishna Mission Association

Q: Who are you?
A: My name is Dibyarka Basu. There is not much to say about me. I am a boy. I read in RKMA Vidyalaya. My hobbies are reading storybooks and watching cricket.

What do you know about 1947?
It was a year that brought much hope to the Indian common people. But the independence of India also brought the partition of Bengal. A catastrophic (pauses, gropes for the word) riot began. It gave the Indian people an opportunity to develop their country, but it gave the political leaders a way of exploiting the country.

Who is to blame?
Mahatma Gandhi is partially involved but I think the real ... was Zinnah[2] [*sic*] ...

How do you know all this?
General information . . . what I hear from people, what I read in books.

Do you study about it in history?
No, our textbooks have nothing on this. Our syllabus is not so much attached with politics.

Do your teachers talk about it?
Our history teacher is not so good, although he has knowledge, but my English teacher in my previous school was very good.

Did you see anything on TV in this connection?
Yes, two or three films . . . I can't remember which. *Gandhi?* Yes. Yes, I know some songs. Which ones? *Bande Matram, Bharat amar janani* ["Long live our Motherland," "India is my Mother"]. On 15 August we have a march or parade, and flag hoisting.

Do your parents tell you about this?
My father does. No, he is not like the textbook.

Do you know anything about your grandfathers?
Yes, he [*sic*] was a professor of English. I heard that he was wise. He lived nearby. The second grandfather I have forgotten. At one time, *at one time* he lived in Bangladesh. I don't know where. His occupation? I don't know.

Would you like to know?
Yes. I am interested.

Are you a Hindu?
Yes.

How is that different to others?
There is no difference. Customs are different. That is not very important. All the gods of all the religions are the same. My father and mother are Hindu *by name.* They celebrate Durga Puja. They worship God Kali. But all the gods are the same.

Do you know any Muslims?
Yes. [He names cricketers, at least four of them.] No, I have no friends. I have one uncle. Not a direct relation. A friend of my father's. No, there is no difference between his house and mine. . . . Yes, the construction is different. The kitchen is very big. There is a big roof. The house is large. They are rich.

Why do Hindus and Muslims fight?
It is a perfect example of stupidity. There is no reason to fight. It is due to orthodoxies. They are stubborn. No, I don't know this from my teachers, but in general . . . but I don't know the way of removal of this.

Would you like to do something about it when you grow up?
It depends on the political situation of the time. There may be no need.

What religious books do you know or have you read?
The Veda [Hindu texts]. We have *shlokas* [Sanskrit verses] in our school.

Amader Gan ["Our Songs"] has Veda *path* [excerpts from the Vedas]. We have
a subject, "Indian culture." We memorize shlokas and learn the meanings.
No, I have not read the Qur'an.

Would you like to read it?
No. I mean I have not decided.

The Muslim school of the first case above sets itself apart from madrasas; in the tradition of the nineteenth-century Muslim reformer Sir Syed
Ahmad Khan, it states its intention to produce a well-rounded, modern, progressive person, but one who is also a good Muslim. To achieve this goal,
the principal and teachers of Qudrutullah depend far more on the guardians of their students to accomplish their purposes than madrasas can.
Qudrutullah guardians are required to actively cooperate in the school's
mission, to complete daily homework and pass periodic exams, and the
guardians in fact do so—or remove their wards to a madrasa. The guardians' failure to meet these standards is exactly what madrasa teachers de-
plore but have to tolerate.

The corollary of this greater cooperation is the undermining of the arts
of memory as practiced in daily life. The school, in performing its job better, co-opts the home, weakens home culture, and weakens a world of intangible traditions, rituals, practices, and role playing that helped—and
continues to help in the case of madrasa children—in the perpetuation of
histories. The modern school's student will not have the time or inclination
to learn, and her guardians will not have the will, the coherence, and sometimes the very courage, to teach seriously in any way an identity and relationship to the past that is different from the officially preferred one. The
project of modernity, secularism, and nationalism becomes a family project, with the child at the vanguard.

Interviews 3 and 4 demonstrate—indeed, highlight—the second process at work. The school's history teaching is imbibed by the child but with
no connection to the child's own identity. Nor does the child have an alternative culture or history. The schools these two students belong to are,
respectively, an old, well-established Christian missionary school, a model
for a kind of modern English-medium institution; and a Hindu reformist
school, which, denominational differences aside, has an Annie Besant[3]
philosophy for producing modern, scientific Hindu citizens. In both cases,
the overwhelming experience of the child is one of homogenization, where
no part of the home culture is acknowledged or tolerated, unless it be targeted for reform. Guardians of these public or missionary schools cooperate with the project of homogenization even more fully than in the case of
the modern Muslim school. Indeed, they do not follow, but lead the school
in its mission, being either products of such institutions themselves or consumed by the ambition of seeing their children "succeed" in a frankly
competitive world. Whatever they retain of an alternative history—as in

the case of the above interviewees, the parents having been refugees from East Bengal in 1947—is consigned slowly to oblivion. All linguistic, regional, sectarian, and caste identities of the child and her family are purposefully erased.

It is perhaps natural for us to regard the socialization effected by Qudrutullah, Loreto, and Ramakrishna Mission Vidyalaya as more successful than that of Jamia Hamidia Rizvia. The Muslim, Christian, and Hindu reformist schools—all claiming to be secular in practice within their sectarian ideological pronouncements—teach students with more professional acumen. They are closer to the model of a modern institution, with less soul-searching and conflict regarding the validity of the model. Their students are better able to answer factual questions regarding their history, and they are altogether better trained in the art of answering questions. As one student responded:

> I think Partition was the fault of some leaders who wanted to satisfy their own interests, like Jinnah; they knew they were in a minority in India, they would never become big leaders—now I'm talking like my textbook—they aroused communal feeling among Muslims. The Congress had to agree. [Were some of the Congress leaders not at fault?] (Pause) Some of the Congress leaders might have also wanted partition but the aim of the Congress was to keep India united so they couldn't openly support that demand.

Both the level of knowledge of the student and her self-consciousness that she sounds like her textbook are noteworthy. Also noteworthy is the reflexive sense of humor of the child in interview 3 as she admits that she would "rather do something else" than fight for her country even to save the clean and pretty Kashmir, or as another child of the same age responded, "I do not want to fight because I might die, and I prefer to be alive than to be dead." Similarly, the self-conscious dignity of interviewee number 4 is notable when he refuses to commit himself to what he would do to resolve the communal question when he grew up: "It would depend on the political situation of the time."

How far the "history" learnt as a subject gets assimilated by the child as part of his or her identity is not possible for me to say conclusively, given our relatively simple ethnography here. The evident indifference in response to questions related to history in general and "Indian history" in particular points to a weak relationship between the subject as studied and the child's sense of the self. The child's world does not incorporate a sense of the nation and its birth. But then, there are the occasional insights that obviously suggest interplay between lessons and personal experiences, which indicate at least the possibility of a strong relationship between the sense of self and the sense of the nation. For instance, a child

of an immigrant father from Pakistan and a non-immigrant mother explained:

> Am I sorry about Partition? My grandfather was a zamindar; he had a lot
> of property. They had to leave all their property. Later on, the government
> gave some of the money to the refugees, not all the money, that would have
> been too much. My grandfather had a really nice library, which they had
> to leave behind. (Pause) My father seems sorry about Partition. Since they
> had a big library, I'm sorry. But (pause) if it hadn't happened, if they'd
> stayed there, our lives would have been different. He wouldn't have met my
> mother, I wouldn't have been born. It must have been very sad for them
> though. My father said my grandfather didn't want to leave.

This interesting philosophical point came quite unselfconsciously to the
child, that what happens in history, when seen from our personal vantage
point, is very likely the best, since if things happened differently, we personally wouldn't be here at all to discuss these questions.

But these glimpses aside, the child in South Asia—not only the disadvantaged working-class child whose school does not teach national history, but also the privileged middle-class child who learns history lessons
well—grows up without a sense of personal certainty about her national
history, where she belongs in it, and what her "duties" within it are. This
is all due to various reasons that I have not discussed here, such as the
unimpressive pedagogic approaches used even in the mainstream nationalist schools, and the absence of all debate about what are the best processes by which the child may be wooed to participate in the construction
of a national identity.

However, these inadequacies provide a vacancy that could possibly be
exploited by those who choose to confront the dilemma described here.
How should we formulate the relationship between our official history
and the senses of history created in routine, everyday ways? That is, how
could one write or talk about the nation, or implicitly assume the nation,
while doing the least possible violence to—indeed, while respecting and
celebrating—other higher- and lower-level histories? How could we educate a child about her nation and yet protect that brilliant innocence that
makes her admit that she would not like to fight for its boundaries because
she "would rather do something else?"

NOTES

1. Zamindars were landowners who served as intermediaries between their
cultivators and the government of India (especially during the periods of Muslim

and British rule), paying the government fixed substantial revenue raised from cultivators.

2. He refers to Muhammed Ali Jinnah, the leader of the Muslim League, who argued for creating Pakistan during the Independence movement, and who was the first prime minister of Pakistan.

3. Annie Besant may be regarded as an archetypical Hindu nationalist, working with the eloquent formula "national progress = religion (Hinduism) + secularism (Western science)." See Kumar 2000 for her educational efforts.

**Walking through Violence:
"Everyday Life" and Anthropology**

Pradeep Jeganathan

AN ETHNOGRAPHIC MAP?

On 31 January 1995, cadres of the Liberation Tigers of Tamil Eelam (LTTE), arguably one of the most sophisticated militant groups in the world, exploded a massive bomb in the heart of Colombo's financial district. Hundreds died, and nearly a thousand people were injured. Several steel-and-glass towers were reduced to blackened shells. The direct consequences of this explosion, though they are important in many ways, do not concern me here. Rather, I am concerned with another kind of consequence of this event.

Let me explicate that concern with an example. A few miles south of the financial district at a busy intersection, Tunmulla, lies the headquarters of the Sri Lankan air force. It is surrounded, in a holdover from another time, by upper-middle-class homes of prominent citizens of Colombo. This neighborhood was not directly affected by the bomb downtown. Yet in the wake of that event, residents renewed with vigor their previous efforts to have the military installation that had been part of the area for many years removed. Why so? The next bomb, they thought, might blow up right next door. That assumption was not unreasonable. Six years previously, a similar bomb had exploded at another military complex, the Joint Operations Command (JOC), located nearby in another upper-middle-class residential neighborhood. Every new bomb that explodes in the city renews the possibility of more violence in areas like Tunmulla. Such places are remapped then, again and again, into new spatial arrangements. New cartographies, predicated on the anticipation of violence, come into being.

In Colombo, bombs, like people, are given names. From the "Pettah" bomb which killed 150 people in the Pettah bus station in the summer of 1986, through the JOC bomb which devastated an entire neighborhood in

1990, to the Wijeratne and Dissanaike bombs that killed politicians in the intervening years, bombs acquire and carry names. A bomb is named after its "target": military installations, government offices, hotels, airports, or politicians. And after the event, once the "target" of the bomb has been "determined," all the other destruction that accompanies the event is folded into that one "thing" that the bomb is thought to have centered on, e.g., the "JOC" or the "Central Bank." That becomes the "target" of the bomb, which then, in turn, becomes known by its name. In the wake of the relocation of these transgressive events into the social cartographies of targets, then, there can arise cartographies that become in turn cartographies of anticipated violence—mappings of a terrifying future.

A map of targets as lived by the residents of Colombo would include a whole host of sites, for example military installations like the air force headquarters, homes of prominent and therefore vulnerable politicians, ports and airports and shopping malls. But such maps are not indiscriminate; such maps of anticipation have a particular logic, constituted recursively by that very logic. For example, they do not include schools and universities, or stadiums and playgrounds in the city, since the LTTE has never attacked such sites, and has not, therefore, made them visible as potential "targets." The targets could be further classified, into "hard" targets, which are well "secured," like the president's official residence, and "soft" targets, like buses or trains, which are hardly "secured" at all. One could in fact extend the classification to include fixed targets, such as buildings, and moving targets: people. Neelan Tiruchelvam, one of my senior colleagues and a well-known liberal intellectual was, one could argue, such a soft, moving target: he was blown up by a suicide bomber in July 1999 on his way to work. It is possible to produce what would be called in anthropological discourse an "ethnographic map" of Colombo as a map of targets, organized spatially and classified through some social or cultural logic. I will not, however, produce such a map here.

Let me elaborate my reasons for refusing to create such a map. My first reason is tied to my concept of the anticipation of violence itself: the tactics that accompany such anticipation do not map out a cartography of violence in a stable way. Given those very tactics, what might be subjected to "violence" shifts, and the targets themselves flitter like shadows across the landscape of the city. "But surely the ethnographic present," an interlocutor steeped in anthropological disciplinarity may respond, "is that analytical construct that allows for such freezing—whatever flickers can be snapped, captured, and made still at a defined moment, a fiction of the present." "And how," I respond, "am I to frame the frozen moment?" It is not my contention that such a freezing is impossible; rather, my refusal to do it is a way to underline the epistemological problems of the framing of the freeze. It is worth stepping back here to note that a frozen moment is not the concern simply of disciplinary anthropologists. Much of social-scientific knowledge does depend on such knowing, which then informs other fields of knowledge as well. Consider any map of a city that has a set of landmarks inscribed on it, which anyone may read and use. Such a map is a framed freeze. How is it to be thought about theoretically?

In the opening passages of his essay "Walking in the City," Michel de Certeau invokes a view of Manhattan from the 110th floor of the World Trade Center (1984: 91–110). In looking down over Greenwich Village, Central Park, Harlem, and Midtown, de Certeau makes a set of remarks about the temporality of New York, noting the contrast "between yesterday's buildings, already transformed into trash cans, and today's urban irruptions that block out its space," and comparing it to Rome: "unlike Rome New York has never learnt the art of growing old by playing on all its pasts. Its present invents itself, from hour to hour" (91). New York and Rome are subjects in these sentences, having describable properties distinct from one another. It may seem, then, that if de Certeau's panoptic analytical eye can claim such a specificity for any urban place such as New York in contrast to another specificity—then Colombo, too, may be mapped in the same way. But as one reads on, de Certeau's invocation of New York seems ironic, for his central point is that this view from above, this panoptic map of New York, if you will, does not and cannot articulate the "everyday"—that layer of life which for him is always fraught with multiplicity and heterogeneity, beneath the cognizance of that kind of knowledge and eluding it. "The 1370 foot high tower that serves as a prow for Manhattan continues to construct the fiction that creates readers, makes the complexity of the city readable, and immobilizes its opaque mobility in a transparent text." (92). That map, de Certeau argues, represents with the full force of the words an impossible vision of knowledge, marking what is left out in a particular frozen frame.

If I am allowed an analogy between the de Certeaurian everyday and the tactics of anticipation[1] given militant bombs, then the drawing of a map may not allow my analysis to encounter the everyday, in this de Certeaurian sense, and it may also not allow for the ethnographic present, in the sense of the frozen frame, that I invoked earlier. If I am to preserve this sense of the everyday, in the de Certeaurian sense of radical heterogeneity, it could well be argued that not only should a panoptic map of the city of Colombo not be drawn, but also the very notion of the ethnographic present itself may stand in question. For if I am to think of the everyday as radical heterogeneity, then how can any stable account of it be possible? De Certeau, it seems to me, plays with this question, claiming a radically different epistemological space for the "everyday," yet he also, with every analytical move, attempts to fill that space, to write the possibility of a descriptive account of it. If we pick up his well-developed suggestion that the practice of the everyday is akin to the enunciation of a speech act, then perhaps anthropology can continue, the pause in its progress being only temporary: the "everyday" is a viable anthropological object. Such, at least, is a possible reading, a reading which will allow our anthropological projects to proceed unhindered. Let me make an incision into the everyday, in this de Certeaurian sense, and test the possibility of such an account.

CHECKPOINTS AND THE EVERYDAY ANTICIPATION OF VIOLENCE

My incision into the impossible map of the everyday locates me at a checkpoint. Colombo is a city of checkpoints, large or small, important or minor, confused or precise, official or unofficial. At its most basic and ordinary, a checkpoint is staffed by low-ranking soldiers, men or women, who will stop the flow of traffic, usually vehicular, to ask questions of the drivers, and then the passengers. The first of these questions is prefaced with a request, most often for a national identification card. I wish to pay attention in some detail to both this request and the questions that follow in an attempt to conceptualize the interaction. But before I do so, let me explicate the location of the "checkpoint" in the ethnographic present, which is, in my account of it, constituted by the "anticipation of violence."

The checkpoint lies at the boundaries of a target. As such, it delineates and focuses practices on the target. If, as I argued earlier, the logic of the anticipation of violence creates a plethora of shifting targets that flicker and move like shadows across the landscape with each explosion or threat, then the checkpoint is an attempt by an agency of the state to control that flickering movement, to announce in no uncertain terms that "this is a target." The irony of this must be more than apparent. Such "checkpointed" targets might be the president's residence in the city, or the residence of the commander of the army, but checkpoints also govern entrances/exits from the city, delineating the city itself as a target. The checkpoint configures practices of anticipation in a double way. On the one hand, to pass through one is to remember why they exist—it is to recall the possibility of a bomb. The few who are in fact carrying or have some knowledge of a bomb would also, I imagine, be anticipating its explosive impact. But on the other hand is another kind of anticipation, that of the soldiers who are checking the flow of traffic and people, asking questions. They, the not-so-diffuse tentacles of the state, are, as I suggested before, anticipating violence in an organized way.

So then, now that we see this location of the checkpoint, in this field of anticipated violence, let me return to the point of it: the everyday. I shall do so, as promised, by considering the question asked at the checkpoint. But before I do so, I warn—as may be becoming clear to the irritated reader —that I will treat the checkpoint not simply as "some thing" in Colombo that I can describe "ethnographically," but rather as a checkpoint in another sense, a site for the interrogation and accounting of anthropology itself.

A CHECKPOINT

The most prominent checkpoint in my everyday life in Colombo used to be the one at Baudhaloka Mawatha. It was located three hundred yards or so from Tunmulla, where the air force headquarters still stands. That entire section of road has been closed, but before it was the checkpoint had been in existence for many years. Its location interrupts a major road that houses a series of state facilities. The Sri Lanka Rupavahini Corporation, which consists of TV studios, telecasting towers, and transmitters, and the Bandaranaike Memorial International Conference Hall, a major convention center, are both further down the road from the checkpoint. By the side of the checkpoint itself are spacious "official" residences of senior state bureaucrats, arranged in order of their rank. At the first section of this road lies the official residence of the governor of the Central Bank, right near the Tunmulla intersection, and next to this is the army commander's residence. Hence the checkpoint. When in Colombo in years past, I took great care to avoid this checkpoint, navigating alternate routes, weaving in and out of the terrain of targets. Another checkpoint is situated north of this one, again on a major road, which curves by an airfield. This road is unavoidable, and I am often stopped there.

The first question one is asked at a checkpoint is "May I see your ID?" It is asked very politely and cautiously, by a soldier in fatigues with a large, visible automatic weapon slung over his back. Not having this card is the privilege of foreigners or the careless citizen, who will then have added questions to answer. A passport may be proffered and deemed acceptable, but it is the national ID card that is requested, not just any form of identification. This is a small, yellow, laminated paper. On one side is a photograph, the date of issue, a long unique number, and the signature of the bureaucrat responsible for issuing the card. On the other side is written, upon a series of dotted lines, the name, sex, date of birth, place of birth, occupation, and address of the holder. This card, unlike a passport, has no expiration date on it, so its renewal is difficult to enforce.

My card is old, issued in 1982, just before I took a national university entrance examination. It lists my occupation as student, my place of birth as Colombo, and my address as my parents' house, which is in a residential district in the city. There is nothing else on this card, there is no line for "nationality," "race," or "ethnicity" or any other such classificatory category. Having asked for my ID and having looked it over, the soldier usually returns it to me, and waves me on. Sometimes he may ask a question like "Do you still live at this address?" or say "This card is very old." Rarely do the questions get more intense. Once at another checkpoint, I was arrested.

What is this check about? What is being checked, and how can we conceptualize theoretically the question that is being asked? At its heart, the question is this: "Are you an enemy of the state, and does your enmity extend to violence upon it or its citizens?" This question is surely a specific form of a more general question: "What is your political identity?" Elaborated, the question might be something like this: "Do you represent a politics which lies outside the bounds of the state, which is insurrectionary, which in its deployment and operation may explode a bomb in the vicinity of a well-known target?" If the soldier decides that the answer is yes, then he may detain you.

But the crucial question is this: "How would that be decided?" How does an account of political identity, which might be an adequate answer to this question, be obtained by quick and polite interrogation? My concern here, let me hasten to add, is with the logic of the question, not with the success or otherwise of these interrogations. It is my claim that following the logic of the question may take us some distance in our appreciation both of the everyday and of anthropology.

An account of the answer to the question "What is your political identity?" is, I argue, read off as a series of interpretations of what are taken to be social or cultural signs on the card. In this, it seems to me, the soldiers participate in the work of anthropology, which through its disciplinary provenance marks privileged access to, and makes authoritative claims about, the "cultural," which is undergirded, secured, or perhaps even simultaneous with the "social." If the soldier concerned can be seen in one sense to be asking an anthropological question, let me qualify quickly that I do not see him as an anthropologist, for he is not a disciplinary practitioner. What I want to analogize here is the form of the question "Who are you?"

The tags on the card, as in "name _____" or "occupation _____," are written in both Sinhala and Tamil. These are both official languages of Sri Lanka at present. The blanks are filled out, however, in one language, as one might expect. My card is filled out in Sinhala. Now this, from the point of view of deciphering the social-cultural, is significant, since some cards are filled out in Tamil. A card filled out in Sinhala—it is handwritten—would mean, of course, that the official who wrote it out could write Sinhala. It would not be certain that he would *be* "Sinhala" in the classificatory sense of the census, since by the state's own rules all state bureaucrats must have some proficiency in Sinhala. That is to say, bureaucrats who are Tamil, in the classificatory sense of the census, may well write Sinhala script. But in the north and east of the country, administrative affairs are conducted in Tamil more often than they might be in the south, so a card written in Tamil may well originate in the north. The address and place of birth on the card are also crucial. They place the holder on a map of Lanka—north, south, east, west. But none of this gives a "conclusive" reading of the holder's social-cultural identity: one can be born in the south, have a card written in Sinhala, and be thought to be "Tamil," or vice versa. Or one might be a Muslim who is Tamil-speaking, but not "Tamil" as such. The name might well prove a clincher—it can be read, again, with an anthropological eye, for the socio-cultural: Sinhala names, Tamil names, Muslim names, and so on. These readings too can confound. Or not. Anthropological logics can often be quite effective.

But what I want to draw attention to is not the confounding or not, as such—which is to say, not the possibility of the socio-cultural being so radically heterogeneous that it defies easy intelligibility, which it seems to me is de Certeau's position, or the position of one critique of the social-scientific knowledge, which is best known as a critique of essentialism.[2] That is not the position I take or wish to develop. Rather, my concern is with *the play* of the two questions. That is to say, the play between the first question, which is the logically prior question, "what is your political identity?" and the second question, "what is your social-cultural identity?" It seems it is crucial to think of it as play, for even after the second question is answered, let us say securely, as in "a Tamil from the north," this does not answer the first question securely. If it did, then the state would simply have to arrest all such persons. This is logically possible, and would then call for a characterization of fascism, but even so it would not answer or put the elaborated form of the first question to rest in a secure way. (Even after the Nazi state arrested its Jewish citizens, it still could conceive of enemies.) Given the state of this play, the answer to the second question only allows a return to the first in a circular way.

In two brilliant and increasingly well known essays, the political philosopher Etienne Balibar theorizes this state of play that modern beings— that is, both us and our interlocutors—operate (Balibar 1991a, 1994).[3] His formulations, I suggest, will illuminate my navigation of these checkpoints. The modern citizen, Balibar argues, is defined by the unique confluence of equality and of the sovereignty of that collective equality. The citizen is the conceptual representation of this confluence, but that duality is an irreducible contradiction. The play is between equality on the one hand and the particular expression of sovereignty, freedom, or liberty on the other. "Equaliberty" is a neologism that Balibar coined to capture this play, which results in the production of an unpredictable excess. Forms of subjection are forms of this excess. To be a citizen is also to be a subject, doubly, paralleling here, of course, Foucault's empirico-transcendental doublet of Man (Foucault 1970: passim; cf. Balibar, 1991a: 51). The citizen is that abstract being of equality that, with the demand of freedom in an insurrectionary sense or its granting, as a right, in a constitutional sense, must be subject, in the double sense of self-subjection and being subject to, that field which Balibar calls "community." In this formulation, "community" is irreducibly modern, since its very form is produced by a play between two modern conditions of "Man," equality and liberty. This community then can take the specific form of the nation, an "ethnic" group, or, say, a political party. The community itself might make claims to egalitarianism, or it might well be hierarchical: that is not crucial to its constitution. What is crucial is the claim that it mediates between equality and freedom. Subjection, in other words, is that which mediates the contradiction of citizenship.[4]

Let us proceed with this insight to the thicket of the checkpoint. Consider the two, necessarily double, operations of subjection. The first is both inscribed on and reinterpreted by the agents of the state on the document of identity I described. There is some social-cultural identity which corresponds to some community, which might be marked as a mix of both ethnic and regional that is produced in the reading of that card. And then there is the cardholder, the navigator of the checkpoint. His self-subjection may or may not match that of the state, but it does exist in some form: once when arrested at a checkpoint, holding in my bag a detailed map of the country which aroused suspicion, I claimed to be a scholar working at a renowned research center, which of course was only one such community I could claim. For the checkpoint to do the work it claims—to check identity—the double play on both sides of the divide must match up: the soldier and I (or whoever is checked) must agree on the resultant answer of the irreducible play between citizen and subject. In this case, it did not work; I was arrested.

But in most cases it seems to work: most people pass through a checkpoint without disagreement, their identities "checked." In just this way are many ethnographies written by disciplinary anthropologists. But surely, we now see the precarious nature of this agreement between checker and checked. For each citizen to position his political affiliation in terms of alliance or enmity with the state is also then to work through his own subjection—and that result, clearly, is not fixed. Surely militants who are on bombing missions would carry false papers! Many who do not, who are in fact arrested, do not have projects of violence they intend upon the state. Yet, the checkpoint persists. The high and almost unimaginable stakes of the massive explosion it entails keeps it in place, a testament not to what it *can* tell us about the identity of those who pass through it, but to what it *cannot* tell us given the irreducible contradictions of citizenship, which are the irreducible contradictions of politics itself.

ACKNOWLEDGMENTS

This essay emerges from notes written for an SSRC/MacArthur workshop organized by Adam Ashforth in Tiburon, California, in April 1997. I would like to thank Jean Comraoff, John Broughton, Craig Calhoun, Michael Gillsenan, and Michael

Watts, for commenting on that version, and Kumari Jayawardena and Jayadeva Uyangoda for commenting on another version presented at the Social Scientists' Association, Colombo, in August 1999. It was presented in this form at the Center for Interdisciplinary Studies, at Virginia Tech University, in April 2001, at an occasion organized by Ananda Abeysekara. I thank him and his colleagues for a most stimulating discussion.This works intersects with, and has gained much from the ongoing work of, Qadri Ismail, and I note with pleasure the innumerable conversations with John Ingham which both calmed and stimulated me immeasurably as I wrote this version. None of this work would be possible without the support of Gloria Goodwin Raheja; my greatest debt, as always, is to Malathi de Alwis.

NOTES

1. For an elaboration of "tactics of anticipation," see Jeganathan 2000.

2. This position is well known; perhaps Ronald Inden's *Imagining India* (1990) could be taken as a good example of it. My thoughts on essences owe much to David Scott's questioning of its critique in *Refashioning Futures: Criticism after Postcoloniality* (1999), p. 9, even though my own critical direction may diverge from his.

3. My reading of both these essays is indebted to Vivek Dhareshwar's engagement with them in "'Our Time': History, Sovereignty, Politics," in *Economic and Political Weekly,* Feb. 11, 1995, 317–324, and "The Postcolonial in the Postmodern: Or, the Political after Modernity," *Economic and Political Weekly,* July 29, 1995, PE104–PE112.

4. In an earlier work, I attempted to work through this contradiction by reading through Marx's "The Jewish Question"; see Jeganathan 1994. I am now persuaded, given Balibar 1994: 46, that Marx is incorrect on this point.

Interviews with High School Students in Eastern Sri Lanka

Margaret Trawick

The school at Anilaaddam[1] is one of the largest in the hinterlands of eastern Sri Lanka, with over eight hundred students in the elementary and high school sections. Its catchment area consists of several villages on the edge of territory held by the Liberation Tigers of Tamil Eelam (LTTE), just across a narrow lagoon from territory controlled by the Sri Lankan Army. For more than eighteen years, the LTTE have been fighting the Sri Lankan government for an independent Tamil-majority state, which would include the area in which Anilaaddam is situated. All the members of the LTTE are Tamils, and many of them come from the eastern hinterlands, including villages in the vicinity of Anilaaddam. The government army consists mainly of Sinhala-speaking men from the southern part of Sri Lanka. The government army is assisted in its war against the LTTE by Tamil paramilitary groups, with names such as EPRLF (Eelam People's Revolutionary Front), TELO (Tamil Eelam Liberation Organization), and PLOTE (People's Liberation Organization of Tamil Eelam). These groups once fought for an independent Tamil Eelam, but now they have joined the Sri Lankan government. Their main job is to find and identify members or suspected members of the LTTE, to capture and kill them if possible. The paramilitary organizations consist of boys recruited from the local Tamil populace. The paramilitaries as well as the LTTE include teenagers in their ranks. Also assisting the army is the STF (Special Task Force of the police). From 1987 to 1989, the IPKF (Indian Peace Keeping Forces) also occupied the area. People who were adults around Anilaaddam during that time report that the IPKF were more brutal even than the Sinhalese in their treatment of Tamils.

The ferocity of the war in Sri Lanka is intense, and Tamil civilians are its principal victims. Habitations close to the border between territories controlled by hostile groups are most vulnerable to being "caught in the crossfire"—a euphemism for direct and intentional attacks by armed organizations and raiding parties on civilians, their homes, stores, and cattle. The people who live in such places are small farmers and agricultural laborers. Many of them are so poor that feeding themselves and their families from day to day is their greatest concern. Malnourishment and its attendant diseases are visible everywhere. The problem of getting food is greatly exacerbated by the war. Such is the situation in Anilaaddam.

I visited the Anilaaddam school in January and February of 1998 to interview students about their experiences of the war. The ultimate goal of the interviews was to learn not just how these young people had been affected by the war, but what choices they had made in the face of this war, and why? What options did they perceive to be available to them? What motivated them to choose one option over another? In particular, what motivated them to join, or not to join, the LTTE?

The year 1987 was a crisis point for people here, the year of the prawn project massacre. During that year, on one day, more than eighty civilian men were captured and summarily executed, because the owner of the prawn farm (a foreign entrepreneur) was suspected of selling kerosene to the local branch of the LTTE. The foreign entrepreneur sued the Sri Lankan government, and the families of the victims received some monetary compensation for their loss. But the memory of the massacre, men being shot in the head, one by one, before one another's eyes on a junction at Anilaaddam, their bodies being hauled off, burnt somewhere, and never recovered, remains vivid in the minds of people who live here.

Again in 1991, the rice mill massacre brought the war home to the people of Anilaaddam in the most horrible way. As a tractor full of Sinhala soldiers was entering the area, it tripped a land mine laid as a trap by the Tigers, and several of the soldiers were killed. The remaining soldiers went on a rampage, killing all the civilians in sight. Some were shot, their bodies thrown in a pit and the bodies burned on the spot. Others sought refuge in a rice mill. They burned to death when the soldiers set the mill on fire. In all, over 160 civilians from in and around Anilaaddam died on that one day.

In between such major disasters, intermittent aerial attacks, shelling, ground attacks, disappearances, and abductions have kept civilians in a state of constant fear. What was always most surprising to me was the way they were able to live their lives, between attacks, in a more or less normal, even celebratory fashion. Anyone born in this area after around 1980 could not clearly remember a time without war. Most of the students in the Anilaaddam school were of this category. A generation was coming of age who could only imagine what peace might be like. Peace for them meant two kinds of freedom: freedom from fear and freedom to move, or to stay where they were, according to their own will. All of them were restricted in their movements by army checkpoints throughout the cleared area across the lagoon, where they had to travel to get medical care if they needed it, or to sell produce in the towns, or to visit relatives, or to get job training, or any of countless other things.

In the midst of all this, some gave up on schooling, but remarkably many—probably the majority—kept faith and continued to attend the impoverished school available to them. When I asked them what the most important experience in their life had been, almost all of them answered either school or the incident of 1987 or 1991, depending perhaps on how they interpreted the question. Several of the students had developed a contingency plan: if the army attacked their area again, they would join the LTTE; if not, they would finish their schooling and live as civilians—or as one boy put it simply, he would join the LTTE or he would live. In fact, the students took it for granted that if they joined the LTTE they would die. They knew this from experience: the siblings and friends they knew who had joined the LTTE had mostly died. They had seen the bodies of those killed in combat. They had no illusions concerning what they were in for if they joined the Tigers. The ones who actually joined were not much different from ordinary teenagers, and were no less realistic in their view of the movement than those who chose not to join—which is to say, who chose not to die at this particular time. Although the students who did not join the Tigers sometimes expressed incomprehension as to why their friends and siblings had joined, they also expressed almost unanimous strong sympathy for the Tigers. The Tigers were people they knew, people of the area; they had no cause to fear them. Moreover, the Tigers did not arbitrarily attack and kill civilians, as the army did. It was clear from what the students said that they had learned and accepted the revolutionary ideology of the LTTE: their analysis of what the war was about and what had to be done for the Tamil people to achieve their freedom. But the students also reported that the Tigers encouraged them, even urged them, to stay in school and finish their degrees. This was a remarkable assertion, given the fact that at that time the local Tigers were engaged in an intensive recruitment campaign, and were openly announcing their serious shortage of manpower. Just three months after these interviews, at a big public performance, an important leader of the military section of the Tigers came onstage and virtually pleaded with parents to let their children join the movement, and with young people not to excuse themselves from service for any but the most serious reasons. Meanwhile, the students reported that about six people from the class ahead of them in school had joined the Tigers the previous year. In other words, even from this school which one might expect to be a strong recruitment base for the Tigers, only a small minority of those eligible had actually joined. Perhaps the students were hiding the truth concerning the number of recruits. But the large number of able-bodied young men and women living in the village who were manifestly not members of the LTTE seemed to bear out the students' claims. There was no evidence at all of forcible recruitment. I think the Tigers knew that forcible recruitment would lead to an ill-disciplined and ineffective fighting force, at best. They already had problems with people they had armed and trained who had used their positions for personal gain and then fled to become informers for the army. The students, too, were all too aware of this problem. It was a problem for them, as well. They knew some of the turncoats personally. They knew some of the members of the anti-LTTE paramilitary groups who roamed the region. They had suffered beatings at checkpoints from these individuals, whom they knew, and who knew them.

The students were in the terrible position of being able to identify members of the enemy groups to the LTTE, and members of the LTTE to the enemy. Whenever a young civilian traveled from the Tiger-held side of the lagoon to the army-held side, he or she could be captured and forced to become an informant. Moreover, if any civilian bore a grudge against another, he or she could falsely report to the army that the other was a Tiger. That the civilian community maintained its integrity under these conditions is a fact worthy of note. We must ask ourselves why Anilaaddam has not become another Pine Ridge or Buffalo Creek.[2]

Historians of a certain bent have often argued, or even assumed, that warfare strengthens a society, by giving people a common cause, toughening them through adversity, and so forth. The Spencerian view of survival of the fittest prevailed throughout the colonial British Empire. The "fittest" in this view were those individuals most capable of fighting and winning —or, on a larger scale, those nations most able to wage war against other nations and conquer them militarily. Colonial historians and indeed anthropologists admired "warlike" peoples, from Maori to Maasai, respecting those who put up a good fight against the colonizers. After conquest these people were recruited into the colonizers' own militaries. Tamils were traditionally not among those people. Those modern Tamils who take pride in the military prowess of the LTTE are (in my view) seeking prestige according to the old Spencerian model. But times have changed and spokesmen for postcolonial world powers represent themselves as despising ethnic warfare.

Moreover, Tamil society in Sri Lanka has been decimated by the war. Thus, anyone who imagines that civilian society in a place like Anilaaddam derives strength from the war itself need only visit the place to be divested of that illusion. Civilian culture in eastern Sri Lanka, including Anilaaddam, is not militant and does not condone violence. For this reason, many civilians express profound ambivalence toward the LTTE. Whether Saiva (worshiping Siva) or Christian, they believe that killing is deeply sinful, and the Tigers, however righteous their cause, however evil their enemy, take this sin upon themselves whenever they take a life. Even some Tigers themselves believe this: to take on this sin is part of their sacrifice. Perhaps this is why they do not talk about an afterlife. They do not expect God to reward them for what they have done. A girl who joins the LTTE perceives herself as having no future. This is not to say she has lost her sense of individual personhood. She has lost hope of personal fulfill-ment, but for what she finds in the movement, and she has lost hope of personal continuation, but for the hope of being remembered. For her, love is all—love in present living hearts, love out of time. Civilian young people are much the same. Many of the students at Anilaaddam expected that they would never see an end to the war. For as long as they lived, they would live in this hell. Some said peace would come when the Tigers won, but no one ventured a guess as to when this would happen. None of these students believed that peace was possible under Sinhala rule. Certainly there could be no peace under army occupation: from these students' point of view, the army was the war. Army weapons killed their fathers, army soldiers raped their sisters and tortured their brothers. Army advances were what they feared. Army checkpoints were what restricted their free-dom. They never said but perhaps they knew what the Tiger leaders also knew, that a military victory by the LTTE was impossible, that long-term army occupation of Tamil areas was a distinct likelihood. Only a deus ex machina might possibly save them, some foreign intervention, some helping hand reaching out from the sky. Some better-off students at pri-vately run schools in town expressed exactly this desire. But the students of Anilaaddam had seen no helping hands reaching down from the sky, and they entertained no dreams that any outsider would save them. This dreamlessness was implicit, I think, in the students' predictions that the war would never end.

Total despair, the lack of a future, is often cited as a cause for disaf-fection among youth, for their displays of cynicism, reckless short-term selfishness, and acts of aimless violence. The students at Anilaaddam faced a grim future indeed. But among these students, despite severe poverty, de-spite exposure to chronic violence, danger, and displacement, despite the destruction of families, despite the urging of people they admired in the LTTE to join in the armed conflict, interpersonal fighting was disdained. Some stated that there was no fighting among students at all, that all were in accord. Some stated that only little kids got into fights. One stated that he had been in fights, but when I asked him, Who wins? he answered that both win. I should have asked him, "What kind of fighting is this, where both sides win?" In my presence, no child over the age of five displayed the slightest antagonism toward any other child. Among high school stu-dents, almost all said they enjoyed sports such as cricket and football, and some were avid players. It may be old-fashioned, but I think it is not un-reasonable to surmise that physical aggression was channeled and disci-plined in this way. The sports contests I watched in March 1998 showed that students took strong pride in being students, that they had what can only be called intense school spirit, and that athletic and academic accomplishment were the arenas in which their pride was asserted. The point here is not to claim that students in these schools never fought among themselves, but that they wanted me to perceive them as above spontaneous fighting. This held true even of those who stated their intention to join the Tigers.

Is there a way to explain such courage? It might be plausibly argued that the children I saw were special, they were the survivors. Of course there were ones who had dropped out of school, succumbed to cynicism. In the Tiger-controlled area, there were one or two wandering bands of little boys. On the army side, I was told by many sources, there were no street children, and indeed I never saw any. The reason was that it was too dangerous to be out on that side after nightfall. Students and adults living on the army side told me that boys who became cynical and dropped out of school early joined one of the movements, for money, for safety, for getting a gun. They got to be the abusers, rather than the abused, but in fact they were not all that safe. On the Tiger side, only Tigers had guns. There were no drugs but alcohol and tobacco, and these were strongly discouraged. Alcohol was confiscated when it was found by Tigers, who poured it on the ground. Thus two sources of violence among civilians were taken away. Plus, as students said, the Tigers themselves encouraged the students to study. Perhaps, then, the Tigers may be awarded partial credit for students walking the line. But even if we gave Tigers full credit, we would be begging the question of where the people as a people, Tigers and civilians, got their strength.

Supporting them all, bearing them up under all conditions, was the earth beneath their feet, which gave their lives beauty, meaning, and sustenance. The culture of regeneration was strong in Anilaaddam, where all the families were farming families. The students of Anilaaddam were proud of what one boy called the tradition of all the people here of cultivation. These embattled and impoverished students loved their family homes and loved growing things. They aspired to be teachers of children if they were fortunate enough to pass their exams.

It seemed to me that they had determined to want only this: to farm the land, even someone else's land, so that they could feed others; and to acquire knowledge, even though they might never use it for their own purposes, so that they could pass it on to others. When I asked them what they wanted to be when they became adults, they never said things like doctor or engineer—the usual answers one would expect from (for instance) middle-class Jaffna Tamils or Indian Tamils. Even when such answers were urged upon them by adults watching the interviews, the young respondents would not pretend to set for themselves more ambitious goals.

Humility of this kind should not be mistaken for absence of self-esteem. If military and political prosecutors of the war in Sri Lanka read this report, they will only learn what they have already been told by other sources:

attacks on Tamil civilians by the army or its supporting paramilitary groups only encourage young people to join the LTTE. Some join because of revolutionary ideals or because of admiration for the members of the LTTE or because of a burning desire to fight back against the military that has abused and humiliated them or, in some cases, because they have decided to die. But others join explicitly because they feel safer as members of the LTTE than as unprotected civilians. This is not so much because the LTTE have the weaponry and the training to fight back, as because the LTTE know in advance of impending army attacks, and they get most of their members to safe places in the jungle before the attacks begin, while they leave civilians to fend for themselves. The Tigers may leave civilians unprotected for the purpose of getting young people to leave civilian life and join them, but more likely it is because they cannot safely convey to the general populace the intelligence reports they have received. Moreover, they have no means of protecting civilians; indeed, fighting back against an army offensive is almost certain to intensify the siege. Especially when the ranks of the LTTE are depleted, they will act with extra caution to preserve the lives of their own members. Their greatest asset is a trained and experienced fighting force, and this takes years to raise. Thus engaging the Tigers in massive bloody battles is not the way to destroy them, as they will avoid such battles if they need to preserve manpower. Terrorizing Tamil civilians is also clearly counterproductive. In the midst of terror a young person will think, If I stay as I am I may die now; if I join the movement I will probably die later. And they will join the movement now. Such a choice is not made impulsively, nor, it would seem in most cases, out of anger. In general, acting in anger is discouraged. Anger is attributed by Tamil people to those who act violently against them, such as the army or the paramilitaries. Anger is not attributed to people one perceives as one's friends. Young people and adults, Tigers and civilians, have no difficulty confessing that they have experienced anger, but no one brags about actions they may have taken in anger, any more than they brag about beating other kids in schoolyard brawls. Hence, even people who have been beaten by the Army, or who have seen kin killed by the Army, do not necessarily respond by joining the Tigers. It is an interesting case of cultural misunderstanding, perhaps, that ordinary Sinhala soldiers assume that someone who has been beaten will join the Tigers for revenge, so that any young Tamil man or woman who bears the scars of beating or torture is almost automatically assumed to be a Tiger. It is as though the Sinhalese cannot conceive of any other response to the brutality of their own comrades. Unbridled anger is, after all, their own response to real or perceived harm done to them. And yet they continue to batter unarmed Tamil civilians, as though inviting retaliation. Human beings can adapt to anything, and the young people of Anilaaddam have adapted to terror. They are prepared to live with terror for the rest of their lives, and to make rational choices in the moments of terror's intensity. They are also prepared to live with peace, and peace is of course what they want most: no more fighting and no more army. They cannot end the fighting and they cannot make the army go away. But in the intervals between moments of terror, the lives they build for themselves are lives of peace.

*   *   *

I interviewed twelve students in the school on three separate days. The students included six boys and six girls, with their ages ranging between 13 and 22. The median age was 16.5 and the average age was 17. Some students were chosen by the teachers and some came and asked to be interviewed while I was there. The interviews were not private; teachers and other students were present. I had a list of questions which I asked each student. Sometimes I would follow up on a statement that a student made; with one or two students certain questions were omitted because they were redundant. I told the students that what they told me would be used in a book I was writing about their experiences of the war, and that I would keep their identities confidential. Nevertheless, under the circumstances it was impossible for me to keep information given by particular students from spreading throughout the school, and thence possibly to the army. The students must have edited what they said to me, not only for this reason, but for the equally serious reason that I was a foreigner intending to represent them to the outside world. The content of the interviews given below will immediately demonstrate to the reader how inadequate formal, tape-recorded interviews can be as a means of trying to learn what people think. At the same time there is no substitute for recording and preserving the exact words of the people whom you are trying to know. Otherwise, as an ethnographer, you have nothing to write down but your own perceptions and memories, and these can be very faulty indeed. Using the words of the students as building blocks, I have attempted to construct a kind of miniature oral history of the war as it has happened in this place, as these young people remember it. In the text below, each paragraph is a string of short sentences, each of which was the response to some question of mine. Here, I have omitted the questions, so that the answers appear as a continuous narrative. I have not changed the words of the respondents, except where necessary for clarity, to fill in what a one-word response was in answer to. In the original interview, the brevity of most responses is even more apparent than it is with my questions deleted. For all these reasons, the text below is not smooth or easy to read. It is raw and rough. But it is exactly the truth of what happened, exactly the words that were said on these days by these people. Among other things, the brief answers reflect the stark quality of the respondents' experiences. They do not speak about the smell of burning flesh, the sight of spattered blood and brains, the screams of men pleading for their lives. And yet from their terse words, we know they have experienced these things. They respond as in a court of law. And we know they do not lie because the Sri Lankan military has confessed to the killings of 1987 and 1991, to the beatings of countless suspected terrorists, and to the bombing of places where terrorists are suspected to be. Though we may trust these students not to lie, we will know that their memories also are imperfect. Some of the events they describe happened when they were very young, and recollections will therefore be hazy. The dates they give for certain events do not always match the dates given by adults for the same events. Discussion of the events with others over the years will also have shaped their memories. And the brevity of responses suggests also that some students were reluctant to say any more to me than they had to. Some probable reasons for such reluctance have already been stated above. Finally, the reader will understand that the topics discussed and the memories evoked are of the most painful kind. Forgetting can be healing, and the last thing I wanted was to unheal these children, to put them in pain again. Hence I did not push them, but tried to let them lead me wherever they wanted to go. For the most part, they did not take the lead. Sometimes they led me to unexpected places.

In total, I asked all the students about a dozen main questions. Space does not allow me to include all the answers to all the questions here. These are the answers I got when I asked my first question: "How have you been affected by the war?"

Student no. 1

. . . My uncle died due to the violence (*vanseyal*) problems. The army shot him. He was running because of some problems in town. They shot him while he was running away. I was thirteen years old then. He was my mother's own brother. He was twenty-two years old. He was not married.

. . . In the land-mine incident in 1991, forty-one civilians in this school were shot dead. They were people from this village. People we knew.

. . . I have been displaced twice in my life, to Arayampathy and to town. Due to the war the army bombed us and we had to move.

Student no. 2

. . . I have no father. Mother is at home. Father was affected by the violence at Pillaiyaaradi [a village adjacent to Anilaaddam] in 1991. I was ten years old then. A land mine exploded and the army got angry and shot him. We were afraid. They were waiting nearby with knives to cut us. They took my father away. They came into our house before and after the bomb blast. When they came into the house, we did nothing. We were afraid. They came into the house, started to cut us and shoot us. But then they left.

Student no. 3

. . . Near our house at the junction, we had a shop. The army destroyed it and the STF [Special Task Force of the Sri Lankan police] looted it earlier.

That was in 1987. We lost two and a half lakhs (rupees 250,000). Now we have built another house on that same land and are living in it. In 1987, I was five years old. I remember that time. At that time, we had prawn farming here. Suddenly they came and shot some people and took my father to the jail. They beat him up there and released him. Then they took all our things and gathered them up and threw them to civilians. We did not see the people who were being shot. They took them away in tractors. My mother cried. Three days after the shooting they took my father to jail. He is living now. He is doing farm work. Because of the STF beating, he was blinded. After that he was operated on in Batticaloa Hospital and now he can see a little. My brothers do the farm work with him.

. . . I am the youngest in my family. I had four older sisters. One died. Due to a small problem, my mother hit her for doing wrong. So she drank oil and died. Oil used for farming. It was a small problem. But she got angry and did it. That was in 1976. I was not born then.

. . . When we speak with the army or the STF, they ask whether we support the LTTE. We say no. Otherwise they will beat us. My older brother was beaten. The Indians (IPKF) beat him. The EPRLF informed on him. They beat him and gave him electrical shocks and everything. Now he is well. He farms. He does not get angry. He is married and has children and all. He can't join the movement.

. . . The last time the army came here was in 1996. They were moving around here. We were hiding. Then they gathered the people and had a meeting at the school. They did not do anything to anyone. They came because the LTTE had hit a camp and took artillery shells from there. The army came to recover those shells. They left immediately. They stayed for only one day. When they were leaving, the LTTE attacked them. A Black Tiger[3] blew himself up. That happened in Kilimalai.

. . . Our family has not been badly affected by the war. The house was lost. No lives were lost. There has been only material loss.

Student no. 4

. . . We have been affected by the war. I have gotten a beating by the army. When there is fighting, when people travel, they capture and beat them. I was fourteen years old then. It was in 1995. When there was fighting, the army came and stayed here. They beat me with sticks. They beat me here, in Anilaaddam, when I was going by bicycle from home, on the road. They caught me and took me alone and beat me. There were fifty or a hundred of them, but only one of them beat me. They said that I supported the LTTE. They released me after the beating. When I came home, my stomach was upset. I went to the hospital. I did not say I was beaten, I said I fell off my bicycle. They believed me. There were no serious wounds. I don't know if they beat people now. Only if you go to the other side of the lagoon (*turai*) will they beat you. We don't go there anymore.

. . . Previously we were living in the fields in Unnichai. Because of the army's arrival there, we moved here to Anilaaddam. Our house and belongings were destroyed, so we came here. . . .

. . . I don't know about land mines. I have heard. It exploded in Pillaiyaaradi. A land mine. In that, the army took eighteen or twenty Tamils and put them in a pit and burnt them alive. The father of one of our friends also died then. He was forty-five or fifty years old. We knew him well. We did not go and see because the army was standing next to the pit.

. . . My mother died due to the violence. She was displaced and shot dead by the army. It happened when I was small, so I can't tell the details.

Student no. 5

. . . I am not more affected than anyone else, but all Tamil people have been affected by the war. At the checkpoints they check our ID cards, they check our clothes and parcels and so forth. They ask if we are Tigers. They beat us. I was beaten in 1997, only last year. They accused me of being a Tiger. They beat me with a baton. They asked me to turn around and they beat me. It lasted for five minutes, then they released me. The army has been to our house. They looked around and asked if there was a Tiger. Then they left. They take us to the camp and make us do work such as loading soil, loading clay. After we do the work, they release us. The army captures people and beats them. If they take about five or six people, they will release one or two. The rest are shot. My mother's younger brother was taken away, he did not come back. The army shot and killed him. I was small then, I don't know what year it happened.

. . . When the army came to our house, it was 1995. They were doing a roundup. They looked around and asked if there was a Tiger and left. My mother, father, older sister, and younger sister were there. They are afraid that there are Tigers, so they come and search. If they capture someone and beat them, they will tell the truth. When they did the roundup, they captured my mother's elder sister's son. They beat him and released him. He did not talk about it. He was wounded on his knee. They tied him upside-down and beat him. He was eighteen. Now he is at home, doing agricultural work.

Student no. 6

. . . My age is thirteen. I was born in 1985. My mother is alive. My father is not. The army shot him in 1987. I do not know why they shot him.

Student no. 7

. . . My mother and father are both alive. Father left. I have two older brothers and three older sisters. I am the youngest. My brothers are in the village. They do not work. Two of my sisters are married. No one in my family has died or been wounded during my lifetime. I live in my mother's house. I have never stayed in any other house. The most important experience in my life is studying. What makes me happy is playing. I go to the movies. That makes me happy. What makes sickness come to me is fever. Grief does not come to me. What makes anger come to me is fighting. I fight with other children when they scold me. When we fight, both win. The most important person in my life is mother. The most important problem in my life is food. Ordinarily what we eat is rice. We get vegetables. We get chicken. We eat one meal a day. My mother goes to work. She sells rice. That work brings our only income. I do not know my father. I do not know why he left. I do not know when he left. I remember him. He was good. He will not come back. When I finish my studies I will work. I have not been affected by the war.

Student no. 8

. . . Mother's mother died of disease. Mother's uncle (*ammaavuda maamaa*) died because of the war. When he was in the paddy fields the army came and shot him. It was five years ago. When the army came to the LTTE base and did a roundup, he too ran away and they shot him. While we were here, they shot him there. The army chased Father's younger brother too into the fields and shot him, at the same time they shot Mother's uncle.

. . . People we know have been taken by the army. They lifted them onto trees and beat them. They threw stones at them. They gave them no food, they made them work, they crushed them, it is said.

. . . Now they [the army] won't come. The LTTE are here, after all. And if they come, there is a river in between. They [army operatives] would dress in white shirts like common people and come and shoot and run. It happened like that in 1997. Now it doesn't. It happened twice. They would just wear a sarong and come. They would wear a sarong and hide the rifle and shoot and run. Now it doesn't happen that way. The LTTE stand at the junction. Therefore they [army] can't come. The LTTE examine people they suspect. They stand also at the ferry launch, to confiscate liquor and pour it out. The LTTE are there, therefore the army doesn't come.

. . . I am not affected by the war, but the people I told you about before were all affected. With that, all the Tamil people have been affected.

Student no. 9

. . . My father died in 1983, when I was a small child. It happened when he tried to settle a street fight. My mother told me about it. She said that when two people were fighting each other, he went in between and was accidentally hurt by a knife and died in the hospital. He was a bus driver for CTB [Ceylon Transporting Board, a government public transport service].

. . . Apart from my father, my three older brothers have died. They joined the LTTE and were shot by the army.

. . . I live now in Anilaaddam, at my sister's house, but this is not my home village. We moved here because the army burned our house. That was in 1987. I was five years old. My mother told me about these things. She said that EP [EPRLF] burned our house because they were angry at my brothers. 1987 was the first year I realized a war was happening in this country, the year they killed the people at the prawn-raising project.

. . . The most important event in my life was the bomb explosion in Pillaiyaaradi. The army came and beat all the people and took some people and put them into the pit made by the bomb explosion and killed them. We ran away to the other side of the lagoon, to Aayirampaaddu. We stayed in a refugee camp. I was about ten years old at the time. I was afraid. We ran away because of fear. It frightened me very much, when they took those people with them. They closed the door of this school and lifted their guns and fired them. We were refugees for ten days, then we returned home. This event changed my thinking. This event was the first one that happened here. There was an incident that happened before at the prawn-raising project, where the army shot and killed several people. But this incident made us refugees. In 1987, although I was very small, I remember what happened. Several of our village people were hurt but none of my relations. The small children were afraid and stayed with their mothers. I am afraid of the army.

. . . I am affected by the war. I do not see any great differences between affected and unaffected people. There are small differences. Those who are unaffected are a little bit richer. The others are poor. The reason for this difference is that there are no brothers or fathers in the families of the affected. If there are brothers and fathers, they can earn money and build a house.

Student no. 10

. . . The bomb blast in Pillaiyaaradi was the most important event of my life. We were in Munaikkaadu when the incident happened. We didn't know much about it immediately. We came to know about the incident later. We didn't run away. My father's brother was shot dead during that incident. After this incident, I came to know about war. Before that, I didn't understand what war was. At that time I was eight years old.

. . . Before 1990, people were talking about the war but I didn't understand well. After the horrible killing of 1990, I came to know about the war.

. . . What causes me fear is this. We are staying on this side [of the lagoon]. The Razeek group [a Tamil paramilitary group working for the army] comes to the bank of the lagoon and sometimes they come into the village and kidnap people. Not on the other side but on this side. Because of this we have no peace at night. They have taken people from this place—not relatives, but people we knew. After they take them, sometimes they release them, but sometimes nobody knows what happens to them. They enter the village of Anilaaddam, in the corner, on this side of the lagoon. They come by small boat. They don't come every day, but occasionally. The

LTTE know about this, but how long can they keep watch for them? If they [the Razeek group] came every day, they [LTTE] could keep watch. But if they come only occasionally, then it is difficult. They [LTTE] don't go every day to the harbor where people travel through, but they go there whenever people travel to the other side through the harbor at night. The Razeek group came last year. December 1997 they came. [This would have been less than two months prior to the date of the interview.] They took one person and released him. Nobody knows what happened to the people taken by them earlier.

Student no. 11

. . . They came to the school and closed the window and seized us and beat us. They fired their rifles. We were very afraid and we threw down our books and ran away. They also beat two teachers and took some people from here and put them in the pit. When they came, we threw down our books and didn't go to our house but ran to the other side and stayed somewhere there and came back to our home the next day.

. . . Now we are staying in our own house in this village. During the first problem we moved and came back when it was over. When the army came and shot and captured people, we went and hid in the paddy fields. Two weeks we stayed there. I was twelve years old at the time. Our whole family went there. It was so hard to get food and water. We slept on the ground. We were afraid.

Student no. 12

. . . The army shot my father's brother's family, in 1992, in a paddy field. When they were all in the paddy field, the army came to round them up. Then they all started to run. At that time the army shot them. We were afraid and we thought our lives were also going to end. Because in that incident, a whole family—father, mother, and a boy were shot dead. It was a great shock. We wept.

. . . Apart from this, in 1987, in the trouble that happened here, about twelve of our relatives were killed, of whom six were our close relatives. I remember it. It was a real shock. Because at that time I was fourteen years old and was able to understand what was happening. I did not know what war was before this incident. It was the first incident here.

. . . We live in Pillaiyaaradi. When the bomb exploded here in 1991, we were displaced to Aayirampaaddu. We faced difficulties there, too, then we moved from there to a paddy field, and from there we came back home. We were refugees for three weeks, because there in Pillaiyaaradi about sixty-five people were killed. They burned our houses. There were no places to stay. Therefore, we too experienced hardship, and for about a month we survived however we could, fleeing from one place to another. The shooting incident in 1987 and the bomb explosion in 1991 were the most important events in my life. They changed my thinking. In this nerve-wracking situation, I thought, what is the point of studying? That feeling arose in my mind. I left my studies for two years and started again after I returned to the village. For the two years that I was out of school I stayed with my parents. But after people said, "You should study," a somewhat better mental state arose in my mind, and I came back to study.

. . . When the land mine exploded in 1991, we were frightened. When classes were going on, we all ran to this very town, to Munaikkaadu, away from our school in Pillaiyaaradi to this school. Here, they took everyone and locked them in this very room [in the school, where I am conducting the interview]. They lifted their rifles and fired them and at that same time and place, they beat the teachers. All of the boys, many people, ran away. Many girls were hurt; they were inside the school. After they took everyone and locked them up, two or three of those [soldiers] who came took many common people and made them raise their hands, and put them in the pit and shot them. They were afraid that a bomb might be here. But a bomb was not here. It exploded over there in the neighboring village. That is why we ran over here, thinking we would be safer.

In the future, if I have the convenience to stay at home, I will stay. If I have to run away, I will have to run away with everyone else.

NOTES

1. The names of all places mentioned in this account have been changed to fictional names by the author.

2. These are two communities in North America that have been so badly damaged by human-inflicted and natural disasters that the people who live in them have all but given up hope of dignified survival. Pine Ridge is an Oglala Lakota Sioux reservation in South Dakota where alcoholism, unemployment, violence, and poverty are rife. The current situation of the Oglala Sioux at Pine Ridge is a consequence of many years of abuse by the U.S. government. Buffalo Creek is a hollow in West Virginia that contained a number of towns and villages roughly the size of Anilaaddam and its neighbors. In 1972, a large dam burst, due to negligent strip-mining practices that had been carried out over decades by the Pittston Coal Co. In a matter of minutes, 118 were dead and over 4,000 people were left homeless. The community never recovered. (See Kai T. Erikson, *Everything in Its Path: Destruction of Community in the Buffalo Creek Flood* [New York: Simon and Schuster, 1976].)

Although the chain of disasters that have afflicted the people of Buffalo Creek and Pine Ridge are monstrous, what has happened to the people in and around Anilaaddam is no less horrible. The question of how the Anilaaddam people have managed to hold out through all these horrors is therefore not a trivial one.

3. Black Tigers are specially trained suicide bombers of the LTTE.

PART SIX

Globalization, Public Culture, and the South Asian Diaspora

South Asian social-cultural life is not bound within the specific locales or regions that constitute geographically what we know as South Asia. Rather, it is in essential respects flowing, mobile, and public. People, ideas, values, commodities, media images, and popular cultural forms flow into, out of, and around South Asia to create what can be considered a "public culture." This public culture is very much a part of South Asians' everyday lives, both for those in the diaspora and for those who live in the villages and cities of South Asia while partaking in localized public or global cultural forms.

Arjun Appadurai and Carol Breckenridge coined the term "public culture" in their 1988 article "Why Public Culture?" They use it to refer to a "zone of cultural debate" (p. 6) within which persons engaging in many areas of study (including history, literature, anthropology, media studies, the arts, and folklore) discuss the relation between a local culture (Indian culture or Tamil culture, for example) and the apparently uniform global or transnational culture that seems increasingly to define a homogeneous cosmopolitan elite culture—the world's urban middle and upper classes who share many of the same tastes and values.[1] Before Appadurai and Breckenridge, Milton Singer called attention to the kinds of public cultural performances so important to understanding South Asia, in *When a Great Tradition Modernizes* (1972). Singer defined cultural performances as the particular instances of cultural organization—such as plays, musical concerts, public lectures, dance performances, weddings, temple festivals—through which Indians, and perhaps all people, think of their culture (pp. 70–72). Through the study of such performances, Singer argued, scholars can piece together understandings about the culture and values of the society in which these performances are produced and consumed.

While Singer was primarily interested in how localized cultural performances could be connected to the study of *Indian* civilization as a whole (that is, how the performances were about, derived from, and creative of that whole), the public culture project situates itself more globally. It looks at the ways nations such as India or Sri Lanka have developed forms of public culture that derive from and draw them into the cosmopolitanism of the rest of the world, at the same time that the global cosmopolitan culture is changed according to (i.e., appropriated by) local cultural forms (Appadurai and Breckenridge 1988: 5). A main thrust of the work of those participating in the public culture debate is to demonstrate that modernization—in South Asia as well as in any so-called "third world" country— need not mean simply global homogenization at the expense of the local culture. Their work, rather, explores the ways in which modernization in, for example, India, is *Indian*, how the meanings and uses of global cultural forms are altered as they are locally (and culturally) consumed and appropriated.

For example, it is now commonplace all over Tamil Nadu, India—in cities, towns, and villages—to watch the Olympics, to wear blue jeans, to buy and eat prepackaged snack foods, and, at least in the larger towns, to eat in fast-food restaurants. Chennai (Madras), the capital city of Tamil Nadu —like Mumbai (Bombay) or New Delhi or Karachi—looks more and more like any city anywhere. Yet at the same time, the consumption of cosmopolitan cultural items may take on culturally unique forms, their Tamil "stamps." For instance, the TV on which people watch sports may be outdoors and common to a community, the gift perhaps of a local politician or other leader; blue jeans may signify a particular form of worldly connection to the "West"; McDonald's joints may sport lamb burgers as well as different aesthetics, meal times, seating arrangements, condiments, etc. As another example, take going to the movies in Tamil Nadu: The audience often throws flowers and other gifts to heroes and deity-characters on the screen; they garland the posters of the stars much as they do the images of gods and politicians. They may even perform rituals for them, and they incorporate film showings into other kinds of rituals (weddings, temple festivals, etc.). The Tamil cinema is a Tamilized cinema.

Studies of public culture and globalization in South Asia have explored such phenomena as: people's relationships to the Indian cinema—now the largest movie-making industry in the world (e.g., Dickey 1993; Derné 2000); Indian television viewing (e.g., Mankekar 1999); the ways international tourism intersects with the lives and imaginations of Mt. Everest Sherpas (e.g., Adams 1996; Ortner 1999); the production of advertising in India (Mazzarella forthcoming); middle-class Nepali youth's experiences of modernity, mass media, and consumer culture (see Liechty, part I and forthcoming); and how an international gerontology and the dynamics of Indian cinema, advertising, and popular medicine are linked to the imagining of aging (Cohen 1998). These works scrutinize equally how public (or global or cosmopolitan or "Western") forms of culture impact upon South Asian people's lives and how various people in South Asia produce, fashion, and reinterpret these forms. Vincanne Adams (1996: 12) writes of "the culture that floats between the two groups of participants"—Westerners and Sherpas—as each produces and uses representations of the other in their lives.

In this part, William Mazzarella discusses one force that has had a profound impact on the nature of globalization in India over the past decade. In 1991 the Congress government of Prime Minister P. V. Narasimha Rao inaugurated a comprehensive program of economic deregulation, which lowered the formerly stringent barriers to foreign trade. As Mazzarella notes, one of the most significant results of this reform was "the sudden presence of hundreds of foreign brands on Indian shelves, television screens, and billboards."

The diasporic flows of South Asian people to and from various parts of the world are also an important part of the making and experiencing of public or transnational cultural forms. As people move—whether by choice, or by necessity as a refugee (Daniel)—they creatively combine and rework the ideas, values, images, and lifeways that constitute what they perceive to be their new site (such as America or Britain) and their homeland (such as India or Sri Lanka).

South Asians have moved in significant numbers at particular historical moments to various locales, including Africa, Fiji, Trinidad, Great Britain, the United States, Canada, and the Middle East. They arrived in East and South Africa mostly as indentured laborers under British colonial rule after 1860. Later, some came as free immigrants. Mahatma Gandhi himself spent several important formative years in South Africa in his mid-twenties, working as a (British-trained) barrister for the civil rights of local Indians. South Asians still make up a significant ethnic group in the region today (see, e.g., du Toit 1990). In fact, the British used South Asians as indentured laborers in many of their sugar-producing colonies, such as British Guiana, Mauritius, Fiji, and Trinidad. John Kelly (1991) investigates the Fiji Indian community under the British in the early 1900s and its efforts to mount an anticolonial Hindu reform society.

South Asians in Britain come from a wide range of class, regional, and religious backgrounds. As members of the British Commonwealth, South Asians—from the subcontinent as well as from East and South Africa—were earlier entitled to stay and work in the United Kingdom for as long as they wished, and many settled there, particularly during the postwar years when Britain was badly in need of extra labor. In the 1960s and '70s, however, amid public concern over the "race problem" in Britain, the United

Kingdom tightened its immigration laws, making it very difficult for South Asians to migrate to the country unless they had close family ties there (Gardner 1995: 35–50; Hall forthcoming). Ethnic census data were collected for the first time in Britain in 1991. According to these figures, people of Indian ethnicity make up the United Kingdom's largest ethnic group, followed by Black Caribbeans and then Pakistanis (Hall forthcoming). Kathleen Hall in this part explores the complex forging of class, racial, and ethnic identities among second-generation British Sikhs. Paula Richman examines a feminist group of mixed-ethnic South Asian and African Caribbean women in Southall, Greater London, as they work on a creative, progressive performance of the Hindu Ramayana. Bhangra music emerged among British-born South Asian youth in the mid-1980s—with its roots in the persistent beat of the traditional north Indian folk dance known as *bhangra* in Punjab—and since then it has flowed between New York, Delhi, Mumbai, Port-au-Prince, Toronto, and other scenes of the South Asian diaspora as a vibrant form of transnational popular culture (Gopinath 1995; Maira 1999).

Prior to 1965, few South Asians were admitted to the United States, although Punjabi men migrated to rural northern California at the turn of the century (from about 1850 to 1930) to help develop California's agriculture as cheap Asian labor (Leonard 1992).[2] Since 1965, when the United States vastly opened up immigration opportunities for people from Asia, the South Asian American community has grown significantly, and in the 2000 U.S. Census "Asian Indians" reached the status of the fastest-growing Asian American group. Until very recently, the majority of South Asians entered the United States as graduate students and highly educated professionals. Now the class backgrounds of South Asian Americans are becoming somewhat more varied, as less professional kin come to join families here, or as laborers are brought over to work in places like the computer sweatshops of California's Silicon Valley. The South Asian American population is still quite "young," and the scholarly work on South Asian Americans has tended to focus on youth and the ambiguities of second-generation identity (e.g., Narayan, this part; Maira 1999). Over the past decade, however, more and more older South Asians have begun to come to the United States, seeking to join their U.S.-settled children in their old age, striving to sustain their visions of family intimacy across generations and now nations.

Since the 1970s, when oil prices boomed and created a host of new job opportunities in the Middle East, many South Asians from Bangladesh, Sri Lanka, and India have migrated also to countries such as Saudi Arabia and Kuwait in search of employment. Men have ended up primarily in low-level oil industry jobs (see Gardner 1995), while women from Sri Lanka have sought work as domestic housemaids (Gamburd 2000). Refugees from war-torn Sri Lanka have also desperately fled to Canada, England, Germany, and the United States—although they are sometimes bluntly expelled from these destinations and returned back to almost certain torture and death, as Daniel's piece here searingly portrays.

The people who make up the South Asian diaspora come, it is clear, from strikingly diverse national, ethnic, and class backgrounds, and move for very different reasons. Some remain in their new places, and others continue to travel regularly back and forth between South Asia and their diasporic homes. Most, whether or not they travel themselves, continue to creatively combine and rework the images, values, goods, and lifeways from what they see as their two or more cultural traditions, transforming each system, and themselves, in the process, and in so doing also creating rich, novel forms of public culture.

* * *

William Mazzarella opens this part with a look at an instance of mass-media advertising in India, taking place as part of the complex phenomenon of globalization. He describes the highly elaborate 1998 visit of the American "supermodel" Cindy Crawford to Mumbai as "brand ambassadress" for a new line of Omega watches. Mazzarella scrutinizes the processes by which Omega CEOs, via Cindy Crawford and other ceremonial performances, strive to establish a "direct connection" between the global brand (Omega) and local "Indian traditions." In such ways, the globalized commodity images that are pouring into and circulating around South Asia summon local people's desires, and draw them into the institutions of transnational consumerism.

Paula Richman asks what happens when the ancient Hindu epic Ramayana travels abroad? In a London community, a feminist group of South Asian and African Caribbean women staged a Ramayana performance, reflecting a precise moment in the history of South Asian immigration to the United Kingdom. Their innovative performance was meant both to critique the racism, labor conditions, electoral politics, and sexism of their local British society and to connect them and their viewers to South Asian cultural traditions. Through her essay, Richman reflects that diaspora is perhaps "less about 'being in exile from home' and more about being tied to two places."

Kathleen Hall's work is also situated in the United Kingdom. She explores the complex ways second-generation British Sikh youth—born in Britain to upwardly mobile families who grew up in the villages of Punjab or the racially divided cities of East Africa—live their lives "in translation," as they negotiate the conflicting cultural worlds of being both "British" and "Sikh."

Kirin Narayan examines second-generation South Asian American lives through their stories. Concepts of diaspora and displacement often go together, Narayan reflects, but what she is interested in exploring here are the ways second-generation South Asian Americans forge their own "emplacement"—strategies of coming to belong somewhere—through telling stories, about themselves, family folklore, and reworked cultural mythology.

Finally, Daniel's piece powerfully, disturbingly, conveys some of what it can be like when the "everyday" dimensions of life are suddenly—poof—gone—because you're a refugee; when you move from homeland not out of choice but in desperation to stay alive; and when you come to a land you have heard and dreamed of as a place of "freedom" but are faced with forces seemingly as brutal and impervious as those you escaped from—such as gang rape in a detention center and the cold bureaucracy of a U.S. judicial and immigration system.

NOTES

1. See also Appadurai 1996; Breckenridge 1995; and the journal *Public Culture*.
2. See also Dasgupta 1998; Leonard 1997; Lessinger 1995; and Women of South Asian Descent Collective 1993 for portrayals of the lives of South Asian Americans.

Cindy at the Taj: Cultural Enclosure and Corporate Potentateship in an Era of Globalization

William Mazzarella

THE PRESIDENT AND THE SUPERMODEL

Hazy late morning on a South Mumbai Saturday in January 1998. On a column directly facing the imposing entrance to the Taj Hotel, a huge mosaic of freshly cut flowers has not yet begun to wilt in the warm, humid breeze blowing in from Back Bay. In tricolor, the mosaic spells: "The Taj Hotel Extends a Hearty Welcoming to Mr. Jacques Chirac, President of the French Republic." Somewhere inside the marbled corridors and lavish air-conditioned suites of the Taj, the president and his entourage, a handful of ministers and businesspeople, hide from the blinding profusion outside.

A few paces away at the water's edge, overlooking the febrile transactions of tourists, hawkers, pickpockets, and beggars, stands Mumbai's most iconic monument: the Gateway of India, a triumphal arch in the calculatedly hybrid colonial style known as "Indo-Saracenic."[1] Completed and inaugurated in 1924, the Gateway was erected to commemorate the arrival and imperial coronation of an earlier head of state, King George V, in 1911. But on this particular January weekend, it is not the European head of state who will go on to preside over the courtly ritual of imperial incorporation that the British adapted from their Mughal predecessors, the *durbar* (Cohn 1983). Instead, that honor will go to a rather different foreign dignitary, who is at this moment also somewhere inside the Taj: the American "supermodel" Cindy Crawford. Both Chirac and Crawford are, in different registers, attempting to establish their own gateways to India. But there is no doubt where the center of attention lies. Even the travel-bleary perma-smoking French reporters who arrived with the Chirac entourage are now falling over themselves to get admitted to the "Cindy Shindig."

Both the president and the supermodel have flown to Mumbai on the wings of a complex phenomenon known as "globalization." In 1991 the Congress government of P. V. Narasimha Rao inaugurated a series of sweeping reforms that helped the brisk rhetoric of "liberalization" and "free markets" to have its brutal way with the increasingly sclerotic discourse of the Nehruvian planned economy.[2] But the austere rhetoric of structural adjustment came accompanied by its riotous alter ego: a veritable carnival of globalized commodity images, hailing Indian desires from television screens, glossy magazine spreads, and metropolitan billboards. Against this background, Chirac and Crawford now appear in Mumbai, seat of Lakshmi, goddess of wealth, as the twin *avataras*[3] of the new global capitalism. Each commands their own specialist public interpreters: Chirac's official meetings and "policy line" will be the subject of "serious" current affairs reportage, while Crawford's progress as "brand ambassadress" for a new line of Omega watches will be rendered breathlessly in the "fluffy" lifestyle sections and gossip columns of the weekend press.

It would be easy to assume that the Crawford/Omega show is a kind of smokescreen; a deployment of seductive consumerist spectacle intended to divert critical attention away from the trade agreements and negotiations that purportedly constitute the "real" process of globalization. But Crawford, I will argue, is far more than a sweetener for the bitter pill of transnational corporate machination. Rather, she is the focal point for a series of rituals—including promotional performances and mass-media advertising—whose purpose is to achieve *cultural enclosure.* If we imagine publicly circulating narratives and symbols as a kind of common property —a "symbolic commons," perhaps—then the process of establishing a brand identity through promotional ritual can be interpreted as an attempt by a corporation to proclaim exclusive ownership of a chunk of this common property.[4] By associating particular meanings with the insignia of their brand, a corporation hopes to sharpen the identity, and thus the value, of their offerings. But as I shall argue, this process is also aimed at managing several tensions that are inherent to globalizing consumerism. There is the tension between the populist tone of the language of consumer empowerment and the paternalistic, almost regal stance of corporate brands. There is also the tension between the transcendent glamour of brand imagery and the prosaic texture of the everyday situations that marketing attempts to infiltrate. Finally, there is the tension between the cultural location of specific groups of consumers and the global profile of the brand. In order to see how these tensions play out in practice, let us step inside the hotel.

INSIDE THE BALLROOM

The Crystal Ballroom at the Taj has been carefully prepared for the occasion. At one end of the long hall stands a low stage, flanked by a large video screen and a dark blue backdrop featuring the Omega logo. Along the left side of the room, long tables bearing product displays have been installed. Television and still photographers from the media are, for the moment, restricted to an area at the rear. Across the center of the floor stand dozens of round tables bearing lacy white tablecloths and vases of red and white roses. Potbellied press hacks, a smattering of actors, models, and mid-level celebrities, and a large contingent of expensively coifed and brightly manicured middle-aged European women are gradually taking their seats. Skirting the walls and darting between tables, thickset dark-suited Omega security men mutter into cell phones, beams of light bouncing off their shaven heads.

The first part of the show revolves around establishing the credentials of the Omega brand. Dramaturgically, it unfolds like this: the image-world of the brand is offered as internally coherent, yet nevertheless lacking the crucial component that the emergence of Cindy Crawford will provide. On the basis of this preliminary work, Cindy Crawford's eventual appearance appears as both a narrative continuation of the story so far and the presence that will overcome the absence at the heart of the brand.

This is what happens: the Omega CEO, Nicolas Hayek, is introduced to the crowd by a sprightly female VJ (video jockey) from the Mumbai wing of the Hong Kong–based music television station Channel V. To the mild yet palpable disappointment of the assembled, Hayek only deigns to make a virtual appearance by video. An awkward, bearded middle-aged man sitting behind a heavy wooden desk somewhere in Europe, he offers the audience the assurance (perhaps paradoxically, under these markedly mediated circumstances) that he and Omega are "so proud to be here with you in India." Abstractedly, somewhat in the manner of a starship commander from a distant galaxy, he adds: "We are proud because we love your country and we love Indians. You are a warm-hearted people, with a great civilization, spirituality, and technological achievement."

Disappointment is blended with confusion, as Hayek preemptively demands: "Why in India? Because India *is* the future. To think about the future we have to be in India." Whether India "*is* the future" in a world-historical sense or, more prosaically, in terms of Omega's continued search for profitable new markets,[5] Hayek has done his bit, and his countenance now gives way to a narrative video presentation which chronicles the heroic rise of Omega from the humble solitary efforts of a nineteenth-century Swiss watchmaker to the dizzying futuristic heights of manned space travel. Having thus established the diachronic dimensions of the brand, the video defers to the VJ: "After that journey into the past, let's now resume with Omega *today*." A third clip ensues, this time extending the brand synchronically, sketching its various contemporary faces and attitudes. The audience is offered a rapid sequence of lifestyle vignettes, each with its own soundtrack, each introduced with explanatory titles: "Omega is Youth." "Omega is Timing." "Omega is Golf . . . Film . . . Apollo13 . . . Bond . . . Space." Still, apparently, there is a gap in the brand, a gap that can evidently only be filled by the physical embodiment of its meaning, because just after the video declares "Omega is *Emotion* . . . " the screen abruptly fades to black. This juncture heralds the moment in the ritual that calls for the presence of its human protagonist.

But before Cindy Crawford can actually appear, two more operations must be performed. The first legitimates the relationship between Omega and Crawford. This step in the proceedings is marked by a deep self-consciousness about the artificiality of commercial endorsement. Crawford must not only be portrayed as *inherently* suited to represent the new Omega line, but also as *actively* and *genuinely* engaged with the product. One of the "suits" that has until now been hiding in the shadows behind the VJ steps forward and is introduced as Michel Sofisti, the president of Omega. "The communication of a product is all about emotion," he tells the crowd. "We do this through our ambassadress; through her personality, she conveys the emotions that the product is all about." What, then, are these emotions? Much as Sofisti's characterization suggests that the product contains its own personality which is then "conveyed" by Crawford, it appears that the product's personality resides in a conceptual space that can only be realized through its association with her. As Omega's publicity puts it: "When we began designing the My Choice watch, which needed to embody elegance, beauty, style, sophistication and excellence, we knew we wanted input from a woman who exudes these same values and qualities. For us, the only woman to do this is Cindy Crawford."[6]

But the relationship is not just a matter of what Sir James Frazer once called "sympathetic magic," an efficacious resonance between similar entities (Frazer 1925). It is, so the press release tells us, no mere "endorsement" but rather a "partnership," an "authentic" relationship. To this end, the promotional materials handed to each member of the Mumbai audience include expensively reproduced photographs of Crawford visiting Omega's Swiss headquarters, famous face attentively inclined at the drawing board, index finger interrogating design details. The relationship thus comes full circle: following Crawford's "input," she no longer simply "conveys the emotions that the product is all about." Rather, "the fine crafting of the My Choice reflects the charm of Cindy's personality." At this point, commercial subject and object seem inextricably intertwined, each amplifying yet also feeding off the other in endless regress.

The crowd is growing restless; after all, they haven't struggled through the smoggy thoroughfares of South Mumbai to gaze at a series of Euro-suits. But still one mediation remains. Before Crawford can appear in the flesh, she must appear on video, again subordinated to the Omega brand narrative, in this case playing the starring role in the global Constellation My Choice television commercial. The clip finds Crawford pouting and preening in front of a small mirror, while inserting the men's version of the watch into a small white gift box. Hair bouncing, she then descends a massive marble staircase (uncannily similar to the one just outside the Crystal Ballroom) and bursts impetuously into what appears to be an extremely select (and, until this point, inviolably male) boardroom meeting: all square jaws, gleaming surfaces, and frowning concentration. An executive looks up, transfixed by the vision that is Cindy. She slides the gift box across the sleek table; he opens it as she lands in his lap. All the while she gazes coyly and conspiratorially into the camera, as a purring voice-over concludes: "Omega—*my* choice."

Model, product, and company thus interwoven in a shining visual fabric, the woman herself appears from behind a curtain at the precise moment that her video image fades from view. The illusion is one of perfect continuity between screen persona and present being, as if Crawford has simply stepped right out of an indeterminate global space of glamour into the concrete coordinates of the here and now. And indeed she *does* seem startlingly indistinguishable from her photographic alter ego. In no small part, this is an effect of her deeply stylized mode of movement and self-projection. As she minces to the lip of the stage, the press photographers, who until this point have been sullenly slouching at the back of the room, surge forward in a frenzy of popping flashbulbs. With practiced, seemingly automatic ease, Cindy (for now she is fully in character) arches, smiles, and moves through a sequence of poses, each held for a few seconds.

On one level, the entire show so far has been structured as a narrative-buildup, preparing the way for, and culminating in, Crawford's physical appearance. At the same time, this preparation has at every step been carefully designed to ensure that the spectacular power of Cindy's actuality will not overwhelm the narratives of the Omega brand, but will rather work to enhance it, infuse it with energy and palpability. To this end, the audience has been offered a series of discrete and reified tableaux, each circumscribing the celebrity of Cindy within the framework of the brand: "Cindy and Omega," the various "faces of Omega," "Omega and India," "Cindy in Geneva." Now here is the latest installment, "Cindy in the Flesh," a tableau that is itself subdivided into a series of discrete profiles, poses, and attitudes.[7] So deliberate and yet instinctive is Cindy's performance that it causes her momentarily to forget herself. As Sofisti answers the VJ's questions, Cindy seeks to maximize the publicity value of these few expensive minutes by switching into her string of poses, this time in a seated variation, making sure to bring her My Choice–encircled arm into the camera viewfinders. When the VJ turns to Cindy, her freeze-frame rhythm has become locked in to the stroboscopic inferno of flashbulbs. Seconds pass before she comes to with a start: "Oh! I'm just modeling while he's talking."

The tensions underlying the ritual become more evident once the floor is opened for questions from the assembled reporters. Most of these are harmless and banal, obeying the tacit feel-good protocol of the performative genre: "Cindy, how do Indian beauties compare with Western beauties?" "Cindy, is there anything in life that you still want to achieve?" "Cindy, do you like India?" These are answered smoothly and in bland kind: "The [Indian] people are wonderful ... such warmth ... there's just *life!*" But one reporter is more curious about the structure of the spectacle itself. He asks why Omega selected Crawford as its "brand ambassadress." "Obviously it's just business," comes the deceptively self-deprecating reply. "They think I'll help them sell more watches. I mean, it's not because they like me!" At this, Sofisti fidgets uncomfortably, and jumps in with a mirthless chuckle: "Well! Of course that's only part of it!"

This apparently innocuous exchange is beginning to point to the heart of the exercise, namely the *collective* elaboration of a set of meanings and impressions that can then be "seized" by the brand and turned into added value and, therefore, premium prices. And yet the interlocutors, celebrity as well as reporters, continue to speak as if these meanings are not being collectively forged but rather exist as objective and inherent properties of Crawford, the brands she endorses, and the products they mark. This is entirely in keeping with the terms of the spectacle so far: Sofisti has, after all, taken pains to explain why and how Cindy and Omega "fit" each other, and how their marriage is based on this compatibility.

Crawford elaborates her policy: she only endorses brands that she likes, brands, furthermore, that "go together." Before she mentions specific names (Revlon and Pepsi) she checks with Sofisti whether these other brand indices may be allowed to intrude, even if only in name, upon the spectacular space that Omega is so expensively and laboriously constructing. (The company president nods with judicious magnanimity.) But the inquisitive journalist remains unsatisfied and persists: what is the logic of her decision to endorse these particular brands? Crawford's apparently improvised answer locates the required coherence in the space of her own celebrity: "Well, I guess that I build up fans. And then those fans want to buy a part of me. With these products they can." Her lone interrogator jumps in, still assuming essential properties, but nevertheless catching the implication of Crawford's statement: "So instead of the product being the star, *you* are the star?" Crawford, by now irritated at his tenacity, snaps back: "I need to use the attention that's focused on me, and lend it to the product." A lull follows the mounting tension of the exchange, as apparently less pointed questions are submitted. But another journalist soon picks up on his colleague's thread, and follows it to its logical conclusion: "Cindy, what is the image that you're trying to project?"

Silence. For a few crucial seconds, Crawford seems entirely stumped. Sofisti glances discreetly at his Omega. So far, the exchange has perpetuated the illusion that the meanings that are being dramatized in the name of Omega (and in the person of Cindy Crawford) are inherent and respective properties of the brand, the products, and the supermodel. Analogously, this last question imputes an intentionality to Crawford that mistakes the long-term processes of public cultural accretion and negotiation that have given rise to the referent system we know as "Cindy Crawford" for the human being seated on the stage.[8] And indeed, in the service of the spectacle, Crawford is obliged to assume that she *is* the creative agent behind her own public image. After the relentless visuality of the foregoing portions of the ritual, it is as if not the audience but Crawford herself is suddenly blindfolded, tentatively exploring the outlines of a "self" that is familiar to everyone but her. Only minutes earlier, basking with practiced ease in the general gaze, there was more than a touch of noblesse oblige to her depiction of sending out little packages of herself in the products she endorsed. Now, however, a tone of American populist humility emerges: "Hmmm . . . I don't know. I'm a real person," she begins. Picking up steam, she ventures: "I'm young. Modern. I'm a businesswoman." The conventionality of kinship is evoked: "I'm just like my sisters, really. They're in different professions, but our approach to life, our *professionalism*, is the same." In homage to the universalizing metaphor for consumerist aspiration, the care of the body, she concludes: "I like to work out."

Here, then, we can see cultural enclosure in action. In a staged ritual setting, generally circulating symbolic elements are seized upon and presented as inherent and perhaps even exclusive properties of the actors, both human and inanimate, celebrity and brand. At the same time, there is the attempt to conjure both hierarchical distance *and* populist appeal. Cindy is both unattainably singular and glamorous *and* at the same time made intelligible through a very prosaic set of references ("I'm a real person . . . I'm just like my sisters really . . . I like to work out"). To the extent that this double identity rubs off on Omega the implication will be that the brand provides a conduit between the prosaic life of the consumer and a rarefied world of transnational glamour. All it takes to follow Cindy through the looking glass and back into the sublime world of the ad is the willingness to be "professional."

It might seem that the proceedings have only made the vaguest of nods to the fact that they are taking place in India. As we shall see, however, Crawford's performance takes place within a larger attempt to gauge the emotional and commercial value of local references. This is true of all global brands. But Omega will take the further step of drawing upon a specifically Indian ritual form to carve out its own gateway to the subcontinent.

A NEW INCORPORATION

Cindy Crawford and Jacques Chirac both arrive in Mumbai by way of Sahar International Airport. To that extent, the Gateway of India, overlooking the docks, is no longer in a position to welcome them. Nevertheless, the Gateway still prefigures the ritual conclusion of Crawford's progress. And the next day in Delhi, it becomes clear that the event in the Crystal Ballroom was only the prelude to a full-fledged, if unwitting, ceremony of imperialist cross-dressing. Just as King George once proceeded from his landing in Bombay to a spectacular ritual of symbolic incorporation in the new imperial capital, so Crawford will, on the Sunday evening, hold her own Delhi durbar.

Crawford's job vis-à-vis Omega is not only to "use the attention that's focused on [her] and lend it to the brand." It is also to act as the symbolic figurehead of a larger ritual of corporate potentateship; Omega, like many other international brands, will invoke the powers of the kings and emperors of old against the authority of the contemporary nation-state, presenting itself as the source and guarantor of much (if not all) that is excellent in earthly life.[9] The durbar, as Cohn (1983) explains, originated as a Mughal ritual of kingship, in which subordinate princes and dignitaries were "incorporated" into the emperor's system of rule. The means of this incorporation was the exchange of symbolically charged precious objects: the person to be incorporated offered gold coins and, in some cases, other valuables. The emperor would reciprocate with a counteroffering that typically took the form of articles of clothing which, when worn by the recipient, literally incorporated him. Starting in the early nineteenth century, the British in India adapted the durbar for their own ends, but tended to impose a narrowly economic calculation on the central act of exchange.

By deploying, in its turn, the form of the durbar, Omega is being both more literal and more culturally calculating about it than most of its competitors. Omega's press release, unsurprisingly, makes no mention of the fact that the British before them sought to appropriate the durbar as a ritual of rule. Rather, it seeks to establish the corporation as the conduit of a direct connection between "Indian tradition" and contemporary Indian glamour: "The two-day celebration [the Omega launch, that is] will culminate in a *Commemorative Durbar*, a procession of horse-drawn carriages bearing Indian royalty and VIP guests from politics, economy and fashion, with all the pomp and splendor of a traditional durbar.[. . .] Historically, the most spectacular durbars were held in the 17th century by the Indian Mogul emperor Shah Jahan, builder of the Taj Mahal [given the location of the Mumbai launch, another thematic tie-in], one of the seven wonders of the world" (Omega 1997, original emphasis).

Omega's self-presentation as the worthiest custodian of its Indian consumer-subjects' interests coincides with the argument that has long been propounded by local advocates of consumer-led "liberalization": that consumerism represents a far more sensitive and efficient mechanism for satisfying the needs of the population than the state-socialist planned economy (see Mazzarella 2001 and forthcoming for extended discussions). The corporation reminds the public that its ties with India predate the independent nation-state itself ("Omega and India—a successful partnership since 1929," proclaims one press release). Portraying itself as going to extreme lengths to maintain customer-subject relations in face of the arbitrary impositions of the government, Omega underscores that it has maintained after-sales service for its Indian customers even during those years when the sale of foreign watches was entirely banned.[10]

The corporation's solicitude for its consumer-constituents' welfare and needs is, once more according to the ancient formula, matched by more public acts of munificence. Sponsorship, like all giving, creates complex relationships: on the one hand, recipients gain publicity, prominence, and recognition. On the other, the donor benefits from an association with the moral and/or aesthetic qualities of the recipients. Either way, the patron is established as a custodian and guardian of particular fields of meaning and cultural practice, which increasingly seem possible only through the patron's grace and favor.

Alongside the launch of My Choice, Omega announces that it will be donating $15,000 to the Archaeological Survey of India and $30,000 to Mother Teresa's Missionaries of Charity. The golden wand also touches NIFT (the National Institute of Fashion Technology) in Delhi, where Omega establishes a series of scholarships. Later in the year, Omega will distribute "Awards for Excellence" to Indian celebrity couples; in the category "Lifetime Achievement," Bollywood legend Amitabh Bachchan and his wife Jaya are honored, while the "Young Achievers" citation is bestowed upon fashion models Arjun Rampal and Meher Jessia, a former Miss India. As Cohn (1983) shows, the British quite consciously used the durbar to elaborate a symbolic hierarchy within which "Indian" motifs and signifiers were at once included, highlighted, and subordinated. Something analogous takes place in Omega's scheme of sponsorship. What is more, the degree to which this sponsorship grapples with overtly "Indian" markers is tightly related to the political economy of the corporation's presence in the country.

As long as the import barriers remain such that only the upper end of (Omega parent company) SMH's product lines can be sold in India, the symbolic emphasis of the company's promotional activities remains focused upon facilitating high-end Indian consumers' access to a global model of excellence which has little to do with specific geographical or cultural markers. The NIFT scholarships, for instance, include trips for two graduates to Omega's Geneva headquarters. The awards presented to the Bachchans and to Rampal and Jessia later in the year, on the other hand, mark the beginnings of a gradual shift toward an association between the Omega brand and contemporary Indian public culture. Even here, however, there is a careful attempt to emphasize the transnational credentials of these Indian honorees: the Bachchans are read a congratulatory message from director Bernardo Bertolucci, while the international experience and standing of Jessia and Rampal is underlined (IPAN 1998).[11]

In an important way, however, the rituals of potentateship available to Omega and its contemporaries are quite different from those once available to the erstwhile empire. Cohn suggests that the British always struggled with an ambiguity at the heart of their adaptation of the durbar: the problematic relationship between the affective politics of spectacle and the bureaucratic rationality that officially legitimated British rule. There were two aspects to this dilemma. First, like Cindy Crawford's appearance on behalf of Omega, the durbar provided a ritually delimited forum for the visual and physical *embodiment* of an otherwise rather abstract power. Second, the durbar allowed for the symbolic *subsumption* of the Indian, allowing at once the appearance of the sovereign's body as the capacious container of all local differences *and* as a locally legitimated source of authority.

At first sight, it might appear that the tension between the affective and bureaucratic politics of sovereignty has, in 1998, simply been resolved by establishing a division of labor: the supermodel takes care of the spectacle, the president represents the apex of an administrative apparatus. What such an explanation misses is the way in which the institutions of transnational consumerism, not least the commercial media, have enabled consumer brand marketing to combine rationalization and spectacle in a powerful, if always unstable, alliance. The site at which these two modes of rule intersect is the brand. As a property of the corporation, the integrity of the brand is jealously guarded and assiduously managed by professional experts, contemporary heirs to ancient priesthoods. At the same time, through its name, logo, and visual signs, embossed on mass-produced objects and disseminated through media networks worldwide, the brand operates as a kind of insignia of value, decorating and incorporating those loyal retainers who, in turn, "consume" it.[12]

In its time, the Gateway of India denoted not simply the intended majesty of British rule, but also its consciousness of the need to define and control borders and boundaries. To be sure, the political boundaries of the colonized domain, but also the boundaries that articulated the symbolic and cultural relationship between the metropolis and the periphery. Architecture was, on one level, a highly tangible and often spectacular exercise in supervised hybridization, a process of cultural admixture in which the colonizing culture, as befitting its lordly universalism, could be seen to encompass and contain that of the colonized.

The globalization of mass consumerism is certainly not reducible to any simple notion of "cultural imperialism," at least insofar as that term is understood as cultural homogenization. But that is not to say that the structures of promotional practice are not deeply indebted to far older techniques of incorporation and cultural management. To that extent, consumer brands are the new gateways. They are the focal points for an attempted coordination of the collective cultural imagination, encouraging local audiences to aspire to a passage through their portals, and promising global corporate capital an entry point into the hearts and minds of millions.[13]

ACKNOWLEDGMENTS

I would like to thank the Social Science Research Council and the American Institute of Indian Studies for providing the material and practical support that made my research in India possible. I would also like to thank Janet Fine for facilitating my participation in the "Cindy Shindig," Jennifer Cole for her always-astute commentaries, and Sarah Lamb and Diane Mines for their excellent editorial suggestions.

NOTES

1. The Indo-Saracenic style was developed in the late nineteenth century, and is predominantly associated with British colonial architects like Sir Swinton Jacob, Major Charles Mant, Henry Irwin, John Begg, and the architect of the Gateway of India as well as the Prince of Wales Museum, George Wittet. The Indo-Saracenic look was explicitly designed as a dramatization and legitimation of British rule, suggesting an incorporation of "Indian" (actually, particularly Mughal) styles under a Gothic vision of the European. Write Lang et al.: "Indo-Saracenic architecture was an effort to provide a visible symbol of an aspect of British policy in India—to show a sense of belonging to India" (1997: 99).

2. In the summer of 1991, the newly elected Congress government, faced with a dire foreign exchange crisis, inaugurated a fairly comprehensive program of economic deregulation, particularly of previously stringent barriers to foreign trade. For the purposes of this article, one of the most important results of the reforms was the sudden presence of hundreds of foreign brands on Indian shelves, television screens, and billboards. A variety of perspectives on the reforms of this period may be found in Bhagwati and Srinivasan (1993), Drèze and Sen (1996), Joshi and Little (1996), and Patnaik (1994).

3. In Hinduism, *avatara* refers to a specific manifestation or incarnation of a deity. So, for example, Krishna is typically acknowledged to be one of the avataras of Vishnu. A useful elementary presentation of this and related issues may be found in Flood (1996).

4. My thinking on the corporate control of public signification owes a great deal to Coombe (1998).

5. Later, press reports will offer more concretely instrumental justifications for the company's presence in India; a board member of Omega's parent company, SMH, tells reporters that "SMH judges the potential of a market on mainly two accounts: the standard of living in the cities and [the] attraction citizens have for gold and other jewelry. The second parameter was found [to be] strongest in India, China and Italy as compared to England and the Scandinavian countries" (Bansal 1998).

6. This quotation appears on Cindy Crawford's official website, at www. cindy.com/about/omega/index.html. Further promotional material may be located at Omega's own website, www.omega.ch/home_quad.html.

7. Roland Marchand (1985) introduced the concept of "tableaux" into the analysis of consumer goods advertising. He proceeded to assemble a copiously documented account of the construction of a "soul" for American consumer goods corporations (Marchand 1998), which shares some themes with my reflections in the present piece on the corporation as potentate.

8. I borrow the term "referent system" from Judith Williamson's seminal 1978 study of the semiotics of advertising.

9. Erik Barnouw (1978) is best known for using the term "potentate" to describe corporations. While I am indebted to his analysis of the intervention of American business into public life, my own discussion here obviously elaborates the metaphor of kingship both in relation to the figure of the *durbar* and in order to make sense of the management of meaning through ritual.

10. Still, a company so clearly focused on the "prestige segment" of Indian consumers will, insofar as it is attempting to set itself up as a fulfiller of Indian needs, encounter a kind of legitimation crisis vis-à-vis a democratically elected government that can always claim to cater to all citizens, rich and poor alike. Omega responds to this problem in two ways. First, it blames the Indian government's restrictive import policy for the fact that it is unable to sell any watch worth less than Rs. 35,000 (about U.S. $830, before retail margins, at 1998 exchange rates) in India. Second, and more interestingly, the corporation attempts to transfigure the exclusivity that marks its pricing and brand image as an "excellence" that is, through "aspiration," potentially available to all. The publicity distributed by Beautiful Boulevard, the flashy South Mumbai boutique that will retail My Choice, similarly figures its offering of these expensive accessories as, relatively speaking, a globalizing move that is at the same time democratizing. Whereas customers would previously have had to journey abroad to acquire the likes of Omega, Beautiful Boulevard aims to "provide Indians with a wide range of world class products without having to leave the shores of India." Indeed, something of a reversal of imperial looting is implied, as the store "has brought home to India the treasures of the world."

11. When the younger Hindi film superstar Shah Rukh Khan is made the new Indian "brand ambassador" for Omega in the Spring of 1999, the announcement is read by many commentators as proof that transnationals have to adapt their advertising to local markets (Skaria 1999, but see Mazzarella, forthcoming, for a critique of this discourse). Few notice the fact that Khan's appointment coincides with Omega being allowed, by virtue of the 1999 budget, to sell much cheaper— and therefore more widely accessible—product lines in India. Nor does Khan in any sense "take over" Omega's brand image as a whole; rather, the local resonances that he adds to the brand, at a particular set of price points, are still subordinated to more "global" faces higher up the status scale.

12. One might illustrate this idea of brand names and/or logos as a kind of insignia simply by pointing to the ways in which they become constitutive parts of goods that are conspicuously worn on consumers' bodies. But perhaps the most extreme example is that of Harley-Davidson motorcycle enthusiasts, who commonly have the corporate insignia tattooed onto their flesh (Aaker 1995).

13. I would emphasize that the question of how "end consumers" actually *respond* to the narratives and images purveyed in promotional rituals is a different matter altogether. Foregrounding "creative" and/or "counterhegemonic" practices of consumption has become a cottage industry in anthropology, not least

since Michel de Certeau's (1984) emphasis on the politics of everyday life was imported into the discipline. However, I would caution against the assumption that such practices have any simple or direct impact on the way promotional rituals are produced and arranged, despite the lip service that marketing practitioners necessarily pay to understanding "the consumer" (see Mazzarella, forthcoming, for a more detailed discussion of this point). For thinking about these matters, we could do far worse than to bring the much-misunderstood writings of Max Horkheimer and Theodor Adorno (Adorno 1991; Horkheimer and Adorno 1972 [1947]) into dialectical tension with the more recent literature on consumer "resistance."

A Diaspora Ramayana in Southall

Paula Richman

Editor's note: The Ramayana is one of Hinduism's oldest and best-loved epic stories. It probably began even as early as 500 B.C.E. as an oral story, but over the centuries has been retold, rewritten, televised, and acted out (theatrical versions are called Ramlila) *in many different languages in many different versions. Richman's article presents us with one such version, what might be called a "postcolonial" version. The story, in briefest synopsis, goes something like this: The King of Ayodhya is childless, but makes a sacrifice from which are born three sons, each to a different wife. Rama is the eldest. Because of jealousy and strife in the palace, Rama's brother Bharata is named king upon their father's death, and Rama—the rightful heir to the throne—is sent into a fourteen-year exile. With him go his wife, Sita, and his loyal youngest brother, Lakshmana. While in exile, Rama defeats and banishes many evil creatures. Finally, with the aid of his monkey friend Hanuman, Rama vanquishes even the evil Ravana, a many-headed demon king who would wreak havoc in the universe and who has lusted after and finally kidnapped Sita. Having saved the kingdom and Sita from the demons, and having lived out his exile, Rama returns triumphantly to Ayodhya, where he reigns as a just and dharmic king. In a controversial episode, not part of all versions, Rama fears that Sita's chastity and purity may have been sullied by Ravana. Doubting Sita, unjustly, he allows her to jump into a fire. But she emerges unscathed—so pure is she—and they rule together as king and queen.*

A longer version of this essay originally appeared in the *Journal of the American Academy of Religion* 67, no. 1 (winter 1999). Reprinted with permission.

What happens when the Ramlila travels abroad? On 19 October 1979, a feminist group of South Asian and African Caribbean women in Southall, Greater London, staged a Ramlila that reflects a precise moment in the history of South Asian immigration to the United Kingdom. The women who produced the play, members of the Southall Black Sisters (SBS),[1] did so to help defray legal costs of friends arrested when they participated in a protest against the neo-Nazi National Front Party. SBS incorporated into their rendition of the Ramlila humorous commentary with a topical slant. In doing so, they linked events portrayed in the performance to the racism, labor conditions, electoral politics, and sexism they encountered in everyday life.

Like traditional Ramlilas, the performance ended with the death of Ravana, King of the Demons, but the SBS Ravana was unique. He sported a huge mask composed of ten heads, upon each of which was drawn a person or symbol that represented an aspect of immigrant life in Britain. Some heads bore pictures of conservative political leaders, while others carried symbols of racism, such as the insignia of the British riot police. The Ramlila performance culminated with fireworks to celebrate the destruction of Ravana, to the accompaniment of cheers from the audience. The Ramlila's dramatic structure, casting practices, and interpretation of Ravana tell us a great deal about the historical moment of its performance.

They also reveal some broader insights about how a religious text can migrate from South Asia to Britain, retain its formal contours, express diverse aspects of the diaspora experience, and continue to be part of the multifaceted Ramayana tradition. SBS produced a Ramlila of great creativity, reflecting in unique ways the specific experiences of those onstage and many of those in the audience, but it also contains elements that are in consonance with what recent scholarship has revealed about the Ramayana tradition in South Asia. In SBS's incorporation of women's perspectives, it echoes aspects of women's folk-song traditions in South Asia (Narayana Rao 1991; Nilsson 2000). Its inclusion of topical humor is part of a long tradition of linking improvisatory commentary to local events (e.g., Blackburn 1996; GoldbergBelle 1989). Its skillful use of multiple frames enables characters to provide metanarrative about themselves and the story (Hess 1993, 2000; Shulman 2000). In short, the SBS created a Ramlila in keeping with long-established trends within Ramayana tradition.

In the past, Western and Indian scholars have paid most attention to authoritative tellings of *Ramkatha* (Rama's story), especially the one attributed to Valmiki (Goldman 1984: 1,6; Pollock 1993: 263). More recently, however, scholars have increasingly turned their attention to oral renditions (Blackburn 1996), commentarial concerns (Hess 2000), and transformations shaped by print culture (Narayana Rao 2000). Such studies have demonstrated the range, diversity, and vitality of non-dominant tellings of Ramkatha. A close examination of the SBS Ramlila reveals a great deal about the capaciousness of the Ramayana tradition; the SBS has recounted and recast the story in relation to their locality, its social structures of dominance, and their concerns about gender.

Recent research has highlighted how many tellings of Rama's story question hierarchies of power (e.g., Freeman 2000; Lutgendorf 2000; Richman 1991; Lamb 1991). Interrogation of gendered representation proves particularly salient in the SBS Ramlila. Unique in its casting practices, its mix of Panjabi and English, and its vision of Ravana, the SBS Ramlila lies squarely in the midst of a Ramayana tradition that is diverse, inventive, and open to questions.

MIGRATION AND SBS

Most early South Asian immigrants to Southall left the subcontinent soon after Partition (1947), arriving in Greater London in the late 1950s. Primarily Sikhs or Hindus and mainly Panjabi speakers, many came from the peasant proprietor class whose members had lost land, savings, and security through the dislocation that accompanied Partition. Upon arrival most were able to obtain jobs only at factories in or near Southall at low pay with long hours and few benefits (Brah 1996; Fryer 1984; Visram 1986; Dhanjal 1976; Lee 1972). In the late 1960s and early 1970s, a new group of South Asians from East Africa arrived in Southall, bringing with them their middle-class urban experience as well as skills as owners of small businesses, enriching the Southall community in many ways (Bhachu 1985; Brah 1996; Institute of Race Relations 1981). Soon after their arrival, however, immigration came under explicit attack by the National Front (NF), a party which presented itself as protecting the "racial purity" of England (Taylor 1978; Hanna 1974; Nugent 1976).

The NF's announcement that it would hold an election meeting on 23 April 1979, in Southall, was the first in a set of events leading to the SBS Ramlila. Just two days before the planned meeting, an NF leader called upon members to emulate the heroes of H. G. Wells's *The Time Machine* and defeat "dark-skinned, hook-nosed dwarfs" (Dummett 1980: 190). Not surprisingly, a large group of protesters from Southall and elsewhere in the country showed up to contest the views of the NF. The presence of the police that day was large as well, with highly visible representation from the Special Patrol Group police, a corps of crack riot police. In the violence that ensued during the meeting and protest, hundred of protesters were injured, one man died, and about seven hundred were arrested. While "mainstream" English-language newspapers such as the *Daily Telegraph* reported the event with the headline "Asian Fury at Election Meeting" and the subheading "40 Police Hurt in Protest over National Front" (24 May 1979), a local newspaper, *Punjab Times*, argued that people of Southall had been reduced to "the status of a British Imperial Colony from that of a town of free citizens" (1 May 1979).

In the aftermath of the event, SBS met to discuss how they should respond. The group contained women of South Asian descent born in Britain, women with South Asian parents who had grown up in East Africa, and women of African Caribbean descent born in Britain or the Caribbean. The Asian community in Southall was larger than the African Caribbean one at that time and each group had different pre-immigration histories. Yet SBS women found that their roots in colonized countries and their current experience of racism and sexism in Britain gave them many shared experiences, issues, and hopes.[2] The founding members of SBS ranged from teenage schoolgirls to young postgraduates and working women.

Earlier, SBS had undertaken a series of community projects to improve the lives of girls and women in Southall and worked with other organizations to combat racism in Greater London. They also staffed an advice center on Saturdays at the Southall Rights Building, volunteering their time to give information about legal issues and immigration laws, as well as providing support to women experiencing difficulties in their families or relationships. Heretofore, male elders and community leaders within the South Asian community had counseled wives to use strategies of avoidance and compliance when dealing with domestic violence and other gender-related issues. SBS felt that women needed advice from other women, especially ones without a vested interest in maintaining the status quo within families.

Some male members of the Southall community greeted the formation of SBS with suspicion. A few saw SBS as troublemakers who threatened the stability of the family structure, especially because they helped women who fled their homes because of domestic violence. Other men felt that the South Asian community should speak as a single group, and SBS would undermine that. Some worried this new group might later siphon funds away from established social service organizations or draw support away from such groups as the Southall Youth Movement, founded in 1976 to combat racist attacks. Nonetheless, SBS-initiated projects, such as picketing the "Miss Southall" beauty contest, won them support in the larger community. Feminist goals in this case had paralleled those of some male-dominated groups who had earlier been suspicious of SBS. After the events on 23 April in Southall, SBS chose a Ramlila as their means to express their solidarity with those arrested and with the larger Southall community.

CONCEPTUALIZING A RAMLILA

Among the stories that hold a special place in South Asian culture, SBS chose Ramkatha because its narrative resources helped them to dramatize their ideal relationship to their community and to express their defiance of British racism. Rama and Sita show their deep commitment to virtue when they save the reputation of Rama's father for truthfulness by going into forest exile. During their stay there, the demon Ravana tricks Rama into leaving Sita alone and then abducts her. After an extended search Rama finds Sita, defeats Ravana in battle, and rescues his wife. This narrative has long been dramatized in South Asia.

Several factors shaped the SBS decision to perform a Ramlila in response to the incidents of 23 April 1979. First, as an anti-racist group, they sought some form of symbolic action that would make visible their outrage about police brutality against the black population of Southall. A benefit performance whose proceeds would be donated to the Southall Legal Defense Fund, an organization helping to defray the legal costs of those charged in the 23 April conflict, seemed an appropriate project. Although the SBS realized that the performance might not raise a large amount of money, they viewed the benefit as a material contribution and an expression of solidarity.

Second, they wanted to undertake a project that would demonstrate publicly their connection to the cultural traditions of their community, as understood by their elders. Such an event would show that criticisms of SBS as divisive to the community were unwarranted. SBS chose a Ramlila because of its link with Divali, a major South Asian festival of lights long popular in north India, in which Hindus commemorated the destruction of a demon.[3] Before communalism in India became as pronounced as it did later, lighting lamps and sharing sweets with one's Hindu and non-Hindu neighbors was common at Divali in many parts of the subcontinent. SBS chose a Ramlila at Divali because of its traditional connections with unity, celebration, and good fortune.

Third, the story of Ravana's destruction resonated strongly with recent events. Ramlila celebrates the victory of good over evil, dramatizing a tale of oppressive rule destroyed by the perseverance of those committed to virtue. At a symbolic level, it could be seen as paralleling Southall resistance to abuse from the British state, and might comfort those recovering from the physical and psychological wounds of policy brutality in April.

Finally, the shared feminist convictions of members of SBS challenged them to find an appropriate way to depict the relationship between Rama and his utterly devoted wife Sita. In most well-known tellings of the story, the portrayal of Sita could be seen as reinforcing patriarchal views of gender. SBS members did not want to stage a play that could be seen as contradicting the feminist tenets of SBS. On the other hand, if they found an appropriate way to incorporate their critical views into the play, it could provide them with an opportunity to share their political convictions with members of their community. At that time, they were the only inside group that could mount a critique of sexist attitudes to improve it, rather than attack it from the outside to disparage South Asian culture, as some racist groups had done.

Therefore, the SBS chose to stage a unique Ramlila that would combine cultural appreciation with cultural critique. Many South Asian members of SBS had participated in Ramlilas during their school years. The SBS decided to produce a Ramlila similar to such plays in general, but differing in ideological goals. This drama would question patriarchal attitudes in the community, but do so in a spirit of affection and celebration.

Immediately complex issues surfaced. Several Marxist SBS members felt that supporting the project would affirm religious ideals (and according to classical Marxist thought, religion is the opiate of the masses, as well as epiphenomenal). Second, as one member asked, "What's the contribution of this play to the African Caribbean community?" The Ramayana was linked primarily with South Asian Hindu culture, so why should African Caribbeans or, indeed, other South Asian religious groups such as Sikhs and Muslims, see it as a meaningful drama for them?[4] In response, the group sought to mount a Ramlila that would strengthen and celebrate the entire Southall black community, and contest patriarchal ideologies at the same time. But this, pointed out another member of the group, might offend orthodox members of the community who would attend expecting a pious reiteration of the story. Would such a performance defeat the goal of bringing the community together? SBS wanted to create a thought-provoking Ramlila that would take into account these multiple concerns (Brah 1988).

Financial and temporal limitations contributed to the improvisational nature of the production. The SBS had virtually no funding and exactly three weeks to prepare the drama to be staged on 19 Friday 1979. SBS received help from many people, including the Indian Workers Association, which loaned them a venue; a Indian classical music teacher who volunteered to provide musical accompaniment to enhance the mood of the scenes; and an Indian restaurant in Southall which provided free sweets to distribute to members of the audience. Samosas, fried dumplings stuffed with spicy potato filling, were donated for sale at the performance as a fundraiser. Several women donated old saris to be sewn into a stage curtain, while others lent jewelry and other props. Many women who were not SBS members helped set up the stage, put out chairs, distribute sweets, and sell tickets. The performance was publicized in local shops and by community groups, as well as some nationally based anti-racist groups. A small notice appeared in the *Southall Gazette* (19 October 1979).

The collaborative manner in which SBS wrote the script, in keeping with its principle of coalitional practices, led to a play whose emphases were intensely debated, critiqued, and revised before the performance. Perminder Dhillon, to whom primary responsibility fell for synthesizing the many ideas for the script, recounted in an interview with me the intensity and excitement of working through and with the many views taken into account in conceptualizing the play (1994 interview). The collaborative manner in which the play developed also meant that the SBS Ramlila represented the views of the group in a way that no performance put together by a single director could.

PERFORMING THE SBS RAMLILA

SBS told Rama's story in ways that would encourage members of the audience to question some widely accepted cultural assumptions about women, but would still contain elements that made the drama clearly recognizable as a Ramlila. The play included the familiar events in the story: Rama's birth, the exile to the forest, the abduction of Sita, and Rama's victory over Ravana. Although the narrative remained fairly standard, certain decisions about casting and framing devices introduced multiple perspectives into the drama.

In contrast to some Indian dramatic traditions where men play both female and male roles (because acting is considered disreputable for women),[5] in the SBS Ramlila women played all the parts. In addition, casting choices deliberately thwarted traditional expectations. For example, Sita was played by a tall Asian woman, while Rama was played by a short African Caribbean woman. This casting undercut notions that the story "belongs" to a single ethnic group. It also subverted a widely held belief that a "proper" wife must be shorter than her husband.

In a manner crucial to its critical edge, the SBS production included a storyteller and two jesters, who mediated between the events depicted and the audience: The storyteller would come onstage, give background for the upcoming scene, and begin to comment on its significance. As she did so, the two jesters would interrupt her, drawing the audience's attention to traditional sayings, pointing out topical parallels, or interrogating certain assumptions about women reflected in the scene. One jester, a South Asian woman fluent in both English and Panjabi, included well-known Panjabi expressions in her speeches. The other jester, an African Caribbean woman, found ways to translate those Panjabi phrases in her comments, mediating for audience members who did not know Panjabi. Both functioned to disrupt the familiar, easy flow of the Ramayana narrative and question stereotypical gender roles in the play.

For an example of how this structure worked, consider how SBS dealt with the birth of Rama and his brothers. After many childless years, Dasaratha performed a special sacrificial rite, as a result of which his three wives conceived and gave birth to male children. What a great celebration the king sponsored! At this moment the first jester said:

Yes, it was like that when my brother was born—a great celebration and my family passed out laddhus [a round sweet made of brown sugar and butter]. But when I was born, they didn't celebrate. My mother said *"Hi Veh Raba, soota mundiyan dha thaba."*

Immediately following the first jester's comments, the second one responded by paraphrasing the Panjabi comment in English, and adding her own economic analysis of the situation:

She said to God "why don't you just throw me a bunch of boys?" Why such jubilation when the son is born, but not the daughter? She must have been worrying about the dowry to be paid for the marriage of a daughter.

The interchange between jesters directs the listeners' attention to the socioeconomic forces that immediately begin to shape parents' attitudes toward their children: It was not a daughter per se that was disagreeable; instead it was the custom of giving dowry for a bride, and thus commodifying her, that allowed such fears about and responses to the birth of daughters to continue.

One performer recalled that her mother brought to the play a grandmother and some elderly aunts who spoke Panjabi and knew little English. They were used to sitting through community meetings conducted in English without understanding them, coming anyway in order to meet friends and feel part of their community. Until the first jester's comment, they had viewed the drama primarily as a pious reiteration of Lord Rama's greatness, enjoying the event in their own terms, as a religious holiday and a chance to socialize. Their perception of the Ramlila received confirmation as they entered the theater and received special Divali sweets. They responded to the first jester's idiomatic Panjabi comments with laughs of recognition; the play called attention to the greater value placed on male babies than female babies, a fact of life with which they were all too familiar. That women outnumbered men in the audience meant many of them had personal experience with the differing ways in which the birth of a girl or a boy was greeted.

The majority of those of South Asian descent who attended the SBS Ramlila spoke English. For example, one member of the cast recalled that her mother brought along not only pious older womenfolk but younger sisters, brothers, and cousins who were fluent in English as a result of their schooling. Thus the second jester's translation of the Panjabi phrase and the dialogue between the two jesters enhanced the process of questioning certain gender assumptions that might otherwise have been received without further reflection.

The jesters included pointedly topical comparisons to show that the relationships in the story were not only ones enacted in some mythic past, but echoed events in the daily life of the audience. In one scene, for example, Sita begged her husband to take her along on his forest exile, but he refused, claiming to her that life would be too harsh for her: her tender lotus-feet might get cut by thorns and bruised by rocks. Sita hit him in the shoulder with a thump and said, "I'm good enough to wear myself out doing all the housework in our home, but not good enough to go to the forest with you?" Submissively, Rama replied, "Whatever you say, my dear." His response parodied the way a "proper" wife is "supposed" to answer her husband's commands.

At another point, when the narrator enumerated the heavy duties that fall to a wife, a jester interrupted, saying, "Yeh, it's a bit like how hard the women at T'walls Factory work, isn't it?" Many South Asian women worked long hours at local factories, and then returned home to cook and clean house. The jester asked why women have to work a shift outside the home, and a shift inside the home as well. The scene also undermined the gender construct of a wife as a weak creature.

The Ramlila presented these topical comments humorously in a non-threatening way, linking them to daily life by referring to familiar places. Among the actors and audience members whom I interviewed, it is this topical humor that has remained most sharply etched in people's memories of the Ramlila. Almost everyone remembered the funny asides of the jesters, a few repeating the Panjabi line quoted above. Several others recited word for word, as a high point of the performance, the line about Sita's tender lotus-feet and its irony; these women had to deal on an everyday basis with multiple pressures and dangerous work environments in factories, laundries, their homes, and during their journeys to and from work. They had little time to worry about their tender lotus-feet.

Members of the cast raised questions about notions of masculinity as well. In a scene set in the forest, for example, Rama's brother Lakshmana heard the calls of wild animals, cowered in fear, and then ran to hide behind Sita, who reassured him, "Don't worry, I'm here." This line would be particularly comic for regular Ramlila-goers because Lakshmana is usually portrayed as a fearless warrior, ready to attack anyone who poses the slightest threat to Rama, Sita, or the kingly lineage.

Towards the end of the Ramlila where Rama battles Ravana, the objects of critique shift from gender relations to the current electoral situation in Southall. As the brief program notes say, "Ravana is killed by Rama. Good wins over evil" (Southall Black Sisters 1979:1). The interpretation of Ravana as Evil Incarnate determined the appearance of Ravana's mask, composed of ten different visual images. Several of the heads were enlarged photographs of specific people, including Enoch Powell, major figures in the NF, a local member of the Ealing council, and even Prime Minister Margaret Thatcher. Other heads represented oppression in more abstract form. For example, the hat worn by riot police was drawn on one head to stand for police brutality. A bobby's black hat over a drawing of a pig symbolized the policing to which the community was subject on a regular basis (Dhillon 1979). Another drawing represented the increasingly restrictive immigration laws which threatened to tear apart families and penalize those whose parents were not born in Britain. The symbolism of Ravana, therefore, encompassed crucial concerns not just of South Asian immigrant communities but of African Caribbean ones as well.

The practice of culminating the Ramlila by burning Ravana in effigy, accompanied by celebratory fireworks, is an ancient and venerable one, symbolizing the conquest of good over evil. In the SBS production, after Rama defeated Ravana, the storyteller told the audience, "I'll see you in the carpark, where we'll finish Ravana off." There SBS set off fireworks, much to the delight of the spectators. In this Ramlila, the destruction of Ravana's effigy symbolized the desire to end racism in Britain. This final message brought together the concerns of the varied members of the audience: Panjabi and English speakers, South Asians and African Caribbeans, people from Southall and anti-Nazi activists that came from afar. The fireworks were a celebratory moment, and they gestured toward a future when all people in Southall could live without fear, humiliation, or deprivation of their rights.

HERE AND THERE

Several of the original SBS members, speaking in the 1990s in interviews with me, look back on the 1979 Ramlila as a moment of singular unity. In the more than two decades since the performance, pan-minority unity has been harder to achieve. Increasing competition for council funding and housing, as well as tensions caused by the financial constraints of the Thatcher and Major years, have tended to put one community in competition with another at times (Baumann 1996: 60–71). Among children of South Asian descent who identify with the cultural heritage of their parents but have grown up in England, some community boundaries have become more clearly marked, at least partially due to political events in India, Pakistan, and Bangladesh. Indira Gandhi's decision to bring troops into the Sikh Golden Temple in Amritsar (1984), the subsequent assassination of Mrs. Gandhi, and the rioting that took the lives of hundreds of Sikhs split Hindus and Sikhs more strongly than ever before. The destruction of the Ramjanmabhumi/Babri Mosque in Ayodhya and the riots that developed in response to it in Pakistan and Bangladesh, as well as in India, tend to make it harder and harder for Hindus and Muslims to carry on coalitional politics. Events surrounding the publication of Salman Rushdie's *Satanic Verses* also took their toll (Asad 1993). Thus, current reflection on the SBS as a moment of unity raises intriguing questions about the notion of diaspora. How is unity in Britain tied to or separate from conceptions of unity in South Asia? Is diaspora less about "being in exile from home" and more about being tied to two places?

Finally, the SBS Ramlila raises intriguing questions about the nature of representation in the context of South Asian immigration. For example, one might ask whose "culture" does the SBS Ramlila represent? It cannot be equated purely with Hindu identity, since key members of the production were African Caribbeans and/or Marxists. Among the South Asians, both Sikhs and Hindus were involved. Nor could it be said to be an exact reflection of the entire Southall South Asian community, since the audience was made up primarily of women. Furthermore, it is possible that some orthodox Hindus might even find the performance "inauthentic" because the play did not linger on auspicious scenes for darshan of Lord Rama, as most pious Ramlilas do. Finally, one could not label it a pristine transportation of a particular Indian regional performance to Britain, since its performers used an eclectic style of script-development and borrowed from a number of dramatic forms.

Rather than arguing that the SBS performance was not a "real" one, one must question the notion of a homogeneous Indian tradition transplanted to England. The Ramayana tradition has long encompassed both authoritative and oppositional tellings (Richman 2000). Authoritative tellings of Ramkatha such as those by Valmiki and Tulsidas tend to reaffirm the power of the king, the priest, and the male patriarchy. In contrast, the SBS self-consciously sought to avoid reaffirming such patriarchal norms. Their oppositional Ramlila suggests ways of overcoming sexism within their own community and racism within the wider British community. The SBS Ramlila represented the diversity of the non-white population in Southall. Its combination of cultural appreciation and cultural critique may mirror the ambiguities and contradictions of other South Asian diaspora communities as well.

ACKNOWLEDGMENTS

I thank Avtar Brah, Perminder Dhillon, Parita Mukta, and several other members of the original Southall Black Sisters, who graciously shared their time and memories with me and gave me suggestions for improving an earlier version of this paper. Leela Fernandez, Michael H. Fisher, and Lakshmi Holmstrom also made helpful comments. I alone am responsible for any errors.

A longer version of this essay, with extensive comparison between this and other women's Ramayanas, first appeared in the *Journal of the American Academy of Religion* 67, no. 1 (winter 1999), pp. 33–57, and was reprinted in a somewhat different form in *Questioning Ramayanas, A South Asian Tradition* (New Delhi: Oxford University Press, and Berkeley: University of California Press, 2000).

NOTES

1. Recently a group whose membership does not overlap with the original group of "Southall Black Sisters" (formed in 1978–79) also adopted the name "Southall Black Sisters." Throughout this article, I refer only to the original Southall Black Sisters.

2. Some comments on the "Black" in "Southall Black Sisters" are also in order here. A number of South Asians and African Caribbeans in Southall viewed themselves as part of a larger black identity, because of their shared history of colonialism and the racist assumptions upon which it rested. The sense of black identity as a unifying force developed in the later 1970s and remained strong in the 1980s; many used the term "black" (and, in some British circles, continue to use it) self-consciously as a political term to indicate unity among various non-white minority groups fighting racism. The term "Asian" had been used to describe Asian immigrants in Kenya and Uganda. Although "Asian," when used to describe people of the Indian subcontinent, is more limited than "black," it still involves unity across boundaries, since it includes people of different nationalities (Indians, Pakistanis), religions (Hindus, Muslims, and Sikhs primarily), and classes (mostly lower and middle class).

3. Divali lasts for four or five days, depending upon the lunar calendar, and falls sometime in October or November each year. Until fairly recently Sikhs shared the celebration of Divali with Hindus, since Guru Amar Das had approved of it for Sikh congregations. In the years of South Asian immigration under discussion in this paper, Sikhs and Hindus in Southall did celebrate Divali together. After Mrs. Gandhi ordered the destruction of the Golden Temple in Amritsar, and then was assassinated by two Sikh bodyguards, the situation changed in Southall and elsewhere. Today, Hindus celebrate Divali and Sikhs celebrate the holiday as the day of Guru Hargobind's release from the Gwalior jail. See Nesbitt 1955.

4. Many Indians in the Caribbean did, however, celebrate Divali and perform Ramlilas. For ethnography and photographs of Ramlila performances in Trinidad, see Niehoff.

5. Examples include *terukuttu* performances in Tamil Nadu, Kathakali plays in Kerala, and the *svarup*s of the Ramnagar Ramlila performance of Varanasi.

British Sikh Lives, Lived in Translation

Kathleen Hall

[I]f . . . the act of cultural translation (both as representation and as reproduction) denies the essentialism of a prior given originary culture, then we see that all forms of culture are continually in a process of hybridity. But for me the importance of hybridity is not to be able to trace two original moments from which the third emerges, rather hybridity to me is the "third space" which enables other positions to emerge. (Bhabha 1990: 211)

Migrant people live their lives within a cultural "third space," a site of social encounters and cultural articulations that engender processes of cultural change characterized by hybridity, fragmentation, and displacement. Within this cultural "third space," cultural orientations and identities are made rather than merely given (Bhabha 1990: 211; Hall 1996: 629). The everyday lives of migrant people are lived through acts of translation, practices of representation, reproduction, and contestation through which they negotiate what are often contradictory cultural influences in their lives. In these acts of translation, "tradition" becomes an object of reflection and reinvention, just as new lifestyles, cultural practices, and identities come to be created.

The article is drawn from my work with second-generation British Sikhs, children of migrants who are forging life paths through everyday acts of cultural translation.[1] These young people often say they feel pulled between "two cultures," pressured to conform to two very different ways of life, one viewed as "Sikh," the other "English." They express their dilemmas in dichotomous terms, while in practice they engage a broad range of cultural influences interwoven in the taken-for-granted fabric of their daily lives. Their tastes in clothing and food, in the television programs they watch and the activities they engage in, all reflect cultural mixing. Yet, if the cultural influences within their lives are multiple and varied, what leads them to feel torn between two distinct and separate cultures?

British Sikhs perceive the cultural influences in their lives in dichotomous terms, I argue, because they encounter in their lives two dominant socializing forces. These socializing forces, within Sikh communities and in British society more generally, work against cultural mixing as they define and reinforce cultural boundaries. They attempt to mold the next generation into particular types of Sikhs and British nationals in order to reproduce the status quo within as well as mark the boundaries between "Sikh" and "British" communities. Acts of translation, then, engage British Sikhs in negotiating two contradictory cultural processes: cultural reproduction, or pressures to maintain the status quo, as well as cultural production, or processes through which individuals negotiate these normative pressures as they create new or reinvent "traditional" identities and lifestyles.

In the section that follows, I describe tensions between forces of cultural reproduction and cultural production in the lives of British Sikhs. I then move on to consider how tensions between these two processes are experienced and negotiated by Sikhs themselves. I portray the experiences of some of the Sikhs I grew to know in Leeds, providing brief portraits of the very different lives they are creating as British Sikhs in England.

BECOMING BRITISH SIKHS

Sikhs as a people are associated historically with Sikhism, a modern religion tracing its origin to the birth of the first Sikh guru, Guru Nanak, in 1469. Their homeland is the Punjab, a state in northern India. Most of their historic shrines are found in the territory on either side of the border separating India from Pakistan, an area that was, prior to Partition, considered part of Punjab. Over the past century, their travels and relocations have created a global Sikh diaspora that stretches from Punjab to Kenya, England to the United States, and Fiji to Singapore.[2]

Many among this first generation to grow up in Britain were born to upwardly mobile families, to parents who came to adulthood in the villages of Punjab or the racially divided cities of colonial East Africa. The life paths of these young people bridge the boundaries of race, ethnicity, and class. In their everyday lives they move through social worlds separated by these boundaries and learn to inhabit the "third space" in between. As they reach adulthood, they fashion lifestyles that reflect a vast range of cultural orientations, from those that celebrate the aesthetic sensibilities of the urban cosmopolitan to others that reassert the value of "tradition" and seek to maintain aspects of Sikh religious and Punjabi cultural heritage.

Growing up in England, British Sikhs imagine their futures in relation to numerous possible identities, potential communal ties, and alternative life paths.[3] Their sense of self is molded by contradictory cultural influences in contrasting social settings and transmitted through multiple forms of media. In their homes, at the Sikh temple (or gurdwara) as well as in religious education classes in British schools, "their culture," "their heritage," and "their religion" are represented in distinctive ways. As members of the South Asian diaspora their sense of what it means to be "Asian," "Indian," or "Sikh" is shaped by ideas and images, film narratives and artistic forms circulating across networks linking Leeds, Vancouver, New York, and Amritsar (Appadurai 1991; Gillespie 1995; Gopinath 1995).[4] As teenagers in a capitalist culture, British Sikhs also consume youth culture commodities that provide myriad cultural styles and subcultural orientations to use in creating adolescent identities (Sharma, Hutnyk, and Sharma 1996; Maira 1999).

Analyses that simply celebrate the creative potential within processes of cultural production and identity formation, however, ignore the cultural constraints as well as the social barriers that they, as the children of immigrants and as racial minorities, frequently face.[5] Social actors, particularly those defined as different, do not produce new cultural forms or make identity choices freely, independently, and in isolation. Identity and lifestyle choices have social consequences in terms of how the dominant society, family members, neighbors, teachers, peers, and co-workers evaluate one another's everyday conduct in relation to particular cultural distinctions, moral codes, and normative standards. To choose to be "traditional" or cosmopolitan can have significant social and personal consequences, in terms of one's status in British society and within British Asian communities.

These constraints are evident in the way young people consistently feel "caught between two cultures." To make sense of the disjuncture between the choices in their lives and the way they perceive these choices, their "choices" need to be considered in relation to the normative pressures that inform them. Many accounts of second-generation South Asians in Britain and in the United States have noted the powerful influence that familial demands for loyalty to traditional cultural ideals can have in young people's lives. Yet, this, I argue, is only part of the picture.

As the first generation to grow up in Britain, second-generation British Sikhs are subject to two explicit projects of social reproduction. They are the focus of attempts on the part of the dominant British national community and the caste status communities within the Sikh population to socialize the next generation. Relations of power and inequality in these status communities are legitimated by normative values and beliefs inscribed within two contrasting ideologies.[6]

An ideology of family honor (or *izzat*) provides the basis for determining a family's position within the status hierarchies that exist within each Sikh caste community. The ideology of family honor gives expression to normative expectations concerning gender relations, modesty among young women, and moral behavior among Sikhs more generally. A family's honor, its status in the caste community, is most influential, perhaps, in determining the family's ability to arrange good marriages for their children, particularly their daughters.

A second ideology, what I call the ideology of British national purity, supports a belief in a pure and homogeneous British nationality (Gilroy 1987). This ideology represents British identity as primordial or given, an identity that cannot be chosen or achieved and must, to survive, be protected and preserved. This construction of Britishness as rooted in time and territory excludes Britain's citizens of color and serves to legitimate racialized boundaries of national belonging. The ideology of British national purity supports a form of "cultural racism" specific to Europe in the era of decolonization, one that has arisen in response to the postcolonial reversal of migratory movements in which ex-colonial peoples from the old colonies have settled in the old metropoles. Articulated within notions of nationalism or national purity, the dominant theme of this form of racism "is not biological heredity but the insurmountability of cultural differences" and "the incompatibility of life-styles and traditions" (Balibar 1991b: 21). This construction of social difference in terms of incommensurable racialized cultural essences informs ongoing processes of cultural reification and corresponding acts of social exclusion that continue to divide the dominant white population from Britain's newest citizens of color.

Each of these ideologies represent communities that are more idealized than real, more imagined than enacted. Each reflects a commonly shared desire for social wholeness, a desire to impose order in a world of cultural flow and flux, to protect boundaries of belonging perceived to be under threat. As conservative forces, they attempt to halt the forward march of social and cultural change. The conflicting demands in these young people's lives are not conflicts between two distinctive bounded cultures. They derive from dominant ideologies that do not reflect the complex and heterogeneous cultural orientations found within Sikh communities and in British society. While not all those identified as "Sikhs" or as "British" may subscribe to these ideological constructs, these ideologies continue to support dominant relations of power, privilege, and authority within Sikh caste communities and in British society. Hence, for many, particularly young people still under the normalizing gaze of family and school authorities, these ideologies police the boundaries of group belonging.

As British Sikhs negotiate the boundaries, social expectations, and constraints supported by the ideologies of British nationalism and of family honor, they develop a sense that they live between two worlds, worlds they frequently refer to as "English" and as "Indian." They associate things "Indian" with being "traditional," and things "English" with being "modern." Yet, in their everyday lives these young people enact a much broader range of lifestyles. Their lives embody a creative tension that engages the dialectics of power and inequality as well as the dynamics of cultural improvisation and transformation. They negotiate these fields of power and meaning through acts of translation. From this interstitial perspective, this "third space," British Sikhs observe and reflect upon different cultural influences, forms of oppression as well as future opportunities; and, in everyday practice, they produce hybrid identities and lifestyles, "traditional," cosmopolitan, and often a mixture of both.

I turn now to the stories of individuals I grew to know in Leeds, England, descriptions that illustrate the range of lifestyles British Sikhs are creating as well as the consequences these young people have encountered in relation to choices they have made. These stories capture their struggles to create new ways of being black and British, Sikh and middle class in England.

BECOMING MODERN TRADITIONAL SIKHS

Kulwant and Amarjit are Ramgarhia Sikhs. Kulwant's family is from Punjab, Amarjit's from Kenya. Both came to Britain before they were five. Their families are middle class. Amarjit's family brought economic and cultural capital from East Africa, Kulwant's has become economically successful since arriving in England. Kulwant is a successful solicitor, Amarjit a radiologist.

Kulwant and Amarjit fell in love as their marriage was being arranged. The couple and their families are very religious and quite active in their respective gurdwaras. Amarjit's family attends the Ramgarhia gurdwara frequented nearly exclusively by East African Sikhs, while Kulwant's family has been active in another temple whose members are largely from Punjab. Neither Kulwant nor Amarjit has taken *amrit pahul* ("nectar of immortality") or, in other words, undergone baptism for initiation into the Khalsa (the order of baptized Sikhs established by the tenth and final Sikh guru, Gobind Singh, in 1699).[7] Yet, they are both Kesdhari Sikhs (Sikhs who retain the *kes*, or uncut hair), and both, for the most part, keep the five symbols (the five Ks) of the Sikh faith: kes, kanga (a comb worn in the hair), kara (a silver bracelet), kachh (a pair of underwear traditionally worn by soldiers), and kirpan (a sword or dagger worn on the side of the body in a holster that wraps diagonally around one shoulder). Kulwant wears a turban, except on Saturdays when he plays cricket.

Kulwant worries a great deal about the survival of the Sikh religion in Britain. He reads widely on the subject of Sikh history and religion and has taught "Sunday school" classes for teenagers at the temple in an attempt to pass on this knowledge to the next generation. Kulwant is concerned that the essential principles of Sikhism are at risk. The young have little knowledge of the faith and, in his view, show little interest in learning. More profoundly, perhaps, he fears that certain practices among the first generation threaten to "Hinduize" Sikhism (a fear, of course, that is hardly new within Sikhism or unique to Sikhs in Britain). Sikh women, in particular, he feels, grant supernatural power to ritual acts, to sounds, to scents and, most critically, perhaps, to particular holy people. In contrast, the essence of Sikhism, for Kulwant, is in its textual base, in the teachings of the original ten Sikh gurus contained in the Sikh holy book, the Guru Granth Sahib. A Sikh's faith, he believes, should be grounded in a rational, literate, and informed understanding of Sikh religious teachings. Kulwant dedicates his free time to reading, teaching, and taking a leadership role at the gurdwara in order to protect the purity of his religious tradition.

Amarjit's everyday life revolves around her family. While she is tremendously close to her own family, she and Kulwant live with his parents. This, for Amarjit, is a source of great ambivalence. She feels fondness and respect for her in-laws and values living in an extended family unit, in which her children are learning Punjabi. Yet, having grown up in Britain, she is frustrated that the elderly people she lives with and cares for are not her relations. While she enjoys the communal nature of family life, the constant flow of relatives and friends through the doors of her in-laws' home, she wishes they would phone before coming and, on arriving, would not expect her to prepare a full Indian meal. Amarjit's ambivalence fuels her fantasies of moving out on their own, of enjoying the kind of domestic privacy that she imagines exists within a British nuclear family.

When I visit Amarjit, our days are spent in perpetual motion, preparing meals and traveling from house to house, gurdwara to gurdwara, children in hand, to be with relatives or to join in the festivities at yet another wedding. Between my visits, her letters tell of new babies born, siblings who have wed, and the deaths of elderly loved ones.

BECOMING COSMOPOLITAN

Devinder was born in Britain. Her parents too are quite religious and active in the Sikh temple. Devinder's parents came to England during the early sixties from a village in Punjab where, as members of the Jat caste, their families were landowning farmers. When her father first arrived, he stopped wearing the turban; but following the storming of the Golden Temple in Amritsar in 1984, he began once again to keep the symbols of the faith.[8] Devinder's family is upwardly mobile. Her father started his own small business and, as the eldest family member, worked to put his brothers (though not his sisters) through university while his own children were young.

During my first stay in Britain, Devinder, the eldest among her siblings, was studying dentistry at Leeds University while living at home. She was a successful student and remains a dutiful daughter. Her appearance at the time reflected her respect for the cultural ideals of her family; her hair was long and plaited, her face was free of makeup and her dress modestly covered her body, usually in a jumper (sweater) and jeans. She never wore a skirt or a dress. Though strongly devoted to her family, she is not religious. Outside of family events and weddings, she avoids the gurdwara and other Asian-specific spaces, where she says she feels awkward and out of place.

Devinder possesses a double consciousness. She is quite aware of differences between how she views herself and how she and her family are seen through the eyes of the dominant British population. This awareness was deepened by a sense of "release" she felt during a visit to India, where, for the first time, she felt English and did not feel marginalized racially.

> *Devinder:* [W]hen I went to India for my holiday it was really funny because I thought that I'd been released. I could walk in the streets and I felt a part of it. Everybody looked like me and behaved like me. It's funny because I never thought I was conscious of it, but I felt suddenly as if I was home. It's silly, isn't it? I've lived here all my life so this should be the place. I mean I was really happy to come back. It was really, really nice to have been there, but I think I was happier just coming back home. But while I was there I had this feeling, you can't imagine.
>
> *K.H.:* Did you feel different in any way from the people that were there?
>
> *Devinder:* Well, yes, I did feel different. . . . I could see by the way I was dressed they knew that I'd come from England. . . . That wasn't the difference—that I could speak English and they couldn't. That's not the point. It's just that if I wore an Indian suit, I suppose, and went somewhere, they wouldn't know where I was from. What's the difference?

Devinder comes from a lower-middle-class family; her academic success has taken her across racial and class boundaries, deepening and refining, in many ways, her understanding of how power relations are legitimated by the signification of social difference. In spite of her academic success at university, she had a profound sense that she did not belong in the white middle-class world of her classmates. Her family and her background did not "fit," did not correspond to the taken-for-granted British norm. The pressures of otherness, of living two lives, at that time permeated her everyday experiences.

> *Devinder:* I've never had a really close English friend like you because nobody else would understand. They can't understand the two different —the fact that I can cope with the way my parents are and still be happy at university. And not totally living the way students are supposed to live. . . . [I'm] two different people. I get into the car to come home, I'm somebody else.
>
> *K.H.:* Is that hard?

Devinder: It depends which side of me dominates. Because there are times when the university side dominates and that interferes with home life. But when I'm at home like I have been for the last four weeks it's going to be harder getting used to going back there. Not consciously, but I suppose I'm just aware of it because you asked me. I wouldn't normally think of it. I mean I'll be successful here, but I want a home in India.

When Devinder finished her course at university, her parents informally initiated the process of arranging or assisting her marriage. A number of frustrating meetings with potential partners ensued. At the point when her patience was about to give out, her father happened to meet a very interesting young Sikh man at a wedding and invited him home to tea. Raj and Devinder met, were very attracted to one another, discovered they had a great deal in common, dated, fell in love, and married. Like Kulwant and Amarjit, Raj and Devinder are of the same caste. Both their families came from villages in Punjab and their fathers have established businesses in England. Raj's father, in particular, has made a great deal of money in manufacturing and export. Raj attended public school (the British equivalent of U.S. "private" school), graduated from university, and is employed by the government. He also is not religious and has never kept a turban—though Devinder's younger sisters were quite taken with the romantic image of Raj on his wedding day, standing tall, handsome, and heroic in his turban.

The couple lived for a short time at Raj's parents' estate in an upper-class village in the country outside London, but they soon decided they preferred the city and purchased their own flat in central London. Marriage has transformed Devinder. A few months after the wedding, I went to visit. When she met me at the train, I didn't recognize her. Her hair was short, her eyes enveloped in a lovely shade of blue, and she was dressed in a knee-length navy skirt, white blouse, tailored jacket, navy tights and heels. Devinder tells me that except for subtle middle-class forms of racism she senses periodically, she now feels that she somehow "fits in." She and Raj have driven through France and across Ireland. They subscribe to the opera, eat out regularly, and catch all the latest art films. And, in between, they visit their families.

BRIDGING THE BORDERLAND

Jas is from a middle-class family. His father, a Ramgarhia Sikh from Punjab, has a university degree. They are quite religious and very active in the Sikh temple. During his high school and university years, Jas blended into a very middle-class English world. He never wore a turban or attended the gurdwara. Recently, Jas decided to grow his hair and begin to wear a turban. This reconnection to his faith came at the same time as his engagement to his white English girlfriend.

These seemingly contradictory developments in Jas's life reflect, in part, the political transformation he has undergone in the last few years. While completing his M.A., Jas became involved in local politics and community organizing, work that he says has "politicized him." While passionate about politics, he remains concerned about the ramifications of his choices. His unease is evident, as he characterizes "getting tunneled" into race work and getting married as "significant crises."

> *Jas:* I'm getting tunneled into another kind of area called race work. That I find unhappy because it's not what I want to do. Being here has been very very useful because it's politicized me, it's given me information about how the system works and how individuals in the system work, etc. etc. But now I'm personally getting labeled into that. And now there's another significant crisis. I'll probably get, not probably, I am getting married to a white woman. . . .
>
> *K.H.:* Are your dad and mom okay with the marriage?
>
> *Jas:* Yes, now they are, yeah. But you know there's all kinds of dilemmas on both sides. You know, it's not just my mom and dad. I think it's . . . it's probably worse for my parents in the sense that in Sikh society marriage brings more friends, gives them more relations.

Imagining raising children with his soon-to-be wife has prompted Jas to think about being a Sikh in a new light. Marrying a non-Sikh, a non-Asian, has given him a heightened sense of why his "tradition" is important to him.

> *Jas:* I've just been on a holiday with my so-called girlfriend at the moment, and one of the questions was, what are we going to do with our kids? Are they going to wear a turban? And I in the ostrich situation say yes. No questions asked, yes. I want my kids . . . I will have no choice for them being black or white, they'll have to be both, they'll have to go into both kind of cultures . . . [T]he minority culture is the culture which I think they will question the most because they will be like this more, they will question that more, because the majority culture is there anyway. . . . I want to keep the identity going. I want them to be, find out about the faith, where they belong. I want to give them this sense of belonging. They belong here, you know, their granddad, their grandparents are in Leeds and Manchester, one happens to be Sikh, one happens to be white. They will both love them, they will.

As he identifies what his children will have to confront in relation to racial, cultural, and religious differences, Jas speaks from the perspective of his own experience. Growing up in Britain, he too developed a double consciousness, a consciousness that his cultural background would be questioned and could not be taken for granted or simply "lived." He has been forced to think critically about his identity, and he has continued to question, to identify with as well as to challenge the ways of his parents' generation. His words reflect an objective distance, a space of self-awareness about his choice to marry outside his "race" and culture, while simultaneously proclaiming, visibly, his identity as Sikh. Proud, he still wonders where it will lead.

> I still, until we get married she can't get involved with the gurdwara, really, we can't go hand and hand, boyfriend and girlfriend. But I think, you know, I think she would take it on. She's the kind of person who would say, well look, I may not become a Sikh, but I will come to the gurdwara. I'll have to dress up and do something. But she's brilliant. I don't personally recognize that sometimes, because I do this ostrich thing. So, yes I think, I feel more powerful, you know, in having a turban. . . . It makes you do certain things. So like here, dressing up, putting the turban on, makes you take care of how you present yourself. It makes you think all the time who you are. There are certain things you wouldn't do in public that you might do otherwise.

Forced when growing up to "think all the time about who you are," Jas has learned to think about who he is in a thoughtful, reflective manner. Becoming politicized and thinking about his tradition through the eyes of his future children have brought Jas back to his community, to an identification with being Sikh, to political activism, and to work with British Sikh youth.

BATTLING RACISM

I grew to know Jaspir quite well during the course of my first stay in Leeds. She was the daughter of a very religious Punjabi Ramgarhia family. Her father has achieved a fair degree of economic mobility, having built a successful business. He was also quite active in both gurdwara and local city politics. Jaspir was a serious, thoughtful, and outspoken college student. We spent hours talking about the dilemmas faced by the second generation, dilemmas about which she was passionately concerned.

After I left Leeds, Jaspir's life-path took a painful turn. She had just taken a "race" job with a local authority in Yorkshire. She was acting on the political principles that her father, as well as her life experiences, had instilled in her: she was engaged in the fight against racism. Jaspir fell in love with a man she met at her job. This would have been difficult enough for her "traditional" family. But the man she chose to love is Afro-Caribbean, and she chose to love him openly, publicly, against her family's wishes. This choice profoundly wounded Jaspir's family and had serious consequences for their standing in the Sikh community. Reacting in pain to their feelings of betrayal, her family disowned Jaspir. When her favorite aunt died, she was not invited to the funeral. Jaspir's act challenged the principles of Sikh family honor, and she is no longer a member of her family.

Jaspir's story brings to light the contradictions in her father's world and the consequences that can result from challenging the status system. In loving a black man, she acted in accordance with the anti-racist ideals for which her father fervently fought, but against the principles of Sikh family honor that he felt were fundamental to his faith. She bravely chose to follow her heart and her politics along a path of resistance, but without her family, she must find the path a lonely one.

BECOMING BRITISH (AND EVENTUALLY AMERICAN)

I remember the first time I saw Ravi. I was sitting in a car with her sister and brother-in-law waiting for her to appear from her medical school lab at Leeds University. We were heading out on the motorway to visit Ravi's sister's family in Cardiff, Wales. "There she is. Finally!" her brother-in-law announced in frustration. I looked up to see a strikingly beautiful young woman with lush black hair in a spotted fake-fur coat, short blue skirt, black lace tights, and funky black and white loafers. She hopped in back with me and we talked all the way to Wales. She complained about school, said she disliked medicine on the whole, and quietly mentioned her white English boyfriend, Ben. They were living together, planned to marry, maybe, but her family had not quite adjusted to the idea just yet.

Ravi, while herself not at all religious, is from a very religious Ramgarhia Sikh family who came to Britain from Kenya. Ravi's parents were both educated within the British colonial educational system and had professional careers both in Kenya and in England. During the days we spent with her sister, Ravi and I continued to talk incessantly as we decompressed —her from university, me from fieldwork—over wine, samosas, and crisps (potato chips). We shared our personal tales of the trials of student life and she taught me all about Leeds—which clubs were "in" and where I could find the best bargains on clothes and Chinese food to die for. She was and remains totally "hip." Her interests and obsessions, activities and travels seldom take her into purely Asian social worlds. She thinks of herself as British and, when "race" is marked, as a black woman. She has been forced to confront racism and sexism often during her medical schooling and in the initial stages of her career. She takes these irritations in stride, avoids incidents when she can, and continues to frame her life, individualistically, around pleasures and accomplishments.

We met a few times at O'Hare airport in Chicago when she was flying through to her residency in Barbados or to see relatives in California. One summer I received an invitation to her wedding at a Unitarian church in New York City, where Ravi and Ben now reside. I was in Britain at the time and could not attend. All of Ravi's relatives, her parents, sisters and brothers, nieces and nephews, and aunts and uncles, flew to New York from Britain and California for the wedding, which, her sister reported, the couple forgot to have videotaped. Ravi and Ben have settled in Manhattan, where they are both practicing medicine.

In forging her life path, Ravi has found ways to subvert the dominant pressures of family honor and of British racism, partially, perhaps, by removing herself completely from the Sikh community in Leeds as well as from Britain itself. Her family has adjusted to her choices, and they have accepted Ben into the fold. Ravi's two older sisters, in contrast, chose to marry Sikh men whom they were introduced to through more "traditional" arrangements. One husband wears a turban while the other does not. Cultural change is taking distinctive forms between as well as within British Sikh families.

CONCLUSION

British Sikhs are paving life paths through everyday acts of translation. They are producing new identities and fashioning novel lifestyles, from the overtly "cosmopolitan" to the decidedly more "traditional." Their stories highlight what many postmodern analyses of hybrid identity formation too often seem to ignore, the constraints and the personal costs associated with cultural mixing, with making choices that directly challenge boundaries of belonging. Through their struggles, old boundaries are slowly becoming blurred, just as new relations of inequality are continuing to emerge, particularly in the form of class differences that increasingly divide the British Asian population. As they raise their children and enjoy their grandchildren, second-generation British Sikhs will continue to reflect on the nature of their culture and their identity in England and will make choices, at each new life stage, that reconfigure their relationship to both. Identities, like culture, are constantly remade in ongoing processes of becoming, processes experienced, in the moment, as everyday acts of being.

ACKNOWLEDGMENTS

The material presented here is drawn from a longitudinal field research project that I began in 1986 and is ongoing. The project has been supported by a Fulbright Fellowship, a Spencer Doctoral Fellowship, a Spencer/National Academy Post Doctoral Fellowship and a University of Pennsylvania Research Foundation Grant. I would also like to take the opportunity to express deep gratitude and warm appreciation to my mentor Bernard Cohn, whose creative inspiration first set me off on this particular path many years ago.

NOTES

1. This piece is taken from a broader study of the social mobility experiences of British Sikhs growing up in Leeds, England (see Hall 1995 and forthcoming).

2. More in-depth analyses of the history of Sikhs in Punjab can be found in McLeod (1997) and Oberoi (1994). For studies of Sikh migrant populations, see Singh and Barrier (1996 and 1999) and Barrier and Dusenbery (1989). My work builds upon the earlier research with first-generation Sikhs in Leeds carried out by Roger Ballard and Catherine Ballard (see Ballard 1989; Ballard and Ballard 1977).

3. In this account, I use the term "South Asian" to refer to people who have migrated from the South Asian subcontinent to various parts of the world and "Asian" or "British Asian" to refer more specifically to South Asians in Britain. "Asian" is the term used in Britain to refer to citizens of South Asian origin, regardless of whether they originally migrated from Pakistan, India, Bangladesh, or East Africa (the homelands of the majority of South Asians in Britain). I also refer to second-generation Sikhs as "British Sikhs" to emphasize their citizenship and cultural identification as British.

4. See Vertovec (1997) for a useful analysis of the concept of "diaspora."

5. Visweswaran (1997), making a distinctive yet related point, has called upon researchers to consider more closely the relevance of class differences to particular South Asian migration histories and settlement experiences.

6. My use of the concept of ideology is similar to what Comaroff and Comaroff, following Raymond Williams (1977: 109), have defined as "an articulated system of meanings, values, and beliefs of a kind that can be abstracted as [the] 'worldview' of any social grouping. Borne in explicit manifestos and everyday practices . . . this worldview may be more or less internally systematic, more or less assertively coherent in its outward forms. But, as long as it exists, it provides an organizing scheme for collective symbolic production" (Comaroff and Comaroff 1991: 24).

7. Men and women keep the Five Ks, but among Punjabi Sikhs, only men wear turbans. Amritdhari Sikhs are those who have undergone baptism by the double-edged sword (*khande-da-amrit*) into the Khalsa (brotherhood). Amritdhari Sikhs are required to adhere to a code of conduct, the Rahit Maryada, which includes keeping the Five Ks. Amritdhari Sikhs have traditionally been distinguished from Sahajdhari Sikhs, who have not been baptized. This distinction was instituted after the tenth guru, Gobind Singh, first elected a segment of the Sikhs to undergo baptism into the Khalsa. Kesdhari Sikhs (those who keep kes) are Sahajdhari Sikhs who keep the five symbols of the faith. Other Sahajdhari Sikhs choose to cut their hair and to practice Sikhism without keeping the symbols. According to McLeod, only about 15 percent of Sikhs are Amritdhari and another 70 percent "heed the principal requirements of the rahit" (McLeod 1999: 64; see also Lal 1999 and Oberoi 1994).

8. It is not possible to provide an adequate account here of the tragic history of "Operation Bluestar" and the assassination of Prime Minister Indira Gandhi. For an analysis of these events and the Khalistani movement more generally, see Tatla (1999) and Axel (2000).

Placing Lives through Stories: Second-Generation South Asian Americans

Kirin Narayan

"Displacement" and "diaspora" are two terms that often move together, hand in hand. Wandering through the terrain of anthropological discourse, diaspora and displacement measure the ways in which the last two decades of theory have complicated the relations between culture and place (Appadurai 1996; Bammer 1994; Gupta and Ferguson 1997; Lavie and Swedenburg 1996). Global flows, ethnoscapes, traveling cultures, and hybridity loomed large in the theoretical landscapes of the 1990s, and form a backdrop for anthropology in the new century, too. In this essay, I will explore a third term that seems to me to skip at the heels of displacement and diaspora, but has not yet been sufficiently recognized at their side: emplacement. By emplacement, I mean the strategies of coming to belong somewhere, as when people in diaspora who have left old homes struggle to make new ones. Emplacement occurs in concrete geographical space, in settling into homes, in the establishment of community resources like specialized grocery stores, and in arenas for gathering, like mosques, gurdwaras, or temples. Also, emplacement is an imaginative process, the orienting of self within multiple frameworks of meaning. Drawing on life stories from second-generation South Asian Americans, I argue here that telling one's own stories, staking out a space for one's own meaning, is a powerful discursive means of emplacement.

RESEARCH BACKGROUND

There is a long history of people of South Asian origin leaving South Asia for different parts of the world, whether on account of trade, movement within the British colonial labor force, indentured labor contracts, or the seeking of new opportunities (Clarke et al. 1990; Tinker 1974). In the United States, a noteworthy South Asian presence can be traced to the early part of the twentieth century, particularly after 1905, and centered on the west coast (Daniels 1989: 11–25). Many of these settlers were Sikhs, who often met strong racial prejudice. After the passing in 1917 and 1924 of immigration bills that excluded most people of Asian origin, the numbers who entered dwindled, and those who were in the United States encountered difficulties in obtaining citizenship and owning land. In 1946, naturalization for those of South Asian background became possible, and also small quotas of immigrants were allowed each year. It was not until 1965, though, that the immigration law was changed, allowing for 20,000 people each year from each country in South Asia, and showing preferences for educated professionals as well as close relatives of citizens and permanent residents (Helweg and Helweg 1990: 58–60). Since then, the flow of immigrants has continued to be tied to the vagaries in immigration laws: the middle-class professional bias of the first flood of immigrants later came to include working-class relatives, and more recently, skilled technological workers on temporary visas have added to the South Asian presence in the United States (Leonard 1997).

Migration and the changed imaginative relationship to countries of origin as well as countries of settlement have been noted as creative forces in modern fiction (cf. Rushdie 1991). In 1994, I published a novel that featured Indians living in the United States (Narayan 1994). What I knew about the South Asian Americans around me was rooted in the randomness of my own experience or the experiences of friends. To my discomfort, though, I found that people seemed to assume that my expertise as an anthropologist of South Asia somehow extended to the materials of my fiction. In a hurry, I set about trying to gain some scholarly credentials in order to be able to answer wider questions about South Asian American experience. Apart from exploring the scholarly literature, I also began to interview people.

I was particularly intrigued by second-generation South Asian Americans, mostly the children of the post-1965 immigrants. As someone of mixed cultural background myself—I grew up in India with a Gujarati father and German-American mother—I saw these second-generation individuals as potential mirrored selves, as twinned others. They looked more "authentically" Indian than I did, yet I also sensed that they were far more American than I. How, I wondered, did they perceive themselves?

Between 1995 and 2000, I periodically taped, wrote down, or simply listened to personal narratives from second-generation Indian and Pakistani Americans who were willing to give me their time. All the young men and women I approached knew they were helping me out on two scores: first, to instruct me as an anthropologist, and second, to give me insight into the character of Indian American Nikhil/Nick, for a second novel that was taking shape on my computer screen. Somehow, asking for help with the character of Nick became an unanticipated rich method for eliciting life stories: Nick served as a catalyst with some (though not all) of the people I interviewed, inspiring the telling of powerful personal stories that could potentially become part of his experience, too.

The twenty people I spoke with at length were all connected in one way or another to the Midwest, and to university life, whether as students, faculty, or the children of faculty: it would be safe to say they were all of middle-class background. All of them had grown up in the United States from at least the age of five onward, though most were born here. They ranged in age from eighteen to forty at the time of the first interview, and had lived before in places as varied as Libya, Palo Alto, Cincinnati, and Ahmedabad. For all these people, I have used pseudonyms and have tried to suppress other identifying markers. I have also, as much as possible, attempted to maintain a dialogue through drafts of writing.

In undertaking these interviews, I have been uncomfortably aware of my own inadequacies in trying to reciprocate for the gift of stories through tea, meals, my own stories, or even advice on subjects ranging from graduate-school applications to romantic dilemmas. The reward has been many new friendships as well as a wealth of new research materials. A disadvantage of remaining in contact with people through time, though, is that life stories are an unstable and contingent genre, subject to change. Whether on account of personal changes, such as marriage or graduation, or political shifts, like the post-Kargil era of strained relations between India and Pakistan, several people I contacted in 2000 said that their perceptions of their own pasts had changed and were we to redo the interviews, I would be likely to learn different stories. One person no longer identified with the term "South Asian American." This essay, then, should be viewed as provisional, representing a period in the late 1990s, among some South Asian Americans based in the Midwest.

Though often mockingly termed "American Born Confused Desis" these young people did not appear to be confused or floundering; rather, they are masters of code-switching, showing different sides and combinations of themselves in different cultural contexts (cf. Ballard 1994: 29–33; Brah 1996: 41–42). Working with an immensely articulate and reflective set of individuals has also made it difficult to muster up the ethnographic authority to transform the delights of the spoken word into written publications. After all, everyone in this group could certainly write to represent themselves and their own story if they wished. I take heart from what twenty-year-old Najma reflected: "See, what's interesting for us is how our own stories might relate to the others of us who grew up here; this is what you can do for us."

NESTED STORIES

Since the 1920s, anthropologists have been interested in life stories as a way to locate cultural generalities and historical forces within the experiences and narrated perceptions of actual people (Langness and Frank 1981). While the term "life history" is often used by anthropologists recording such narratives, I prefer to use "life story" in order to draw attention to the fragmentary, constructed, varied, and contextually evoked nature of the stories people tell about themselves (cf. Peacock and Holland 1993: 368). The kinds of stories that people narrate about themselves are not only retrospective, organizing memories, but also prospective, laying down frameworks of meaning that may guide actions in the future (Bruner 1987). Also, as I argue here, the telling of stories is a form of imaginative emplacement.

The life stories of second-generation South Asian Americans located at the confluence of different cultural influences suggests that it may be useful to think of life stories as conglomerates of different sorts of narratives, some personal, some collective. In this essay, I examine three classes of stories that emerged from my transcripts: (1) stories told about oneself; (2) the reframing of preexisting family folklore, for example tales a parent might have told about him- or herself, or prior ancestors; (3) the retelling of larger cultural stories, like myths or folktales, as part of one's own experience.

Personal Experience

Personal narrative formed the largest frame for the tales I elicited, with occasional family stories or oral traditions nested inside. The life stories I heard resonated strongly with other research on second-generation South Asian American lives (e.g., Agarwal 1991; Bacon 1996; Maira 1998). The content of the stories was shaped by several important vectors: South Asian region of parents' origin, United States region of upbringing and the South Asian presence there, era of upbringing (for example, the 1960s versus the 1980s), gender, and sexual orientation, all of which were differentially experienced depending on the other shaping forces.

Despite all the diversity in particulars, many stories had a similar shape. Conflict between the South Asian and the American sides of self through childhood tended to reach a miserable pitch of anger, depression, denial, or repression in middle-school years. In college, there was usually self-discovery, with the developing of new strategies for being South Asian and American, too. Yet even as this resulted in a greater sense of personal integration, manifest in the telling of the stories, almost everyone I talked to also referred to an ongoing compartmentalization between the self they were creating of their own and the self that was more oriented toward family. (The one marked exemption was Najma, of Pakistani background, whose parents were so open-minded and tolerant that she felt she could confide to them about any struggle.) Many of the people I spoke to, then, felt duplicitous with their parents. As Sudam said, reflecting on how he couldn't tell his parents about his girlfriend, who though also Indian American was from a different caste and region: "I'm one person with family, another person with friends. I lead totally different lives. It's too complicated to explain to each side, so I don't bother." Note, however, that in frankly narrating the tensions he faced between his parents and friends, Sudam used the space of a story to bring the two sides of his life together.

Humor was often emphasized in these accounts, though the humor could verge on the bitter. Reflecting on what India represented to her as a Gujarati child in Indiana, Medha stated:

> *Medha:* I really hated it. I really hated being Indian. I wanted to shed anything that was Indian about myself—other than clothes, because Indian clothes are cool!
>
> *KN:* Did you wear the clothes to school?
>
> *M:* I would. I would wear the *pyjāma*. But I would wear a different blouse. Yeah. I would wear the Indian clothes to school. But I wanted to shed anything that was Indian, because I always got the constant "Girls in India don't do that, and it doesn't matter what people here do. You're Indian and that's your culture. And this is what you do, and as long as you're in this house you're going to abide by the Indian culture." And everything was so Indian culture, American culture, there was no possibility of merging.

Like many young women I talked to, Medha felt her brother had not been as conflicted and depressed by the gulf between gender expectations coming from the Indian parents, and American peers. Similarly, Asha, who grew up in a Gujarati family in Milwaukee, reflected that her own brother was more comfortable in his Indianness than she was: "You know, like, he *can* be Indian because he doesn't face a lot of the same things that I do as a woman in being more Indian. You know, for me to be more Indian would be to give up things. For him to be more Indian is actually to get—to earn some privilege, and I don't think he sees that."

Young men were usually aware that things were harder for their sisters. The men too spoke of their own sense of being suspended between Indianness or Pakistani-ness and Americanness, represented as polarities. Vasant, who grew up in Santa Clara, California, in the 1960s, described how he sought to cover up his difference, to "do everything to fit in and not rock the boat in any way"—excelling in sports, he found, was one way of finding acceptance as an American male. Arjun talked of growing up in Cleveland fascinated by American history, "even the esoteric details and stuff, and that I think was part of country-loving, you know. Like in some ways, I felt like if I learned this stuff, maybe, you know, then they would accept me or something like that."

For men as well, parents could be a repressive force, guiding their decisions from what to major in to social interaction. Though girls were supervised more, and more haunted by middle-class, upper-caste nationalized images of chaste Indian women (cf. Maira 1998), for men too issues of dating and sexuality were a recurring node of inner confusion as well as overt conflict with parents.

One of Dinesh's favorite stories, "a classic," in his own words, was a suspenseful and dramatic account of how, when he was visiting home from college, his parents had discovered something subversive in his room and were so upset that they telephoned him at the party he was at with his non–South Asian friends, asking him to return home. He imagined that they had found his stash of dope, but it turned out that they had unearthed an unopened and signed condom given to him as a joke gift from a girl at graduation. "Do you use condoms?" his father asked. Though relatively sexually inexperienced, Dinesh responded with bravado, saying, "All the time!" which led to his parents' lamentations over the possibility of arranging his marriage.

Manjeet described his confrontations with his parents in terms of their being Indian, and him, challenging their authority, as American.

> I couldn't date. It would seem strange for me to date somebody, you know. Go out on a date with some—some girl, or go out with a girl? Or even, like, stay out late . . . my mom would say that in our culture we don't go out with girls. Or we don't, you know, we don't—we don't kiss girls. . . . You know basically, just, "No, you can't do that!" [laughing]
>
> And I would be, like, "WHY?"
>
> She's like, "You can't do it."
>
> And I would be like, I would be like, being an American, wanting to know the reason why I can't do this, you know?
>
> And my dad's, like, "There's no reason why. Just deal with it."
>
> It's like, I realized—I probably came to accept arbitrary rules, you know, by my parents over me, and the fact that me doing this, like, hurt my mom so much that she can't even tell why it hurts her, you know? She doesn't really know why. It's just like, it's bad. And so I have to realize that if I want to do it, I'm gonna have to hurt her in order to do it.

America, then, represented a challenging of preexisting traditions, and was set up in opposition to "our culture" as perceived by parents. The issue of parents' construction of the homeland, a different kind of nostalgic emplacement, would be the subject of a different essay (cf. Ganguly 1992; Prashad 1996). Indeed, one could view the tension between South Asian–born parents and their America-raised children as being partly the result of their different placements within imaginative landscapes of meaning in terms of what "India," "Pakistan," or "the United States" might represent.

Yet such placements, of course, were not fixed, but could change with time, and be evoked differently in different contexts. Asha, for example, responded to my question of what India meant to her by saying, "Well, mainly family. . . . I mean until I was old enough to understand geography, I always thought that India was one of the states in the United States." After all, she said, they went to what her mother called India-na to visit her mother's brothers in what Asha and her brother imitated as "Indian-a-police." It was only as she grew older that the family network of meaning stretched, and she realized that India was a faraway place.

All the life stories I heard featured powerful moments of revelation, when the speaker saw a new way of placing himself or herself in a semiotic or contextual field that balanced allegiances toward both peers and parents. For Kavi, who grew up in a Jain family in New Jersey, self-understanding came through observing a recent immigrant from India at her high school in the 1980s.

> There was this one kid who for some reason I always think of. He was a freshman, I guess I was a junior. He could not speak English at all, and he was very very small. He looked like he was eleven. He was very small, a very very thin child. He had this huge book bag.
>
> Anyway, I just remember seeing him, and he always sat completely by himself, and no one talked to him. One day I remember seeing him—like I said it didn't erupt in violence most of the time—but I saw him mostly being pushed and sort of shoved out of the way.
>
> I said something like "Why don't you just leave him alone." I guess the epithet then was "Gandhi." I don't understand why that became a curse word. I remember them saying that and saying about him dressing badly. Or something. And I said, "Why don't you just leave him alone!" Because this child, this kid really, he was really just sad, he was always alone and he was so tiny really so vulnerable. And I remember these kids turning to me and saying, "This is nothing to do with you," because I don't have any kind of accent.
>
> And I remember that for me—and I could be rewriting the past—I remember that being for me a pivotal time that I stopped trying so hard to like hide away being Indian, and starting to realize that these were the kinds of people, that was what was making me angry, and not my family. Because I did spend time being ashamed of my family. The fact that my parents had accents, that they didn't really eat at American restaurants, they didn't know how to do that. You know, dinner somewhere, they didn't exactly know how to go about things. The whole money issue was always hard. But anyway, this was when I stopped feeling so bad about myself and just realizing that there were a certain kind of people I just really didn't like.

Such moments of revelation often emerged in a series, as the speaker discovered different ways of bridging and mingling multiple cultures rather than experiencing them as an opposition framed by parents. For some, this meant learning more about South Asia, whether by taking classes in college, or by joining a Hindu student group, like Parvati, or by traveling alone rather than with parents to India or Pakistan, like Dinesh, Arjun, and several other men. For others, this meant becoming knowledgeable and active in larger U.S. minority issues, or becoming involved in political action (cf. Matthew and Prashad 1999/2000). Shankar, for example, had grown up in a Milwaukee suburb, feeling "very white." During his second semester at the University of Wisconsin, though he was pressured by a prestigious accelerated pre-med program, he also began taking classes "that expanded how I looked at where I was, and the stories that I heard, and who I talked to." Among the classes he took was one on race and ethnicity that sensitized him to subtle racism around him as well as educating him on historical inequalities.

In a good-natured parody, Jyoti, who grew up in Cleveland in a family with south Indian roots, outlined two strategies of finding a new balance—becoming more Indian, or becoming more knowledgeable as a United States minority—as "two kinds of stories."

> There are the kids who love their culture and do bhangra dance and say *"chalo, chalo"* [let's go] to each other on the street. They talk to each other in Hindi. There are tons of kids like this in Berkeley. Like I was by the Xerox machine in Berkeley, and this girl came up to me, and she said something to me in Gujarati. I said, "I don't know what you're saying." She said, "Why don't you speak your language?" I said, "Because I'm not Gujarati." But she was born here! So there are those kinds of South Asian second-generation kids. When they tell stories, they tell stories of like, going to the Indian parties, and how Mom does *puja* [worship] in the house, and this and that, about their Indianness, you see what I mean? And then there's MY kind of South Asian.

To illustrate what she meant about her kind of South Asian, Jyoti told me a story about she and her friend Sumitra swapping stories about the first time that their mothers cut their hair and wore Western clothes in their professional lives. She also humorously recounted being mistaken as an "Indian from India" by fellow Americans when she was traveling in Varanasi (resulting in a quip from her mother, who, alluding to the pervasive presence of doctors of Indian origin in the United States, said: "You should have asked them who their doctor is!"). Jyoti reflected:

> I think our stories are all about how we negotiated being Indian and being American, and finding a DIFFERENT balance. I think of my balance as sort of—I'm loath to say it—more assimilationist. See, our stories aren't just about being more Indian in America, they're about being American AND Indian.

Family Stories

As Stuart Hall has noted, "[I]dentities are the names we give to the different ways we are positioned by, and position ourselves within, the narratives of the past" (1990: 225) One of the main sites that the past is transported within diasporas is in family stories. Jean Bacon has explored what she terms the "family idiom" in her account of Indian American assimilation within the United States: that is, orientations shared within families that surfaced in the themes or styles through which parents and children told of their lives in interviews (Bacon 1996: 78). While I ideally would have interviewed the parents of the people I spoke with to gain a sense of how family stories and orientations are transmitted, even without the input of parents, it was clear that the identity of most individuals drew ballast from family stories.

The form of family story most often told involved tracing the routes of arrival: how it happened that the parents emigrated and the person was born here. Given the class background of most of the people I talked to, the story of immigration was also often one of parental accomplishment, often resulting in pressure for children to do well, too. As Sudam said, "Yeah, for me, I feel I am a total overachiever. That's my middle name." Later he commented, "I want to be a little bit more relaxed, but I'm really driven to make my mark on history." When I countered by asking, "Where does that come from?" Sudam responded, "I don't know. My dad was very ambitious. He did lots of activities, he was a student leader. It died off as he grew older. But I think he made a solid impact on this." He then went on to tell the story of how his father arrived in the Chicago area in 1972 as a trained physician.

Bina, a graduate student who grew up in the Chicago area, described how she thought of herself in terms of her family, starting with a tale that was often repeated to her when she visited India and sat on an outdoor swing with her maternal grandmother, mother, and aunts.

> I have wonderful stories that have been passed on to me. I'll start with my grandmother because that's really the one I know well. . . . My grandmother, when she was about four, I guess, her father died leaving her mother widowed with two daughters. As you probably know, her mother had to shave her head and wear a red sari and that kind of thing, and it was just really, really—she couldn't leave the house, so they were basically penniless and they didn't have any money. So my grandmother, who by the time she was six was in school, because of her good grades, she was able to get a scholarship, and with that money they started saving. And eventually that was the money that would put her sister through a wedding. So my grandmother really used her intelligence and scholarship and all that to bring the family together, and there's a lot more to that story, but basically she worked really hard. . . . She became a lawyer, so she was able to claim land. . . . She was able to use that land—sold it, and then with that money they were able to survive. My grandmother, then, really is brilliant and has used her intelligence all her life to survive. So a lot of her stories are really about using what you can in your life, given your station in life, but completely restrictive because she was a woman. And this was something that I've been told so many times as a child.

These stories about accomplishments on Bina's mother's side were offset by negative examples from her father's side, where his sisters all appeared to be trapped in unsupportive marriages. These diverging legacies have made Bina determined to excel in her education, and to support herself.

Sometimes the lineage evoked through stories could go back several centuries. Manjeet, for example, told me of his grandfather who migrated from the Punjab, living apart and sending back remittances for fifty years. In an almost offhand way, he also revealed his Sikh family's lineage of healing:

> My dad would tell us stories about Guru Gobind Singh coming to Gobind-pur, that's why the village is named after him, you know? The crippled— crippled man being on the ground. And him taking the knife they use to cut the wheat with and it going back and forth between him and the man. And it's called *"bāgbi,"* I think, I'm not sure. Then—then him getting up. And being able to walk. And now any—everybody—every male from the village who's named —— can do this. Any male. . . . So people come from all over the country to our house for us to do this to them . . . —the healing of Sikhs.

Manjeet went on to tell me of how a Sikh taxi driver from New York came all the way to Cincinnati so Manjeet's father could exchange a steak knife back and forth, and so heal the man's back.

Sometimes, though, family stories could also be repressive, particularly when they involved comparison with other South Asian kids. Everyone seemed to grow up hearing about the successes of cousins, or even of South Asian American peers. Medha spoke with disdain of the stories her mother told of her cousin back in Gujarat. She'd talk, said Medha,

> [a]bout how my cousin could cook a meal for eighty people when she was eight years old, or something like that. Things like that. Or how she had this beautiful long dark thick hair. It was just like "all Indian girls are sup-posed to have long luscious hair." And I came to really detest that. I hated all the comparison. I couldn't understand. To me it was very clear, "I'm liv-ing in America, OF COURSE I'm not going to be like my cousin." But it seemed like they just couldn't get that!

Retelling her mother's story, Medha reframed it with her own punch line. This reading of new meanings into older stories is common to any transmission of folklore, but perhaps in an immigrant context the frames change faster. Kavi, for example, now a graduate student in a humanities discipline, noted the conventionality in her middle-class family: no art, no books. "Can we be an extended family who don't do anything different?" she asked. Scanning family stories for resonances to her own restless desire to break free, live alone, and pursue a higher degree in a non-science-related field, she could at first find only minor rebellion, like a cousin in Uttar Pradesh eating Chinese food. Then she found kinship with her grandmother.

My grandmother was nineteen. After my father had been born, she tried to commit suicide, and she threw herself off the roof, and she ended up hurting her hip and her leg, and she's been crippled ever since. That's some spark of acting out that hasn't reappeared in my generation! What I'm doing is totally incomprehensible to the majority of my family.

In this retelling, then, Kavi took a skeleton out the family closet, reappropriating it as a courageous protest.

Mythology and Folktales

Given the rich profusion of oral traditions in South Asia, it is no surprise that folktales and mythology surfaced in family contexts in the United States, too. Zeynab, for example, recalled how her Pakistani mother would tell assorted family stories as well as folktales as she drove the children to appointments across the city where they lived.

> *Zeynab:* I guess I've heard some of the stories over and over. I think I remember them differently as a child than I did when I was older. A lot of them were about a mother's devotion to her child. There was one that used to make me cry *every* time I heard it, and then, there were . . .
> *KN:* What was that?
> *Z:* That one was about . . . a mother whose husband had died in the war. Independence. Fighting for Independence. And she had to raise the son. Alone. You know, working in other people's houses. She used to clean their clothes, scrub their floors, a very hard life. And she did it just because she wanted to give her son a good life with all the things that he would need.
> So the son grows up with everything he wants and he falls in love with a woman. And the woman is very *chālāki,* very. . . .
> *KN:* Sly, clever.
> *Z:* Very sly. And also very selfish. She was very resentful of her mother-in-law's love for the son. He had fallen head over heels in love with her. I mean, he was, you know, *dīvāna* [crazily in love], right? So he wanted to marry her. . . . So the woman says I'll marry you only if you kill your mother and bring me her heart. And so the young boy *eventually* succumbs. He became so overwhelmed with his passion for this woman that one night he goes and kills his mother and he takes out the heart. And then he's walking to his lover's home and he trips over a rock and he falls. And then, a voice, his mother's voice comes from the heart and says, "Son, are you okay?"

Zeynab's mother's voice, speaking Urdu, had left powerful traces on the texture of this poignant story. Zeynab said, "Oh! I used to cry and cry and cry when I heard that. . . . I think that in a lot of ways, you know, I did see my mother in that role because she had really made a lot of sacrifices for all of us. I mean, she had literally given her life to us." The use of folktales like this, then, could serve as a powerful link between generations, inspiring reflection not just on larger meanings but also on relationships between parents and their children.

It was at the level of religious folklore that the most difference between backgrounds was apparent, with second-generation South Asian Americans being differentially exposed to different bodies of mythology by parents or even grandparents. While parents' hope often appears to have been inculcating a firm sense of nationalized religious identity, second-generation individuals appeared to sometimes adapt such stories in creative, even resistant ways. Medha, for example, found a new strength and confidence after going off to college, and began challenging her parents on a variety of subjects, including Hindu mythology.

> There are stories about Prahlad who had this awful father who was against God and wanted to proclaim himself as God and Prahlad would have none of that and he was disobeying his father because he knew there was something better. I want to say to my parents, "So when I disobey you it's because I *know* that there's something better, it's not because I want to throw it in your face." And that's not something they want me to see in that story! What they want me to see in that story was "Oh, he was so devoted to God that even though his father was doing all his to him, he was still devoted to God." We definitely have different interpretations of things and they are very rigid. That doesn't work well with the lifestyle that I have made for myself here.

Another strategy was to bring together imagined characters from different cultural settings. Shankar confessed that he identified with the god Shiva, whose name he carried. As he reported, "They said, well, this god has a cobra around his neck. I always had a fascination with snakes. I used to in first grade watch as many snake shows and documentaries as I could." At the same time, he also had admired Superman, and at one point had identified with Superman so strongly that he adopted blue contact lenses, like Christopher Reeve. "Not because I wanted to be white-like but because of the contrast, dark skin, blue eyes."

The *Amar Chitra Katha* mythological comic books were pressed upon most of Hindu children by their parents. Arjun, who grew up in Ohio, learned his Indian stories from these comic books, or from his mother reading aloud Hindu myths. He drew on these story characters to illustrate his own sense of dislocation. For example, he identified strongly with the tragic unacknowledged brother Karna in the Mahabharata epic "because of his kind of outcaste . . . birth . . . his outcaste background." While Shankar had Hindu gods and comic-book superheroes coexisting in his imagination as a child, Arjun actually mingled them together, inventing a hybrid mythology, "like Batman and Bheem [a strong brother in the Mahabharata]."

[S]uperheroes were a part of my imagination. My mythology if you want to call it. So I was thinking to myself, "Yeah, I have this secret society, a secret association, a secret identity that nobody here understands or can figure out." And it's kind of—in a way, like the alter ego of a Batman. Like when he goes into the bat cave, you know, nobody . . . knows about his secret life. . . .

So it was that sort of thing, for me. And that was my way—I think—at the time, of understanding my religion, my difference, my ethnicity. Because at the time, of course, you have no vocabulary. You have no concepts. So this is the way I thought of it. At that moment, I think it was a positive valuation of my situation.

THE USES OF STORIES

Too often, anthropologists fixate on the particular life-story texts they have gathered and neglect to inquire what other situations these stories are used in, and what forms of cultural politics manifest in narrations (cf. Rosenwald and Ochberg 1992). After the interviews, I tried to get back to different people I had talked to in an attempt to better understand the wider life of their stories. Here are a few of their responses:

Najma wrote on e-mail that she tells stories about her experience to "just about anyone who I feel can relate. Mostly, I feel, because I want someone to help me through this experience where I feel few can truly understand and give me meaningful advice . . . " Similarly Vina stated, "To me, intimacy is about sharing secrets. I don't tell these stories much, just sometimes to close friends. And, also to my therapist." Zeynab also felt that her memories were precious and personal. Since she had told her stories as gifts to me, my challenge has been to incorporate her articulate voice in my writings for a larger audience in a way that will hopefully not make her feel too exposed.

The women, then, mostly seemed to concur on storytelling as relating to the creation of intimacy or the assumption of preexisting intimacy. Jyoti, though, one of the most hilarious of all the storytellers, wrote that she loved telling stories "because I like to entertain people, I use them to explain myself, I use them to fill in open spaces in conversation . . . "

The men whom I was able to get answers from also had varying views. At one extreme was Dinesh, an exuberant performer of his own tales, who said on the phone, "I tell stories for shock value. Like my condom story is a classic, I tell it to Americans [meaning white Americans] if they ever say their parents are too strict. With Indian kids I love to tell stories about my drug use. Like, you know, it's all about subverting expectations."

Shankar, though, who is younger and more cautious, reported that he did not tell his stories much to others: mostly his strategy was to ask questions, and listen. He said that he wished that he knew "more Indian kids" to share these stories of growing up with, so they could support each other.

Vasant, who grew up in the 1960s with virtually no South Asian American peers to identify with, most poignantly articulates how telling stories functions as emplacement within a changing social landscape. I first spoke to him in 1997 as South Asian American undergraduates were a growing presence on campus, *chai* appeared in coffee-shops, *bindis* showed up on rock stars' foreheads, and *mahendi* (henna) became available in temporary tattooing kits at Walgreens. Looking back in 1999, he said, "I never told anyone those stories about growing up before. When I told you these stories it was a form of catharsis, I guess. But it raised questions, too: what intersections had made it possible to say now what wasn't possible to say before?"

CONCLUSIONS

Using the term "emplacement," I want to call attention to the *process* of staking out space rather than to *any single moment of fixed arrival.* After all, there are multiple spaces and multiple strategies by which people make space in the world for their distinctive experience. In a brilliant article critiquing the invention of authenticity in the South Asian diaspora, Radhakrishnan points out that the mutation of an "Indian" identity into an "ethnic" or hyphenated American one reminds us to question whether "identities and ethnicities are not a matter of fixed and stable selves but rather the results and products of fortuitous travels and recontextualizations?" (1994: 222).

Life stories among second-generation South Asian Americans worked as emplacement in two ways. First, the very act of making narrative coherence appeared to be a way of integrating conflicting identities. If elements did not fit together anywhere else, they were made to do so in the stories. Telling stories that bridge different arenas of diasporic experience becomes a powerful way of placing the self, and finding new ground for being a culturally mixed but not necessarily mixed-up person.

Second, by telling these stories, inserting distinctive experience into a wider social arena, life stories, like ethnic literature more generally, can be a powerful vehicle of asserting "I'm Here" (cf. Ling 1991). Whether the stories are told to friends, therapists, or nosy anthropologists, the act of telling is also a way of taking others along on the journey that one has lived, with emotional, social, and political consequences. I believe that the same narrative impulse that underlies oral storytelling about lives also permeates the vibrant short story, memoir, and essay collections addressing South Asian American experience that burgeoned in the 1990s (Dasgupta 1998;

Gupta 1999; Ratti 1993; Rustomji-Kerns 1994; Srikanth and Maira 1996; Women of South Asian Descent Collective 1993).

Sharing drafts of this essay with those I interviewed, the concept of emplacement appears to resonate with their experience. Dinesh rephrased my central argument, saying, "See, this emplacement is all about accepting that you don't belong anywhere but the space that you make." In an e-mail, Vasant emphasized the psychological importance of emplacement by reflecting that his need to tell the stories rose from a boiling over of "the feelings of fatigue from a constantly floating state of UNplacement (a condition of feeling like I belong nowhere, so it's not even 'displacement' because that assumes one felt emplaced at some point in the past)."

These comments underscore the importance of stories in this era of multiple identifications, multiple locations, multiple possible sites of return. For those of us who span so many selves and spaces that it seems we can never rest from the work of building bridges back and forth and back again, perhaps the only momentary home is in stories. Making and remaking stories, we frame our own shelters to house the divergent meanings we carry around. Sharing, spreading, claiming distinctiveness, or making alliances with stories, we stake out new spaces in the power-laden, shifting contours of multicultural landscapes.

ACKNOWLEDGMENTS

I am grateful for support from the University of Wisconsin Graduate School, particularly in the form of a Vilas Associateship Faculty Award, an H. I. Romnes fellowship, and a faculty development grant that have enabled me to explore new directions in my research. I am deeply indebted to every kind person who gifted me with time, stories, and critical readings. In honoring confidentiality, I cannot thank you all by name here. Audiences at the Wisconsin South Asia Meetings, the American Folklore Society, the University of Wisconsin, Cornell University, and the University of California at Riverside have all helped in shaping this essay. Special thanks to Regina Bendix, Veena Dwivedi, Sarah Lamb, Maria Lepowsky, Diane Mines, Seema Rao, Hemant Shah, Deepak Sharma, and Nina Tayyib for sustained insights and editorial suggestions.

Unexpected Destinations

E. Valentine Daniel

Editors' note: E. Valentine Daniel, in his book Charred Lullabies, *attempts to understand some of the causes and effects of the
civil war in Sri Lanka, in particular some of the toll that the war
has taken upon Sri Lanka's Tamil population as well as upon the
nation itself. In this excerpt from chapter 6, Daniel discusses some
of the kinds of experiences that Tamil refugees from Sri Lanka
(see part V) have when they flee their nation in search of refuge
elsewhere. We enter his book at a point where Daniel has been discussing three "phases" of Sri Lankan Tamil migration to Britain.
The first phase, Phase 1 immigrants, are "the elite." They were
upper-class Sri Lankans who migrated well before the civil war,
either during or in the wake of colonial rule, often to obtain advanced professional and graduate degrees. By staying in England,
this group severed their ties to Sri Lanka and became British citizens. Phase 2 immigrants are those who came not as elites, but as
students from a variety of class backgrounds in the 1960s and
1970s. Facing unemployment at home and locked out of universities, which had imposed a quota system that worked to the disadvantage of many Tamil students, they found England to be a
viable alternative for pursuing education as well as employment.
Many were disappointed to find that the jobs available to them,
and for which they were often overqualified, were frequently limited to the service sector, such as in gas stations or convenience
stores. Phase 3, the phase that this selection focuses upon, consists
of "refugees," those who beginning in the 1980s fled Sri Lanka in
order to stay alive.*

The early arrivals of Phase 3 had still been those with at least some means: the means to leave before Britain began tightening her laws, before the Immigration Carrier's Liability Act was passed,[1] before racketeers got into the act of facilitating the asylum-seeker's escape with false papers at high cost, before the price for getting to Heathrow went from under four hundred British pounds to more than five thousand. The "success stories" with petrol stations and retail stores that one is likely to hear from asylum-seekers apply mainly to those early arrivals who came to Britain before 1985. For the very poor—increasingly the profile of the average Tamil arriving at Heathrow during the latter part of the 1980s—the new exorbitant passage was bought for only one family member through his or her family's going deeply into debt, in some instances after selling house and possessions. No longer could the one who entered Britain raise enough money to pay back his or her own debt, let alone raise enough to pay the going price for chancy "illegal" exits and entries of other members of the family. And even if and when this was possible, the pits and snares were too many and far too hazardous. There are cases known to the London-based Joint Council for the Welfare of Immigrants in which middlemen—also Tamils—have abandoned groups of Tamils at "transit points" in such faraway places as Bangkok and Nairobi, after these same middlemen absconded with the five thousand plus pounds' "setup money" they received from their charges. Such a middleman takes them to an apartment or a room and tells them to stay put—lest they be caught by the authorities—until he makes arrangements for the next leg of the journey to London or some other Western capital. The room or apartment in question is locked from the outside to ensure double protection. The anxious and frightened group waits, at times for days, until hunger and/or suspicion gets the better of them and they break loose or start screaming for help. Some such desperate and penniless escapees are then offered, by yet another set of racketeers, the opportunity to become drug couriers as a means of buying their way back onto the road to asylum. A refugee who gave me the above account concluded it by saying:

> You ask me about Tamil nationalism. There is only Tamil internationalism. No Tamil nationals. Never was. Never will be. This is Tamil internationalism. Being stuck in a windowless room in Thailand, or a jail in Nairobi or Accra or Lagos or Cairo or America. Or being a domestic servant in Singapore or Malaysia for a rich Tamil relative. Being part of a credit card racket in London. Crossing Niagara Falls into Canada. I am told there is even a Tamil fisherman on a Norwegian island near the North Pole. All internationals. And don't forget the briefless barrister at Charing Cross who tries to hawk his specialty as an immigration lawyer to anyone who is gullible enough to believe him. He is a Tamil too.

The African destinations were explained to me as follows by yet another informant:

> No one plans on ending up in Africa. This happens because of drug-pushing middlemen. Customs in African airports are not that strict. And most of the airport officials are bribed by other agents.
> Q. Who are these agents? Tamils?
> A. They are. Mainly members of PLOTE.[2] They are caught and deported from European ports back to their last stop, usually Nigeria.

The African connection was widely explained in the following manner: Middlemen in Thailand or Pakistan buy desperate Tamils tickets to African destinations, giving them a package of drugs and a promise of a final European or Canadian destination. The Tamils' only obligation is to hand over the package to an African courier in Africa. Unlike Tamils, Africans are willing to carry their drugs in a form undetectable by European customs: stuffed in a condom that is then swallowed. Because of this method, Africans passed through customs with ease until recently, when a swallowed condom burst in a courier's stomach. The courier was rushed to the hospital where he died, and an autopsy exposed the game. Even though the Tamil role in the Africans' trafficking of drugs has achieved widely held folkloric truth, I have been able neither to confirm nor to disconfirm this story with any Tamil who has directly participated in this dangerous activity. It is known, however, that the use of drugs is strictly prohibited not only by the general Tamil cultural strictures and the opprobrium it could bring upon those who violate them, but also by the moral policing of the LTTE. Drugs are meant for Europeans. The money that is believed to result from the sale of drugs is meant for the war effort in Eelam.

The story of Tamil asylum-seekers' ending up in the United States is a curious one. The number of asylum-seekers who have been granted asylum in the United States over the past decade is around a dozen, more than half of whom are Sinhalas who fled the government's crackdown on dissidents in the south of the island. It is widely known in the Tamil community that it is virtually impossible to get asylum in the United States. Almost none who sought asylum in the United States had intended to do so in the first place, but had been trapped in transit on their way to Canada, where they had hoped to find refuge. The story of Shanmugam is both unique and typical and is worth recalling in some detail.

Shanmugam was a twenty-eight-year-old Tamil whom I came to know in 1989 through a human rights attorney in Seattle, who asked me if I would serve as an expert witness at his hearing before an immigration judge. According to Shanmugam and affidavits sent on his behalf by justices of the peace and other prominent citizens of Jaffna, he was the son of

a farmer. He had an older sister and a younger brother. He was unconnected with any of the several Tamil militant groups operating in Jaffna.
But he was persecuted by two Tamil militant groups, members of the Indian Peace-Keeping Forces, and the Sri Lankan army. He had bullet marks
on his foot and shoulder where he had been shot by an EPRLF[3] guard. He
finally fled Sri Lanka in fear of his life. Now let me continue the narrative
based on his account to his attorney and me, and to the court.

From 1980 until the riots of 1983 he lived with his married sister in a
suburb of Colombo. He had moved from Jaffna to Colombo because he
wanted to prepare himself for the G.C.E. (Advanced Level) exams by attending a private "tutory" in Colombo. In 1983, Sinhala mobs attacked his
brother-in-law's home by setting fire to it. His sister had left for Jaffna, to
deliver, as is customary, her first child in her mother's home. His brother-
in-law, who tried to face the mob and dissuade them from attacking his
house, was killed. Shanmugam jumped out of a back window and over the
garden wall and fled the scene. After spending several weeks in refugee
camps in Colombo, he joined an exodus of Tamil refugees and went to
Jaffna by boat.

Back in Jaffna, he and his younger brother tried their best to hide from
recruiters from the various Tamil militant groups combing Jaffna for volunteers who would be trained to fight the Sri Lankan state. In 1985, his
seventeen-year-old brother disappeared, leaving behind a note inform-
ing his parents that he was joining the liberation struggle. In 1986, Shanmugam was taken in for questioning by members of the Sri Lankan army.
After two weeks of considerable beating and torture, and interventions by
the then government agent and his pleading mother, he was released to his
parents. Then came the Indo–Sri Lankan Peace Accord by the terms of
which the Indian army occupied northern and eastern Sri Lanka so as to
restore peace between the Tamils and the Sri Lankan state. A few months
after the LTTE had declared its battle against the Indian army, members of
the Indian army took him in for questioning. The solitary confinement and
beatings lasted for a week. Again, he was released. Again, Shanmugam attributes his release to his mother's indefatigable pleadings with the Indian
commander. No sooner was he released than he was captured by the LTTE
and taken in for questioning. This time the questions were about what he
had told the Indians and what he knew about the whereabouts of his
brother. In response to the first question he told them all that he remembered. As for his brother's whereabouts, he said that he knew nothing,
not even which militant group he had joined. During the first week of his
confinement, he was relentlessly tortured. During the second week, even
though the questions continued, he was treated well by the Tigers.

The very day he was released by the Tigers, he was recaptured by the
Eelam People's Revolutionary Liberation Front. The EPRLF was a Tamil
militant group that came under the good graces of the Indian forces and

was given a certain measure of civil and military authority over the citizens of Jaffna. But members of this group also abused their authority, had alienated many Tamils of the north, and came to be seen as the lackeys of the occupying Indians. According to Shanmugam, the torture under the EPRLF was the most severe. First, they were convinced that he had gone voluntarily to the LTTE to divulge details of the interrogation by the Indians, and wanted to know what he had told them. Second, convinced that his younger brother was with the Tigers, they were keen on capturing him for the Indians, who were by now at war with the Tigers. After several weeks of incarceration, torture, and interrogation, Shanmugam managed to escape. He fled Jaffna and after several days of walking through the jungle, he reached Mannar. From there he bought his passage on a speedboat and reached India. From India he informed his parents of his safety and his whereabouts. He knew that it would be only a matter of time before one of the militant groups, if not the Indian authorities, would catch up with him. While in Madras, he learned that he could get a forged passport and a ticket to Canada. Through labyrinthine means he informed his parents of his plans to buy a passport and leave for Canada. A month later, his mother and sister sold all their jewelry, and his father sold most of their land; through equally labyrinthine means they sent him $5,000. With this money he was able to buy a forged passport at a discounted price and to pay a travel agent, who supplied an air ticket, arranged the route of his flight, and provided him with a contact who knew someone in Vancouver, B.C.; the contact would help him learn the ropes for applying for and obtaining asylum in Canada. The only thing he was told he needed to remember was to destroy his passport and flush it down the toilet of the airplane just before landing in Vancouver. His passport was red in color, Malaysian, and was quite worn from considerable use. It seemed as if it had belonged to a Malaysian businessman.

Shanmugam was routed through Hong Kong and, unlike his compatriots who were stranded in Bangkok, did not have to leave any of the airports en route until he reached Seattle. All that he had seen of the countries through which his flight pattern took him were the airports' transit lounges. In Seattle, all passengers had to disembark and go through U.S. customs before continuing on their flight to Vancouver. No one had warned him of this wrinkle in his itinerary. Even before he got to the long line in front of the customs officer's high table with his tin trunk in hand, he was apprehended by another officer and taken in for questioning. He told them his story. He told them that he had no intention of remaining in the United States but wanted to reach Canada. When given the choice of either being sent back by the next available flight or being incarcerated until he received a hearing where the odds of his repatriation to Sri Lanka were almost assured, Shanmugam chose the latter. This is a short and sweet version of the more detailed, horrendous tale he had told his lawyer and me, and later a court over which a judge by the name of Kahn presided.

A particular episode of the court hearing merits retelling because it illustrates yet another aspect of refugees' predicament that goes unreported: Shanmugam spoke no English and understood almost none. To assist him, the court had hired a South Asian living in Seattle who had been certified by Berlitz as qualified to translate English into Tamil and vice versa. Under cross-examination, Shanmugam had just finished describing the burning of his sister's house in Colombo and the murder of his brother-in-law.

DEFENDANT: And then I ran through the side streets, to avoid the mobs.
PROSECUTOR: Who were these mobs made up of?
TRANSLATOR: (Renders an intelligible translation in a form of Tamil heavily accented by Malayalam.)
DEFENDANT: Sinhalas.
TRANSLATOR: Sinhalas.
JUDGE: Were there policemen on the street?
TRANSLATOR: (Translates the question correctly into Malayalam. The defendant strains to follow him and then answers.)
DEFENDANT: Police and army.
TRANSLATOR: Yes.
JUDGE: Did they help you?
TRANSLATOR: (Translates question into Malayalamized Tamil, but the defendant seems to follow the drift of the question, and responds.)
DEFENDANT: No. They hit me with their rifles. And when I fell down, they kicked me with their boots and said, "Run, Tamil, run."
TRANSLATOR: Yes.

At this point I told the defense attorney that the translation was incorrect, and he conveyed this to the judge.

JUDGE (to defense attorney): Your expert witness is an expert on Sri Lanka. But the translator is an expert in the language spoken and accordingly has been certified by Berlitz. Is your expert witness certified by Berlitz as an expert in . . . Tamil?
DEFENSE ATTORNEY (after seeing me shake my head): No, Your Honor.

Almost immediately after asking the prosecutor to continue, the judge interrupted the prosecutor, asking the court recorder to stop recording the proceedings and turn off the tape recorder. Off the record, the judge asked me to render what I thought was the correct translation of the defendant's response to his question.

EXPERT WITNESS: He said that the police and soldiers did not help him but hit him with the butts of their rifles and, when he fell down, kicked him with their boots and said, "Run, Tamil, run."

JUDGE (to Berlitz translator): Is that correct?

TRANSLATOR (now realizing that there is a native speaker of Tamil in the courtroom): Yes, Your Honor.

At another point in the hearing:

PROSECUTOR: Are you a Malaysian?

TRANSLATOR: (Renders an intelligible translation.)

DEFENDANT: No.

PROSECUTOR: What is your nationality?

TRANSLATOR: Tamil or Sinhala?

DEFENDANT: Tamil.

TRANSLATOR: Tamil.

PROSECUTOR: So you believe in a separate Tamil nation in Sri Lanka?

TRANSLATOR: Do you want a Tamil nation (*tēśam*)?

DEFENDANT: No. I don't even have a country (translatable as "a place to which I belong").

TRANSLATOR: No.

Malayalam is a language spoken in southwest India. Linguists estimate that its breakaway from early Tamil occurred around the thirteenth century. The mutual intelligibility between modern Malayalam and modern Tamil is akin to that between Italian and Spanish. Imagine a monolingual Italian-speaker certified by Berlitz as one who speaks and understands Spanish, and appointed to serve as translator in a court of law between English-speaking attorneys and judge and a monolingual Spanish-speaking defendant. Such was Shanmugam's predicament.

As a postscript to this memorable trial I might add that Judge Kahn rendered his judgment against the defendant. In his judgment he thanked me for my testimony and for educating the court on the recent history of the ethnic tensions in Sri Lanka. But he declared that in the final analysis, he was compelled to take the word of his State Department in meting out his judgment. According to the State Department, "there was no fear of persecution in Sri Lanka."

After two years we learned that Judge Kahn's judgment had been upheld by higher courts. Shanmugam was sent back to Sri Lanka. His family came to meet him at the Colombo airport. They claim to have seen him arrive at customs and then to have waited for him to emerge. But he never came out. After several hours of waiting and inquiries and receiving different kinds of answers, they tried to console themselves by saying that their having seen him briefly must have been only an illusion. Other inquiries pointed toward Sri Lanka's Special Defense Forces, who, it was said, had whisked him off to the notorious Fourth Floor for interrogation. Whatever the case may be, Shanmugam has been neither seen nor heard from since that day.

While waiting for his appeal, Shanmugam had learned Spanish from co-detainees who had come from countries such as El Salvador, Guatemala, and Nicaragua. The detention center was a small international community of card-playing, Ping-Pong batting, story-swapping, language-learning males. Far fewer women were apprehended at the border, and when they were, most of them chose to return to Sri Lanka or managed to get themselves bailed out by relatives in the United States and then found their way to Canada. But there were children who were arrested and detained and whose story needs to be told, if only because of the uniquely dangerous situation into which they are thrown by a well-meaning legal system. Two such cases merit our attention.

AND CHILDREN

Karunaharan was sixteen years old. He too, like Shanmugam, had his asylum-seeking trip to Canada cut short at the U.S. customs in Seattle. He came from a middle-class family in Jaffna and had, until his escape, attended the prestigious secondary school of Jaffna College along with his older sister. One day when he and his sister were walking back home from school, they were stopped by a Sikh soldier of the Indian Peace-Keeping Forces. He was told to wait on the road while his sister was taken into a house occupied by some Indian army officers. Within minutes of her disappearance behind the closed door of the house, he heard his sister's screams. He ran to the side window of the house, and through a crack he saw his sister "being shamed."[4] Then he ran to the front door, which was being guarded by two grinning Indian soldiers, and tried to get access. He was kicked by one of them, and he fell to the ground unable to breathe. Then he heard his sister's screams become muffled, and grow fainter and fainter, and then he heard her no more. He thought that he was dying. Then he thought that his sister was dead. He sat up and wiped his mouth. There was blood. The place of the two soldiers who were guarding the door had been taken over by two others. And finding them engrossed in their own conversation, he crept back to the window just in time to see his sister being shot in the back. He sneaked back to the main road, and when he reached it, he heard a second shot. He ran home sobbing and screaming. After that incident, his parents managed to get him on a flight to Canada, which brought him into Seattle's detention center instead.

Karunaharan was not an adult and therefore was put in a detention center for children, where his co-detainees were streetwise American teenagers who were incarcerated for crimes that ranged from selling drugs to aggravated assault, to robbery, and even rape. Bright as he was and as much as he tried to adjust to the ethos of the place, his middle-class village background in conservative Jaffna had not prepared him for this. He was gang-raped the very first night and beaten up the next. His attorney succeeded in persuading the judge to release him to the custody of a Tamil citizen in the Seattle area in whose charge he was to be kept until his next hearing. He eventually crossed the border into Canada and was granted asylum there.

Shoba was ten years old when the Indian troops came to Jaffna to keep the peace. When I interviewed her with her attorney in Seattle, she was thirteen. According to her, the Indian soldiers whom the citizens of Jaffna had welcomed with garlands had, within a few months, become enemies of all the people, excepting those who joined the "EP" or supported them. (People in her neighborhood secretly called the EPRLF "EP" and rhymed it with *nāi pī*, "dog shit.") The EPRLF ranked foremost among organizations conceiving of a state based on socialist principles of equality: equality for all castes, both sexes, the Tamils of the various regions, and the Sinhalas. But when given the power of the gun and command by their Indian superiors, low-ranking cadres in particular became drunk with power and patrolled the streets intimidating the citizens. When an EPRLF officer rode in his car, other vehicles had to pull over to the edge of the road; when an EPRLF cadre walked along a street, ordinary citizens had to step to the side, even into a ditch if that was the only side left to the road. Those who refused to grant the respect due were taken in and punished or even beaten on the spot. Schoolchildren whose parents were not open supporters of the EP were especially afraid of running into uniformed members of the movement. They usually rode their bikes and chose side lanes and byways to make their way between home and school. One day Shoba and her friends were returning from school on their bikes laughing over a joke that her friend had cracked, when they suddenly ran into an EP commander with his assistants. They all quickly got off their bikes. The girl who had cracked the joke was her best friend, the class comic and very smart. She was so taken aback by the armed "soldiers" that she just got off her seat, did not have time to wheel the bike to the side of the road, and so stood astride her bike as if in shock—but still had a smile on her face because of her joke. One of the EP men jerked her off her bike. While the other threw the bike to the side of the road and smashed it, the commander ordered the man who had hold of her to take her to the field and made her kneel down. While Shoba and her schoolmates looked on in terror, the commander gave them a lecture about respect and the EPRLF, and then turned toward her kneeling friend and shot her in the head. Then he put his gun in his holster saying, "Let this be a lesson to you." The children pushed their bikes home, sobbing in silence for fear of being heard by the "soldiers," who continued on their promenade.

When she reached home, she broke into hysterical sobs. Her mother and father shook her to make her speak, tell them what had happened. Finally, her father, who had never spanked her, slapped her in order to calm her down. Then she told them what had happened. Her father warned them to expect trouble. "An old woman has shot an Indian officer," he told her. The Indian army had ordered the residents of a neighborhood to vacate their houses, so that they, in response to a tip-off, could carry out a search for Tigers and their weapons. The old woman had refused to leave; she merely huddled in a corner and whimpered in terror. Since the North Indian soldiers did not know Tamil, a compassionate South Indian officer—a Malayalee—went into the woman's low-doored hut and bent down to assure her in the little Tamil he knew that she would be safe under his protection, and pleaded with her to leave with him. The woman pulled out a machine gun that had been concealed by the drape of her sari and shot the officer to death. She in turn was riddled with bullets by the two Indian *jawāns* who had been waiting outside.

Even though the killing of the officer had taken place in another area of the peninsula, it was widely known that whenever a soldier was killed, the army would go on a rampage. This was truer of the Sri Lankan army during their earlier occupation, but it happened with the Indians as well. Shoba's father also had heard that those neighborhoods which "stole electricity" by jerry-rigging connections to the main line were thought to be LTTE sympathizers who were rewarded with LTTE expertise. Shoba maintained that this was not true, that ever since the onset of fuel and electricity rationing, citizens all over Jaffna had resorted to devices for beating the restrictions. As predicted by her father, that afternoon around four o'clock, soldiers came to the neighborhood. Most men had been tipped off to the Indians' arrival and had fled. The soldiers ordered everybody to step out of their homes, and the homes were searched. After the search was finished, the residents, all of them women, were told to go back in. Then a soldier came out of a house dragging a woman and her infant son. Shoba ran into the backyard to peek through the palm-frond fence and see what was happening. The senior officer asked the woman where the man of the house was. She said she did not know. He shot her dead. She fell backwards still holding onto her infant. When her hands let loose of her child and fell to her side, the child, still seated on her stomach, started to scream. The soldiers first left the child and his dead mother on the ground and walked out the front gate. A few moments later, one of the soldiers returned and shot the infant with one bullet. Suddenly there was not a sound to be heard.

That was the night her parents decided to send her out of the country. She had a cousin in Canada, and that would be her destination. But she had no passport. They managed to get her a forged passport, in which her age was recorded as eighteen rather than thirteen. She was too young to travel alone. So they found a naturalized Canadian relative and changed her name to read as if she were his wife; they then traveled to Canada as husband and wife. When they were apprehended in Seattle, it was clear that she was younger than eighteen and much too young to be married. Confessions were wrung out of them with ease. She and her partner were arrested. The partner posted bail and left for Canada. Fortunately for Shoba, there was a guard who, sensing the danger she faced in juvenile detention, pleaded with the judge to release her to the custody of someone—she herself was willing—who would take care of the young girl until her hearing. (In several instances, guards who have seen the danger that these children are in have volunteered to take them into their own homes.) The attorney assigned to defend Shoba got in touch with a Tamil family he knew and asked them if he might request that the judge release her to their custody. The male head of the family said that they would have been only too glad to help but feared to get drawn into anything that could signal their presence to the LTTE members who were operating in Europe and Canada, and who were very aggressive fund-raisers for the cause of Eelam. They did not want their name to appear on any LTTE list for fear that this would instigate the Sri Lankan government to harass and persecute family members who still remained on the island. Next, the lawyer contacted an Estate Tamil family that had intermarried with the Sinhalas. This family willingly and gladly took in Shoba, saying that Estate Tamils were still Indian Tamils and therefore had nothing to fear from a Sri Lankan movement such as the LTTE. After two weeks, they flew with her to Ithaca, where she was handed over to a Sri Lankan Tamil Catholic priest who took her across the Niagara bridge into Canada; there she applied for asylum and was met by her cousin. Before she crossed over, the priest asked her what she planned to do in Canada. Her answer: "Keep away from anyone who talks about Eelam or Sri Lanka or motherland."

Children much younger than Karunaharan and Shoba, as young as five years old, have been put onto planes unaccompanied by any adult and sent to Germany and Switzerland. The German and Swiss news media featured these arrivals in their headline stories. While some kind German and Swiss citizens rushed to adopt them, others described this as a new "wave" and called the children economic refugees. I expressed my puzzlement to a German woman at these children's being called "economic refugees." She saw what was happening as being quite straightforward, based on "confessions" by the children themselves. Most of the children who arrived at one of these country's airports, when asked where their parents were, would say, "Mommy said for me to go and that she will come soon and join me." That was the evidence: a mother's ruse to claim the right to emigrate to the country as a parent, once the child was naturalized! That the child would have to grow up to adulthood before being able to sponsor his or her parent, which would take as many as thirteen more years, did not seem like much of an issue. What this woman told me in an interview in Heidelberg was of course repeated more than once over the German and Swiss media. Many of the kind souls who offered to adopt these children, on the one hand, could not believe the cruelty of their parents, on the other: that they could lie to their children when they knew that they had neither plans nor possibility of following their children. The second group is no closer to the truth than the first.

Unfortunately or otherwise, most South Asian parents choose to hide the truth when the truth, they opine, is likely to cause immediate pain, sorrow, and sadness. This is so with terminally ill patients from whom the nature of their illness is concealed as long as possible by both physician and relatives. This is especially true of parents and children. A mother who is about to administer her child some bitter medicine will not hesitate to lie about its bitterness. The mother who sent off her unaccompanied child to Switzerland or Germany most probably did not have the luxury of reflecting on the long-range psychological trauma that such deceptions would wreak on her child. The story of one woman who had dispatched her child in such a manner and whom I had the opportunity to interview in Sri Lanka is likely to have been a typical variant of the accounts of other mothers (and, in a few instances, fathers) who resorted to such desperate actions.

Punitham lost her father, both brothers, and two of her four children. Left with only a son and a daughter, she decided to somehow or other get at least her son to safety. She knew that it would be only a matter of time before the next shell would fall or the next bullet would hit. She was determined to send her child to any country and have fate take over. Her choice for him was between certain death in Sri Lanka and a chancy life somewhere else. The only country that would not return her child, she had heard, was Germany. So she sold all her possessions and got her son a ticket. She could not get herself to tell her son the truth. How could she be so cruel? How could she tell him that he was never going to see her again, that she would most probably be killed, and that he most likely would be able to live? If she had told him that, how could he have left her behind and gone with the stranger whom he called "uncle," who took him to the airport? The only gift she thought that she could give him was the gift of life. And she is glad that she gave that to him. But otherwise, she says, "there isn't a day that goes by that I don't pray for him, and weep for him. He was my only son. He is my only son. I am glad he did not die for Sri Lanka or for Eelam. Maybe he will remember Tamil. That is enough. He will be a German-Tamil. That is enough." Economic refugee, indeed!

The Disaggregation of Identity

Many of the men who, having left their wives and children, came to Great Britain after 1985 came to escape death. Now they hold little hope of seeing their families again. They live in a state of heightened anxiety bounded by a seven-year limit: by the end of the seventh year they must, by law, be notified as to whether their application for asylum has been accepted. Many, unable to bear the strain, have returned home regardless of the consequences awaiting them, some to meet their death there. Others have gone back to Sri Lanka after learning that the reason for their having left that country in the first place no longer exists: their families have been wiped out by one armed group or another. The intransigence of British authorities and the scale of British xenophobia and racism vis-à-vis refugees (as evidenced by the frequent headlines of London's tabloids) are astounding when one realizes that between 1979 and 1989 Great Britain, with a population of almost 58,000,000, admitted only 54,935 refugees, a mere 0.09 percent of the total population. Of these only 7,910 were Sri Lankans (Turner 1996). If white Britain's reluctance to give refuge to asylum-seekers is astounding, Phase 1 Tamils' willingness to share in this sentiment is ironic, but also understandable. They, like the white Britons, believed in a nation and a nationalized past. In the case of Phase 3 refugees, the more urgently they needed a nation or a national past, the more authentically they encountered its unavailableness. The more obtrusively this unavailableness pressed itself upon the lives of these refugees, the more the nation and a national past revealed itself as something just occurrent and nothing more. The national past had been loosened from its hitherto unexpressed inclusion in the background practices of these Tamils. The nationalized past became an isolated property, a cipher.

By the beginning of the 1990s, further changes were observed in the composition of the more recent asylum-seeking cohort. Now, not only did young men and women who had escaped the Sri Lankan and Indian armies seek asylum in Britain, but war-hardened and disenchanted militants, escaping tyrannous militant groups of their own, were arriving in London. This group introduced a climate of suspicion on the one hand and a pervasive cynicism on the other. The most prominent target of this cynicism was the nation. I have witnessed arguments between these Tamils and their fellow Tamils who had embarked upon the project of finding and establishing their national past in which the former thought that the distant past which obsessed their fellow nationalists was irrelevant at best and a sign of derangement at worst. The only past they knew and cared enough not to want to be caught in was the recent past of war, rape, torture, and death that they had just escaped. Phase 3 Tamils have also begun to establish new alliances and to adopt new attitudes toward identity and difference that are now marking them off from Phase 1 Tamils in unprecedented ways. A series of examples will illustrate my point.

A number of Phase 3 Tamils who began at the petrol pump moved up to managing the petrol station and the attached "mini-markets," and then on to acquiring small grocery stores run by Ugandan Indians whose children now have no interest in inheriting their parents' businesses. Along with entailing late hours and hard work, the running of these shops presents a unique problem in customer relations. In Sivapalan's case, for instance, one of his customers is an older English woman who comes to his shop every day to ask him why he sells these nasty-smelling and strange-looking things, and why he does not take it all and go back to where he came from. Sivapalan smiles and checks out the items she buys—because they are inexpensive in his shop—and wishes her a good day. I asked him what he felt. He said, "Hate!" and then added, "But I also know we will win and they will lose." I did not press him to unpack that statement but let it bask in its polyvalence. Sivapalan, and other Tamil shop owners like him, have another interesting customer in the young Afro-Caribbean British male. Some of these young men—"at least one per night"—walk into his shop and pick up a pack or two of beer, presenting, however, only a packet of chewing gum at the cash register. When asked about the beer, the young man boldly declares, knowing full well that everyone knows otherwise, that he brought the beer from outside and owes money only for the gum he bought at this store. Sivapalan takes the money for the chewing gum and lets him go. This practice is so well known that it even piques the sympathetic ire of Phase 1 Tamils, who wonder why the Tamil shopkeeper does not inform the police. Phase 3 Tamils consider this kind of advice a sign of the utter ignorance of Phase 1 Tamils, and of the distance that separates the two groups. For one thing, the policeman is their foremost enemy. In support of these sentiments Phase 3 Tamils supplied me with stories of police racism, injustice, and violence too numerous to recount here. As one Tamil put it, "The policemen of the world should have a country of their own." For another, the shopkeepers find the rage of their "law-abiding" Phase 1 counterparts amusing and out of place. Even I was impressed by the equanimity with which these shopkeepers reacted to these blatant acts of shoplifting. Even though these Tamils did not extend alliances of interpersonal relations to the Afro-Caribbean Britons, they extended them alliances of understanding. They did not see them as breaking the law but as having broken with the law. To this extent their experience was a common one.

Tamils have little to do with the Afro-Caribbean community, a group whose "urban ways" they cannot relate to, people who, in their view, "give the family low priority." However, they find African immigrants much more compatible allies. Not only do many of the latter share Phase 3 Tamils' asylum-seeking status; they also have "rural values." That these new links of affect materialize may be illustrated by the following incident.

Sahitharan was a twenty-nine-year-old asylum-seeker from Sri Lanka. He was waylaid by a group of young whites and bashed to death in London's Eastham. Several of the London-based organizations working for refugees organized a protest march. Over 4,000 people of all ethnic groups joined the march. But there were only 150 Tamils, all from Phase 3. The largest non-Tamil representation at the rally was made up of black Africans. It is of interest that the trustees—all Phase 1 Tamils—of the Wimbledon Hindu temple denied the organizers of the march the right to hang posters on the temple premises. Their reason? "We do not want to antagonize the white community."

Other alliances have been forged among Phase 3 Tamils that have become more vital than any they ever had with their fellow Tamils of the other phases or the separatists/nationalists at home. Most of these alliances span across national boundaries to fellow asylum-seekers in other European countries who have fled both the nationalist Sri Lankan army and the equally nationalist Tamil militant groups. To the immigrant Tamils, the nationalized past that each of these groups is frantically trying to construct is something they have broken away from in the same manner that they feel they have broken with the law. Alliances have also extended to other refugees fleeing other national pasts, and a keen interest is shown in organizations such as Amnesty International whose scrutiny transcends national boundaries.

NOTES

1. This act made it the responsibility of air and sea carriers to ensure that their passengers carried valid papers. Failure to do so made the carrier liable to heavy fines.

2. The People's Liberation Organization of Tamil Eelam is one of the several Tamil liberation movements that were born in the mid-1980s. This group never did engage in combat either with the Indian or with the Sri Lankan state. But it became quite wealthy through investments made in Bombay and the running of a passport-forging shop in that same city. The drug-pushing charge is quite widely leveled against this group, but I have been able neither to confirm nor to disconfirm it. Its leader, Uma Maheswaran, was killed by a member of the LTTE in 1989, after which the liberation-of-Eelam activists of this group have become extinct for all intents and purposes. The fragmented financial empire, I understand, continues to flourish.

3. The Eelam People's Revolutionary Liberation Front, a militant separatist group that, since the 1987 pact between India and Sri Lanka, has given up its demand for a separate state and has participated in government-arranged elections.

4. *Kēvaluppaṭuttinārkaḷ*, a euphemism for rape.

REFERENCES

Aaker, F. David. 1995. *Building Strong Brands.* New York: Free Press.

Abraham, Taisha, and Malashri Lal. 1995. *Female Empowerment: Impact of Literacy in Jaipur District, Rajasthan.* New Delhi: Har-Anand Publications.

Abrahams, Roger D., and Barbara Babcock. 1977. The Literary Uses of Proverbs. *Journal of American Folklore* 98: 85–94.

Abrams, Philip. 1985. Chola Meykkirttis as Literary Texts. *Tamil Civilization* 3, no. 2–3: 1–5.

———. 1988. Notes on the Difficulty of Studying the State (1977). *Journal of Historical Sociology* 1, no. 1: 58–59.

Abu-Lughod, Lila. 1985. Honor and the Sentiments of Loss in a Bedouin Society. *American Ethnologist* 12: 245–261.

———. 1986. *Veiled Sentiments: Honor and Poetry in a Bedouin Society.* Berkeley: University of California Press.

———. 1993. *Writing Women's Worlds: Bedouin Stories.* Berkeley: University of California Press.

Adams, Kathleen M., and Sara Dickey, eds. 2000. *Home and Hegemony: Domestic Service and Identity Politics in South and Southeast Asia.* Ann Arbor: University of Michigan Press.

Adams, Vincanne. 1996. *Tigers of the Snow and Other Virtual Sherpas: An Ethnography of Himalayan Encounters.* Princeton, N.J.: Princeton University Press.

Adorno, Theodor. 1974. *Minima Moralia: Reflections from a Damaged Life.* London: NLB.

———. 1991. *The Culture Industry: Selected Essays on Mass Culture.* London: Routledge.

Agarwal, Bina. 1994. *A Field of One's Own: Gender and Land Rights in South Asia.* Cambridge: Cambridge University Press.

Agarwal, Priya. 1991. *Passage from India: Post-1965 Indian Immigrants and Their Children.* Palo Verdes, Calif.: Yuvati Publications.

Ahmed, Akbar S. 1980. *Pukhtun Economy and Society: Traditional Structure and Economic Development in a Tribal Society.* Boston: Routledge and Kegan Paul.

Ahmed, Akbar S., and Z. Ahmed. 1981. "Mor" and "Tor": Binary and Opposing Models of Pukhtun Womanhood. In *The Endless Day: Some Case Material on Asian Rural Women,* T. S. Epstein and R. A. Watts, eds., pp. 31–46. Oxford: Pergamon Press.

Ali, Daud. 1996. Regime of Pleasure in Early India: A Genealogy of Practices at the Cola Court. Unpublished doctoral dissertation, Department of History, University of Chicago.

Ali, Mohammad, Mohammad Moniruzzaman, and Jahangir Tareq, eds. 1994. *Bangla Academy Bengali-English Dictionary.* Dhaka: Bangla Academy.

Allen, Nicholas. 1974. The Ritual Journey, a Pattern Underlying Certain Nepalese Rituals. In *Contributions to the Anthropology of Nepal,* C. von Fürer-Haimendorf, ed., pp. 6–22. Warminster, England: Aris and Phillips.

Alter, Joseph S. 1992a. The Sannyasi and the Indian Wrestler: The Anatomy of a Relationship. *American Ethnologist* 19, no. 2: 317–336.

———. 1992b. *The Wrestler's Body: Identity and Ideology in North India.* Berkeley: University of California Press.

———. 1993. The Body of One Color: Indian Wrestling, the Indian State, and Utopian Somatics. *Cultural Anthropology* 8, no. 1: 49–72.

———. 1995. The Celibate Wrestler: Sexual Chaos, Embodied Balance, and Competitive Politics in North India. *Contributions to Indian Sociology* 29, nos. 1 and 2: 109–131.

———. 2000. *Gandhi's Body: Sex, Diet, and the Politics of Nationalism.* Philadelphia: University of Pennsylvania Press.

Amin, Shahid. 1995. *Event, Metaphor, and Memory: Chauri Chaura 1922–1992.* Berkeley: University of California Press.

Anand, Mulk Raj. 1990 [1970]. *Untouchable.* New York: Penguin.

Anderson, Benedict. 1991 [1983]. *Imagined Communities.* New York and London: Verso.

Anderson, Jon W. 1982. Cousin Marriage in Context: Constructing Social Relations in Afghanistan. *Folk* 24: 7–28.

Appadurai, Arjun. 1981. *Worship and Conflict under Colonial Rule: A South Indian Case.* Cambridge: Cambridge University Press.

———. 1986. Is Homo Hierarchicus? *American Ethnologist* 13: 745–761.

———. 1990. Topographies of the Self: Praise and Emotion in Hindu India. In *Language and the Politics of Emotion,* Catherine A. Lutz and Lila Abu-Lughod, eds., pp. 92–112. Cambridge: Cambridge University Press.

———. 1991. Global Ethnoscapes: Notes and Queries for a Transnational Anthropology. In *Recapturing Anthropology,* Richard G. Fox, ed. Santa Fe, N.Mex.: School of American Research Press.

———. 1996. *Modernity at Large: Cultural Dimensions of Globalization.* Minneapolis: University of Minnesota Press.

Appadurai, Arjun, and Carol Breckenridge. 1976. The South Indian Temple:

Authority, Honor, and Redistribution. *Contributions to Indian Sociology*, n.s. 10, no. 2: 187–211.

———. 1988. Why Public Culture? *Public Culture* 1, no. 1: 5–9.

———. 1989. On Moving Targets. *Public Culture* 2, no. 1: i–iv.

Asad, Talal. 1993. *Genealogies of Religion: Discipline and Reasons of Power in Christianity and Islam.* Baltimore: Johns Hopkins University Press.

Axel, Brian K. 2000. *The Nation's Tortured Body: Violence, Representation, and the Formation of a Sikh "Diaspora."* Durham, N.C.: Duke University Press.

Aziz, Barbara. 1976. Views from the Monastery Kitchen. *Kailash* 4, no. 2: 155–167.

Babb, Lawrence A. 1975. *The Divine Hierarchy: Popular Hinduism in Central India.* New York: Columbia University Press.

———. 1986. *Redemptive Encounters: Three Modern Styles in the Hindu Tradition.* Berkeley: University of California Press.

Bacon, Jean. 1996. *Life Lines: Community, Family, and Assimilation among Asian Indian Immigrants.* New York: Oxford University Press.

Bakhtin, Mikhail M. 1981. *The Dialogical Imagination: Four Chapters by Bakhtin,* Michael Holquist, ed. Austin: University of Texas Press.

Balibar, Etienne. 1991a. Citizen Subject. In *Who Comes after the Subject?* Eduardo Cadava, Peter Conner, and Jean-Luc Nancy, eds. London: Routledge.

———. 1991b. Is There a "Neo-Racism"? In *Race, Nation, Class: Ambiguous Identities,* Etienne Balibar and Immanuel Wallerstein, eds. London: Verso.

———. 1994. "Rights of Man" and the "Rights of the Citizen": The Modern Dialectic of Equality and Freedom. In *Masses, Class, Ideas,* James Senson, trans. London: Routledge.

Ballard, Roger. 1989. Differentiation and Disjunction amongst the Sikhs in Britain. In *The Sikh Diaspora,* N. Gerald Barrier and Verne A. Dusenbery, eds. Columbia, Mo.: South Asia Publications.

———. 1994. Introduction: The Emergence of Desh Pardesh. In *Desh Pardesh: The South Asian Presence in Britain,* Roger Ballard, ed., pp. 1–34. London: Hurst and Company.

Ballard, Roger, and Catherine Ballard. 1977. The Sikhs: The Development of South Asian Settlements in Britain. In *Between Two Cultures: Migrants and Minorities in Britain,* James L. Watson, ed. Oxford: Basil Blackwell.

Balsamo, Anne. 1996. *Technologies of the Gendered Body: Reading Cyborg Women.* Durham, N.C.: Duke University Press.

Bammer, Angelika, ed. 1994. *Displacements: Cultural Identities in Question.* Bloomington and Indianapolis: Indiana University Press.

Bandyopadhyay, Hiranmoy. 1970. *Udbāstu.* Calcutta: Sahitya Sangsad.

Bandyopadhyay, Sandeep. 1993. *Deśbhāg, Deśtyāg.* Calcutta: Anustup.

Bansal, Rajita. 1998. India to Be among Six Omega Locations. *Indian Express,* 27 January.

Bardhan, Kalpana, ed. and trans. 1990. *Of Women, Outcastes, Peasants, and Rebels: A Selection of Bengali Short Stories*. Berkeley: University of California Press.

Barnes, Nancy. 1987. Buddhism. In *Women in World Religions*, Arvind Sharma, ed., pp. 105–133. Albany: SUNY Press.

———. 1994. Women in Buddhism. In *Today's Women in World Religions*, Arvind Sharma, ed., pp. 137–170. Albany: SUNY Press.

Barnouw, Erik. 1978. *The Sponsor: Notes on a Modern Potentate*. New York: Oxford University Press.

Barrier, N. Gerald, and Verne A. Dusenbery, eds. 1989. *The Sikh Diaspora*. Columbia, Mo.: South Asia Books.

Barth, Fredrik. 1959. *Political Leadership among Swat Pathans*. London: Athlone Press.

———. 1981. *Features of Person and Society in Swat: Collected Essays*. London: Routledge and Kegan Paul.

Bartholomeusz, Theresa. 1992. The Female Mendicant in Buddhist Sri Lanka. In *Buddhism, Sexuality, and Gender*, Jose Cabezon, ed., pp. 37–64. Albany: SUNY Press.

Basu, Nirban. 1994. *The Working Clss Movement: A Study of Jute Mills of Bengal, 1937–47*. Calcutta: K. P. Bagchi and Company, Booksellers and Publishers.

Bateson, Gregory, and Margaret Mead. 1942. *Balinese Character: A Photographic Essay*. Special Publication of the New York Academy of Sciences, vol. 11. New York: Ballantine Books.

Bauman, Richard, and Charles L. Briggs. 1990. Poetics and Performance as Critical Perspectives on Language and Social Life. *Annual Review of Anthropology* 19: 59–88.

Baumann, Gerd. 1996. *Contesting Culture: Discourses of Identity in Multi-Ethnic London*. Cambridge: Cambridge University Press.

Bayly, C. A. 1983. *Rulers, Townsmen and Bazaars: North Indian Society in the Age of British Expansion, 1770–1870*. Cambridge: Cambridge University Press.

Beidelman, Thomas O. 1959. A Comparative Analysis of the Jajmani System. *Monographs of the Association for Asian Studies* 8.

Benedict, Ruth. 1934. *Patterns of Culture*. Boston: Houghton Mifflin.

Béteille, André. 1965. *Caste, Class, and Power: Changing Patterns of Stratification in a Tanjore Village*. Berkeley: University of California Press.

———. 1991. The Reproduction of Inequality: Occupation, Caste, and Family. *Contributions to Indian Sociology*, n.s. 25, no. 1: 3–28 (January).

Bhabha, Homi. 1990. The Third Space. In *Identity*, J. Rutherford, ed. London: Lawrence and Wishart.

———. 1994. *The Location of Culture*. New York: Routledge.

Bhachu, Parminder. 1985. *Twice Migrants: East African Sikh Settlers in Britain*. London: Tavistock Publications.

Bhadra, Gautam. 1985. Four Rebels of Eighteen Fifty-Seven. In *Subaltern*

Studies IV: Writings on South Asian History and Society, Ranajit Guha, ed., pp. 229–275. Delhi: Oxford University Press.

Bhagwati, Jagdish, and T. N. Srinivasan. 1993. *India's Economic Reforms.* New Delhi: Government of India, Ministry of Finance.

Blackburn, Stuart. 1988. *Singing of Birth and Death: Texts in Performance.* Philadelphia: University of Pennsylvania Press.

———. 1996. *Inside the Drama-House: Rama Stories and Shadow Puppets in South India.* Berkeley: University of California Press.

Boesen, Inger W. 1980. Women, Honour, and Love: Some Aspects of the Pashtun Woman's Life in Eastern Afghanistan. *Afghanistan Journal* 7, no. 2: 50–60. Also in *Folk* 21/22 (1979–80): 229–239.

———. 1983. Conflicts of Solidarity in Pashtun Women's Lives. In *Women in Islamic Societies: Social Attitudes and Historical Perspectives,* Bo Utas, ed. London: Curzon Press.

Bolin, Anne. 1992. Vandalized Vanity: Feminine Physiques Betrayed and Portrayed. In *Tattoo, Torture, Mutilation, and Adornment,* Frances E. Mascia-Lees, and Patricia Sharpe, eds., pp. 79–99. Albany: SUNY Press.

Bourdieu, Pierre. 1977a. *Outline of a Theory of Practice.* Richard Nice, trans. Cambridge: Cambridge University Press.

———. 1977b. The Economics of Linguistic Exchanges. *Social Science Information* 16: 645–668.

———. 1984. *Distinction.* Richard Nice, trans. Cambridge: Harvard University Press.

Bowen, Donna Lee, and Evelyn A. Early. 2002. *Everyday Life in the Muslim Middle East: Second Edition.* Bloomington: Indiana University Press.

Brah, Avtar. 1988. A Journey to Nairobi. In *Charting the Journey: Writings by Black and Third World Women,* Shabnam Grewal et al., eds., 74–88. London: Sheba Feminist Publishers.

———. 1996. *Cartographies of Diaspora: Contesting Identities.* London: Routledge.

Breckenridge, Carol A., ed. 1995. *Consuming Modernity: Public Culture in a South Asian World.* Minneapolis: University of Minnesota Press.

Breman, Jan, Arvind N. Das, and Ravi Agarwal. 2001. *Down and Out: Labouring under Global Capitalism.* Delhi: Oxford University Press.

Briggs, Charles. 1985. The Pragmatics of Proverb Performance in New Mexican Spanish. *American Anthropologist* 87: 793–810.

———. 1993. Metadiscursive Practices and Scholarly Authority in Folkloristics. *Journal of American Folklore* 106: 387–434.

Bruner, Jerome. 1987. Life as Narrative. *Social Research* 54: 11–32.

Burke, Kenneth. 1973. *A Philosophy of Literary Form.* Berkeley: University of California Press.

Butalia, Urvashi. 1993. Community, State, and Gender: On Women's Agency during Partition. *Economic and Political Weekly* 28 (17 April): 1634–1647.

Caplan, Lionel. 1984. Bridegroom Price in Urban India: Class, Caste, and "Dowry Evil" among Christians in Madras. *Man,* n.s. 19: 216–233.

——. 1987. *Class and Culture in Urban India: Fundamentalism in a Christian Community.* Oxford: Clarendon Press.

Carrithers, Michael. 1983. *The Buddha.* Oxford: Oxford University Press.

Central Bureau of Statistics. 1994. *Statistical Pocketbook.* Kathmandu: CBS.

Chakrabarty, Dipesh. 2000. *Rethinking Working-Class History: Bergal, 1890–1940.* Princeton, N.J.: Princeton University Press.

Chatterjee, Partha 1993. *The Nation and Its Fragments: Colonial and Post-Colonial Histories.* Princeton, N.J.: Princeton University Press.

——. 1989. Colonialism, Nationalism, and Colonialized Women: The Contest in India. *American Ethnologist* 16: 622–633.

Chaturvedi, Subhadra. 1995. Whether Inheritance to Women Is a Viable Solution to the Dowry Problem in India. *Journal of South Asia Women Studies* 1, no. 1: 17–23.

Chaube, Ram Gharib. 1894. Pachara Song—Chuhar Mal the Dusadh Hero Marrying a Brahman Girl. *North Indian Notes and Queries* 4: 62–63.

Chen, Martha A. 2001. *Perpetual Mourning: Widowhood in Rural India.* Philadelphia: University of Pennsylvania Press.

Chen, Martha A., ed. 1998. *Widows in India: Social Neglect and Public Action.* New Delhi: Sage.

Chen, Martha A., and Jean Drèze. 1992. Widows and Health in Rural North India. *Economic and Political Weekly* 27: WS-81–WS-92.

——. 1995a. Recent Research on Widows in India: Workshop and Conference Report. *Economic and Political Weekly* 30: 2435–2450.

——. 1995b. Widowhood and Well-being in Rural North India. In *Women's Health in India: Risk and Vulnerability,* Monica Das Gupta, Lincoln C. Chen, and T. N. Krishnan, eds., pp. 245–288. Bombay: Oxford University Press.

Chowdhry, Prem. 1994. *The Veiled Women: Shifting Gender Equations in Rural Haryana 1880–1990.* Delhi: Oxford University Press.

Clarke, Colin, Ceri Peach, and Steven Vertovec, eds. 1990. *South Asians Overseas: Migration and Ethnicity.* Cambridge: Cambridge University Press.

Clifford, James. 1997a. Spatial Practices: Fieldwork, Travel, and the Disciplining of Anthropology. In *Anthropological Locations,* Akhil Gupta and James Ferguson, eds., pp. 185–222. Berkeley: University of California Press.

——. 1997b. *Routes: Travel and Translation in the Late Twentieth Century.* Cambridge: Harvard University Press, 1997.

Cohen, Lawrence. 1998. *No Aging in India: Alzheimer's, the Bad Family, and Other Modern Things.* Berkeley: University of California Press.

Cohn, Bernard S. 1968. Notes on the Study of Indian Society and Culture. In *Structure and Change in Indian Society,* Milton Singer and B. S. Cohn, eds., pp. 3–28. Chicago: Aldine.

——. 1983. Representing Authority in Victorian India. In *The Invention of Tradition,* Eric Hobsbawm and Terence Ranger, eds. Cambridge: Cambridge University Press.

———. 1984. The Census, Social Structure, and Objectification in South Asia. *Folk* 26: 25–49.

———. 1985. The Command of Language and the Language of Command. In *Subaltern Studies IV: Writings on South Asian History and Society,* Ranajit Guha, ed., pp. 276–329. Delhi: Oxford University Press.

———. 1987a. *An Anthropologist among the Historians and Other Essays.* New Delhi: Oxford University Press.

———. 1987b. The Census, Social Structure, and Objectification. In *An Anthropologist among the Historians and Other Essays.* New Delhi: Oxford University Press.

Comaroff, Jean, and John Comaroff. 1991. *Of Revelation and Revolution.* Vol. 1. Chicago: University of Chicago Press.

Conley, Dalton. 1999. *Being Black, Living in the Red: Race, Wealth, and Social Policy in America.* Berkeley: University of California Press.

Coombe, Rosemary. 1998. *The Cultural Life of Intellectual Properties: Authorship, Appropriation and the Law.* Durham, N.C.: Duke University Press.

Crapanzano, Vincent. 1996. "Self"-Centering Narratives. In *Natural Histories of Discourse,* Michael Silverstein and Greg Urban, eds., pp. 106–130. Chicago: University of Chicago Press.

Cre-A. 1992. *Kriyāviṉ Taṟkālat Tamiḻ Akarāti* [Dictionary of Contemporary Tamil]. Madras: Cre-A.

Crook, John, and Henry Osmaston. 1994. *Himalayan Buddhist Villages.* New Delhi: Motilal.

Crooke, William. 1888. *A Rural and Agricultural Glossary for the N.-W. Provinces and Oudh.* Calcutta: Superintendent of Government Printing.

———. 1896. *The Tribes and Castes of the North Western Provinces and Oudh.* Calcutta: Superintendent of Government Printing.

———. 1914. The Holi: A Vernal Festival of the Hindus. *Folk-Lore* 25: 55–83.

———. 1979. *A Glossary of North Indian Peasant Life.* Shahid Amin, ed. Delhi: Oxford University Press.

Csordas, Thomas. 1983. The Rhetoric of Transformation in Ritual Healing. *Culture, Medicine and Psychiatry* 7: 333–376.

Csordas, Thomas, and Arthur Kleinman. 1990. The Therapeutic Process. In *Medical Anthropology: A Handbook of Theory and Method,* T. M. Johnson and C. Sargent, eds., pp. 11–25. New York: Greenwood Press.

Cutler, Norman. 1987. *Songs of Experience: The Poetics of Tamil Devotion.* Bloomington: Indiana University Press.

Daniel, E. Valentine. 1984. *Fluid Signs: Being a Person the Tamil Way.* Berkeley: University of California Press.

———. 1993. Tea Talk: Violent Measures in the Discursive Practices of Sri Lanka's Estate Tamils. *Comparative Studies in Society and History* 15, no. 3: 568–600.

———. 1996. *Charred Lullabies: Chapters in an Anthropography of Violence.* Princeton, N.J.: Princeton University Press.

Daniel, E. Valentine, and J. M. Peck. 1996. *Culture and Contexture: Explora-*

tions in Anthropology and Literary Studies. Berkeley and Los Angeles: University of California Press.

Daniels, Christine. 1994. Defilement and Purification: Tibetan Buddhist Pilgrims at Bodhnath, Nepal. D.Phil Thesis, Faculty of Anthropology and Geography. Oxford University.

Daniels, Roger. 1989. *History of Indian Immigration to the United States: An Interpretive Essay.* New York: The Asia Society.

Dargyay, Eva. 1987. The Dynasty of Bzang-la (Zanskar, West Tibet) and Its Chronology: A Reconsideration. In *Silver on Lapis: Tibetan Literary Culture and History,* Christopher Beckwith, ed., pp. 13–32. Bloomington, Ind.: The Tibet Society.

———. 1988. Buddhism in Adaptation: Ancestor Gods and Their Tantric Counterparts in the Religious Life of Zanskar. *History of Religions* 28, no. 2: 123–134.

Dargyay, Eva, and Lobsang Dargyay. 1980. Vorlaufiger Bericht Uber Zwei Forschungreisen Nach Zangskar (West-Tibet). *Zentralasiatische Studien* 14, no. 2: 85–114.

Das, Veena. 1995. National Honour and Practical Kinship: Of Unwanted Women and Children. In *Critical Events: An Anthropological Perspective on Contemporary India.* Delhi: Oxford University Press.

———. 1996. Language and the Body: Transactions in the Construction of Pain. *Daedalus* 125, no. 1: 67–91.

Das Gupta, Buddhadev. 1992. *Tāhāder Kathā* (motion picture).

Das Gupta, Somdev. 1986. Once a Refugee, Always a Refugee. *Statesman* (Calcutta), 28 March.

Dasgupta, Shamita Das, ed. 1998. *A Patchwork Shawl: Chronicles of South Asian Women in America.* New Brunswick, N.J.: Rutgers University Press.

Davis, Richard. 1985. Chola Meykkirttis as Literary Texts. *Tamil Civilization* 3, no. 2–3: 1–5.

———. 1991. *Ritual in an Oscillating Universe: Worshiping Siva in Medieval India.* Princeton, N.J.: Princeton University Press.

———. 1995. Introduction: A Brief History of Religions in India. In *Religions of India in Practice,* Donald Lopez, ed. Princeton, N.J.: Princeton University Press.

de Certeau, Michel. 1984. *The Practice of Everyday Life.* Berkeley: University of California Press.

Denny, Frederick. 1987. *Islam.* San Francisco: HarperCollins Publishers.

Dendaletche, Claude, ed. 1985. *Ladakh, Himalaya Occidental: Ethnologie, ecologie.* Pau: Acta Biologica Montana.

Derné, Steve. 1995. *Culture in Action: Family Life, Emotion, and Male Dominance in Banaras, India.* Albany: SUNY Press.

———. 2000. *Movies, Masculinity, and Modernity: An Ethnography of Men's Filmgoing in India.* Westport, Conn.: Greenwood Press.

Des Chene, Mary. 1991. Relics of Empire: A Cultural History of the Gurkhas, 1815–1987. Ph.D. dissertation, Stanford University.

Desjarlais, Robert. 1992. *Body and Emotion: The Aesthetics of Illness and Healing in the Nepal Himalayas.* Philadelphia: University of Pennsylvania Press.

Dhanjal, Beryl. 1976. Sikh Women in Southall. *New Community* 5, no. 1–2: 109–114.

Dhillon, Perminder. 1979. They're Killing Us in Here. *Spare Rib*, n.p.

Dickey, Sara. 1993. *Cinema and the Urban Poor in South India.* Cambridge: Cambridge University Press.

———. 2000. Permeable Homes: Domestic Service, Household Space, and the Vulnerability of Class Boundaries in Urban India. *American Ethnologist* 27, no. 2: 462–489.

Dirks, Nicholas B. 1987. *The Hollow Crown: Ethnohistory of an Indian Kingdom.* Cambridge: Cambridge University Press.

———. 1990. History as a Sign of the Modern. *Public Culture* 2, no. 2: 25–32.

———. 1992. Castes of Mind. *Representations* 37: 56–78.

———. 1997. The Policing of Tradition: Colonialism and Anthropology in Southern India. *Comparative Studies in Society and History* 39, no. 1: 182–212.

Dollfus, Pascale. 1989. *Lieu de neige et de genévriers: Organisation sociale et religieuse de communautes bouddhistes du Ladakh.* Paris: CNRS.

Doniger, Wendy O'Flaherty. 1980. *Women, Androgynes, and Other Mythical Beasts.* Chicago: University of Chicago Press.

Dooling, Richard. 1999. Diary of an Immortal Man: A Chronicle of My First 150 Years. *Esquire* (May): 80–89.

Dorson, Richard M. 1968. *The British Folklorists: A History.* Chicago: University of Chicago Press.

Dow, James. 1986. Universal Aspects of Symbolic Healing: A Theoretical Synthesis. *American Anthropologist* 88: 56–69.

Drèze, Jean, and Amartya Sen. 1996. *India: Economic Development and Social Opportunity.* Delhi: Oxford University Press.

Driver, Edwin D., and Aloo E. Driver. 1987. *Social Class in Urban India: Essays on Cognitions and Structures.* Leiden: E. J. Brill.

du Toit, Brian M. 1990. *Aging and Menopause among Indian South African Women.* Albany: SUNY Press.

Dube, Leela. 1988. On the Construction of Gender: Hindu Girls in Patrilineal India. *Economic and Political Weekly* (30 April): 11–19.

Dube, Saurabh. 1998. *Untouchable Pasts: Religion, Identity, and Power among a Central Indian Community, 1780–1950.* Albany: SUNY Press.

Dummett, Michael, ed. 1980. *Southall 23 April 1979: The Report of the Unofficial Committee of Enquiry.* London: National Council for Civil Liberties.

Dumont, Louis. 1970. *Homo Hierarchicus.* Chicago: University of Chicago Press.

———. 1980. *Homo Hierarchicus: The Caste System and Its Implications.* Complete revised English edition. Chicago: University of Chicago Press.

——. 1986 [1957]. *A South Indian Subcaste: Social Organization and Religion of the Pramalai Kallar.* Delhi: Oxford University Press.

Eaton, Richard Maxwell. 1993. *The Rise of Islam and the Bengal Frontier, 1204–1760.* Berkeley: University of California Press.

Eck, Diana. 1981. *Darshan: Seeing the Divine in India.* Chambersburg, Pa.: Anima Books.

Epstein, Scarlett. 1973. *South India: Yesterday, Today, and Tomorrow.* New York: Holmes and Meier Publishers.

Fabian, Johannes. 1986. *Language and Colonial Power.* Berkeley: University of California Press.

Fabricius, Johann Philip. 1972. *Tamil and English Dictionary.* 4th ed., revised. Tranquebar, Tamil Nadu, India: Evangelical Lutheran Mission Publishing House.

Falk, Nancy. 1980. The Case of the Vanishing Nuns: The Fruits of Ambivalence in Ancient Indian Buddhism. In *Unspoken Worlds: Women's Religious Lives,* Nancy Falk and Rita Gross, eds., pp. 207–224. San Francisco: Harper and Row.

Featherman, David L., and Robert M. Hauser. 1978. *Opportunity and Change.* New York: Academic Press.

Feld, Steven. 1982. *Sound and Sentiment.* Philadelphia: University of Pennsylvania Press.

Fernandes, Leela. 1997. *Producing Workers: The Politics of Gender, Class, and Culture in the Calcutta Jute Mills.* Philadelphia: University of Pennsylvania Press.

Flood, Gavin. 1996. *An Introduction to Hinduism.* Cambridge: Cambridge University Press.

Forbes, Geraldine. 1996. *Women in Modern India.* Cambridge: Cambridge University Press.

Foucault, Michel. 1970. *The Order of Things.* New York: Vintage.

——. 1973. *Madness and Civilization: A History of Insanity in the Age of Reason.* New York: Vintage.

Frank, Jerome. 1974. *Persuasion and Healing: A Comparative Study of Psychotherapy.* New York: Schocken Books.

Frazer, James, 1925. *The Golden Bough: A Study in Magic and Religion.* London: Macmillan.

Freeman, [John] Rich[ardson]. 2000. Thereupon Hangs a Tail: The Deification of Vali in the Teyyam Worship of Malabar. In *Questioning Ramayanas: A South Asian Tradition,* ed. Paula Richman, pp. 187–220. Berkeley: University of California Press.

Freitag, Sandria. 1991. Crime in the Social Order of Colonial North India. *Modern Asian Studies* 25: 227–262.

Fryer, Peter. 1984. *Staying Power: The History of Black People in Britain.* London: Pluto Press.

Fuller, Christopher J. 1987. The Hindu Pantheon and the Legitimation of Hierarchy. *Man,* n.s. 23: 19–39.

———. 1989. Misconceiving the Grain Heap: A Critique of the Concept of the Indian Jajmani System. In *Money and the Morality of Exchange,* Jonathon Parry and Maurice Bloch, eds. Cambridge: Cambridge University Press.

———. 1992. *The Camphor Flame: Popular Hinduism and Society in India.* Princeton, N.J.: Princeton University Press.

Fuller, Christopher J., ed. 1997. *Caste Today.* Oxford: Oxford University Press.

Fürer-Haimendorf, Christoph von. 1976. A Nunnery in Nepal. *Kailash* 4, no. 2: 121–154.

Gamburd, Michele Ruth. 2000. *The Kitchen Spoon's Handle: Transnationalism and Sri Lanka's Migrant Housemaids.* Ithaca, N.Y.: Cornell University Press.

Ganguly, Keya. 1992. Migrant Identities: Personal Memory and the Construction of Selfhood. *Cultural Studies* 6: 27–50.

Gardner, Katy. 1995. *Global Migrants, Local Lives: Travel and Transformation in Rural Bangladesh.* New York: Oxford University Press.

Geertz, Clifford. 1960. *The Religion of Java.* Chicago and London: University of Chicago Press.

———. 1968. *Islam Observed: Religious Development in Morocco and Indonesia.* Chicago: University of Chicago Press.

———. 1973. *The Interpretation of Cultures.* New York: Basic Books.

Geetha, V., and S. V. Rajadurai. 1995. Eighth World Tamil Conference: Of Cardboard History and Discursive Space. *Economic and Political Weekly* 30, no. 4: 201–203.

Ghosh, Gautam. 1998. God Is a Refugee: Nationality, Morality, and History in the 1947 Partition of India. In *Partition, Unification, Nation: Imagined Moral Communities in Modernity,* Gautam Ghosh, ed. Special Issue of *Social Analysis* 42, no. 1: 33–62.

Giddens, Anthony. 1987. *Social Theory and Modern Sociology.* Stanford, Calif.: Stanford University Press.

Gillespie, Marie. 1995. *Television, Ethnicity, and Cultural Change.* London: Routledge.

Gilroy, Paul. 1987. *There Ain't No Black in the Union Jack.* London: Hutchinson.

Gold, Ann Grodzins. 1992. *A Carnival of Parting.* Berkeley: University of California Press.

———. 1996. Khyal: Changed Yearnings in Rajasthani Women's Songs. *Manushi* 95: 13–21.

———. 2001. Counterpoint Authority in Women's Ritual Expressions: A View from the Village. In *Jewels of Authority: Women, Text, and the Hindu Tradition,* Laurie L. Patton, ed., pp. 177–201. New York: Oxford University Press.

Gold, Ann Grodzins, and Bhoju Ram Gujar. 1994. Drawing Pictures in the Dust: Rajasthani Children's Landscapes. *Childhood* 2: 73–91.

———. 2002. *In the Time of Trees and Sorrows: Nature, Power, and Memory in Rajasthan.* Durham, N.C.: Duke University Press.

GoldbergBelle, Jonathan. 1989. Clowns in Control: Performances in a Shadow Puppet Tradition in South India. In *Oral Epics in India,* Stuart Blackburn et al., eds., pp. 118–139. Berkeley: University of California Press.

Goldman, Robert P. 1984. *The Ramayana of Valmiki: An Epic of Ancient India.* Vol. 1. Princeton, N.J.: Princeton University Press.

Gombrich, Richard. 1971. *Precept and Practice.* Oxford: Clarendon Press.

———. 1988. *Theravada Buddhism: A Social History from Ancient Benares to Modern Colombo.* New York: Routledge.

Gombrich, Richard, and Gananath Obeyesekere. 1988. *Buddhism Transformed: Religious Change in Sri Lanka.* Princeton, N.J.: Princeton University Press.

Good, Anthony. 1991. *The Female Bridegroom: A Comparative Study of Life-Crisis Rituals in South India and Sri Lanka.* New York: Oxford University Press.

Good, Byron J. 1994. *Medicine, Rationality, and Experience: An Anthropological Perspective.* Cambridge: Cambridge University Press.

Gopinath, Gayatri. 1995. "Bombay, U.K., Yuba City": Bhangra Music and the Engendering of Diaspora. *Diaspora* 4, no. 3: 303–321.

Gossen, Gary. 1973. Chamula Tzotzil Proverbs. In *Meaning in Mayan Languages,* M. S. Edmonson, ed., pp. 205–233. The Hague: Mouton.

Gough, Kathleen. 1989. *Rural Change in Southeast India: 1950s to 1980s.* Delhi: Oxford University Press.

Gould, Harold. 1958. The Hindu Jajmani System: A Case of Economic Particularism. *Southwestern Journal of Anthropology* 16: 434.

Graham, Laura. 1993. A Public Sphere in Amazonia? The Depersonalized Collaborative Construction of Discourse in Xavante. *American Ethnologist* 20, no. 4: 717–741.

Gray, John N., and David J. Mearns. 1989. *Society from the Inside Out: Anthropological Perspectives on the South Asian Household.* New Delhi: Sage Publications.

Grima, Benedicte. 1992. *The Performance of Emotion among Paxtun Women: "The Misfortunes Which Have Befallen Me."* Austin: University of Texas Press.

Gross, Rita. 1993. *Buddhism after Patriarchy: A Feminist History, Analysis, and Reconstruction of Buddhism.* Albany: SUNY Press.

Gupta, Akhil. 1995. Blurred Boundaries: The Discourse of Corruption, the Culture of Politics, and the Imagined State. *American Ethnologist* 22, no. 2: 375–402.

Gupta, Akhil, and James Ferguson, eds. 1997. *Culture, Power, and Place: Explorations in Critical Anthropology.* Durham, N.C.: Duke University Press.

Gupta, Ranajit Das. 1994. *Labour and Working Class in Eastern India.* K. P. Bagchi and Company, Booksellers and Publishers.

Gupta, Sangeeta, ed. 1999. *Emerging Voices: South Asian American Women Redefine Self, Family, and Community.* New Delhi: Sage.

Gutschow, Kim. 1995. The Power of Compassion or the Power of Rhetoric? A Report on Sakyadhita's Fourth International Conference on Buddhist Women. *Himal* 8, no. 6: 18–21.

———. 1997. Unfocussed Merit-Making in Zangskar: A Socio-Economic Account of Karsha Nunnery. *The Tibet Journal* 22, no. 2: 30–58.

———. 1998. An Economy of Merit: Women and Buddhist Monasticism in Zangskar, Northwest India. Ph.D. dissertation, Department of Anthropology, Harvard University.

———. 2000. A Novice Ordination for Nuns: The Rhetoric and Reality of Female Monasticism in NW India. In *Women's Buddhism, Buddhism's Women: Tradition, Revision, Renewal,* Ellison Findly, ed., pp. 103–118. Boston: Wisdom Press.

Hall, Kathleen. 1995. "There's a Time to Act English and a Time to Act Indian": The Politics of Identity among British-Sikh Teenagers. In *Children and the Politics of Culture,* Sharon Stephens, ed. Princeton, N.J.: Princeton University Press.

———. Forthcoming. *Lives in Translation: Sikh Youth and British Cultural Citizenship.* Philadelphia: University of Pennsylvania Press.

Hall, Stephen S. 2000. The Recycled Generation. *New York Times Magazine* (January 30, 2000): 30–35, 46, 74, 78–79.

Hall, Stuart. 1990. Cultural Identity and Diaspora. In *Identity: Community, Culture, Difference,* J. Rutherford, ed., pp. 222–237. London: Lawrence and Wishart.

———. 1996. The Question of Cultural Identity. In *Modernity,* Stuart Hall et al., eds. Oxford: Blackwell.

Hancock, Mary. 1999. *Womanhood in the Making: Domestic Ritual and Public Culture in Urban South India.* Boulder, Colo.: Westview Press.

Hanna, Max. 1974. The National Front and Other Right-wing Organizations. *New Community* 3: 1–2, 49–55.

Haraway, Donna. 1991. *Simians, Cyborgs, and Women: The Reinvention of Nature.* New York: Routledge.

Harper, Edward B. 1959. Two Systems of Economic Exchange in Village India. *American Anthropologist* 61: 760–778.

Havnevik, Hanna. 1990. *Tibetan Buddhist Nuns.* Oslo: Norwegian University Press.

Helweg, Arthur, and Usha Helweg. 1990. *An Immigrant Success Story: East Indians in America.* Philadelphia: University of Pennsylvania Press.

Herzfeld, M. 1992. History in the Making: National and International Politics in a Rural Cretan Community. In *Europe Observed,* Joao de Pina-Cabral and John Campbell, eds., pp. 93–122. London: Macmillan.

Hess, Linda. 1993. Staring at Frames Till They Turn into Loops: An Excursion through Some Worlds of Tulsidas. In *Living Banaras: Hindu Religion in Cultural Context*, Cynthia Humes and B. Hertel, eds., pp. 73–101. Albany: SUNY Press.

———. 2000. Lovers' Doubts: Questioning the Tulsi Ramayan. In *Questioning Ramayanas: A South Asian Tradition*, ed. Paula Richman. Berkeley: University of California Press.

Hiltebeitel, Alf, ed. 1989. *Criminal Gods and Demon Devotees: Essays on the Guardians of Popular Hinduism*. Albany: SUNY Press.

Holmberg, David. 1989. *Order in Paradox: Myth, Ritual, and Exchange among Nepal's Tamang*. Ithaca, N.Y.: Cornell University Press.

Holmstrom, Mark. 1976. *South Indian Factory Workers: Their Life and Their World*. New Delhi: Allied.

Horkheimer, Max, and Theodor Adorno. 1972 [1947]. *The Dialectic of Enlightenment*. New York: Continuum.

Horner, Isabelle. 1930. *Women under Primitive Buddhism*. London: George Routledge and Sons.

———. 1992. *The Book of the Discipline (Vinaya Pitaka)*. Vol. V: *Cullavagga*. Oxford: Pali Text Society.

Hussein, Aamer. 1999. *Hoops of Fire: Fifty Years of Fiction by Pakistani Women*. London: Saqi Books.

Ian, Marcia. 1993. *Remembering the Phallic Mother*. Ithaca, N.Y.: Cornell University Press.

———. 1995. How Do You Wear Your Body? Bodybuilding and the Sublimity of Drag. In *Negotiating Lesbian and Gay Subjects*, Monica Dorenkamp and Richard Henke, eds., pp. 71–88. New York: Routledge.

Ibbetson, Denzil C. J. 1882. *Memorandum on Ethnological Inquiry in the Panjab*. 2nd ed. Pamphlet P/V 188, India Office Library.

———. 1883. *Report on the Settlement of the Panipat Tahsil and Karnal Parganah of the Karnal District, 1872–1880*. Allahabad: Pioneer Press.

———. 1916. *Panjab Castes: Being a Reprint of the Chapter on "The Races, Castes, and Tribes of the People" in the Report on the Census of the Panjab Published in 1883*. Lahore: Superintendent of Government Printing.

Illaih, Kancha. 1996. Productive Labour, Consciousness and History: The Dalitbahujan Alternative. In *Subaltern Studies IX: Writings on South Asian History and Society*, Shahid Amin and Dipesh Chakrabarty, eds., pp. 165–200. Delhi: Oxford University Press.

Inden, Ronald. 1990. *Imagining India*. Oxford: Basil Blackwell.

Inglis, Steven. 1985. Possession and Pottery: Serving the Divine in a South Indian Community. In *Gods of Flesh, Gods of Stone: The Embodiment of Divinity in India*, Joanne Punzo Waghorne and Norman Cutler, eds., in association with Vasudha Narayanan. Chambersburg, Pa.: Anima Books.

Institute of Race Relations. 1981. *Southall: The Birth of a Black Community*. London: Institute of Race Relations.

IPAN. 1998. Amitabh and Jaya Bachchan Presented "Omega Award for Excellence: Lifetime Achievement." www.ipan.com/press/98nov/3011oma.htm

Irvine, Judith. 1993. Mastering African Languages: The Politics of Linguistics in Nineteenth-Century Senegal. *Social Analysis* 33: 27–43.

Jackson, Michael. 1996. *Things As They Are: New Directions in Phenomenological Anthropology.* Bloomington: Indiana University Press.

Jacobson, Doranne. 1982. Purdah and the Hindu Family in Central India. In *Separate Worlds: Studies of Purdah in South Asia,* Hanna Papanek and Gail Minault, eds., pp. 81–109. Delhi: Chanakya.

Jacobus, Mary, Evelyn Fox-Keller, and Sally Shuttleworth. 1990. *Body/Politics: Women and the Discourses of Science.* New York: Routledge.

Jaini, Padmanabh S. 1979. *The Jain Path to Purification.* Berkeley: University of California Press.

Jeffery, Patricia, and Roger Jeffery. 1996a. *Don't Marry Me to a Plowman! Women's Everyday Lives in Rural North India.* Boulder, Colo.: Westview Press, and New Delhi: Vistaar.

———. 1996b. Delayed Periods and Falling Babies: The Ethno-physiology and Politics of Pregnancy Loss in Rural North India. In *The Anthropology of Pregnancy Loss,* Rosanne Cecil, ed., pp. 17–37. Oxford: Berg Publishers.

Jeffery, Patricia, Roger Jeffery, and Andrew Lyon. 1987. Contaminating States: Midwifery, Childbearing, and the State in Rural North India. In *Women, State, and Ideology: Studies from Africa and Asia,* Haleh Afshar, ed., pp. 152–169. London: Macmillan.

———. 1989. *Labour Pains and Labour Power: Women and Childbearing in India.* London: Zed Books.

Jeffrey, Robin. 1997. Tamil: "Dominated by Cimema and Politics." *Economic and Political Weekly* 32 (8 February): 254–56.

Jeffery, Roger. 1997. Tamil: Dominated by Cinema and Politics. *Economic and Political Weekly* 32: 254–256.

Jeffery, Roger, and Alaka M. Basu, eds. 1996. *Girls' Schooling, Women's Autonomy, and Fertility Change in South Asia.* New Delhi: Sage Publications.

Jeffery, Roger, and Patricia Jeffery. 1993. Traditional Birth Attendants in Rural North India: The Social Organization of Childbearing. In *Knowledge, Power, and Practice: The Anthropology of Medicine and Everyday Life,* Shirley Lindenbaum and Margaret Lock, eds., pp. 7–31. Berkeley: University of California Press.

———. 1996. What's the Benefit of Being Educated? Girls' Schooling, Women's Autonomy, and Fertility Outcomes in Bijnor. In *Girls' Schooling, Women's Autonomy, and Fertility Change in South Asia,* Roger Jeffery and Alaka M. Basu, eds., pp. 150–183. New Delhi: Sage Publications.

———. 1997. *Population, Gender, and Politics: Demographic Change in Rural North India.* Cambridge: Cambridge University Press.

Jeffery, Roger, Patricia Jeffery, and Andrew Lyon. 1984. Female Infanticide and Amniocentesis. *Social Science and Medicine* 19: 1207–1212.

Jeganathan, Pradeep. 1994. The Task of Theory. In *An Introduction to Social Theory,* Radhika Coomaraswamy and Nira Wickremasinghe, eds. Delhi: Konark Press.

——. 2000. On the Anticipation of Violence. In *Anthropology, Development, and Modernities: Exploring Discourses, Counter-tendencies, and Violence.* Alberto Acre and Norman Long, eds. London: Routledge.

Joshi, Vijay, and I. M. D. Little. 1996. *India's Economic Reforms, 1991–2001.* Delhi: Oxford University Press.

Kakar, Sudhir. 1981. *The Inner World: A Psycho-analytic Study of Childhood and Society in India.* New Delhi: Oxford University Press.

——. 1990. *Intimate Relations: Exploring Indian Sexuality.* Chicago: University of Chicago Press.

——. 1995. *The Colors of Violence: Cultural Identities, Religion, and Conflict.* Chicago: University of Chicago Press

Kapadia, Karin. 1995. *Siva and Her Sisters: Gender, Caste, and Class in Rural South India.* Boulder, Colo.: Westview Press.

Kapferer, Bruce. 1983. *Celebration of Demons.* Bloomington: Indiana University Press.

——. 1997. *The Feast of the Sorcerer: Practices of Consciousness and Power.* Chicago: University of Chicago Press.

Kavoori, Purnendu S. 1999. *Pastoralism in Expansion: The Transhuming Herders of Western Rajasthan.* New Delhi: Oxford University Press.

Kelly, John D. 1991. *A Politics of Virtue: Hinduism, Sexuality, and Counter-colonial Discourse in Fiji.* Chicago: University of Chicago Press.

——. 1995. Diaspora and World War, Blood and Nation in Fiji and Hawai'i. *Public Culture* 7: 475–497.

Kerin, Melissa. 2000. From Periphery to Center: Tibetan Women's Journey to Sacred Artistry. In *Women's Buddhism, Buddhism's Women: Tradition, Revision, Renewal,* Ellison Findly, ed., pp. 319–338. Boston: Wisdom Press.

Kersenboom, S. 1995. *Word, Sound, Image: The Life of a Tamil Text.* Oxford: Berg Publishers.

Kinsley, David. 1986. *Hindu Goddesses: Visions of the Divine Feminine in the Hindu Religious Tradition.* Berkeley: University of California Press.

Klein, Anne. 1985. Primordial Purity and Everyday Life: Exalted Female Symbols and the Women of Tibet. In *Immaculate and Powerful: The Female in Sacred Image and Social Reality,* Clarissa W. Atkinson, Constance H. Buchanan, and Margaret R. Miles, eds. Boston: Beacon Press.

Kleinman, Arthur. 1988. *Rethinking Psychiatry.* New York: Free Press.

Knipe, David. 1989. Night of the Growing Dead: A Cult of Virabhadra in Coastal Andhra. In *Criminal Gods and Demon Devotees: Essays on the Guardians of Popular Hinduism,* Alf Hiltebeitel, ed. Albany: SUNY Press.

Kolenda, Pauline. 1987a. Living the Levirate. In *Dimensions of Social Life,* Paul Hockings, ed., pp. 45–67. Berlin: de Gruyter.

——. 1987b. *Regional Differences in Family Structure in India.* Jaipur: Rawat Publications.

Kroskrity, Paul V. 1998. Arizona Tewa Kiva Speech as a Manifestation of

Linguistic Ideology. In *Language Ideologies: Practice and Theory,* B. B. Schieffelin, K. A. Woolard, and P. Kroskrity, eds. New York: Oxford University Press.

Kroskrity, Paul V., ed. 2000. *Regimes of Language.* Santa Fe, N.Mex.: School of American Research Press.

Kuipers, Joel. 1990. *Power in Performance: The Creation of Textual Authority in Weyewa Ritual Speech.* Philadelphia: University of Pennsylvania Press.

Kulkarni, V. G. 1993. The Middle-Class Bulge. *Far Eastern Economic Review* 156, no. 2 (January 14): 44–46.

Kumar, Krishna. 1991. *Political Agenda of Education: A Study of Colonialist and Nationalist Ideas.* New Delhi: Sage Publications.

Kumar, Nita. 1988. *The Artisans of Banaras.* Princeton, N.J.: Princeton University Press.

———. 2000. *Lessons from Schools: The History of Education in Banaras.* New Delhi: Sage Publications, and New York: Routledge.

Laderman, Carol. 1987. The Ambiguity of Symbols in the Structure of Healing. *Social Science and Medicine* 24: 293–301.

———. 1991. *Taming the Wind of Desire: Psychology, Medicine, and Aesthetics in Malay Shamanistic Performance.* Berkeley: University of California.

Laderman, Carol, and Marina Roseman, eds. 1996. *The Performance of Healing.* New York: Routledge.

Lal, Bhai Harbans. 1999. Sahajdhari Sikhs: Their Origin and Current Status within the Panth. In *Sikh Identity: Continuity and Change,* Pashuara Singh and N. Gerald Barrier, eds. New Delhi: Manohar.

Lamb, Ramdas. 1991. Personalizing the Ramayan: Ramnamis and Their Use of the Ramcaritmanas. In *Many Ramayanas: The Diversity of a Narrative Tradition in South Asia,* Paula Richman, ed. Berkeley: University of California Press.

Lamb, Sarah. 2000. *White Saris and Sweet Mangoes: Aging, Gender, and Body in North India.* Berkeley: University of California Press.

Lang, Jon, et al. 1997. *Architecture and Independence: The Search for Identity— India 1880 to 1980.* New Delhi: Oxford University Press.

Langness, L. L., and Gelya Frank. 1981. *Lives: An Anthropological Approach to Biography.* Novato, Calif.: Chandler and Sharp.

Lapierre, Dominique, and Larry Collins. 1975. *Freedom at Midnight.* New York: Simon and Schuster.

Lavie, Smadar, and Ted Swedenburg. 1996. *Displacement, Diaspora, and Geographies of Identity.* Durham, N.C.: Duke University Press.

Lawrence, Bruce, and Carl Ernst. 2001. *Burnt Hearts: The Chishti Sufi Order in South Asia and Beyond.* Surrey, England: Curzon Press.

Lee, Trevor. 1972. Immigrants in London: Trends in Distribution and Concentration, 1961–71. *New Community* 2, no. 2: 145–158.

Leonard, Karen Isaksen. 1992. *Making Ethnic Choices: California's Punjabi Mexican Americans.* Philadelphia: Temple University Press.

———. 1997. *The South Asian Americans*. Westwood, Conn.: Greenwood Press.

Lessing, Ferdinand. 1951. Calling the Soul: A Lamaist Ritual. *Semitic and Oriental Studies* 11: 263–284.

Lessinger, Johanna. 1995. *From the Ganges to the Hudson: Indian Immigrants in New York City*. Boston: Allyn and Bacon.

Levinson, David. 1996. *Religion: A Cross Cultural Dictionary*. New York: Oxford University Press.

Lévi-Strauss, Claude. 1950. The Effectiveness of Symbols. In *Structural Anthropology*, pp. 167–185. New York: Basic Books.

Levy, Robert I. 1990. *Mesocosm: Hinduism and the Organization of a Traditional Hindu City*. Berkeley: University of California Press.

Lewis, Oscar. 1955. Peasant Culture in India and Mexico: A Comparative Analysis. In *Village India: Studies in the Little Community*. Chicago: Midway Reprint Edition, 1986.

Lexicon. 1982. *Tamil Lexicon*. 6 vols. Madras: University of Madras.

Li, Yuchen. 2000. Ordination, Legitimacy, and Sisterhood: The International Full Ordination Ceremony in Bodhgaya. In *Innovative Buddhist Women: Swimming against the Stream*, Karma Lekshe Tsomo, ed., pp. 168–200. Richmond, Surrey, England: Curzon Press.

Liechty, Mark. 1994. Fashioning Modernity in Kathmandu: Mass Media, Consumer Culture, and the Middle Class in Nepal. Ph.D. dissertation, University of Pennsylvania.

———. 1995. Modernization, Media, and Markets: Youth Identities and the Experience of Modernity in Kathmandu, Nepal. In *Youth Cultures: A Cross-Cultural Perspective*, Vered Amit-Talai and Helena Wulff, eds., pp. 166–201. London: Routledge.

———. 1996. Kathmandu as Translocality: Multiple Places in a Nepali Space. In *Geography of Identity*, Patricia Yaeger, ed., pp. 98–130. Ann Arbor: University of Michigan Press.

———. 2001. Women and Pornography in Kathmandu: Negotiating the "Modern Woman" in a New Consumer Society. In *Images of the "Modern Woman" in Asia: Global Media/Local Meanings*, Shoma Munshi, ed. London: Curzon Press.

———. 2002. *Class as Cultural Practice: Consumption, Media, and the Making of Middle-Class Culture in Kathmandu*. Princeton, N.J.: Princeton University Press.

Lindholm, Charles. 1982. *Generosity and Jealousy: The Swat Pukhtun of Northern Pakistan*. New York: Columbia University Press.

Lindholm, Charles, and Cherry Lindholm. 1979. Marriage as Warfare. *Natural History* 88, no. 8: 11–21.

Ling, Amy. 1991. I'm Here: An Asian Woman's Response. In *Feminisms: An Anthropology of Literary Theory and Criticism*, Robyn R. Warhol and Diane P. Hendl, eds., pp. 738–745. New Brunswick, N.J.: Rutgers University Press.

Lopez, Donald. 1995. Foreigners at the Lama's Feet. In *Curators of the Buddha: The Study of Buddhism under Colonialism*, Donald Lopez, ed., pp. 251–296. Chicago: University of Chicago Press.

———. 1998. *Prisoners of Shangri-La: Tibetan Buddhism and the West*. Chicago: University of Chicago Press.

Lopez, Donald, ed. 1995. *Religions of India in Practice*. Princeton, N.J.: Princeton University Press.

Lowe, Marie R. 1998. *Women of Steel: Female Bodybuilders and the Struggle for Self-Definition*. New York: New York University Press.

Luard, C. E., n.d. *Central Indian Proverbs*. MSS. Eur. E. 139, India Office Library.

Ludden, David, ed. 1996. *Contesting the Nation: Religion, Community, and the Politics of Democracy in India*. Philadelphia: University of Pennsylvania Press.

Lutgendorf, Philip. 2000. The Shabari Episode in Multiple Ramayanas. In *Questioning Ramayanas: A South Asian Tradition*, ed. Paula Richman. Berkeley: University of California Press.

Lyall, J. B. 1874. *Report of the Land Revenue Settlement of the Kangra District*. Panjab. Lahore: Central Jail Press.

Maira, Sunaina Marr. 1998. Chaste Identities, Ethnic Yearnings: Second-Generation Indian Americans in New York. Ph.D. thesis, Graduate School of Education, Harvard University.

———. 1999. Identity Dub: The Paradoxes of an Indian American Youth Subculture (New York Mix). *Cultural Anthropology* 14, no. 1: 29–60.

Malinowski, Bronislaw. 1965 [1948]. *Coral Gardens and Their Magic*. Bloomington: Indiana University Press.

Malkki, Liisa. 1992. National Geographic: Rooting of Peoples and the Territorialization of National Identity among Scholars and Refugees. *Cultural Anthropology* 7, no. 1: 24–44.

Mani, Lata. 1984. The Production of an Official Discourse on Sati in Early Nineteenth-Century Bengal. In *Europe and Its Others*, Francis Barker, ed., pp. 89–127. Colchester, England: University of Essex.

———. 1989. Contentious Traditions: The Debate on Sati in Colonial India. In *Recasting Women: Essays in Colonial History*, Kumkum Sangari and Sudesh Vaid, eds., pp. 88–126. New Delhi: Kali for Women.

———. 1998. *Contentious Traditions: The Debate on "Sati" in Colonial India*. Berkeley: University of California Press.

Mankekar, Purnima. 1999. *Screening Culture, Viewing Politics: An Ethnography of Television, Womanhood, and Nation in Postcolonial India*. Durham, N.C.: Duke University Press.

Manu. 1991. *The Laws of Manu*. Wendy Doniger, trans., with Brian K. Smith. New York: Penguin.

March, Kathryn. 2002. *"If Each Comes Halfway": Meeting Tamang Women of Nepal* (with CD of original Tamang songs). Ithaca, N.Y.: Cornell University Press.

Marchand, Roland. 1985. *Advertising the American Dream: Making Way for Modernity, 1920–1940*. Berkeley: University of California Press.

———. 1998. *Creating the Corporate Soul: The Rise of Public Relations and Corporate Imagery in American Big Business*. Berkeley: University of California Press.

Marriott, McKim. 1976. Hindu Transactions: Diversity without Dualism. In *Transaction and Meaning: Directions in the Anthropology of Exchange and Symbolic Behavior*, Bruce Kapferer, ed., pp. 109–142. Philadelphia: Institute for the Study of Human Issues.

———. 1990. Constructing an Indian Ethnosociology. In *India through Hindu Categories*, McKim Marriott, ed., pp. 1–39. New Delhi: Sage Publications.

Marriott, McKim, and Ronald Inden. 1977. Toward an Ethnosociology of South Asian Caste Systems. In *The New Wind*, Kenneth David, ed., pp. 227–238. The Hague: Mouton Publishers.

Martin, Dan. n.d. *Calling, Hooking, and Ransoming: Popular Tibetan Rituals for Recovering Lost Souls*. Unpublished Paper.

Marx, Karl. 1994a [1932]. The German Ideology, Part I. In *Karl Marx: Selected Writings*, Lawrence H. Simon, ed. Indianapolis, Ind.: Hackett Publishing Company.

———. 1994b [1859]. Preface to A Contribution to the Critique of Political Economy. In *Karl Marx: Selected Writings*, Lawrence H. Simon, ed. Indianapolis, Ind.: Hackett Publishing Company.

Matthew, Biju, and Vijay Prashad, eds. 1999/2000. *Satyagraha* in America: The Political Culture of South Asian Americans. *Amerasia Journal* 25, no. 3.

Mayaram, Shail. 1991. Criminality or Community? Alternative Constructions of the Mev Narrative of Darya Khan. *Contributions to Indian Sociology* 25: 57–84.

Mazzarella, William. 2001. Citizens Have Sex, Consumers Make Love: Marketing KamaSutra Condoms in Bombay. In *Asian Media Productions*, Brian Moeran, ed. Honolulu: University of Hawai'i Press.

———. Forthcoming. *Shoveling Smoke: Advertising and Globalization in Contemporary India*. Durham, N.C.: Duke University Press.

Mbembe, A. 1992. Provisional Notes on the Postcolony. *Africa* 62, no. 1: 3–37.

McDaniel, June. 1989. *The Madness of the Saints: Ecstatic Religion in Bengal*. Chicago: University of Chicago Press.

McHugh, Ernestine L. 1989. Concepts of the Person among the Gurungs of Nepal. *American Ethnologist* 16, no. 1: 75–86.

———. 2001. *Love and Honor in the Himalayas: Coming to Know Another Culture*. Philadelphia: University of Pennsylvania Press.

McLeod, Hew. 1997. *Sikhism*. London: Penguin Books.

McLeod, W. H. 1999. The Turban: Symbol of Sikh Identity. In *Sikh Identity:*

Continuity and Change. Pashuara Singh and N. Gerald Barrier, eds. New Delhi: Manohar.

Mead, G. H. 1934. *Mind, Self, and Society: From the Standpoint of a Social Behavioralist*. Chicago: University of Chicago Press.

Mehta, Rama. 1981. *Inside the Haveli*. New Delhi: Arnold-Heinemann.

Menon, Ritu. 1998. *Borders and Boundaries: Women in India's Partition*. Delhi and New Brunswick, N.J.: Rutgers University Press, 1998.

Miller, Barbara D. 1981. *The Endangered Sex: Neglect of Female Children in Rural North India*. Ithaca, N.Y.: Cornell University Press.

———. 1987. Female Infanticide and Child Neglect in Rural North India. In *Child Survival*, Nancy Scheper-Hughes, ed., pp. 95–112. Dordrecht, Holland: D. Reidel Publishing. Reprinted in Caroline B. Brettell and Carolyn F. Sargent, eds., *Gender in Cross-Cultural Perspective*, pp. 492–505. Upper Saddle River, N.J.: Prentice-Hall, 2001.

Mines, Diane P. 1990. Hindu Periods of Death "Impurity." In *India through Hindu Categories*, McKim Marriott, ed. New Delhi: Sage.

———. 1997a. From Homo Hierarchicus to Homo Faber: Breaking Convention through Semeiosis. *Irish Journal of Anthropology* 2: 33–44.

———. 1997b. Making the Past Past: Objects and the Spatialization of Time in Tamilnadu. *Anthropology Quarterly* 70, no. 4.

———. In press. Waiting for Vellalakantan. In *Tamil Geographies: Cultural Constructions of Space and Place in South India*, Martha Selby and Indira Peterson, eds. Albany: SUNY Press.

Minturn, Leigh. 1993. *Sita's Daughters: Coming Out of Purdah*. New York: Oxford University Press.

Mistry, Rohinton. 1992. *Such a Long Journey*. New York: Vintage Books.

———. 1997 *A Fine Balance*. New York: Vintage Books.

Moon, Vasant. 2001. *Growing Up Untouchable in India: A Dalit Autobiography*. Gail Omvedt, trans. New York: Rowman and Littlefield.

Moore, Pamela L. 1997. *Building Bodies*. New Brunswick, N.J.: Rutgers University Press.

Mukhopadhyay, Carol Chapnick, and Susan Seymour. 1994. Theoretical Introduction. In *Women, Education, and Family Structure in India*, Carol Chapnick Mukhopadhyay and Susan Seymour, eds., pp. 1–33. Boulder, Colo.: Westview Press.

Mumford, Stan. 1989. *Himalayan Dialogue: Tibetan Lamas and Gurung Shamans in Nepal*. Madison: University of Wisconsin Press.

Murthy, Anantha U. R. 1989. *Samskara: A Rite for a Dead Man*. 2nd ed. Oxford: Oxford University Press.

Naim, C. M. 1999. Discussant Comments. "Tensions and Transformations in Lament Genres" panel, South Asia Conference, Madison, Wis., 1999.

Nanda, Serena. 1999. *Neither Man nor Woman: The Hijras of India*. Belmont, Calif.: Wadsworth.

Nandy, Ashis. 1980. *At the Edge of Psychology*. New Delhi: Oxford University Press.

———. 1995. *The Savage Freud and Other Essays on Possible and Retrievable Selves*. New Delhi: Oxford University Press.

———. 1983. *The Intimate Enemy*. New Delhi: Oxford University Press.

Narayan, Kirin. 1994. *Love, Stars, and All That*. New York: Pocket Books, and New Delhi: Penguin India.

———. 1997. Singing from Separation: Women's Voices in and about Kangra Folksongs. *Oral Traditions* 12: 23–53.

Narayana Rao, Velcheru. 1991. A Ramayana of Their Own: Women's Oral Tradition in Telugu. In *Many Ramayanas: The Diversity of a Narrative Tradition in South Asia*, P. Richman, ed., pp. 114–136. Berkeley: University of California Press.

———. 2000. The Politics of Telugu Ramayanas: Colonialism, Print Culture, and Literary Movements. In *Questioning Ramayanas: A South Asian Tradition*, Paula Richman, ed., pp. 159–185. Berkeley: University of California Press, and New Delhi: Oxford University Press.

Nath, Shaileswar. 1980. *Terrorism in India*. New Delhi: National Publishers.

Nehru, Jawaharlal. 1995. *The Discovery of India*. New Delhi: Nehru Memorial Fund.

Nelsen, Kristina. 1985. *The Art of Reciting the Qur'an*. Modern Middle East Series, no. 11. Austin: University of Texas Press.

Nesbitt, Eleanor. 1955. Panjabis in Britain: Cultural History, and Cultural Choices. *South Asia Research* 15, no. 2: 221–240.

Niehoff, Arthur, and Juanita Niehoff. 1960. *East Indians in the West Indies*. Publications in Anthropology, no. 6. Milwaukee: Milwaukee Public Museum.

Nigam, Sanjay. 1990a. Disciplining and Policing the Criminals by Birth, Part 1: The Making of a Colonial Stereotype—The Criminal Tribes and Castes of North India. *Indian Economic and Social History Review* 27, no. 2: 131–164.

———. 1990b. Disciplining and Policing the Criminals by Birth, Part 2: The Development of a Disciplinary System, 1871–1900. *Indian Economic and Social History Review* 27, no. 3: 257–287.

Nilsson, Usha. 2000. Grinding Millet but Singing of Sita: Power and Domination in Awadhi and Bhojpuri Women's Songs. In *Questioning Ramayanas*, Paula Richman, ed., pp. 137–158. Berkeley: University of California Press.

Nugent, Neill. 1976. The Anti-immigration Groups. *New Community* 5, no. 3: 302–310.

Oberoi, Harjot. 1994. *The Construction of Religious Boundaries: Culture, Identity, and Diversity in the Sikh Tradition*. Chicago: University of Chicago Press.

O'Brien, Edward. 1881. *Glossary of the Multani Language Compared with Punjabi and Sindhi.* Lahore: Punjab Government Civil Secretariat Press.

———. 1882. *Report of the Land Revenue Settlement of the Muzaffargarh District of the Punjab, 1873–1880.* Lahore: Central Jail Press.

Oldham, C. E. A. W. 1930. The Proverbs of the People in a District (Shahabad) of Northern India. *Folklore* 41: 320–344.

Omega. 1997. Press release for Indian launch of Omega Constellation My Choice.

Omvedt, Gail. 1993. *Dalits and the Democratic Revolution: Dr. Ambedkar and the Dalit Movement in Colonial India.* New Delhi: Sage Publications.

Ortner, Sherry L. 1973. Sherpa Purity. *American Anthropologist* 75: 49–63.

———. 1989. *High Religion: A Cultural and Political History of Sherpa Buddhism.* Princeton, N.J.: Princeton University Press.

———. 1991. Reading America: Preliminary Notes on Class and Culture. In *Recapturing Anthropology: Working in the Present*, Richard G. Fox, ed. Santa Fe, N.Mex.: School of American Research Press.

———. 1995. Resistance and the Problem of Ethnographic Refusal. *Comparative Studies in History and Society* 37, no. 1 (January): 173–193.

———. 1996. *Making Gender: The Politics and Erotics of Culture.* Boston: Beacon Press.

———. 1998. Identities: The Hidden Life of Class. *Journal of Anthropological Research* 54, no. 1 (Spring): 1–17.

———. 1999. *Life and Death on Mt. Everest: Sherpas and Himalayan Mountaineering.* Princeton, N.J.: Princeton University Press.

Pandey, Gyan. 1983. Rallying round the Cow: Sectarian Strife in the Bhojpuri Region, c. 1888–1917. In *Subaltern Studies II: Writings on South Asian History and Society*, Ranajit Guha, ed., pp. 60–129. Delhi: Oxford University Press.

Pandian, M. S. S. 1992. *The Image Trap: MG Ramachandran in Film and Politics.* New Delhi: Sage Publications.

Parry, Jonathan. 1994. *Death in Banaras.* Cambridge: Cambridge University Press.

Parry, Jonathan, Jan Breman, and Karin Kapadia, eds. 1999. *The Worlds of Indian Industrial Labour.* Contributions to Indian Sociology. Occasional Studies, 9. New Delhi: Sage.

Patnaik, Prabhat. 1994. International Capital and National Economic Policy: A Critique of India's Economic Reforms. *Economic and Political Weekly*, March 19.

Paul, Diane. 1985. *Women in Buddhism: Images of the Feminine in Mahayana Tradition.* Berkeley: University of California Press.

Peabody, Norbert. 2000. Collective Violence in South Asia. *American Ethnologist* 27, no. 1: 167–177.

Peace, Adrian. 1984. Constructions of Class, Images of Inequality: The

Middle Class and the Urban Poor in a North Indian City. *Urban Anthropology* 13, no. 2–3: 261–294.

Peacock, James L., and Dorothy C. Holland. 1993. The Narrated Self: Life Stories in Process. *Ethos* 21: 367–383.

Petech, Luciano. 1977. *A Kingdom of Ladakh.* Rome: Instituto per il Medio ed Estremo Oriente.

——. 1998. Western Tibet: Historical Introduction. In *Tabo: A Lamp for the Kingdom—Early Indo-Tibetan Buddhist Art in the Western Himalayas,* Deborah Klimburg-Salter, ed. London: Thames and Hudson.

Peterson, I. V. 1989. *Poems to Siva: The Hymns of the Tamil Saints.* Delhi: Motilal Banarsidass Publishers.

Pinney, Christopher. 1990. Colonial Anthropology in the "Laboratory of Mankind." In *The Raj: India and the British, 1600–1947,* C. A. Bayly, ed., pp. 252–263. London: National Portrait Gallery.

Pollock, Sheldon. 1993. Ramayana and Political Imagination in India. *Journal of Asian Studies* 52, no. 2: 261–297.

Prakash, Gyan. 1981. *Bonded Histories: Genealogies of Labor Servitude in Colonial India.* Cambridge: Cambridge University Press.

——. 1991. Becoming a Bhuinya: Oral Traditions and Contested Domination in Eastern India. In *Contesting Power: Resistance and Everyday Social Relations in South Asia,* Douglas Haynes and Gyan Prakash, eds., pp. 145–174. Berkeley: University of California Press.

Prashad, Vijay. 1996. Desh: The Contradictions of "Homeland." In *Contours of the Heart,* R. Srikanth and S. Maira, eds., pp. 225–236. New York: Asian American Workshop.

Purser, W. E., and H. C. Fanshawe. 1880. *Report of the Revised Land Revenue Settlement of the Rohtak District of the Hissar Division in the Panjab.* Lahore: W. Ball.

Radhakrishnan, R. 1994. Is the Ethnic "Authentic" in the Diaspora? In *The State of Asian America,* K. Aguilar-San Juan, ed., pp. 219–223. Boston: South End Press.

Rafael, Vicente L. 1993. *Contracting Colonialism: Translation and Christian Conversion in Tagalog Society under Early Spanish Rule.* Durham, N.C., and London: Duke University Press.

Raheja, Gloria Goodwin. 1988. *The Poison in the Gift: Ritual, Prestation, and the Dominant Caste in a North Indian Village.* Chicago: University of Chicago Press.

——. 1995. The Limits of Patriliny: Kinship, Gender, and Women's Speech Practices in Rural North India. In *Gender, Kinship, Power: A Comparative and Interdisciplinary History,* M. J. Maynes and Ann Waltner, eds. London and New York: Routledge.

——. 1999. The Illusion of Consent: Language, Caste, and Colonial Rule in India. In *Colonial Subjects: Essays on the Practical History of Anthro-

pology, Peter Pels and Oscar Salemink, eds., pp. 117–152. Ann Arbor: University of Michigan Press.

Raheja, Gloria Goodwin, and Ann Grodzins Gold. 1994. *Listen to the Heron's Words: Reimagining Gender and Kinship in North India.* Berkeley: University of California Press.

Raman, Sita Anantha. 1996. *Getting Girls to School: Social Reform in the Tamil Districts 1870–1930.* Calcutta: Stree.

Ramanujan, A. K. 1970. Towards an Anthology of City Images. In *Urban India: Society, Space, and Image*, R. G. Fox, ed., pp. 224–244. Monograph and Occasional Papers Series, Monograph no. 10. Durham, N.C.: Duke University Program in Comparative Studies on Southern Asia.

———. 1975 [1967]. *The Interior Landscape: Love Poems from a Classical Tamil Anthology.* Bloomington: Indiana University Press.

———. 1981. Three Hundred Rāmāyaṇas: Five Examples and Three Thoughts on Translation. In *Many Ramayanas: The Diversity of a Narrative Tradition in South Asia*, Paula Richman, ed. Berkeley: University of California Press.

———. 1985. *Poems of Love and War.* New York: Columbia University Press.

———. 1986. Two Realms of Kannada Folkore. In *Another Harmony: New Essays on the Folklore of India*, Stuart Blackburn and A. K. Ramanujan, eds. Berkeley: University of California Press.

———. 1992 [1981]. *Hymns for the Drowning: Poems for Visnu by Nammalvar.* New York: Penguin Books.

Rao, M. S. A. 1989. Some Conceptual Issues in the Study of Caste, Class, Ethnicity, and Dominance. In Francine R. Frankel and M. S. A. Rao, eds., *Dominance and State Power in Modern India*, pp. 21–45. Delhi: Oxford University Press.

Ratti, Rakesh, ed. 1993. *A Lotus of Another Color: An Unfolding of the South Asian Gay and Lesbian Experience.* Boston: Alyson Publications.

Ray, Raka. 2000. Masculinity, Femininity, and Servitude: Domestic Workers in Calcutta in the Late Twentieth Century. *Feminist Studies* 26, no. 3: 691–718.

Riaboff, Isabelle. 1997. *Le Roi et le moine: Figures et principes du pouvoir et de sa légitimation au Zanskar* (Himalaya occidental). Ph.D. thesis, Laboratoires d'ethnologie et de sociologie comparatif, Université de Paris X.

Richman, Paula, ed. 1991. *Many Ramayanas: The Diversity of a Narrative Tradition in South Asia.* Berkeley: University of California Press, and New Delhi: Oxford University Press.

———. 2000. *Questioning Ramayanas: A South Asian Tradition.* Berkeley: University of California Press, and New Delhi: Oxford University Press.

Risley, H. H. 1891. *The Tribes and Castes of Bengal.* Calcutta: Bengal Secretariat Press.

———. 1907. *Manual of Ethnography for India: General Instructions, Definitions, and Ethnographic Questions.* Calcutta: Bengal Secretariat Press.

———. 1908. *The People of India.* Calcutta and London: Thacker, Spink.

Rosaldo, Michelle. 1980. The Use and Abuse of Anthropology. *Signs* 5, no. 3: 389–417.

Roseman, Marina. 1991. *Healing Sounds from the Malaysian Rainforest.* Berkeley: University of California Press.

Rosenwald, George C., and Richard L. Ochberg, eds. 1992. *Storied Lives: The Cultural Politics of Self-Understanding.* New Haven, Conn., and London: Yale University Press.

Roy, Beth. 1994. *Some Trouble with Cows: Making Sense of Social Conflict.* Berkeley: University of California Press.

Roy, Manisha. 1992. *Bengali Women.* Chicago: University of Chicago Press.

Roy Choudhury, P. C. 1966. *Bihar District Gazetteer/Shahabad.* Patna: Secretariat Press.

Rozario, Santi. 1992. *Purity and Communal Boundaries: Women and Social Change in a Bangladeshi Village.* London: Zed Books.

Rushdie, Salman, 1991. *Imaginary Homelands: Essays and Criticism.* London: Granta Books.

Rustomji-Kerns, Roshni, ed. 1994. *Living in America: Poetry and Fiction by South Asian American Writers.* Boulder, Colo.: Westview Press.

Sahlins, Marshall. 1985. *Islands of History.* Chicago: University of Chicago Press.

Said, Edward. 1978. *Orientalism.* New York: Pantheon Books.

Sarkar, Sumiti. 1983. *Modern India: 1885–1947.* New Delhi: Macmillan India.

Sato, Ikuya. 1991. *Kamikaze Biker: Parody and Anomy in Affluent Japan.* Chicago: University of Chicago Press.

Schieffelin, Edward. 1976. *The Sorrow of the Lonely and the Burning of the Dancers.* New York: St. Martin's Press.

———. 1985. Performance and the Cultural Construction of Reality. *American Ethnologist* 12: 704–724.

Schuh, Dieter. 1976. *Urkunden und Zendschreiben aus Zentraltibet, Ladakh, und Zanskar. Monumenta Tibetica Historica.* Band 2, 4. St. Augustin: VGH Wissenschaftsverlag.

———. 1983. *Historiographische Dokumenta aus Zans-dkar.* Sankt Augustin: Archiv für Zentralasiatische Geschichts-Forschung Heft 6.

Scott, David. 1999. *Refashioning Futures: Criticism after Postcoloniality.* Princeton, N.J.: Princeton University Press.

Sedgwick, Eve Kosofsky. *Between Men: English Literature and Male Homosocial Desire.* New York: Columbia University Press, 1985.

Seitel, Peter. 1977. Saying Haya Sayings: Two Categories of Proverb Use. In *The Social Use of Metaphor: Essays in the Anthropology of Rhetoric,* J. David Sapir and J. Christopher Crocker, eds., pp. 75–99. Philadelphia: University of Pennsylvania Press.

Seizer, Susan. 1995. Paradoxes of Visibility in the Field: Rites of Queer Passage in Anthropology. *Public Culture* 8, no. 1: 73–100.

——. 2000. Roadwork: Offstage with Special Drama Actresses in Tamil-nadu, South India. *Cultural Anthropology* 15, no. 2: 217–259.

Seymour, Susan C. 1975. Some Determinants of Sex Roles in a Changing Indian Town. *American Ethnologist* 2, no. 4: 757–769.

——. 1976. Caste/Class and Child-Rearing in a Changing Indian Town. *American Ethnologist* 3, no. 4: 783–796.

——. 1980. *The Transformation of a Sacred Town: Bhubaneswar, India.* Boulder, Colo.: Westview Press.

——. 1988. Expressions of Responsibility among Indian Children: Some Precursors of Adult Status and Sex Roles. *Ethos* 16, no. 4: 355–370.

——. 1999. *Women, Family, and Child Care in India: A World in Transition.* Cambridge: Cambridge University Press.

Shakabpa, Tsepon. 1967. *Tibet: A Political History.* New Haven. Conn.: Yale University Press.

Sharma, O. P. 1994. *Universal Literacy: A Distant Dream (Based on the Census Data).* New Delhi: Kar Kripa Publishers.

Sharma, O. P., and Robert D. Retherford. 1993. *Literacy Trends in the 1980s in India.* Faridabad: Government of India Press.

Sharma, Sanjay, John Hutnyk, and Ashwani Sharma. 1996. Introduction. In *Dis-Orienting Rhythms: The Politics of the New Asian Dance Music,* Sanjay Sharma, John Hutnyk, and Ashwani Sharma, eds. London: Zed Books.

Shulman, David Dean. 1985. *The King and the Clown in South Indian Myth and Poetry.* Princeton, N.J.: Princeton University Press.

——. 2000. Bhavabhuti on Cruelty and Compassion. In *Questioning Rama-yanas: A South Asian Tradition,* Paula Richman, ed., pp. 49–82. Berkeley: University of California Press.

Shweder, Richard A., and Edmund J. Bourne. 1984. Does the Concept of the Person Vary Cross-Culturally? In *Culture Theory: Essays on Mind, Self, and Emotion,* Richard A. Shweder and Robert A. LeVine, eds., pp. 158–199. Cambridge: Cambridge University Press.

Singer, Milton. 1972. *When a Great Tradition Modernizes: An Anthropological Approach to Indian Civilization.* Chicago: University of Chicago Press.

Singh, Pashaura, and N. Gerald Barrier, eds. 1996. *The Transmission of Sikh Heritage in the Diaspora.* New Delhi: Manohar.

——. 1999. *Sikh Identity: Continuity and Change.* New Delhi: Manohar.

Sisson, Richard, and Leo E. Rose. 1990. *War and Secession: Pakistan, India, and the Creation of Bangladesh.* Berkeley: University of California Press.

Skaria, George. 1999. The Indianization of the Transnational. *Business Today,* 7 July.

Skorupski, John. 1976. *Symbol and Theory: A Philosophical Study of Theories of Religion in Social Anthropology.* Cambridge: Cambridge University Press.

Snellgrove, David, and Tadeusz Skorupski. 1980. *The Cultural Heritage of Ladakh: Zangskar and the Cave Temples of Ladakh.* Warminster, Wiltshire, England: Aris and Phillips.

Solon, Gary. 1992. Intergenerational Income Mobility in the United States. *American Economic Review* 83, no. 2 (June): 393–408.

Southall Black Sisters. 1979. The Traditional Story of Ramayana. One-page program distributed at the Ramlila, 19 October.

Spivak, Gayatri Chakravorty. 1995. Translator's Preface. In *Imaginary Maps: Three Stories by Mahasweta Devi*, pp. xxiii–xxix. New York and London: Routledge.

Sponberg, Alan. 1992. Attitudes toward Women and the Feminine in Early Buddhism. In *Buddhism, Sexuality, and Gender*, Jose Cabezon, ed. Albany: SUNY Press.

Srikanth, Rajni, and Sunaina Maira, eds. 1996. *Contours of the Heart: South Asians Map North America*. New York: Asian American Workshop.

Srinivas, M. N. 1976. *The Remembered Village*. Berkeley: University of California Press.

Srivastava, Manoj. 1998. Promoting Adult Literacy in India through State-Society Synergy: A Comparative Study of Mass Literacy Campaigns in Kerala and Bihar. Master's paper in Professional Studies, International Development, Cornell University.

Stokes, Eric. 1978. *The Peasant and the Raj: Studies in Agrarian Society and Peasant Rebellion in Colonial India*. Cambridge: Cambridge University Press.

———. 1986. *The Peasant Armed: The Indian Rebellion of 1857*. Oxford: Clarendon Press.

Stone, Linda, and Caroline James. 1995. Dowry, Bride-Burning, and Female Power in India. *Women's Studies International Forum* 18, no. 2: 125–135. Reprinted in *Gender in Cross-Cultural Perspective*, Caroline B. Brettell and Carolyn F. Sargent, eds., pp. 307–316. Upper Saddle River, N.J.: Prentice-Hall, 2001.

Suleri, Sara. 1989. *Meatless Days*. Chicago: University of Chicago Press.

Tambiah, Stanley J. 1990. *Magic, Science, Religion, and the Scope of Rationality*. Cambridge: Harvard University Press.

———. 1991 [1986]. *Sri Lanka: Ethnic Fratricide and the Dismantling of Democracy*. Chicago: University of Chicago Press.

Tapper, Nancy. 1987. Direct Exchange and Brideprice: Alternative Forms in a Complex Marriage System. *Man* 16: 387–407.

Tatla, Darshan Singh. 1999. *The Sikh Diaspora: The Search for Statehood*. London: Routledge for University College, London.

Taylor, Stan. 1978. The National Front: Anatomy of a Political Movement. In *Racism and Political Action in Britain*, Robert Miles and Annie Phizacklea, eds., pp. 124–146. London: Routledge.

Temple, R. C. 1914. *Anthropology as a Practical Science*. London: G. Bell and Sons.

Tharu, Susie, and K. Lalita, ed. 1991. *Women Writing in India 600 B.C. to the Present*. Vol. I. New York: Feminist Press.

Thiruchendran, Selvy. 1997. *Ideology, Caste, Class, and Gender.* New Delhi: Vikas.

Tinker, Hugh. 1974. *A New System of Slavery: The Export of Indian Labour Overseas 1830–1902.* Oxford: Oxford University Press.

Tolen, Rachel. 1996. Between Bungalow and Outhouse: Class Practice and Domestic Service in a Madras Railway. Ph.D. dissertation, University of Pennsylvania.

———. 2000. Transfers of Knowledge and Privileged Spheres of Practice: Servants and Employers in a Madras Railway Colony. In *Home and Hegemony: Domestic Service and Identity Politics in South and Southeast Asia,* Kathleen M. Adams and Sara Dickey, eds., pp. 63–86. Ann Arbor: University of Michigan Press.

Trawick, Margaret Egnor. 1986. Internal Harmony in Paraiyar Crying Songs. In *Another Harmony: New Essays on the Folklore of India,* Stuart Blackburn and A. K. Ramanujan, eds., pp. 294–344. Berkeley: University of California Press.

———. 1988. Spirits and Voices in Tamil Songs. *American Ethnologist* 15: 193–215.

———. 1990. *Notes on Love in a Tamil Family.* Berkeley: University of California Press.

———. 1991. Wandering Lost: A Landless Laborer's Sense of Place. In *Gender, Genre, and Power in South Asian Expressive Traditions,* Arjun Appadurai, Frank J. Korom, and Margaret A. Mills, eds. Philadelphia: University of Pennsylvania Press.

Trust Deed of Narayana Guruviah Chetty's Charities. 1968 (Reprinted). Chennai: Narayana Guruviah Chetty's Estate and Charities.

Tsering, Tashi, and Philippa Russell. 1996. An Account of the Buddhist Ordination of Women. *Cho Yang* 1, no. 1: 21–30.

Tsomo, Karma Lekshe. 1988. *Sakyadhita: Daughters of the Buddha.* Ithaca, N.Y.: Snow Lion Press.

———. 1996. *Sisters in Solitude.* Albany: SUNY Press.

Turner, Victor. 1967. *The Forest of Symbols.* Ithaca, N.Y.: Cornell University Press.

Ullrich, Helen. 1987. Marriage Patterns among Havik Brahmins: A Twenty-Year Study of Change. *Sex Roles* 16, no. 11/12: 615–635.

———. 1994. Asset and Liability: The Role of Female Education in Changing Marriage Patterns among Havik Brahmins. In *Women, Education, and Family Structure in India,* Carol Chapnick Mukhopadhyay and Susan Seymour, eds., pp. 187–212. Boulder, Colo.: Westview Press.

Unnithan, Maya, and Kavita Srivastava. 1997. Gender Politics, Development, and Women's Agency in Rajasthan. In *Discourses of Development: Anthropological Perspectives,* R. D. Grillo and R. L. Stirrat, eds., pp. 157–181. New York: Berg.

Upadhyay, Anita, et al. 1995. *Prerṇā gīt aur chetan nāre.* Jaipur: Rajasthan Prauṛh Íikṣaṇ Samiti.

van der Veer, Peter. 1994. *Religious Nationalism: Hindus and Muslims in India.* Berkeley: University of California Press.

van der Veer, Peter, and Hartmut Lehmann. 1999. *Nation and Religion: Perspectives on Europe and Asia.* Princeton: Princeton University Press.

van Willigen, John, and Narender K. Chadha. 1999. *Social Aging in a Delhi Neighborhood.* Westport, Conn.: Bergin and Garvey.

Vanita, Ruth, ed. 2001. *Queering India: Same-Sex Love and Eroticism in Indian Culture and Society.* New York: Routledge.

Vanita, Ruth, and Saleem Kidwai, eds. 2000. *Same-Sex Love in India: Readings from Literature and History.* New York: St. Martin's Press.

Vatuk, Sylvia. 1980. Withdrawal and Disengagement as a Cultural Response to Aging in India. In *Aging in Culture and Society,* Christine Fry, ed., pp. 126–148. New York: Praeger.

——. 1990. "To Be a Burden on Others": Dependency Anxiety among the Elderly in India. In *Divine Passions: The Social Construction of Emotion in India,* Owen Lynch, ed., pp. 64–88. Berkeley: University of California Press.

——. 1995. The Indian Woman in Later Life: Some Social and Cultural Considerations. In *Women's Health in India: Risk and Vulnerability,* Monica Das Gupta, Lincoln C. Chen, and T. N. Krishnan, eds., pp. 289–306. Bombay: Oxford University Press.

Vertovec, Steven. 1997. Three Meanings of "Diaspora," Exemplified among South Asian Religions. *Diaspora* 6, no. 3: 277–299.

Visram, Rozina. 1986. *Ayahs, Lascars, and Princes.* London: Pluto.

Visweswaran, Kamala. 1997. Diaspora by Design: Flexible Citizenship and South Asians in U.S. Racial Formations. *Diaspora* 6, no. 1: 5–29.

Vivek Dhareshwar. 1995a. "Our Time": History, Sovereignty, Politics. *Economic and Political Weekly,* February 11, 317–324.

——. 1995b. The Postcolonial in the Postmodern: Or, the Political after Modernity. *Economic and Political Weekly,* July 29, 104–112.

Wadley, Susan S. 1975. *Shakti: Power in the Conceptual Structure of Karimpur Religion.* The University of Chicago Studies in Anthropology Series in Social, Cultural and Linguistic Anthropology, no. 2.

——. 1994. *Struggling with Destiny in Karimpur, 1925–1984.* Berkeley: University of California Press.

——. 1995a. No Longer a Wife: Widows in Rural North India. In *From the Margins of Hindu Marriage: Essays on Gender, Religion, and Culture,* Lyndsey Harlan and Paul Courtright, eds., pp. 90–118. New York: Oxford University Press.

——. 1995b. The "Village Indira": A Brahman Widow and Political Action in Rural North India. In *Women in India: Two Perspectives,* Doranne Jacobson and Susan S. Wadley, eds., pp. 225–250. Delhi: Manohar.

———. 2001. The Village in 1998. In *Behind Mud Walls: Seventy-five Years in a North Indian Village,* by William Wiser and Charlotte Wiser. Revised and expanded edition. With chapters by Susan S. Wadley. Foreword by David G. Mandelbaum. Berkeley: University of California Press, 2001.

Wadley, Susan S., and Bruce W. Derr. 1993. Karimpur Families over 60 Years. In *Family, Kinship and Marriage in India,* Patricia Oberoi, ed., pp. 393–415. Delhi: Oxford University Press.

Warner, Michael. 1990. *Letters of the Republic: Publication and the Public Sphere in Eighteenth-Century America.* Cambridge: Harvard University Press.

Watters, David. 1975. Siberian Shamanistic Traditions among the Kham-Magars of Nepal. *Contributions to Nepalese Studies* 2: 123–168.

Weber, Max. 1958 [1920–21]. *The Protestant Ethic and the Spirit of Capitalism.* Talcott Parsons, trans. New York: Charles Scribner's Sons.

———. 1968. The Distribution of Power within the Political Community: Class, Status, Party. In Max Weber, *Economy and Society,* vol. 2, Guenther Roth and Claus Wittich, eds. New York: Bedminster Press.

Wilce, James M. 1998. *Eloquence in Trouble: The Poetics and Politics of Complaint in Bangladesh.* New York and Oxford: Oxford University Press.

———. 2000. The Poetics of "Madness": Shifting Codes and Styles in the Linguistic Construction of Identity in Matlab, Bangladesh. *Cultural Anthropology* 15, no. 1: 3–34.

Williams, Raymond. 1977. *Marxism and Literature.* London: Oxford University Press.

Williamson, Judith. 1978. *Decoding Advertisements: Ideology and Meaning in Advertising.* London: Marion Boyars.

Willis, Jan. 1985. Nuns and Benefactresses: The Role of Women in the Development of Buddhism. In *Women, Religion, and Social Change,* Y. Haddad and E. Findly, eds. Albany: SUNY Press.

Willis, Paul. 1977. *Learning to Labour: How Working Class Kids Get Working Class Jobs.* Aldershot, U.K.: Grover.

Wilson, J. 1898. *Grammar and Dictionary of Western Panjabi, As Spoken in the Shahpur District, With Proverbs, Sayings, and Verses.* Lahore: Punjab Government Press.

Wiser, Charlotte V. 1978. *Four Families of Karimpur.* Foreign and Comparative Studies Program, South Asian Series, no. 3, Syracuse University.

Wiser, William H. 1958 [1936]. *The Hindu Jajmani System: A Socio-economic System Interrelating Members of a Hindu Village.* Lucknow: Lucknow Publishing House.

Wiser, William, and Charlotte Wiser. 2001. *Behind Mud Walls: Seventy-five Years in a North Indian Village.* Revised and expanded edition. With chapters by Susan S. Wadley. Foreword by David G. Mandelbaum. Berkeley: University of California Press.

Wolpert, Stanley. 1982. *A New History of India.* 2nd ed. Oxford: Oxford University Press.

Women of South Asian Descent Collective, ed. 1993. *Our Feet Walk the Sky: Women of the South Asian Diaspora.* San Francisco: Aunt Lute Books.

Yalman, Nur. 1962. The Ascetic Buddhist Monks of Ceylon. *Ethnology* 1, no. 3: 315–328.

Zelliot, Eleanor. 1992. *From Untouchable to Dalit: Essays on the Ambedkar Movement.* New Delhi: Manohar.

CONTRIBUTORS

JOSEPH S. ALTER is Associate Professor of Anthropology at the University of Pittsburgh. His most recent publications are *Gandhi's Body: Sex, Diet, and the Politics of Nationalism* (2000) and *Knowing Dil Das: Stories of a Himalayan Hunter* (1999). He is currently doing research on the medicalization of yoga and the relationship between science, yoga, and nationalism in modern India.

J. BERNARD BATE is Assistant Professor of Anthropology at Yale University, where he teaches on South Asia, language, politics, and gender. He is currently working on an historical ethnography of Tamil oratory in Christian and Saivite sermons and early democratic practice, 1847–1919.

E. VALENTINE DANIEL is Professor of Anthropology and Director of the Southern Asian Institute at Columbia University. He is best known for two of his books, *Fluid Signs: Being a Person the Tamil Way* (1987) and the more recent *Charred Lullabies: Chapters in an Anthropography of Violence* (1996).

ROBERT DESJARLAIS is Associate Professor of Anthropology at Sarah Lawrence College. He is the author of two books, *Body and Emotion: The Aesthetics of Illness and Healing in the Nepal Himalayas* (1992) and *Shelter Blues: Sanity and Selfhood among the Homeless* (1997).

SARA DICKEY is Professor of Anthropology at Bowdoin College and has carried out research on film watching, politics, domestic service, and class identities in South India. She is the author of *Cinema and the Urban Poor in South India* (1993) and co-editor of *Home and Hegemony: Domestic Service and Identity Politics in South and Southeast Asia* (2000).

GAUTAM GHOSH is Assistant Professor of Anthropology and a member of South Asia, History, and Folklore graduate groups at the University of Pennsylvania. His publications include "God Is a Refugee."

ANN GRODZINS GOLD is Professor of Religion and Anthropology at Syracuse University. Her research in North India has included studies of pilgrimage, world renunciation, women's expressive traditions, environmental change, and children's environmental knowledge. Her most recent book, co-authored with Bhoju Ram Gujar, is *In the Time of Trees and Sorrows: Nature, Power, and Memory in Rajasthan* (2002).

BENEDICTE GRIMA received her Ph.D. in folklore from the University of Pennsylvania and an M.A. in Iranian studies from the University of Paris, where she studied Pashto at the Oriental Institute. She is the author of *The Performance of Emotion among Paxtun Women* (1992) and is currently working on a second book, *Understanding Pashtun Women: Their Stories, Their Lives,* as she teaches Pashto at the University of Pennsylvania.

KIM GUTSCHOW teaches anthropology and religion at Brandeis University. Her book, *Gendered Illusions: Buddhism and the Ascetic Life in Kashmir,* is under contract with Harvard University Press, and she has published on Buddhism, gender, sexuality, exchange, the politics of irrigation, and Tibetan medicine.

KATHLEEN HALL is Assistant Professor in the Education, Culture, and Society program of the University of Pennsylvania's Graduate School of Education. Her ongoing work with Sikh youth in England is the focus of a forthcoming book, *Lives in Translation: Sikh Youth and British Cultural Citizenship,* to be published by the University of Pennsylvania Press.

PATRICIA JEFFERY is Professor of Sociology at the University of Edinburgh. Her recent publications include *Appropriating Gender: Women's Activism and Politicized Religion in South Asia,* co-edited with Amrita Basu (Routledge, 1998), and a new edition of her 1979 book *Frogs in a Well: Indian Women in Purdah* (Manohar, 2000).

ROGER JEFFERY is Professor of Sociology of South Asia at the University of Edinburgh. His recent publications include (with Patricia Jeffery) *Population, Gender, and Politics: Demographic Change in Rural North India* (Cambridge University Press, 1997) and (with Nandini Sundar) *Branching Out: Joint Forest Management in Four Indian States* (Oxford University Press, 2001).

PRADEEP JEGANATHAN is Assistant Professor of Anthropology and Global Studies in the College of Liberal Arts and a MacKnight–Land Grant Professor at the University of Minnesota, Minneapolis. He is co-editor (with Qadri Ismail) of *Unmaking the Nation* (1995) and (with Partha Chatterjee) of *Subaltern Studies* 11 (2000).

NITA KUMAR's research interests and publications include artisans, community, identity, and social change (*The Artisans of Banaras,* 1988); methodology (*Friends, Brothers, and Informants,* 1992); women and feminism in India (*Women as Subjects,* 1994; *Mai,* 2000); and children and education (*Lessons from Schools,* 2000; *The Educating of India,* forthcoming).

SARAH LAMB is Associate Professor of Anthropology at Brandeis University. She is the author of *White Saris and Sweet Mangoes: Aging, Gender, and Body in North India* (2000) and is currently doing research on the transcultural lives of older immigrants from India in the United States.

MARK LIECHTY is Assistant Professor of Anthropology and History at the University of Illinois at Chicago. He is the author of *Class as Cultural Practice: Consumption, Media, and the Making of Middle-Class Culture in Kathmandu* (2002) and co-editor of the journal *Studies in Nepali History and Society*.

MCKIM MARRIOTT, whose base is in Anthropology and the Social Sciences College of the University of Chicago, has researched cultures of South Asia for five decades, mainly through residing in the rapidly changing small communities of Uttar Pradesh and Maharashtra. He edited *Village India* (1955) and *India through Hindu Categories* (1990) and has written extensively on caste and other aspects of social organization.

WILLIAM MAZZARELLA is Assistant Professor of Anthropology at the University of Chicago. His book *Shoveling Smoke: Advertising and Globalization in Contemporary India* is forthcoming from Duke University Press.

DIANE P. MINES is Assistant Professor of Anthropology at Appalachian State University in Boone, North Carolina. She has authored several articles on ritual, caste, and politics in rural Tamil Nadu, including "Hindu Nationalism, Untouchable Reform, and the Ritual Making of a South Indian Village" (*American Ethnologist*, 2002).

MATTISON MINES is Professor of Anthropology at the University of California at Santa Barbara. He is the author of *Public Faces, Private Voices: Community and Individuality in South India* (1994), *The Warrior Merchants: Textiles, Trade, and Territory in South India* (1984), and numerous articles reporting his field and historical research in Tamil Nadu.

SERENA NANDA, Professor Emerita of Anthropology at John Jay College of Criminal Justice (CUNY), is the author of *Neither Man nor Woman: The Hijras of India* (1999) and *Gender Diversity: Crosscultural Variations* (2000). She is also co-author of texts in cultural anthropology and on cultural pluralism and law.

KIRIN NARAYAN is Professor of Anthropology and Languages and Cultures of Asia at the University of Wisconsin at Madison. She is author of *Storytellers, Saints, and Scoundrels: Folk Narrative in Hindu Religious Teaching* (1989), *Mondays on the Dark Night of the Moon: Himalayan Foothill Folktales* (1997), and also a novel, *Love, Stars, and All That* (1994).

STEVEN M. PARISH is Associate Professor of Anthropology at the University of California at San Diego. He is the author of *Moral Knowing in a Hindu*

Sacred City (1994) and *Hierarchy and Its Discontents: Culture and the Politics of Consciousness in Caste Society Culture* (1996).

JEAN-LUC RACINE is Senior Fellow at the Centre for the Study of India and South Asia in Paris. He has edited *Calcutta 1905–1971: Au Coeur des Créations et des Révoltes du Siècle* (1997) and *Peasant Moorings: Village Ties and Mobility Rationales in South India* (1997). He is co-author, with Viramma and Josiane Racine, of *Viramma, Life of an Untouchable* (1994).

JOSIANE RACINE resides in Paris and conducts research on popular culture in Tamil Nadu, South India. She is co-author, with Viramma and Jean-Luc Racine, of *Viramma, Life of an Untouchable* (1994).

GLORIA GOODWIN RAHEJA is Professor of Anthropology at the University of Minnesota. She is the author of *The Poison in the Gift: Ritual, Prestation, and the Dominant Caste in a North Indian Village* (1988), co-author (with Ann Grodzins Gold) of *Listen to the Heron's Words: Reimagining Gender and Kinship in North India* (1994), and editor of *Songs, Stories, Lives: Gendered Dialogues and Cultural Critique* (forthcoming). She is currently writing on the relationship between colonial ethnography and administrative practice in nineteenth-century India.

PAULA RICHMAN, Irvin E. Houck Professor in the Humanites and Chair of the Religion Department at Oberlin College, has published *Extraordinary Child: Poems from a South Indian Devotional Genre* (1997), as well as edited and contributed to *Questioning Ramayanas: A South Asian Tradition* (2000). She is currently completing a monograph on Ramayanas in modern Tamil.

SUSAN SEIZER is Assistant Professor of Anthropology and Gender and Women's Studies at Scripps College in Claremont, California. She is currently writing an ethnography of the Special Drama acting community that focuses on the artists' various strategic responses to the social stigma of their profession.

SUSAN SEYMOUR is the Jean M. Pitzer Professor of Anthropology at Pitzer College and author and editor of several books, including *Women, Family, and Child Care in India: A World in Transition* (1999), *The Transformation of a Sacred Town: Bhubaneswar, India* (1980), and (co-edited with Carol C. Mukhopadhyay) *Women, Education, and Family Structure in India* (1994).

MARGARET TRAWICK is a sociocultural anthropologist who has done extensive ethnographic research in Tamil Nadu and more recently in Sri Lanka. In the past she has written about indigenous systems of healing, Saiva poetics, folk songs, and the condition of untouchability in India. Her best-known work is *Notes on Love in a Tamil Family* (1990). Her current research is about children's responses to armed conflict.

RUTH VANITA is Associate Professor of Liberal Studies and Women's Studies at the University of Montana. Formerly Reader in English, Delhi University, she was founding co-editor of *Manushi*, India's first feminist journal, for thirteen years, and is also the author of *Sappho and the Virgin Mary: Same-Sex Love and the English Literary Imagination* (1996) and co-editor (with Saleem Kidwai) of *Same-Sex Love in India: Readings from Literature and History* (2000).

VIRAMMA was a Dalit agricultural laborer and a midwife in Karani, a village in southeast India. She passed away in her village in 2000.

SUSAN S. WADLEY is Ford Maxwell Professor of South Asian Studies at Syracuse University. Her work deals with gender, oral traditions, and social change in rural north India. She is the author of *Struggling with Destiny in Karimpur, 1925–1984* (1994) and has updated the classic *Behind Mud Walls* by William and Charlotte Wiser to include materials on Karimpur in the late 1990s.

JIM WILCE is Associate Professor of Anthropology at Northern Arizona University, and studies language, interaction, illness, and madness. He is the author of *Eloquence in Trouble: The Poetics and Politics of Complaint in Rural Bangladesh* (1998) and "The Poetics of 'Madness'" (2000).

INDEX

Page numbers in italics refer to illustrations.

270; and family destinies, 18; and generosity, 79; and Jainism, 231; and low castes, 179
Kartikkai, Tamil festival of, 194, 198n2
Kashmir: and aftermath of Partition, 304; children's knowledge of, 351; nuns and monastic renunciation in, 261–72
Kathmandu, Nepal: Buddhist nunneries, 264; Thamel street-youth culture, 37–46
Kelly, John, 383
Kerala, India, historic Christian and Jewish communities in, 233
Kerin, Melissa, 273n12
Khan, Shah Rukh, 398n11
Khan, Sir Syed Ahmad, 353
Kharrals (caste), 206–207, 208
kinship ties and charitable giving, 74–77
Kishan Garhi, India, 249, 259n1. *See also* festival of Holī
Klein, Anne, 273n6
kolams (patterns in powder), 128, 131n8
Kolkotta, India: and Partition, 327, 328, 329, 333; schools, history, and memory in, 349–53, 354
Komati Chettys (caste), 71, 80n2
Korea, Buddhism in, 231, 263
Krishna: and festival of Gobardhan Divālī, 254, 260nn3,16; and festival of Holī, 249–59; temples of, 239; as universally recognized, 236
Ksatriyas, 167
Kuipers, Joel, 212n2
Kumar, Nita, 88, 96
kung fu films, 43, 46n3

Ladakhi Nuns Association, 271
Lakshmi, 84
Lal, Malashri, 91–92, 99n11
lamas, 276
laments. *See* tuneful laments and Muslim prayer in Bangladesh
Laos, Buddhist nuns in, 263
Lévi-Strauss, Claude, 281
Levy, Robert, 181–83
Lewis, Oscar, 130n7
Liberation Tigers of Tamil Eelam (LTTE): bombings in Colombo, 357, 358; civilian feelings toward, 369–71; military strength and survival of fittest, 369; recruitments, 368–69; students' motivations for joining, 367, 368–69; students' stories of, 375, 376, 377; and Tamil refugees, 443, 444, 449, 450
life stages, Hindu: and aging, 65, 67n9; women's, 67n9
Lindholm, Charles, 48
literacy: and education of boys, 86, 98n4; and family honor, 97, 99n13; and Rajas-

thani women, 86–87, 89. *See also* education
Lopez, Donald, 261–62, 272n2
LTTE. *See* Liberation Tigers of Tamil Eelam (LTTE)

McLeod, W. H., 424n7
madness, 292–94, 301
Madras City, India, and will of Narayana Guruviah Chetty, 69–80
madrasás, 33, 338–41, 343–47, 348, 353
Madurai, India: class mobility in, 214–26; and praise poetry in Tamil newspapers, 311–23; and Special Drama, 122, *124,* 128, 130nn2,4
Mahavira, 230
"mahilā vikās," 92
Malinowski, Bronislaw, 250, 281
Mangaldihi, West Bengal, 56–67
Marchand, Roland, 398n7
marriage: and Buddhist nuns, 270; changes in, 106–11, 113; education and, 106–11; and family class status, 221–23, 224, 225; weddings and Muslim tuneful prayers, 298–99; weddings and ritual performances, 253–54. *See also* arranged marriages
Marriott, McKim, 169–70, 324n3
Marx, Karl, 217
Marxism and diaspora Ramlila, 405
masculinity: and modernity, 143–44, 145; and wrestling, 133–34, 138, 141–45
mass media: advertising and brand identity, 388–94, 396–97, 398nn11–12; Hindi films, 146–57; self-peripheralization, 39–41; Western images and street culture in Kathmandu, 39–43, 45–46, 46n3
māyā: and aging, 59–63, 65; and caste, 63; as illusion, 59–60; as increasing with age, 61–63; as problematic, 61–63, 65; as ties and attachment, 59–61; as valued and sought, 60–61
Mayaram, Shail, 212n7
Mazumdar, R. C., 332, 336n21
Mead, G. H., 77
Mead, Margaret, 277
Meos (caste), 206, 208, 212n7
meykkīrtti inscriptions, 316–17
Middle East, South Asian migration to, 384
Mines, Diane, 76, 171
modernity: advertising and consumerism, 387–97; and aging, 64–65; and Buddhist monasticism, 261, 271–72; and disapproval of tuneful laments, 292, 301, 302n2; and education, 88, 89, 92–98, 102, 106–107; history and memory, 345–46; and marriage expectations, 106–15; and masculinity, 143–44, 145; and public cul-